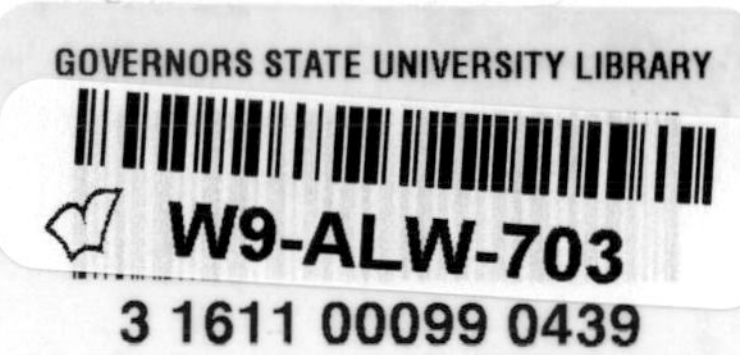
GOVERNORS STATE UNIVERSITY LIBRARY
W9-ALW-703
3 1611 00099 0439

Young Children with Special Needs

THIRD EDITION

Young Children with Special Needs

Warren Umansky

Children's Clinic
Augusta, Georgia

Stephen R. Hooper

The Clinical Center for the Study of Development and Learning
University of North Carolina School of Medicine

Merrill,
an imprint of Prentice Hall

Upper Saddle River, New Jersey Columbus, Ohio

Cover photo: © Jeffry W. Myers/H. Armstrong Roberts
Editor: Ann Castel Davis
Production Editor: Linda Hillis Bayma
Copy Editor: Genevieve d'Arcy
Photo Researcher: Linda Gray
Design Coordinator: Karrie M. Converse
Text Designer: John Edeen
Cover Designer: Brian Deep
Production Manager: Deidra M. Schwartz
Director of Marketing: Kevin Flanagan
Marketing Manager: Suzanne Stanton
Advertising/Marketing Coordinator: Julie Shough

This book was set in Garamond by Carlisle Communications, Ltd. and was printed and bound by Quebecor Printing/Book Press. The cover was printed by Phoenix Color Corp.

Photo credits: Scott Cunningham/Merrill, pp. 75, 188, 333, 340, 360; Custom Medical Stock Photo, p. 350; Laura Dwight, p. 80; Courtesy of Nancy Fallen, p. 178; Courtesy of Stephen Hooper, pp. 45, 46; Courtesy of Intellitools, pp. 329, 330, 332; Courtesy of Lekotek of Georgia, pp. 308, 320; Courtesy of Jean Patz, pp. 170, 191; Courtesy of Prentke Romich Company, p. 334; Courtesy of Rebecca Pretzel, pp. 43, 44, 355; Barbara Schwartz/Merrill, pp. 18, 156, 166, 221, 276; Courtesy of Tina Smith, p. 400; Courtesy of Sunburst Communications, p. 331; Anne Vega/Merrill, pp. 30, 33, 62, 72, 85, 94, 159, 193, 230, 247, 266, 279, 368, 372, 393; Tom Watson/Merrill, p. 214; Todd Yarrington, pp. xvi, 210, 284, 376, 384.

Library of Congress
Cataloging-in-Publication Data

Umansky, Warren.
Young children with special needs / Warren Umansky and Stephen R. Hooper. — 3rd ed.
p. cm.
Rev. ed. of: Young children with special needs / Nancy H. Fallen, Warren Umansky. 2nd ed. c1985.
Includes bibliographical references and index.
ISBN 0-13-612052-0
1. Handicapped children—Education—United States. 2. Perceptual-motor learning. 3. Child development—United States. I. Hooper, Stephen R. II. Fallen, Nancy H. Young children with special needs. III. Title.
LC4031.U425 1998
371.91'0973—dc21 97-24506
CIP

Printed in the United States of America

10 9 8 7 6 5 4 3 2

ISBN: 0-13-612052-0

PRENTICE-HALL INTERNATIONAL (UK) LIMITED, *LONDON*
PRENTICE-HALL OF AUSTRALIA PTY. LIMITED, *SYDNEY*
PRENTICE-HALL CANADA INC., *TORONTO*
PRENTICE-HALL HISPANOAMERICANA, S.A., *MEXICO*
PRENTICE-HALL OF INDIA PRIVATE LIMITED, *NEW DELHI*
PRENTICE-HALL OF JAPAN, INC., *TOKYO*
PEARSON EDUCATION ASIA PTE. LTD., *SINGAPORE*
EDITORA PRENTICE-HALL DO BRASIL, LTDA., *RIO DE JANEIRO*

To Jean and our children, Derrick, Aaron, and Neely, who make the sun shine 24 hours a day. To my father, a model of kindness and parental support. And to the students, children, and parents who have taught me so very much.

W. U.

To Lindsay Rae and Madeline Grace, whose persistent intolerance for this process constantly forced me to focus on why we were doing this book in the first place. To Mary for her constant love and support. And to my mother, Virginia Rebecca, whose strength has impacted on me in ways that she will never know.

S. R. H.

Foreword

Within 30 years the interdisciplinary field of early intervention has gained the reputation as one of the most cohesive, technically sophisticated, and transactional professional specialties within the spectrum of human services. Using creative "grass roots" approaches, early interventionists have crafted a blend of developmentally-based perspectives and practices that have been field-validated in diverse settings with diverse groups of families and young children with special needs. Early interventionists have tackled ingeniously the many problems that underscore the complex interactions among biological, developmental, social, and environmental factors in neurodevelopmental disabilities. It is arguable that no other human service field has shown such ambition and such commitment to quality and effectiveness. High-quality early education and child care are beneficial; early intervention is effective. These outcomes are a tribute to the many interdisciplinary professionals in early intervention and their partnerships with families.

Several introductory textbooks in the field of early intervention or early childhood special education have both chronicled and influenced the evolution of this professional specialty. One of the best of these resources has been *Young Children with Special Needs;* this revised edition maintains the quality of the previous editions and parallels the quality and expertise of the current and future leaders whose energy and commitment will be sparked by its content. Umansky and Hooper have generated a superb product that reviews past accomplishments in the field and lights the way for new directions. The content effectively promotes the integrated interdisciplinary standards that have resulted in these accomplishments culled from the "best practice" position statements of such professional organizations as the National Association for the Education of Young Children (NAEYC), The Division for Early Childhood of CEC; the American Speech, Hearing, and Language Association (ASHA); and the National Association of School Psychologists (NASP): family-centered; interdisciplinary; culturally-competent; community-based; developmentally-appropriate; inclusive; treatment-focused; resource-based; and disability-sensitive. Students will profit from a pedagogic device that effectively links content and application through the use of selected case studies. This revised text is logical and readable as the reader is led through three sections that encompass such topics as a review of the field, the developmental basis of disability; family-professional collaboration; the major developmental domains; teaching and intervention; assessment-intervention linkages; technology in early intervention; and future trends.

The challenges are immense for early interventionists; children and families face a much wider array of risks than those evident in the early "compensatory" intervention studies in the 1960s and 1970s. Some of the most effective markers for future leaders in early intervention will be ingenuity; technological expertise; a commitment to family-centered and community-based interventions; teamwork skills that foster interagency and interprofessional collaboration; a blended knowledge of medical and developmental issues; and a flair for reasoned and passionate advocacy for families. Perhaps above all, true future leaders will project a savvy knack for systems change, coupled with a slightly subversive attitude regarding the institutional barriers to helping families and young children with special needs, especially as funding for early intervention relies on the healthcare sector. The 1998 edition of *Young Children with Special Needs* will stand as one of the "lighthouses" for professional preparation in early intervention that will enable future leaders to meet and overcome these challenges in the best interests of some of the youngest and most vulnerable members of our society.

Stephen J. Bagnato, Ed.D
Associate Professor of Pediatrics & Psychology
Director, Early Childhood Partnerships
Child Development Unit
Children's Hospital of Pittsburgh
The UCLID Center at the University of Pittsburgh

Preface

It has been almost 20 years since the first edition of *Young Children with Special Needs* was published, and there was little history to present about the field at that time. How early childhood special education has grown since then! From the first few experimental personnel preparation programs, there have grown dozens. From a few demonstration early intervention programs for preschoolers in each state, there have grown thousands of programs, and early intervention is mandatory in every state for eligible children beginning at birth. From a few experimental curricula and homemade materials, there has grown an industry geared to serving the needs of young children with disabilities and their families. Chapter 1 of the current edition documents this history of early childhood special education that was absent a brief two decades ago when this book first appeared.

The key to successful early intervention has not changed over the years, however. At the center of successful early intervention are competent professionals who are knowledgeable about children, families, and the tools of intervention, and who apply that knowledge in a sensitive and skillful way. The first three chapters in this text provide the reader with an introductory knowledge base about the field, about factors that influence development, and about families. We have made a great effort to present the very latest information and to challenge the reader to think beyond the facts.

This third edition of *Young Children with Special Needs* contains many organizational and philosophical differences from the past editions. We now place greater emphasis on the reader's gaining a deep and broad perspective of how children develop as they do and what can go wrong. For the sake of clarity and consistency, we have standardized terminology. For example, we use the term *early interventionist* to refer to the many different professionals, including and most specifically the early childhood special educator, who provide early intervention services. Most chapters have been realigned to emphasize the information that is most important for early interventionists and to provide as broad a perspective as possible to the reader. Philosophically, we see development as the basis of assessment and diagnosis; it is the foundation upon which interventions are built. The early interventionist who knows child development can feel confident and be supportive of children's and parents' needs. To this end, Chapters 4 through 8 of this text provide the information necessary to make the reader comfortable and confident in his or her knowledge of how children develop. Some of the chapters, such as that on sensorimotor development, have been expanded dramatically. The assessment chapter has been completely rewritten. The emphasis now is on the array of assessment approaches and the process of assessment rather than on instruments. Needless to say, this represents yet another area that has seen significant progress over the past two decades. The new intervention chapter incorporates and expands on material from the program planning and intervention chapters in the earlier edition. We have deleted the chapter on play and integrated the most important elements into other chapters. This change does not imply a disregard for the importance of play, but rather it should be viewed as an attempt to address the extraordinary impact that play can have on all aspects of child development. A new chapter on technology has been added to reflect the elevated role of computers and other technological aids in the education of young children and their families. We also have rearranged the chapters to reflect a knowledge-content-application approach. We believe that the current format is more logical and more conducive to incremental learning by the reader. We have added an epilogue to the text in which we comment on some of the more critical and controversial issues that are raised in the other chapters. We hope this discussion will become the basis for reflection and further investigation by the reader.

The modifications in this edition either reflect what early interventionists have said about the importance of a specific issue and their need for more comprehensive knowledge, or they reflect our own impressions of what early interventionists need to know. In either case, the material often is complex and technical. But mastery of the information will lead to mastery on the job. Any redundancy in information among chapters is intentional, because it reflects both the natural overlap in material from one developmental area to another and that repetition facilitates learning.

We are indebted to our contributors, whose hard work, knowledge, and judgment have resulted in a comprehensive, relevant, and concise text. We would like to express appreciation to these fine professionals who reviewed our manuscript: David W. Anderson, Bethel College; Martha Cook, University of Alabama; Barbara Lowenthal, Northeastern Illinois University; and Phyllis Mayfield, University of Alabama. Special thanks to Ann Davis, Linda Bayma, Genevieve d'Arcy, Linda Gray, and Carol Sykes at Prentice Hall. We all have worked to produce an edition that will continue to be helpful to those who work with young children with special needs and those who want to know more about them.

Warren Umansky

Stephen R. Hooper

Contents

1

Introduction to Young Children with Special Needs

Warren Umansky

There is mounting evidence that early intervention can have a markedly positive effect on the development of infants and preschoolers with some types of disabilities. Partly because of the influence of professional and advocacy organizations, such as the Council for Exceptional Children, the United Cerebral Palsy Association, the Society for Autistic Children, and the Epilepsy Foundation of America, decision makers have become more responsive to the needs of children with disabilities and children who are at risk for disabilities. In addition, the experiences of agencies that offer early intervention programs have contributed to an atmosphere of urgency. These experiences have revealed such benefits of early intervention as long-term savings in program costs as children's needs for complex and expensive services decrease with time.

Not everyone is convinced that early education is successful or necessary, however. Certainly the goal of early childhood special education is an ambitious one: to intervene during the early years to prevent or lessen the effects of harmful biological or environmental influences on a child's development and learning. And it is the broad scope of early education efforts that has provided fuel for the fires of both proponents and skeptics.

The idea of early education did not develop overnight; rather, it evolved slowly and on many fronts simultaneously. For example, animal research conducted by Harlow (1974) with monkeys and by Denenberg and his colleagues (Denenberg, 1981; Denenberg et al., 1981) with rats and rabbits related characteristics of early experience to the animals' subsequent behavior and development. Rats that were raised in a complex environment with visual stimulation were found to have brains that were different from those of rats raised in an impoverished environment (Rosenzweig, et al., 1969). The preponderance of evidence from psychological research supports the significant impact of early experience on development (Haddad & Garralda, 1992; Lizardi, Klein, Ouimette, & Riso, 1995): Enriched experiences can maintain or accelerate development, and deprivation and abusive experiences can contribute to retarded or deviant development.

Medical research has contributed further evidence of the effects of early experiences on development. The effects of nutrition on brain growth and mental development have been found to be significant (Leibowitz, 1991; Read, 1982). Malnourished children tend to develop at a retarded rate and exhibit learning and behavioral deficits as they get older (Galler, Ramsey, Solimano, & Lowell, 1983a; Galler, Ramsey, Solimano, Lowell, & Mason, 1983b; Ricciuti, 1993). Prenatal malnutrition may have a particularly negative impact on the later development of children (Morgane, Austin, Borzino, & Tonkiss, 1993); however, the adverse effects of malnutrition may be overcome by sensory stimulation. Several studies (Winick, Meyer, & Harris, 1975; Yatkin, McLaren, Kanawati, & Sabbach, 1971) revealed that the rate of development and intelligence of severely malnourished children improved to normal ranges when social stimulation was supplemented by individual attention.

In theory, as in practice, attention has focused on early experiences. The works of Freud (1965), Erikson (1963), and Piaget and Inhelder (1969) portray a building-block concept of development in which development is viewed as a structure made up of different levels. The strength and integrity of the lower levels of the structure—the early years—are necessary for stability as more levels are added. Similarly, this chapter lays the foundation for a logical and supportable approach to the education of young children with special needs. Subsequent chapters focus on characteristics of these children and the process for providing high-quality services to them (and their families) to maximize their development and independence.

A Rationale for Early Childhood Special Education

Particularly during times of economic hardship and competition for limited resources, programs that remain and grow are often those with advocates who present the most logical and compelling arguments. Many arguments can be made for committing resources to the education of young children with special needs. Programs throughout the country that have served these children provide firsthand evidence of the benefits of doing so.

Legislation

Until the last half of this century, education for exceptional children was primarily a local and state concern. The federal government made few specific commitments to children with special needs. Its first commitment to special education was the establishment in 1864 of Gallaudet College for the Deaf in Washington, DC, but it was not until 1930 that the federal government directly addressed the issue of special education and established a Section on Exceptional Children and Youth in the Office of Education of the Department of Health, Education, and Welfare. The needs of young children were also addressed through the Children's Bureau of the same department.

The federal government's role in special education remained limited, however, until the 1960s. It did support programs for exceptional children by (1) supplying matching funds to state and local agencies, (2) granting funds for research in all areas of exceptionality, (3) disseminating information, (4) providing consultative services to state and local groups, and (5) distributing fellowships for the training of professionals in all areas related to special education (Kirk & Gallagher, 1983), but a major turning point for federal support of education came in 1965, when Congress passed the Elementary and Secondary Education Act (ESEA). This act and its subsequent amendments (1) made available to schools large amounts of money with which to serve children from 3 to 21 years of age who were educationally disadvantaged and who were disabled, (2) created the Bureau of Education for the Handicapped, and (3) funded research and demonstration projects to improve special education services.

The Handicapped Children's Early Education Assistance Act of 1968 represented the first major federal recognition of the specific importance of early education. The purpose of this legislation was to support model programs throughout the nation that would demonstrate exemplary practices and share their information with others. The act established the Handicapped Children's Early Education Program (HCEEP) to administer and provide technical support for 3-year demonstration programs, called *First Chance* projects. Over the years, this act also funded outreach programs and a Technical Assistance and Development System (TADS) to assist these projects. Now called *NEC*TAS* and engaged in technical assistance, publication, and other support activities, the system continues to be located at the University of North Carolina at Chapel Hill. HCEEP, now called the *Early Education Program for Children with Disabilities* (EEPCD), continues to fund exemplary model programs.

Several hundred other demonstration programs have been funded over the years since 1968. Many former demonstration programs still receive funds to help other agencies adopt their documented models for delivering services to young children with special needs in other geographical areas. Two large studies of demonstration projects have evaluated the projects' efforts in meeting their goals. A Battelle Institute report (1976), although criticized for lack of stringent research procedures, cited developmental gains in children beyond those that would have been expected had intervention not been provided. Subsequent to that study, Littlejohn & Associates (1982) followed up on programs and children who once had been part of the First Chance network and found that 84% of the programs continued to serve children when eligibility for federal funding expired. The outcomes for the children who had been served in the programs also appeared to be favorable. The legislative incentive offered in 1968, then, recognized the importance of the early years, and it appears that mandate has been exercised prudently and effectively. The continued growth of early childhood programs and their benefits to children affirms the logic of this incentive.

Other federal legislation has acknowledged the need for early intervention as well. The Economic Opportunity and Community Partnership Act of 1974 and subsequent amendments to the law required Head Start programs in each state to serve a minimum of 10% children with disabilities. In addition, 14 Resource Access Projects were funded to provide training and technical assistance for improved services to children with disabilities in Head Start programs. In 1994 and 1995, more than 98,000 children with disabilities were served in Head Start programs.

In 1974, amendments to the Education of the Handicapped Act required states without conflicting laws to establish a plan to identify and serve all children with disabilities from birth to 21 years of age. The same philosophy and a similar age range were included in Public Law (P.L.) 94–142, the Education for All Handicapped Children Act of 1975. (Unfortunately, few states fell within this act's mandate because of state laws that defined an older mandatory school age.) In addition, priorities for serving children were established such that states first had to serve school-age children who were receiving no education, then children with severe disabilities who were in inappropriate placement, and, finally, preschool children. Nevertheless, several states passed local legislation to serve young children with special needs. Texas, for example, made programs available from birth to children who needed special services. California offered state funds to any school system that served preschool-aged children with disabilities. Virginia maintained a statewide technical assistance system for preschool teachers of children with disabilities and reimbursed the school system for a large portion of the teachers' salaries. P.L. 94–142 is viewed by some as one of the major pieces of legislation ever passed that has motivated states to provide high-quality education to children with special needs. Amendments to the original law have further expanded and refined services.

P.L. 94–142 contains numerous provisions that apply to children with disabilities of all ages and some that apply to preschool-aged children specifically. Some of the requirements of the original law follow:

1. Public education agencies must ensure that all children who need special education and related services are identified and evaluated.
2. Parents have numerous procedural safeguards that protect the rights of each child with a disability to a free and appropriate education. These safeguards include the rights of parents to do the following:
   a. Review the child's educational records.
   b. Obtain an independent evaluation of the child.
   c. Receive written notice before the school begins the special education placement process.
   d. Request a hearing before an impartial hearing officer to challenge placement or program decisions.
3. The child must receive a comprehensive multidisciplinary educational assessment. Various types of intellectual, social, and cultural information must be considered in the assessment. The process must be repeated at least every 3 years.
4. An individualized education plan (IEP) must be written for every child in special education. Development of the document is a joint effort of school personnel and the parent. The IEP must be reviewed at least annually.
5. To the maximum extent possible, children with disabilities must be educated with their nondisabled peers. Special classes and separate schools can be used only when the nature or severity of the child's disability prohibits education in a more normal setting (Kirk & Gallagher, 1983).

P.L. 94–142 also provided Preschool Incentive Grants to states that identified preschool children in need of special education services. The act allowed states to receive up to $300 for each 3- to 5-year-old child in addition to the funds the act already made available to all children with disabilities. In actuality, considerably less than that amount was available for each child with disabilities; only about an additional $100 was provided by the federal government to states for each identified 3- to 5-year-old in need of special education services.

Legislative action during the past 25 years has left little doubt about the federal commitment to young children with special needs. A major step was taken by Congress in 1986 with the passage of P.L. 99-457. In addition to continuing authorization for services to preschool children with disabilities from age 3 under Section 619 of Title B of the law (the Preschool Grants Program), Title H of the law provided incentives to states to serve children from birth who had special needs or were at risk for later problems. The law specified an increased role for families in services to children from birth through 2 years of age and introduced the individual family service plan (IFSP), which is the equivalent of the IEP but must consider the needs of the whole family relative to the child. States that adopted this initiative were required to have 14 components in place based on a time line specified by the law wherein states had to be prepared to provide full services to infants and toddlers by the fifth year of funding. By the 1993–94 school year, all states were required to assure full implementation. The 14 components required by P.L. 99–457 are presented in Figure 1.1.

In 1991, Congress reauthorized funds for special education programs as the Individuals with Disabilities Education Act (IDEA). This revision of the original law made services for the 3-to-5-year-old population mandatory for states rather than optional. A subsequent authorization changed the funding formula to increase the

FIGURE 1.1 The 14 minimum components of the Public Law 99–457 Part H

1. A definition of "developmentally delayed" to be used by the state in carrying out the program.
2. A timetable for making appropriate services available to all eligible children in the state.
3. Performance of comprehensive multidisciplinary evaluations to determine needs of children and families.
4. Development of individualized family service plans and the provision of case management services.
5. A comprehensive child find and referral system.
6. A public awareness program.
7. A central directory of services, experts, research, and demonstration projects.
8. A comprehensive system of personnel development.
9. A single line of authority in a lead agency designated or established by the governor.
10. A policy pertaining to contracting or making arrangements with local service providers.
11. A procedure for timely reimbursement of funds.
12. Procedural safeguards.
13. Policies and procedures for personnel standards.
14. A system for compiling data regarding the early intervention programs.

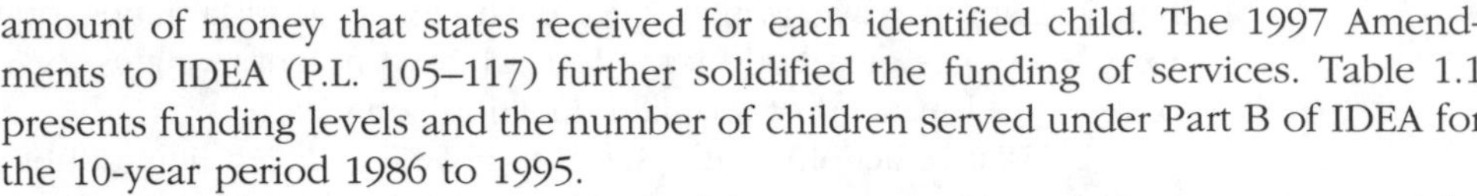

amount of money that states received for each identified child. The 1997 Amendments to IDEA (P.L. 105–117) further solidified the funding of services. Table 1.1 presents funding levels and the number of children served under Part B of IDEA for the 10-year period 1986 to 1995.

About 600,000 children with disabilities ages 3 through 5 are now served by preschool programs supported by IDEA. Over 150,000 infants and toddlers through age 2 and their families currently are receiving early intervention services under Part H of IDEA; Table 1.2 presents the settings in which infants and toddlers receive such services. IDEA provides other services that are beneficial to young children with special needs and their families. For example, the law provides continued funding for demonstration service projects (formerly First Chance projects), for research projects and demonstration personnel training projects, and for research institutes of early intervention. During the 1993–94 school year, 116 projects were funded. These included 34 model demonstration projects, 45 outreach projects, 21 in-service training projects, 4 experimental projects, 6 research institutes, 5 statewide data system projects, and 1 national technical assistance center. A description of these projects is presented in Figure 1.2. Finally, IDEA provides funds to states for personnel preparation programs and specifies that each state must have a Comprehensive System of Personnel Development (CSPD) plan to prepare its personnel.

The successful application of other federal laws to young children with special needs offers further support for the rights of these children to early education opportunities. Section 504 of the Rehabilitation Act of 1973 prohibits discrimination

TABLE 1.1 Summary of the Preschool Grants Program, Section 619, Part B, of the Individuals with Disabilities Education Act

FISCAL YEAR	APPROPRIATIONS (IN MILLIONS OF DOLLARS)	NUMBER OF CHILDREN SERVED	AMOUNT ALLOCATED PER CHILD (IN DOLLARS)
1986	28	261,000	110
1987	180	265,000	679
1988	201	288,000	697
1989	247	323,000	769
1990	251	352,000	713
1991	292	367,000	797
1992	320	398,000	804
1993	326	441,000	738
1994	339	479,000	708
1995	360	528,000	683

Source: From *Progress in Providing Services to Young Children with Special Needs and Their Families: An Overview to and Update on Implementing the Individuals with Disabilities Education Act (IDEA)* (NEC*TAS notes No. 7) (p. 16) by P. L. Trohanis, 1995, Chapel Hills, NC: NEC*TAS. Copyright 1995 by NEC*TAS. Reprinted by permission.

TABLE 1.2 Number of Infants and Toddlers in Different Settings Receiving Services Under Part H of the Individuals with Disabilities Education Act as of December 1, 1992

SETTING	NUMBER OF CHILDREN
Early intervention classroom	36,486
Family day care	698
Home	40,826
Hospital (inpatient)	8,096
Outpatient service facility	37,390
Regular nursery school/day care	4,441
Residential facility	105
Other settings	10,982
All settings	139,021

Source: From *Seventeenth Annual Report to Congress on the Implementation of the Individuals with Disabilities Education Act* (p. 47) by the U.S. Department of Education, 1996, Washington, DC: U.S. Government Printing Office.

on the basis of disability in any state or local government program or activity that receives federal funds. A regulation added in 1977 specifies the applicability of Section 504 to public school districts and other recipients of federal funds in education, health, and social services. These agencies, including schools, must ensure that children with disabilities are not excluded from services or denied benefits. Title II of the Americans with Disabilities Act of 1990 provides similar protection of rights.

In 1994, Congress passed the Goals 2000: Educate America Act. As of April 1995, 45 states had received funds under the Goals 2000 Act. States may use the funds in any number of ways to meet the goals of improved academic achievement and greater parental and community involvement. The justification for early intervention support under Goals 2000 is Goal 1, that all children will start school ready to learn.

Clearly, there is now tangible evidence to support the prudence of government involvement in early childhood intervention. While government action initially was a response to pressure from advocacy groups and legislators with family members or friends with disabilities, federal and state legislative and regulatory activities currently reflect growing acceptance of early education.

Empirical Evidence

Factors that cause impairment in a child are present even before birth. The gene pool of the mother and father as well as the level and extent of prenatal care contribute to the outcome of pregnancy. Research literature continues to identify specific factors that have an impact during pregnancy and influence the subsequent health and well-being of the child. Intervention in the areas of maternal nutrition

FIGURE 1.2 Focus of representative projects funded through IDEA (fiscal year 1994)

DEMONSTRATION PROJECTS (34)
- Unique needs of children with low-incidence disabilities, such as deaf/blind
- Use of technology to enhance services for young children with disabilities
- Multidisciplinary intervention services
- Interagency collaboration in provision of services
- Family and professional collaboration
- Examination of differing service delivery models
- Coordination between public and private agencies
- Curriculum and materials development
- Services for infants with special health needs

OUTREACH PROJECTS (45)
- Replication of demonstration projects in various geographical locations with diverse populations

IN-SERVICE TRAINING PROJECTS (21)
- Improvement of skills for personnel already involved in providing services to young children with disabilities

EXPERIMENTAL PROJECTS (4)
- Language instruction
- Intervention in inclusive versus segregated settings
- Bilingual/bicultural training for preschoolers who are deaf
- Paraprofessional training systems

RESEARCH INSTITUTES (6)
- Cost and effectiveness of early intervention
- Intervention for children affected by parental substance abuse
- Challenges and barriers to preschool inclusive service delivery
- Developmental care and intervention in the neonatal intensive-care unit
- Influences on service patterns and utilization in early intervention and preschool programs
- Barriers to inclusion in educational, cultural, and community contexts

STATEWIDE DATA SYSTEM PROJECTS (5)
- Expand states' capabilities for tracking and linking services for children with disabilities

NATIONAL TECHNICAL ASSISTANCE CENTER (1)
- NEC*TAS at Chapel Hill provides a variety of support services to projects funded through IDEA

Source: Summarized from *Seventeenth Annual Report to Congress on the Implementation of the Individuals with Disabilities Education Act* by the U.S. Department of Education, 1996, Washington, DC: U.S. Government Printing Office.

and child-rearing attitudes have yielded optimistic results (Badger, 1981; Ramey & Bryant, 1982). Further, revelations from the Human Genome Project offer hope of prenatal identification and even prenatal treatment for many genetically based disorders. The Human Genome Project is a 15-year, federally funded program whose goal is to identify the functions of each of the 100,000 human genes.

Once a child is born with a disabling condition, of course, a different set of factors must be dealt with. The accumulating evidence indicates that results of efforts to remediate or attenuate children's deficits also can be successful.

Investigations of early intervention have focused on two major groups of children: those who exhibit developmental deficits as a result of environmental factors and those who are disabled as a result of biological factors. These two groups of children comprise the majority of the special education population in public school programs. A question that must be asked is: If these children had been identified and served earlier, could something have been done to make special education placement less likely or, at least, to reduce the severity of the children's problems? While more evidence exists to support the benefits of early intervention for children at environmental risk (Ramey & Ramey, 1994), research that supports services for young children with biological impairments also is growing. This body of research is riddled with procedural problems such as small sample size, lack of comparison groups, a short period of intervention, and poorly defined intervention procedures (Gallagher, 1991). Even when these problems are considered, however, early intervention with biologically impaired children appears to be effective for maintaining or accelerating their rate of development (Blair, Ramey, & Hardin, 1995; Boyce, Smith, Immel, & Casto, 1993; Fewell & Oelwein, 1991). Various components of early intervention may have greater impact than others (Shonkoff, Hauser, Krauss, & Upshur, 1992).

The earliest study of contemporary importance concerning children at environmental risk was the classic work of Skeels (1966). A group of children in an institutional facility were moved to an orphanage where they received individualized attention from older residents, in contrast to the considerable deprivation experienced by the children who remained in the institution. As time passed, children who remained in the original setting showed an average decrease in measured intelligence while children in the new setting showed significant increases in measured intelligence, apparently as a result of the greater attention they received.

Research on the influence of early education received great impetus when prominent scholars such as Bloom (1964) and Hunt (1961) emphasized the sensitive nature of children's earliest years. Federal funding of programs to serve disadvantaged preschool children provided researchers with an opportunity to explore the application of their theories through various approaches to early intervention. In the mid–1970s, a group of individuals who had directed these model programs gathered to review the progress of the children they had served. The Consortium for Longitudinal Studies (1978) issued several reports based on their review (Lazar & Darlington, 1982). Longitudinal results also were reported independently for the Perry Preschool Project in Michigan (Schweinhart & Weikart, 1980) and the DARCEE Project in Tennessee (Gray, Ramsey, & Klaus, 1982). The Consortium for Longitudinal

Studies and Perry Preschool reports described the following outcomes for children who had received early intervention compared to children who had not:

1. The number of special education placements and children who were retained in grade was significantly smaller for the early intervention groups when they entered school.
2. These children attained higher achievement test scores and were more committed to school.
3. Members of this group were less likely to show delinquent behavior outside of school or to get into legal trouble.

These are the more conservative outcomes of early intervention, representing the human aspect of the benefits. That is, children are more productive and perform better within and outside of school when they receive early intervention. The other aspect of the benefits is equally meaningful. Significant financial gains are realized as a result of serving preschoolers with disabilities from the youngest age possible. Studies on the cost-effectiveness of early intervention generally are in agreement that schools quickly recover the costs of early intervention through savings in the lesser amount of special services required and in less retention in grade. The cumulative cost of serving a child through age 18 decreases in proportion to how early intervention begins (Wood, 1981). Savings to society continue after and outside of school. Children who receive early intervention are less likely than those who do not to use public funds for maintenance in prison, for welfare payments, or for unemployment compensation. They are more likely to obtain gainful employment after school and to pay taxes (Weber, Foster, & Weikart, 1978).

Palmer (1983), one of the Consortium for Longitudinal Studies members, urged caution in interpretation and generalization of the results. Gray (1983), another member, responding to comments that the outcome of her own project did not match the enthusiastic results of some other projects, placed intervention into perspective by noting that the families with whom her project worked had multiple and severe problems, including extreme poverty. She also noted that, compared with the amount of time a project child spent in impoverished surroundings, "the total input from our program occupied about two-thirds of one percent of the waking hours of the participants from birth to 18 years" (p. 128).

Several contemporary longitudinal studies provide additional insight into the influences of early intervention. For example, in a review of results of three long-term studies of children from low-income and undereducated families, Ramey and Ramey (1994) concluded that

> Maternal intelligence is a key factor in children's intellectual development, especially when these children are not provided with intensive early intervention. Fortunately, children whose mothers have low IQs respond positively to intensive, high-quality early intervention, which leads to a dramatic reduction in their rates of mental retardation during the intervention program. (p. 1066)

Another study followed a large cohort of infants living in poverty (Bradley, Whiteside, Mundfrom, & Casey, 1994). The Infant Health and Development Program found that, at 3 years of age, certain home factors and participation in the early intervention program differentiated those children who showed early signs of coping with environmental demands ("resiliency") from those who did not. The latter group was identified as having a poorer developmental prognosis. A study of specific types of early intervention with a low-birth-weight subgroup of this cohort found that the treatment group had significantly higher IQ scores than the children who did not receive early intervention services (Brooks–Gunn, McCarton, Casey, & McCormick, 1994).

A summary review of the evidence supports the benefits of early intervention on both personal and financial levels. More systematic research on biologically impaired children is needed, but the available evidence suggests a justification for early intervention. Of course, one must weigh anticipated outcomes against the intensity and duration of the intervention, and the intervention approach must be clearly delineated (see Chapter 11).

Ethical Considerations

Individuals with special needs are likely to be dependent on others throughout their lives. Their dependence can be extremely burdensome financially and in terms of the quantity of resources. The cost of maintaining one person who is disabled in a state institution, for example, can exceed $50,000 per year. Within the community, adults with disabilities often require special housing, transportation, health services, sheltered employment or work training, food and clothing subsidies, and other support. The constant dependence of the individual on others and the inability to break away from the dependency promotes what Sameroff (1979) has called "learned incompetence." Continued dependence also contributes to negative attitudes on the part of the public toward people with disabilities. When so much public money is spent on expensive services for a small percentage of the population, a society under economic stress often looks for a scapegoat. The problem is compounded when resources are channeled to individuals with disabilities when it is too late to do more than support a subsistence level of living. Certainly, the evidence shows only limited success for intervention with older school-aged children and adults with disabilities.

The ethical arguments for early intervention, then, encompass three issues: (1) preventing the child from learning incompetence by promoting greater independence, (2) removing the continued burden to society by reducing the child's long-term needs for intensive and expensive resources, and (3) changing the public's attitudes toward individuals who are disabled by demonstrating the success of early intervention programs in decreasing their dependence on public support.

Ethical considerations in support of early childhood special education should be as important as empirical evidence. The forces that motivated passage of the Americans with Disabilities Act and those that refocused the attention of Americans on the future of our youth appear to be maintaining momentum to support educational opportunities for young children with special needs. But this trend could change quickly because Congress and the states reconsider funding and priorities on a regular basis. Early childhood special educators and early interventionists play a critical and challenging role in this advocacy process as well as being competent deliverers of high-quality services. They are in a position that demands both the persuasive discourse and oratory of a journalist and the controlled militarism of one who has seen battles on the front lines. The challenge is keen, but the outcomes are tangible and offer a significant contribution to individuals and to society.

The Early Childhood Special Educator

Teacher Roles

The professional who works with young children with special needs and their families is called by many titles and wears many hats: those of teacher, social worker, psychologist, counselor, and public relations person. This is not always by design, but often out of necessity. The early childhood special educator may, after all, work in a public school classroom, in a center-based program operated by a nonschool agency, in a clinical setting, in a consulting capacity, or in the home, and he or she works with a population with which few people have much experience. Consequently, the teacher becomes the resource for the parent, for education colleagues, and for community agency personnel.

The teacher has several primary tasks. Ultimate responsibility for program planning and implementation belongs to the teacher, who may base the intervention approach on a central theoretical scheme or on a more generalized eclectic scheme. (See Chapter 11 for a discussion of program models.) In either case, the teacher should be able to justify the particular program used with any child.

Program implementation for a young child often demands identification of the many factors that influence development and learning. Recognition of the importance of the home environment and family members in this process frequently draws early intervention programs toward a homebound model, but, as we shall see, there are many ways to make an impact on a young child.

The role of early childhood special educators encompasses great diversity and requires certain personal qualities: quick thinking, flexibility, diplomacy, scholarship, and an inner drive for accomplishment. The daily schedule of an early childhood special educator in a school system reflects the uniqueness of the job:

> *The first thing I do when I arrive in the morning is to go over the daily schedule with my "parapro" (paraprofessional), Ken. He's the best; I couldn't do without him! We have two groups of six parents and their children who come into school three times each week. One group comes Monday, Wednesday, and Friday; the other group Tuesday, Thursday, and Friday. Fridays get a little hairy, but it does the parents and kids so much good to get together with each other.*

So my "parapro" and I start the day reviewing what we will do with the morning group. They are here from 9 until 11:30 and get our total attention during that time. From 11:30 to 12, we talk over what occurred, jot down notes, and transfer any data we collected to the kids' folders. It really helps for us to keep an ongoing record of the kids' progress just so we can feel we're making a difference. And the parents really appreciate it, too.

We usually brown-bag lunch at one of the local agencies in the area or go out for lunch with a few of the welfare caseworkers, public health nurses, school psychologists, or whoever is available. It helps us to know what's going on in other agencies and it sure helps for them to know us. A lot of our kids use other community resources, and it's nice to be able to pick up the phone and say, "Hi, Nick. Enjoyed lunch yesterday. By the way, I think Ms. Jones is having some problems again with Toni's braces. I'd appreciate it if you'd give her a call today." It works! And our colleagues around town do the same with us. Martha called me yesterday because she knew Ken had a visit scheduled with one of our mutual families. Martha wanted Ken to remind the family about their appointment at the orthopedic clinic next week. Happy to do it! It's also a lot more efficient than professionals tripping over each other trying to get to the family. Some of our families are followed by five or more agencies. Can you imagine all those visitors coming and going in your home!

Well, Ken and I each have two home visits scheduled for the afternoon. One of my visits today is to screen a new child for the program. The others are to continue working through our curriculum with the children and families.

I head back to school today after the visits for a staffing on another new child. Sometimes the special education director runs the staffing, but I'll be running this one. I was a little scared the first few times I ran staffings. I've settled in now and just try to get the parent and the other people there to share their thoughts on what the child needs. Everyone's concern for the child and desire to do the best thing usually come through loud and clear. And I think that some of my colleagues who hadn't thought much about serving disabled preschoolers are becoming really strong advocates for the program!

Today's a little longer day than usual. I speak to a church group this evening. They have a lot of kids in their neighborhood who have dropped out of school or have graduated but don't have jobs. I think I'd like to use some of them on a volunteer basis in our class. Maybe after they're trained, they'll be able to get a good job at a local childcare center. The programs need good people, and we could sure use a few extra sets of trained hands around our kids.

No question about it, it's a challenging job. But we love it. Ken and I enjoy working with the children, of course, but the opportunities to work with

> *parents and other community people make us feel that we're doing the most efficient job of addressing the total needs of the kids and helping to change community attitudes, too.*

The early interventionist who works with the infant and toddler program of the community public health agency also brings his or, in this case, her own perspectives:

> *Sometimes my first visit with the child and parent is in the hospital right after the child is born. When an obvious disability is identified, the physician or hospital social worker calls us to begin the process of parent education and preparation for what is likely to be ahead. Having a young child of my own has made me a lot more sensitive to how I approach the parents. I recognize their many months of building happy expectations for a healthy baby, their desire but sometimes reluctance to accept and love the child, and the complications resulting from the impact that early medical interventions (neonatal intensive care units, technological devices, and limited physical contact, for example) may have on the parent-child relationship. And we talk about these issues. We talk about how I can help the family when the baby gets home and start talking about other family and community support resources that are available.*

Teacher Competencies

It is relatively easy to see that an untrained person will not do well in the tasks just described. The complex roles that early childhood special educators take on require careful training and ongoing clarification of professional responsibilities (Buysse & Wesley, 1993). Certain minimum entry-level skills and knowledge are necessary to do an adequate job. Experience as well as further knowledge and skill allows the teacher to meet the challenges of the position with confidence and competence.

The complexity of the teacher's role may be thought of as a matrix with at least four dimensions:

1. the age of the child may range from newborn to 5 years or older
2. the setting may be a hospital, the home, a clinic, a special preschool classroom, a parent-child group, or an inclusive setting with nondisabled children and children with disabilities together
3. the individuals involved in the intervention may be the child, the parents and other family members, community agency personnel, health professionals, and others representing a variety of cultures and backgrounds
4. the task may be assessment, intervention, counseling and education, evaluation, report writing, case management, or coordination of a staffing

Even without complete agreement among professionals about the order of importance of skills and knowledge (Hanson & Lovett, 1992), several competencies stand out logically for the early childhood special educator, as one teacher tells us:

> *I couldn't believe all I was called upon to do and all I felt that I needed to do. It helps to enjoy the work and to be really committed to it. I believe it was Weikart (1981) who found that one's commitment to whatever approach is used is more closely related to the child's outcome than any one particular approach over another. Of course, the interventionist should know child development backward and forward and be ready to be amazed when a child does something unexpected!*
>
> *I think I know what I'm doing. Each time I interact professionally with a child or parent or colleague I know what I want to accomplish and I have a plan to accomplish it. I also keep some alternate plans in my "back pocket." Flexibility helps!*
>
> *I find it important to speak several languages, also. A language for parents and volunteers that is free of the professional jargon. Jargon can lose them really quickly. And there are the languages of the other professionals. I've learned a lot about occupational therapy, speech therapy, physical therapy, medications, and all types of physical and health problems that my kids have. I've had to if I am to keep my credibility with my colleagues. They've learned my language, too. I like the continuous learning aspect of the job anyway. It does a lot to prevent burnout.*
>
> *Screening and assessing kids came pretty easy to me because I had done a lot in my university training program. I learned about a few more testing instruments pretty quickly, which let me concentrate on the child and parent instead of the test manual during a testing session. The school psychologist hasn't had much experience testing really young kids, so we work together most of the time. Testing young kids is tough even when you know what you're doing. I want to be sure we do everything possible to get an accurate assessment, so it's good that we work together.*
>
> *What blew me away the most in my job was a late night call I got from one of my parents. We had become close—it happens when you go into people's homes regularly and share their emotional highs and lows. Her child had been in the hospital with respiratory complications. The child had just died and I was the first person that the mom had thought to call. I wasn't prepared for that moment and was pretty disappointed that I couldn't do more. But maybe the fact that I was there to listen was enough for the parent at the time. I at least know now how, ideally, to deal with a situation like that—what to say, what to do. I've done some reading and talking to people about it.*

It's a difficult balance to maintain when you work with parents of kids with disabilities. You want to remain objective but you need to give them support and get them actively involved in supporting their kids. I've got lots more learning to do but I'm sure working on it.

I get a lot of satisfaction out of seeing how far the classroom part of the program has progressed. It's taken a bunch of work to make the parents feel comfortable with me and with each other, and I think they could run the program themselves now (with a little guidance every once in a while). The routine we established for the sessions has helped. We try hard to model for the parents and to give them good feedback when they interact with their kids. Our parents also are becoming better able to identify the resources that they and their children need in the community. They seem more confident calling the health department or physician or counseling center, for example. I hope that we've helped to build their skills to mobilize community resources. Just as we're trying to teach the children to be more independent in making choices and decisions, we're trying to make parents less dependent upon us. That's not easy and sometimes I feel so tempted to make the call for the parent or handle a child's temper tantrum or bring toys into the home or do for the parents what they are ready to do for themselves. It's taken some time for me to know how fast to move with different families, and I still make mistakes. But I feel pretty comfortable now discussing my fallibility with the parents and they understand!

The early childhood special educator must have a broad knowledge base and diverse skills. For a good foundation, teachers must know where to seek needed information and skill-building experiences. Above all, they must recognize their own limitations. Teachers should use to the maximum extent possible public and university libraries, teacher centers, and community resource people.

Over the course of the past several years, communities have made efforts to offer programs to young children with disabilities in the same settings as their nondisabled peers. This movement toward capitalizing on inclusive settings has demanded an examination of the practices used by programs that serve young children.

The National Association for the Education of Young Children (NAEYC) published a position paper in 1991 entitled *Developmentally Appropriate Practice in Early Childhood Programs Serving Children from Birth to Age 8* (Bredekamp, 1991). This document of general philosophy and program guidelines for early childhood educators led to the publication of a similar document for early childhood special educators by the Division for Early Childhood (DEC) of the Council for Exceptional Children. *DEC Recommended Practices: Indicators of Quality in Programs for Infants and Young Children with Special Needs and Their Families* (DEC Task Force on Recommended Practices, 1993) provides the early childhood special educator with excellent guidelines against which to evaluate one's philosophy, knowledge, and skills. There are many similarities between the developmentally appropriate practices (DAP) presented by NAEYC and DEC. However, the philosophical differences, characterized by a developmental approach in early childhood education (ECE) versus a remedial-prescriptive approach in early childhood special education (ECSE), have spurred considerable debate in the literature (Fox, Hanline, Vail, & Galant, 1994; Odom & McEvoy, 1990). The differences, however, do not appear to be an impediment for either discipline to work together for the good of each child and family. Furthermore, the changing faces of both ECE and ECSE within the community setting encourage a drawing together of the content of both documents:

> Analyses of the components of DAP reveal that practices valued by ECSE are not incompatible with what has been stated as important in educating typically developing children. In the areas of curriculum, adult-child interaction, and developmental evaluation, the practices that are important to ECSE fit within the breadth of what is considered developmentally appropriate. Furthermore, there appears to be a trend in ECSE, with a growing empirical base, to move towards interventions that reflect the practices articulated by NAEYC and away from a narrow, remedial approach to early intervention. (Fox, Hanline, Vail, & Galant, 1994, p. 253)

The unity of ECE and ECSE is reflected in the collaborative position paper by DEC, the Association of Teacher Educators, and NAEYC entitled *Personnel Standards for Early Education and Early Intervention* (1994). This document offers a framework for the preparation of professionals to serve a unique population and a standardization of minimum competencies. The competent early childhood special educator is one who:

- is knowledgeable about child development and disabilities
- follows a theoretical intervention model and can justify the approach
- supports and responds to children and parents but promotes their independence
- adapts quickly to new and demanding situations
- administers and interprets preschool test instruments
- interacts productively with colleagues, children, and parents
- evaluates program success routinely and systematically
- utilizes available resources to better understand and meet the needs of children and their families
- functions well in a variety of settings
- adapts to the cultural differences of families
- encourages and accepts input related to development and modification from families and other sources

Young Children with Special Needs and Their Families

Who Are Young Children with Special Needs?

IDEA defines children with disabilities as those children with mental retardation, hearing impairments including deafness, speech or language impairments, visual

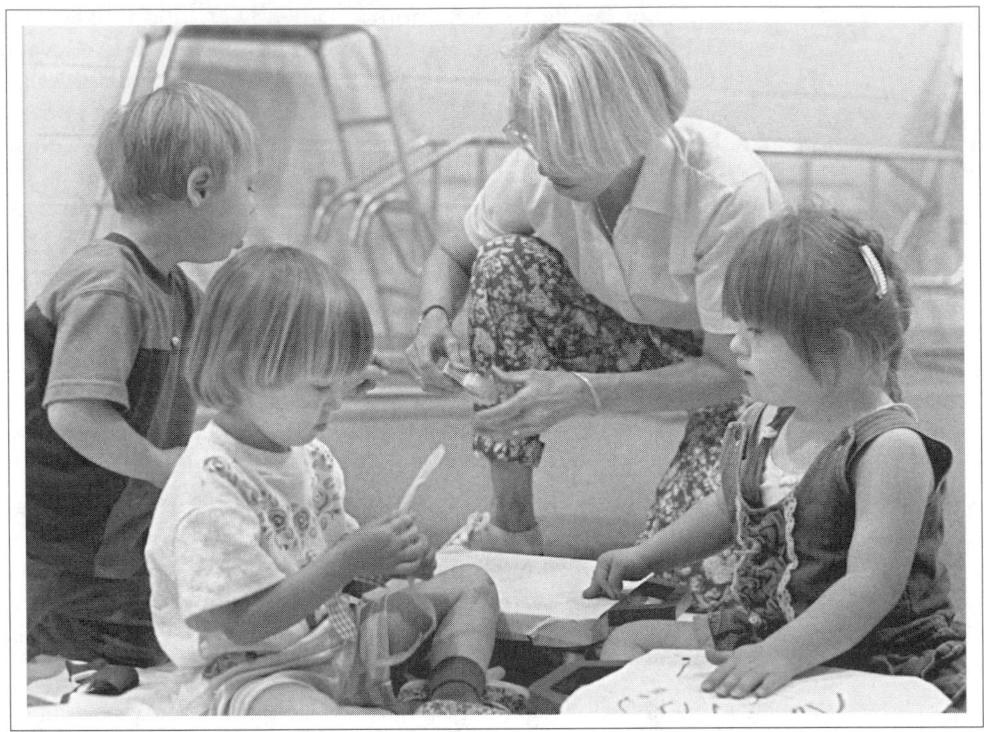

For children with disabilities, legislation and research have provided support for early intervention services.

impairments including blindness, serious emotional disturbance, orthopedic impairments, autism, traumatic brain injury, other health impairments, specific learning disabilities, deaf-blindness, or multiple disabilities, and who because of those impairments need special education and related services (34 CFR, Ch. 111, Section 300.7 (a) (1), p. 13). Any child from birth through 21 years of age who meets the specific criteria for any of these categories may be eligible for services. For infants and toddlers, states also may choose to serve, under Part H of IDEA, children who are at biological or environmental risk for one of the specified disabilities. For children from 3 years of age, under Part B of IDEA, states may serve children who are experiencing "developmental delays" as defined by the state using objective measures of physical, cognitive, social-emotional, and adaptive development. The 1997 Amendments to IDEA changed the limitation on the use of the "developmental delay" category to age 9.

There is a sound rationale for serving young children in at-risk and developmentally delayed categories. The range of variations in development is considerable, even in a group of children of the same chronological age, sex, and ethnic group (Wolff, 1981). In some children, the variation is so extreme that identification of a problem is relatively easy. In such cases, a child may clearly fit into a category described by IDEA. However, Behr and Gallagher (1981) propose that a more flexible definition is needed for young children who might have special needs not so much as a result of the extent of the developmental variation as of the type of variation. This would include those children who, prior to their third birthday, have a "high probability of manifesting, in later childhood, a sensory motor deficit and/or mental handicap which may be the result of a birth defect, disease process, trauma, or environmental conditions present during the prenatal and/or postnatal periods" (p. 114).

The advantage of a more flexible definition for young children with special needs, in particular, is that more serious impairments can be prevented by serving a child early. Children from poor environments are overrepresented in special education classes in the public schools relative to their number in the general population. Successful efforts have been reported with many different high-risk populations to prevent minor developmental delays from becoming serious impairments (Brooks-Gunn, McCarton, Casey, & McCormick, 1994; Campbell & Ramey, 1994; Meyer-Probst, Teichmann, Hayes, & Rauh, 1991). By offering incentives to serve young children prior to the appearance of a clearly identifiable disability, the government thus may prevent more serious impairments as children grow up.

In our discussions in this text, we approach children's needs from a developmental perspective. A framework of normal development underlies descriptions of how children vary from the normal pattern and what programmatic modifications are helpful to support learning. We also have included information on how specific types of disabilities influence development in each skill area. Table 1.2 indicates the number of young children by disability area who are receiving special education under IDEA. A brief description of these disability areas follows.

Mental Retardation (Intellectual Disability). The definition of *mental retardation* used most often was developed by the American Association on Mental Deficiency (AAMD): Mental retardation refers to significantly subaverage general intellectual functioning existing concurrently with deficits in adaptive behavior and manifested during the developmental period (Grossman, 1977, p. 7).

Intellectual functioning has traditionally been assessed by performance on intelligence tests. Figure 1.3 shows the theoretical distribution of scores on a standardized intelligence test. It has become commonplace to provide labels for different levels of retardation. A score between 1 and 2 standard deviations below the mean (70–85) characterizes a borderline intellectually subnormal child. Mentally retarded children are those who score greater than 2 standard deviations below the mean of 100, an intelligence quotient of less than approximately 70. The levels of retardation are

Mild or educable mental retardation	55–69 IQ*
Moderate or trainable retardation	40–54 IQ
Severe mental retardation	25–39 IQ
Profound mental retardation	Below 25 IQ

* IQ = (mental age/chronological age) × 100

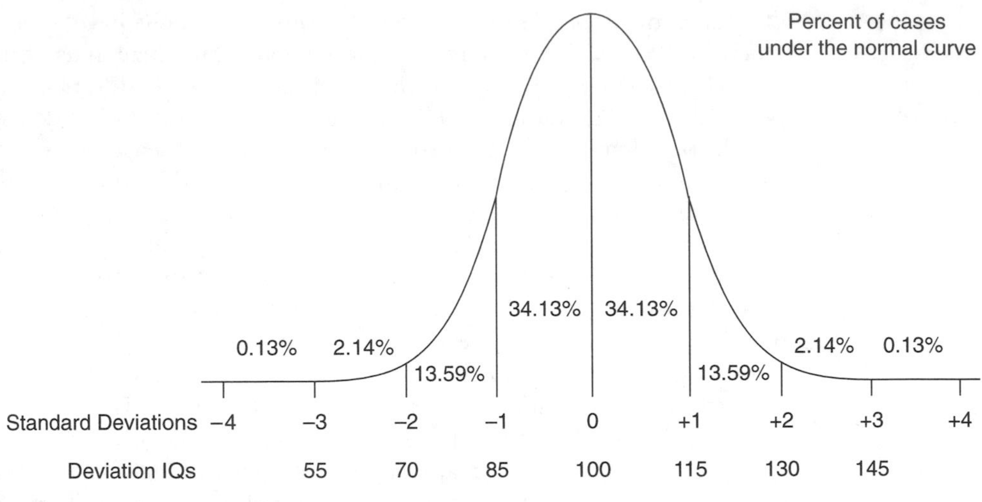

FIGURE 1.3 The theoretical distribution of IQ scores

The AAMD recently modified the definition of *mental retardation* to abolish levels based on cognitive dysfunction, as described previously, to differentiate cases of mental retardation based on "needed levels of support (MacMillan, Siperstein, & Gresham, 1996). It appears, however, that categorization based on the original definition persists and that the newer definition has been largely ignored.

Adaptive behavior describes a child's ability to deal with worldly demands. This may encompass components of communication skills, self-help skills, social skills, and psychomotor skills. Demands vary from setting to setting. A child therefore may show deficits in adaptive behavior and be considered mentally retarded in some settings but not in others. What constitutes mental retardation, however, is both subaverage intellectual functioning *and* deficits in adaptive behavior.

The characteristics of a child who is mentally retarded depend predominantly on the child's mental age, which is derived from an intelligence test. The more severely mentally retarded a child is, the greater the disparity between mental age and chronological age will be. Children of the same chronological age, then, may display very different characteristics. Mental age, more than chronological age, reflects a child's current level of ability and determines educational needs. It should be noted that few standardized intelligence tests are available and statistically sound for preschool children, particularly for infants and toddlers. Consequently, other strategies and instrumentation may be employed to measure the intellectual capabilities of these children.

Hearing Impairments. Hearing losses are characterized by degree and type. Hearing is measured in units of intensity (i.e., loudness) and frequency (i.e., pitch). A child with normal hearing can hear sounds as soft as 0 to 25 decibels (dB) within a frequency range of approximately 40 to 4000 hertz (Hz). Most conversational speech has an intensity of about 55 dB and a frequency range of 500 to 2000 Hz. A child with a hearing loss of greater than 40 dB will probably miss a considerable amount of spoken information; a profound loss of greater than 90 dB will severely disable a child.

A hearing loss may be conductive or sensorineural. Conductive losses are caused by interference with the sequence of sound vibrations reaching the auditory nerve. Sensorineural losses are caused by defects in the inner ear or in the auditory nerve, which transmits electrical impulses to the brain for interpretation.

Hearing impairments may result from infection during the prenatal or postnatal period, from an accident, or from exposure to certain prescription drugs. The severity of the impairment depends on the degree of loss and the age of onset. A mild loss may allow a child to benefit completely from an auditory environment. A more severe loss may require alternative communication systems and modifications to the environment. In addition, a hearing loss that occurs prior to a child's learning language requires greater environmental modifications than a loss that occurs after mastery of language. Deafness is defined in IDEA as a hearing impairment that is so severe that a child is impaired in processing linguistic information through hearing, with or without amplification, and that the child's educational performance is thus adversely affected. Further discussion of hearing impairments is provided in Chapter 7.

Speech and Language Disorders. Because of differences in the rates of development of young children, it is difficult to clearly define what is and what is not a disorder. Certainly, some structural and functional aspects stand out as being atypical. For example, a child with a cleft palate who uses no words at 4 years of age or whose language is limited to repetition of what others say clearly can be categorized as having disordered speech and language. But the absence of certain speech sounds at times may reflect a disorder and at other times not. Great care must be taken in identifying a child as fitting this category, particularly when cultural diversity and environment play such critical roles in forming children's speech and language patterns.

Impairments of speech and language frequently accompany other disabilities and, in fact, may be the first suggestion of problems. Children with hearing impairments, cerebral palsy, emotional disturbances, or mental retardation all may exhibit atypical speech and language.

The ability of a child to communicate functionally is a requirement for independent living. A child who is unable to express needs and wants or to interact verbally and appropriately with other children and adults is at a serious disadvantage. Consequently, speech and language disorders must receive careful attention as soon as problems are identified.

Visual Impairments. A child is considered to be blind if visual acuity is poorer than 20/200 in the better eye after correction or if the field of vision is limited to an angle of less than 20 degrees. A child with partial sight has an acuity of less than 20/70 but greater than 20/200. An acuity of 20/200 indicates that a child can see at 20 feet what a person with normal vision can see at 200 feet.

In education, children often are categorized in terms of their potential as either print or braille readers. Preschool children with visual impairments whose vision is too poor for them to benefit from even large-print materials should begin a program that sensitizes them to tactile learning materials. This provides an introduction to subsequent learning of pre-braille and braille reading skills.

Most problems in young children are attributable to prenatal factors. Infections, such as rubella, and certain hereditary factors may manifest themselves in blindness at birth or create a likelihood that a child will require special education services.

Serious Emotional Disturbance. The causes of severe emotional disturbance in young children are not well understood. Some experts attribute such problems to environmental factors and others to neurological or chemical factors. Strategies used to remediate emotional disturbance usually reflect the theoretical orientation of the program staff. Some programs may adjust the child's diet, others may restructure her physical environment, and still others may plan her interactions with other objects and people. It is most likely, however, that emotional disturbance encompasses many different types of problems, some biologically based and others environmentally based. Certainly, the variety of behaviors that characterize a child with emotional disturbance may be quite diverse: anxiety, withdrawal, aggression, impulsiveness, extreme fear, and so on. Diagnosis is based on the frequency, duration, and intensity of these behaviors.

Serious emotional disturbance is defined in IDEA as a condition exhibiting one or more of the following characteristics over a long period of time and to a degree that adversely affects a child's educational performance:

- an inability to learn that cannot be explained by intellectual, sensory, or health factors
- an inability to build or maintain satisfactory interpersonal relationships with peers and teachers
- inappropriate types of behavior or feelings under normal circumstances
- a general pervasive mood of unhappiness or depression
- a tendency to develop physical symptoms or a physical focus associated with personal or school problems

Orthopedic Impairments. The category of orthopedic impairments is so broad that it is difficult to identify many general characteristics. Any condition that interferes with the health or normal functioning of bones, joints, or muscles qualifies as an orthopedic impairment. Defects such as spina bifida, club feet, or cerebral palsy may be present at birth; other problems, such as amputations, may occur later in childhood.

Causes of orthopedic impairments are as diverse as the problems themselves. Some are a result of hereditary factors and some are a result of the influence of infection or toxic substances on the mother, particularly during the first trimester of pregnancy. Other impairments may be traced to birth injuries or to diseases or accidents after birth.

Many children with orthopedic impairments require no special education services. Adaptive equipment for some children may help them function independently in a normal setting. Special education staff may help children adjust to their impairment and adapt to the demands of their environment.

Other Health Impairments. Based on the definition in IDEA, children in this category have limited strength, vitality, or alertness as a result of chronic or acute health problems related to a heart condition, tuberculosis, rheumatic fever, nephritis, asthma, sickle cell anemia, hemophilia, epilepsy, lead poisoning, leukemia, diabetes, or other conditions that adversely affect a child's educational performance.

Recent amendments to IDEA added two categories of disability: autism and traumatic brain injury. As defined by the law, *autism* is a developmental disability that significantly affects verbal and nonverbal communication and social interaction, is generally evident before age 3, and adversely affects a child's educational performance. Other characteristics often associated with autism are engagement in repetitive activities and stereotyped movements, resistance to environmental change or change in daily routines, and unusual responses to sensory experiences.

The law defines *traumatic brain injury* as an acquired injury to the brain caused by an external physical force, resulting in total or partial functioning disability or psychosocial impairment, or both, that adversely affects a child's educational performance. Although this definition appears to be fairly simple in its presentation, a plethora of issues surround this disability category (e.g., type of brain injury, severity of brain injury, and age at time of injury). In fact, this special education classification may be especially challenging for the early interventionist, particularly in regard to understanding the nature of recovery from a traumatic brain injury as well as specialized rehabilitation and intervention techniques.

The Family and the Community

It is difficult for even the experienced professional to have an accurate understanding of the dynamics of families with young children who are disabled. Prospective parents who have waited so many months for the birth of a baby may suddenly find that the child does not even approximate their idealized expectations. The amount of stress imposed on the family may depend upon how radically parental expectations are violated (Cummings, 1976; Cummings, Bayley, & Rie, 1966; Dyson, 1993; Powers, 1993). The degree of family stress is related to the specifics of the child's disability, with the greatest stress occurring in families with children who are most severely disabled (Wallander & Noojin, 1995). An outgrowth of dealing with the multiple needs of such children is isolation from normal community activities and interactions (Ehrmann, Aeschleman, & Svanum, 1995). A review of the literature, however, indicates that many important questions remain to be answered (Murphy, 1982).

Consider for a moment the parents for whom every feeding session is a struggle because the child thrusts the food out with her tongue as soon as the parent spoons it in, or the parents who must still change diapers on their 4½-year-old child, or the parents who must keep constant vigilance over their 3-year-old, who sleeps only 2 hours per night and is on the move the remainder of the time! One teacher describes her experiences with families coping with disabled children:

> *I don't ever spend time anymore feeling sorry for myself. One of the first families I worked with cured me of that, and it's been reinforced by family after family. Myrna had twin boys. Both were deaf and had cleft palates and hip problems. John also had a cleft lip and a congenital cataract. Myrna was in an auto accident recently and has had medical problems of her own. She's spent most of her time since I've known her running from doctor to doctor and clinic to clinic for John and James. I bet she's had more experience with community agency people than anyone in the state. And she's shared with me a lot of her frustrations about the "hurry up and wait" games and not getting understandable answers from professionals. Yep, she's been through a lot, and I hope her struggles will make things easier for those who follow.*
>
> *Myrna's husband left soon after the kids were born so she has been pretty much on her own. The kids are 5 years old now, and she's still shuttling them to the speech and hearing clinic regularly for hearing aid checks and to the medical center for monitoring of their cleft palate surgery, making sure they get to school, and trying to keep the house in order. I've never seen happier kids or a mom who could cope the way Myrna has. Sometimes when I'm driving in my car, I just think about her and wonder how she's handled it. I go crazy if my checkbook doesn't balance! Myrna's really given me an education. I hope I've helped her.*
>
> *Another family that sticks out in my mind has taught me a lot, also. Vicky and Larry's daughter is 2 years old now and has Down syndrome. Her pediatrician recommended immediately after birth that Annie be institutionalized "for her own good and the good of the other children." Imagine that! It's been a tough few years for the family but somehow they manage to come through crisis after crisis a bit stronger and more reflective. Annie has had heart and respiratory problems, and Vicky spends most of her nights keeping watch while Larry gets some rest. He works the first shift at a local plant and rushes home after work to help feed Annie and the other kids, run errands, and handle chores. I don't think Vicky and Larry have been out alone together since Annie was born. They're still scared to leave her with a babysitter, and they have no relatives in the area. I've watched her for a few hours on a couple of nights so that the rest of the family could go out and eat casually at a restaurant. But those moments have been few for them. Mostly, it's feed, change diapers, run to doctors, come to school, and start the cycle again. Vicky and Larry have recently relaxed enough to talk with some of the other parents. I believe it's helped. Hopefully, they'll begin swapping childsitting chores and give each other support.*

Sometimes I feel very limited. At other times I know I'm very limited. It's clear to me that I don't know about a child until I know about the child's family. And often the only way to help the child is to help the family. This takes getting to know and understand, as much as possible, about the family and home environment. Fortunately, there have been some good folks working in the community who have been more than willing to get me through some rough moments and to help me get families through even more trying times. I remember people telling me about how I should stay away from Cathy Sue at the health department or Jimmy at the welfare office because they're so tough to work with. But these very colleagues—and I choose the word carefully—are my best friends now and some of the strongest advocates for my kids and families.

It's taken me a long time to be comfortable visiting homes routinely, but there's no other way to do my job well. At first, I also thought I was wasting my time stopping by different community agencies to say hello. But it's all helped; it really has. Parents need to know that I'm not interested in their child just as a clinical entity—because it's my job—but that I care about them, the whole family and the child together. Agency people also need to know that I take my job seriously. It makes them feel that their jobs are as important as they really are! I think I've made a difference.

IDEA mandates parent-related activities. Parents must approve individualized testing of their child, must be invited to and may attend the program staffing, must approve the child's special education program and placement, and have the right to question and challenge decisions that are made for the child. In addition, the needs of the family are a central point of the IFSP:

> The evidence indicates that the family is the most effective and economical system for fostering and sustaining the development of the child. . . . Without family involvement any effects of intervention, at least in the cognitive sphere, appear to erode rapidly once the program ends. In contrast, the involvement of the parents as partners in the enterprise provides an on-going system which reinforces the effects of the program while it is in operation, and helps to sustain them. (Bronfenbrenner, 1974, p. 55)

Summary

The proliferation of early childhood special education programs represents a significant sociological and educational event. The long-term impact of early intervention has been demonstrated in terms of human and financial resources. Furthermore, early intervention offers opportunities to prevent or reduce deficits in children and stress in their families. However, the effectiveness of early intervention efforts depends to a great extent on the competence of the early childhood special educator. The diversity of children, families, and communities poses both problems and challenges. The ability of the teacher to apply a broad base of knowledge, to communicate well with families and other professionals, to utilize available resources effectively, and to monitor progress, maximizes the ultimate benefits of programs for children.

The first years of children's lives are the most important for establishing a foundation for later learning. Young children with special needs require careful attention by trained individuals to ensure a path of development that, as closely as possible, parallels that of nondisabled children. This is achieved by providing for the child's physical and biological needs and by providing an environment rich in opportunities to learn. While legal and ethical precedents have spawned an increase in the number of programs available, only the commitment of knowledgeable and skilled professionals can assure that a high level of quality accompanies the increase in services.

References

Badger, E. (1981). Effects of a parent education program on teenage mothers and their offspring. In K. Scott, T. Field, & E. Robertson (Eds.), *Teenage parents and their offspring*. New York: Grune & Stratton.

Battelle Institute of Columbus, Ohio. (1976). *A summary of the evaluation of the Disabled Children's Early Education Program.* Columbus: Author.

Behr, S., & Gallagher, J. J. (1981). Alternative administrative strategies for young disabled children: A policy analysis. *Journal of the Division for Early Childhood, 2,* 113–122.

Blair, C., Ramey, C. T., & Hardin, J. M. (1995). Early intervention for low birth weight, premature infants: Participation and intellectual development. *American Journal on Mental Retardation, 99,* 542–554.

Bloom, B. (1964). *Stability and change in human characteristics.* New York: Wiley.

Boyce, G. C., Smith, T. B., Immel, N., & Casto, G. (1993). Early intervention with medically fragile infants: Investigating the age-at-start question. *Early Education and Development, 4,* 290–305.

Bradley, R. H., Whiteside, L., Mundfrom, D. J., & Casey, P. H. (1994). *Journal of Clinical Psychology, 23,* 425–434.

Bredekamp, S. (1991). *Developmentally appropriate practice in early childhood programs serving children from birth through age 8.* Washington, DC: National Association for the Education of Young Children.

Bronfenbrenner, U. (1974). *A report on longitudinal evaluations of preschool programs. Volume II: Is early intervention effective?* DHEW Publication No. (OHD) 76–30025. Washington, DC: U.S. Department of Health, Education, and Welfare.

Brooks-Gunn, J., McCarton, C. M., Casey, P. H., & McCormick, M. C. (1994). Early interventions in low birth weight premature infants: Results through age 5 years from the Infant Health and Development Program. *Journal of the American Medical Association, 272,* 1257–1262.

Buysse, V., & Wesley, P. W. (1993). The identity crisis in early childhood special education: A call for professional role clarification. *Topics in Early Childhood Special Education, 13,* 418–429.

Campbell, F. A., & Ramey, C. T. (1994). Effects of early intervention on intellectual and academic achievement: A follow-up study of children from low-income families. *Child Development, 65,* 684–698.

Consortium for Longitudinal Studies. (1978). *Lasting effects after preschool.* (Final report of HEW Grant 90c–1311.) Denver: Education Commission of the States.

Cummings, S. T. (1976). The impact of the child's deficiency on the father: A study of fathers of mentally retarded and of chronically ill children.

American Journal of Orthopsychiatry, 46, 246–255.

Cummings, S. T., Bayley, H. C., & Rie, H. E. (1966). Effects of the child's deficiency on the mother: A study of mothers of mentally retarded and of chronically ill children. *American Journal of Orthopsychiatry, 36,* 595–608.

DEC Task Force on Recommended Practices. (1993). *DEC Recommended Practices: Indicators of quality in programs for infants and young children with special needs and their families.* Reston, VA: Council for Exceptional Children.

DEC, the Association of Teacher Educators, NAEYC. (1994). *Personnel standards for early education and early intervention.* Reston, VA.: Author.

Denenberg, V. H. (1981). Hemispheric laterality in animals and the effects of early experience. *Behavioral and Brain Sciences, 4,* 1–49.

Denenberg, V. H., Zeidner, L., Rosen, G. D., Hofman, M., Garbanati, J. A., Sherman, G. F., & Yutzey, D. A. (1981). Stimulation in infancy facilitates interhemispheric communication in the rabbit. *Brain Research, 227,* 165–169.

Dyson, L. L. (1993). Response to the presence of a child with disabilities: Parental stress and family functioning over time. *American Journal of Mental Retardation, 98,* 207–218.

Ehrmann, L. C., Aeschleman, S. R., & Svanum, S. (1995). Parental reports of community activity patterns: A comparison between young children with disabilities and their nondisabled peers. *Research in Developmental Disabilities, 16,* 331–343.

Erikson, E. H. (1963). *Childhood and society.* New York: Norton.

Fewell, R. R., & Oelwein, P. L. (1991). Effective early intervention: Results from the Model Preschool Program for children with Down syndrome and other developmental delays. *Topics in Early Childhood Special Education, 11,* 56–68.

Fox, L., Hanline, M. F., Vail, C. O., & Galant, K. R. (1994). Developmentally appropriate practice: Applications for young children with disabilities. *Journal of Early Intervention, 18,* 243–254.

Freud, A. (1965). *Normality and pathology in childhood: Assessments of development.* New York: International Universities Press.

Gallagher, J. J. (1991). Longitudinal interventions: Virtues and limitations. *American Behavioral Science, 34,* 431–439.

Galler, J. R., Ramsey, F., Solimano, G., & Lowell, W. E. (1983a). The influence of early malnutrition on subsequent behavioral development, II: Classroom behavior. *Journal of the American Academy of Child Psychiatry, 22,* 16–22.

Galler, J. R., Ramsey, F., Solimano, G., Lowell, W. E, & Mason, E. (1983b). The influence of early malnutrition on subsequent behavioral development, I: Degree of impairment in intellectual performance. *Journal of the American Academy of Child Psychiatry, 22,* 8–15.

Gray, S. W. (1983). Controversies or concurrences: A reply to Palmer. *Developmental Review, 3,* 125–129.

Gray, S. W., Ramsey, B. K., & Klaus, R. A. (1982). *From 3 to 20: The Early Training Project.* Baltimore: University Park Press.

Grossman, H. J. (Ed.). (1977). *Manual on terminology and classification in mental retardation.* Baltimore: American Association on Mental Deficiency.

Haddad, P. M., & Garralda, M. E. (1992). Hyperkinetic syndrome and disruptive early experiences. *British Journal of Psychiatry, 191,* 700–703.

Hanson, M. J., & Lovett, D. (1992). Personnel preparation for early interventionists: A cross-disciplinary survey. *Journal of Early Intervention, 16,* 123–135.

Harlow, H. F. (1974). Syndromes resulting from maternal deprivation. In J. H. Cullen (Ed.), *Experimental behavior: A basis for the study of mental disturbance.* New York: Wiley.

Hunt, J. McV. (1961). *Intelligence and experiences.* New York: Ronald Press.

Kirk, S. A. & Gallagher, J. J. (1983). *Educating exceptional children* (4th ed.). Boston: Houghton Mifflin.

Lazar, I., & Darlington, R. (1982). Lasting effect of early education. *Monographs of the Society for Research in Child Development, 47,* (Serial No. 495).

Leibowitz, G. (1991). Organic and biophysical theories of behavior. *Journal of Development and Physical Disabilities, 3,* 210–243.

Littlejohn & Associates, Inc. (1982). *An analysis of the impact of the Disabled Children's Early Education Program.* Washington, DC: Author.

Lizardi, H., Klein, D. N., Ouimette, P. C., & Riso,

L. P. (1995). Reports of the childhood home environment in early onset dysthymia and episodic major depression. *Journal of Abnormal Psychology, 104,* 132–139.

MacMillan, D. L., Sipperstein, G. N., & Gresham, F. M. (1996). A challenge to the viability of mild mental retardation as a diagnostic category. *Exceptional Children, 62,* 356–371.

Meyer-Probst, B., Teichmann, H. H., Hayes, A., & Rauh, H. (1991). Follow-up of a cohort of risk children from birth into adolescence: The Rostock Longitudinal Study. *International Journal of Disability, Development, and Education, 38,* 225–246.

Morgane, P. J., Austin, L. R., Borzino, J. D., & Tonkiss, J. (1993). Prenatal malnutrition and development of the brain. *Current Directions in Psychological Science, 17,* 91–128.

Murphy, M. A. (1982). The family with a disabled child: A review of the literature. *Developmental and Behavioral Pediatrics, 3,* 73–82.

Odom, S. L., & McEvoy, M. A. (1990). Mainstreaming at the preschool level: Potential barriers and tasks for the field. *Topics in Early Childhood Special Education, 10,* 48–61.

Palmer, F. (1983). The continuing controversy over the effects of early childhood intervention: A perspective and review of Gray, Ramsey, and Klaus's From 3 to 20: The Early Training Project. *Developmental Review, 3,* 115–124.

Piaget, J., & Inhelder, B. (1969). *The psychology of the child.* New York: Basic Books.

Powers, L. E. (1993). Disability and grief: From tragedy to challenge. In G. H. S. Singer & L. E. Powers (Eds.). *Family, disability, and empowerment: Active coping strategies for family interventions.* Baltimore: Paul H. Brookes.

Ramey, C. T., & Bryant, D. M. (1982). Evidence involving prevention of developmental retardation during infancy. *Journal of the Division for Early Childhood, 5,* 73–78.

Ramey, C. T. & Ramey, L. R. (1994). Which children benefit the most from early intervention? *Pediatrics, 94(2),* 1064–1066.

Read, S. (1982). Malnutrition and behavior. *Applied Research in Mental Retardation, 3,* 279–291.

Ricciuti, H. N. (1993). Nutrition and development. *Current Directions in Psychological Science, 2,* 43–46.

Rosenzweig, M. R., Bennett, E. L., Diamond, M. C., Wu, Su-Yu, Slagle, R.W., & Saffron, E. (1969). Influence of environmental complexity and visual stimulation on development of occipital cortex in rats. *Brain Research, 14,* 427–445.

Sameroff, A. J. (1979). The etiology of cognitive competence: A systems perspective. In R. B. Kearsley & I. E. Sigel (Eds.), *Infants at risk: Assessment of cognitive functioning.* Hillsdale, NJ: Erlbaum.

Schweinhart, L. J. & Weikart, D. P. (1980). *Young children grow up: The effects of the Perry Preschool Program on youths through age 15.* Ypsilanti, MI: High Scope Educational Research Foundation.

Shonkoff, J. P., Hauser, C. P., Krauss, M. W., & Upshur, C. C. (1992). Development of infants with disabilities and their families: Implications for theory and service delivery. *Monographs of the Society for Research in Child Development* (Serial No. 230).

Skeels, H. M. (1966). Adult status of children with contrasting early life experiences. *Monographs of the Society for Research in Child Development* (Serial No. 105).

Trohanis, P. L. (1995). *Progress in providing services to young children with special needs and their families: An overview to and update on implementing the Individuals with Disabilities Education Act (IDEA)* (NEC*TAS Notes No. 7). Chapel Hill, NC: NEC*TAS.

U.S. Department of Education (1996). *Seventeenth annual report to Congress on the implementation of the Individuals with Disabilities Education Act.* Washington, DC: Author.

Wallander, J. L. & Noojin, A. B. (1995). Mothers' reports of stressful experiences related to having a child with a physical disability. *Children's Health Care, 24,* 245–256.

Weber, C. U., Foster, P. W., & Weikart, D. P. (1978). *An economic analysis of the Ypsilanti Perry Preschool Project,* Ypsilanti, MI: High Scope Educational Research Foundation.

Weikart, D. P. (1981). Effects of different curricula in early childhood intervention. *Educational Evaluation and Policy Analysis, 3,* 25–35.

Winick, M., Meyer, K. K., & Harris, R. (1975). Malnutrition and environmental enrichment by early adoption. *Science, 190,* 1173–1175.

Wolff, P. H. (1981). Normal variation in human maturation. In K. J. Connolly & H. F. R. Prechtl (Eds.), *Maturation and development: Biological and psychological perspectives.* Clinics in Developmental Medicine No. 77/78. Spastics International Medical Publications. Philadelphia: Lippincott.

Wood, M. M. (1981). Costs of intervention programs. In C. Garland, N. W. Stone, J. Swanson, & G. Woodruff (Eds.), *Early intervention for children with special needs and their families.* Monmouth, OR: WESTAR.

Yatkin, U. S., McLaren, D. S., Kanawati, A. A., & Sabbach, S. (1971). Undernutrition and mental development: A one-year follow up. In D. S. McLaren and N. J. Daghir (Eds.), *Proceedings of the 6th Symposium on Nutrition and Health in the Near East.* Beirut: American University.

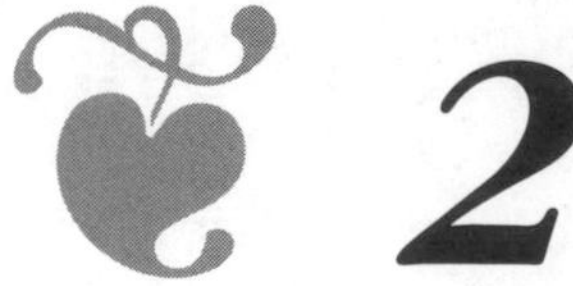

2

Developmental Stages and Factors Affecting Development

Stephen R. Hooper and Rebecca Edmondson

A sound knowledge of normal growth and development is essential for anyone interested in children, particularly for those who work with children in educational and developmental programs. For the student aspiring to work with young children with special needs, as well as for professionals already engaged in clinical practice serving such children, an understanding of normal growth and development provides a foundation with which to adequately meet all children's needs. Not only does such knowledge contribute to an understanding of how normal children develop, but it also provides a basic measure for recognizing children with all kinds of exceptionalities and appropriately addressing their needs. Further, this knowledge base facilitates an understanding of the plethora of factors that can impinge on a child's developmental progress.

This chapter provides an overview of the basic processes and principles of development. In addition to discussing definitional issues and specific stages of child development through the preschool years, selected risk factors that can impede development are highlighted.

Definitional Issues and Processes

Several questions arise in any attempt to define *development*. "Is there a time frame for the development of a specific behavior or repertoire of behaviors?" "How much change is needed in a behavior before it is recognized as development?" "Are there componential aspects to development?" How one conceptualizes human behavior and its development is a determining factor in how it is defined.

Definition

At its most fundamental level, development involves change. This change must be cumulative and systematic, however, and random change is not considered to be developmental in nature. Whereas the concept of *growth* refers to the addition of new components or skills through the appearance of new cells, *development* refers to the refinement, improvement, and expansion of existing skills through the refinement of cells already present (Schuster, 1992). More specifically, three basic criteria must be met before change can be considered to be development:

- The change must be orderly—not random fluctuations of behavior.
- The change must result in a consistent modification in behavior.
- The change must contribute to a higher level of functioning in the individual.

When a specific change in behavior satisfies these three criteria, development has occurred.

Development may be either qualitative or quantitative. For example, increases in height, weight, creativity, activity level, and vocabulary are quantitative changes; that is, they are directly measurable. Progression toward maturity and the integration of complex physiological and psychological processes are qualitative changes; that is, it is more difficult to gain exact measure of these changes, but we do notice them. We see both types of change when children's shoes no longer fit, when they run faster and jump higher, when their increased proficiency in language helps them control their surroundings and their behaviors in a more accomplished manner, and when old toys and games lose their fascination in favor of new friendships and increased social contacts.

With these definitional components in mind, it also becomes important to distinguish between development and maturation. The concept of maturation is similar to that of development in that skills and functions are refined and improved over time. The concepts differ, however, in that maturation refers to the unfolding of personal characteristics and behavioral phenomena through the processes of growth and development. The concept of maturation reflects the final stages of differentiation of cells, tissues, and organs in accordance with a genetic blueprint wherein full or optimal development of a specific skill is achieved (Schuster, 1992).

Individual Differences

Another factor to consider in relation to development is the concept of individual differences. Children develop at different rates, and this in turn creates individual differences. Again, these differences can be either qualitative or quantitative. For children in any preschool classroom setting, the differences in temperament, personality, intelligence, achievement, and physical factors such as height and weight are noteworthy and reflect a wide range of normal variation. Some children grow rapidly and others grow more slowly. There also are racial and gender developmental variations. During the fetal stage, for example, females mature faster than males do, especially in skeletal development. At birth, the skeletal development of females is about 4 weeks ahead of that of males, and African-American children show more rapid skeletal maturation than Caucasian children do (Lowrey, 1986; Tanner, 1989).

It is important to understand that the concept of individual differences is the basis upon which one child is compared to another. It also is the fundamental premise in the development of standardized educational and psychological tests. An understanding of individual differences provides the foundation for recognizing normal variations as well as extreme differences among children, and thus for identifying those who may have special needs. In general, understanding of the various developmental levels is enhanced by familiarity with the concept of individual differences.

Principles of Development

Although children develop at different rates, and thus there exist inter-individual differences, a single child can show more rapid change in some developmental areas than in others; thus, intra-individual differences also exist. Regardless of the perspective, however, there are certain principles of development that apply to all children. These include the following:

- Development progresses in a step-by-step fashion. It is orderly, sequential, and proceeds from the simple to the complex. Each achieved behavior forms the foundation for more advanced behaviors.
- Rates of development vary among children as well as among developmental areas in a single child.
- Development is characterized by increasing specificity of function, or differentiation, as well as integration of these specific functions into a larger response pattern. A good example of this principle is the infant startle reflex. When an infant is startled, his entire body tenses and his arms move out to the side. With age, this reflex becomes integrated into more specific behavioral patterns such that a startled preschooler will tense only the shoulder and neck muscles.
- Neurological development contributes significantly to the acquisition of physical skills in young children. Physical development proceeds in

Normal variation is the rule in the development of a young child.

cephalocaudal and proximodistal directions. *Cephalocaudal development* describes the progression of body control from the head to the lower parts of the body. For example, an infant will achieve head, upper trunk, and arm control before lower trunk and leg control. *Proximodistal development* describes progress from the central portions of the body (i.e., the spinal cord) to the distal or peripheral parts. In this developmental progression, gross motor skills and competencies precede fine-motor skills. This developmental progression continues throughout early childhood, with upper trunk control being achieved first, then arm control, and finally finger control. According to this principle, each change in the child's development should be increasingly refined.

- Development of any structure follows a sequential pattern; however, there appear to be specific times during development in which a developing structure is most sensitive to external conditions. These sensitive periods, or critical periods, are the time during which a specific condition or stimulus is necessary for the normal development of a specific structure. Conversely, these periods also represent times when a structure may be most vulnerable to disruption (O'Rahilly & Muller, 1992). The concept of critical periods has created much debate in theoretical circles, particularly with respect to parent-infant bonding (Anisfeld et al., 1983) and language development (Lenneberg, 1967).
- All development is interrelated. Although it is convenient for the student or child practitioner to discuss development in terms of discrete developmental areas such as motor skills, development in other areas such as social-emotional or communication functions does not cease, nor is it necessarily separate from other areas. The student or child practitioner must recognize how different areas of development are interrelated to understand how a particular child develops.
- Development is influenced by heredity and environment. Although there is much discussion by experts in the field about which is more important, there is no doubt that they both play a role in a child's development. A child's genetic inheritance provides the basic foundation for many physical and personality attributes, but the influences of social, cultural, and familial variables also contribute to development.

Processes of Development

An understanding of development requires resolution of a fundamental question: Do we develop primarily because we learn from our surroundings (environment) or because we are predisposed to grow in certain ways (heredity)? An explanation of each position provides an interesting framework for examining contemporary theories of child development.

Heredity.

Heredity describes the inborn attributes of an organism. The view that behavior and development are primarily directed by heredity, or nature, was initially set forth by Jean Jacques Rousseau in the 18th century. Rousseau was a French philosopher who believed that a child's growth and development were ultimately determined by nature, and that the child's surroundings had little influence on development. According to this viewpoint, nature provides the primary guidance for healthy growth and development. In the 20th century, this philosophy has been advocated by Gesell (Gesell & Ilg, 1943), Jensen (1980), and others.

Environment. The position that environment is primarily responsible for how a child develops can be traced to the work of 17th-century British philosopher John Locke. Locke resurrected many of the teachings of Aristotle in describing the mind of an infant as a *tabula rasa,* or "blank slate." Locke believed that all of an individual's experiences contribute to filling the blank slate. The child was perceived as a passive receiver of information and thus easily shaped by environmental influences.

In the 20th century, John Watson (1924) and many other theorists (e.g., Skinner, 1961) have been strong advocates for the environmentalist position. Watson was a prominent force in American psychology and adhered almost exclusively to the nurture philosophy of the nature-nurture controversy. The basic tenets of his thinking are revealed in one of his earlier works (Watson, 1924):

> Give me a dozen healthy infants, well-formed, and my own specified world to bring them up in, and I'll guarantee to take any one at random and train him to become any type of specialist I might select—doctor, lawyer, merchant, chief, and yes, even beggar man and thief, regardless of his talents, penchants, tendencies, abilities, vocations, race of his ancestors. (p. 104)

Watson represented an extreme environmentalist position which downplayed biological influences on development and truly emphasized Locke's *tabula rasa* philosophy.

Interaction of Heredity and Environment. As a resolution to these seemingly opposing positions, common sense dictates that neither heredity nor environment alone explains a child's normal growth and development. Heredity does not dominate development, nor are environmental influences solely responsible for one's personality, talents, or physical abilities. It seems that an interaction between these two positions most likely accounts for development. Although the interaction between heredity and environment is well accepted from a contemporary viewpoint, the exact degree of interaction remains a mystery. The task for observers of child behavior and development should be to focus on describing the specific aspects of each philosophical position that may be affecting the development of any particular child.

 *Periods of Development*

This section explores the development of a child from conception through the early childhood years, including the prenatal period, the neonatal period, infancy, toddlerhood, and the preschool period. To complement the other chapters in this text, the emphasis here is placed on the prenatal and neonatal periods, although later developmental periods also will be described briefly. We begin with a brief review of some of the key biological foundations of development starting at the very beginning—the time of conception.

Conception

Conception occurs when a sperm fertilizes an ovum, or egg. This union can take place only within approximately a 10- to 24-hour period after ovulation. The period of ovulation, which corresponds to the release of an egg from an ovary, occurs in 28- or 29-day cycles in sexually mature females. In general, there are about 90 hours per cycle when fertilization can occur (Flynn, 1989). It is at this time of fertilization, or conception, that growth and development begin.

Cell Division, Chromosomes, and Genes. After union of the sperm and egg, the fertilized egg begins to divide. Levitan (1988) estimates that approximately 44 geometric divisions of a single cell are required to transform it into a physiologically independent infant. In approximately 9 months, the single-celled fertilized ovum is transformed into a system of over 15 trillion cells, each with a similar genetic composition, yet different with respect to their specific functions (Levitan, 1988).

Cell division occurs by two processes, each serving a different function in development of the embryo. The first process is that of mitosis, in which a cell divides in half, thereby forming two new cells. It is through continuous cell division that a single cell evolves into a complex individual. Mitosis continues in body cells for one's entire life span; it contributes to growth as well as to replacement of dead and damaged tissue.

The second process of cell division is meiosis, which prepares a new cell for reproduction of the entire organism. Meiosis is a cell division that involves two highly specialized sex cells called *gametes*. These gametes are the ovum and the sperm, which are different from other cells in their chromosomal structure. When regular cells are formed, they contain 46 chromosomes arranged in 23 pairs. However, when the sex cells are formed, the chromosome pairs split so that the resulting sex cell has only 23 unpaired chromosomes. The gametes have a shorter life span than regular cells because they are missing a complete set of 46 chromosomes. They gain a full set of chromosomes, and consequently increase their life expectancy, only when the sperm fertilizes the egg (Vogel, 1986).

Chromosomes are hairlike particles of protein located in the nucleus of every cell. Each chromosome contains thousands of genes distributed in a balanced way among the pairs of chromosomes. Each gene carries coded information that combines to create unique human beings. It is precisely these informationally loaded particles that have been utilized in exploring revolutionary treatments involving gene replacement therapy for such genetic disorders as cystic fibrosis.

Genes may be either dominant, and always express their trait, or recessive, and express their trait only when paired with another recessive gene carrying the same coded information. For example, two tall parents, both carrying recessive genes for shortness in height, may have a short child if the recessive gene of each parent combines to form their child's gene for determining height. In this case, the child will not be as tall as the parents. This is an example of the genetic genotype. However, if one or both genes for tallness are transmitted, then the dominant gene will prevail and the child will be tall like the parents. This is an example of the genetic phenotype. The process of cell division, and the involvement of the chromosomes and genes, are contributors to the hereditary construction of the individual. These processes and structures provide the blueprint for the unfolding of development.

Although specific types of genetic risk factors and inheritance mechanisms will be discussed later in this chapter, it is important to note that alterations in the chromosomes can contribute to a variety of birth defects as well as to spontaneous termination of the pregnancy. In fact, approximately 25% to 40% of conceptions are spontaneously terminated even before a woman knows that she is pregnant, and another 15% to 20% are spontaneously terminated after the woman knows about the pregnancy. At least half of these spontaneous abortions have been deemed secondary to chromosomal abnormalities, and they typically occur within the first trimester of pregnancy (O'Rahilly & Muller, 1992). This stands in stark contrast to the 0.6% frequency of chromosomal abnormalities in liveborn infants and the 4% to 12% rate in stillborn infants.

Prenatal Development

Prenatal refers to the time from conception to birth. The prenatal period may be divided into three stages. The first stage is called the *germinal stage* and lasts for about 2 weeks. The *embryonic stage* is next and lasts from about 2 to 8 weeks. The third stage, the *fetal stage,* follows and continues until birth. Although the variation of ovulation among women, as well as within the same woman, creates minor difficulties in accurately dating the pregnancy (Moore, 1988), this sequence of prenatal development holds true for all children.

Germinal Stage.

The cell created by the union of the sperm and the egg is the zygote. Within 36 hours of fertilization mitosis begins, and this single cell rapidly divides. During the beginnings of mitosis the zygote slowly moves down the fallopian tube toward the uterus. This process takes about 3 to 4 days. Once its destination is reached, the zygote has transformed into a liquid-filled structure called a *blastocyst,* which floats in the uterus for about 24 to 48 hours. Mitosis continues and some of the cells of the blastocyst begin to clump on one side to form the embryonic disk. This is the group of cells from which the baby will develop.

As the embryonic disk thickens, it begins to divide into three layers: the ectoderm, the endoderm, and the mesoderm. The ectoderm is the upper layer of cells in the embryonic disk and ultimately will become the epidermis, nails, hair, teeth, sensory organs, and central nervous system. The lower layer of cells, the endoderm, will eventually become the child's digestive system, respiratory system, and various other internal organs. The mesoderm is the last of the three layers to develop. It will evolve into the dermis, muscles and connective tissue, the skull, and parts of the circulatory and reproductive systems. The remaining parts of the blastocyst will create the prenatal structures required for intrauterine life. These include the placenta, which will nourish and protect the developing infant; the umbilical cord, which will connect the placenta to the developing child; and the amniotic sac, which will house the baby for the entire prenatal period. The outer layer of the blastocyst, called the trophoblast, eventually will produce microscopic, hairlike structures called *villi*. These villi adhere to the uterine lining until the blastocyst is totally implanted. Once uterine implantation is complete, the germinal stage is over, and the embryonic period begins.

Embryonic Stage. This stage of development actually has been divided into 23 separate stages termed *Carnegie Stages*. It is beyond the scope of this chapter to review each of these stages in detail (for a review, see O'Rahilly & Muller, 1992); the main point to note is that during the embryonic stage, the *embryo,* as it is now called, experiences rapid growth. The amniotic sac, placenta, and umbilical cord are fully developed, and mitosis has progressed to the point that the embryo resembles a miniature human being. During this period, the developing embryo is extremely sensitive to toxic and infectious agents. Nearly all major birth defects, such as malformed limbs, cleft palate, blindness, and deafness, occur during this period or slightly after, but typically within the first 3 months of pregnancy (O'Rahilly & Muller, 1992). In fact, as noted earlier, many embryos spontaneously abort when their defects are markedly severe.

By the end of this period, at about 8 weeks, the embryo has a beating heart, the beginnings of a skeleton, and a rapidly growing brain. This tiny developing human is now only about 1 to 1½ inches long and weighs about 1⁄30 of an ounce, but it clearly has begun to show distinct human characteristics (Moore & Persaud, 1993). For example, the head and brain are now visible, with the head accounting for approximately one half the length of the fetus, and a thin pink skin covers the body.

Fetal Stage. The fetal stage begins with the development of the first bone cell, which is produced from the cartilage of the developing skeleton at about 8 to 9 weeks. The embryo now becomes a fetus. This final stage of the prenatal period lasts until birth, and it is during this time that the organism experiences the most extensive rate of growth in its lifetime. The length of the fetus increases until normal body proportions are achieved, and all internal systems and organs continue to increase their efficiency. At the end of the third month, the fetus is approximately 3 inches long and is humanlike. Its musculature is developing, and some spontaneous movements may be noted by the mother. Eyelids, teeth, fingernails, toenails, and external genitalia begin to form, and the gender is easily distinguished. During the fourth month the fetus grows another 1 to 2 inches in length and begins to develop hair, called lanugo, on its body. The eyelids begin to blink, the mouth begins to open, and the hands are capable of grasping. The fifth month is characterized by the mother typically feeling the fetus move for the first time. Eyebrows and hair appear, and the skin begins to take on the human shape. The length of the fetus is now roughly 10 inches. At the end of the second trimester, the fetus has eyes that can open, taste buds on the tongue, and a functional respiratory system; it also is capable of making crying sounds. The fetus now weighs approximately 1½ pounds, and life outside of the uterus is possible.

The final trimester is a period of further growth and development of the fetus. This is manifested in greater structural differentiation and definition. At this point the fetus is viable; that is, its respiratory system and central nervous system are developed to a point at which it could survive outside of the uterine environment. This growth continues until the point of delivery, or birth, typically somewhere between weeks 37 to 40 of the pregnancy. Figure 2.1 presents a month-by-month summary of the growth and development during the prenatal period.

The Birth Process

As delivery time nears the mother's calcium level drops. This decrease is particularly marked in the pelvic area so that the mother's pelvis can be extended as widely as possible to accommodate the fetus. Simultaneously, muscles around the uterus and cervix become larger and more flexible also to accommodate the fetus during birth. In preparation for birth the fetus rotates in the womb so that it will be born head first. This rotation is triggered by hormonal action in the mother and is the first indication of the onset of labor. If fetal rotation does not occur, the baby will be born feet first. This awkward type of delivery is called a *breech delivery* and occurs in about 3% to 4% of births (Kauppila, 1975), with increased frequency noted in preterm deliveries (i.e., 14% at 29 to 32 weeks gestation) (Haughey, 1985). A breech delivery can cause anoxia (i.e., a lack of oxygen), intracranial hemorrhage, and transient lowering of the fetal heart rate, particularly in the premature infant (Schifrin, 1982). While a breech delivery typically is not of major consequence to outcome, some association has been made to abnormalities in the child, with central nervous system anomalies being noted most frequently (Mazor, Hagay, Leiberman, Biale, & Insler, 1985). In addition, nearly half of all cases of hydrocephalus, myelomeningocele, Prader-Willi syndrome, and trisomy are associated with breech presentation (Westgren & Ingemarsson, 1988).

Other factors that can affect the baby include pressure in the birth canal, the use of forceps during delivery, and the sedation of the mother. This latter factor can be critical because the baby's immature liver and excretory systems experience difficulties eliminating maternal medications and anesthesia from the body. This may contribute to sedation and, consequently, to a baby who initially may be less responsive to environmental stimulation—including its parents (Murray, Dolby, Nation, & Thomas, 1981).

When there is a possibility of an abnormal delivery, a Caesarian section can be performed. In this procedure, the mother's abdomen and uterus are surgically opened, and the baby and placenta are removed. This procedure eliminates many of the risks associated with an abnormal delivery for the mother as well as for the child. One factor that can indicate the need for a Caesarian section is postmaturity. *Postmaturity* refers to a baby being postterm, or after the 41st week. About 9% of babies are born after the 41st week of gestation (Haesslein, 1987). Although most

FIGURE 2.1 A month-by-month summary of development in the prenatal period

First Month *(1 to 4 weeks after conception)*
Conception, rapid growth
Fertilized egg imbeds in uterine wall
Differentiation of individual from accessory structures
Three germ layers differentiated
Rudimentary body parts formed
Cardiovascular system functioning
Yolk sac begins to diminish

Second Month *(5 to 8 weeks)*
Formation of head and facial features
Very rapid cell differentiation and growth
Beginning of all major external and internal structures
External genitalia present, but gender not discernible
Heart functionally complete
Some movement by limbs
Yolk sac incorporated into the embryo
Weight: 1 gm

Third Month *(9 to 12 weeks)*
Eyelids fused, nail beds formed
Teeth and bones begin to appear
Kidneys begin to function
Some respiratory-like movements exhibited
Begins to swallow amniotic fluid
Grasp, sucking, and withdrawal reflexes present
Moves easily (not felt by mother)
Gender distinguishable
Weight: 30 gm (1 oz)

Fourth Month *(13 to 16 weeks)*
Much spontaneous movement
Moro reflex present
Rapid skeletal development
Meconium present
Uterine development in female infant
Downy hair (lanugo) appears on body
Weight: 120 gm (4 oz)

Fifth Month *(17 to 20 weeks)*
Begins to exchange new cells for old, especially in skin
"Quickening"—fetal movement felt by mother
Vernix caseosa appears
Eyebrows and head hair appear
Skeleton begins to harden
Strong grasp reflex present
Permanent teeth buds appear
Heart sounds can be heard with a stethoscope
Weight: 360 gm (12 oz)

Sixth Month *(21 to 24 weeks)*
"Miniature baby"
Extrauterine life first possible (but very unlikely)
Mother may note jarring but rhythmic movements of infant indicative of hiccups
Body becomes straight
Fingernails appear
Skin has a red, wrinkled appearance
Alternates periods of sleep and activity
May respond to external sounds
May try to find comfortable position
Weight 720 gm (1½ lb)

babies show no permanent signs of being postmature, largely because of routine and careful prenatal monitoring, some postmature babies do not obtain sufficient nutrients and oxygen from the placenta to meet the demands of labor (Korones, 1986), and thus brain injury or death can occur.

Neonatal Period

The neonatal period is the transitional time from intrauterine to independent existence. It is defined as approximately the first 4 weeks after delivery. The neonatal period is possibly the most tenuous in a human's lifetime. Of the nearly 4 million babies who are born alive annually in the United States, approximately 1% die

FIGURE 2.1 Continued

Seventh Month *(25 to 28 weeks)*
Respiratory system and central nervous system sufficiently developed that many babies may survive with excellent and intensive care
Eyelids reopen
Assumes head-down position in uterus
Respiratory-like movement
Weight: 1,200 gm (2½ lb)

Eighth Month *(29 to 32 weeks)*
Begins to store fat and minerals
Testes descend into scrotal sac in male
Mother may note irregular, jerky, cryinglike movements
Lanugo begins to disappear from face
Skin begins to lose reddish color
Can be conditioned to environmental sounds
Exhibits good reflex development
Good chance of survival if born
Weight: 2,000 gm (4 lb)

Ninth Month *(33 to 36 weeks)*
Continues fat deposits
Body begins to round out
Increased iron storage by liver
Increased development of lungs
May become more or less active because of space tightness
Excellent chance of survival if born
Lanugo begins to disappear from body
Head hair lengthens
Weight: 2,800 gm (6 lb)

Tenth Month *(37 to 40 weeks)*
Lanugo and vernix caseosa both begin to disappear
High absorption of maternal hormones
Skin becomes smooth, plump
Firming of skull and bones
Continued storage of fat and minerals
Ready for birth
Weight: 3,200 to 3,400 gm (7 to 7½ lb)

Source: Adapted from "Antenatal Development" by C. S. Schuster, 1992. In C. S. Schuster and S. S. Ashburn (Eds.), *The Process of Human Development: A Holistic Approach,* 3rd ed. (pp. 60–70). Philadelphia: J. B. Lippincott. Adapted with permission of S. S. Ashburn.

within the first 24 hours, 1% die within the first week, and 1% die within the first year. Behrman and Kliegman (1983) note that an infant experiences a greater risk of death during the first 7 days of life than at any other time during the next 65 years.

The average newborn enters the world weighing between 5½ and 9½ pounds, with the overall average being about 7 to 7½ pounds. About 90% of newborns are approximately 18 to 22 inches in length, with the average being about 20 inches (O'Rahilly & Muller, 1992). The baby's size is associated with a variety of factors including parental size, race, sex, maternal nutrition, and overall maternal health. Male newborns tend to be slightly longer and heavier than their female counterparts, and the first child in the birth order generally weighs less than any of the siblings who follow (Lowrey, 1986). The skin of newborns—even African-American infants—is pale, because it is so thin. The skin also may be covered with lanugo, a light, fuzzy body hair, or vernix caseosa, an oily fluid that protects the baby from infection. Both of these substances disappear shortly after birth.

The skeletal system of the neonate is not totally developed, and consequently many of the bones are soft and pliable. For example, the fontanelles, or soft spots in the head, are the gaps between the bones in the skull that permit the skull bones to overlap during the birth process and allow for additional brain growth. The posterior fontanelle gradually closes up through the third month of life, while the anterior fontanelle is closed by 18 months of age (Behrman & Vaughan, 1987).

The respiratory system of the newborn must adapt to a gaseous environment. Although the newborn consumes about twice the amount of oxygen as an adult does (Hubbell & Webster, 1986), respiration tends to be rapid, shallow, irregular, and unsynchronized, with the abdomen doing more work than the chest does. The neonate may make peculiar wheezing and coughing sounds because the entire respiratory system is underdeveloped and inexperienced with the demands of the extrauterine environment. The digestive and circulatory systems also must make the transition to independent functioning. The visual system is incomplete because of underdevelopment of the retina and optic nerve; however, the newborn's eyes can follow a moving light as well as a moving target. In general, neonates can see best at a distance of about 7½ inches. There also seems to be a preference for visually following human faces more than any other type of object (Maurer & Maurer, 1988). The neonate also maintains physiological reactivity to sound intensity, as indicated by increased heart rate and motor activity, as well as an orienting reflex in which the baby turns in the direction of the sound stimulus. The other senses of olfaction, taste, and tactile sensitivity also are intact (Maurer & Maurer, 1988). For example, the neonate is capable of distinguishing among sweet, sour, and bitter tastes, as well as distinguishing the odor of its mother's breast milk (MacFarland, 1975). Motor skills of the neonate are mainly characterized by primitive reflexes and random gross motor activity. Reflexes are automatic inborn behaviors of which the newborn has many. Further discussion of reflexes and motor development is provided in Chapter 4.

Infant Period

Infancy describes the growth and development of the child from about the fourth week through the second year of life. The infant experiences rapid physical growth during this time. The birth weight doubles by the fifth month and triples by the end of the first year, and the infant gains about 5 to 6 pounds per year for the next several years (Lowrey, 1986). The infant grows approximately 10 inches by the end of the first year and 3 inches per year for the next several years (Bondy, 1980). In addition to weight and length, head circumference is an important physical feature to measure at regular intervals. Changes in head circumference are important because they denote brain growth. During the first year of life, head circumference increases from 13 or 14 inches at birth to about 17 or 18 inches, with most of this growth occurring during the early months of development. The circumferences of the chest and abdomen are about the same in the neonate, but during infancy the chest circumference becomes larger than that of the abdomen. Deciduous, or primary, teeth appear at about 6 to 8 months and continue to erupt until all 20 are in place by toddlerhood. The skeletal structure of the infant hardens, and the musculature increases in weight and density. Typically, African-American children show more

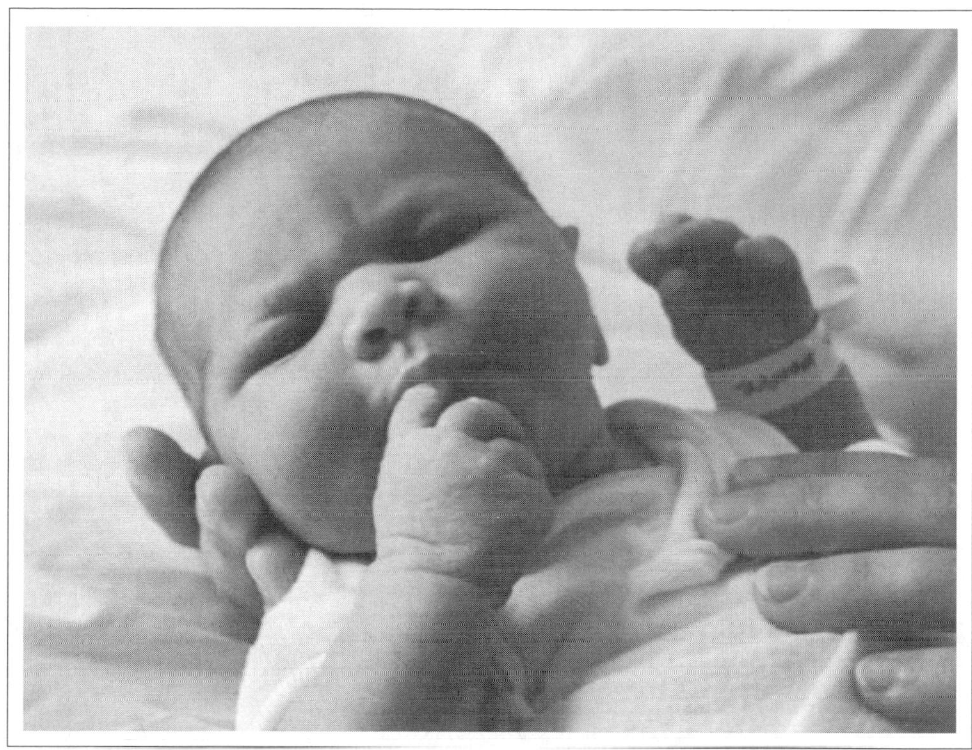

Infants begin learning about themselves and their environments as early as the first day of life.

rapid skeletal growth than Caucasian children do, and the bones of females generally grow faster than those of males (Lowrey, 1986; Tanner, 1989).

Another manifestation of infancy is the apparent disappearance or integration of many of the primitive reflexes into the baby's developing nervous system. This occurs as the cerebral cortex matures and begins to exert control over the lower central nervous system. This control is accomplished, in part, by a process called *myelinization*. Myelin is a soft, white substance that coats and protects many nerve cells. It allows for rapid transmission of neural messages from the brain to other parts of the body. Myelinization begins in utero at about the fourth gestational month, with some neural pathways (e.g., the brain stem) being fully myelinated by the 30th gestational week (Amand, Phil, & Hickey, 1987); however, myelinization is not complete at birth (Willis & Widerstrom, 1986). Although it will not be basically complete until approximately 6 years of age, by 6 months many of the cortical fibers have been sheathed with myelin, thus facilitating greater cortical control and enabling the infant to achieve various developmental milestones such as sitting-up, grasping, walking, and various cognitive and adaptive skills necessary for maturation (Tanner, 1989).

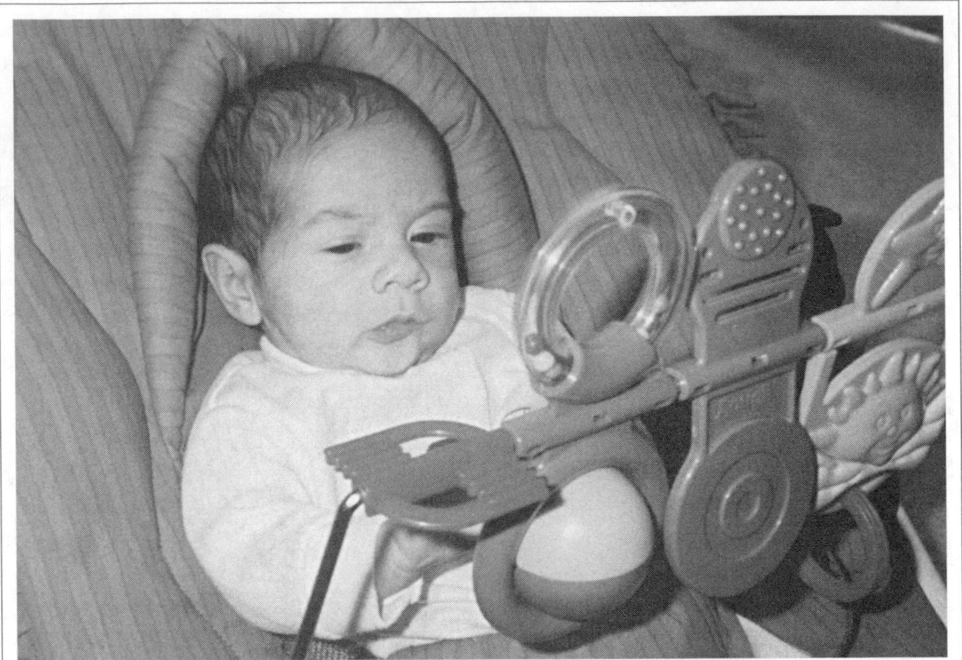

During infancy, children continue to learn about their surroundings through all of the sensory modalities.

Toddler Period

The toddler period generally encompasses development during the second and third years of life. Strang (1969) has labeled this period "the first adolescence." It is a transitional time between infancy and early childhood, just as adolescence links childhood to adulthood. The toddler period is characterized by a slowing of physical development, although the toddler maintains a growth rate faster than any subsequent period except adolescence. At age 2 the average toddler is 32 to 35 inches tall and weighs approximately 25 to 30 pounds. The child now is capable of maintaining an upright physical posture, and development in all areas becomes more refined. Brain growth reaches about four-fifths of its ultimate adult weight by age 2, and it is closer to its mature size than any other body part is by age 3 (Black & Puckett, 1996; Lowrey, 1986).

Bones continue to calcify and harden with the composition of wrists and ankles changing from cartilage to bone. Nonetheless, the toddler still has a larger proportion of cartilage than hard bone in her body, making possible skeletal damage resulting from disease or poor diet. A toddler normally has a full set of baby teeth by age 2. Muscle and fat tissues develop slowly during this period, with fatty tissue growth actually decreasing up to about age 2½ when it again begins to increase. Motor development improves; well-balanced walking, jumping, and climbing without adult assistance are quite common. Fine muscle control is evident in the child's finger coordination in learning to handle pencils, crayons, and paintbrushes.

Memory and language skills also show significant gains during this period. The child learns the names of people, objects, and places and can recall them for later use. In the language domain, the child moves from word combinations at age 2 to sentences at age 3. Words and actions become more coordinated near the end of the toddler period. Social-emotional development moves from adult-assisted activities to more independent social-emotional activities, with play being exploratory and egocentric in nature. Self-help and adaptive behaviors also emerge during toddlerhood, with the major one being toilet training. In general, the toddler begins to use thought, language, movement, and emotions in a coordinated fashion and is learning to gain verbal control over actions (Tinsley & Waters, 1982).

Preschool Period

The preschooler continues to experience refinement in growth patterns, particularly in physical structures and motor skills. Self-help skills, such as dressing, toileting, and language usage, become a regular part of day-to-day behaviors. Sex differences

Play during the toddler period is increasingly exploratory and self-directed.

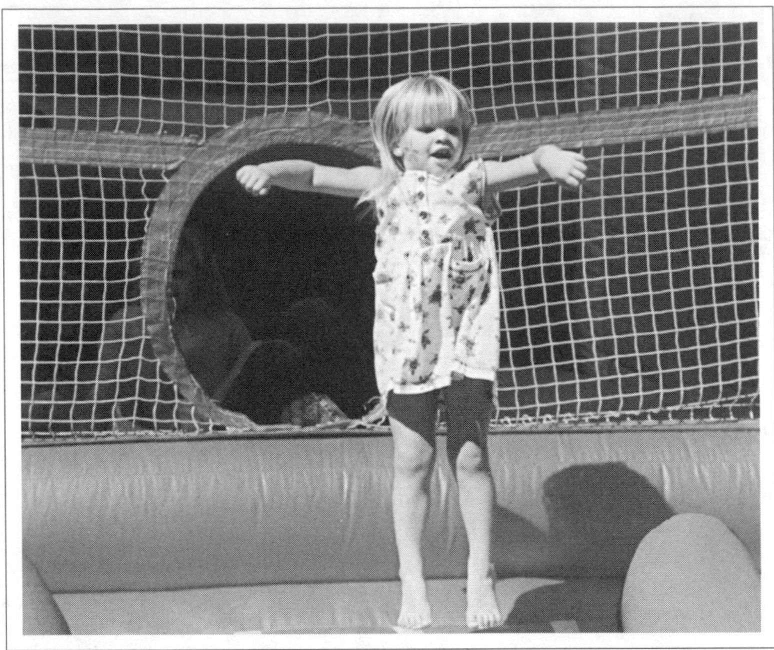

In the preschool period children continue to gain a sense of self-mastery and self-confidence.

are minimal, although boys usually weigh more and have more muscle tissue than girls do. The head reaches about 90% of its adult size and the brain about 75% of its adult weight by the end of the preschool years (Lowrey, 1986; Tanner, 1989).

The preschool child is willing to try new games, tricks, and stunts, and self-confidence in this realm is growing. Preschoolers are excited about their surroundings and are curious enough to ask "Why?" questions. Speech and language skills have become more grammatically correct, and the child uses language in a functional manner. Social-emotional development is characterized by increased child-to-child and child-to-adult interactions as fears, fantasies, and a sense of self-respect emerge. Much of the preschooler's developmental activity forms the foundation for the social and learning challenges to be encountered when formal schooling begins around age 6 (Black & Puckett, 1996).

Factors Affecting Development

Although the unfolding of the developmental process is a fairly remarkable set of events, there are many factors that can influence the viability of the developing embryo and the subsequent condition of the young child. Some of these factors, such as maternal age and parity, exist prior to conception; some, such as maternal nutrition, substance use during pregnancy, and maternal illness, exist at or following conception, but prior to birth; some, such as prematurity and low birth weight, appear at the time of birth; and others, such as failure to thrive and child abuse or neglect, exist after birth. Many of these factors are interrelated, such as when poor maternal nutrition during the prenatal period or prematurity contributes to low birth weight; however, these factors will be considered separately for the purposes of discussion. Further, it is important to note that this section is not meant to be an exhaustive listing of factors that can disrupt development; it is intended merely to illustrate the many possible factors that can disrupt the developmental process.

Maternal Age and Parity

Maternal age and parity (i.e., number of pregnancies) provide clues relating to the course of development of the fetus. Women between the ages of 20 and 35 are in the prime of their childbearing years, although today more women are waiting until their mid-30s or early 40s to have children. Although the risks during pregnancy are still small, they do increase with advancing age. For instance, the risk of Down syndrome increases with age, with rates being approximately 1 in 10,000 for 20-year-old mothers; about 3 in 1,000 for 35-year-old mothers; and 1 in 100 for 40-year-old mothers (Eisenberg, Murkoff, & Hathaway, 1991). Mothers who are 35 or older also may be at increased risk for high blood pressure, diabetes, cardiovascular disease, preterm labor, and postpartum hemorrhage. In some older mothers, a decrease in muscle tone and joint flexibility may contribute to more difficult labor, but this may not be a problem for women who have maintained good physical condition prior to and during pregnancy.

Not only mothers over the age of 35, but also pregnant teenagers are more likely to have high-risk pregnancies. Reasons for the increased risk may include limited prenatal care and poor nutrition, as well as a number of negative social and emotional consequences. This combination of factors may increase the teenage mother's chances of premature labor and delivery of a low-birth-weight child. Both teenage and older mothers have a greater likelihood of developing toxemia (Batshaw & Perret, 1992). Children of adolescent mothers also are at greater risk for a number of physical, emotional, and cognitive problems (Smith, 1994).

Regardless of the mother's age, the first birth carries an added risk because all of the maternal systems involved in pregnancy and delivery have yet to be tested. Subsequent births less than 2 years apart and after the third child also carry additional risks (Apgar & Beck, 1972; Holley, Rosenbaum, & Churchill, 1969), although many of these risks have been linked to poor prenatal care (Blondel, Kaminsky, & Breart, 1980).

Paternal Factors

Until recently it was believed that a father's responsibility in the reproductive process was solely to fertilize the egg and that the male had no involvement in how the child develops in utero. This may not be an accurate reflection of the paternal role, however. It was discovered during this century that the father's sperm decides the sex of the baby, and in the last few decades it has been suggested that an older father's sperm might contribute to birth defects such as Down syndrome (Abroms & Bennett, 1981). Just as in the case of the eggs of the older mother, the undeveloped sperm of the older father have had longer exposure to environmental hazards or teratogens and, consequently, might contain altered or damaged genes or chromosomes (Eisenberg et al., 1991). Ongoing research is still needed to provide greater clarification in this regard, particularly as it may apply to genetic counseling (Hook, 1987). In addition, it has been postulated that a father's sperm may be a vehicle for transporting drugs, such as cocaine, to the egg during fertilization (Yazigi, Odem, & Polakoski, 1991). Therefore, many obstetricians are now considering paternal age and related factors (e.g., substance abuse) as risk factors to development in addition to the age of the mother.

Maternal Nutrition

Over 25 years ago, the Food and Nutrition Board published a landmark report entitled *Maternal Nutrition During the Course of Pregnancy* (National Research Council, 1970), which examined the relationship between nutrition and the course and outcome of pregnancy. This report made recommendations for weight gain and nutritional intake during pregnancy. It also suggested that women should be concerned about their nutritional habits from puberty through the childbearing years because these habits can help prepare the mother for childbirth. Adequate maternal nutrition is important to the health of the expectant mother as well as to that of her unborn child. Poor maternal nutrition will affect the child by not sufficiently meeting the nutritional requirements of the developing fetus and by weakening the mother and, consequently, the intrauterine environment (Herbert, Dodds, & Cefalo, 1993).

During pregnancy, many substances are exchanged between mother and baby as their blood passes through the placenta. Thus, dietary intake by the mother influences the developing fetus. Both quality and quantity of nutrient intake required by a woman increase during pregnancy. Qualitative deficiencies relate to the imbalance of proteins, vitamins, and minerals in the mother's diet. Quantitative deficiencies are simply those in which the mother lacks sufficient caloric intake. A review of data on nutrient intakes during pregnancy indicates that, on the average, women probably meet their recommended daily allowance (RDA) for protein, thiamin, riboflavin, niacin, and vitamins A, B12, and C. Expectant mothers are less likely to meet requirements for folacin, iron, calcium, zinc, magnesium, and vitamins B6, D, and E. This does not necessarily mean that a woman's diet is deficient, however, as many of the RDA requirements are somewhat generous. While a sensible, balanced diet is considered the optimal way for an expectant mother to pass nutrients to her baby, vitamin and mineral supplementation is common.

For example, for women who are on restricted diets, are carrying more than one fetus, are very young, use drugs, or have poor prepregnancy nutritional status, selective supplementation may be warranted. For women who regularly follow suggested dietary guidelines, iron and folacin appear to be the primary nutrients for which requirements cannot be met reasonably by diet alone. The RDA for iron during pregnancy is more than twice as high as the average daily intake. Further, a deficiency in folate in the expectant mother's diet has been associated with neural tube defects (Smithells et al., 1983) and orofacial clefts (Shaw, Lammer, Wasserman, & O'Malley, 1995). In fact, the United States Public Health Service now recommends that all females of childbearing age consume 0.4 mg of folic acid every day during the periconceptual period; that is, one month before conception through the third month of pregnancy (Centers for Disease Control, 1995). In addition, the Department of Health and Human Services and the Food and Drug Administration (FDA) recently announced that many foods in the U.S. will be fortified with folic acid to prevent birth defects (FDA, 1996).

Poor prenatal care and insufficient food intake both are associated with poor pregnancy outcomes. Between the 1960s and 1980s it became common for doctors to recommend a gestational weight gain averaging 24 pounds or more rather than the 20 pounds or less recommended prior to the 1960s. Contemporary best practices suggest a range of weight gain for pregnant women based upon prepregnancy weight-for-height. This change in recommended weight gain for expectant mothers has been accompanied by an increase in mean birth weight of their infants and a reduction in low birth weight (Institute of Medicine, 1990; Susser, 1991). A large body of evidence indicates that gestational weight gain during pregnancy, particularly during the second and third trimesters, is an important determinant of fetal growth. For example, inadequate nutritional intake during the last trimester can permanently reduce the number of brain cells by as much as 40%, and improved nutritional intake after such a period of malnourishment will not increase the number of brain cells (Winick, 1971).

In general, low weight gain during pregnancy is associated with intrauterine growth retardation, which in turn can have adverse consequences for subsequent growth and possible neurobehavioral problems. It also increases the risk of infant mortality. Women with total individual weight gains of less than 22 pounds were two to three times more likely to have growth-retarded full-term babies (Luke, Dickinson, & Petrie, 1981). Conversely, excessive weight gain in pregnancy can be associated with high birth weight and, secondarily, prolonged labor, shoulder dystocia, Caesarean delivery, birth trauma, and asphyxia (Institute of Medicine, 1990).

The Special Supplemental Food Program for Women, Infants and Children (WIC), which is administered by the U.S. Department of Agriculture, has had an increasing impact on the provision of food to low-income pregnant women since 1974 (Rush, 1988). In addition to food or food vouchers, WIC provides education, counseling, and referrals for women who meet state criteria for nutritional risk during pregnancy and the early childhood years of their babies. This program has had a positive impact on the health of pregnant mothers from lower socioeconomic strata and their babies: about a 25% reduction in low birth weight infants and a 44% reduction in very low birth weight infants (U.S. General Accounting Office, 1992).

Substance Use During Pregnancy

Substance use during pregnancy is an area of serious concern, with contemporary estimates suggesting a prevalence of about 11% (Chasnoff, 1991). This figure could be even higher given that many expectant mothers do not report their use of illegal substances. This issue was brought to the fore during the early 1960s when a number of babies were born with no limbs and with other malformations because their mothers had taken thalidomide, a German-made tranquilizer to control vomiting during pregnancy. About 20% of the pregnant women who took thalidomide gave birth to babies with birth defects. This incident dramatically underscored the risks involved in taking any drug during pregnancy. While detrimental effects have been suggested for a variety of drugs, such as heroin, marijuana, and lysergic acid diethylamide (LSD), it is difficult to document the individual impact of these specific substances because many users of illegal drugs experiment with a variety of substances, not to mention variants of the same drug. Many women who use illicit drugs often place their babies at additional risk resulting from poor nutrition and lack of adequate prenatal care.

In general, the specific effects of a drug on a developing fetus are determined by a number of factors. These include the dosage level and the stage of pregnancy during which the drug is taken. In fact, drugs with addictive properties, such as heroin, can cross the placenta barrier and cause the baby to be born addicted to that particular substance. Unfortunately, the infant then must go through withdrawal symptoms similar to those of adult addicts to get the drug out of its system. For the sake of the unborn child, the use of any drug for recreational purposes during the prenatal period should be avoided. This precaution should be extended to include both over-the-counter and prescription drugs, and all medications should be used only when they are recommended by the mother's physician.

Alcohol. Alcohol is the drug most frequently used by women in the United States, with alcohol abuse present in 1% to 2% of all pregnant women in the United States. Estimates suggest that approximately 40,000 infants born each year are affected by prenatal alcohol exposure (National Council on Alcoholism and Drug Dependence, 1990). A number of detrimental short- and long-term effects have been associated with prenatal alcohol use. Some of the most consistent manifestations of significant alcohol exposure are intrauterine growth deficiency, low birth weight, cardiac defects, microcephaly, shortened fetal length, and subsequent cognitive delays (Abel, 1989).

A distinct cluster of characteristics, termed *Fetal Alcohol Syndrome* (FAS), has been identified in infants of alcoholic mothers. These characteristics include (a) pre- and postnatal growth retardation, (b) abnormalities of major organ systems such as the heart and liver, (c) central nervous system abnormalities including microcephaly, mental retardation, or specific neurodevelopmental delays, and (d) distinctive facial characteristics (e.g., short palpebral fissures, a thin upper lip, a flattened and elongated philtrum, minor ear anomalies, and micrognathia) (Shubert & Savage, 1994). These latter features are illustrated in Figure 2.2. The incidence of FAS is approximately 2.2 per 1,000 live births (Abel & Sokol, 1987), and it is estimated that thousands more children may exhibit fetal alcohol effects (FAE); that is, they have some, but not the full range, of FAS characteristics. Barbour (1990) has noted that children with FAE may show a variety of maladaptive behaviors, learning disabilities, speech and language problems, hyperactivity, and attention deficit hyperactivity disorder.

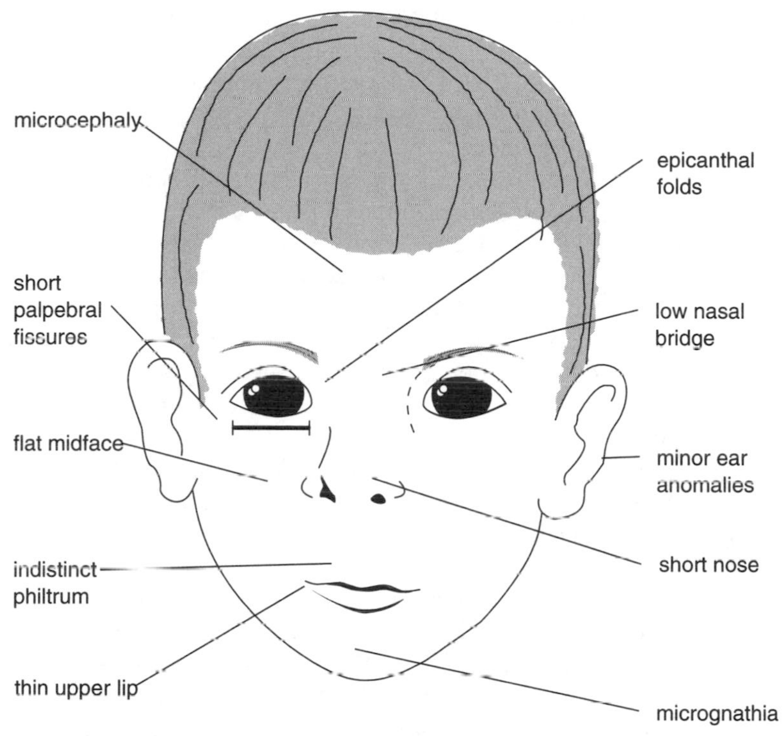

FIGURE 2.2 Distinctive facial characteristics of FAS

Source: Reprinted with permission from the King County Medical Society, Seattle, WA.

Along with fragile-X syndrome in males, FAS is one of the leading known causes of mental retardation in the United States (Abel & Sokol, 1987). Current research also indicates that there may be a dose-response relationship to development; that is, detrimental effects on development seem to increase with the amount and frequency of alcohol consumption (Day & Richardson, 1991). In general, there may be no safe level of alcohol consumption during pregnancy (O'Rahilly & Muller, 1992), although it appears that moderate-to-high levels of alcohol consumption early in pregnancy cause the most severe of problems. A woman is thought to be at increased risk of delivering a baby with FAS when her daily alcohol intake exceeds 80 grams of alcohol per day (10 grams = one glass of wine or half a pint of beer). In fact, fetal growth may be compromised by as little as 40 grams of alcohol per day (Shubert & Savage, 1994). It is thought that one of the primary mechanisms of damage occurs when high blood concentrations of alcohol hinder the transfer of amino acids and other necessary nutrients from the mother to the fetus, thus contributing to fetal hypoxia, subsequent decreased brain weight, and perhaps brain abnormalities. The rate at which alcohol is metabolized also may contribute to these anomalies (Autti-Ramo & Granstrom, 1991).

Tobacco. One million babies are estimated to be at increased risk for low birth weight because their mothers smoke cigarettes (Floyd, Zahniser, Gunter, & Kendrick, 1991). In fact, smoking is one of the most preventable causes of low birth weight babies, yet at least 25% to 30% of pregnant women in the U.S. continue to smoke throughout pregnancy (Benowitz, 1991; Kanwit & Brunel, 1987). The potential impact of this problem has led to the identification of Fetal Tobacco Syndrome (FTS) (Nieburg, Marks, McLaren, & Remington, 1985). This syndrome is characterized by (a) mothers who smoke five or more cigarettes per day, (b) no maternal history of hypertension in pregnancy, (c) fetal growth retardation at term, and (d) no other causes of intrauterine growth retardation. A likely mechanism for FTS involves the vasoconstrictive properties of nicotine. Nicotine actually binds to fetal hemoglobin and, consequently, reduces oxygen availability to the fetus (Longo, 1976).

There have been additional risks associated with smoking during pregnancy including spontaneous abortion, premature delivery, and stillbirth later in pregnancy (Kleinman & Madans, 1985). More recent concern also has focused on the effects of passive exposure to smoking, and correlations have been made to delays in intellectual, academic, and social-emotional development (Rush & Callahan, 1989). Infants whose mothers were exposed to passive smoking also have been found to be at increased risk for illnesses such as pneumonia, bronchitis, laryngitis, and otitis media (Floyd et al., 1991).

As is suspected with alcohol, a strong dose-response relationship seems to exist for smoking; that is, the more a woman smokes during pregnancy, the greater the likelihood that her baby will have low birth weight (Cnattingius, 1997). In fact, Cnattingius reported that the incidence of low birth weight is significantly higher for infants born to women who smoke than for those born to women who do not. More specifically, the rate is higher not only for women who smoke more than 10 cigarettes per day, but also for women who smoke less than 10 cigarettes per day. Further, Cnattingius (1997) reported that age is a significant mediating factor affecting these rates. For example, the risk of a baby being small for his gestational age is about two-fold for teenage mothers who smoke compared to teenage mothers who do not smoke, but the rate more than doubles to about 4.5 times for women over 40 years of age who smoke during pregnancy. Despite these findings, only about 25% of women who smoke stop smoking during pregnancy, and it may be even more difficult to encourage older smokers to quit than younger ones. Nonetheless, smoking remains one of the most preventable risk factors, and quitting smoking even as late as the seventh or eighth month of gestation has a positive influence on an infant's birth weight (Rush & Cassano, 1983).

Other Substances. Since the mid-1980s a number of studies have examined the impact of prenatal cocaine exposure on infant development. Early reports suggested that cocaine use during pregnancy was associated with a host of adverse effects spanning a continuum of severity from significant physical and neurological impairments to very subtle neurobehavioral differences. More recent studies, however, have been less conclusive, in part because of complex methodological issues (Zuckerman & Frank, 1994). The direct impact of cocaine is difficult to document because of its many variants, the concern that women using cocaine are likely to be using other drugs concomitantly, including tobacco, and the problem that there often are coexisting environmental factors of poverty and malnutrition, which can lead to less than optimal pregnancy outcomes. Nonetheless, studies have linked cocaine exposure to smaller babies, either as a result of early delivery or intrauterine growth retardation, or both (Frank, Bresnahan, & Zuckerman, 1993; Robins & Mills, 1993).

Heroin use by expectant mothers also has received recent attention. The use of heroin during pregnancy is associated with decreased birth weight and length (Little et al., 1990), along with other perinatal and postnatal complications. Heroin quickly crosses the placenta, so if the mother is addicted, the infant is too. This addiction results in neonatal withdrawal symptoms affecting both the central and autonomic nervous systems (Strauss & Reynolds, 1983). Symptoms frequently include tremulousness and hyperirritability, a high-pitched cry, and possible sleeping and eating disturbances. Methadone maintenance often is recommended for heroin-addicted women in conjunction with adequate prenatal care, and it has been shown to reduce the incidence of medical complications resulting from prematurity (Kaltenbach & Finnegan, 1987). Although the use of methadone during pregnancy also may have some early effects on the baby, long-term developmental problems are not suspected.

Maternal Illness

Some diseases minimally affect the expectant mother but can devastate her unborn child. Diseases and infections have the greatest influence during the first trimester, when the major body systems are being formed. The effects of rubella on the mother, for example, may be mild or even go unnoticed; however, the unborn child may experience heart malformation or disease, microcephaly, retardation, vision and hearing deficits, or death. There is now a vaccine for rubella that can be administered to prepubescent females to prevent this from becoming a factor during pregnancy. Other maternal illnesses contracted during the prenatal period, such as venereal diseases, toxoplasmosis, toxemia, pica, chicken pox, mumps, measles, scarlet fever, tuberculosis, and urinary tract infections, also may cause children to have various intellectual, motor, physical, or sensory differences or deficits.

Diabetes. With an incidence of between 1.5% to 11.3%, diabetes in expectant mothers can have negative affects on their infants (Magee, Walden, Benedetti, & Knopp, 1993). In pregnancy, there are two main forms of diabetes: gestational diabetes mellitus (GDM) and pregestational diabetes mellitus (PGDM). GDM generally is limited to pregnancy and is not considered to be a maternal disease; it usually is resolved about 6 weeks after the birth of the baby (Ezra & Schenker, 1996). GDM occurs in about 2% to 3% of pregnancies (Herbert et al., 1993).

In contrast, PGDM is a maternal disease that can begin to exert an impact on the pregnancy at the point of conception, particularly if the mother-to-be has not achieved adequate glycemic control (Kitzmiller et al., 1991). This impact may be seen in the form of major and minor abnormalities in the fetus, with the incidence of major abnormalities falling between 5% and 13% (Gotto & Goldman, 1994; Omori et al., 1994). Although these abnormalities can involve nearly all of the body systems (Cousins, 1983), in particular there is a 2-to-19 times higher risk of central nervous system disruption (Reece & Hobbins, 1986) and a 4-to-7 times higher risk of cardiac anomalies (Ferencz, Rubin, McCarter, & Clark, 1990). The most frequent central nervous system malformation is anencephaly (i.e., no brain) followed by spina bifida (Reece & Hobbins, 1986). More generally, infants born to diabetic mothers tend to be larger, heavier, and born somewhat earlier than infants of nondiabetic mothers; they also tend to be more prone to critical levels of hypoglycemia (i.e., low blood sugar) after birth (Ezra & Schenker, 1996). Women with poorly controlled PGDM also experience a higher rate of spontaneous abortion (Katz & Kuller, 1994).

One of the most significant fetal complications of GDM or PGDM is macrosomia (i.e., "large body," or an absolute birth weight of 4000–4500 grams), which occurs 10 times more frequently in infants with diabetic mothers than in infants with nondiabetic mothers. Macrosomia can lead to birth trauma, such as brachial plexus palsy, and asphyxia in labor secondary to difficulties in extracting the baby from the mother. Approximately 25% of fetuses born to diabetic mothers have macrosomia (Spellacy et al., 1985).

A number of etiological factors have been described as contributing to the formation of congenital abnormalities in babies of women with diabetes. These include metabolic abnormalities, such as hyperglycemia (i.e., high blood sugar levels), hypoglycemia (i.e., low blood sugar levels), and hyperinsulinemia (i.e., high insulin levels); hyperketonaemia (i.e., high ketone concentrations), and general genetic susceptibility. While a description of these etiological factors is beyond the scope of this chapter, the main point to note is that one of the key factors necessary for fetal development is glucose. For the fetus, glucose is completely derived from the blood circulation of the mother via diffusion through the placenta. Therefore, the condition of the mother's metabolic system is a critical determinant in fetal growth. Circulating glucose levels that are too high or too low force the fetus to adjust to these conditions because it is completely dependent upon these circulating levels, and this condition sets the stage for the potential of the abnormalities just described (Aerts, Pijnenborg, Verhaeghe, Holemans, & Van Assche, 1996).

Acquired Immunodeficiency Syndrome. One of the most fatal conditions that infants can acquire from their mothers is acquired immunodeficiency syndrome (AIDS). AIDS in young children primarily is the result of congenital or perinatal maternal transmission to the fetus or newborn infant. Transmission of the AIDS-causing virus, the Human Immunodeficiency Virus (HIV), affects about 30% to 50% of infants born to HIV-infected mothers (Fallon, Eddy, Wiesner, & Pizzo, 1989). This transmission also can occur across the placenta, via breast milk, or from intimate contact with other body secretions (Gonik & Hammill, 1990). Not only can development in cognitive, physical, and social domains become slowed or arrested, but actual deterioration of previously achieved skills and milestones also can occur (Crocker, 1992). In addition, the mortality rate is high for these infants, with a median survival rate of approximately 38 months once the child exhibits symptoms of the virus. Although most infected infants may appear to be healthy at birth, symptoms reportedly can occur as early as 8 months of age (Scott et al., 1989), and the incubation period seems to be much shorter in young children than in adults (Rubinstein, 1986). The leading cause of death in HIV-positive children is opportunistic infections secondary to a compromised immune system (Hammill & Murtagh, 1993). Even those children who are fortunate enough to remain uninfected by the virus face a life filled with uncertainty because of their mother's infection.

Maternal Emotional State

The emotional state of the mother does not directly affect her developing child. It has been suggested, however, that the hormonal releases that accompany emotions, particularly those associated with stress and anxiety, affect the baby both before and after birth (Herrenkohl, 1988). These hormonal releases have been associated with the neuroanatomical and biochemical organization of the brain of the fetus as early as 8 weeks following conception. Peptic ulcers related to maternal stress also have been found in newborns (Herrenkohl, 1988).

Stress creates changes in the nervous system that contribute to reduced blood flow to the uterus and, consequently, reduced flow of nutrients and oxygen to the fetus. One of the hormones triggered by increased stress is cortisone. Cortisone is a recognized teratogen to body organs, especially the organs of the reproductive system (Schuster, 1992). Herrenkohl (1988) has noted that the "prenatal stress syndrome" may contribute to the feminization and demasculinization of male offspring, and it may contribute to reproduction dysfunctions in females. More generally, women who are highly anxious or who experience prolonged stress have complicated deliveries, spend about 5 more hours in labor, and have more spontaneous abortions and premature births than their relaxed counterparts. The presence of malformations in babies of mothers with critical stress during the first trimester is higher than in babies of mothers with lower levels of stress (Stott, 1971). Examination of other maternal lifestyle variables has the potential to provide new insights about the effects of maternal emotional states on the fetus (Nathanielsz, 1995).

Blood Incompatibility

Early in pregnancy all women are tested to determine blood type (A, B, AB or O) and Rh factor (positive or negative). If a woman's blood type is Rh positive (which is true of approximately 85% of women), or if both she and the baby's father are Rh negative, there is no cause for concern. If the mother is Rh negative and the father is Rh positive, however, the baby could inherit the father's positive blood type, which could cause a problem during pregnancy or at the time of delivery if the condition is not treated. When the baby's blood enters the Rh-negative mother's circulatory system during delivery, amniocentesis, or the turning of a breech baby, the mother's body produces antibodies to destroy the "foreign substance" in a natural protective immune response. The antibodies are intended to attack the baby's blood cells in the mother's circulatory system, but they can cross the placenta and destroy the fetus' Rh-positive blood cells. These antibodies may not be a problem during a first pregnancy, but they can lead to serious hemolytic or Rh disease in subsequent newborns. When there is a high level of antibodies produced by the mother, many of the fetus' red blood cells are destroyed, eventually leading to severe anemia or possible fetal death. If this condition is left untreated, live births can be complicated by severe jaundice, which can lead to mental retardation, hearing loss, or cerebral palsy.

Fortunately, hemolytic disease of the newborn can be prevented most of the time by injections of gamma globulin, or RhoGam. RhoGam acts to prevent the mother's immune system from reacting to the fetus' red blood cells and producing antibodies. At 28 weeks an expectant Rh mother who shows no antibodies in her blood receives an injection of RhoGam, and another dose is administered within 72 hours of delivery (i.e., delivery, miscarriage, abortion, amniocentesis, or bleeding during pregnancy) if the baby is Rh positive. If it is determined that the Rh mother has begun producing antibodies during pregnancy and that her blood is incompatible with the fetus' blood, maternal antibody levels are carefully monitored. When the incompatibility is severe, which is rare, a fetal transfusion of Rh-negative blood may be necessary. In most cases, however, a transfusion is not necessary or can be done at the time of delivery.

Genetic Abnormalities

Although most babies are born healthy and develop normally, approximately 3% to 4% have defects that are detected prenatally, at birth, or within the first few years of life (National Society of Genetic Counselors, 1989). Some birth defects are inherited, some are a result of environmental influences, and others are attributable to the interaction of heredity and environment. Families with a history of genetic abnormalities may wish to consider genetic counseling, testing, or both as part of their family planning process. It may be important for an expectant couple to be aware of any increased risk so they can consider the possibility of prenatal screening. Parents of a child with developmental difficulties may decide, along with their pediatrician, to have a karyotype (i.e., chromosomal analysis) performed or to have other, more sophisticated genetic testing conducted to diagnose current problems.

Abnormalities caused by hereditary factors are of three types: autosomal inheritance, X-linked inheritance, and defective chromosomes. Table 2.1 (on pages 58–59) provides examples of problems resulting from the three types of genetic abnormalities, their causes, their characteristics, and what is known about the developmental course of individuals with the abnormality.

Autosomal inheritance is a natural process by which traits are transmitted from parents to their children. Two autosomal patterns of inheritance include the autosomal recessive pattern and the autosomal dominant pattern, of which the chances of inheritance are equal for males and females. For an autosomal recessive disorder to occur, both parents must be carriers of a defective recessive gene and transmit this gene to their child; the risk of occurrence is 25% for each conception, as shown in Figure 2.3. Carriers are not usually clinically symptomatic.

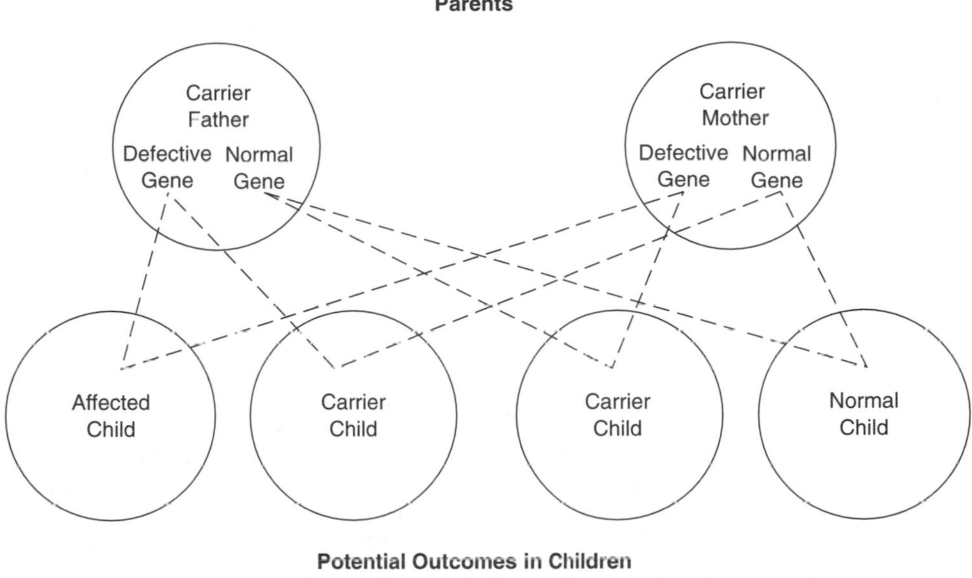

FIGURE 2.3 Pattern of an autosomal recessive disorder

One example of the autosomal type of inheritance pattern is phenylketonuria (PKU). PKU is an inherited inborn error of metabolism for which infants are routinely screened at birth. It is a condition whereby the body is unable to process adequately the food it consumes, particularly with respect to a component of protein called *phenylalanine*. The fetus is unaffected by this metabolic defect prior to birth because excess materials pass freely from child to mother via the placenta (Ensher & Clark, 1994). Following birth, however, and without treatment, the body accumulates excess phenylalanine within tissues, which causes central nervous system damage including mental retardation by one year of age. Early identification of PKU can lead to restriction of the intake of phenylalanine in the diet within the first few weeks of life. Although this special diet may need to continue indefinitely, it has been proven to be effective in preventing adverse outcomes.

Autosomal dominant disorders are different from autosomal recessive disorders in that the individual has the disease when he has a single abnormal gene and thus the risk of transmission is increased to 50%. Autosomal dominant disorders usually involve structural abnormalities (Batshaw & Perret, 1992). This type of inheritance pattern can be seen in Figure 2.4.

An example of the autosomal dominant pattern is neurofibromatosis. Neurofibromatosis is one of the most common genetic disorders, with an incidence rate of approximately 1 per 3,000 births. One of the common signs of this disorder is the presence of large tan spots, or "cafe-au-lait" spots, on the skin. These spots often are present at birth, and they may increase in size, number, and pigmentation with age. Small benign tumors under the skin may appear at any age, and other tumors may be present in and damage major neurological systems; tumors in the

TABLE 2.1 Examples of Genetic Abnormalities

ABNORMALITY	CAUSE/EARLY DETECTION	CHARACTERISTICS	DEVELOPMENTAL COURSE
AUTOSOMAL INHERITANCE			
Cystic fibrosis	Recessive gene/prenatal testing	Glands controlling production of mucus, sweat, tears, and saliva function incorrectly and make breathing difficult. Coughing, recurring pneumonia, large appetite, small size, and enlarged fingertips are symptoms.	Increased risk of severe respiratory infection; possible future candidate for gene therapy.
Phenylketonuria (PKU)	Recessive gene located on chromosome #12/ possible prenatal DNA analysis and routine newborn screening	Inborn error of metabolism; newborn lacks ability to process phenylalanine found in products like milk. If left untreated, can cause mental retardation.	Dietary restriction of phenylalanine beginning in infancy minimizes any effects.
Sickle-cell anemia	Recessive gene/prenatal screening and blood test after birth	Shortage of red blood cells causes pain, damage to vital organs, possible death in childhood or early adulthood.	Chronic illness; often treated medically but there is no cure.
Tay-Sachs disease	Recessive gene/prenatal screening	Progressive nervous system disease that allows a toxic product to accumulate in the brain as a result of enzyme deficiency. Leads to brain damage and death.	Normal development until 6 months of age. Neurological deterioration includes seizures, blindness, mental retardation and death by age 5.
Achondroplasia	Dominant gene/prenatal testing	Disproportionately short stature, relatively large head, short limbs, trident hand, normal intelligence.	Possible delay in developmental milestone attainment; occasional deafness.
Marfan's syndrome	Dominant gene/no prenatal testing at this time; usually diagnosed by physical exam	Tall, thin with hypermobile joints; long, thin spiderlike fingers; spinal curvature, dislocated eye lens.	Prone to lung collapse with high incidence of heart and blood vessel defects; associated with ADHD and learning disabilities.
Neurofibromatosis	Dominant gene; linked to chromosome #17/no prenatal tests; diagnosis based on physical exam	Multiple "cafe-au-lait" spots on body; small nerve tumors on body and skin; some affected persons may have large heads, scoliosis, or variety of bone defects.	No known treatment. Wide variability in expression; may be associated with mild mental retardation or learning disabilities.
X-LINKED INHERITANCE			
Color blindness	X-linked recessive gene	Red-green color blindness	No known cure.
Hemophilia	X-linked recessive gene	Blood lacks important clotting factor	Blood clotting factor is needed to stop bleeding.

TABLE 2.1 Examples of Genetic Abnormalities (Continued)

ABNORMALITY	CAUSE/EARLY DETECTION	CHARACTERISTICS	DEVELOPMENTAL COURSE
			Frequent hospitalizations and chronic problems. No known cure.
Duchenne muscular dystrophy	X-linked recessive gene/ prenatal testing	Normal development until 6 to 9 years of age; then muscular weakness appears and progresses	Progressive disease affecting all muscles including heart and diaphragm; usually results in death during young adulthood.
Fragile-X syndrome	X-linked fragile site/ chromosomal testing available pre- and postnatally	Possibly the most common hereditary form of mental retardation in males, with associated physical features of prominent jaw, large ears and testes.	Children may have associated behavioral problems, hyperactivity, and some autistic-like features.
DEFECTIVE CHROMOSOMES			
Cri du chat syndrome	Deletion on top portion of #5 chromosome	Microcephaly, widely spaced eyes, small chins, and high-pitched cry ("cat cry"); severe retardation.	No known cure.
Down syndrome	Extra chromosome of 21st pair/prenatal testing	Cognitive deficits, hypotonia, facial characteristics, short stature, congenital heart disease.	Developmental progress appears to slow.
Klinefelter's syndrome	Extra X chromosome (45XXY)/prenatal testing	Male child with inadequate testosterone production resulting in abnormal sexual development. Usually tall, slender, with breast development and small genitalia. Close to normal intelligence.	Psychological and psychiatric abnormalities; small percentage has mental retardation, language delays. Medical treatment involves administration of male hormones.
Turner's syndrome	Missing X chromosome (XO or 45X)/prenatal testing	Only disorder associated with survival despite loss of chromosome. All are female, very short, and have webbed necks, widely spaced nipples, and nonfunctional ovaries. Usually of normal intelligence, with visual perceptual difficulties.	Majority of girls have learning disabilities; medical treatment with hormones.
XYY syndrome	Extra Y chromosome/ prenatal testing	Usually tall with normal sexual development but low intelligence. Aggressive behavior; severe acne.	Associated with behavioral problems and learning disabilities. No known cure.

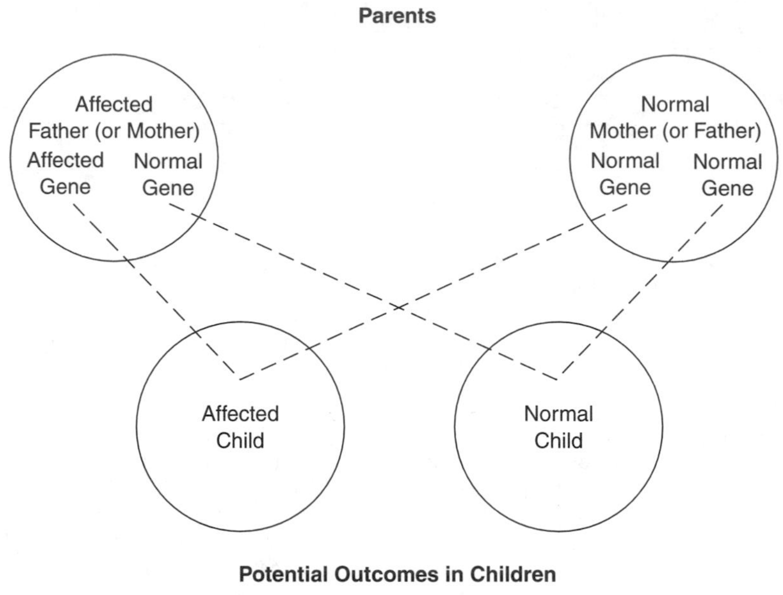

FIGURE 2.4 Pattern of an autosomal dominant disorder

auditory nerve, for example, result in hearing impairment or deafness. The degree of involvement in any single case can vary widely, ranging from relatively few problems to significant learning problems. Currently, there is no prenatal test that can detect neurofibromatosis; the diagnosis is made by physical exam.

The second form of genetic inheritance of abnormalities is referred to as *sex-linked,* or *X-linked,* because it involves genes located on the X, or female, chromosome. With this type of disorder females typically are carriers and males are affected. One variant of an X-linked inheritance pattern can be seen in Figure 2.5.

An example of an X-linked inheritance pattern is fragile-X syndrome. As noted in Table 2.1, fragile-X syndrome is the leading cause of inherited mental retardation in males (Sherman, 1991). The prevalence of mental retardation in males is about 1 per 1,250 compared to about 1 per 2,500 for females. As its name implies, this abnormality relates to a mutation at the bottom of the X chromosome. This mutation can result in a variety of behavioral, emotional, and learning problems (Cohen, 1995; Hagerman, 1996) ranging from subtle learning problems in mildly affected children to severe levels of mental retardation. Both males and females are affected by this disorder, although females tend to have less impairment (Hagerman et al., 1992).

The third type of genetically inherited abnormalities is caused by chromosomal malformations in which chromosomes are added to or deleted from the normal 23 pairs or they are broken. Any of these disruptions can result in birth defects or death. The incidence of chromosomal aberrations is about 0.4%. Autosomal chromosomal abnormalities usually lead to mental retardation and are characterized by distinct physical characteristics (Batshaw & Perret, 1992). Down syndrome is an

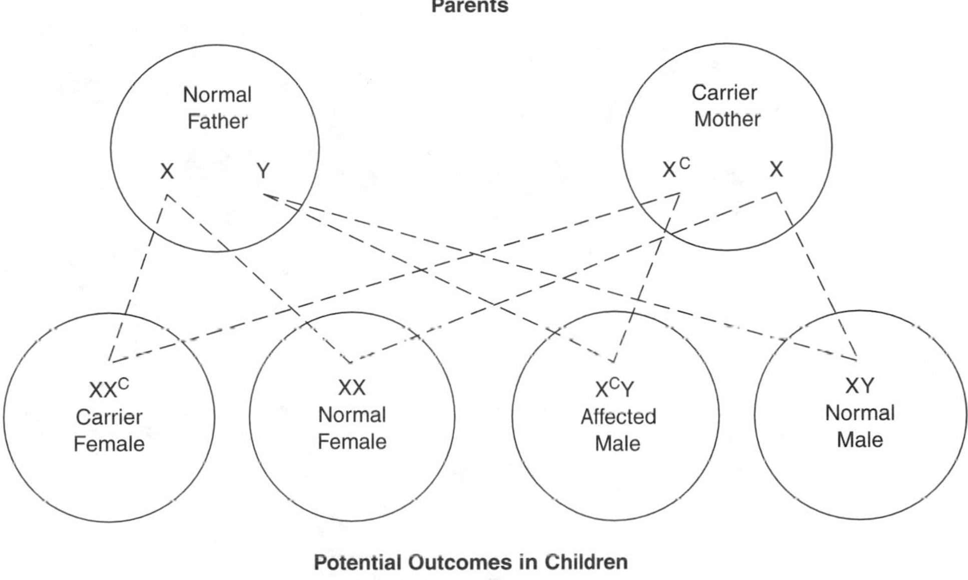

FIGURE 2.5 Example of an X-linked disorder inheritance pattern

example of this type of genetic abnormality, with an incidence rate of about 1 in 770 live births. As noted earlier, this rate tends to increase for expectant mothers over the age of 35. The diagnosis of Down syndrome is typically made on a clinical basis and then confirmed by obtaining a karyotype (Pueschel, 1994); however, prenatal testing also can determine its presence. Selected physical features include a variety of minor anomalies (e.g., flat nasal bridge and short fifth finger), although most individuals manifest only some of these features (Pueschel, 1994). More severe involvement of musculoskeletal, hematological, neurological, endocrine, and cardiac systems also are common (McBrien, Mattheis, & Van Dyke, 1996). Although children diagnosed with Down syndrome tend to show pervasive developmental delays, they also manifest steady rates of development with appropriate educational and family interventions.

Prematurity and Low Birth Weight

Historically, the risk factors of prematurity and low birth weight have been used interchangeably. Certainly, these factors are intimately related in that prematurity tends to be a cause of low birth weight; however, it is important to note that infants born prematurely do not always have low birth weight and, conversely, infants with low birth weight are not always born prematurely. In fact, about 33% of babies with a birth weight of less than 2,500 grams are actually small for their gestational age, perhaps secondary to placental insufficiency. Placental insufficiency reduces the flow of oxygen and nourishment to the fetus (Behrman, 1992).

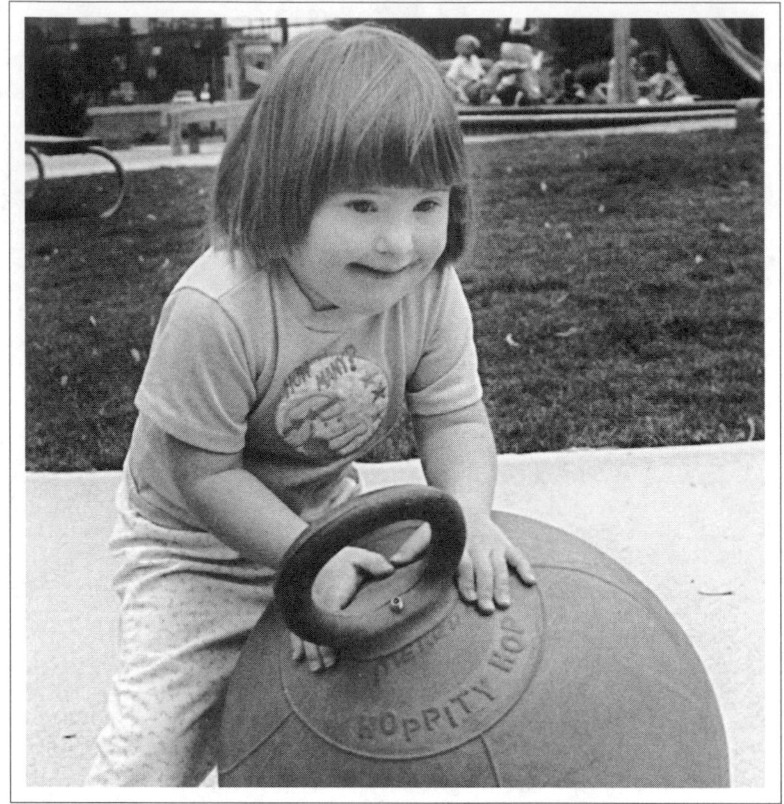

Development is a process of using one's basic skills in new ways, in new settings, and with new materials.

A baby is defined as premature if the period of gestation is less than 37 weeks (Korones, 1986). In the United States about 11% of newborns are classified as premature (Paneth, 1995), although the births of twins and babies with diabetic mothers inflate this figure somewhat because prematurity is an expected outcome in these cases (Lin, Verp, & Sabbagha, 1993). While most babies born after 36 weeks usually experience few problems and have good survival rates, babies born before this time can experience a myriad of problems and risks, including heightened mortality. Currently, most infants who are born at about 6-months gestation do survive, while of those born at 23 weeks about 15% survive, and of those born at 22 weeks and below very few survive (Allen, Donohue, & Dusman, 1993).

Many preterm infants manifest spasmodic and weak reflex movements and crying, show periods of apnea (i.e., not breathing), have problems maintaining body temperature, and may require respiratory assistance until the lungs mature. Lanugo and vernix may still cover the body of the preterm infant. Cerebral hemorrhaging, or bleeding in the brain, also is common in these infants. Improved medical technology has increased the survival rate of premature babies; however, as we shall see with the low birth weight babies, this higher survival rate has increased the vulnerability of surviving premature infants to a host of developmental abnormalities.

Many professionals consider fetal birth weight to be one of the most important indices in the prediction of fetal outcome (Pollack & Divon, 1992). In general, a baby is deemed to be small at birth because it was born too soon (i.e., prematurity), because it grew too slowly in utero (i.e., it is small for its gestational age), or because of a combination of these two factors. More specifically, an infant is viewed as having low birth weight if it weighs less than 2,500 grams, or about 5 pounds, 8 ounces. It has been estimated that, at present, about 7% of all infants are born with low birth weight (Wegman, 1993), with about one half of these births reflecting neonatal deaths (Pollack & Divon, 1992).

Survival rates for infants born with low birth weight have improved dramatically over the past decade, with infants weighing over 1,000 grams having a survival rate of over 90%, and infants weighing 751 to 1,000 grams (i.e., about 1 lb., 10 oz. to 2 lb., 3 oz.) having a survival rate approaching 80%. Infants with birth weights of 501 to 750 grams (i.e., 1 lb., 2 oz. to 1 lb., 10 oz.) have about a 50% chance of survival at present (Tsang, Lucas, Uauy, & Zlotkin, 1993). Infants weighing less than 500 grams at birth rarely survive, although some cases have been reported (Pleasure, Dhand, & Kaar, 1984).

As a general rule of thumb, the further from the 2,500-gram criterion the infant is, the greater the problems it experiences. The closer to the 2,500-gram birth weight criterion the infant is, the better the prognosis. While most low birth weight children function within the normal range across a variety of domains when compared to normal birth weight children, these children tend to show higher rates of mental retardation, cerebral palsy, blindness and deafness, psychomotor problems, school failure, subnormal growth, and related health problems (Hack, Klein, & Taylor, 1995). In fact, cognitive factors, such as intelligence level (IQ), show a direct relationship to birth weight; that is, as birth weight declines, so does IQ (Breslau et al., 1994). Further, school-age children who had birth weights of less than 2,500 grams are nearly 50% more likely than their normal counterparts to be receiving some form of special education (Lewit, Baker, Corman, & Shiono, 1995).

Other complications of prematurity and low birth weight also have been shown to have an impact on later development. For example, children born prematurely, with very low birth weight ($\leq$ 1,500 grams), or both, are at risk for chronic lung disease because of their lack of lung maturity. In fact, lung disease is the most common chronic illness among very low birth weight infants who survive the neonatal period, with an estimated prevalence of between 22% to 26% (Kraybill, Bose, & D'Ercole, 1987). Infants with lung immaturity require mechanical ventilation for at least 30 days or longer (Kraybill et al., 1987). Outcome studies of infants born with chronic lung disease indicate that this condition is associated with an increased risk for developmental abnormalities over and above the problems attributed to very low birth weight (Farel, Hooper, Teplin, Henry, & Kraybill, in press; O'Shea et al., 1996). In fact, some of these developmental abnormalities have contributed to learning difficulties even at 10 to 12 years of age (Vohr et al., 1991).

The use of surfactant has become part of the routine treatment for infants with immature lungs, and its use has increased the survival rate of infants with chronic lung disease (Fujiwara, 1996); however, research to this point suggests that it has not lowered the risk for chronic lung disease nor its associated morbidity (Schwartz, Luby, Scanlon, & Kellogg, 1994).

Another problem resulting from prematurity and low birth weight involves the flow of oxygen to the fetus. Anoxia results from a lack of oxygen during the birth process, while hypoxia results from a reduced flow of oxygen. These conditions can occur during prolonged labor, when excessive pressure can rupture a blood vessel in the brain (intraventricular hemorrhage), or during the birth process when the umbilical cord can become tangled or restricted. In each case, oxygen flow to the baby is disrupted and brain damage can result. In fact, chronic hypoxia has been found to be the cause of at least 60% of postnatal fetal deaths (Manning, Morrison, Lange, & Harman, 1982). In many instances, hypoxia and anoxia cause damage in the motor areas of the brain, and a variety of motor disorders can occur. These disorders as a group are called *cerebral palsy*. Although most babies who experience anoxia or hypoxia do not suffer mental retardation or central nervous system involvement, the risk is higher for these babies than for their problem-free counterparts (Ensher & Clark, 1994).

Failure to Thrive

Failure to thrive (FTT) is a chronic, potentially life-threatening disorder of infancy and early childhood. It strikes as many as 3% to 5% of all infants under one year of age (Mitchell, Gorrell, & Greenberg, 1980) and accounts for 1% of all pediatric hospitalizations (Berwick, 1980). The criteria used to diagnose FTT have been described as a "quagmire of factors" (Drotar, 1983), but generally the term refers to infants and young children whose weight is persistently below the third percentile for age on appropriate standardized growth charts (Berwick, 1980). In the past, some researchers (e.g., Homer & Ludwig, 1981) suggested that three etiological categories were necessary to describe the causation of FTT: organic, nonorganic, and a combination of these. Most cases are of the combined type, however, and the organic-versus-nonorganic distinction is not used by most pediatricians practicing today (Alexander, 1992). Regardless of etiology, the common trait for all infants with FTT is the inadequate intake, retention, or utilization of calories. In addition to medical malnutrition, many of these children show poor physical growth; delayed motor, language, and cognitive skills; and emotional listlessness (Homer & Ludwig, 1981).

Although adequately controlled studies in FTT are rare, it appears that the prognosis is more favorable for the child's physical growth than for cognitive growth (Berwick, 1980). Sturm and Drotar (1989) noted in their longitudinal study of 59 infants with FTT that about 67% of their group achieved normal growth parameters at age 3 years; however, intellectual functioning for the group tended to fall within the borderline range. With respect to treatment, the earlier and more vigorous the intervention is, particularly when the parents are involved and multiple etiological factors are considered, the better the chances of recovery from FTT (Spinner & Siegel, 1987).

Child Abuse and Neglect

In addition to the medically based factors that can influence development, child abuse and neglect can exert a significant influence on the developing child. In 1993, the National Committee to Prevent Child Abuse determined that approximately 2.9 million children in the United States had been identified or reported as being victims of child abuse and neglect (Association for Respite Care and Health, 1994). Abuse can come in several forms: physical, sexual, and psychological. All represent a significant and profound assault on a developing child. Child abuse occurs across racial, ethnic, and socioeconomic groups, and it may be difficult to recognize. Physical abuse and neglect may be the easiest forms to detect; other forms may be manifested by a child's internalizing (e.g., depression and anxiety) or externalizing (e.g., conduct problems) behaviors.

Because the circumstances under which abuse occurs vary dramatically from case to case, and because data are often based on retrospective or speculative information, it is difficult to determine a direct causal relationship between detrimental developmental outcomes and various forms of abuse. Nonetheless, child abuse and neglect have been associated with negative short-term and long-term effects on children's physical development and mental health.

For example, physical abuse in infancy can result in scarring or other deformities, as well as in problems such as mental retardation, seizures, cerebral palsy, or blindness following head trauma (e.g., "shaken baby" syndrome). Neglect of young children puts them at increased risk for poisoning, burns, cuts, and similar types of injuries (Rosenberg & Krugman, 1991). Abuse and neglect during infancy also have been associated with difficulties in the regulation of emotions, poor attachment, language delays, and problems with peers (Cicchetti & Rogosch, 1994). Maltreatment in childhood may lead to behavioral or psychiatric problems that manifest themselves in childhood or adulthood. Conditions such as post-traumatic stress disorder, depression, anxiety, personality disorders, self-injurious behaviors, substance abuse, eating disorders, interpersonal difficulties, and other forms of psychopathology also have been linked to child abuse (Briere & Elliot, 1994; Rosenberg & Krugman, 1991). Indeed, young children with special needs may be at increased risk for abuse and neglect because of the very nature of their needs and disabilities (Alexander & Sherbondy, 1996; Ammerman, Hersen, Van Hasselt, Lubetsky, & Sieck, 1994).

Summary

The development of an individual from conception through childhood is a complex unfolding that is influenced by the processes of heredity and environment. Numerous theories have been proposed to explain how this process occurs; however, no single theory appears to provide a satisfactory explanation for all the intricate events that comprise development. Certainly, children inherit many characteristics from their parents. The environment also shapes the way children behave, how and what they learn, and their rate of development. Selected aspects of the environment may impact neurological growth and development as well.

Stages of development are characterized by major milestones. The division and differentiation of the fertilized egg cell are the most important events during the early gestational period. Later in gestation, major organ systems are refined so that the fetus is prepared for entry into the world. During the gestational period, the developing mother's experiences also are key contributors to this process. For example, food and beverage intake, exposure to toxic substances and disease, and other activities of the mother have an impact on intrauterine life.

Once born, the child's interactions with the environment and the quality of parental care appear to be critical influences on the child's development. Furthermore, observations of developing children over time reinforce the concept that areas of development are interrelated. For example, language development and cognitive skills parallel each other in many ways, and in turn both of these are further influenced by a child's physical health, social-emotional development, family dynamics, school, and cultural expectations. No single theory integrates all of the factors of child development; a holistic perspective of the child more readily lends itself to understanding the multitude of factors that are involved in development. In reading the following chapters, it is important to consider how each area of development affects the others. With an understanding of the complexity of these phenomena, the early childhood special educator or early interventionist will be prepared to identify and address the many needs that young children with disabling conditions have.

References

Abel, E. L. (1989). *Fetal alcohol syndrome: Fetal alcohol effects.* New York: Plenum Press.

Abel, E., & Sokol, R. (1987). Incidence of fetal alcohol syndrome and economic impact of FAS-related anomalies. *Drug and Alcohol Dependency, 19,* 51–70.

Abroms, K. I., & Bennett, J. W. (1981). Age dispersion of parents of Down and non-Down syndrome children. *American Journal of Mental Deficiency, 86,* 204–207.

Aerts, L., Pijnenborg, R., Verhaeghe, J., Holemans, K., & Van Assche, F. A. (1996). Fetal growth and development. In A. Dornhorst & D. R. Hadden (Eds.), *Diabetes and pregnancy: An international approach to diagnosis and management* (pp. 77–97). New York: John Wiley & Sons.

Alexander, R. C. (1992). Failure to thrive. *APSAC Advisor, 5,* 1–13.

Alexander, R. C., & Sherbondy, A. L. (1996). *Child abuse and developmental disabilities.* In M. L. Wolraich (Ed.), *Disorders of development and learning: A practical guide to assessment and management* (2nd ed.) (pp. 164–184). Boston: Mosby.

Allen, M. C., Donohue, P. K., & Dusman, E. E. (1993). The limit of viability—neonatal outcome of infants born at 22 to 25 weeks' gestation. *New England Journal of Medicine, 329,* 1597–1601.

Amand, K. J. S., Phil, D., & Hickey, P. R. (1987). Pain and its effects in the human neonate and fetus. *New England Journal of Medicine, 317,* 1321–1329.

Ammerman, R. T., Hersen, M., Van Hasselt, V. B., Lubetsky, M. J., & Sieck, W. (1994). Maltreatment in psychiatrically hospitalized children and adolescents with developmental disabilities: Prevalence and correlates. *Journal of the American Academy of Child and Adolescent Psychiatry, 33,* 567–576.

Anisfeld, E., Curry, M. A., Hales, D. J., Kennell, J. H., Klaus, M. H., Lipper, E., O'Conner, S., Siegel, E., & Sosa, R. (1983). Maternal-infant bonding: A joint rebuttal. *Pediatrics, 72,* 569–572.

Apgar, V., & Beck, J. (1972). *Is my baby all right? A guide to birth defects.* New York: Trident Press.

Association for Respite Care and Health Factsheet No. 36 (Sept. 1994). *Abuse and neglect of children with disabilities.* Chapel Hill, NC: Chapel Hill Training-Outreach Project.

Autti-Ramo, I., & Granstrom, M. (1991). The psychomotor development during the first year of life of infants exposed to intrauterine alcohol of various duration: Fetal alcohol exposure and development. *Neuropediatrics, 22,* 59–64.

Barbour, B. G. (1990). Alcohol and pregnancy. *Journal of Nurse-Midwifery, 35,* 78–85.

Batshaw, M. L., & Perret, Y. M. (1992). *Children with disabilities.* Baltimore: Paul H. Brookes.

Behrman, R. E. (1992). *Nelson textbook of pediatrics* (14th ed.). Philadelphia: W. B. Saunders.

Behrman, R. E., & Kliegman, J. M. (1983). Jaundice and hyperbilirubinemia in the newborn. In R. E. Behrman, V. C. Vaughan, & W. E. Nelson (Eds.), *Nelson textbook of pediatrics* (12th ed.) (pp. 378–381). Philadelphia: W. B. Saunders.

Behrman, R. E., & Vaughn, V. C. (1987). *Nelson textbook of pediatrics* (13th ed.). Philadelphia: W. B. Saunders.

Benowitz, N. L. (1991). Nicotine replacement therapy during pregnancy. *Journal of the American Medical Association, 266,* 3174–3177.

Berwick, D. (1980). Nonorganic failure to thrive. *Pediatric Review, 1,* 265.

Black, J. K., & Puckett, M. B. (1996). *The young child: Development from prebirth through age eight.* Upper Saddle River, NJ: Prentice Hall.

Blondel, B., Kaminsky, M., & Breart, G. (1980). Antenatal care and maternal demographic and social characteristics: Evolution in France between 1972 and 1976. *Journal of Epidemiology and Community Health, 34,* 157–163.

Bondy, A. S. (1980). Infancy. In S. Gabel & M. T. Erickson (Eds.). *Child development and developmental disabilities.* Boston: Little, Brown.

Breslau, N., DelDotto, J. E., Brown, G. G., Kumar, S., Ezhuthachan, S., Hufnagle, K. G., & Peterson, E. L. (1994). A gradient relationship between low birth weight and IQ at age 6 years. *Archives of Pediatric and Adolescent Medicine, 148,* 377–383.

Briere, J. N., & Elliott, D. M. (1994). Immediate and long-term impacts of child sexual abuse. *The Future of Children: Sexual Abuse of Children, 4,* 54–69.

Centers for Disease Control (1995, March). Prevention program for reducing risk for neural tube defects: South Carolina, 1992–1994. *Morbidity & Mortality Weekly Report, 44(8),* 141–142.

Chasnoff, I. (1991). Drugs, alcohol, pregnancy, and the neonate—pay now or pay later. *Journal of the American Medical Association, 266,* 1567–1568.

Cicchetti, D., & Rogosch, F. A. (1994). The toll of child maltreatment on the developing child. *Child and Adolescent Psychiatric Clinics of North America, 3,* 759–772.

Cnattingius, S. (1997). Maternal age modifies the effect of maternal smoking on intrauterine growth retardation but not on late fetal death and placental abruption. *American Journal of Epidemiology, 145,* 319–323.

Cohen, I. L. (1995). A theoretical analysis of the role of hyperarousal in the learning and behavior of fragile-X males. *Mental Retardation and Developmental Disabilities Research Reviews, 1,* 286–291.

Cousins, L. (1983). Congenital anomalies among infants of diabetic mothers: Etiology, prevention, prenatal diagnosis. *American Journal of Obstetrics and Gynecology, 147,* 333.

Crocker, A. C. (1992). Human immunodeficiency virus infection. In M. D. Levine, W. B. Carey, & A. C. Crocker (Eds.), *Developmental-Behavioral pediatrics* (2nd ed.) (pp. 271–275). Philadelphia: W. B. Saunders.

Day, N. L., & Richardson, G. A. (1991). Prenatal alcohol exposure: A continuum of effects. *Seminars in Perinatology, 15,* 271–279.

Drotar, D. (1983, August). *Outcome in failure to thrive: Implications for prevention.* Kennedy Center Lecture Series at Peabody College of Vanderbilt University, Nashville, TN.

Eisenberg, A., Murkoff, H. E., & Hathaway, S. E. (1991). *What to expect when you're expecting.* New York: Workman.

Ensher, G. L., & Clark, D. A. (1994). *Newborns at risk: Medical care and psychoeducational intervention* (2nd ed.). Gaithersburg, MD: Aspen Publishers, Inc.

Ezra, Y., & Schenker, J. G. (1996). The diabetic fetus. In F. A. Chervenak & A. Kurjak (Eds.), *The fetus as a patient*. New York: John Wiley & Sons.

Fallon, J., Eddy, J., Wiesner, L., & Pizzo, P. (1989). Human immunodeficiency virus infection in children. *Journal of Pediatrics, 114,* 1–27.

Farel, A., Hooper, S. R., Teplin, S., Henry, M., & Kraybill, E. (in press). Very low birthweight infants at 7 years: An assessment of the health and neurodevelopmental risk conveyed by chronic lung disease. *Journal of Learning Disabilities*.

Ferencz, C., Rubin, J. S., McCarter, R. J., & Clark, E. B. (1990). Maternal diabetes and cardiovascular malformations: Predominance of double outlet right ventricle and truncus arteriosus. *Teratology, 41,* 319.

Floyd, R. L., Zahniser, C., Gunter, E. P., & Kendrick, J. S. (1991). Smoking during pregnancy: Prevalence, effects, and intervention strategies. *Birth, 18,* 48–53.

Flynn, A. M. (1989). Natural family planning. In M. Filshie & J. Guillebaud (Eds.), *Contraception: Science and practice*. Boston: Butterworths.

Food and Drug Administration (February 29, 1996). *Folic acid to fortify U.S. food products to prevent birth defects*. Press release.

Frank, D. A., Bresnahan, K., & Zuckerman, B. (1993). Maternal cocaine use: Impact on child health and development. *Advances in Pediatrics, 40,* 65–99.

Fujiwara, T. (1996). Surfactant therapy for neonatal respiratory distress syndrome. In F. A. Chervenak & A. Kurjak (Eds.), *The fetus as a patient*. New York: Parthenon.

Gesell, A., & Ilg, S. (1943). *The infant and child. The culture of today*. New York: Harper Brothers.

Gonik, B., & Hammill, H. A. (1990). AIDS in pregnancy. *Seminars in Pediatric Infectious Disease, 1,* 82–88.

Gotto, M. P., & Goldman, A. S. (1994). Diabetic embryopathy. *Current Opinions in Pediatrics, 6,* 486.

Hack, M., Klein, N. K., & Taylor, H. G. (1995). Long-term developmental outcomes of low birth weight infants. *The Future of Children, 5,* 176–196.

Haesslein, H. C. (1987). Diseases of fetal growth. In K. R. Niswander (Ed.), *Manual of obstetrics: Diagnosis and therapy* (3rd ed.). Boston: Little, Brown.

Hagerman, R. J. (1996). Fragile-X syndrome. In M. L. Wolraich (Ed.), *Disorders of development and learning. A practical guide to assessment and management* (2nd ed.). Boston: Mosby.

Hagerman, R. J., Jackson, C., Amiri, K., Silverman, A. C., O'Connor, R., & Sobesky, W. (1992). Fragile-X girls: Physical and neurocognitive status and outcome. *Pediatrics, 89,* 395–400.

Hammill, H. A., & Murtagh, C. (1993). AIDS during pregnancy. In R. A. Knuppel & J. E. Drukker (Eds.), *High-risk pregnancy. A team approach*. Philadelphia: W. B. Saunders.

Haughey, M. J. (1985). Fetal position during pregnancy. *American Journal of Obstetrics and Gynecology, 153,* 885–886.

Herbert, W. N. P., Dodds, J. M., & Cefalo, R. C. (1993). Nutrition in pregnancy. In R. A. Knuppel & J. E. Drukker (Eds.), *High-risk pregnancy. A team approach* (2nd ed.). Philadelphia: W. B. Saunders.

Herrenkohl, L. R. (1988). The impact of prenatal stress on the developing fetus and child. In R. L. Cohen (Ed.), *Psychiatric consultation in childbirth settings: Parent- and child-oriented approaches*. New York: Plenum Medical Books.

Holley, W. L., Rosenbaum, A. L., & Churchill, J. A. (1969). *Effects of rapid succession of pregnancy*. In *Perinatal factors affecting human development*. Pan-American Health Organization, Pan-American Sanitary Bureau, Regional Office of World Health Organization.

Homer, C. & Ludwig, S. (1981). Categorization of etiology of failure to thrive. *American Journal of the Disabled Child, 735,* 848.

Hook, E. B. (1987). Issues in analysis of data on paternal age and 47, +21: Implications for genetic counseling for Down syndrome. *Human Genetics, 77,* 303–306.

Hubbell, K. M., & Webster, H. F. (1986). Respiratory management of the neonate. In N. S. Streeter (Ed.), *High-risk neonatal care*. Rockville, MD: Aspen Publishing.

Institute of Medicine, National Academy of Sciences (1990). *Nutrition During Pregnancy*. Washington, DC: National Academy Press.

Jensen, A. R. (1980). *Bias in mental testing*. New York: Free Press.

Kaltenbach, K., & Finnegan, L. P. (1987). Perinatal and developmental outcome of infants exposed to methadone in utero. *Neurotoxicology and Teratology, 9,* 311–313.

Kanwit, E., & Brunel, L. E. (1987). Prenatal care. In K. R. Niswander (Ed.), *Manual of obstetrics: Diagnosis and therapy* (3rd ed.). Boston: Little, Brown.

Katz, V. L., & Kuller, J. A. (1994). Recurrent miscarriage. *American Journal of Perinatology, 11,* 386.

Kauppila, O. (1975). The perinatal mortality in breech deliveries and observations on affecting factors: A retrospective study of 2227 cases. *Acta Obstetrica et Gynecologica Scandinavica, 39* (Supplement), 1–79.

Kitzmiller, J. L., Gavin, L. A., Gin, G. D., Jovanovic-Peterson, L., Main, E. K., & Zigrang, W. D. (1991). Preconception care of diabetes: Glycemic control prevents congenital anomalies. *Journal of the American Medical Association, 265,* 731.

Kleinman, J., & Madans, J. H. (1985). The effects of maternal smoking, physical stature, and educational attainment on the incidence of low birth weight. *American Journal of Epidemiology, 121,* 832–855.

Korones, S. B. (1986). *High-risk newborn infants: The basis for intensive nursing care* (4th ed.). St. Louis: C.V. Mosby.

Kraybill, E. N., Bose, C. L., & D'Ercole, A. J. (1987). Chronic lung disease in infants with very low birthweight: A population-based study. *American Journal of Diseases of Children, 141,* 784–788.

Lenneberg, E. H. (1967). *Biological foundations of language.* New York: Wiley.

Levitan, M. (1988). *Textbook of human genetics* (3rd ed.). New York: Oxford University Press.

Lewit, E. M., Baker, L. S., Corman, H., & Shiono, P. H. (1995). The direct cost of low birth weight. *The Future of Children, 5,* 35–56.

Lin, C. L., Verp, M. S., & Sabbagha, R. E. (1993). *The high-risk fetus: Pathophysiology, diagnosis, and management.* New York: Springer-Verlag.

Little, B. B., Snell, L. M., Klein, B. R., Gilstrap, L. C., Knoll, K. A., & Breckenridge, J. D. (1990). Maternal and fetal effects of heroin addiction during pregnancy. *Journal of Reproductive Medicine, 35,* 159–162.

Longo, L. D. (1976). Carbon monoxide: Effects on oxygenation of the fetus in utero. *Science, 194,* 523–525.

Lowrey, G. H. (1986). *Growth and development of children* (8th ed.). Chicago: Year Book Medical.

Luke, B., Dickinson, C., & Petrie, R. H. (1981). Intrauterine growth: Correlation of maternal nutritional status and rate of gestational weight gain. *European Journal of Obstetrics, Gynecology, and Reproductive Biology, 12,* 113–121.

MacFarland, A. (1975). Olfaction in the development of social preferences in the human neonate. *Ciba Foundation Symposium (33).* New York: Elsevier.

Magee, M. S., Walden, C. E., Benedetti, T. J., & Knopp, R. H. (1993). Influence of diagnostic criteria on the incidence of gestational diabetes and perinatal morbidity. *Journal of the American Medical Association, 269,* 609.

Manning, F. A., Morrison, I., Lange, I. R., & Harman, C. (1982). Antepartum determination of fetal health: Composite biophysical profile scoring. *Clinics in Perinatology, 9,* 285–296.

Maurer, D., & Maurer, C. (1988). *The world of the newborn.* New York: Basic Books.

Mazor, M., Hagay, Z. J., Leiberman, J., Biale, Y., & Insler, V. (1985). Fetal abnormalities associated with breech delivery. *Journal of Reproductive Medicine, 30,* 884–886.

McBrien, D. M., Mattheis, P. J., & Van Dyke, D. C. (1996). Down syndrome. In M. L. Wolraich (Ed.), *Disorders of development and learning: A practical guide to assessment and management* (2nd ed.) (pp. 316–345). Boston: Mosby.

Mitchell, W., Gorrell, R., & Greenberg, R. (1980). Failure to thrive: A study in a primary care setting. *Pediatrics, 65,* 971.

Moore, K. L. (1988). *The developing human: Clinically oriented embryology* (4th ed.). Philadelphia: W. B. Saunders.

Moore, K. L., & Persaud, T. V. N. (1993). *The developing human: Clinically oriented embryology.* Philadelphia: W. B. Saunders.

Murray, A. D., Dolby, R. M., Nation, R. L., & Thomas, D. B. (1981). Effects of epidural anesthesia on newborns and their mothers. *Child Development, 52,* 71.

Nathanielsz, P. W. (1995). The role of basic science in preventing low birth weight. *The Future of Children, 5,* 57–70.

National Council on Alcoholism and Drug Dependence (1990). *NCADD fact sheet: Alcohol-related birth defects.* New York: Author.

National Research Council Committee on Maternal Nutrition/Food and Nutrition Board (1970). *Maternal nutrition during the course of pregnancy: A summary report.* Washington, DC: U.S. Government Printing Office.

National Society of Genetic Counselors (November, 1989). *Prenatal Genetic Counseling Fact Sheet.* Wallingford, Pennsylvania: Author.

Nieburg, O., Marks, J. S., McLaren, N. M., & Remington, P. L. (1985). The fetal tobacco syndrome. *Journal of the American Medical Association, 253,* 2998–2999.

Omori, Y., Minei, S., Testuo, T., Nemoto, K., Shimizu, M., & Sanaka, M. (1994). Current status of pregnancy in diabetic women. A comparison of pregnancy in IDDM and NIDDM mothers. *Diabetes Research and Clinical Practice, 24* (Supplement), 273.

O'Rahilly, R., & Muller, F. (1992). *Human embryology and teratology.* New York: Wiley-Liss.

O'Shea, T. M., Goldstein, D. J., deRegnier, R., Sheaffer, C. I., Roberts, D. D., & Dillard, R. G. (1996). Outcome at 4 to 5 years of age in children recovered from neonatal chronic lung disease. *Developmental Medicine and Child Neurology, 38,* 830–839.

Paneth, N. S. (1995). The problem of low birth weight. *The Future of Children, 5,* 19–34.

Pleasure, J. R., Dhand, M., & Kaar, M. (1984). What is the lower limit of viability? Intact survival of a 440 g infant. *American Journal of Diseases in Children, 138,* 783–785.

Pollack, R. N., & Divon, M. Y. (1992). Intrauterine growth retardation: Definition, classification, and etiology. *Clinical Obstetrics and Gynecology, 35,* 99–113.

Pueschel, S. M. (1994). Down syndrome. In S. Parker & B. Zuckerman (Eds.), *Behavioral and developmental pediatrics.* New York: Little, Brown.

Reece, E. A., & Hobbins, J. C. (1986). Diabetic embryopathy: Pathogenesis, prenatal diagnosis, and prevention. *Obstetrics and Gynecology Surveillance, 41,* 325.

Robins, L. N., & Mills, J. L. (Eds.) (1993). Effects of in-utero exposure to street drugs. *Journal of Public Health, 83* (Supplement), 8–32.

Rosenberg, D. A., & Krugman, R. D. (1991). Epidemiology and outcome of child abuse. *Annual Review of Medicine, 42,* 217–224.

Rubinstein, A. (1986). Pediatric AIDS. *Current Problems in Pediatrics, 16,* 361–409.

Rush, D. (1988). Evaluation of the Special Supplemental Food Program for Women, Infants, and Children. *American Journal of Clinical Nutrition Supplement, 48,* 512–519.

Rush, D., & Callahan, K. R. (1989). Exposure to passive cigarette smoking and child development. *Annals of New York Academy of Sciences, 562,* 74–100.

Rush, D., & Cassano, P. (1983). Relationship of cigarette smoking and social class to birth weight and perinatal mortality among all births in Britain, 5–11 April 1970. *Journal of Epidemiology and Community Health, 37,* 249–255.

Schifrin, B. S. (1982). The fetal monitoring polemic. *Clinics in Perinatology, 9,* 399–408.

Schuster, C. S. (1992). Antenatal development. In C. S. Schuster & S. S. Ashburn (Eds.), *The process of human development: A holistic life-span approach* (3rd ed.). Philadelphia: J. B. Lippincott.

Schwartz, R. M., Luby, A. M., Scanlon, J. W., & Kellogg, R. J. (1994). Effects of surfactant on morbidity, mortality, and resource use in newborn infants weighing 500 to 1,500 g. *New England Journal of Medicine, 330,* 1476–1489.

Scott, G. B., Hutto, C., Makuch, R. W., Mastrucci, M. T., O'Connor, T., Mitchell, C. D., Trapida, E. J., & Parks, W. D. (1989). Survival in children with perinatally acquired human immunodeficiency virus type I infection. *New England Journal of Medicine, 321,* 1791–1796.

Shaw, G. M., Lammer, E. J., Wasserman, C. R., & O'Mally, C. D. (1995). Risks of orofacial clefts in children born to women using multivitamins containing folic acid periconceptionally. *Lancet, 346,* 393–396.

Sherman, S. L. (1991). Epidemiology. In R. J. Hagerman & A. Cronister-Silverman (Eds.), *Fragile-X syndrome: Diagnosis, treatment, and research.* Baltimore: Johns Hopkins University Press.

Shubert, P. J., & Savage, B. (1994). Smoking, alcohol, and drug abuse. In D. K. James, P. J. Steer, C. P. Weiner, & B. Gonik (Eds.), *High-risk pregnancy: Management options.* Philadelphia: W. B. Saunders.

Skinner, B. F. (1961). *Cumulative record* (enlarged ed.). New York: Appleton-Century-Crofts.

Smith, T. M. (1994). Adolescent pregnancy. In R. J. Simeonsson (Ed.), *Risk, resilience, and prevention: Promoting the well-being of all children.* Baltimore: Paul H. Brookes.

Smithells, R. W., Nevin, N. C., Seller, M. J., Sheppard, S., Harris, R., Read, A. P., Fielding, D. W., Walker, S., Schorah, C. J., & Wild, J. (1983). Further experience of vitamin supplementation for prevention of neural tube defect recurrences. *Lancet, 1,* 1027–1031.

Spellacy, W. N., Miller, S., Winegar, A., and Peterson, P. Q. (1985). Macrosomia—Maternal characteristics and infant complications. *Obstetrics and Gynecology, 66,* 158–161.

Spinner, M. R., & Siegel, L. (1987). Nonorganic failure to thrive. *Journal of Preventative Psychiatry, 3,* 279–287.

Stott, D. H. (1971). The child's hazards in utero. In J. G. Howells (Ed.), *Modern perspectives in International child psychiatry.* New York: Brunner/Mazel.

Strang, R. (1969). *An introduction to child study.* New York: Macmillan.

Strauss, M. E., & Reynolds, K. S. (1983). Psychological characteristics and development of narcotic-addicted infants. *Drug and Alcohol Dependence, 12,* 381–393.

Sturm, L., & Drotar, D. (1989). Prediction of weight-for-height following intervention in three-year-old children with early histories of nonorganic failure to thrive. *Child Abuse and Neglect, 13,* 19.

Susser, M. (1991). Maternal weight gain, infant birth weight, and diet: Causal sequences. *American Journal of Clinical Nutrition, 53,* 1384–1396.

Tanner, J. M. (1989). *Foetus into man: Physical growth from conception to maturity* (rev. ed.). Cambridge, MA: Harvard University Press.

Tinsley, V. S., & Waters, H. S. (1982). The development of verbal control over motor behavior: A replication and extension of Luria's findings. *Child Development, 53,* 746–753.

Tsang, R. C., Lucas, A., Uauy, R., & Zlotkin, S. (1993). *Nutritional needs of the preterm infant: Scientific basis and practical guidelines.* Philadelphia: Williams & Wilkins.

United States General Accounting Office (1992). *Early intervention: Federal investments like WIC can produce savings.* Washington, DC: Author.

Vogel, F. (1986). *Human genetics: Problems and approaches* (2nd ed.). New York: Springer-Verlag.

Vohr, B. R., Garcia-Coll, C. T., Labato, D., Ynis, K. A., O'Dea, C., & Oh, W. (1991). Neurodevelopmental and medical status of low-birthweight survivors of bronchopulmonary dysplasia at 10–12 years of age. *Developmental Medicine and Child Neurology, 33,* 690–697.

Watson, J. (1924). *Behaviorism.* New York: Norton.

Wegman, M. E. (1993). Annual summary of vital statistics—1992. *Pediatrics, 92,* 743–754.

Westgren, L. M., & Ingemarsson, I. (1988). Breech delivery and mental handicap. *Baillieres Clinical Obstetrics & Gynecology, 2,* 187–194.

Willis, W. G., & Widerstrom, A. H. (1986). Structure and function in prenatal and postnatal neuropsychological development: A dynamic interaction. In G.W. Hynd & J. Obrzut (Eds.), *Child neuropsychology (Vol. 1).* New York: Academic Press.

Winick, M. (1971). Cellular growth during early malnutrition. *Pediatrics, 47,* 969.

Yazigi, R. A., Odem, R. R., & Polakoski, K. L. (1991). Demonstration of specific binding of cocaine to human spermatozoa. *Journal of the American Medical Association, 266,* 1956–1959.

Zuckerman, B., & Frank, D. A. (1994). Prenatal cocaine exposure: Nine years later. *Journal of Pediatrics, 124,* 731–733.

Zuckerman, B., Frank, D. A., Hingson, R., Amaro, H., Levenson, S. M., Kayne, H., Parker, S., Vinci, R., Aboagye, K., Fried, L. E., Cabral, H., Timperi, R., & Bauchner, H. (1989). Effects of maternal marijuana and cocaine use on fetal growth. *New England Journal of Medicine, 320,* 762–768.

3

Partnerships with Families

Zolinda Stoneman and Jeanette E. Manders

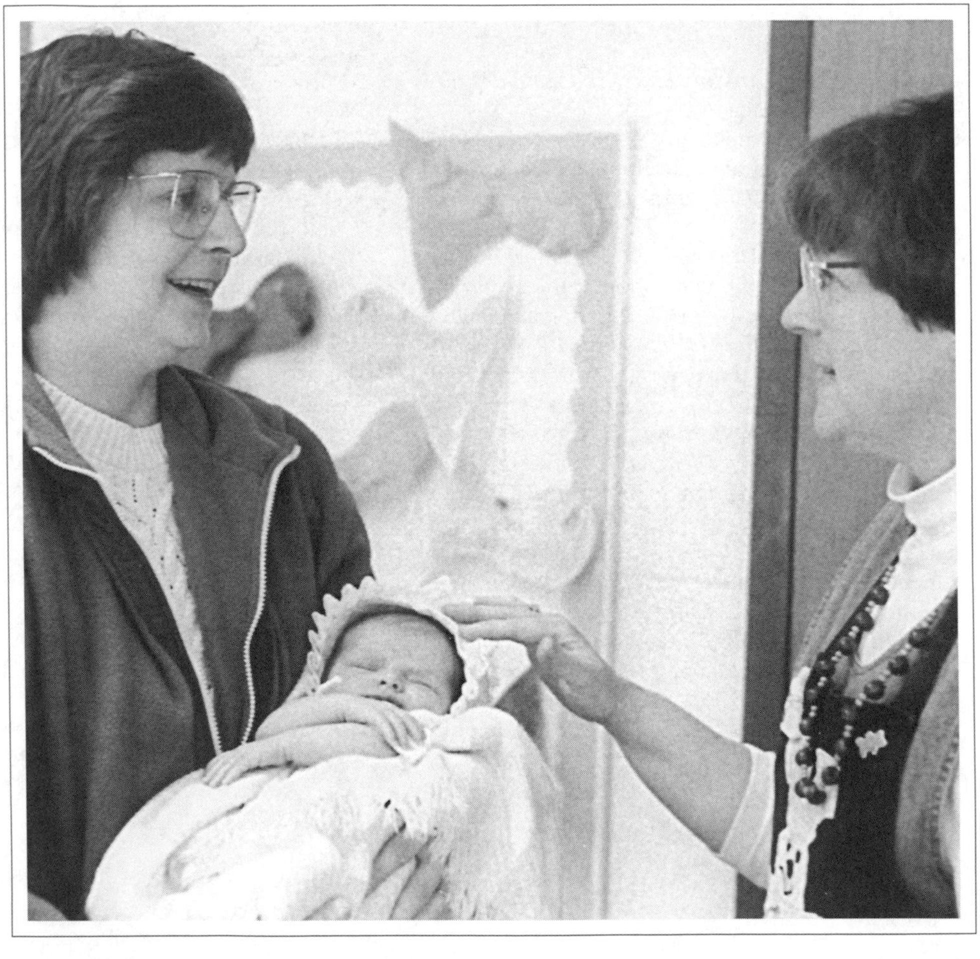

In the past decade, there has been a dramatic change in the role of families in programs for young children with disabilities. An emphasis on parent involvement has given way to a family-centered approach, in which families have the power to direct the services that they and their children receive. Families are the first, and most important, teachers of young children. For many years, this realization prompted educators and other professionals to emphasize parent involvement in infant and preschool programs. Parents were encouraged to attend educational and support-oriented meetings, to assist the teacher in the preschool classroom, to implement intervention programs at home, and to provide information about the child and family to early childhood educators. It was believed that parent involvement would serve the best interests of young children. This approach to parent involvement retained professional control of services and programmatic decisions. Rather than being decision makers, parents' traditional roles have been those of information providers and interventionists who reinforce aspects of the service program at home (Morsink, Thomas, & Correa, 1991).

Recent changes in the role of families are the direct result of federal legislation. When P.L. 99–457 (subsequently reauthorized as the Individuals with Disabilities Act, or IDEA) was enacted into law in 1986, the role of families in the development and implementation of programs for young children with disabilities was radically enhanced. Part H of this act, which focuses on children from birth through 2 years of age, codified into law the requirement that each family be offered a central role in its child's early intervention program. This requirement formally recognizes the family as the most important constant in each child's life, and the family environment as the richest context for social, emotional, cognitive, and physical development. The role of the service delivery system and service providers is seen as that of supporting the family. Part H further strengthens this concept by the use of language such as "family-centered" and "family-focused" care, and by the development of individualized family service plans (IFSPs) (Safer & Hamilton, 1993). The IFSP allows for the expansion of the intervention focus to include families as well as their children.

Part B of IDEA, which focuses on services to preschool children (ages 3–5) with disabilities, also stresses the important roles to be played by families. Parents of preschool children are given a significant role in the design and evaluation of services provided to their children; they are partners with the schools in developing individualized education plans (IEPs). Clearly, the rights, roles, and responsibilities of parents of children with disabilities have been greatly changed and expanded in the past decade. In family-centered programs, families control the early intervention process. This change in the role of families has created a need for early intervention professionals who (a) embrace family-centered values, (b) understand family systems, (c) accept diversity among families, and (d) have the attitudes and skills necessary to work in partnership with families. The remainder of this chapter is organized around these four themes.

Family-Centered Values

Implementing family-centered approaches to intervention requires a dramatic shift in the way that many professionals think about families. To be successful, the interventionist must hold a set of attitudes, or values, that place the needs and desires of the family at the center of the intervention process. This value system is counter to the child-centered approach historically endorsed by early intervention professionals, regardless of disciplinary background. Professional training programs, including those in early intervention, have concentrated on teaching students how to be experts in a particular content area (Racino, O'Connor, & Walker, 1993). Family-centered approaches require that professionals relinquish this "expert" role, instead creating a partnership with families in which both the professional and the family member have equal status.

Early intervention services based on family-centered values have four defining characteristics: (a) the family is actively included in decision making and planning, (b) services and support are developed for the whole family, not just for the child, (c) family priorities guide the goals and services, and (d) the preference of the family concerning its level of participation in the program is respected (Murphy, Lee, Turnbull, & Turbiville, 1995). Each of these characteristics is discussed briefly in the following paragraphs.

Families as Decision Makers

In family-centered programs, families hold the power to make key decisions about their children. Professionals believe that families are capable of making wise and responsible decisions about their children and about the family as a whole. Parents are encouraged to take a leadership role on the intervention team rather than acting as passive participants (McBride, Brotherson, Joanning, Whiddon, & Demmitt, 1993). Family decisions are respected, even when they conflict with the recommendations of professionals.

Support for the Whole Family

Forest and Pearpoint have noted that "families who . . . do not have support systems for all their members cannot adequately build support around their children" (1992, p. 77). Support for the whole family, including the mother, father, siblings, and extended family members, recognizes that family members are interdependent and that the development of the child with a disability is enhanced when the family is strong and all members' needs are respected. Even in the most compromised circumstances, all families have strengths (Dunst, Trivette, & Deal, 1988). Interventionists using family-centered approaches value the family and focus on identifying and enhancing family strengths and capabilities. The needs of mothers, fathers, and

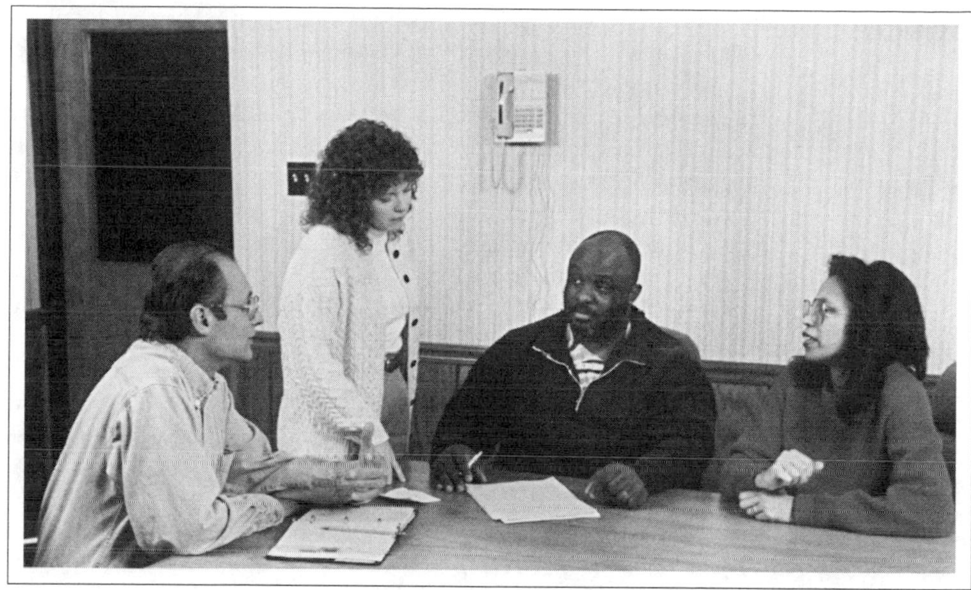

Parents should be encouraged to take a leadership role on the intervention team.

siblings are considered, as well as the needs of other family caregivers. Natural support systems (e.g., friends, relatives, and members of the clergy) are utilized to assist the family in achieving its goals.

Family Priorities Guide Goals and Services

In family-centered early intervention programs, services reflect the choices and preferences of families and are tailored to meet their needs. Goals on the IFSP and the IEP are selected by the family. Family members have the opportunity to be actively involved in all aspects of their child's program, including assessment, writing the program plan, selecting appropriate services and service providers, implementing the intervention, and evaluating the outcomes of the intervention. Parents are asked their ideas about how to accomplish targeted goals and about existing family resources for carrying out intervention activities (e.g., transportation and child care). The interventionist works with parents to generate intervention options and lets the family members decide which options best fit their resources and desires (McWilliam & Winton, 1990).

The Preferred Level of Family Involvement Is Respected

Some families prefer to be actively involved in all aspects of their children's programs; others want professionals to plan and implement the intervention with little family involvement. In family-centered intervention programs, all families are given the option of controlling their children's programs. Not all families want this level of responsibility. The extent to which they choose to engage in intervention activities may vary greatly among families and change over time. For example, some parents may decline a particular service in order to have time for the family to participate in much-needed recreation or leisure or to engage in other nondisability-related activities. The importance of such activities for the resilience and well-being of all family members is recognized, and their choices are validated.

Family members have the right to have minimal participation in their child's program, if that is their choice, without being viewed as "bad" or "uninterested" parents. Interventionists are respectful of family routines and commitments, and they schedule evening meetings, weekend home visits, and so on to accommodate the family's schedule (McBride et al., 1993). Interventions are developed that fit within the daily routines of the child and family (McWilliam & Winton, 1990). Families are not pressured into any choice of services, nor are they denied those services at a later date if their needs change.

The Family as a System

In addition to adopting a family-centered values base, it is important that early interventionists appreciate the systemic nature of the family. A family is more than a collection of individual members. Families are organized networks of interpersonal relationships. Family-systems theory recognizes that there are complex interconnections among family members. In the family system, many roles and rules guide individual and family functioning. Within the larger system of the family are subsystems made up of smaller groups of family members. For example, there may be a husband and wife subsystem, a parent and child subsystem, a grandparent and parent subsystem, and a sibling subsystem, all within the same family. The members of these subsystems have strong influences on each other. Each subsystem also has influences on other subsystems and on the family as a whole. Thus, change or intervention in one part of the family can affect the entire family system (Minuchin, 1974). A change in the relationship between the parent and one child, for example, might affect the marriage and the relationships between siblings as well. Similarly, when events impact one member of a family, all family members are changed in some way.

This conceptualization of the family as a system is important when intervention programs for young children are being planned. As noted by Seligman and Darling (1989), "Strategies need to be considered within the context of the other subsystems so that the resolution of one problem does not bring about the emergence of others" (p. 7). For example, failure to consider what effect multiple forms of time-consuming, out-of-home therapy may have on the relationship between the child and her sibling, or on the relationship between her parents, may limit the extent to which therapy can be successful. The addition of stress-creating therapy or intervention demands also may create conflict in the marital relationship(s), or in the relationships between siblings. When families alter their schedules to include additional teaching or therapeutic activities, this alteration can have a direct positive effect on the functioning of the child, but at the cost of family harmony and cohesion. In such a case, the child with the disability may achieve short-term benefits from the additional teaching or therapy, but, in the long term, the developmental progress of this child may be compromised by the stress and conflict created in the child's family. It is important that service providers monitor the extent to which families are being asked to perform specific duties, and that they recognize that overburdening in one area of family functioning can negatively impact functioning in another area to the overall detriment of the child and family (Seligman & Darling, 1989).

To function as a family system, individual family members are assigned roles and responsibilities. Rules are developed about how family members are to behave in those roles. Service providers who wish to deliver the most appropriate and helpful services to families of children with disabilities must be aware of the assigned roles and family rules unique to each family. This often entails spending time talking with all possible family members in an informal, open, and respectful manner before suggesting interventions. In general, families will be most open to suggestions, interventions, and changes that most closely fit their already-established values and behaviors. The following sections of this chapter discuss the family roles often filled by parents, spouses, siblings, the child with a disability, and members of the extended family. Changes in the family system over time (the family life cycle) also are discussed.

Parental Roles

Even with the recent major societal changes in the roles of women, many two-parent families still divide family responsibilities based on traditional gender roles in order to decrease ambiguity and clarify task responsibility. In part because of the specialized care sometimes required, one parent—often the mother—may assume primary responsibility for the care of the child with a disability (Breslau, 1983). Married mothers of children with disabilities may be less likely to work than mothers who do not have children with disabilities (Breslau, Salkever, & Staruch, 1982). It is important to note, however, that in some families the father is the primary caretaker of the child, while other families are headed by a single-parent father.

Early interventionists often use the term *parents* when, in practice, they mean *mothers* (Pearl, 1993). It is vital that fathers be supported in their efforts to participate in their children's intervention programs, consistent with their preferred roles or levels of involvement. This may mean scheduling meetings when fathers can attend or communicating directly with a father over the phone rather than immediately asking to speak with the mother. Some reasons that have been given for resistance to meeting "family goals" that have been determined in individualized family service plans have included a lack of paternal input and support, and paternal priorities that differ from maternal priorities (Pearl, 1993). It is important that service providers talk directly with both mothers and fathers about their preferred roles in the home and in intervention, and determine whether the roles they have assumed are based on their own choices or have been imposed upon them by the service delivery system.

Parents of children with disabilities often are expected to function as educators, speech therapists, physical therapists, medical technicians, advocates, service planners, and in numerous other roles not usually assumed by family members. Parents are asked to perform these other duties, sometimes to the exclusion of the primary role of all parents—that of nurturer. Asking parents to perform such a complex array of duties can have unanticipated negative consequences, sometimes interfering with the formation of healthy attachment and normal parent-child relationships. Expecting that parents perform painful physical exercises, certain behavior modification strategies, or intensive educational strategies may have short-term benefits for the child, but it also may disrupt important aspects of the child's family environment. Creating expanded parent-role expectations can be especially problematic in single-parent families in which a second caregiver is not available to share added tasks and responsibilities.

Marital Roles

Parents are partners with each other as well as parents to their children. The relationship between parents is a very important predictor of overall family functioning. Marital satisfaction and harmony have been associated with more-positive parental attitudes, less-strict beliefs about child discipline, more-sensitive father-child interaction, and fewer feelings of parental annoyance with the child than those experienced by parents with less-satisfying relationships (Stoneman & Brody, 1993). Marital security and satisfaction have been identified as key variables in successful maternal coping and resistance to disorganization in families with children with disabilities (Friedrich, 1979; Nihira, Mink, & Meyers, 1981).

Some marriages experience additional stressors related to parenting a child with a disability (Wright, Matlock, & Matlock, 1985). It is important to recognize, however, that many marriages are not adversely affected by disability, and many become even stronger (Lambie & Daniels-Mohring, 1993; Longo & Bond, 1984). Two main parental characteristics that are associated with positive marital adjustment are a healthy and supportive marital relationship prior to the identification of a disability and the strengths of the individual spouses (Abbott & Meredith, 1986). The importance of the marital relationship must be recognized, and service providers should support the maintenance of healthy marital partnerships through the provision of services, such as respite care, that allow the couple to spend time away from caretaking or disability-related duties. Similarly, for single parents, it is important to recognize the parent's need for time away from child-related responsibilities and to support the parent in maintaining a healthy network of social relationships.

Sibling Roles

Brothers and sisters serve as teachers, caretakers, friends, and playmates to each other. The relationships between the siblings in families of children with disabilities are very similar to all sibling relationships. Few differences have been found in the levels of play, social activities, or conflict. In fact, siblings have been found to be very good at choosing play materials and activities that allow for extended social interaction with their brothers and sisters with mental retardation (Stoneman, Brody, Davis, & Crapps, 1987). In general, the level of adjustment of siblings of children with disabilities tends to be reflective of the attitudes and feelings of their parents (Powell & Gallagher, 1993). Siblings benefit when parents are open and supportive in talking with siblings about the brother or sister with a disability.

Brothers and sisters of children with disabilities do have developmental needs of their own that can be addressed by early intervention. During home visits, it is helpful for the interventionist to include siblings in ongoing activities, listen to the siblings' communications, and provide play materials for siblings as well as for the child with a disability. By actively including siblings in the visit, interventionists can help siblings understand that they are an important part of the family, worthy of the interventionist's time and attention. Services designed specifically for brothers and sisters can help normalize feelings and fears, increase family communication, and highlight family strengths (Powell & Gallagher, 1993). Resources such as the Sibling Need and Involvement Profile (SNIP), (Fish, McCaffrey, Bush, & Piskur, 1995) and Sibshops (Meyer, Vadasy, & Fewell, 1985) are useful tools that can be used to explore siblings' levels of awareness, feelings, and desired roles and responsibilities. Both resources include helpful reading lists for parents, siblings, and service providers. Sibling support groups can help children share their experiences as well as realize that there are many other children in similar family situations.

Stoneman and Brody (1982) provide several suggestions for families with children with disabilities and their siblings. These include assigning siblings child-care or household responsibilities that are consistent with their levels of maturity. While such tasks can increase siblings' feelings of competence and self-esteem and also can help alleviate parental overload, care should be taken that the assigned responsibilities do not overburden siblings or limit their development in other areas, such as academic achievement or peer relationships. Siblings are often very good at teaching their brothers and sisters as well as modeling and reinforcing desired skills and behaviors. Allowing siblings without disabilities to assume teaching roles can be beneficial for all involved. It also is important to recognize areas in which the child with a disability may have greater skills than her siblings and encourage her to teach those skills to her brothers and sisters. Such opportunities serve to teach and reinforce skills for each of the siblings, as well as to help build self-esteem.

It is important for families, and for interventionists, to recognize the needs of siblings and to avoid an exclusive focus on the child with the disability or on disability-related issues and activities. Teachers and service providers should consider the impact of goals and strategies on siblings while planning services, and recognize the importance of family involvement in nondisability-related activities, including leisure time. Children without disabilities need the freedom and support from their families to pursue their own interests and activities.

Although there is still much to learn about the brothers and sisters of children with developmental disabilities, we do know that, given appropriate support and

The adjustment level of siblings of children with disabilities tends to be reflective of the parents' attitudes and feelings.

opportunities, sibling relationships in these families are characterized by many of the same strengths and challenges found in all other families. Brothers and sisters of children with disabilities can benefit from the expanded opportunities for role enactment and personal growth when the family system responds positively to the child with a disability.

The Role of the Child with a Disability

Parents, siblings, grandparents, and other family members develop relationships with the child with a disability based on their understanding of who the child is and what her unique qualities are. Families can be very good at adapting roles to fit the strengths and needs of each family member, including the child with a disability. To support the full inclusion of the child with a disability within the family, it is important that all family members have frequent and informal opportunities to interact with the child in the same way that they interact with the other children in the family. Such opportunities might include baby-sitting, picnics, family visits, vacations, or bedtime rituals such as reading and storytelling. These naturally occurring family interactions allow for the development of a more complete image of the child, independent of the disability.

The formation of a holistic view of a child, along with clear and accurate information about the disability, reduces the possibility that the child will be labeled as the "vulnerable," "needy," or "special" one in the family and will have areas of strength and potential go unrecognized. Interventionists can promote this holistic perspective by frequently engaging in conversations with family members regarding characteristics of the child that are not directly related to the disability, including the child's strengths, interests, and personality traits. Of course, to support this family view, it is important that the interventionist know the child well enough to have developed a personal perception of the whole child. An interventionist who cannot see beyond the child's disability cannot support a family in taking a more holistic view. Because of the daily opportunities that family members have to get to know their child with a disability in multiple contexts, it is often the members of the family who naturally develop a comprehensive, holistic view of the child. Ironically, it can be the family's task to help the interventionist see beyond the disability and appreciate the complexity of the whole child.

Parents often form their expectations for their children based on information given to them by doctors, interventionists, educators, and various other professionals. This is particularly true during infancy and early childhood. It is frequently the case, however, that unambiguous answers regarding the implications of the disability for the child's health or development are not available. Such a situation can be particularly difficult for family members as they seek to define the child's role in their lives. Some members may be reluctant to form strong bonds with a child with a life-threatening medical condition or discouraged from doing so by well-intentioned friends, relatives, or professionals. Others may be unsure of what role to give a child who is frequently out of the home because of treatments or hospitalization, or whose developmental progress is in question. In the past, many service providers presented worst-case scenarios as fact in order to prepare families for what might lie ahead. While it was intended to save the family pain or disappointment later, this practice has functioned to limit child outcomes and jeopardize the formation of healthy attachments in the family. Service providers must be straightforward regarding the limitations of available knowledge, and provide parents and other family members the opportunity to talk about the challenges associated with living with such uncertainty. Parent and sibling support groups can be particularly useful in these circumstances. As with all children, those with disabilities frequently shape their own roles in their families by their interests, personalities, and talents. The unique characteristics of each child must be recognized and celebrated.

The Role of the Extended Family

Increased family mobility and an emphasis on independence rather than interdependence have functioned to limit extended family networks as sources of support (Santelli, Turnbull, Lerner, & Marquis, 1993). Many families, however, do continue to rely on extended family members to provide emotional and practical help with child rearing. Support from other family members has been found to have greater positive effects on the behavior and attitudes of mothers of children with disabilities than does support either from friends or from members of the community (Crnic, Greenberg, Ragozin, Robinson, & Basham, 1983). In some families, including those with young single parents or parents with multiple life stresses, grandparents may be the primary caregivers for the child with a disability. Thus, it is important that interventionists ask specific questions regarding the involvement of extended family members and their attitudes and behaviors toward the child. Grandparents, aunts, uncles, and other relatives often have emotional and informational needs related to the child's disability that could be met through involvement in early intervention. Additionally, they frequently have unique perspectives on the child and can be sources of additional information for the interventionist, as well as sources of family support. All people identified as members of the family should be offered the opportunity to participate in support groups, educational activities, or IFSPs when such involvement is desired by the parents.

The Family Life Cycle

In understanding the family as a system, it is important to consider how that system changes over time. It has long been accepted that children develop in orderly and predictable stages (Erikson, 1963; Piaget, 1952). Theorists now recognize that families also change through a series of predictable events and developmental milestones; this ongoing change is the family life cycle. A six-stage family life cycle has been proposed by Carter and McGoldrick (1980) to describe the sequence of change in family development: (a) the newly married couple, (b) families with young children, (c) child-rearing families, (d) families with adolescents, (e) families launching children, and (f) families in later life. Obviously, many families, such as single-parent families and those headed by grandparents, do not follow these six stages; nonetheless, the stage model of family development provides an important context for thinking about the changes experienced over time by families of young children with disabilities.

Each stage of family development is marked by a plateau period and a transitional period (Carter & McGoldrick, 1980; Lambie & Daniels-Mohring, 1993). Plateau periods are characterized by relative stability in roles and events. For example, families of infants develop roles, rules, and routines that guide and facilitate the day-to-day functioning of the family during that particular stage. Transitional periods begin when some life event necessitates change in the structure or function of the family. Many life events can be expected, such as the birth of a child or the first day of kindergarten. Others are unexpected, such as an unplanned teen pregnancy or the early death of a spouse (Lambie & Daniels-Mohring, 1993). While transitions are often periods of increased anxiety, uncertainty, or a sense of loss (Olson, et. al., 1983), events that are expected or on time tend to cause less stress than those that are unexpected or occur at unusual points in the life cycle (Walsh, 1982).

The birth or diagnosis of a child with a disability is usually an unexpected life event. Family members may react in a variety of ways. Possible parental responses include denial, blame, fear, guilt, grief, withdrawal, rejection, and acceptance (Berger, 1987). Grief, or mourning, often has been addressed as a common response to learning that a child has a disability, in part as a result of cultural norms that maintain health and ablebodiedness as necessary for happiness and acceptance (Powers, 1993). Grief is sometimes viewed as the result of a family's attempt to cope with the loss of the "perfect" child they anticipated during pregnancy (Patterson, 1988). It should be noted, however, that theories regarding grief or chronic sorrow as they are related to disability have been challenged by some interventionists who view these feelings as the result of negative and pessimistic attitudes regarding the effects of disability on the lives of children and families. Indeed, many family members do not report feelings of loss, grief, or sorrow.

Family members vary in their initial responses to the diagnosis or birth of a child with a disability, and responses can change over time. There is no single "correct" or permanent reaction. Services and levels of involvement that are necessary at one stage of coping or decision making may be viewed as unnecessary, intrusive, or disrespectful at another stage. For example, some parents may be highly active and involved in planning and decision making immediately following the initial diagnosis of a disability, and later they may wish to alter their roles to allow them more time to focus on other aspects of their child's life. Other parents may want more time to make decisions or define their roles, gradually increasing their levels of involvement. Service providers must be careful to monitor such changes and adjust their roles accordingly.

Relatively few controlled studies have been conducted to examine the initial responses of family members to the discovery that their child has a disability, and so we have very limited information on the variety of reactions experienced by parents or other family members and the factors contributing to differences in these experiences (Powers, 1993). It is clear, however, that not all families are alike, and that it is inappropriate to make assumptions about what families or individual members of a family are feeling or experiencing, without first talking with them and listening to their communications.

Transitions in the family life cycle can be particularly stressful for families of children with disabilities for a number of reasons. First, when feelings of loss or grieving are experienced, they may need to be addressed at each stage of child and family development (Hollins, 1985). Milestones such as self-feeding, walking, talking, and toilet training, which provide a sense of accomplishment and satisfaction for family members, may be delayed or never occur, renewing feelings of sadness or grief. Second, families of children with developmental disabilities often must begin making plans for later stages in the family life cycle much sooner than other families do. For example, families of infants with disabilities are often encouraged to engage in estate planning, because of the legal complexities of guardianship and wills for children with disabilities. Third, when a child is found to have a disability, an extensive network of service providers becomes active almost immediately (e.g., social workers, doctors, therapists, and early interventionists). Normative transitions, such as entering school, are marked by the involvement of new and often larger systems of service provision. Many families need ongoing support in defining roles, relationships, and responsibilities within these systems, and in renegotiating these as needs and circumstances change throughout the family life cycle. For this reason, it has been recommended that interventionists function as "consultants to the system," by helping families understand and negotiate issues associated with service provision systems (Imber-Black, 1987).

Parents of children with disabilities face all of the typical demands associated with parenting, as well as the additional challenges posed by parenting a child with a disability. The first choice of social support for many parents is other parents in similar situations (Boukydis, 1984). To meet this need, Parent-to-Parent programs began in the early 1970s and quickly expanded. Today, there are over 350 Parent-to-Parent programs in the United States and many in other countries (Santelli, 1992). The success of the programs is based on the personalized support for new members offered by well-trained veteran parents who have children with similar disabilities or who share similar life experiences (Santelli, Turnbull, Lerner, & Marquis, 1993). The shared information and emotional support received by the family reduce isolation and support active involvement and decision making related to disability issues.

Family Diversity

Early interventionists are called upon to serve families representing a wide variety of situations, backgrounds, and philosophies. Two ways in which families may differ from others that are of particular importance to service providers are family membership and cultural identity. Awareness and respect for family diversity in these areas are critical to the provision of sensitive and effective services. Both of these areas of family diversity are discussed in the following sections of this chapter.

Family Membership

In addition to rules about what family members are expected to do and how they are expected to behave, families also have rules about who is included as part of the family. These boundaries help define the roles and responsibilities of family members, and they also determine who has access to private activities and information within the family. Boundaries are determined by each family and are often strongly influenced by culture. For example, findings from numerous studies indicate that African-Americans tend to have larger, more extensive family networks and tend to emphasize the importance of extended family relationships (Sudarkasa, 1980).

Historically, the provision of human services has been based on the traditional definition of a family as a married couple with children living in the same household. Families in today's society, however, are of many different types and have many different structures, including nonmarital relationships and parenting partnerships, families with single parents in the home, blended families with stepparents, families raising adopted or foster children, and multigenerational households. Indeed, one recent definition describes *family* as "any group of people who are related legally or by blood, or who are perceived to be family by the members" (Thomas 1992, p. 36). Thus, service providers in early intervention must be prepared to recognize and honor each family's unique boundaries and definition of membership. Such recognition entails taking time to get to know each family's structure and individual members and allowing for the participation of all family members in meetings. It is important to value the contributions of each member, including nonmarital partners, extended kin, friends, and religious and community leaders.

Cultural Identity

The culture of a family is a primary determinant of the family's structure, membership, values, and beliefs. Even families that do not identify with a specific cultural

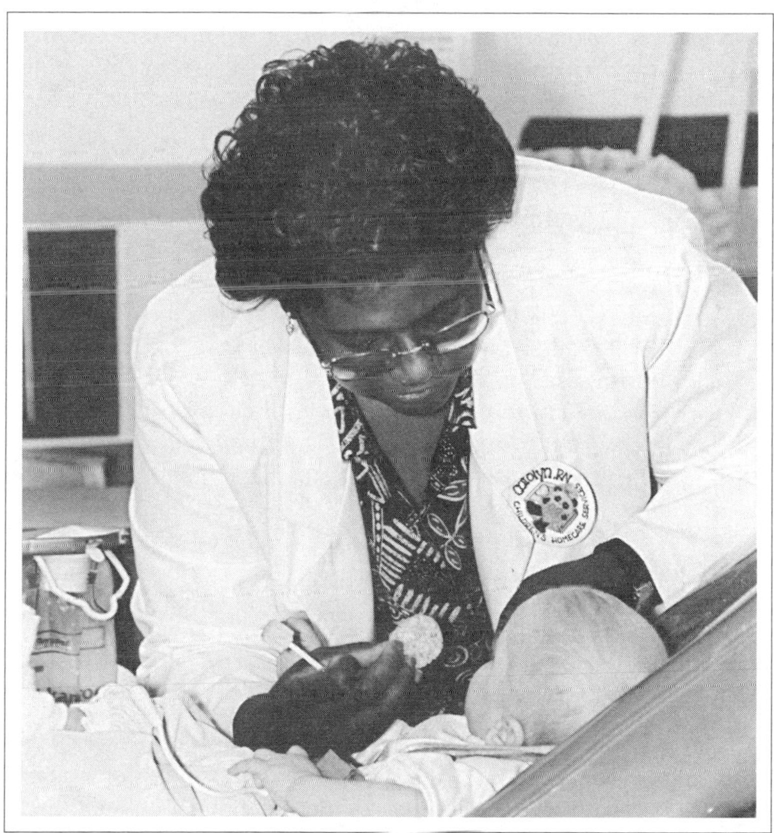

It is critical that service providers have an understanding and appreciation of each family's cultural identity.

group may be strongly influenced by a particular group (Lynch & Hanson, 1992). It is critical that service providers have an understanding and appreciation of each family's cultural identity and an awareness of the implications for service provision.

It is not necessary for an interventionist to know everything about a particular culture in order to provide sensitive and appropriate services (Lynch & Hanson, 1992). Cultural competence is more reflective of a set of personal characteristics rather than factual knowledge. Service providers who are open and eager to learn, respectful of differences, and willing to conduct thoughtful self-examinations and make personal changes are most capable of developing cultural competence. These traits allow interventionists to identify and use cultural resources, strengthen their relationships with families, and provide the most effective services. A focus on the development of these traits rather than on the acquisition of detailed knowledge of a culture also discourages service providers from overgeneralizing or stereotyping families based on their membership in a cultural group. All families are unique, and any one family may be as different from a family in its own cultural group as it is from a family in another cultural group (Wayman, Lynch, & Hanson, 1990).

While in-depth knowledge of a specific culture is not a requirement for the provision of culturally sensitive services, it is important to have an awareness of some of the fundamental aspects of each culture in the communities we serve. Lynch and Hanson (1992) have several suggestions to guide interventionists in gathering information:

- Find out specific information about the cultural practices regarding child rearing and beliefs about health, healing, disability, causation, and help seeking. Expect variations in desired levels of involvement and parent-professional collaboration.
- Identify people willing to serve as interpreters, mediators, or guides to a culture rather than relying exclusively on families to provide this information.
- When working with families with limited proficiency in English, use as few written forms as possible, and then only in the family's language. Learn some basic vocabulary such as common words and greetings in the family's language.
- Allow for additional time to build relationships with families and learn about their resources, concerns, and priorities before moving on to the next steps in the process. Rely on the family, the interpreter, and your own instincts to determine how and when to proceed.

Other suggestions include the following:

- Ask the parents about others who are supportive or who take part in decision making in the family and, with their permission, invite them to participate in conversations and meetings. This may include community or religious leaders.
- Seek opportunities to observe families as a learner rather than as an assessor or interventionist (Rounds, Weil, & Bishop, 1994). Participate in informal

conversations and observations that may not be directly related to disability issues to gain a more holistic perspective on the family and culture.

- Conduct ethnographic interviews with families during which members are allowed to define what is important for the interventionist to know about their culture and own experiences (Rounds, Weil, & Bishop, 1994).
- Complete a thorough and honest self-assessment regarding your own feelings about cultural differences and your willingness to learn or change. Two useful resources for such reflection include the Ethnic Competence Skill Model (Ho, 1992) and *Strategies for Working with Culturally Diverse Communities and Clients* (Randal-David, 1989).

Attitudes and Skills for Effective Work with Families

In addition to a recognition of the importance of families in the lives of children with disabilities, an awareness of how families function as systems, and a genuine respect for family diversity, a number of other skills and attitudes have been identified as necessary for service providers to work effectively with families. Dunst and Trivette (1994) define effective helping as an

> act of enabling individuals or groups (e.g., a family) to become better able to solve problems, meet needs, or achieve aspirations by promoting the acquisition of competencies that support and strengthen functioning in a way that permits a greater sense of individual or group control over its developmental course. (p. 160)

Characteristics of service providers that promote effective helping as defined above include respect, realism, good listening skills, the provision of support rather than direction, and the ability to be flexible and do whatever it takes.

Be Respectful

Respect for the family is the hallmark of all positive and effective intervention efforts and is an important aspect of all other necessary service provider characteristics. Respect is created and sustained by a fundamental belief in the importance of families and trust in the ability of families to make the most appropriate choices for the lives of their children. Early interventionists demonstrate respect when they ask families what they see as priority areas for intervention before offering their own opinions and when they offer their own opinions in a way that allows parents to comfortably disagree (McWilliam & Winton, 1990). Service providers who respect families honor their decisions, lifestyles, values, beliefs, and efforts to care for their children, even when this entails supporting choices the service provider would not have made.

Be Realistic

It is sometimes easy for interventionists to forget that parents have other roles and responsibilities in addition to parenting a child with a disability. The day-to-day demands of rearing children and managing careers, finances, and households, as well as meeting other family responsibilities, can sometimes be overwhelming. Even more is demanded of parents of children with disabilities, and it is demanded for a longer period of time.

Parents of children with disabilities are often expected to be "superparents" who attend meetings; work in their children's classrooms; advocate for their children's rights and needs; implement home-based intervention programs; collect daily data; attend workshops; support other parents; plan and implement IFSPs, IEPs, and home-based therapy programs; and transport their children to see doctors, therapists, educators, and other service providers. It is in this context that demands placed on families of children with disabilities should be evaluated.

Most families welcome the opportunity to participate in planning meetings, obtain multiple services for their children, and implement home-based intervention plans. For some families, however, these extra parenting tasks become overwhelming. When families are overburdened with intervention plans that they cannot possibly implement, or when such plans have negative impacts on other areas of family functioning, members often feel guilty and discouraged and may avoid contact with the service provider whom they feel they have failed. Without sensitivity for the multiple pressures and demands placed on families by the provision of services and other life factors, families that decline or fail to complete services may be labeled as "resistant" or thought to care less for their children than they should. It is important to consider the many aspects of a family's day-to-day life when suggesting services or levels of involvement.

Be a Good Listener

Listening skills are critical for successful work with families. To be effective, service providers must want to hear what family members have to say and be truly interested in understanding each family's unique needs and concerns. While family members are talking, the service provider must concentrate fully on what they are saying. This means paying careful attention to what is being communicated and being sensitive to both verbal and nonverbal cues. Service providers must watch and listen for feelings that are presented, as well as for factual information. It is often helpful to repeat what you hear family members say in your own words so that they are aware that you are listening and have the opportunity to correct or clarify your interpretation. Whenever possible, make notes after, rather than during, conversations, and review any notes with the family. Allow ample time for conversations to occur, and refrain from rushing in to fill silences in conversation. Important information is often revealed after a period of silence.

Service providers should be keenly sensitive to how their negative attitudes or disagreements with a family may be communicated, either directly or in more subtle ways. Such thoughts can undermine family confidence and responsibility, causing members to feel inadequate, unimportant, or defensive, and seriously limiting the extent to which services will be utilized or effective. Professionals who always keep the overall goal of family empowerment in mind and who derive personal rewards from seeing families become more competent and self-sustaining are most likely to provide the most appropriate and effective services (Dunst & Trivette, 1994).

The provision of services to families of children with disabilities often necessitates the involvement of numerous service providers, many of whom have access to confidential and intimate information about the families. Boundary conflicts can arise between the family and the service delivery system when service providers fail to recognize the roles and rights of all family members, or when professionals intrude too far into the lives of families. For example, in professional attempts to conduct family assessments, the parents of children with disabilities are sometimes asked very personal questions about their marital satisfaction and functioning, financial status, and family relationships. Such assessments can be viewed by the family as intrusive and unhelpful unless they are approached with sensitivity and a clear statement of purpose (Malone, Manders, & Stewart, in press; Slentz & Bricker, 1992). Questions about family coping and marital adjustment are often unnecessary and can send the message that the interventionist believes that because the child has a disability, the parents must have problems as well (Slentz & Bricker, 1992). On the other hand, some families want to share this personal information with the interventionist. Sensitive communication and good listening skills allow the interventionist to understand the family's feelings and to be responsive to their desired level of disclosure.

Be a Support to the Family

Family members are the primary caregivers for all children, including children with disabilities. In the past, family roles were often usurped and replaced by professional involvement when the presence of a disability was identified in a child. After many years of excluding families in favor of more "objective" or "effective" professional intervention, there is a new and growing acknowledgment that the interventionist's role is to support, rather than to replace, the family. Dunst and Trivette (1994) maintain that helping relationships must be based on a philosophy of empowerment that assumes all families to be competent, identifies barriers to the practice of that competence that exist in the service system, and gives the family credit for attained success. They make a number of suggestions for help-giving behaviors based on this philosophy:

- Communicate a sincere sense of caring, warmth, and encouragement. Support is much easier to accept when it is offered by someone who is perceived to have a positive attitude and be genuinely invested in helping.
- Offer support based on the needs and goals identified by the family. Services are more likely to be accepted and successfully completed when they are clearly connected with the goals and wishes of the family.
- Encourage the family's use of natural support networks when they are available; these include friends, neighbors, community and church resources, and extended family relationships. Involvement with these

sources of support can enhance a sense of connection and community, normalize the need for support as something common to all families, and decrease reliance on paid service provision. Additionally, natural support networks are often more stable and convenient to families, because they usually exist in the families' own neighborhoods or communities.

- Help the family identify and successfully solve small problems or achieve short-term goals before moving on to tackle more difficult or long-range issues. Such successes bolster the self-esteem and confidence of family members and validate their investment in the intervention process.
- Highlight successes. When goals have been achieved or needs met, emphasize these experiences and the active, significant roles played by family members. These successes and the accompanying sense of control are critical to the maintenance of desired change.

Be Flexible: Do Whatever It Takes

The *Statement in Support of Families and Their Children,* published by the Center on Human Policy (1987), states that family services should be "flexible, individualized, and designed to meet the diverse needs of families." The policy introduces the principle of "whatever it takes," representing the idea that interventionists working with families must be creative and adaptable, and not limit their actions or services to those prescribed by the service system. Implementing family-centered early intervention requires a willingness to create positive visions for the future with families and to listen to and share their dreams. The next step is to do whatever it takes to join in partnership with families to work toward achieving their goals for themselves and for their young children with disabilities.

Summary

It is both natural and desirable for interventionists to be excited about their chosen profession and to be confident of their abilities to serve children with disabilities and their families. Most have worked for years to acquire the knowledge and skills required of professionals. It is also natural for service providers to care deeply about the families and children they serve and to have their own values and beliefs about what is best for them. Indeed, it would be very difficult for service providers to continue to work successfully without clear ideas about what is important and a high level of investment in their own roles in the intervention process. There will be times, however, when family choices, goals, practices, or values will be different from those of the professional. This is not undesirable; rather, it is one of the primary reasons for the provision of family-guided services. The major change from past practice to current practice is the response of the interventionist to these differences in viewpoint. In these instances, the wishes of the family should be honored, except in the rare cases in which to do so would be to put the child at risk for abuse or neglect.

More than a decade after the enactment of P.L. 94–142, states across the nation are still struggling to turn the promise of family-centered intervention into reality for families and young children. We have made much progress, but there is still much work to be done. Progress toward this goal will be enhanced when a new generation of early intervention professionals are trained to embrace family-centered values, understand family systems, accept the diversity among families, and have the attitudes and skills necessary to work in partnership with families.

References

Abbott, D., & Meredith, W. (1986). Strengths of parents with retarded children. *Family Relations, 135,* 371–375.

Berger, E. H. (1987). *Parents as partners in education: The school and home working together* (2nd ed.). Upper Saddle River, NJ: Merrill/Prentice Hall.

Boukydis, C. F. (1984, October). *The importance of parenting networks.* Paper presented at the Parent Care Conference, Salt Lake City, UT.

Breslau, N. (1983). Care of disabled children and women's time use. *Medical Care, 21,* 620–629.

Breslau, N., Salkever, D., & Staruch, K. (1982). Women's labor force activity and responsibilities for disabled dependents: A study of families with disabled children. *Journal of Health and Social Behavior, 23,* 169–183.

Carter, E. A., & McGoldrick, M. (1980). *The family life cycle: A framework for family therapy.* New York: Gardner Press.

Center on Human Policy (1987). *Statement in support of families and their children.* Syracuse, New York: Author.

Crnic, K. A., Greenberg, M. T., Ragozin, A., Robinson, N., & Basham, R. (1983). Effects of stress and social support on mothers of premature and full-term infants. *Child Development, 54,* 209–217.

Dunst, C. J., & Trivette, C. M. (1988). Helping, helplessness, and harm. In J. Witt, S. Elliott, & F. Gresham (Eds.), *Handbook of behavior therapy in education.* New York: Plenum Press.

Dunst, C. J., & Trivette, C. M. (1994). What is effective helping? In C. J. Dunst, C. M. Trivette, & A. G. Deal (Eds.), *Supporting and strengthening families, Vol. 1: Methods, strategies and practices.* Cambridge, MA: Brookline Books.

Dunst, C. J., Trivette, C. M., & Deal, A. G. (1988). *Enabling and empowering families.* Cambridge, MA: Brookline Books.

Erikson, E. (1963). *Childhood and society.* New York: W. W. Norton.

Fish, T., McCaffrey, D., Bush, K., & Piskur, S. (1995). *SNIP: Sibling Need and Involvement Profile.* Columbus, OH: The University of Ohio, Nisonger Center University-Affiliated Program for Persons with Developmental Disabilities.

Forest, M., & Pearpoint, J. (1992). Families, friends, and circles. In J. Nisbet (Ed.), *Natural supports in school, at work, and in the community for people with severe disabilities.* Baltimore, MD: Paul H. Brookes.

Friedrich, W. (1979). Predictors of the coping behavior of mothers of handicapped children. *Journal of Consulting and Clinical Psychology, 47,* 1140–1141.

Ho, M. K. (1992). *Minority children and adolescents in therapy.* Newbury Park, CA: Sage.

Hollins, S. (1985). Families and handicap. In I. Craft, J. Bicknell, & S. Hollins (Eds.), *Mental handicap: The multidisciplinary approach.* London. Baillier Tindall.

Imber-Black, E. (1987). The mentally handicapped in context. *Family Systems Medicine, 5,* 428–445.

Lambie, R., & Daniels-Mohring, D. (1993). *Family systems within educational contexts.* Denver, CO: Love Publishing.

Longo, D. C., & Bond, L. (1984). Families of the handicapped child: Research and practice. *Family Relations, 33,* 57–65.

Lynch, E. W., & Hanson, M. J. (1992). *Developing cross-cultural competence: A guide for working with young children and their families.* Baltimore, MD: Paul H. Brookes.

Malone, M., Manders, J., & Stewart, S. (in press). A rationale for family therapy specialization in early intervention. *Journal of Marital and Family Therapy.*

McBride, S. L., Brotherson, M. J., Joanning, H., Whiddon, D., & Demmitt, S. (1993). Implementation of family-centered services: Perceptions of families and professionals. *Journal of Early Intervention, 17,* 414–430.

McWilliam, P. J., & Winton, P. (1990). *Brass tacks: A self-rating of family-centered practices in early intervention.* Chapel Hill, NC: University of North Carolina at Chapel Hill, Frank Porter Graham Child Development Center.

Meyer, D. J., Vadasy, P. F., & Fewell, R. R. (1985). *Sibshops: A handbook for implementing workshops for siblings of children with special needs.* Seattle, WA: University of Washington Press.

Minuchin, S. (1974). *Families and family therapy.* Cambridge, MA: Harvard University Press.

Morsink, C. V., Thomas, C. C., & Correa, V. I. (1991). *Interactive teaming: Consultation and collaboration in special programs.* Upper Saddle River, NJ: Prentice Hall.

Murphy, D. L, Lee, I. M., Turnbull, A. P., & Turbiville, V. (1995). The family-centered program rating scale: An instrument for program evaluation and change. *Journal of Early Intervention, 19,* 24–42.

Nihira, K., Mink, I. T., & Meyers, C. E. (1981). Relationship between home environment and school adjustment of TMR children. *American Journal of Mental Deficiency, 186,* 8–15.

Olson, D., McCubbin, H., Barnes, H., Larsen, A., Muxen, M., & Wilson, M. (1983). *Families: What makes them work.* Beverly Hills, CA: Sage.

Patterson, J. M. (1988). Chronic illness in children and the impact on families. In C. S. Chilman, E. W. Nunnally, & F. M. Cox (Eds.), *Chronic illness and disability.* Beverly Hills, CA: Sage.

Pearl, L. (1993). Providing family-centered early intervention. In W. Brown, S. K. Thurman, & L. Pearl (Eds.), *Family-centered early intervention with infants and toddlers: Innovative cross-disciplinary approaches.* Baltimore, MD: Paul H. Brookes.

Piaget, J. (1952). *The origins of intelligence in children.* New York: International Universities Press.

Powell, T. H., & Gallagher, P. A. (1993). *Brothers and sisters: A special part of exceptional families.* Baltimore, MD: Paul H. Brookes.

Powers, L. E. (1993). Disability and grief: From tragedy to challenge. In G. H. S. Singer & L. E. Powers (Eds.), *Families, disability, and empowerment: Active coping strategies for family interventions.* Baltimore, MD: Paul H. Brookes.

Racino, J. A., O'Connor, S., & Walker, P. (1993). Conclusion. In J. A. Racino, P. Walker, S. O'Connor, & S. J. Taylor (Eds.), *Housing, support, and community: Choices and strategies for adults with disabilities.* Baltimore, MD, Paul H. Brookes.

Randal-David, E. (1989). *Strategies for working with culturally diverse communities and clients.* Washington, DC: Association for the Care of Children's Health.

Rounds, K. A., Weil, M., & Bishop, K. K. (1994). Practice with culturally diverse families of young children with disabilities. *Families in Society: The Journal of Contemporary Human Services, 75,* 3–15.

Safer, N. D., & Hamilton, J. L. (1993). Legislative context for early intervention services. In W. Brown, S. K. Thurman, & L. Pearl (Eds.), *Family-centered early intervention with infants and toddlers: Innovative cross-disciplinary approaches.* Baltimore, MD: Paul H. Brookes.

Santelli, B. (1992). *Parent-to-Parent National Survey Project.* Paper presented at the National Parent-to-Parent Conference, Phoenix, AZ.

Santelli, B., Turnbull, A., Lerner, E., & Marquis, J. (1993). Parent-to-Parent programs: A unique form of mutual support for families of persons with disabilities. In G. H. S. Singer & L. E. Powers (Eds.), *Families, disability, and empowerment: Active coping strategies for family interventions.* Baltimore, MD: Paul H. Brookes.

Seligman, M., & Darling, R. (1989). *Ordinary families, special children: A systems approach to childhood disability.* New York: Guilford Press.

Slentz, K. L., & Bricker, D. (1992). Family-guided assessment for IFSP development: Jumping off the family assessment bandwagon. *Journal of Early Intervention, 16,* 11–19.

Stoneman, Z., & Brody, G. (1982). Strengths inherent in sibling interactions involving a retarded child: A functional role-theory approach. In N. Stinnett, B. Chesser, J. DeFrain, & P. Knaub (Eds.), *Family strengths: Positive models for family life.* Lincoln, NE: University of Nebraska Press.

Stoneman, Z., & Brody, G. H. (1993). Sibling relations in the family context. In Z. Stoneman & P. W. Berman (Eds.), *The effects of mental retardation, disability, and illness on sibling relationships*. Baltimore, MD: Paul H. Brookes.

Stoneman, Z., Brody, G. H., Davis, C. H., & Crapps, J. M. (1987). Mentally retarded children and their older siblings: Naturalistic in-home observations. *American Journal on Mental Retardation, 92,* 290–298.

Sudarkasa, N. (1980). African and Afro-American family structure: A comparison. *Black Scholar, 11(8),* 37–60.

Thomas, M. B. (1992). *An introduction to marital and family therapy: Counseling toward healthier families across the lifespan*. Upper Saddle River, NH: Prentice Hall.

Walsh, F. (1982). *Normal family processes*. New York: Guilford Press.

Wayman, K. L., Lynch, E. W., & Hanson, M. J. (1990). Home-based early childhood services: Cultural sensitivity in a family-systems approach. *Topics in Early Childhood Special Education, 10(4),* 56–75.

Wright, L. S., Matlock, K. S., & Matlock, D. T. (1985). Parents of handicapped children: Their self-ratings, life satisfactions, and parental adequacy. *The Exceptional Child, 32,* 37–40.

4

Sensorimotor Development

Jean A. Patz and Carole W. Dennis

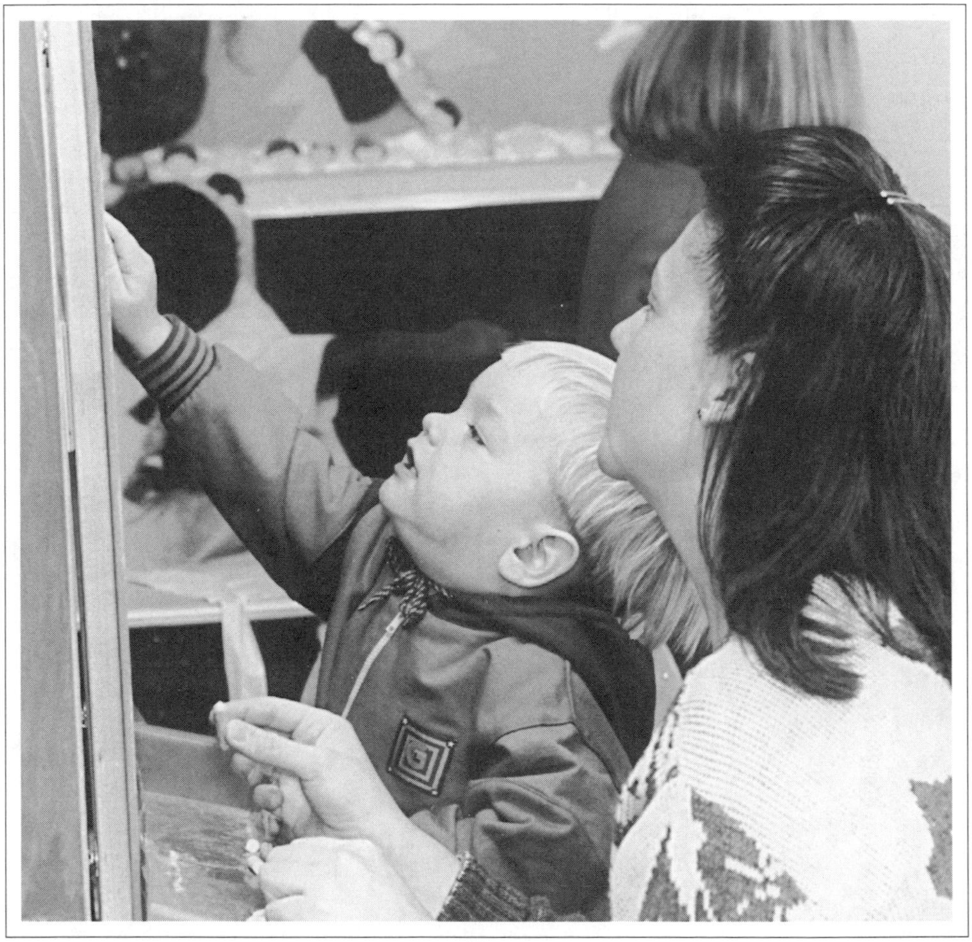

Sensorimotor development represents a child's growing proficiency in producing movement that is appropriate to current sensory stimuli and environmental demands. Its significance in the developing child is multifaceted. Through the development of sensorimotor skills, the child gains feelings of self-control, competence, and self-esteem. The ability to control one's own body in the immediate physical environment is primary to the development of feelings of mastery and motivation.

In addition, sensorimotor skills support the development of abilities in the areas of cognition, communication, adaptive skills, and social and emotional competence in the typically developing child. For example, by manipulating objects in their hands, children learn a great deal about perceptual properties of objects, and they can experiment with cognitive concepts such as object permanence, classification, and conservation.

Sensorimotor skills also allow the expression of skills in other domains. Most assessments of cognition, language development, self-care skills, and socialization in the very young child require the demonstration of some type of sensorimotor behavior. For example, the behaviors an infant develops that indicate attachment to and separation from the primary caregiver are considered to be important milestones of social and emotional development. These behaviors all require some type of motor output (turning toward, gazing at, and smiling at the caregiver; moving away from the caregiver; and returning to the caregiver for comfort).

Those who work with young children who experience difficulties in motor control face several challenges. To help improve such children's sensorimotor development, it is important for the early interventionist to understand where delays exist and to hypothesize why they have occurred so that an appropriate intervention plan can be developed. Because motor deficits affect other aspects of development, it is not enough merely to attempt to improve sensorimotor skills: It is equally important to consider the impact of adaptation and compensation in relation to task mastery. The use of compensatory techniques for impaired function, as well as adaptation of social and educational activities, adaptation of the environment, and the provision of specific adaptive equipment will have far-reaching implications for the overall development of the child.

Principles of Neuromotor Development

The emergence of sensorimotor skills in the developing infant is an extraordinary process. While most of us view a newborn as being helpless, a typical infant is born with all of the requirements necessary for movement. Infants appear to be born with an intrinsic motivation to move and, despite the lack of coordination typical of movement in early infancy, there appears to be some mechanism whereby infants can exert rudimentary control over their environments. In this section of the chapter, some of the theoretical rationales that motor specialists utilize to explain motor development are discussed.

Theoretical Models of Neuromotor Development

The Neuromaturational Model. The neuromaturational model, advocated by Gesell and Amatruda (1947), attempts to explain the progression of motor development as the result of maturation of the central nervous system. According to this model, which is well accepted by physical and occupational therapists, movement progresses from primitive, reflexive control to voluntary control of movement (Piper & Darrah, 1995).

Reflexive Control of Movement. For many years, motor development was viewed in light of Sherrington's (1947) study of reflexes, which suggested that normal human movement was the result of the summation of preprogrammed reflexes (Piper & Darrah, 1995). Reflexes are automatic, stereotypical movement patterns that are triggered by sensory stimuli such as touch, stretching of specific muscle groups, the position of the head in relation to the body, and the position of the head in relation to gravity. It is still believed that many of the infant's earliest movements are reflexive in nature and mediated by subcortical areas of the central nervous system. Reflexes are thought to have a discrete function in development. For example, when an infant's cheek is touched, he turns his head toward the touch in a rooting response, which is necessary for suckling and, consequently, survival among mammals. In addition, when an infant is lying on his back and a caregiver grasps his forearms and gently pulls upward, the infant responds by pulling his head and arms toward the center of his body (in a flexion response), much as a baby monkey must do to hang onto its mother as she swings from tree to tree.

Volitional Control of Movement. While most movement specialists today do not believe that the reflex model is sufficient to explain all aspects of motor control, early reflexes do appear to allow the infant to experience movement without conscious control, thus providing the possibility for use of the movement volitionally in the future. For example, when an infant turns his head to the left side, the asymmetrical tonic neck reflex is triggered, which promotes extension of his left arm out to the side of his body. If this movement results in contact with an environmental object, other sensory mechanisms are triggered: The body's proprioceptive system registers the position of the limb, the tactile system registers the feel of the object, and the visual system records the optical image of the hand touching the object. As this sequence of movement and feedback is repeated, the infant gradually begins to associate the movement pattern with the sensory rewards just noted and eventually learns to control this pattern volitionally through control of higher cortical centers of the central nervous system (Piper & Darrah, 1995). When volitional control is possible, the reflex becomes integrated; in other words, the reflex is overridden by conscious movement. When the infant repeats a volitional movement pattern over and over again, myelination of the neural connections that imprint the movement pattern occurs, resulting in fast, automatic movement that requires no conscious thought for its execution. Myelination is the developmental process whereby nerve fibers are insulated with a waxy sheath, allowing rapid, efficient neural transmission.

In addition to the concept that purposeful, controlled, and voluntary movement evolves from primitive, reflexive movement, the neuromaturational model embraces several other assumptions: that motor development progresses in a head-to-foot (cephalocaudal) direction, that movement control occurs in a proximal-to-distal sequence (from the center of the body toward the extremities), and that movement occurs in a predictable, sequential pattern among typically developing children (Piper & Darrah, 1995). While these assumptions still guide much of current therapeutic practice, some important exceptions to the model have been demonstrated.

The early domination of reflexively based movement has been questioned by Touwen (1978), who argues that even neonates have variability of movement, and Thoman (1987), who has demonstrated very early control of movement in premature neonates. Furthermore, the concept of proximal-to-distal control has been called into question by studies indicating that differential acquisition of motor skills may occur as a result of the type of movement valued in a specific cultural group (Super, 1976). In addition, Fetters, Fernandes, and Cermak (1988) have demonstrated through kinematic recordings that infants develop proximal and distal skills simultaneously when learning to reach for a block.

Hierarchical Model. The development of volitional control, as described in the neuromaturational model, parallels the earliest hierarchical models of motor development, wherein the highest level of central nervous system motor control, the cerebral cortex, governs lower levels of the central nervous system (Mathiowetz & Haugen, 1994). In children who have suffered specific brain injuries (as occurs in cerebral palsy), the higher systems are unable to override early, primitive reflexes, and these children may not be able to move with volitional control. In these children, primitive reflexes may not become integrated and subsequent movement is stereotypical. When the higher centers of the central nervous system are unable to function as a result of injury, lower level reflexes are released. In children and adults who suffer brain injuries as a result of trauma, movement that was previously under volitional control may again be reflexively controlled following the injury.

More recent hierarchical models have regarded movement as controlled by an executor in the central nervous system that determines the motor plan to be used in response to specific sensory stimuli. An effector then carries out this preprogrammed motor plan without alteration (Mathiowetz & Haugen, 1994). This model also incorporates anticipatory movement in which the muscles begin contracting in anticipation of a given movement.

Systems Model. The neuromaturational model and the hierarchical model of motor development share a common basic assumption: Motor development occurs as a function of structural change in the central nervous system, primarily change from lower-level control to higher-level control. While the systems model of motor development does not dispute the requirement of structural change for motor development, it holds that neuromaturation is insufficient to explain motor development (Thelen & Ulrich, 1990). Motor development, like many other areas of development, is part of an open system that is responsive to events occurring within other domains such as motivation, experience, and spatial orientation. In this model, the child is able to modify a motor plan while it is being enacted in response to specific task constraints and environmental events, rather than relying on a preprogrammed motor plan (feed-forward) in its entirety or relying on feedback produced by the movement (Mathiowetz & Haugen, 1994; Piper & Darrah, 1995). In a feedback mechanism, incoming sensory stimuli result in initiation or modification of movement. In a feed-forward mechanism, the child may initiate movement in response to sensory stimuli, but once the movement has begun, it is not modified. Feedback is used when the child is learning new skills that require careful monitoring, such as using a spoon to scoop up pudding. Feed-forward applies to movements that have been learned and practiced so the movements become more automatic. Scooping with a spoon may become a feed-forward movement in the older child. Both feedback and feed-forward are used to produce coordinated, goal-directed movement.

Gross Motor and Postural Skills: Typical Development

The First Year

Typical full-term infants are born in a position of physiological flexion, or flexion of utero, which parallels the infants' posture in the cramped space they occupied just prior to birth. The infant's head, legs, and arms tend to be drawn toward the center of the body. This early posture allows the infant to gather some basic information about his own body: The hands are in close proximity to the mouth, allowing oral exploration, and the infant can see the hands and other parts of the body. This may be contrasted with the position of prematurely born infants, whose extremities tend to hang away from the body (in extension). These infants require special positioning to allow bodily exploration and optimal motor development.

Extension. Because of the flexor position of the full-term infant's body at birth, the most likely option for movement is extension, in which the head and limbs move away from the body. Many primitive reflexes (including the Moro reflex, the asymmetrical tonic neck reflex, and the tonic labyrinthine reflex) support the development of movement and strength in extension, thus preparing the infant for early functional behaviors. The infant uses extension to hold his head in an upright position when he is held, and later to turn and lift his head when placed on his tummy. This extensor control moves from the head in a downward direction, allowing the infant to shift his weight back toward the pelvis and to raise his upper trunk off of the floor when placed in a tummy-lying position (prone), thus moving his arms underneath his body to support his weight on his elbows. As this extension continues to move downward, the infant is able to support his weight on his hands, with his arms extended, shifting his weight down to the pelvis. At about the same time in development, the infant becomes able to use this extension in the trunk to lift head, chest, arms, and legs off of the floor in an airplane posture. By pushing with one arm and pulling with the other, the infant learns to pivot to attain toys that are out of reach.

Flexion. Continuous with this process of developing extension is the development of flexion, or moving body parts toward the center of the body. The newborn is already in flexion, so not much more movement is possible in flexion until the infant attains some skills in extension. Once the infant can extend his head against gravity, then he can begin to balance it in an upright position by using both flexion and extension. When the infant is able to reach away from his body while lying on his back (supine), the infant learns to bring his hands back toward the center of the body, allowing oral exploration, visual regard, and hand-to-hand play. This play in flexion and extension in the supine position prepares the infant for increased control in the prone position, thus allowing the infant to maintain stability, or control, when shifting weight to free one arm to reach for a toy. The infant develops this ability to shift weight first from an on-elbows position and later from an extended-arms position.

Similar control in flexion is achieved in the lower half of the body as the supine infant raises his legs against gravity to kick, lifts his feet to his hands, and finally lifts his feet to his mouth in play. This control gained in the supine position prepares the infant to move from the prone position into a position on his hands and knees.

Coactivation and Rotation. Typically developing infants develop postural control along the continuum of control in extension, control in flexion, control of both flexion and extension together (coactivation), which is necessary for postural stability, and rotation (the turning of one body part on another). This pattern of development repeats itself at each stage of the developmental sequence. For example, when a prone infant lifts his head to an angle of 20 degrees from the horizontal, extension is primarily used. However, when the infant balances his head at 90 degrees in a prone or upright position, he must exert control of both flexion and extension, or coactivation, and in order to turn his head to look at objects in the environment, the infant must develop rotation, which incorporates differential control of flexion and extension. By about 6 months of age, the infant's body follows the head, and rolling from the stomach to the back occurs; shortly thereafter, rolling develops from the back to the stomach. While early rolling is characterized by the body moving as a whole, later it becomes segmental, with rotation occurring at the head, neck, trunk, and pelvis.

Another example of this continuum of control further along in the developmental sequence is when an infant is first placed in a sitting position and the trunk leans forward and is held upright primarily by extension of the muscles of the back. Through play in a supine position, including raising the head to look at the body, bringing the hands to midline, and bringing the feet toward the hands, the infant develops control of the muscles of the abdomen in flexion, so that the infant is able to gradually utilize both extension and flexion for sitting in an upright, balanced position. In addition, the infant must develop control in rotation in order to turn the head and trunk to reach for toys in the environment.

The ability to attain a position on the hands and knees is necessary to develop control in flexion and extension of the whole body, so that the infant can move into a sitting position (the infant pushes back and slightly to the side with the arms), rock on his hands and knees, and creep (move forward on hands and knees). The infant gains additional control of flexion and extension when exploring on his hands and knees in preparation for the transition to standing. Most infants learn to move into a standing position using furniture at first, pulling upward with the arms while pushing into extension with both legs. Later the infant learns to bring one leg forward and push up, allowing the other leg to follow. This builds differentiated control in each leg in preparation for cruising along furniture and, finally, walking.

When an infant first attains a standing position, strong extension occurs throughout the body to remain upright. First movements in standing are stiff, with the child swaying the body slightly from side to side to gain initial forward mobility. When the child is able to utilize flexion in this upright position for coactivation, control improves and the child can advance one leg and then the other reciprocally. Later, as rotation gradually develops, the child ultimately will walk with the counterrotation and arm swing that characterize mature walking. With full rotation, as one leg swings forward, the arm on the same side swings backward. Walking and other early developmental milestones are presented in Table 4.1.

Protective and Equilibrium Reactions. In each of the developmental patterns just described, early loss of balance results in protective reactions. For example, when a child begins to fall when sitting, the arms extend to break the fall. Similarly, loss of balance in standing results in a stepping reaction that is protective. Mature movement, however, is characterized by the use of equilibrium reactions. Equilibrium reactions allow the infant to shift weight smoothly and efficiently while maintaining the center of gravity. These reactions consist of subtle automatic postural adjustments that allow the infant to remain upright while moving without exerting conscious effort, thus freeing the child to interact with objects and people in the immediate environment.

Toddler and Preschool Development

The continuing development of gross motor (large muscle) skills among toddlers and preschool children is dependent upon the postural skills mastered earlier, as

TABLE 4.1 Gross Motor Skills and Mean Ages of Acquisition in Infants

POSITION	MEAN AGE OF ACQUISITION*	GROSS MOTOR SKILL
Prone	less than 1 month	lifts head momentarily in prone, asymmetrically
	2½ months	bears weight on forearms (elbows ahead of shoulders)
	4½ months	bears weight on hands, arms extended
	6 months	rolls from prone to supine, without rotation
	7½ months	crawls on tummy
	8½ months	creeps on hands and knees, reciprocally
Supine	1 month	balances head in midline in supine
	2½ months	brings hands to midline in supine
	4½ months	brings feet to hands
	5½ months	rolls from supine to prone, without rotation
	6½ months	rolls from supine to prone, with rotation
Sitting	5 months	sits alone briefly
	6½ months	sits alone steadily
	8 months	moves from sitting to four-point (hands and knees)
Standing	8 months	pulls to stand at furniture
	8½ months	pulls to stand through half-kneel position
	10½ months	stands alone momentarily
Walking	9 months	cruises around furniture, without rotation
	11 months	walks independently, five steps
	11½ months	rises from supine to four-point to standing
	12 months	maintains squatting position

* Note that the age reported is the mean age of acquisition of the infants in the sample. Most skills were attained by 90% of the infants studied within 2 to 3 months after the mean age.

Source: Adapted from *Motor Assessment of the Developing Infant* by M. C. Piper & J. Darrah, 1995, Philadelphia: W. B. Saunders. Copyright 1995 by W. B. Saunders. Adapted by permission.

well as on the environmental experiences afforded to the child. As children develop increased strength, balance, endurance, and coordination, they are able to increase their motor schemata in relation to environmental demands. Continuing development of differentiated control of the body, or the ability to use one limb alone or use both flexion and extension in different joints of the same extremity, allows the child to gain higher-level motor skills, such as the control of flexion and extension to allow stooping to the floor. Equilibrium reactions become more mature, so that the lateral weight shift to allow standing on one foot in the toddler is replaced in the preschooler with a mature rotational pattern throughout the trunk. Movements become smoother and more controlled as refined equilibrium reactions are called into action, and protective skills such as reaching out with the arms or legs are used only when falls are imminent. Children master more difficult motor skills, such as climbing stairs, jumping, hopping, and running. Each of these skills has a predictable pattern of maturity as well. For example, independent stair climbing is first mastered by holding the railing and advancing the feet in a step-to-step progression, with lateral weight shift and minimal trunk rotation. Later the child can utilize a reciprocal progression of the feet, without needing to hold the railing for balance and demonstrating a smooth diagonal weight shift with trunk rotation. Acquisition of higher-level motor skills has been demonstrated to parallel acquisition of early motor skills (Roberton & Halverson, 1984). When ball throwing is a new skill, for example, the arm moves while the trunk remains stable. As this skill improves, however, the trunk rotates in conjunction with arm and shoulder movements to add efficiency, speed, and force to the action. Table 4.2 provides a list of toddler and preschool gross motor skills and the age at which children typically attain them.

Once children have mastered the basic movement skills, repetition allows smooth performance of specific motor patterns and combinations of these motor patterns. Preschool children enjoy practicing their skills, challenging themselves, and mastering the environment. Children begin to use these skills in simple social games, such as Duck, Duck, Goose and Tag, in which movements must conform to changing speed and position of the other children playing. Beginning at about age 4, movement patterns are combined for mastery of galloping and, later, skipping. As movements are sequenced for learning more-complex tasks, adequate motor planning, or praxis, is required. Praxis is the ability to plan and execute a skilled movement (Goodgold-Edwards & Cermak, 1989). Praxis demands adequate sensory capabilities to provide feedback about the correctness of a given motor attempt and to allow adaptation to environmental demands during execution of the motor plan.

TABLE 4.2 Gross Motor Skills and Expected Ages of Acquisition in the Toddler and Preschooler

AGE OF ACQUISITION	GROSS MOTOR SKILL
15 months	creeps up steps
18–23 months	creeps down steps backwards
24–29 months	jumps off floor 2 inches using both feet
2–2½ years	climbs stairs and descends stairs with both feet on each step
2–2½ years	descends stairs with both feet on each step
2½–3 years	climbs stairs, alternating feet
3–3 years	descends stairs, alternating feet
3–5 years	hops on one foot
4–5 years	gallops
5–6 years	skips, alternating feet
6–7 years	walks four steps on 4-inch balance beam

Sources: Bayley Scales of Infant Development: Second Edition. Copyright © 1993 by The Psychological Corporation. Adapted and reproduced by permission. All rights reserved. "Bayley Scales of Infant Development" is a registered trademark of The Psychological Corporation. Adapted from the *Peabody Developmental Motor Scales,* by M. R. Folio and R. R. Fewell. Copyright by Pro-Ed, Austin, TX. Adapted by permission.

Gross Motor and Postural Skills: Atypical Development

The failure of a child to attain developmental milestones on time may be cause for concern for parents and professionals. Often, the observant parent or nonprofessional friend may notice that the child's movements don't look quite right, or that he may seem floppy or stiff. In addition to being aware of atypical posture, observers may note that transitions from one position to another are not possible or are accomplished in unusual ways. Figure 4.1 indicates movement patterns that may signal motor delays and the need for additional assessment of sensorimotor skills.

Variations in Early Motor Development

The sequence of development just described is fairly uniform and predictable for typically developing infants who are exposed to similar experiences; however, developmental variations may be noted when conditions are different. For example, infants who have experienced thoracic surgery may find play in the prone position (on the tummy) uncomfortable and may have weak abdominal control. These children may fail to learn to move from a position on hands and knees to a sitting position or to develop the ability to creep when they are expected to, and they may move about by scooting in a sitting position. Transitions to standing are often not developed in the typical manner and the child may learn to walk before he is able to move to and from the floor. Because of an unbalanced development of flexion and extension, good control in coactivation and rotation may not occur and these children may be quite fearful of movement.

Variations in musculoskeletal development, postural tone, and sensory processing, as well as variations in the child's physical and social environment, may alter development of motor skills. Some of the problems that may occur are discussed in the following paragraphs.

Disorders of Postural Tone

Variations in muscle tone are frequently seen in children with delayed sensorimotor development. Muscle tone is the degree of tension that exists in a muscle when it is at rest. Postural tone may range on a continuum from hypotonicity to hypertonicity or it may fluctuate. Each of these conditions is discussed in more detail later in this chapter. The condition of postural tone in children with traumatic head injuries follows a more transitional and dynamic versus static process. Initially, the involved extremities may, for example, be flaccid (completely lacking tone) with a gradual increase over time to hypertonicity. While not all children with motor delay exhibit atypical tone, some generalizations can be made with respect to those who do. Children diagnosed with cerebral palsy may have any type, degree, or distribution of

FIGURE 4.1 Movement Patterns That May Signal Postural and Gross Motor Development Delays

PRONE
- newborn assumes position of relative extension, rather than flexion of utero
- infant is unable to lift head off floor by 3 months
- infant maintains a uniform posture; no variety of position or movement in prone
- infant is unable to balance head in a midline position by 5 months
- arms remain pulled into flexion, close to infant's body by 4 months
- infant is unable to assume a position of support on both forearms by 5 months, or on hands by 7 months

SUPINE
- infant is unable to balance head at midline by 4 months
- infant remains in extended position, unable to lift legs from floor, past 6 months
- infant maintains a consistently asymmetrical posture

CREEPING
- infant is unable to crawl on tummy by 8 months
- infant is unable to creep, or utilizes one of the following patterns:
  - commando crawling: pulling self forward on elbows, legs extended
  - bunny creeping: arms and legs move together bilaterally, rather than reciprocally
  - creeps with exaggerated turning of head as arm on same side extends

SITTING
- sits with rounded head, neck, and back past 6 months
- infant is unable to sit independently for extended periods by 9 months
- infant is able to sit, but falls when he or she turns head or reaches for objects past 10 months
- infant is able to sit, but posture is characterized by one of the following:
  - narrow base of support (posterior pelvic tilt, trunk rounded, and head hyperextended)
  - wide base of support (legs spread wide, or habitual sitting in a W pattern)
- infant is unable to prevent falls by extending arms to front, side, and back by 12 months
- infant is unable to move into and out of sitting from other positions by 12 months or uses unusual movement patterns to change position

STANDING AND WALKING
- child is unable to stand independently by 14 months or walk independently by 15 months
- child bears weight on toes, rather than flat on feet
- child stands with significant knee hyperextension or swayback (lordosis) beyond 15 months

TODDLER AND PRESCHOOL SKILLS
- child has met most early milestones, but walking is stiff, unsteady, or met with many falls
- child has difficulty with activities requiring single-limb stability, such as climbing stairs, standing on one foot, and hopping
- child has mastered most basic skills, but has more difficulty than peers when learning new, sequenced motor tasks
- child appears clumsy when compared with typically developing peers

Source: Used with permission of Carole W. Dennis.

atypical tone depending on the site and extent of central nervous system dysfunction. Children with Down syndrome typically have varying degrees of hypotonia, or low muscle tone, throughout the body. Some children diagnosed with learning disabilities and mental retardation may have mild hypotonia, resulting in clumsiness.

Hypertonia. *Hypertonia* refers to tight muscles or spasticity; postural tone thus is increased. Hypertonia is characteristic of the spastic and rigid subtypes of cerebral palsy, but the degree of tone can range from mild to severe involvement. Distribution of hypertonia in the body can vary from child to child. Patterns typically seen include increased tone in one extremity (monoplegia), one side of the body such as the right arm, right leg, and right side of the trunk (hemiplegia), all four extremities (quadriplegia), or primarily in the lower extremities with some mild involvement in the upper extremities (diplegia).

Hypertonia reduces mobility and range of motion, potentially leading to deformities such as contractures (permanent shortening of muscles around a joint) scoliosis (curvature of the spine), or hip dislocation. Hypertonia often results in characteristic problems with posture and movement. For example, when spasticity is present in an upper extremity, as in hemiplegia, the arm tends to be pulled into a flexion pattern, with the elbow, wrist, and fingers flexed, the arm turned inward (internal rotation), the forearm rotated downward (pronated), and the thumb pulled toward the palm of the hand (Figure 4.2). When spasticity is present in the lower extremities, the legs tend to assume a position of extension (straightening) with the hips adducted and internally rotated. The hamstring muscles at the back of the upper leg are often tight and tend to rotate the pelvis backward (posterior pelvic tilt), resulting in compensatory rounding of the trunk (Figure 4.3) and extension of the head and neck in sitting. Sensorimotor deficits in children with increased tone are more fully covered in the discussion of cerebral palsy later in this chapter.

Clonus may be present along with spasticity. Clonus is a hyperactive stretch reflex consisting of repetitive, jerky movements occurring most commonly at the wrist or ankle when the muscles are put on stretch. Associated reactions (mirror movement in the opposite limb) may occur on one side of the body when there is excessive effort on the other side.

Hypotonia. *Hypotonia* refers to decreased, low muscle tone that occurs symmetrically throughout the body. Low muscle tone is characteristic of hypotonic cerebral palsy, prematurity in the first months (Hunter, 1996), myelomeningocele, which is a form of spina bifida (Hinderer, Hinderer, & Shurtleff, 1995), and many conditions associated with mental retardation, including the following syndromes: Down syndrome, Cri du chat syndrome, fragile X syndrome, Prader-Willi syndrome, and early Rett syndrome (McEwen, 1995). Children with hypotonia have difficulty moving against gravity. Parents may describe the quality of such children's tone as "floppy," "double-jointed," or "like that of a rag-doll." Excessive range of motion (hypermobility) occurs at the joints. When a child with hypotonia is positioned in

FIGURE 4.2 Atypical posturing in a preschool-age child with left spastic hemiplegic cerebral palsy. The effort of work with the right hand further increases muscle tone in the left extremity, causing the left arm to pull toward the body with elbow flexion, deviation of the wrist, and fisting of the hand.
Source: Used by permission of Jean Patz.

supine or prone, the lower extremities exhibit wide hip abduction and external rotation, frequently termed the "frog-leg" position (Figure 4.4). Children with low muscle tone tend to assume a characteristic posture when standing, with the legs hyperextended or locked at the knees, pelvis rotated forward (anterior pelvic tilt), lumbar spine in lordosis (swayed back), and thoracic spine in kyphosis (rounded back) (Figure 4.5).

Sensory Processing Disorders

Sensory difficulties that influence motor skill development may include problems in the registration, discrimination, processing, and organization of sensory stimuli. Skillful execution of motor skills requires sensory input to plan what action needs to occur, as well as sensory feedback to plot the action that has occurred and to help determine whether that action was successful. Children with cerebral palsy, particularly those with hemiplegia, may be unable to identify that the involved

FIGURE 4.3 Poor sitting position in a toddler with spastic diplegic cerebral palsy. Note the posterior pelvic tilt, rounded back, adducted legs with toe clawing, resulting in a narrow base of support and requiring the use of one arm to maintain balance.
Source: Used by permission of Jean Patz.

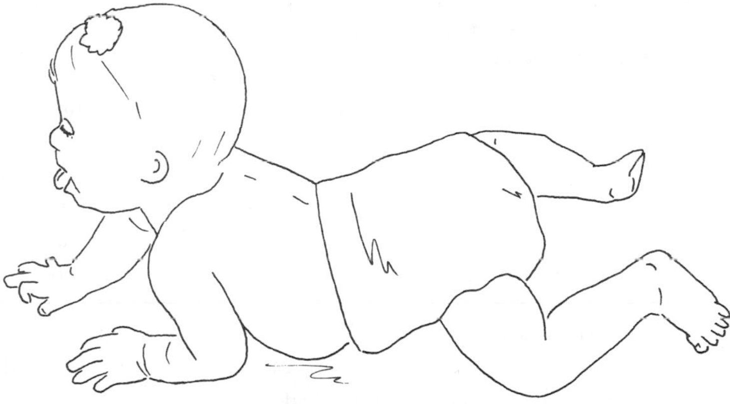

FIGURE 4.4 Low muscle tone in a year-old child with Down syndrome. Note the widely spread legs, poor trunk control, and immature weight-bearing on arms, which interfere with play and crawling.
Source: Used by permission of Jean Patz.

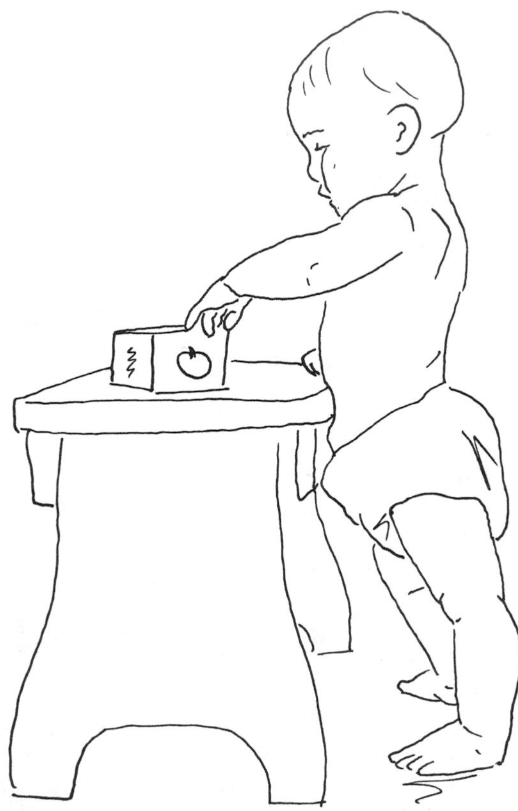

FIGURE 4.5 Supported standing in a toddler with low muscle tone. Note how the child leans into the supporting surface, with locked knees, anterior pelvic tilt, lordosis of lumbar spine, and shoulder instability.
Source: Used by permission of Jean Patz.

extremity has been touched, or they may have difficulty describing the nature of the touch or identifying where on the body it occurred; this represents problems with registration and discrimination. Difficulties with the processing and organization of sensory stimuli may be seen in children with pervasive developmental disorders including autism (which is described later in this chapter), in some children with learning disabilities, and in children raised in situations devoid of sufficient sensory stimulation.

Children raised in situations in which social and environmental interactions are severely restricted may suffer from sensory deprivation. Adequate sensory stimulation is necessary for typical development to occur. Much of an infant's early experience is sensory in nature, resulting in the formation of neural connections in the brain; neurons that do not form connections with other neurons will die (Vander Zanden, 1997). The results of sensory deprivation have been highlighted recently in institutionalized children in Romania, where sensory and motor deficits have been well documented (Haradon, Bascom, Dragomir, & Scripcaru, 1994; Sweeney & Bascom, 1995).

Motor coordination disorders such as developmental dyspraxia, or difficulty with motor planning, are a common problem in children with mental retardation, learning disabilities, and autism. Acquisition of specific, complex motor tasks such as skipping, tying shoes, cutting with scissors, and handwriting may be especially difficult for children with motor planning problems. Children with developmental dyspraxia may have difficulty integrating sensory information from their own bodies with environmental information, and often they cannot adapt their motor behavior to changing environmental demands (Goodgold-Edwards & Cermak, 1989). Deficient sensory processing is also implicated in children with developmental coordination disorder, which refers to motor incoordination in children when no known physical disorder exists (Willoughby & Polatajko, 1995). More information about children with developmental dyspraxia and developmental coordination disorder is provided later in this chapter.

Gross Motor and Postural Skills: Intervention

Positioning the Child

Postural control is central to the development of most sensorimotor skills and often represents the initial consideration in intervention. For very young children who have problems with postural tone, simple environmental modifications may promote successful interaction with the environment and may help to prevent the development of habits of atypical posture and movement. For example, placing rolled towels under the head and extremities of an infant in supine with hypotonia will facilitate bringing the head, hands, and legs toward midline. This will support the child's visual and tactile exploration of his own body in midline, which many consider to be the first position of learning. For the child with hypertonia, primitive reflexes often dominate the prone and supine positions, making volitional movement difficult. Placement in the side-lying position may eliminate the influence of tonic reflexes by minimizing the effects of gravity on postural tone, allowing the child to move with greater freedom and control.

For children with the need for postural control in higher positions, adaptations to infant seats, strollers, highchairs, classroom tables and chairs, toilet seats, and even swings may greatly improve the child's functional success. Simple seating modifications may provide better posture and allow more optimal function. Figure 4.6 provides an illustration of simple postural modifications to typical preschool furniture, including a seat belt, a back insert to reduce seat depth, footrests, and a cut-out table.

When home-made adaptations are not practical, special adaptive equipment may be purchased commercially. Wheelchairs, for example, are typically used for postural support by children with severe motor impairments. In such cases, it is imperative that all members of the assistive technology team consider mobility

FIGURE 4.6 Seating modifications to typical preschool chairs designed to enhance fine motor function.
Source: Used by permission of Jean Patz.

needs, transfer capabilities, communication needs, and the support necessary for feeding and fine motor (small muscle) activities. Family concerns must be foremost: Family members may benefit from a lightweight chair that they can carry in their car and can get into their home. Depending on the services available and the problems that need to be addressed, the assistive technology team may include the developmental pediatrician, the physical and occupational therapists, the speech and language pathologist, the orthopedist, the rehabilitation technology supplier, the early interventionist, and the family. The interventionist should be knowledgeable about how to handle children when placing them in and out of adapted positioning devices to reduce the influence of atypical tone or primitive reflexes, if these are present. The interventionist also should know about the application of seating accessories for wheelchairs such as anterior chest supports, lap trays, and headrests.

Power wheelchairs may be prescribed for children whose cognitive capabilities are at the 2-year level or higher. Carlson and Ramsey (1995) provide a concise review of the developmental benefits of power wheelchair provision to young children with disabilities. The use of power wheelchairs has been found to result in increased communication and peer interaction, increased interaction with objects in the environment, increased motivation for independent mobility, and decreased family perceptions of the child's helplessness. Scull (1996) discusses additional benefits of power mobility for children as young as 2 years of age. The assistive technology team, the child, and the family determine the best method to access the power wheelchair, depending on the child's physical and cognitive readiness. Wheelchair controls can be activated by any part of the body: pushing a joystick with the hand or extremities, pressing switch controls mounted on a headrest with the head, moving a chin cup, blowing into a sip-and-puff control, or activating a tongue-touch control plate (newAbilities Systems Inc., 1994) placed on a child's palate.

Modifying Task Demands

When postural control interferes with task performance, it is often a simple matter to alter the way in which the task is presented to allow greater success for the child with special needs. For example, simply positioning necessary materials close to the child will alleviate the need for significant body adjustment by the child. Through the use of positioning aids and classroom personnel, children with significant postural and gross motor deficits can be included in most classroom activities.

Fostering the Development of Postural and Gross Motor Control

When postural control is significantly impaired, the physical or occupational therapist may develop a treatment program keyed to the specific needs of the individual child. Treatment programs may include activities to promote more-normal muscle tone, to maintain range of motion, and to improve the ability to utilize protective and equilibrium reactions in functional activities. Because different underlying mechanisms may cause postural deficits in children, the early interventionist should not implement a motor program without strong guidance from these professionals.

When providing self-initiated mobility to a young child is not possible, educational professionals must do their best to provide the child with as much control as possible over his interactions with the environment. For example, promoting and responding to communicative attempts by young children with significant motor impairment will allow them some ability to direct others to move them through the environment or to bring the environment to them. In addition, it is important to position these children on a level with peers to foster social interaction and to make the environment as accessible to them as possible.

For children with mild motor impairments, such as those with developmental motor disorders, modifying activities to lessen motor demands may be particularly helpful. Children with problems with motor coordination are often cognizant of their difficulties and see their performance in motor activities as inferior to those of their peers. They may avoid engaging in activities with other children because of fear of failure and therefore limit their ability to improve their motor skills performance. Children with motor incoordination may find relative success in activities that provide the opportunity for practice and that do not require constant interaction with changing environmental conditions. The special physical educator may be especially helpful to classroom teachers in finding ways to modify motor tasks for success.

For children with specific medical diagnoses, such as cerebral palsy, spina bifida, and juvenile rheumatoid arthritis, it is important to consult with the physical and occupational therapists before instituting a program to improve gross motor skills acquisition. This is because there are often contraindications for movement that must be considered and methods of improving skills for each child must be established.

For children with mild-to-moderate motor impairment, perhaps the most important step in improving skills is a firm understanding of the present motor, sensory, and cognitive capabilities of the child. When the goal of an activity is motor performance, the activity should be structured so that it represents the "just-right challenge," or the point at which the task is just difficult enough to entice the child to try to succeed, but not so difficult so as to result in poor performance or failure (Koomar & Bundy, 1991).

Fine Motor Skills: Typical Development

Fine motor skills are comprised of precise movements of the hands and fingers, supported by stability of the trunk and control of the shoulder girdle and arms, for purposeful object use. Other motor components that are necessary for children to carry out complex movements related to object use include the skilled, preferred use of one hand (hand preference), the ability to use two hands together, and the ability to perform different tasks with each hand. In addition to motor control, fine motor skills require adequate cognition and sensory processing of tactile, proprioceptive, and visual information. Proprioception provides information through the muscles and joints about the position of one body part in relation to the body as a whole. The child integrates all of this sensory information to form accurate perceptions of object characteristics (such as size, weight, and position) in relation to the environment and to the self. These sensory integrative skills are necessary for planning fine motor movements and for visual motor integration.

Fine motor control is defined as a child's ability to functionally reach, grasp, and release objects for purposeful manipulation of toys and tools. Development in each of these areas is supported by a child's increasing control in flexion, extension, coactivation, and rotation of the shoulder girdle, forearm, and hand. The foundational components of reach, grasp, and release mature within the first 2 years, allowing for development of higher-level manipulative skills in the toddler and preschool-aged child.

Reach

Reaching is the movement of the arm toward an object. Components for the development of reach are mature by approximately 12 to 15 months of age (see Table 4.3 for milestones related to reach). When a newborn is placed on his stomach, his arms are flexed and close to the body. Weight is centered mostly on the head and shoulders. As extension develops from head to toe, the infant learns to lift and turn his head. The infant then progresses from bearing his weight on his forearms to pushing up on extended arms, which helps to develop stability in the shoulder girdle for reach. The ability to free an arm for reaching occurs when the infant can stabilize the pelvis and shift his weight toward one side, thus unweighting an arm for reach.

Arm movements of the newborn in supine are random and disorganized, and the ability to look at his hands has not yet developed. At 2 months of age, when the infant turns his head to one side, the arm on that same side extends while the opposite extremities flex as a result of the influence of the asymmetrical tonic neck reflex. This provides the first visual connection between the eyes and the arm. Swiping with one hand occurs as the infant is able to look at interesting faces and objects. Reach progresses from this random swiping to purposeful reaching with both arms together. When the infant is supine, the surface of the floor or crib provides stability to the shoulder girdle. Two-handed reaching is replaced as the infant matures by the use of one arm in a direct approach toward an object. This demonstrates the ability to differentiate one arm from the other. Further refinement occurs when the infant is able to supinate the forearm while

TABLE 4.3 Development of Reach

AGE OF ACQUISITION	FINE MOTOR SKILLS
2 months	arms activate upon sight of object
3 months	infant swipes at objects
	hands to midline
4 months	bilateral reach
	infant contacts object
5 months	infant underreaches
6 months	infant overreaches
	infant reaches in prone on forearms
	circular reach in sitting with one arm
7 months	infant reaches in prone on extended arms
	direct reach in sitting with one arm
12 months	forearm supination with reach

Source: Adapted from *Developmental Hand Dysfunction: Theory, Assessment and Treatment,* by R. Erhardt, 1994, San Antonio, TX: Therapy Skill Builders. Copyright 1994 by Therapy Skill Builders. Adapted by permission.

reaching (Erhardt, 1994). Supination, which is a critical component of controlled use of the thumb and fingers, is the ability to rotate the forearm so that the thumb moves in an upward direction and the object within the hand is clearly visible to the infant.

Grasp

Grasp is the attainment of an object with the hand. Grasp is usually described according to the placement of the object held within the hand; however, wrist stability and forearm rotation are important factors that affect grasp. Grasp on an object is reflexive during the first 2 to 3 months; an infant does not have voluntary control of grasp. In the earliest forms of voluntary grasp, the object is held in the palm on the ulnar (little finger side) of the hand. This is called an *ulnar palmar grasp,* corresponding to the position of the ulna bone in the forearm. During this stage of development, the wrist is usually somewhat flexed, indicating lack of development of extension to stabilize the wrist. The forearm is rotated so that the palm and thumb are turned downward (forearm pronation). Over the next few months, grasp of small objects progresses from the ulnar side of the hand to the middle of the palm (palmar grasp). Development continues so that the infant gains control of the radial side of the hand, corresponding to the radius bone in the forearm (radial palmar grasp), and finally to the thumb and digits (radial digital grasp). For tiny objects, such as a pellet, very young children will attempt to rake the object with the fingers and trap it against the palm. A mature pincer grasp reflects the ability to pick up a small, pellet-sized object between the tips of the index finger and thumb, with the other fingers flexed and the wrist held in slight extension (Figure 4.7). A fine pincer grasp indicates that the child has developed the ability to use one side of the hand actively while the other side is quiet, to hold the wrist stable in slight extension, and to rotate the thumb to allow opposition of the index finger. The development of grasp patterns is provided in Table 4.4.

The developmental sequence of pencil grasp progresses from immature grasps to transitional grasps to mature patterns (Schneck & Henderson, 1990). Initially, a child uses an immature palmar grasp on a crayon. Movement is initiated at the shoulder and the entire arm moves as a unit when scribbling. Immature pencil grasps include holding the pencil in the palm of the hand with the fingers flexed around the pencil shaft and with the forearm turned in pronation (Figure 4.8) or supination. In transitional grasps, movement is initiated from the wrist and forearm. The dynamic tripod grasp, the most commonly used mature grasp, incorporates dynamic and precise alternating movements of the index finger, middle finger, and thumb during writing, with the ring finger and little finger stabilized in flexion (Long, Conrad, Hall, & Furler, 1970; Rosenbloom & Horton, 1971) (Figure 4.9). The wrist is stable and the space between the thumb and index finger is rounded, forming an open web space. Young children tend to hold the pencil in the middle of the shaft, while mature finger placement is closer to the tip of the pencil.

FIGURE 4.7 Pincer grasp in a 2-year-old child. Note the tip-to-tip prehension and open web space.
Source: Used by permission of Jean Patz.

Release

Release is the purposeful letting go of an object held within the hand. Voluntary release begins when the infant mouths toys, transferring objects from hand to mouth to hand. At this stage the infant releases toys by stabilizing the object in the mouth and pulling it with the opposite hand or releasing it against a surface. Direct transfer from hand to hand occurs by approximately 7 months (Erhardt, 1994). Active release occurs by 10 to 11 months along with the development of object permanence, as the child purposefully drops objects from the highchair, for example, with full arm, wrist, and finger extension (Case-Smith, 1995). Excessive finger extension upon release, which is typical at this stage of development (Figure 4.10), results from a lack of stability in the fingers. As shoulder, elbow, and wrist stability develop, the child demonstrates less finger extension when releasing objects. Erhardt (1994) indicates that controlled release of a cube and pellet into a small opening develops by 12 months and 15 months, respectively. As control of release continues, the child is able to place objects into small containers, build towers, and release a ball. Table 4.5 presents the developmental progression for release skills.

TABLE 4.4 Development of Grasp

AGE	CUBE/PENCIL	PELLET
1 month	hands mostly fisted grasp reflex	
3 months	hands mostly open grasp reflex diminishes ulnar digits; brief grasp	
4 months	ulnar palmar grasp	
5 months	palmar grasp	
6 months	radial palmar grasp	raking grasp
7 months	radial palmar grasp	inferior scissors grasp
8 months	radial digital grasp active palmar arches	scissors grasp
9 months	radial digital grasp	inferior pincer grasp
10 months		pincer grasp
12 months	palmar grasp on crayon	fine pincer grasp
15 months	pincer grasp ulnar fingers stabilized	
3–4 years	adult grasp on spoon begins	
4–5 years	static tripod grasp on pencil	
5–6 years	dynamic tripod grasp on pencil	

Source: Adapted from *Developmental Hand Dysfunction: Theory, Assessment and Treatment,* by R. Erhardt, 1994, San Antonio, TX: Therapy Skill Builders. Copyright 1994 by Therapy Skill Builders. Adapted by permission.

FIGURE 4.8 Pronated palmar grasp on a crayon in a 2-year-old child. Note that the writing arm moves as a unit, while the left hand supports the paper.
Source: Used by permission of Jean Patz.

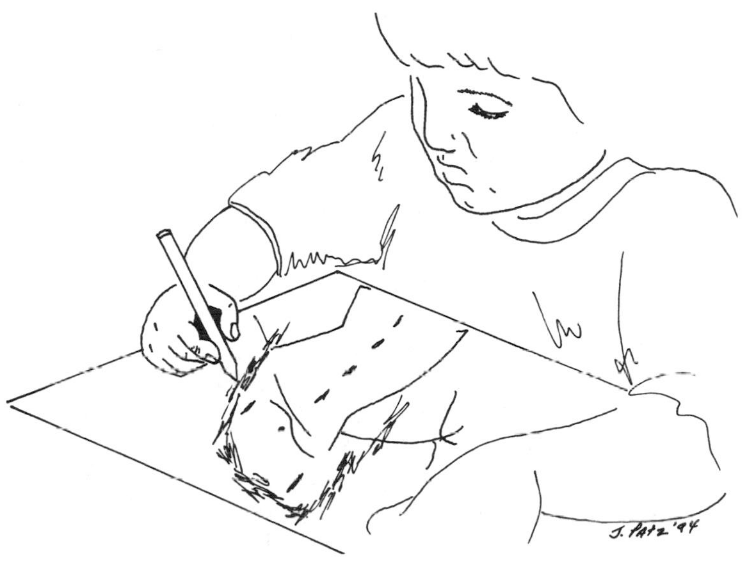

FIGURE 4.9 Tripod grasp on a marker with slight forearm supination, wrist extension, thumb and finger opposition, and an open web space.
Source: Used by permission of Jean Patz.

FIGURE 4.10 Age-appropriate finger extension upon release of a cube.
Source: Used by permission of Jean Patz.

Toddler and Preschool Fine Motor Development

Manipulation

This section addresses how young children combine reach, grasp, and release to perform functional tasks, such as those involved in play, prewriting, and cutting with scissors. The focus is on tasks that often are problematic for young children with special needs, including the use of both hands to manipulate objects, the development of hand preference, and the ability to move an object within the hand.

Bilateral Development. Asymmetry is noted in an infant's arm movements during the first few months of life. The infant begins to move his arms together at approximately 3 months of age when the hands are brought to the chest in midline. Bilateral activities include reaching with two hands at 4 to 5 months, transferring from hand to hand by 6 to 8 months, and clapping hands or banging objects together by the end of the first year (symmetrical bilateral movements). Between 12 and 18 months of age, the child utilizes one hand for manipulation and the other for stabilization (Case-Smith, 1995; Exner, 1996); for example, holding a bucket while pouring sand with a shovel or stabilizing a bowl while scooping with a spoon (differentiated asymmetrical movements). The ability to use opposing hand and arm movements for highly differentiated activities (simultaneous manipulation) emerges at approximately 18 to 24 months and matures by 2 to 3 years of age (Exner, 1996). Stringing beads (Figure 4.11) and

TABLE 4.5 Development of Voluntary Release Skills

AGE	SKILL
0–2 months	no voluntary release; avoiding-response reflex
3 months	involuntary release of objects
5 months	indirect transfer from hand to mouth to hand
6 months	beginning direct transfer
7 months	successful hand-to-hand transfer; releases objects against a surface
8 months	clumsy release into large container
9 months	controlled release into large container
10 months	drops object from highchair; object permanence
12 months	precise release with cube; minimal finger extension
	begins graded hand opening; begins to stack blocks
15 months	precise release of pellet into small container; builds tower
2–3 years	smooth, graded release of objects

Source: Adapted from *Developmental Hand Dysfunction: Theory, Assessment and Treatment,* by R. Erhardt, 1994, San Antonio, TX: Therapy Skill Builders. Copyright 1994 by Therapy Skill Builders. Adapted by permission.

cutting with scissors are examples of the complementary use of both hands. By 3½ to 4 years of age, a child can hold scissors correctly and rotate the forearm to guide the scissors; the child is able to move the paper in coordination with cutting by 6 years of age (Lopez, 1986). Development of bilateral hand skills is outlined in Table 4.6.

Hand Preference. Development of hand preference allows the child success with precise control of one hand for skilled tasks. A clear hand preference becomes apparent during the preschool years (Gesell & Ames, 1947; Harris & Carlson, 1988; McManus, Ski, Cole, Mellon, Wong, & Kloss, 1988; Tan, 1985). A history of a strong hand preference before 1 year of age may be indicative of a motor deficit.

In-hand Manipulation. While grasp patterns capture children's ability to statically hold objects, to use objects efficiently in many daily tasks children must

FIGURE 4.11 Complementary use of both hands as seen in stringing beads.
Source: Used by permission of Jean Patz.

TABLE 4.6 Bilateral Hand Skills Development

AGE	FINE MOTOR SKILL
1 month	alternating arm movements; asymmetry
3 months	brings hands to midline; symmetry
5 months	bilateral, simultaneous reach and holding of objects
7 months	bilateral manipulation; transferring a toy from hand to hand
9–10 months	coordinated bilateral and symmetrical manipulation; banging blocks together
12–18 months	one hand manipulates, one stabilizes; coordinated asymmetry; scribbling while stabilizing the paper, holding a piggy bank while inserting a coin
2 years and beyond	dissociated, simultaneous manipulation; complementary use of both hands; threading beads, buttoning, tying shoes

Source: Adapted from "Grasp, Release, and Bimanual Skills in the First Two Years of Life" by J. Case-Smith, 1995. In A. Henderson and C. Pehoski (Eds.), *Hand Function in the Child: Foundations for Remediation,* St. Louis: Mosby. Copyright 1995 by Mosby. Adapted by permission.

be able to move objects within the hand. For example, a child who is given several coins will pick them up with his fingertips and transfer them to his palm one at a time (translation). When stringing beads, a child needs to move the end of the string in his fingers for more accurate placement (shift), and when using a key, a child may need to rotate the key in his hand so that the correct end faces the keyhole (rotation). Exner (1996) proposes that these "in-hand manipulation skills" represent a higher level of fine motor skill than grasp alone. These skills begin to emerge between 12 and 18 months of age. A key time for development is from 2 to 4 years of age, with increasing speed and efficiency of in-hand manipulation skills occurring after age 4. Development of in-hand manipulation is provided in Table 4.7.

Fine Motor Skills: Atypical Development

When considering atypical fine motor development, it may be helpful to conceptualize three distinct areas of concern. The first is the ability to use the body as a stable base, or a foundation for arm use. The second is the development of the basic components of reach, grasp, and release. The third is the combined use of these components for object manipulation in functional activities such as play and self-feeding. Although problems may exist in postural control in addition to reach, grasp, and release, often fine motor difficulties are not identified until the child demonstrates problems integrating these skills for object manipulation. Parents may find that they have difficulty selecting toys for the child because the child is unable to play with age-appropriate toys. Problems may be noted when the child is expected to use two hands together to manipulate toys or to use objects as tools.

TABLE 4.7 Development of In-hand Manipulation

AGE	SKILLS
12–15 months	begins finger-to-palm translation (picks up small pieces of food and hides them in hand)
2–2 1/2 years	palm-to-finger translation (moves small piece of food from palm to fingertip) and simple rotation (90 degrees or less)
3–3 1/2 years	skill in finger-to-palm translation, begins shift and complex rotation
3 1/2 to 5 1/2 years	skill in shift (moves crayon by sliding fingers to tip) and complex rotation (180 to 360 degrees, as in turning a pencil from writing end to eraser end)

Source: Adapted from "Development of Hand Skills" by C. Exner, 1996. In J. Case-Smith, A. Allen, & P. Pratt (Eds.), *Occupational Therapy for Children* (3rd ed.), St. Louis: Mosby. Copyright 1996 by Mosby. Adapted by permission.

Fine motor difficulties may result from atypical postural tone, sensory processing deficits, poor motor planning, perceptual difficulties, and cognitive delay. Red flags suggestive of fine motor problems (Figure 4.12) can alert a teacher to potential difficulties in postural control, reach, grasp, release, and manipulation.

As noted earlier, a child with hypertonia resulting from cerebral palsy may sit with a posterior pelvic tilt, resulting in a rounded trunk and limited ability to raise the arms. Such a child may compensate by elevating his shoulder and leaning forward when reaching for objects, rather than extending the arm, as a result of decreased range of motion. In addition, shoulder retraction and elevation (pulling back and raising the shoulders) may limit the ability to bring the hands to midline. Tremors may be a red flag indicating the possibility of specific neuromotor problems or generalized weakness.

Low tone proximally in the trunk interferes with upright sitting, which limits the range available to reach forward. If trunk rotation has not developed as a result of poor proximal stability, reach across the midline will be affected. The child subsequently is forced to reach with the hand closest to the object. The child may have difficulty stabilizing his arm against gravity to reach for objects.

Wrist stability in slight extension is needed for mature grasping patterns; poor proximal control of the trunk, shoulder, elbow, and forearm affects the ability to control the wrist and subsequently the hand for grasp. Wrist flexion with ulnar deviation resulting from increased muscle tone (Figure 4.13) interferes with fine motor control. Thumb adduction into the palm, a pattern seen in children with more involved neuromotor dysfunction, prevents any oppositional use of the thumb.

Persistent use of the entire hand in an immature palmar grasp indicates that the child cannot differentiate one side of the hand from the other. Inability to isolate the index finger to point (in a child who is cognitively ready for this skill) may be a red flag indicating poorly differentiated movements; the child may not

FIGURE 4.12 Red flags suggestive of fine motor problems

REACH
- inability to bring the hands to midline after 4 months of age
- motor inability or lack of interest in reaching for objects by 6 months of age
- tremors upon reach
- inaccurate or indirect reaching after 9 months of age

GRASP
- continual fisting of the hands with thumb in palm beyond 3 months of age; hands are typically open by three months
- lack of variety of grasp patterns to accommodate size and shape of objects
- lack of ability to isolate the index finger for pointing after 10 to 12 months of age
- persistence of a palmar grasp beyond 12 months of age
- lack of supination of the forearm
- lack of development of a pincer grasp by 15 months of age
- awkward grasp on the pencil during manuscript or cursive writing; thumb wrapped around pencil; presses too hard when writing
- refusal to use eating utensils during preschool years

RELEASE
- excessive dropping of objects
- inability to actively transfer (coordinate grasp and release) after 6–7 months
- unable to stack a few blocks after 15–18 months

MANIPULATION
- strong preferred use of one hand under 1 year of age (hand preference is generally not seen before 12 months of age)
- poor visual attention to toys
- inability or unwillingness to manipulate toys; cannot play with age-appropriate toys
- extreme difficulty learning how to manipulate scissors by age 3–4 years or later; inability to coordinate after much instruction (dependent on exposure)
- lack of a hand preference by first grade; continual switching of hands while eating or using a pencil
- frequent dropping of objects
- poor handwriting skills
- difficulty copying from the chalkboard

PARENTAL CONCERN
- difficulty choosing toys for the child

Source: Used by permission of Jean Patz.

have the motor ability to separate one finger from the others. The lack of development of rotational patterns, which is typical in children with fine motor delay, also interferes with a mature grasp. For example, the lack of forearm rotation in supination makes it difficult for the child to mechanically use mature grasps and to see and learn about the object grasped as the palm faces downward. Also, limited rotation in the proximal joints of the fingers, and particularly the thumb, interrupts the finger-to-thumb opposition needed to grasp small objects or a pencil.

A child with poor hand use may develop compensatory patterns during grasp that are not efficient or precise. For example, a child with hypotonia will have difficulty with finger stability in the fine pincer grasp as a result of increased mobility in the joints. In addition, a child with hypotonia or poor sensation in the hand may grip a pencil by wrapping the thumb tightly over the pencil shaft instead of oppos-

FIGURE 4.13 Child with spastic quadriplegic cerebral palsy with similar atypical positioning in both arms resulting from increased tone. Note elbow flexion, forearm pronation, wrist flexion, and ulnar deviation upon grasp with a built-up handled spoon.
Source: Used by permission of Jean Patz.

ing the tips of the thumb and index finger on the pencil. With this type of compensatory pencil grip, key clues include a closed web space, lack of distal finger movements during pencil use, and heavy markings with occasional tearing of the paper. Poor motor planning, or dyspraxia, may be suspected when a child with no apparent motor dysfunction has more difficulty than expected learning how to grasp tools such as scissors, pencils, or eating utensils after repeated instruction.

Persistence of a primitive grasp pattern, fisting of the hand, exaggerated wrist flexion, limited thumb extension, or lack of forearm supination may all interfere with controlled release. Exner (1996) notes that "the quality of voluntary release can be no better than the quality of the grasp" (p. 296). Fisting of the hand, typically seen in children with neuromotor dysfunction, prevents voluntary opening of the hand for release. The inability to bring the hands to the midline will inhibit direct hand-to-hand transfer of an object, the first stage of release. Poor proximal stability of the wrist and lack of forearm supination prevent control in midposition for precise release.

During the toddler and preschool years, a child may demonstrate continued resistance to using age-appropriate tools such as scissors, a pencil, or a spoon and instead prefer direct contact with his hands, or a child may prefer to play with the toys of younger children. A child who has difficulty manipulating objects within one hand will use compensatory patterns rather than in-hand manipulation skills. Common compensatory substitution patterns include assistance in object manipulation by supporting the object with the other hand, the chest, or a table surface. These children frequently drop objects.

Fine Motor Skills: Intervention

When considering intervention for the young child with fine motor needs, the most efficient approach is to address first that which will make the greatest difference in the functional performance of the child. The child's position needs to be considered first. Often, by simply improving the child's posture, better performance will result. Next, the objects used in performance of the task and the nature of the task itself need to be examined. Perhaps different objects or different placement of the objects will result in better success, or perhaps the task can be done in a simpler way. When these have been considered yet problems remain, the interventionist needs to plan how to foster improved development of fine motor skills.

Positioning the Child

As noted earlier, adapted seating, including such items as a hard back and hard seat insert, abductor wedge, seat belt, lateral trunk supports, anterior chest support, or lap tray may be indicated for a child who cannot sit independently because of poor trunk control. Working on sitting with stability and on hand skills simultaneously is counterproductive for a child with poor trunk control. Depending on the child's degree of involvement, appropriate positioning during fine motor tasks may include side lying, prone or supine lying, sitting, or standing.

In the older child who is embarking on prewriting or writing skills, ideal positioning includes a chair height that allows the child to place his feet firmly on the floor and a desk height approximately 2 inches above the bent elbow at 90 degrees when the child is seated symmetrically and erect (Benbow, 1995). A child may lean into the table if the surface is too low; a table that is too high tends to turn the arms inward and thumbs downward, resulting in poor control and opposition of the thumb and index finger (Exner, 1995).

Positioning of Objects

How an object is presented to the child can make a difference in postural control. If a child demonstrates atypical head hyperextension when sitting (Figure 4.14), for example, the early interventionist can present objects close to the child below chin level to promote active head flexion (Figure 4.15). Placing objects at the child's midline is important, particularly for children with central nervous system dysfunction, to minimize the influence of persistent primitive reflexes such as the asymmetrical tonic neck reflex. Optimal placement of the paper during writing tasks can be determined by having the child grasp his hands in the midline while resting on the desktop and prepositioning for the paper under the writing arm so it slants parallel to that arm (Benbow, 1990).

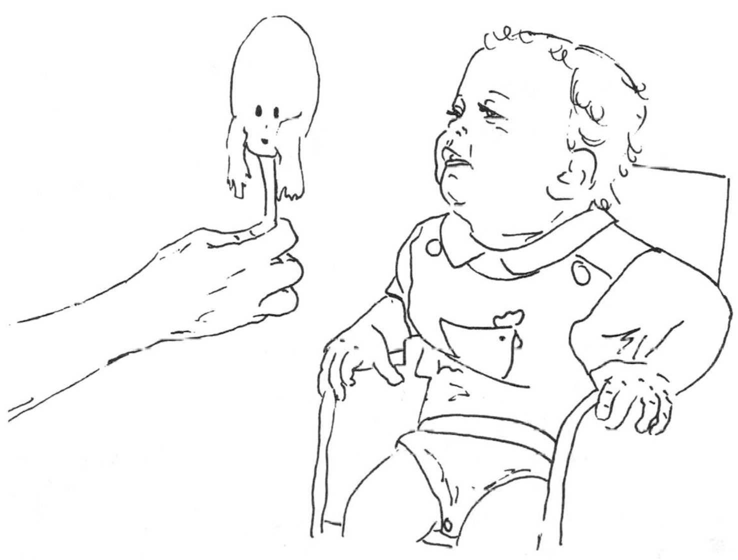

FIGURE 4.14 Inappropriate object presentation to toddler with spastic diplegic cerebral palsy, reinforcing shoulder retraction, and head and neck hyperextension.
Source: Used by permission of Jean Patz.

FIGURE 4.15 Improved presentation of object below eye level, fostering appropriate head, trunk, and upper extremity control.
Source: Used by permission of Jean Patz.

Fine Motor Materials

Larger toys may assist the child who has a poor grasp or weak grasp. Large lacing beads, easy-grip pegs, and knobbed puzzles are available commercially and from special-order catalogs. A variety of beginner puzzles have single shapes with vegetables, fruits, animals, geometric figures, or flowers. The knob provides a 1-inch clearance for ease in grasp. Switch-activated toys are particularly useful for children with restricted arm use. Switches can be activated with any part of the body such as the head, arm, foot, or knee. See Chapter 9 for a discussion of these devices.

Prewriting Adaptations

Adaptations may be needed to assist the child in holding a pencil with a more mature pattern. Pencil grips come in a variety of shapes, sizes, and textures. Pencil grips available include pear-shaped grips to guide placement of the index finger and thumb and prevent cramping, Super-Grips® for large, ½-inch-diameter pencils, bulb-design built-up grips, triangular pen grips, and round rubber or soft foam grips.

Adjustable-angle tabletops can assist the child in maintaining a more upright posture during prewriting or writing activities. Nonslip mats may be used to stabilize a child's writing paper, or self-adhesive strips can be used to wrap around utensils or other tools for a better grip.

Prewriting Programs. There are a number of resources that can assist the interventionist in developing a prewriting program for preschool-aged children. For example, Klein's (1990a) illustrated book describes typical prewriting development, the necessary prerequisite skills, and suggestions for intervention. Witt and Klein (1990) have compiled activities that address kinesthetic and sensory awareness needed for the development of writing and school readiness, and Levine (1995) has developed a visual analysis of the normal components necessary for prewriting as well as scissor skills from birth to 6 years of age.

Scissor Skills

Equipment for Scissor Skills. Appropriate scissors should be selected to address the child's needs. For children who have not developed handedness, scissors for use with either the right or left hand are indicated to avoid frustration. Care should be taken to select scissors that cut well; many standard scissors sold for children's use do not. Four-loop training scissors have an extra pair of loops placed adjacent to the child's rings; the interventionist places a hand over the child's for extra guidance. Another type of training scissors, the double-loop or training scissors, have an extra pair of loops placed vertically to the child's loops. The interventionist holds the distal loops while the child holds the proximal loops. This can be useful for a child who is tactually defensive (or who finds touch uncomfortable) to the interventionist's hand touching the child's (Klein, 1990b). Loop scissors consist of one large, flexible loop that the child with poor or weak grasp can easily squeeze.

Prescissor Programs. An illustrated workbook for preschool and school-aged children that is designed to foster prescissor skills has been developed by Klein (1990b). Schneck and Battaglia (1992) suggest precutting activities to develop eye-hand coordination, hand strength, and fine-motor dexterity in children who are not ready to use scissors. Activities include modeling clay for building strength and manipulating squeeze toys or squirt guns for opening and closing the hand, as well as bilateral activities such as snapping and unsnapping pop beads, sewing cards, or stringing beads. If the child has poor coordination because of tremors or jerkiness, the interventionist can provide external stabilization to the shoulder, arm, forearm, or wrist while cutting. This can be gradually weaned. When the child begins cutting, Schneck and Battaglia (1992) suggest using long, narrow strips of paper and increasing the width as the child's skills develop.

Oral Motor Skills: Typical Development

Oral motor development incorporates coordinated movements of the jaw, tongue, lips, and cheeks during sucking, swallowing, munching, chewing, spoon-feeding and cup drinking. In addition to the motor control necessary for feeding, it is important to consider positioning of the child's head in relationship to the body and to gravity, positioning of the person feeding the child in relationship to the child, positioning of the bottle, cup, or spoon and the selection of types and textures of food that are suitable for the developmental level of the child. As noted earlier in relation to the development of fine and gross motor skills, sensory processing skills also are necessary for feeding so that the child can respond appropriately to the texture and temperature of food in the mouth. The nature of oral motor skills required is quite different, for example, when a raw apple is eaten from when pudding is eaten. Higher-textured foods provide the sensory stimulus for the development of more-mature oral motor skills. Developmental eating milestones from birth through 2 years of age are listed in Table 4.8.

Positioning During Meals

Normally, an infant enjoys being held in a semireclined position during feedings. By the age of 7 months, most infants can sit independently in a highchair with support provided by the seat belt or tray; most children can sit in a small chair by 18 months of age (Morris & Klein, 1987). These positions parallel the development of oral structures as well as oral motor skills. Most infants can safely be fed in a reclined position because the relationship of the oral structures to one another makes it unlikely that aspiration, the passage of liquids into the lungs, will occur (Case-Smith & Humphrey, 1996). As an infant approaches 12 months of age, however, the throat elongates and additional space is created between the base of the

TABLE 4.8 Development of Oral Motor Skills

AGE	SKILLS
1 month	wraps tongue around nipple with strong grasp; positioned semi-reclined when fed
4–6 months	introduced to cereals and pureed and strained baby food
5 months	munches on a cracker; vertical tongue and jaw movements
6 months	jaw and tongue remain still when spoon approaches; introduced to a cup
7 months	lateral tongue movements develop for beginning chewing; can sit upright in high chair, support needed
8 months	eats mashed or junior foods; actively uses upper lip to clear food off spoon
9 months	lateral border of lips seal on nipple, no liquid loss
12 months	eats table food coarsely chopped
15 months	handles cup drinking well; consecutive sips from cup
18 months	eats meat and raw vegetables; can sit in small chair, support needed only for safety
2–3 years	tongue can cross midline when chewing; tongue tip elevation occurs during drinking; jaw stability during cup drinking

Source: From *Pre-Feeding Skills* by S. Morris and M. Klein, 1987, San Antonio, Texas: Therapy Skill Builders.

tongue and the epiglottis, which covers the trachea during swallowing. This provides a greater opportunity for aspiration to occur when a child is in a reclined position because of the effect of gravity on foods; by this age, children should begin to move to a more upright position. An upright position facilitates the ability to handle solid foods safely, to chew, and to drink from a cup.

Sucking

The rooting reflex, which the newborn exhibits from birth to 3 months of age, enables the child to locate the source of food. The infant's head turns toward the stimulus and he opens his mouth when touched around the oral area. Reflexive swallowing occurs with the suck-swallow reflex, which diminishes around 2 to 4 months of age (Connor, Williamson, & Siepp, 1978). Positional flexion predominates. Sucking pads assist in the sucking process by providing lateral cheek stability. A healthy, full-term infant has the ability to initiate suckling, maintain a strong grasp on the nipple using an extension-retraction pattern of the tongue, and ingest the required amount of liquid efficiently within 20–30 minutes (Morris & Klein, 1987). Liquid loss may be apparent as a result of incomplete development of a lateral lip seal around the nipple and wide yet rhythmical jaw excursions. According to Morris and Klein, the mature sucking pattern emerges around 6 to 9 months of age. This involves a cupped configuration of the tongue and vertical up-and-down tongue movements, creating negative intraoral pressure resulting from smaller jaw gradations and complete lip closure around the nipple. Nutritive and nonnutritive sucking rates differ.

Sucking on a bottle occurs at approximately one suck per second with few rests and long bursts of sucking, while nonnutritive sucking is faster, with two sucks per second and shorter bursts and pauses (Sameroff, 1973; Wolff, 1968).

Swallowing

Morris and Klein (1987) discuss the tongue, jaw, and lip movements during the oral phase of swallowing. Initially, tongue extension-retraction is utilized during swallowing and suckling; swallowing occurs after every second or third suck. Tongue movement changes at 6 to 8 months of age from slight protrusion to a vertical pattern, and finally to tongue tip elevation around 2 years of age as jaw stability develops (Morris & Klein). At this stage, no liquid loss occurs and the lips remain closed with this efficient pattern of swallowing. The pharyngeal phase begins when the bolus moves through the pharynx, triggering the swallow reflex; the final phase involves passage of liquid or food through the esophagus into the stomach (Logemann, 1983).

Protective mechanisms to prevent aspiration of liquid or food include elevation of the soft palate to close off the nasal cavities and backward movement of the epiglottis to cover the airway. A sphincter at the top of the stomach prevents reflux, or back-up of food contents up the esophagus and into the pharynx.

Munching and Chewing

Munching occurs around 5 to 6 months of age as food is simply mashed up against the palate with vertical tongue and jaw movements when the child manipulates a cracker (Morris & Klein, 1987). Food stays in the front of the mouth at this stage of development, because lateral tongue and circular jaw movements have not developed. Tongue lateralization and circular or rotary jaw movements, which are needed to carry food to the side of the mouth and pulverize it for chewing, begin at around 7 to 8 months, with mature chewing abilities developing by 2 years of age (Morris & Klein, 1987).

Morris and Klein (1987) outline the developmental progression of the introduction of solids. Time lines for the introduction of solid foods vary according to pediatricians' recommendations and families' culture, beliefs, and past experiences. Children are introduced to cereals and pureed or strained baby foods at around 4 to 6 months of age. Ground or mashed table foods, referred to as "lumpy solids," are generally introduced at approximately 8 months, followed by coarsely chopped table food at around 1 year of age. Most meats and some raw vegetables are appropriate for an 18-month-old eating coarsely chopped table food.

Spoon-feeding

The ability to quiet the tongue and jaw upon seeing the spoon approach occurs at around 6 months of age (Morris & Klein, 1987). This resting posture is important for preparing the mouth to receive food. Another important milestone during spoon-feeding is the child's ability to actively use the upper lip to clear food from the spoon; this begins at around 7 to 8 months of age (Morris & Klein, 1987).

Cup Drinking

Cup drinking generally begins at around 4 to 6 months of age as the mother holds a cup up to the child's mouth for a taste. The infant uses a suck-swallow pattern on the cup initially. Because jaw stability has not yet developed, liquid loss occurs, necessitating use of a cloth or bib under the child's chin. The parent may offer cups with spouted lids initially to avoid spillage; the child uses more of a sucking pattern when drinking from this type of cup. Gradually, jaw stabilization develops, allowing closure of the lips on a regular cup rim. Jaw stability progresses from wide vertical jaw movements to biting on the cup rim for stability at 15 to 18 months. The child achieves mature internal jaw stability at approximately 24 months (Morris & Klein, 1987). Movement of the tongue changes from the up-and-down pattern noted in sucking to a simple tongue protrusion pattern during the first year, followed by mature elevation of the tip of the tongue by 2 years (Morris & Klein, 1987). Initially, the child takes individual sips; continuous swallowing, or taking several sips in succession, indicates a more mature swallowing pattern. The child drinks successfully from a cup held by the person feeding him by 12 to 15 months of age, and will do so with no liquid loss by 2 years of age. Chapter 5 further discusses development of self-feeding from a cup.

Oral Motor Skills: Atypical Development

In the preceding section, the oral motor components of positioning, sucking, swallowing, chewing, spoon feeding, and cup drinking were described. Atypical oral motor development may occur when there are problems with tone, which affect the oral musculature in the same way as it affects postural and motor skills. Sensitivity to texture and temperature may also result in resistance to eating or difficulties coping with different foods. For some children, prematurity, illness, gastroesophageal reflux, or surgical intervention can result in an interruption in normal feeding procedures. For these children, the discomfort associated with alternative feeding methods such as nasogastric and gastrostomy tube feedings and lack of appropriate oral stimulation may result in complicated behavioral issues related to feeding. In addition, parents and interventionists need to keep in mind that some medical conditions and medications may result in diminished appetite. Any of these problems can contribute to poor intake and low weight gain. The following section provides information that may be helpful in determining the need for further evaluation. Figure 4.16 summarizes this information.

Positioning

Poor positioning or postural control of the child resulting from atypical tone can have a considerable impact on all feeding functions. An infant who is consistently

FIGURE 4.16 Red flags suggestive of oral motor problems

POSITIONING
- parent has difficulty holding or positioning the child in a chair during meals
- child is extremely fussy when held
- child has trouble sitting independently during meals as a result of poor postural control (independent sitting generally occurs by approximately 8 months)

SUCKING
- persistent difficulty initiating sucking when hungry and alert
- weak grasp or suction on the nipple when hungry and alert; poor intake
- consistently takes too long to complete a bottle when hungry and alert—more than 40–60 minutes
- frequent choking or gagging when drinking from bottle or breast
- tongue pushes nipple out of mouth involuntarily
- persistent, involuntary biting on the nipple
- parent feels the need to cut a hole in the bottle nipple to increase intake
- parent has difficulty finding a nipple that the child will consistently use

SWALLOWING
- coughing during or after eating and drinking
- history of aspiration pneumonia
- gurgly voice
- frequent vomiting
- persistent drooling beyond the teething phase of 6 to 18 months
- open mouth posture; excessive loss of liquid

CHEWING
- persistence on only baby food (strained, pureed, or mashed) beyond 12–15 months (strained or pureed food is generally offered between 3 and 8 months; mashed by 8 months, followed by coarsely chopped regular food by 12–15 months)
- negative reaction to solid foods such as crying or spitting; "picky eater"
- lack of tongue lateralization; therefore, food stays in the front of the mouth after the first year; food loss
- persistent choking or gagging on solid food
- consistent asymmetry of the tongue, jaw, and lips during chewing, crying, or smiling

SPOON-FEEDING
- persistent, involuntary biting or clamping down on the spoon
- tongue involuntarily and forcefully pushes spoon out of the mouth on a consistent basis
- persistent choking or gagging when being spoon-fed
- inability to clear or wipe thickened food off the spoon with the upper lip after 9–12 months of age

CUP DRINKING
- excessive liquid loss beyond 1 year of age when drinking from a cup held by the caregiver
- coughing during or after drinking thin liquids from a cup
- difficulty transitioning from the bottle to a cup at a developmentally appropriate age
- inability to get enough liquid in by cup; history of dehydration
- report from the parent that cup drinking is stressful
- inability of a child over 1 year of age with at least 2 months of cup-drinking experience to take consecutive sips

Source: Used by permission of Jean Patz.

difficult to hold, seems extremely fussy when held, or prefers being left alone may have positioning problems related to atypical postural tone or a dysfunctional sensory system. Caregivers may report that the child's body feels limp or stiff and that they don't have enough hands to support the child during eating. A child's need for additional support in sitting upright beyond the 8-to-12-month level is cause for concern because independent sitting generally develops by 6 to 8 months.

Poor postural alignment is not conducive to swallowing. Head hyperextension tends to place the oral structures in a position incompatible with normal swallowing. The atypical posture mechanically opens the airway, placing a child at risk for aspirating foreign material. This in turn may lead to aspiration pneumonia.

Sucking

Many factors can interfere with sucking skills, including structural deformities, weakness resulting from poor health, poor oral motor control resulting from central nervous system dysfunction, and behavioral issues stemming from inadequate sensory processing. Absent or weak oral reflexes can impede the sucking process. Tongue thrust, or protrusion, which is seen in some children with cerebral palsy and Down syndrome, interferes with sucking as the tongue is either bunched as a result of increased tone or flat as a result of low tone, making it difficult for the tongue to wrap around the nipple to assist in channeling the liquid back in the mouth for swallowing. The thrusting motion of the tongue may push the nipple out of the mouth. Presence of an abnormal tonic bite reflex sets off a biting-versus-sucking response on the nipple. A tonic bite reflex, an atypical clamping of the jaw in response to stimulation on the gums or teeth, is an abnormality seen in children with more severe neuromotor dysfunction. Increased tone can create retraction of the upper lip, making it difficult to achieve lip closure around the nipple. An open mouth posture resulting from hypertonia or hypotonia prevents jaw and lip approximation around the nipple. All of these factors can increase feeding times.

Swallowing

Children with neuromotor dysfunction are at risk at all stages of swallowing. A multidisciplinary team is crucial for the diagnosis and treatment of gastroesophageal reflux and aspiration. Poor oral motor control resulting from atypical tone makes it difficult for a child to collect the bolus and time the swallow. Problems may also occur in the pharyngeal and esophageal phases of swallow. Coughing may be a sign of direct or indirect aspiration of food or liquid into the airway. Aspiration can occur without coughing as well; this is termed "silent aspiration." Frequent burping or vomiting may be an indication of reflux. Delayed or atypical oral motor control can contribute to an open mouth posture which fosters drooling. A persistently soaked bib beyond the time when teething occurs can indicate oral motor dysfunction.

Chewing

A child's inability or refusal to progress from pureed or strained baby food to more highly textured food beyond the 12-to-15-month level after repeated introductions of solids warrants further investigation, although this is dependent on culture and medical advice. A child manipulates food between the molar surface when chewing; inefficient chewing would be suspected if food remained in the front of the mouth and resulted in food loss. Consistent choking when solids are given after the expected developmental range is also cause for concern. Poor oral motor control, such as that evidenced by tongue thrusting in children with cerebral palsy or Down syndrome (Figure 4.17), may appear to be purposeful spitting when in fact it is an involuntary tongue protrusion that expels food from the mouth. A child's difficulty carrying food back in the mouth to swallow combined with forward protrusion of the tongue can cause excessive food loss.

A child may not have the oral motor capabilities to maneuver food laterally between the molars for chewing and then back for swallowing. Persistent gagging may indicate a hyperactive gag reflex seen in some children with central nervous system dysfunction. Consistent negative reaction (e.g., crying, turning the head away, or spitting) to chunky or solid foods may indicate a strong food preference. However, the resistance may be accounted for by a more serious condition, such

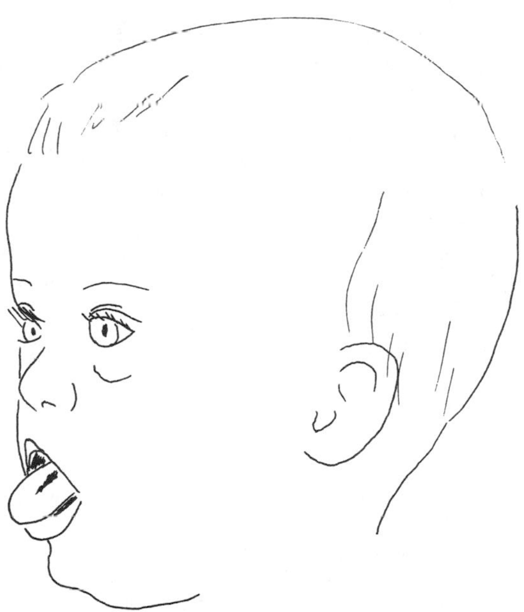

FIGURE 4.17 Tongue thrust in a child with Down syndrome.
Source: Used by permission of Jean Patz.

as oral hypersensitivity, which occurs when a child is unable to tolerate the tactile qualities of the food, or oral motor dysfunction. Asymmetry in oral movements may be a symptom of motor dysfunction on one side of the body, as in spastic hemiplegia, whose signs include an uneven smile, asymmetrical mouth posture when crying, and persistent pocketing of food on one side of the mouth. Another indicator that must not be ignored is the level of stress related to feeding solids to their child that parents report.

Spoon-feeding

One should question why a child with cerebral palsy consistently bites down on a spoon with clenched jaws. This may be a sign of a tonic bite reflex, which is a form of tactile hypersensitivity (Morris & Klein, 1987). Once stimulated by the contact of the spoon on the teeth, a child with tonic bite reflex has difficulty releasing the bite. A parent may unknowingly stimulate the tonic bite again by attempting to pull the spoon out of the child's clenched mouth.

Cup Drinking

Morris and Klein (1987) discuss various factors that cause difficulties with cup drinking. These include oral motor delay, which can cause a primitive sucking pattern on the cup; atypical tone, which can result in poor oral motor control; and abnormalities in sensory processing, which can lead to oral hypersensitivity. Typically, a child loses liquid when he begins to drink from a cup. Excessive loss beyond the first year may indicate poor development of jaw stability, tongue control, or lip closure. One might be alerted to the possibility of aspiration if liquids are given by cup in a safe and effective manner and the child demonstrates a persistent cough. If the cup has been introduced in the normal developmental time frame and the child repeatedly refuses to drink from a cup, then one might suspect oral motor dysfunction, oral hypersensitivity, delayed development, or behavioral resistance. Parents are generally the first to notice difficulties in feeding their child. If the parent seems to be experiencing stress related to giving the child a drink from a cup, further investigation is warranted.

Oral Motor Skills: Intervention

During intervention with oral motor skills, it is important to consider the need for multiple team members, including the parents, physician, occupational therapist or speech and language pathologist, nutritionist, nurse, and early interventionist. Consultation from appropriate personnel regarding possible food allergies and swallowing irregularities may be necessary.

Positioning the Child

If the child must be held for feeding, he needs to be placed in as upright a position as possible, with the head in a slight bit of flexion, the arms supported forward (not behind the feeder's back), and the hips bent at approximately 90 degrees (Figure 4.18). The person feeding the child cradles the child's head in the crook of his elbow and can actively move that arm to counteract tonic head hyperextension. The feeder can cross his leg to create a seat for the child, which places the hips in flexion.

Positioning of the Feeder

Positioning of the feeder is important as well. Generally, the feeder needs to sit directly in front of the child and at eye level to foster symmetry and to decrease the influence of abnormal primitive reflexes. The feeder should avoid sitting to the side, particularly if the child has cerebral palsy, as this might elicit tonic posturing from the influence of the asymmetrical tonic neck reflex (Figure 4.19). The plate of food

FIGURE 4.18 A grandfather holding his grandson for feeding, supporting the child's head with his arm while maintaining the child's arms forward and supporting the child's hips in flexion. The child has severe spastic quadriplegic cerebral palsy.
Source: Used by permission of Jean Patz.

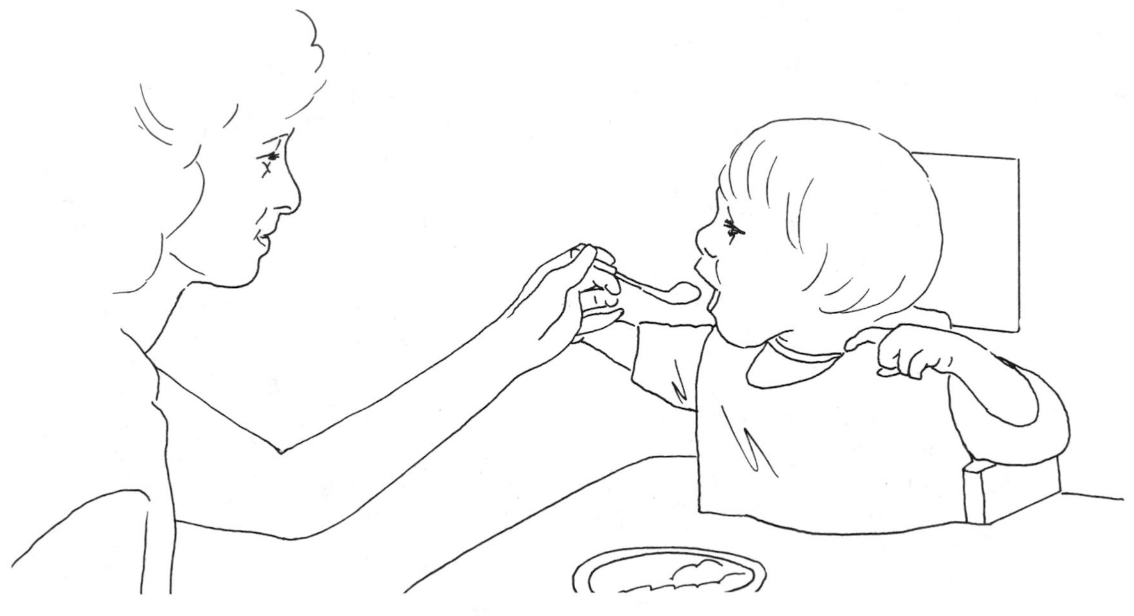

FIGURE 4.19 Inappropriate spoon presentation from the side, which triggers the expression of the asymmetrical tonic neck reflex in a child with spastic quadriplegia cerebral palsy. The feeder should sit directly in front of the child and at eye level to foster more normal tone and position for better success with eating.
Source: Used by permission of Jean Patz.

is placed on the side of the feeder's dominant hand for efficiency when feeding. The person feeding the child needs to ensure her own comfort in a suitable chair.

Fostering the Development of Oral Motor Skills

Sucking

Intervention addressing sucking problems needs to be orchestrated by a team of specialists because the program may include therapy to decrease the influence of atypical postural and oral tone, inhibit persistent oral reflexes, or modulate sensory problems. Medical issues are ruled out prior to initiation of any program addressing sucking problems in infants. Intervention may address the type of equipment used to foster more efficient sucking from a bottle. Characteristics of nipples such as the type, configuration, size, and ease of flow are evaluated. Various choices of bottles are available. For example, angled-neck bottles, available commercially, allow the child to be fed in a more upright position, thus reducing air intake and decreasing head hyperextension. Suggestions for positioning may be indicated to enhance a neutral or slightly forward flexion of the head needed for sucking from

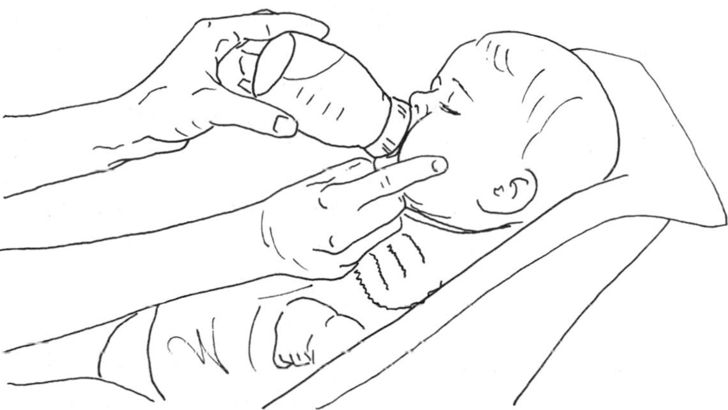

FIGURE 4.20 Jaw support provided to an infant with a weak suck. The lateral surface of the middle finger supports the jaw, while the index finger and thumb support the infant's cheeks.
Source: Used by permission of Jean Patz.

the breast or bottle. Oral facilitation techniques such as jaw support (Figure 4.20) may be warranted to provide better oral stability during sucking.

Swallowing

Intervention for swallowing dysfunction is addressed by professionals skilled in oral motor evaluation and intervention. When aspiration is medically diagnosed, intervention can range from thickening the child's food or liquid texture to gastrostomy feeding. Educational staff members need to be informed of any precautions regarding oral intake. If a child does have a swallowing disorder, feeding should occur when the child is positioned in as upright a position as possible. Jaw support may be provided by the feeder to create a more closed mouth posture, which is needed for effective swallowing. Thickened textures of food and liquid give the child more time to control the bolus and coordinate the swallow. Johnson and Scott (1993) have developed a resource guide addressing assessment and intervention for management of drooling.

Chewing

Children can easily choke on small pieces of food; therefore, caution is required when carrying out any program related to chewing. It is essential that a professional trained in oral motor assessment and intervention be consulted for recommendations. Chewing requires coordinated movements of the tongue, jaw, lips, and cheeks. Given the complexity of chewing, children with severe oral motor problems may not acquire this skill, thus necessitating adjustments to the type of food given.

Intervention addresses interfering factors such as tongue thrust, tongue retraction, jaw thrust, tonic bite reflex, lip retraction, jaw instability, and oral hypersensitivity (Morris & Klein, 1987).

A change in food texture may be needed to foster chewing development. The therapist may move the child from low-textured foods such as cereals and strained or ground foods, which do not require chewing, to foods thickened with baby cereals, rice cereal, and dehydrated fruit flakes and lumpy soft foods including cottage cheese and mashed macaroni and cheese (Morris & Klein, 1987). Foods that melt in the mouth, such as graham crackers, are used when the child has progressed to the stage of beginning to orally manipulate small pieces. Foods that make noise when they are crunched, such as cereal bits, can be fun for the child; however, these can present a choking hazard depending on the size. The feeder has to provide special handling techniques to assist the child who has oral motor difficulties to accept and manipulate the more-textured food.

Because chewing intervention usually requires diet texture changes, intervention includes techniques to help the child adjust to this new sensory experience. If a child exhibits oral hypersensitivity, tolerating more highly textured food will be a major challenge.

The therapist can assist in training the interventionist and parents in jaw control management. The interventionist also needs to be aware of the sensory and proprioceptive components of providing jaw control. It can be uncomfortable for the child to experience an adult's hand providing jaw control on his face while eating. The interventionist should be sensitive to the temperature of her own hand as well as how much pressure is exerted. A cold hand may startle the child. A light touch can be noxious to a child who has overly sensitive responses to touch, while a firm hold might restrict necessary jaw movements; therefore, moderation is recommended.

Diet Texture

The primary goal related to diet texture is that the child will handle and tolerate developmentally appropriate food texture or the highest texture possible. The primary goal for the parent is to prepare the appropriate food texture to accommodate the child's oral motor capabilities. The interventionist needs to know what texture has been recommended for the child. Adjusting food texture for a child with special needs is not the responsibility of a teacher, given the possibility of choking, gagging, or aspirating. Consistency of liquid and food texture depends on the level of oral motor competency, which is determined by an occupational therapist or speech pathologist who has performed a thorough oral motor and pharyngeal evaluation. This is done in consultation with the pediatrician and nutritionist, if one is available. Recommendations will then be shared with the parents and school personnel to incorporate them into the goals of the Individualized Family Service Plan (IFSP) or Individualized Education Plan (IEP). It is best to use the same texture both at home and at school.

Spoon-feeding

A proper approach with the spoon can promote a more normal head position for better swallowing. Head control is enhanced because the child will actively practice flexion of the head (chin tuck) with each bite presented. More effective swallowing is possible as a result of greater mouth closure which allows upper-lip closure on the spoon.

When spoon-feeding a child, the feeder should sit in front of the child at eye level to encourage midline positioning of the head and to discourage head hyperextension. Jaw support is provided if indicated and recommended. When the feeder approaches from below chin level, the child looks slightly down, creating a chin tuck. This can be done with each presentation of a spoon during a meal, giving the child multiple opportunities to bend his head and visually focus on the object. Also, it is important to bring the spoon close enough to the child so that he actively tucks the chin instead of jutting the chin forward to approach a spoon offered too far away. The feeder waits for the child to actively flex the head slightly (chin tuck) to clear food from the spoon. The spoon is inserted and removed in a horizontal fashion to encourage lip closure instead of wiping the spoon in an upward fashion, which negates the need for active lip closure on the spoon.

This is also helpful for a child with cerebral palsy who has a tonic bite reflex, because the approach avoids stimulating the teeth upon spoon removal. The feeder should avoid pulling the spoon out of the child's mouth once the tonic bite reflex has been elicited, because this will further strengthen the response. Instead, the feeder should try to relax the child's tonic posture of the body and jaw by slowly moving the child into a more flexed position and applying slight pressure on the temporomandibular joint or simply wait for the child to relax. A calm and quiet feeding environment is also helpful, because these children overrespond to sensory stimulation. Coated spoons are recommended to protect the child's teeth and provide a soft biting surface to reduce stimulation.

Many different types of spoons are available from various medical supply companies to address the needs of each child. These include coated spoons, shallow-bowled spoons, built-up-handled spoons, weighted spoons, adjustable-angle spoons, swivel spoons, and spoons with horizontal or vertical palm grips for children with weak or absent grasp. A universal cuff may provide a means to hold different utensils; this is a strap wrapped around the palm of the hand with a pocket to hold utensils in place.

Cup Drinking

Intervention techniques will depend on the oral difficulties encountered. Each child's treatment plan will be customized to fit his needs. For example, if a child has an abnormal tonic bite reflex that interferes with cup drinking, then oral desensitization techniques are done initially. Introduction of a cup into play situations prior to initiation of cup drinking is recommended so that the child will have seen and handled a cup.

General principles can be applied to teaching cup-drinking skills. Positioning the cup appropriately ensures that the child does not have to wait too long to drink, which could set off abnormal tongue thrusting. The feeder tips the cup enough so that the liquid is close to the rim prior to bringing the cup to the mouth. Cut-out cups are usually recommended to foster a more normal head position. The cut-out portion allows space for the nose when the cup is tipped up to prevent head hyperextension, which can interfere with swallowing.

Thickened liquids are used initially to slow the flow for ease in swallowing. Commercial thickeners are available; it is difficult, however, to maintain the desired consistency. Age-appropriate foods such as strained baby fruit, rice cereal, mashed bananas, and yogurt can be mixed with the liquid. It is important for the interventionist to prepare the recommended thickness of liquid.

Handling techniques to provide jaw control should be used when recommended if the difficulty is an open-mouth posture. The feeder should approach the child slowly with the cup to avoid eliciting any primitive or abnormal oral movements. The uncut side of the cup, opposite the cut-out portion, is placed on the midsection of the lower lip, not between the teeth. A small amount of liquid is poured slowly into the child's mouth to encourage one sip at a time when the child is first learning the skill; the amount is increased gradually to foster consecutive swallowing. If jaw control is recommended, the feeder maintains the jaw control until the child swallows the liquid. The child's reactions should be observed continuously to monitor what he can handle.

Sensorimotor Development in Children with Special Needs

In this section, common exceptionalities that result in atypical sensorimotor development are discussed. The anticipated developmental progression of motor skills in children with these exceptionalities also is provided. It is important to recognize that the common exceptionalities presented here are subsumed under the educational classifications described in Chapter 1. For example, Down syndrome typically is included under the classification of Mental Retardation, while cerebral palsy may fit within one of several classifications (e.g., orthopedic impairment).

Cerebral Palsy

Cerebral palsy is a group of nonprogressive disorders of movement and posture caused by damage to an immature brain (Batshaw & Perret, 1992). As noted previously, abnormalities of muscle tone characterize cerebral palsy. Because of atypical postural tone, children with cerebral palsy do not experience normal movement and develop compensatory patterns of movement and posture that may further impede their progress. Cerebral palsy is often accompanied by some degree of mental retardation, and sensory deficits may be present as well.

Gross Motor Development. Postural problems that accompany cerebral palsy were discussed earlier in this chapter. A child with spastic quadriplegia generally experiences extensor tone in the lower extremities with flexor tone predominating in the upper extremities. The persistence of primitive reflexes results in the child being pulled into gravity and, therefore, having great difficulty moving against gravity in the prone and the supine positions. It is usually difficult for the child to raise his head and trunk off of the floor when in prone. If rolling is mastered, it is characterized by limited rotation through the trunk with posturing of the arms in flexion and the legs in extension (Figure 4.21). In floor sitting, the pelvis is pulled into a posterior tilt. Compensatory trunk flexion results in further compensatory neck and head hyperextension to maintain balance in sitting (as was shown in Figure 4.3). A W sitting position, in which the legs are internally rotated with the knees together and the lower legs to the side of the body, may be favored by the child because it provides improved stability and frees the arms for use. However, this position is discouraged for several reasons: It may promote dislocation of the hips, it limits trunk rotation in sitting, and it does not require the child to use the lower extremities to assist in maintaining posture, which is necessary for later walking. In crawling, the child pulls his body forward with his arms close to the body, while the legs usually remain extended and adducted (straightened and together). Some children move on the floor by lying in supine and pushing with the feet, while arching the body into extension.

Children with spastic diplegia typically creep in a "bunny hop" pattern, with arms and legs moving together in a bilateral, symmetrical pattern rather than reciprocally. When these children walk, the increased extensor tone in the lower

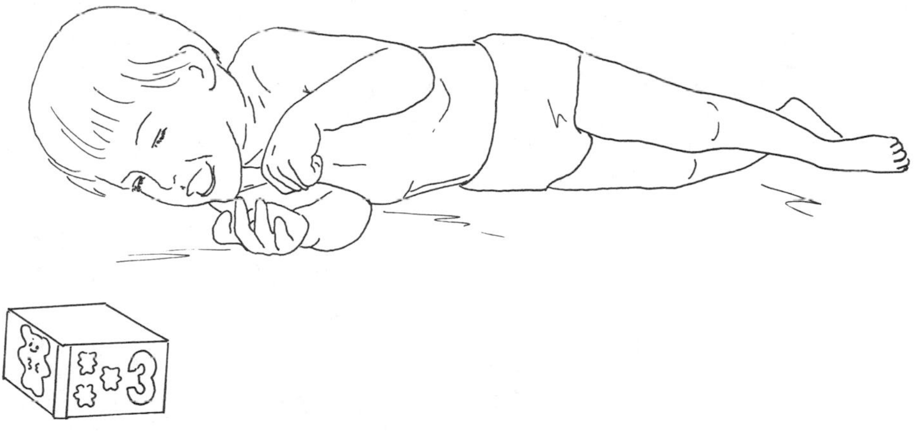

FIGURE 4.21 "Log" rolling in a 4-year-old child with spastic quadriplegic cerebral palsy. Note the extensor tone in the lower body, with flexor tone in the upper extremities.
Source: Used by permission of Jean Patz.

extremities results in adduction and internal rotation, with the legs moving in a pattern of circumduction. Often, the ankles are braced to prevent walking on the toes. The upper extremities, though only mildly involved, often pull into a high guard position as a result of associated reactions, or overflow.

Children with hemiplegia have increased tone on one side of the body, resulting in asymmetrical posture and movement. These children typically master the early gross motor developmental milestones and are very mobile. High-level preschool skills are difficult for them, but children with hemiplegia often try to do all that their peers do. The involved ankle is often braced to maintain muscle length, to help break up the extensor tone in the leg, and to promote walking with the foot flat on the floor.

Children with athetosis have fluctuating muscle tone and variable motor capabilities. Some children with athetosis learn to walk independently, but many never advance beyond moving on the floor. Their posture is very unstable and movements are asymmetrical and uncontrolled, because the fluctuating tone makes it very difficult for them to control flexor and extensor muscles together for coactivation. It is very difficult for a child with athetosis to maintain a midline position because of asymmetrical movement and persistence of the asymmetrical tonic neck reflex.

Fine Motor Development. Fine motor dysfunction in children with cerebral palsy may be caused by tonal abnormalities, sensory deficits, and existence of primitive postural reflexes such as the asymmetrical tonic neck reflex (ATNR) "fencing posture" (Figure 4.22). For example, if the ATNR is present because of delayed integration, turning the head to the side dictates increased tone, thus creating extension in the extremities on the face side and increased flexion on the skull side. This makes it difficult for the child to bring his hands together or maintain visual attention to the hand engaged in an activity that requires elbow flexion, such as bringing a cup to the mouth (Erhardt, 1994). Hypertonia restricts the range of motion available during reach; shoulder retraction, which also is often present, prevents forward movement for reach. Hypotonia, on the other hand, may prevent lifting the arms up against gravity to meet in the midline or to reach. A child who has variable or fluctuating postural tone demonstrates difficulty in grading movements for reach; minimal control is noted in the midranges, or midposition. The child will attempt to minimize involuntary movements by using compensatory stabilizing patterns such as elevating the shoulders to stabilize the head for eye-hand coordination during reach, locking the elbows in hyperextension, or adducting and internally rotating the arms to assist in distal control.

Flexor spasticity in the arm interferes with grasp patterns because of increased elbow flexion, forearm pronation, wrist flexion with ulnar deviation, and thumb adduction (as was shown in Figure 4.2). These problems interfere with the child's ability to see what is grasped and with the thumb-to-fingertip opposition needed to prehend small objects or maintain grasp on a pencil. A child with decreased or variable tone uses primitive grasp patterns such as the palmar grasp for stabilization.

Bilateral (two-handed) control needed during manipulation may be affected by the existence of tonal abnormalities. A child with spastic hemiplegia displays

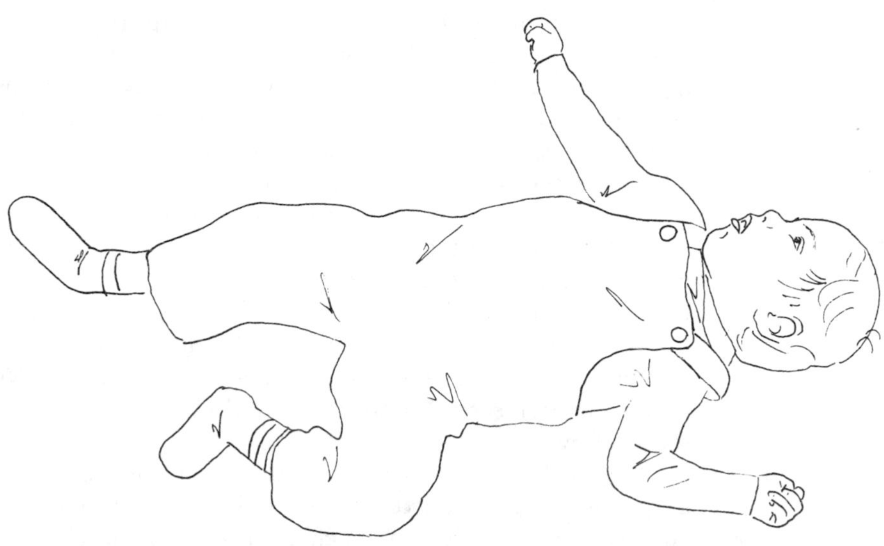

FIGURE 4.22 Asymmetrical tonic neck posture in a child with spastic quadriplegic cerebral palsy. The persistence of this primitive reflex will prevent the child from rolling.
Source: Used by permission of Jean Patz.

asymmetry in movement as a result of both motor and sensory involvement. Unilateral posturing, or postures seen on one side of the body, may include shoulder depression, flexor spasticity of the arm, extensor spasticity of the leg, retracted and elevated pelvis, lateral flexion and backward rotation of the trunk, and lateral neck flexion (Connor, Williamson, & Siepp, 1978). As a child with spastic hemiplegia manipulates objects with the noninvolved hand, overflow or associated reactions may be noted in the involved extremity. Typically, the child disregards or neglects the involved upper extremity because of poor sensory awareness in that arm. Additionally, restricted active movement and posturing of the involved side behind the noninvolved side reinforces this neglect. Exaggerated movements may eventually develop in the noninvolved extremity because of overuse of compensatory patterns with that arm (Connor et al., 1978). A child with hemiplegia may not tolerate being touched on the involved arm and will resist any attempts to integrate that arm into fine motor activities.

Oral Motor Development. Children with cerebral palsy may exhibit a number of characteristics that may interfere with voluntary and involuntary motor control necessary for eating. These may include atypical postural and oral tone and movement, persistent primitive postural reflexes (e.g., asymmetrical tonic neck reflex) and oral reflexes (e.g., gag, rooting, and sucking reflexes), sensory deficits (hyposensitivity or hypersensitivity), pharyngeal involvement (which can cause aspiration), or esophageal involvement leading to reflux.

Hypertonia in the oral area can cause restricted oral movements (e.g., difficulty opening the mouth) that interfere with eating. Oral asymmetry and atypical oral motor patterns can include tongue thrusting, jaw thrusting, and lip retraction leading to an excessive amount of feeding time and poor food intake. Mature oral movements such as isolated, lateral tongue movement needed in chewing may not develop in the presence of atypical tongue and jaw thrust accompanying increased tone. An example of oral hypersensitivity is the presence of a tonic bite reflex.

Hypotonia in the oral area may cause sluggish oral movements. An open-mouth posture prevents a good lip seal on a cup, nipple, or spoon and results in drooling and food and liquid loss. Oral motor skills are delayed; the child persists on a bottle or low-textured foods well beyond the expected range of development. The tongue protrusion pattern, tongue thrust with a flattened configuration, interferes with food intake and channeling liquid and solids posteriorly for swallowing.

A child with variable or fluctuating tone, as with athetoid cerebral palsy, may exhibit involuntary, uncontrolled, extraneous oral movements. The child has difficulty sustaining movements such as maintaining lip closure on a nipple or cup rim and controlling midrange movements of the tongue, jaw, and lips. Proximal stability of the head and trunk is lacking, making it difficult for the child to remain still for feeding. A greater degree of tongue thrust or jaw thrust occurs as a result of involuntary movements.

Motor Incoordination Disorders

Developmental Dyspraxia. *Developmental dyspraxia* is impairment in the ability to plan nonhabitual motor tasks, which results in clumsiness; this is not a problem with motor execution but with motor planning (Cermak, 1991). The child uses excessive effort and energy to figure out complex motor tasks such as buttoning, cutting with scissors, tying shoelaces, riding a bicycle, writing, blowing his nose, skipping, hopping, and playing on playground equipment. Referral to occupational therapy for children with developmental dyspraxia usually centers around handwriting difficulties, delayed independence in self-care activities, or poor self-esteem (Missiuna & Polatajko 1995).

Somatodyspraxia. The term *somatodyspraxia* (Ayres, 1989) refers to a specific type of developmental dyspraxia caused by dysfunction in the ability to discriminate tactile information. Children with somatodyspraxia have impaired tactile and proprioceptive processing, which interferes with learning new motor tasks. Once the skill is learned, the child can accomplish the task, but generalization to other similar activities is difficult (Cermak, 1991). The clinical picture of somatodyspraxia includes clumsiness, poor discrimination of tactile information, poor sequencing and timing of movements, difficulty learning self-care activities such as buttoning, problems in gross motor and fine motor activities including handwriting, and inadequate body schema (Cermak, 1991). These children have minimal oral motor problems related to feeding; oral problems are more commonly associated with oral dyspraxia. Poor motor planning may affect self-feeding skills, for example, by causing difficulty using utensils. Reliance on finger feeding may therefore persist for an extended period of time to avoid frustration with utensils. Other characteristics may include sloppiness, poor attention span, and the inability to sit through an entire meal.

Early motor milestones such as crawling and walking are reported as age-appropriate for children with somatodyspraxia, but they have difficulty with tasks such as manipulating fasteners, using scissors, and other novel motor tasks. A skilled observer often can recognize problems in the preschool years, but typically the disorder is not identified until the early school years, when demands on time, organization, and participation increase (Cermak, 1991; Levine, 1987). Early diagnosis can help prevent some of the difficulties and frustration that these children may encounter. The diagnosis of somatodyspraxia is usually made by an occupational therapist after the analysis of results from clinical observations, pertinent historical information, and standardized testing using the Sensory Integration and Praxis Tests (SIPT) (Ayres, 1989). The SIPT is a standardized assessment tool measuring sensory integrative functions in children who are 4 years of age and older. Poor self-esteem, disorganization, manipulative behavior, and low frustration tolerance are other behavioral characteristics associated with somatodyspraxia (Cermak, 1991).

Developmental Coordination Disorder. According to the American Psychiatric Association's *Diagnostic and Statistical Manual of Mental Disorders* (1994), motor deficits associated with developmental coordination disorder are not neurologically based (i.e., do not result from physical disorders). Such deficits include significant delays in acquiring typical motor milestones (development is below intellectual capabilities), clumsiness in the execution of motor skills, difficulty with handwriting tasks, and poor performance in sports. The motor impairment significantly impedes functional self-care activities and academic achievement. The term *developmental coordination disorder* is relatively new, and many researchers still refer to the incoordination sometimes seen in young children using other terms, including *developmental apraxia* (or *dyspraxia*) and *somatodyspraxia* (David, 1995).

Autism

While the identifying features of autism and other pervasive developmental disorders are primarily related to qualitative deficits in communication and social interaction, atypical responses to sensory stimuli and stereotypical motor movements also are common diagnostic findings.

Sensory Processing. A number of sensory anomalies involving registration, modulation, and response to sensory stimuli have been described in children with autism. Volkmar, Cohen, and Paul (1986) reported that most parents described their young children with autism as being hyporeactive to sound and pain stimulation, yet hyperreactive to visual, tactile, and auditory stimuli. The apparent contradiction in responsivity to auditory stimuli may be explained by reports that children with autism may not respond to verbal commands and may have difficulty processing auditory information, but they may become very upset at the presence of specific environmental sounds or of loud or unusual auditory stimuli (e.g., a vacuum cleaner or door bell). Other frequent sensory manifestations are a fascination with some visual stimuli (e.g., rotating fans and moving lights), an apparent insensitivity to pain, a tendency to lick or smell objects, and an aversion to specific foods (Rapin, 1988). Differences in tactile processing may be seen in avoidance or obsession with specific textures of objects or foods or the avoidance of touch to particular body parts. Because of the sensory processing difficulties often present in children with autism, sensory integrative therapy, which is a method of improving registration, modulation, and adaptation to sensory input (Ayres, 1985), has been suggested as an intervention approach (Grandin, 1995; Siegel, 1996).

Gross and Fine Motor Development. Gross and fine motor development in young children with autism, although often the most successful area of development (Cox, 1993), is nonetheless often significantly delayed (Watson & Marcus, 1986). These children may appear to be physically agile and often do quite well in activities such as completing puzzles and block designs, but they may have difficulties in tasks requiring the planning and sequencing of movement (e.g., pedaling a tricycle, drawing, and folding a paper). The ability of children with autism to gather accurate information about their own bodies through proprioception and the bodies of others, through visual perception—both of which are required for imitation of motor movement—is questionable. Young children with autism are notably poor at imitating the behavior of others, which some feel may be primary to the problems of socialization and communication inherent in children with autism (Meltzoff & Gopnik, 1993).

Specific deficits related to motor development that have been noted in children with autism include decreased postural tone, toe walking, drooling, clumsiness, delayed onset of walking (Rapin, 1988), decreased balance, incoordination, and poor finger-to-thumb movements (Jones & Prior, 1985). Stereotypic motor movements are commonly seen among children with autism. These may involve hand and arm flapping, finger flicking, rocking, and body spinning. There are two divergent schools of thought regarding the function of these behaviors. Lovaas, Newsom, and Hickman (1987) feel that stereotypic movements represent the child's attempt to achieve a state of optimum arousal. King and Grandin (1990), on the other hand, speculate that these behaviors serve the function of calming an overaroused system. Although self-injurious behavior, which is not uncommon in children with autism, has been described as an attempt at communication or a response to frustration (Van Bourgondien, 1993), it might also represent an inability to cope with intense sensory discomfort. Temple Grandin (1995), in her description of sensory problems in individuals with autism, explains that severe sensory processing problems may result in great bodily discomfort. Deep pressure stimulation has been reported to be effective in dealing with overarousal in children and adults with autism (Grandin, 1995; Nelson, 1984).

Oral Motor Development. While no specific problems in oral motor development have been noted in the literature, many parents report that their children with autism have eating problems. Children with autism may limit their diet to particular foods and food textures, which may be related to atypical tactile, gustatory, or olfactory processing. Pica, which is the eating of inedible substances, is common, and is felt by some to be caused by impaired taste perception in children with autism (Van Bourgondien, 1993).

Down Syndrome

Down syndrome is a genetic disorder that results from a chromosomal abnormality causing a number of physical and cognitive anomalies (Blackman, 1997). Children with Down syndrome typically have low muscle tone, short stature, and some degree of mental retardation. A number of health problems may accompany this disorder such as congenital heart disease, visual deficits, and lowered resistance to infection. Instability between the first two cervical vertebrae, or atlantoaxial subluxation, occurs in a small percentage of children with Down syndrome. X-rays of the neck are often recommended to rule out this condition because, in rare instances, pressure on the head and neck may result in damage to the spinal cord (Blackman, 1997).

Gross Motor Development. While gross motor delays are typical in children with mental retardation, the degree of delay is greater in Down syndrome than in retardation caused by other factors. While typically developing children begin to walk without support anywhere from 9 to 17 months, children with Down syndrome begin to walk from 13 to 48 months (Cunningham, 1982). In general, the age of acquisition of developmental milestones is late, and the range of ages in which skills may be acquired is also great. The quality of movement in children with Down syndrome is characterized by symmetrical movements with limited variability, poor balance, and rotation. It is felt that these problems are caused by low muscle tone and limited coactivation around the joints (Lauteslager, 1995), resulting in poor stability at the shoulders and hips and leading to limited ability to shift weight in many developmental positions. In infancy, resistance against gravity is minimal, and range of motion is greater than in typically developing children. Children with Down syndrome tend to utilize atypical posture in static positions, such as sitting in which the legs tend to be widely abducted, or spread apart, providing a wide base and eliminating the need for weight shift. In sitting, children with Down syndrome tend to avoid rotating the trunk to retrieve objects, but they may lean far forward with a rigid trunk or scoot in the sitting position to move toward a desired object. Atypical movement patterns are often observed when such children move from one position to another. Movement often occurs in straight planes, with limited trunk rotation. For example, while the typical child moves from sitting to a modified side-sitting position to the hands-and-knees position, children with Down syndrome are more likely to vault forward over their legs into the hands-and-knees position (Lauteslager, 1995). In walking, they are more likely to have their legs widely abducted and utilize lateral trunk movements to achieve weight shift for much longer periods of time than typically developing children do. Few children with Down syndrome develop the mature counterrotation and arm swing present in most typically developing 6-year-old children.

It further may be hypothesized that, while the movement patterns of young children with Down syndrome are efficient based upon their musculoskeletal features, the stereotypical development results in further delays in the future. For example, when typically developing children move from sitting to four-point, they gain much practice with trunk rotation and thus gain more-developed equilibrium reactions, more strength, and more variability of movement to prepare them for higher-level skills, such as walking. Children with Down syndrome often do not have the same range of experiences in sitting and do not gain the same degree of control before learning to walk, so walking is constrained to follow a similar pattern. Therefore, intervention is often focused on tone building and facilitation of coactivation, weight shift, and rotation in movement activities, allowing the child to experience greater variability of movement.

Fine Motor Development. Children with Down syndrome have short, stubby fingers. Their hands have small, slender bones with poor calcification, low-set thumbs, and delayed development of the carpal bones causing initial instability in the hand (Benda, 1969). As in gross motor skills development, the child with Down syndrome is likely to use bilateral, symmetrical movements of the upper extremities instead of differentiated movements, with minimal use of trunk rotation to support efficient reach. Low muscle tone results in hypermobility in the proximal finger and thumb joints which interferes with grasp. Grasp patterns may be immature, particularly thumb and index finger opposition, with poor differentiation of finger use and poor prepositioning of the hand for grasp. Cognitive limitations also affect fine motor skill development. Edwards and Lafreniere (1995) provide a good overview of assessment and intervention strategies to use with children with Down syndrome.

Sensory Processing. Some researchers have suggested that children with Down syndrome may have deficits in receiving sensory information. Cole, Abbs, and Turner (1988) found that the Down syndrome population displayed an inability to adapt grip forces to characteristics of objects which they felt was unrelated to hypotonia. In addition, the skin of children with Down syndrome may be thick and dry, possibly impairing sensation as age increases (Edwards & Lafreniere, 1995).

Oral Motor Development. Delays in oral motor skills in cases of Down syndrome result from cognitive, motor, and sensory delays from mental retardation, hypotonia, and oral hyposensitivity. Inadequate postural control may result in head hyperextension, which can interfere with safety in swallowing. During eating, infants may exhibit a poor suck resulting from the hypotonia or general weakness from other medical conditions such as associated heart abnormalities. An open-mouth posture and tongue thrusting lead to excessive drooling and poor oral intake. As the child matures, delayed chewing with a lack of progression to more highly textured food, as well as poor spoon-feeding and cup-drinking skills, may become more apparent.

A Framework for Meeting Sensorimotor Needs

Models of Service Delivery

Meeting the needs of children with sensorimotor impairment can be accomplished in a number of different ways. Each model of service delivery has specific strengths that, depending upon the needs of the child, the skills of team members, and the nature of the organization providing services, may be considered most appropriate for the individual child. Evaluation of the needs of the child is the first step in service provision.

Evaluation. The evaluation must include both a quantitative and a qualitative evaluation of sensorimotor performance, and it should be interpreted in light of the child's functioning in problem-solving, communication, self-care, and social and emotional development. In the case of the interdisciplinary team, evaluation may be accomplished by a group of professionals, each assuming responsibility for specific areas of function, in an arena setting or with separate appointments in the home, school, and clinic. Examples of broad-based assessments that might be used to evaluate young children include the Battelle Developmental Inventory (Newborg, Stock, Wneck, Guidubaldi, & Svinicki, 1984), the Early Intervention Developmental Profile (Rogers et al., 1981), the Hawaii Early Learning Profile (Furuno et al., 1984) for children 0 to 3 years of age, and the Help for Preschoolers Assessment Strands, Charts, and Checklists (VORT Corporation, 1995) for children 3 to 6 years of age. These assessments provide information on a child's functioning in self-care, gross motor, fine motor, cognitive, and social and emotional development. In some settings in which a transdisciplinary approach is used—which is becoming more favored, particularly in the provision of early intervention services—a team-based contextual evaluation may be preferred, such as the Transdisciplinary Play-Based Assessment (Linder, 1990). If concerns exist in the sensorimotor areas, the motor specialist on the team may conduct a more in-depth evaluation. Some assessments designed specifically to measure gross and fine motor skills development include the Peabody Developmental Motor Scales for children from birth through 7 years (Folio & Fewell, 1983), and the Bruininks-Oseretsky Test of Motor Proficiency for children from 4½ to 14½ years of age (Bruininks, 1978). In addition to using standardized and criterion-referenced assessment tools, occupational and physical therapists are skilled in the qualitative evaluation of motor skills and sensory processing. A clinical evaluation by the therapist will identify contributing factors that may interfere with motor functioning, such as atypical postural tone, decreased or increased range of motion, atypical movement patterns and components, poor musculoskeletal integrity, inadequate positioning for function, and disorders in sensory registration, discrimination, and tolerance.

Service Delivery

The needs of the child and the family are considered in light of community and agency resources to determine a service program to meet the needs of the child. When a child has specific sensorimotor needs, the appropriate specialist from the team (e.g., the physical therapist or the speech and language pathologist) must determine how services should be provided. The occupational therapist views the child within his physical, social, and cultural environment in a holistic way, examining the processes whereby the environment influences the child's performance of functional activities in such areas as self-care, play, and schoolwork. The occupational therapist addresses issues related to feeding, dressing, positioning, handwriting, and psychosocial needs, and often is very helpful in adapting tasks and the environment for optimal function. Occupational therapists must be certified by the American Occupational Therapy Association, with many states requiring a license to practice. An occupational therapist may be prepared at the basic bachelor's level or at the master's level, while a certified occupational therapy assistant holds a certificate or associate's degree.

Physical therapists are concerned with children's function related to posture and movement. Physical therapists address issues related to mobility and gross motor skill acquisition, and often provide adaptive equipment to support these functions. Physical therapists in practice today may have been prepared at the bachelor's or master's level, although in the future, a master's degree will be required to enter the field. A physical therapy assistant holds an associate's degree. Physical therapists and assistants must be licensed by the state in which they practice.

Special physical educators work with children who "cannot benefit from or safely participate in a regular physical education program" (Jansma & French, 1994, p. 3). This is a specialty area within physical education designed to serve children with special needs. Such teachers may be involved in adapting physical education activities for students or providing programs that foster development of fitness and gross motor skills, or that help to correct specific problems related to posture and body movement.

Intervention by the physical or occupational therapist may be provided through direct therapy, monitoring, consultation, or a combination of these models (Dunn & Campbell, 1990). However, decisions should be made based upon a careful analysis of the child, family, and school situation rather than upon staff availability or what has been done in the past (Palisano, Campbell, & Harris, 1995).

Direct Therapy. Intervention that is individually designed and carried out by the therapist with one child or a group of children is referred to as *direct therapy*. This may occur within a natural environment, such as the child's home, the educational classroom, or the cafeteria, or it may occur in an isolated environment, such as a therapy room. Isolated therapy in a school setting should be provided only when the service the child requires is inappropriate in the natural environment.

Monitoring. When the motor specialist designs a service plan to meet a child's needs but another person (such as a classroom aide) is trained to carry out the activities, the specialist remains responsible for the implementation of the plan. This is done through monitoring whereby the therapist maintains contact with the child and alters the intervention as necessary to accommodate problems or changes.

Consultation. In the consultation model, the motor specialist provides her expertise to another person or program to address concerns identified by that person. In this model, the specialist no longer assumes responsibility for the intervention plan. For example, the occupational therapist may have expertise in developing handwriting programs for children with mild motor delays, but direct services specific to individual children may not be required.

Summary

This chapter has presented typical sensorimotor development in infants and young children, including the acquisition of postural and gross motor skills, fine motor skills, and oral motor skills. Some of the situations and conditions that may result in atypical sensorimotor development were described, and guidelines to help the early interventionist determine when motor development is not following the expected trajectory were provided. Some suggestions for intervention with children who have sensorimotor deficits were given, with indications of when the help of a motor specialist is indicated.

Early interventionists are often the first to observe motor deficits, particularly in children with mild-to-moderate impairment, because they have the benefit of seeing the child with other children of the same age. When an early interventionist has concerns regarding the sensorimotor development of a child, careful observation of the child is required in order to clearly articulate the reason for concern. A discussion of these concerns with the intervention team will help the early interventionist determine when additional evaluation is necessary, and who should perform the evaluation.

It is important for the early interventionist to gather as much information from the motor specialists on the team as possible so that they have a good understanding of the sensorimotor needs of the child. It is equally important for the early interventionist to inform the motor specialist (therapist or special physical educator) about the child's function in the home and classroom to aid the motor specialist in understanding the skills the child needs to be able to perform successfully. Only when there is the opportunity for open and ongoing communication among the family, early interventionist, and motor specialist can sensorimotor intervention be optimal.

References

American Psychiatric Association. (1994). *Diagnostic and statistical manual of mental disorders* (4th ed.). Washington, DC: Author.

Amundson, S., & Weil, M. (1996). Prewriting and handwriting skills. In J. Case-Smith, A. S. Allen, & P. Nuse Pratt (Eds.), *Occupational therapy for children* (3rd ed.). St. Louis: Mosby.

Ayres, A. J. (1985). *Sensory integration and the child.* Los Angeles: Western Psychological Services.

Ayres, A. J. (1989). *Sensory Integration and Praxis Tests.* Los Angeles: Western Psychological Services.

Batshaw, M., & Perret, Y. (1992). *Children with disabilities: A medical primer* (3rd ed.). Baltimore: Paul H. Brookes.

Bayley, N. (1993). *Bayley Scales of Infant Development* (rev. ed.). New York: Psychological Corporation.

Benbow, M. (1990). *Loops and other groups: A kinesthetic writing system.* San Antonio, TX: Therapy Skill Builders.

Benbow, M. (1995). Principles and practices of teaching handwriting. In A. Henderson & C. Pehoski (Eds.), *Hand function in the child: Foundations for remediation.* St. Louis: Mosby.

Benda, C. D. (1969). *Down syndrome: Mongolism and its management.* New York: Grune & Stratton.

Blackman, J. A. (1997). *Medical aspects of developmental disabilities in children birth to three* (3rd ed.). Gaithersburg, MD: Aspen Publishers.

Bruininks, R. (1978). *Bruininks-Oseretsky Test of Motor Proficiency.* Circle Pines, MN: American Guidance Service.

Carlson, S. J., & Ramsey, C. (1995). Assistive technology. In S. K. Campbell (Ed.), *Physical therapy for children.* Philadelphia: W.B. Saunders.

Case-Smith, J. (1995). Grasp, release, and bimanual skills in the first two years of life. In A. Henderson & C. Pehoski (Eds.), *Hand function in the child: Foundations for remediation.* St. Louis: Mosby.

Case-Smith, J., & Humphrey, R. (1996). Feeding and oral motor skills. In J. Case-Smith, A. S. Allen, & P. Nuse Pratt (Eds.), *Occupational therapy for children* (3rd ed.). St. Louis: Mosby.

Cermak, S. (1991). Somatodyspraxia. In A. Fisher, E. Murray, & A. Bundy (Eds.), *Sensory integration: Theory and practice.* Philadelphia: F.A. Davis.

Cole, K., Abbs, J., & Turner, G. (1988). Deficits in the production of grip forces in Down syndrome. *Developmental Medicine and Child Neurology, 30,* 752–758.

Connor, F., Williamson, G., & Siepp, J. (1978). *Program guide for infants and toddlers with neuromotor and other developmental disabilities.* New York: Teachers College Press.

Cox, R. D. (1993). Normal childhood development from birth to five years. In E. Schopler, M. E. Van-Bourgondien, & M. M. Bristol (Eds.), *Preschool issues in autism.* New York: Plenum Press.

Cunningham, C. C. (1982). *Down syndrome: An introduction for parents.* London: Souvenir Press.

David, K. S. (1995). Developmental coordination disorders. In S. K. Campbell (Ed.), *Physical therapy for children.* Philadelphia: Saunders.

Dunn, W., & Campbell, P. H. (1990). Designing pediatric service provision. In W. Dunn (Ed.), *Pediatric occupational therapy.* Thorofare, NJ: Slack.

Edwards, S., & Lafreniere, M. (1995). Hand function in the Down syndrome population. In A. Henderson & C. Pehoski (Eds.), *Hand function in the child: Foundations for remediation.* St. Louis: Mosby.

Erhardt, R. (1994). *Developmental hand dysfunction: Theory assessment treatment.* San Antonio, TX: Therapy Skill Builders.

Exner, C. (1996). Development of hand skills. In J. Case-Smith, A. Allen, & P. Pratt (Eds.), *Occupational therapy for children* (3rd ed.) St. Louis: Mosby.

Fetters, L., Fernandes, B., & Cermak, S. (1988). The relationship of proximal and distal components in the development of reaching. *Physical Therapy, 68,* 839–845.

Folio, M. R., & Fewell, R. R. (1983). *Peabody Developmental Motor Scales.* Allen, TX: DLM Teaching Resources.

Furuno, S., O'Reilly, K., Hosaka, C. M., Zeisloft, B., & Almann, T. (1984). *Hawaii Early Learning Profile.* Palo Alto, CA: VORT.

Gesell, A., & Amatruda, C. (1947). *Developmental diagnosis* (2nd ed.). New York: Harper & Row.

Gesell, A., & Ames, L. E. (1947). The development of handedness. *The Journal of Genetic Psychology, 70,* 155–175.

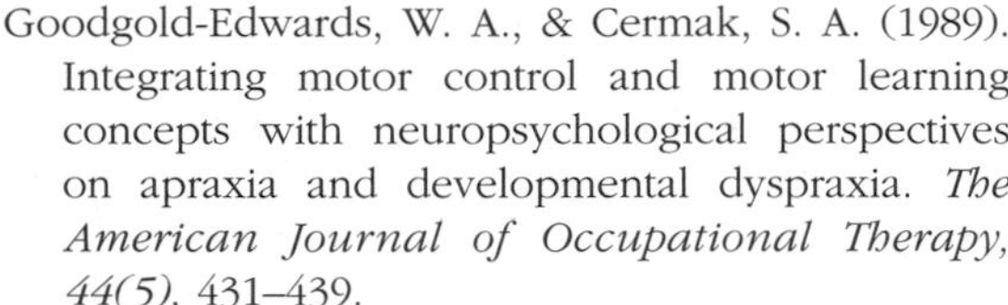

Goodgold-Edwards, W. A., & Cermak, S. A. (1989). Integrating motor control and motor learning concepts with neuropsychological perspectives on apraxia and developmental dyspraxia. *The American Journal of Occupational Therapy, 44(5),* 431–439.

Grandin, T. (1995). *Thinking in pictures.* New York: Doubleday.

Haradon, G., Bascom, B., Dragomir, C., & Scripcaru, V. (1994). Sensory functions of institutionalized Romanian infants. *Occupational Therapy International, 1,* 250–260.

Harris, L. J., & Carlson, D. F. (1988). Pathological left-handedness: An analysis of theories and evidence. In D. L. Molfese & S. J. Segalowitz (Eds.), *Brain lateralization in children: Developmental implications.* New York: Guilford Press.

Hinderer, K. A., Hinderer, S. R., & Shurtleff, D. B. (1995). Myelodysplasia. In S. K. Campbell (Ed.), *Physical therapy for children.* Philadelphia: Saunders.

Hunter, J. (1996). The neonatal intensive care unit. In J. Case-Smith, A. S. Allen, & P. N. Pratt (Eds.), *Occupational therapy for children* (3rd ed.). St. Louis: Mosby.

Jansma, P., & French, R. (1994). *Special physical education.* Upper Saddle River, NJ: Prentice Hall.

Johnson, H., & Scott, A. (1993). *A practical approach to saliva control.* Tucson, AZ: Therapy Skill Builders.

Jones, V., & Prior, M. R. (1985). Motor imitation abilities and neurological signs in autistic children. *Journal of Autism and Developmental Disorders, 15,* 37–46.

King, L. J., & Grandin, T. (1990). *Attention deficits in learning disorder and autism: A sensory integrative treatment approach.* Workshop presented at the Conference Proceedings of the Continuing Education Programs of America, Milwaukee, WI.

Klein, M. (1990a). *Pre-writing skills* (rev. ed.). San Antonio, TX: Therapy Skill Builders.

Klein, M. (1990b). *Pre-scissor skills* (3rd ed.). San Antonio, TX: Therapy Skill Builders.

Koomar, J. A., & Bundy, A. C. (1991). The art and science of creating direct intervention from theory. In A. G. Fisher, E. A. Murray, & A. C. Bundy (Eds.), *Sensory integration.* Philadelphia: F. A. Davis.

Lauteslager, P. E. M. (1995). Motor development in young children with Down syndrome. In A. Vermeer & W. E. Davis (Eds.), *Physical and motor development in mental retardation.* New York: Karger.

Levine, K. (1995). *Development of pre-writing and scissor skills: A visual analysis* [Videocassette]. San Antonio, TX: Therapy Skill Builders.

Levine, M. (1987). Motor implementation. In M. Levine (Ed.), *Developmental variation and learning disorders.* Cambridge, MA: Educators Publishing Service.

Linder, T. W. (1990). *Transdisciplinary play-based assessment: A functional approach to working with young children.* Baltimore: Paul H. Brookes.

Logemann, J. (1983). *Evaluation and treatment of swallowing disorders.* San Diego: College-Hill Press.

Long, C., Conrad, P., Hall, E., & Furler, S. (1970). Intrinsic-extrinsic muscle control of the hand in power and precision handling. *Journal of Bone and Joint Surgery, 52–A,* 853–867.

Lopez, M. (1986). *Developmental sequence of the skill of cutting with scissors in normal children 2 to 6 years old.* Unpublished master's thesis, Boston University.

Lovaas, O. I., Newsom, C., & Hickman, C. (1987). Self-stimulatory behavior and perceptual reinforcement. *Journal of Applied Behavior Analysis, 20,* 45–68.

Mathiowetz, V., & Haugen, J. B. (1994). Motor behavior research: Implications for therapeutic approaches to central nervous system dysfunction. *American Journal of Occupational Therapy, 48(8),* 733–745.

McEwen, I. (1995). Mental retardation. In S. K. Campbell (Ed.), *Physical therapy for children.* Philadelphia: Saunders.

McManus, I. C., Ski, G., Cole, D. R., Mellon, A. F., Wong, J., & Kloss, J. (1988). The development of handedness in children. *British Journal of Psychology, 6,* 257–273.

Meltzoff, A., & Gopnik, A. (1993). The role of imitation in understanding persons and developing a theory of mind. In S. Baron-Cohen, H. Tager-Flusberg, & D. J. Cohen (Eds.), *Understanding other minds: Perspectives from autism.* New York: Oxford University Press.

Missiuna, C., & Polatajko, H. (1995). Developmental dyspraxia by any other name: Are they all just clumsy children? *The American Journal of Occupational Therapy, 49(7),* 619–627.

Morris, S., & Klein, M. (1987). *Pre-feeding skills: A comprehensive resource for feeding development.* San Antonio, TX: Therapy Skill Builders.

Nelson, D. L. (1984). *Children with autism.* Thorofare, NJ: Slack.

newAbilities Systems, Inc. (1994). *newAbilities UCS1000™ with Tongue-Touch Keypad™* [Brochure]. Palo Alto, CA: Author.

Newborg, J., Stock, J. R., Wneck, L., Guidubaldi, J., & Svinicki, A. (1984). *Battelle Developmental Inventory.* Chicago: Riverside Publishing.

Palisano, R. J., Campbell, S. K., & Harris, S. R. (1995). Clinical decision making in pediatric physical therapy. In S. K. Campbell (Ed.), *Physical therapy for children.* Philadelphia: Saunders.

Piper, M. C., & Darrah, J. (1995). *Motor assessment of the developing infant.* Philadelphia: W. B. Saunders.

Rapin, I. (1988). Disorders of higher cerebral function in preschool children. Part II: Autistic spectrum disorder. *American Journal of Diseases of Children, 142,* 1178–1182.

Roberton, M. A., & Halverson, L. D. (1984). *Developing children—their changing movement. A guide for teachers.* Philadelphia: Lea & Febiger.

Rogers, S. J., Donavan, C. M., D'Eugenio, D. B., Brown, S. L., Lynch, E. W., Moersch, M. S., & Schafer, D. S. (1981). *Early Intervention Developmental Profile.* Ann Arbor, MI: University of Michigan Press.

Rosenbloom, L., & Horton, M. (1971). The maturation of fine prehension in young children. *Developmental Medicine and Child Neurology, 13,* 3–8.

Sameroff, A. (1973). Reflexive and operant aspects of sucking behavior in early infancy. In J. Bosma (Ed.), *Oral sensation and perception: Development in the fetus and infant.* Bethedsa, MD: U.S. Department of Health, Education, and Welfare, National Institutes of Health.

Schneck, C., & Battaglia, C. (1992). Developing scissor skills in young children. In J. Case-Smith & C. Pehoski (Eds.), *Development of hand skills in the child.* Rockville, MD: American Occupational Therapy Association.

Schneck, C., & Henderson, A. (1990). Descriptive analysis of the developmental progression of grip position for pencil and crayon control in nondysfunctional children. *American Journal of Occupational Therapy, 44,* 890–893.

Scull, S. A. (1996). Mobility and ambulation. In L. A. Kurtz, P. W. Dowrick, S. E. Levy, & M. L. Batshaw (Eds.), *Handbook of developmental disabilities.* Gaithersburg, MD: Aspen.

Sherrington, C. S. (1947). *The integrative action of the nervous system.* New Haven: Yale University Press. (Original work published 1906.)

Siegel, B. (1996). *The world of the autistic child.* New York: Oxford University Press.

Super, C. M. (1976). Environmental effects on motor development: The case of African precocity. *Developmental Medicine and Child Neurology, 18,* 561–567.

Sweeney, J. K., & Bascom, B. B. (1995). Motor development and self-stimulatory movement in institutionalized Romanian children. *Pediatric Physical Therapy, 7,* 124–132.

Tan, L. E. (1985). Laterality and motor skills in four-year-olds. *Child Development, 56,* 119–124.

Thelen, E., & Ulrich, B. D. (1990). Dynamic processes in learning to walk. *Monographs of the Society for Research in Child Development, 56(1),* 36–46.

Thoman, E. (1987). Self-regulation of stimulation by prematures with a breathing blue bear. In J. J. Gallagher & C. T. Ramey (Eds.), *The malleability of children.* Baltimore: Paul H. Brookes.

Touwen, B. C. L. (1978). Variability and stereotypy in normal and deviant development. In C. Apley (Ed.), *Care of the handicapped child.* Clinics in Developmental Medicine, No. 67. Philadelphia: J. B. Lippincott.

Van Bourgondien, M. E. (1993). Behavior management in the preschool years. In E. Schopler, M. E. Van Bourgondien, and M. M. Bristol (Eds.), *Preschool issues in autism.* New York: Plenum Press.

Vander Zanden, J. W. (1997). *Human development* (6th ed.). New York: McGraw-Hill.

Volkmar, F. R., Cohen, D. J., & Paul, R. (1986). Classification and diagnosis of childhood autism. *Journal of the American Academy of Child Psychiatry, 25,* 190–197.

VORT Corporation (1995). *HELP for preschoolers.* Palo Alto, CA: Author.

Watson, L. R., & Marcus, L. M. (1986). Diagnosis and assessment of preschool children. In E. Schopler & G. Mesibov (Eds.), *Social behavior in autism.* New York: Plenum Press.

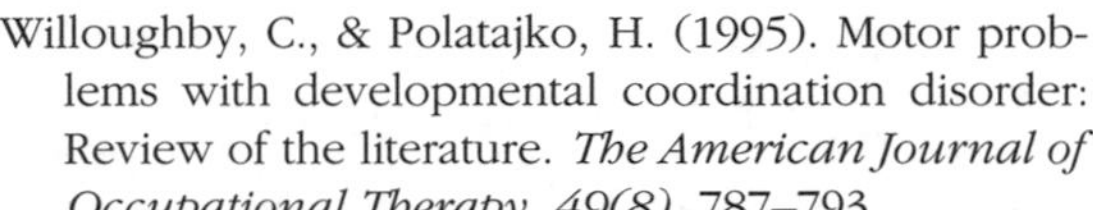

Willoughby, C., & Polatajko, H. (1995). Motor problems with developmental coordination disorder: Review of the literature. *The American Journal of Occupational Therapy, 49(8),* 787–793.

Witt, B., & Klein, M. (1990). Prepare: An interdisciplinary approach to perceptual-motor readiness. San Antonio, TX: Therapy Skill Builders.

Wolff, P. (1968). The serial organization of sucking in the young infant. *Pediatrics, 42,* 943–955.

5

Teaching Self-Help Skills

John Langone

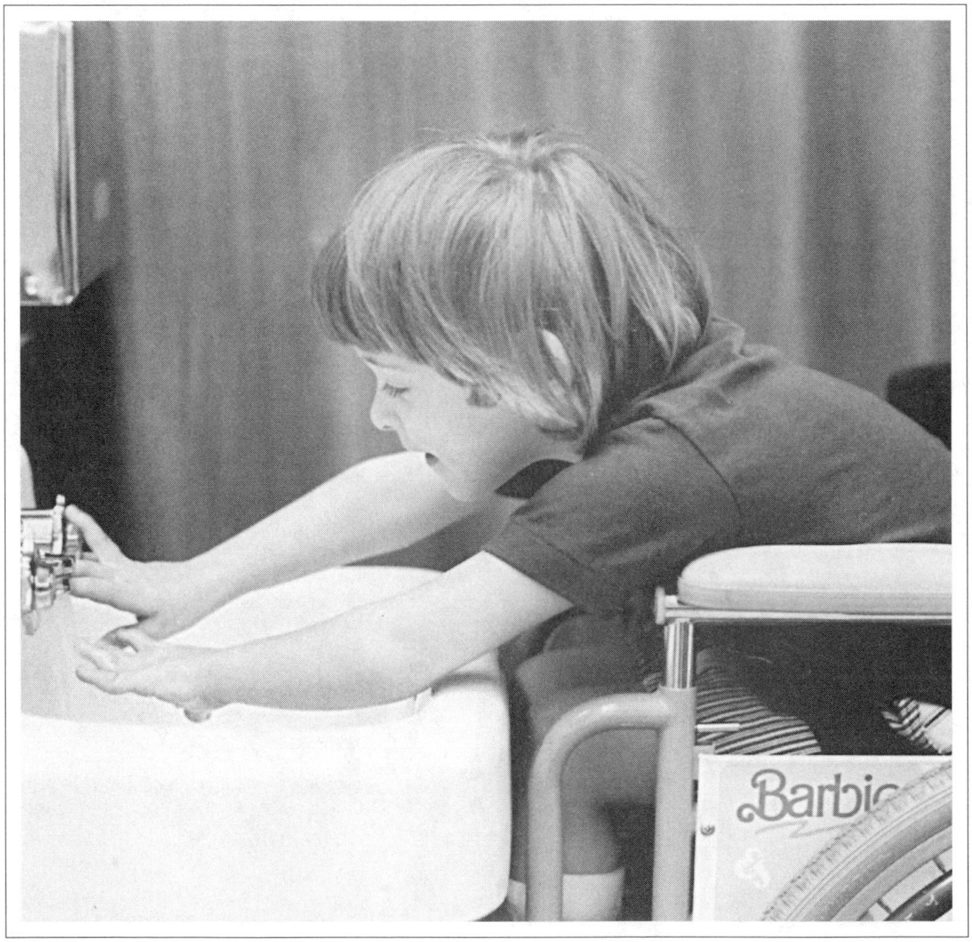

Caring for the daily living needs of children during their first years of life consumes considerable family time. This time can be highly productive when parents see it as an opportunity for quality interactions, which can result in parent-child bonding and a chance for parents to provide rich models for developing language. Many parents use diaper-changing times, for example, to provide their children with soothing conversation (language models). They also use this time to play with their children and to help them feel secure. Mealtimes provide similar opportunities, and they can be joyous experiences. Unfortunately, these times more frequently are stressful for parents of children who have disabilities, and such parents need support from others to help them cope with the unique demands of daily activities.

Self-help skills, including eating, dressing, grooming, and toileting, comprise an important part of everyone's day. Careful teaching of these skills is crucial for helping children to become independent. For children with intellectual and physical challenges, the ability to adequately care for their personal needs or to participate in this process is vital for their placement in community settings as adults. Consequently, the teaching of self-help skills should be an important component of all early intervention programs.

A child's early years is the best time for acquiring basic self-help skills. Toddlers who are learning cause-and-effect relationships begin to associate the uncomfortable feeling of soiled or wet diapers with the need to use the bathroom. As they continue to develop, children assert their independence by wanting to do things for themselves. Preschoolers are avid imitators who enjoy watching and mimicking others who are close to them. By understanding these traits, early interventionists can capitalize on the young child's sensitive learning periods when training in self-help skills can be most effective (Davis & Brady, 1993).

This chapter provides information for interventionists who work with children in center-based programs or with parents in home-based settings. While the preceding chapter focused on program development, adaptive equipment, and positioning considerations required by children with significant physical and neuromuscular challenges, this chapter focuses on facilitating and teaching self-help skills to children with special needs who **do not** have such significant disabilities. In addition, this chapter addresses only eating, toileting, and dressing skills.

Chapter 4 described how motor development can directly impact a child's functioning. In addition to specific types of motor disorders, aberrant motor development negatively impacts the day-to-day activities in a child's life. Tasks that most of us think nothing about, such as brushing our teeth and buttoning a jacket, can be extremely difficult—if not impossible—for many young children with special needs. As was noted in the Preface, this text contains some necessary redundancies; this chapter and Chapter 4 contain some of these. While this chapter focuses on several key self-help skills, it is important to recognize the interdependence of these skills and motor development.

Considerations Involved in Developing Intervention

An important part of the early interventionist's job is to support parents of children with special needs, because together the home and preschool or center-based program are the primary settings in which self-help skills are taught. Also, through collaboration, early interventionists and parents can carefully structure situations so that young children can practice these skills elsewhere (Westling & Fox, 1995). For example, even though classrooms have self-contained bathrooms, interventionists should plan times when children use other bathrooms in the school or center. This allows children to generalize their skills by using them in a variety of settings. Parents can use similar strategies by allowing their children to practice self-help skills at the homes of relatives and friends and when on other family outings.

Locations for Teaching Self-Help Skills

Community-based instruction is an important component of all programs for children with disabilities and provides many opportunities for children to learn and practice skills in natural settings (Langone, 1990). Some parents, for example, may wish to have their children enroll in a beginning swimming class sponsored by a recreation department. This environment can be an excellent place to teach independent toileting and dressing skills that are in line with parents' goals for their children. When taking children on a trip to the zoo, early interventionists also should take the time to point out to children similarities in bathroom facilities. Self-help skills can be taught wherever these skills would naturally be practiced (Noonan & McCormick, 1993). People use bathroom facilities, change their clothes, and eat in many different places; consequently, when teaching these skills to children who have special needs, it is important to instruct them in the locations where they will ultimately be expected to complete the tasks (Brown et al., 1979).

The variety of locations in which to teach skills to young children is more limited than it is for older children because they have less access to the community than older learners do. Infants and toddlers spend most of their time at home or in some type of out-of-home child care. Therefore, these environments require careful attention when one is designing activities to teach adaptive skills. All environments in which children spend their time are important, and an emphasis on one to the exclusion of others can decrease the effectiveness of the total program.

The home should be the primary focus for intervention for a young child. A child may require food or drink only twice during the school day, while at home, a child may engage in some form of eating or drinking two or three times more than that each day. Similarly, the child will probably have a need to use the toilet more frequently at home.

Who Teaches Self-Help Skills?

Many people are in a position to teach self-help skills to young children with special needs. Parents are the primary instructors of their young children, and the role

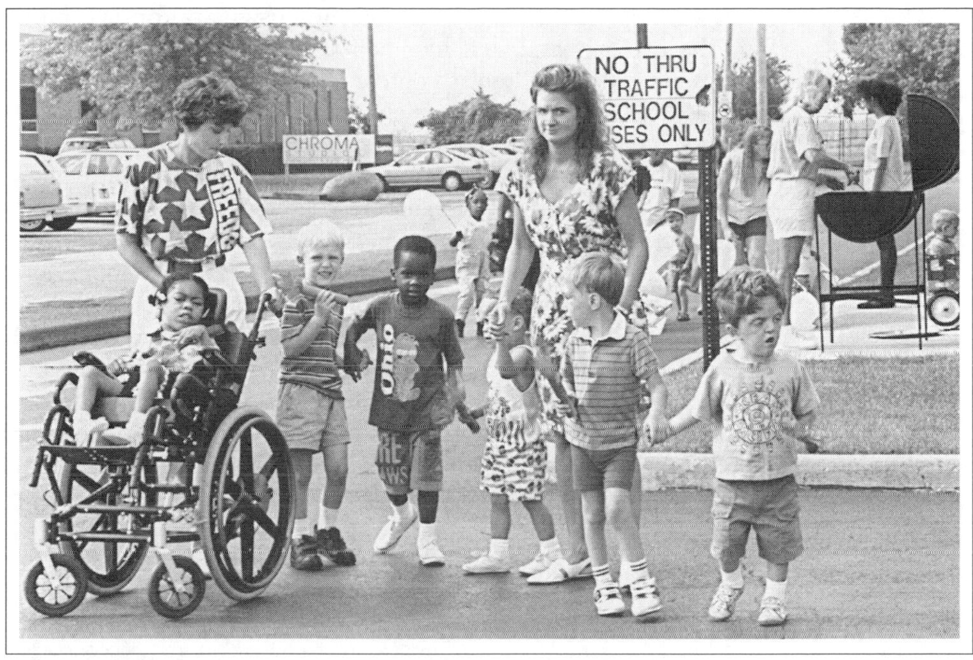

Children should learn and have opportunities to practice skills in real-world settings.

of the interventionist is to provide support for their efforts. When a child's special needs require techniques or devices not available to parents, the interventionist can work with the parents to design an instructional regimen and secure equipment that best meets the family's needs. All programs for teaching self-help skills to young children in schools or center-based programs should be a direct extension of strategies being carried out at home. In unique cases in which family members are unable or unwilling to take the lead in teaching self-help skills at home, school or center-based program, staff members provide the primary instruction. Even in these cases, however, the interventionist should continue to encourage the family members to become involved in the instruction and reinforcement of these important skills.

For young children who have significant physical challenges and developmental disabilities, physical therapists (PTs), occupational therapists (OTs), and speech-language pathologists (SLPs) become important members of the transdisciplinary team. These professionals are skilled in designing strategies and prescribing adaptive equipment that help children with significant challenges to overcome their limitations and maximize their abilities. PTs and OTs also can prescribe physical movement and strength exercises that help children develop the prerequisite motor skills for increasing their independence. SLPs can offer guidance about a child's oral motor abilities as they relate to independent eating. Often, PTs, OTs, and SLPs work directly with children and their families. In other cases, they work on a consultative basis with teachers and staff members to design appropriate programs for children, train the teachers and staff members to use the strategies or adaptive equipment, then monitor the children's progress.

Teachers who have many children in their classes cannot do all things for all students at once. Instruction in eating and toileting skills, for example, often requires longer individual attention than do most preacademic tasks. Well-trained and committed paraprofessionals and volunteers can be a valuable asset to any program. Such aides should be chosen carefully. A person's willingness to do the work is insufficient qualification for such an important job; the teacher should require documentation of the person's ability and desire to deal with messy diapers and potties, difficult feeding situations, and related experiences. When possible, the teacher should have an opportunity to observe the potential volunteer or paraprofessional work with children. The teacher's responsibility is to always monitor staff members when they care for a child's basic bodily functions and not leave staff members unobserved for long periods of time. Although well-developed skills need not be expected at the outset, a desire to learn and a positive, consistent manner with children may be indicators of good potential.

Factors Influencing Self-Help Development

How children with special needs perform in comparison to a standard developmental sequence of skills gives interventionists an idea of strengths and gaps in development. For example, bladder and bowel control usually occur between a child's second and third birthday (Leach, 1977; Westling & Fox, 1995). A 4-year-old child with cognitive delays may not yet have attained this developmental milestone, but the gap may be a result of a lack of communication skills (gestural and verbal) rather than an inability to learn toileting skills. If the child is taught the communication skills necessary to alert adults of her need to use the bathroom (e.g., "I have to potty!"), the delay may disappear and the child can move on to more-advanced toileting skills. The interventionist must be aware of the variety of factors that may contribute to a child's performance in order to analyze how best to help remediate problems. Clearly, a given lag in development may have many causes, both organic and environmental in nature. Information about these causes offers guidance for planning appropriate intervention.

General Motor and Self-Help Skill Development

Certain motor skills, including a child's ability to control parts of her body, are important precursors for self-help skill development (Bigge, 1991). For example, the ability to grasp an object and bring it to the mouth is necessary for finger feeding and usually appears around the seventh month. Similarly, children who can sit unsupported and use their hands for manipulating objects gain abilities useful for mastering several other self-help skills. When children pass the age at which these developmental milestones should appear but do not, intervention may be required. When children master the prerequisite motor skills, mastery of the associated self-help skills should follow (Cook, Tessier, & Klein, 1996). If a child cannot achieve these prerequisite motor skills because of severe physical challenges, adaptations using specialized equipment recommended by PTs or OTs can help to compensate for or replace the undeveloped skills.

Table 5.1 presents the major developmental milestones for self-help skills and associated prerequisite motor skills. Interventionists can use this information as a guide for comparing a child's performance in relation to a normative group.

Organic Factors

Many organic factors can hinder the normal development of self-help skills in children who have special needs. These factors often relate to the persistence of lower-level skills resulting from slow development of or damage to the central nervous system. More-severe problems are manifested in the persistence of primitive reflexes or in the existence of abnormal muscle tone that interferes with normal voluntary motor control, as was discussed in Chapter 4.

Increased, decreased, or variable muscle tone resulting from central nervous system dysfunction is an important factor when developing self-help skill instruction for children with significant physical challenges (Bigge, 1991). Teachers and other direct-care interventionists need the assistance of PTs and OTs to design the appropriate interventions. Interventionists should work closely with them to tailor interventions to each child's educational goals and objectives as delineated on the Individual Family Service Plan (IFSP) or the Individualized Education Program (IEP).

Environmental Factors

Most young children who demonstrate delays in self-help skill development do not suffer from significant neuromuscular problems. Instead, their problems often result from a complex interaction between their innate cognitive abilities and their environment. Teachers have no control over the biological determinants of a child's intellectual development. The environmental factors that influence a child's learning, however, can be modified by intervention.

Modeling of and feedback by parents about appropriate skill performance are the most influential factors in developing self-help skills in young children with disabilities (Snell & Farlow, 1993). The patience that parents and teachers exhibit in tolerating very slow progress also can have an impact on how well these children develop (Snell & Farlow, 1993). A child with moderate cognitive delays and no physical challenges still may require a great deal of teaching time before being able to master even basic self-help skills, and problems intensify as the severity of disability increases. It is difficult to fault parents who find it easier to feed or dress their child rather than engage in a time-consuming and frustrating teaching process. Consequently, the interventionist may have to provide considerable support to the parents. Sometimes the interventionist may suggest that parents complete a task for the child to avoid frustration on the part of both the parents and the child. At other

TABLE 5.1 Developmental Sequence of Self-Help Skills

AGE	MOTOR SKILLS RELATING TO SELF-HELP SKILL DEVELOPMENT	EATING SKILLS	TOILETING SKILLS	DRESSING AND GROOMING SKILLS
Birth–3 months	Moro reflex Asymmetric tonic neck reflex Vigorously kicks legs By 3 months, raises head for short periods Head lag begins to disappear when pulled to sitting position Grasps objects only when placed in hand	Oral reflexes (e.g., sucking) present at birth Tongue thrusts when solids are presented		
3 months–6 months	By 6 months, primitive reflexes are disappearing Begins to prop self up Begins to sit in highchair unsupported	Begins to hold bottle with little or no assistance Begins to swallow from cup May eat some solids; sucks from spoon May bring objects to mouth if placed in hands Basic chewing begins to appear		
6 months–9 months	Begins crawling and progresses to appropriate crawling skills Begins to right body Rolls from supine to prone Can sit unsupported in highchair Supports self in sitting position with arms forward Sits alone without support	Can hold bottle alone and brings bottle to mouth Can hold and eat a cookie independently Begins chewing Eats infant foods Uses scissors grasp to pick up some foods Sucks food from spoon		

9 months–1 year	Crawls well Creeps Sits up with ventral push Sits for longer periods Turns side-to-side when sitting Good coordination when reaching for close objects	Controls drooling More control over lips, tongue, and jaw Feeds self finger foods	Pays attention to acts of elimination	Holds arm out for sleeve
1 year–1½ years	Uses opposite hand for support when reaching for objects	Chews appropriately Grasps spoon and demonstrates some use Holds cup by handle and can lift to mouth for a sip	Begins to indicate when elimination has occurred Begins to sit on potty	Takes off shoes Takes off socks Tries to put on shoes
1½ years–2 years	Reaches for objects with one hand without using the other for support	Begins to suck using a straw Begins to chew food with mouth closed Uses spoon with fewer accidents Uses cup with fewer accidents	Communicates need to go to the toilet	Finds large armhole Shows preference for certain clothes Enjoys attempting to brush teeth, modeling adult
2 years–2½ years	Can imitate simple movements using arms and legs	Holds small cup in one hand Holds fork and begins to spear food	Bladder trained during the day	Begins to remove pull-down garments Buttons large front buttons

TABLE 5.1 Developmental Sequence of Self-Help Skills, continued

AGE	MOTOR SKILLS RELATING TO SELF-HELP SKILL DEVELOPMENT	EATING SKILLS	TOILETING SKILLS	DRESSING AND GROOMING SKILLS
2½ years–3 years			Becomes more routine and establishes set times for elimination Seats self on toilet Attempts to wipe after toileting	Attempts to wash hands when assisted Uses better tooth-brushing movements Wipes nose with tissue Opens front and side buttons Closes front snaps
3 years–4 years	Sits with dorsal push	Chews and swallows before speaking Begins to serve self finger foods Holds spoon with fingers	Is regularly dry at night Adjusts clothing during toileting	Washes and dries hands Disposes of paper towels and tissues Bathes self with minimal supervision Wets brush and applies toothpaste Attempts to comb hair Needs minimal assistance when dressing Begins to lace shoes Distinguishes between front and back of clothes items Buttons series of buttons Buckles belt

times, however, it may be best to allow sufficient time for the child to attempt the task. Parents with poor caregiving skills may themselves need to be taught what and how to teach their child, and parents and teachers may have very different ways of teaching self-help skills. In families with many members, each may have a different approach to feeding children, toilet training them, and so on. These inconsistencies in approach within a family and between home and school can be a severe hindrance for children with special needs. The communication between the caregivers and the interventionist is critical if children with delays are to gain basic self-help skills. Children also will benefit from systematic and consistent teaching approaches (Bailey & Wolery, 1992).

Interventionists should be familiar with typical and delayed developmental patterns of motor and self-help skills. With a knowledge of organic and environmental factors that hinder development, interventionists are more likely to seek help from other professionals and then apply prescribed strategies to help children learn and grow. The following factors should be considered by the interventionist:

- Certain motor skills are precursors of self-help skills.
- A child's abilities to sit unaided, to reach for and grasp objects, and to visually track objects are necessary for mastery of self-help skills. If a child has physical challenges, a physical therapist and occupational therapist may recommend positioning techniques and/or adaptive equipment to compensate for or replace the necessary motor skills.
- Deficits in motor development should receive the immediate attention of trained PTs and OTs. The self-help skill development of typical children (e.g., chewing some food by 9 months) can be an important guide for identifying deficits in young children with developmental delays.
- Abnormal postural tone and persistence of primitive reflexes interfere with voluntary, purposeful movement. Children with these problems often are seen by PTs and OTs.
- Difficulties in sucking, swallowing, biting, and chewing, which can be indicators of neuromuscular or structural impairments, can interfere with normal development of self-feeding skills. PTs and OTs can provide interventionists and parents with positioning and instructional strategies that will reduce the effects of these problems and help the child participate in more-natural mealtime routines (Mills & Hedges, 1983).
- Delays in neuromuscular maturity alter the time line for a child's accomplishment of toilet training. If the child cannot voluntarily control the anal sphincter and abdominal muscles at the expected time, toileting accidents are likely to persist. Voluntary muscle control is a prerequisite of bladder and bowel control.
- An effective program for teaching self-help skills gives consideration to the child's environment. Training programs should help the family learn to be consistent in their teaching methods and to use good modeling. In addition, professionals can assist parents to secure or construct adaptive equipment.

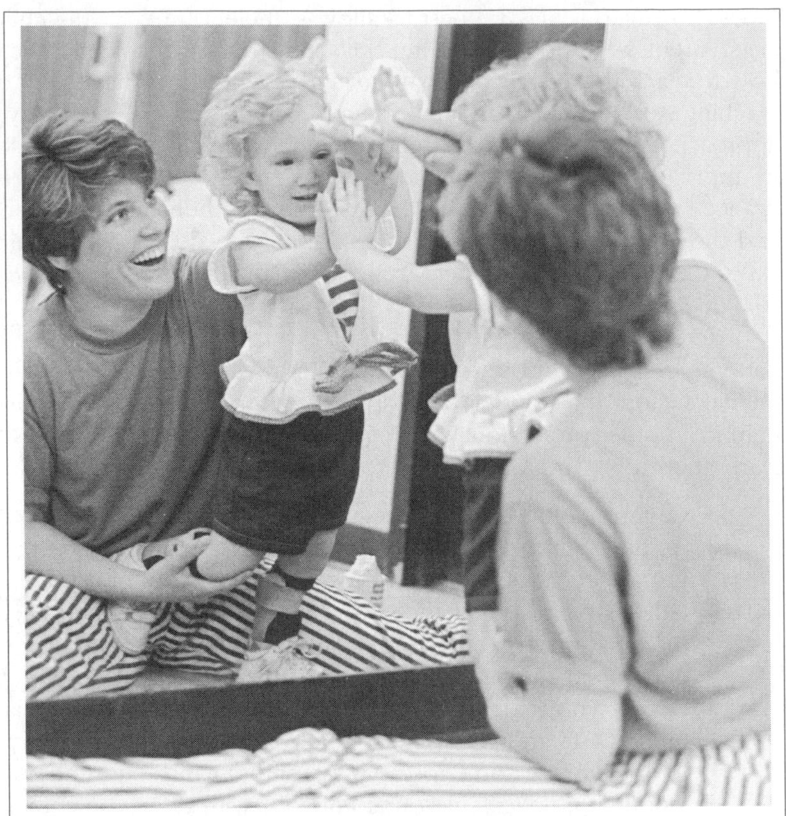

Modeling and feedback of appropriate skill performance are the most influential factors for children's development of self-help skills.

Assessment of Self-Help Skills

Two levels of assessment are available to the interventionist. General assessment provides information to identify a child's major deficit areas. Specific assessment procedures are more detailed. Using a task analysis of the target behavior, the interventionist can pinpoint the child's specific strengths and weaknesses (Howell, Kaplan, & O'Connell, 1979). At a general level of assessment, self-help scales help detect whether a child has a deficit in broad areas, such as toileting and dressing. Because a self-help behavior scale is not sensitive enough to identify how the child will do on specific tasks, the interventionist must task analyze those areas, then observe the child's performance at each step of the sequence in the task analysis. This is a specific level approach and allows the interventionist to collect a more thorough profile of the child's skills.

General Level Assessment: Self-Help Performance

Commercially produced self-help performance scales have two purposes: (1) to assist professionals in identifying children needing special education services (e.g., those who have mental retardation), and (2) to help professionals in identifying deficits in those skills that are important for independent living. Self-help scales allow the user to broadly assess a child's performance on a task, based on observations by the person completing the scale of the child performing or trying to perform the skill (Drew, Hardman, & Logan, 1996).

Self-help scales can be either norm-referenced or criterion-referenced measures. Norm-referenced measures help establish how far children deviate from their same-age peers in the performance of certain skills. These instruments, therefore, can help identify children as having developmental delays. Criterion-referenced measures assist in determining how far from a certain skill level a child is currently performing. The primary concern when using these instruments is not how a child compares with other children, but how well the child performs a specific set of skills.

The value of self-help scales is their use in screening children who may have deficits in certain areas. Most scales are well organized and efficient, and they provide a good way to identify a child's major problem areas. As with any assessment instrument, self-help scales may be misused if professionals attempt to employ them for more than their intended purpose. Such scales can be highly subjective instruments (Helton, Workman, & Matuszek, 1982; Thomas, 1996). Professionals often rate a child based on what they think the child can do rather than by observing the child engaged in the task. Obviously, this severely limits the usefulness and accuracy of results obtained from these instruments.

Using self-help scales as screening devices can provide information concerning suspected deficit areas in self-help skills. For young children, norm-referenced scales are of limited use because the norms of many scales were established with older children. Criterion-referenced measures may be more useful for toddlers and preschoolers. These instruments provide teachers with a profile of children by comparing them to performance expectancies for self-help skills at their age level. Table 5.2 presents a list of frequently used self-help behavior scales. This list may assist early interventionists in choosing an instrument that matches their needs.

General Level Assessment: Environmental Evaluation

Evaluation of a child's level of self-help skill performance involves more than an assessment of current performance of those skills. Assessing the child's performance in relation to specific characteristics of the home is also critical (Brown et al., 1979; Westling & Fox, 1995).

A survey of the home can promote greater home-school interaction; it provides a wealth of information concerning materials, techniques for teaching, and routines

TABLE 5.2 Sample of General Level Assessment Instruments Used to Measure Self-Help Skills

ASSESSMENT INSTRUMENTS	AGE COVERED BY SCALE	REFERENCE	MEASUREMENT TECHNIQUES	SCORES OBTAINED	PRIMARY USE	CONTENT COVERED BY SCALE	COMMENTS
Adaptive Behavior Evaluation Scale (Hawthorne Educational Services, Inc.) 1988	4½ years to 21 years	Norm-referenced	Interview	Scaled scores for each category	Classification decisions	Family; community; peer relations; nonacademic school roles; self-maintenance	Categories may have some use with young children.
Battelle Developmental Inventory Screening Test (Riverside Publishing Co.) 1984	Birth to 8 years	Norm-referenced	Standardized test items, interview, and observation	Domain scores, component scores, and cluster scores	Screening and programming	Personal-Social; affective motor domain; communication domain; cognitive domain	Good for identification of developmental strengths and weaknesses.
Denver II (Denver Developmental Materials, Inc.) 1990	Birth to 6 years	Norm-referenced	Interview and observation	Scaled scores	Screening	Personal-Social; fine motor; language; gross motor	Can be quickly administered for a general estimate of developmental delays.
Developmental Profile II (Western Psychological Services) 1986	Birth to 9 years	Norm-referenced	Interview	Age scores	Screening	Physical scale; self-help scale; social scale; academic scale; communication scale	The self-help scale includes both survival and self-care items for rating.
Early Screening Profiles (American Guidance Service) 1990	2 years to 6 years	Norm-referenced	Interview	Scaled scores	Screening	Self-help-Social for parents and teachers	Allows teachers an opportunity to interview parents.

Hawaii Early Learning Profile (HELP) (Vort Corp.) 1988	0–3 years; 3–6 years	Criterion-referenced	Interview and observation	Age scores	Programming	Self-help; including oral motor, dressing, self-feeding, grooming, and toileting	A thorough instrument that helps build program objectives.
Preschool Developmental Profile (The University of Michigan Press) 1991	3 years to 6 years	Norm-referenced	Observation	Scaled scores	Screening	Self-help	Can provide a relatively fast screening for developmental delays.
Preschool Evaluation Scale (Hawthorne Educational Services, Inc.) 1992	Birth to 35 months; 36 months to 72 months	Norm-referenced	Observation	Scaled scores	Screening and programming	Large muscle; small muscle; cognitive; thinking; expressive language; social-emotional; self-help	Designed to help identify young children who are developmentally delayed.
Revised Brigance Diagnostic Inventory of Early Development (Curriculum Associates, Inc.) 1991	Birth to 7 years	Criterion-referenced	Observation	Age scores	Diagnostic/ programming	Cognitive; thinking; expressive language; social-emotional; self-help	Has an increased self-help section from previous version.

The goal of instruction is to make children more independent and to normalize performance in the home and school settings.

that may influence a child's attainment of self-help skills. For example, if the parents use an adaptive toilet seat for their young child that fits on the top of the commode, it simplifies the child's training if the same type of equipment is used at school. Furthermore, teaching children beginning eating skills in school with certain types of food may not transfer to the home if the family's diet consists of other food types. Particularly during the early stages of skill acquisition, it is preferable to keep the teaching strategies and the materials as consistent as possible. Therefore, a survey of the child's home can help identify materials and settings that can be replicated or simulated in the school setting, if necessary. In addition, it will assist in planning a realistic and individualized program. Figure 5.1 and Table 5.3 provide examples of information obtained from a home survey that may guide the interventionist in making a comprehensive assessment of a child's current level of performance.

Figure 5.1 includes the locations where teaching of self-help skills may occur at home. The interventionist may conclude, for example, that the child can learn self-feeding skills under three different conditions. In the TV room, different types of food can be served and different tables are available. Similarly, the kitchen and dining room may provide different elements that allow the teaching of different dimensions of self-feeding skills.

The most useful information obtained from the home survey is found in Table 5.3, which directs the interventionist and parents to identify materials and other elements used with the child at home. Knowing that the parents use bar soap to wash their child's hands, for example, may encourage the interventionist also to use it and

FIGURE 5.1 Identifying areas of the home where teaching self-help skills can occur

Environment:	Home
Skill Area:	Self-care
Skill 1:	Eating
Locations:	Kitchen
	Dining room
	TV room (snacks)
Skill 2:	Toileting
Locations:	Bathroom (downstairs)
	Bathroom (upstairs)
Skill 3:	Dressing and grooming
Locations:	Bathroom (downstairs)
	Bathroom (upstairs)
	Bedroom

TABLE 5.3 Sample List of Considerations Important for Developing a Home-School Self-Help Program

SKILL AREAS	ENVIRONMENTAL STIMULI
Dressing	Does not own shoes with laces
	Pants held closed with Velcro fasteners or elastic
	All shirts are pullovers
Grooming	Uses bar soap to wash hands—parents complete task
	Hair washed in kitchen sink (no spray)
	Baths, no shower—parents complete task
Eating	Child is given all finger foods
	Parents use spoon to feed some items
	Drinks from safety cup with assistance of parents

thus speed up the child's learning to wash her hands at school. Parents will find it easier to adapt to the instructional system if it parallels their practices at home. In addition, the child has a better chance of generalizing learned skills. As the child progresses, planned variation can be introduced to increase the range of the child's skills.

Specific Level Assessment: Task Analysis

Specific level or curriculum-based assessment procedures relating to self-help skills generally involve the use of a task analysis format. Task analyses of the self-help areas can be purchased commercially (e.g., Ferneti, Lent, & Stevens, 1974), found in reference books (e.g., Anderson, Hodson, & Jones, 1975), or developed by interventionists. Developing one's own task sequences is a good learning experience and yields instruments that may be more easily applied to specific children and teaching materials.

Task analysis of self-help skills is the process of breaking down a skill area into its component parts, sometimes called *subskills* (Cook et al., 1996). Task sequences can be versatile tools in both the assessment and instructional phases of the program. During assessment, the interventionist can observe the number of subskills that a child completes toward accomplishment of a larger task. During instruction, the interventionist can use task analysis as a guide for presenting the subskills in the appropriate sequence and for applying teaching strategies to help the child in accomplishing each subskill.

Figure 5.2 presents a sample task analysis for toileting skills. In this case, an interventionist assessing the entry behavior of a child carefully records the child's performance in each of the 16 steps. If the child needs assistance to complete a subskill, this fact is noted. When this specific level of assessment is completed, the subskills that must be addressed and the order in which to teach them become clear.

A unique feature of task analyzing self-help skills involves the use of backward, forward, or mixed chaining procedures (Bailey & Wolery, 1992; Sailor & Guess, 1983). Chaining capitalizes on the interdependency of the subskills; that is, one step must be accomplished before the next step can be performed. Once the child learns the chain, each completed step triggers the attempt to complete the following step. For example, step 3 in Figure 5.2 requires the child to undo her belt.

FIGURE 5.2 Task analysis for toileting skills

SKILL: DEFECATES IN TOILET

Task Sequence*

1. Put lid up
2. Place seat down
3. Undo belt, snaps, zipper
4. Pull pants down to knees or ankles
5. Back to toilet and sit
6. Elimination
7. Locate toilet paper
8. Tear off desired length
9. Fold or bunch paper
10. Wipe properly
11. Use more paper if necessary
12. Stand
13. Pull up pants
14. Fasten snaps, zipper, belt
15. Flush toilet
16. Place lid down

*Modifications can be made for different types of clothing, a toilet without a lid, and a toilet whose lid and seat have been left in the upright position.

Step 3 becomes a prerequisite for step 4, because the child cannot pull down her pants until she unfastens her belt, snaps, and zipper.

Forward chaining (beginning with step 1) provides the most useful assessment information for developing instructional programs. Backward chaining (beginning with the last step of the task sequence) is more useful for instructional purposes because it allows the child to experience immediate success. For example, a child learning to independently eat finger foods would receive assistance from the parent or interventionist to lift the food to her mouth and take a bite. This strategy immediately provides reinforcement for the child to successfully complete this last step. For young children with special needs, chaining becomes an important procedure because of the cues inherent in the process. Generally, any subskill can be broken down into additional components. For step 3, in Figure 5.2, for example, the child must have mastered the following additional subskills before she can undo her belt, snaps, and zipper:

- use of a lateral pincer grasp
- use of a pincer grasp
- use of a three-finger grasp

At the completion of the assessment phase, the interventionist should develop a list of strengths and weaknesses gained from the specific level assessment procedures. Table 5.4 provides an example of a self-help section of an IEP that reflects the child's present level of performance. With this information, the staffing team can pinpoint the annual goals and short-term objectives that are appropriate for the child.

TABLE 5.4 Sample Self-Help Section of an IEP

PRESENT LEVEL OF PERFORMANCE	ANNUAL GOAL STATEMENTS	SHORT-TERM OBJECTIVES	EVALUATION PROCEDURES
STRENGTHS			
Uses all types of grasping skills (e.g., pincer grasp).	The student will initiate and complete the toileting process and decrease accidents.	The student will signal, using a hand gesture, the need to use toilet facilities.	Data are recorded every 30 minutes concerning whether pants are wet or dry.
Manipulates buttons, zippers, and fasteners.	The student will chew foods.	Given five different solid foods, including breads, meats, and vegetables, the child will chew each item a minimum of three times before swallowing.	Chart used for recording the number of times the child chews each food item. Data are recorded for probes taken once every minute.
WEAKNESSES			
Has frequent toileting accidents.			
Occasionally throws food.			
Does not chew food.			

Intervention Strategies

There are two distinct yet related components to developing a program for teaching self-help skills to young children with special needs. The first component is to decide what to teach and to structure this information into meaningful goals and objectives. These goals and objectives are then included on the child's IFSP or IEP. The second component involves deciding on the best instructional strategies to use that will reach the goals and objectives. It is critical that interventionists work closely with parents and other professionals when developing the goals, objectives, and the instructional strategies.

Program Goals and Objectives

Annual goals in the area of self-help skills are generated from the information collected during assessment. Interventionists then link the goals to each child's identified needs. A child's annual goals may resemble the following:

EATING

1. Holds bottle independently
2. Finger feeds
3. Scoops food with regular or adaptive spoon
4. Holds cup and puts it down independently
5. Drinks using a straw

DRESSING

1. Puts on a pullover shirt
2. Puts on a buttoned shirt
3. Unfastens belt, snaps, and zipper

GROOMING

1. Washes face and hands with bar soap and water
2. Brushes hair
3. Washes toothbrush

TOILETING

1. Indicates need to use bathroom with words or by pointing
2. Controls bowel and bladder between toilet trips
3. Uses toilet independently

Once appropriate annual goals are chosen, the next step in the program development process is to translate the goals into short-term objectives. Each annual goal will have at least one short-term objective as a component. Table 5.4 illustrates this process.

FIGURE 5.3 Task analysis for chewing solid foods

Skill: Chewing Solid Foods

✓ = COMPLETE
— = INCOMPLETE

TASK SEQUENCE

1. Chew soft food with prompt one time
2. Chew soft food with no prompt one time
3. Chew soft food with prompt two times
4. Chew soft food with no prompt two times
5. Chew medium food with prompt
6. Chew medium food with no prompt
7. Chew solid food with prompt
8. Chew solid food with no prompt

After short-term objectives are identified, the child's progress toward the stated outcome is monitored. If the child fails to make progress toward the objective, it may be necessary to task analyze the skills required for its accomplishment. Figure 5.3 provides an example of a task sequence for chewing solid foods. Each step of a task sequence can become a written objective.

Parent Involvement During Intervention

Parent participation is vital to the success of all early intervention programs. Parent support is especially important with self-help skills because of the number of times a day and the many different settings in which these skills are used. Parents, therefore, may have the most opportunities for teaching self-help tasks. Unfortunately, not all parents have the skills needed to teach their child using the systematic techniques tailored to the child's unique needs. Interventionists can model procedures and skills that parents can use to help their children (Allen, 1980). This allows the parents to see how the techniques are carried out. Interventionists should both model the procedures and observe parents using them. For example, an interventionist may visit a home at mealtimes for a week to teach the parents how to manually guide their child through the eating process. The interventionist should demonstrate, then watch the parents (or the person who feeds the child) and help them refine their techniques. Videotaping parents teaching their children is a form of feedback that may help parents improve their instructional skills. A videotape can be used to compare techniques and may help parents in making the changes necessary to increase the effectiveness of their teaching strategy.

Parent involvement in a program has several dividends. It provides the child with a more consistent program and increased chances to maximize progress. In addition, a close parent-staff relationship may provide interventionists the opportunity to assist parents in developing more-positive attitudes toward their child (Stanhope & Bell, 1981) and toward training for independence. Parents of children with disabilities may find it easier to do a task for their children than to help them in repeated attempts to complete the task independently. Helping parents understand that children need opportunities to explore, practice, fail, and succeed is an essential component of all programs. However, it also is important to understand and empathize with the feelings of frustration that parents have.

Parents may need help in understanding the role of positive reinforcement in teaching young children. Unfortunately, the characteristics of some self-help skills may stimulate negative parental responses. For example, a 4-year-old child who continues to have toileting accidents may generate angry responses from her parents, especially after repeated attempts to toilet train the child have failed. Food throwing, regurgitation, and drooling also may provoke unpleasant parental responses. Valuable guidance for working with families in a positive and supportive manner to overcome the frustration and disappointment these experiences often provoke was provided in Chapter 3.

Intervention Strategies: Feeding Skills

Before school-aged children with special needs can learn more-advanced skills associated with eating (e.g., restaurant skills), they must have mastered the basics: chewing, drinking from a cup, eating finger foods, and using utensils properly. The more skills that are mastered during the toddler and preschool years, the more opportunities that are available to students who have disabilities. These additional opportunities help them to develop a larger repertoire of more-advanced behaviors. Young children with disabilities may need instruction in eating and drinking skills if they are not making successful progress toward developing these skills. A close relationship between the parents and interventionist increases the probability that a child will learn independence in using self-help skills.

There is a considerable amount of literature describing good feeding techniques and self-help equipment (e.g., Magnusson & Justen, 1981; Morris & Klein, 1987; Stainback, Healy, & Stainback, 1977; Westling & Fox, 1995) as well as research reports presenting techniques with which to teach self-feeding skills to children with disabilities (e.g., Azrin & Armstrong, 1973; Berkowitz, Sherry, & Davis, 1971). However, children may not be getting enough direct instruction in these skills. For example, Bailey, Harms, and Clifford (1983) observed 40 preschool programs, half of which served children with disabilities, and found that few of the teachers used mealtimes to teach and reinforce independent eating skills. Interventionists must develop an appreciation for the importance of these and similar skills and be willing to spend time teaching them.

Scheduling Instruction. Young children with special needs may require multiple teaching sessions every day to learn new feeding skills. Consequently, interventionists must find more opportunities than the single lunch period during the school day or infrequent visits to the home. One solution is to include parents in the program and expand the teaching to every meal every day. An additional option was developed by Azrin and Armstrong (1973); their minimeal plan breaks down larger meals into small portions presented in short sessions every hour. The child eats the same amount of food, but the number of sessions for teaching eating skills is multiplied five or six times.

In school, lunch periods often are hectic affairs, and the use of the minimeal may not be consistently possible. Another approach is to assign a volunteer or paraprofessional to work with one child during an early lunch each day and teach eating skills 10 to 15 minutes before the regular period begins (Langone, 1990). Bailey and Wolery (1992) further suggest that in preschool programs in which teachers are directly involved with feeding students with motor impairments, other volunteers, such as foster grandparents and high school students, can provide the assistance for teaching feeding skills. When children have motor impairments or other related medical concerns, however, all adults participating in the feeding process must be instructed and supervised periodically by a PT or OT.

Finger Feeding and Drinking from a Cup. Before children can begin to use utensils, they must first learn to bring food to their mouths with their fingers (Westling & Fox, 1996). Finger feeding is a developmentally important skill for all children and becomes critical for the improvement of more-advanced motor skills. Finger feeding also leads to advanced eating and drinking skills. Similarly, drinking from a cup allows children practice in gaining more-advanced motor skills that also will be used for more-advanced activities.

Teaching children with disabilities eating and drinking skills is best accomplished at the beginning of the meal, when they are hungry. Using foods and drinks that parents have at home increases children's motivation to become more independent. Many children with disabilities can learn to eat with their fingers and drink from a cup with little assistance; in such cases, interventionists may need only to help them refine their skills. For children with disabilities who have motor impairments, however, interventionists may need to provide increased assistance. Interventionists also may need to provide increased assistance for children who do not appear to understand the eating process.

Behavioral teaching procedures include tools that both parents and interventionists can use to help children learn to independently finger feed and drink from a cup. The system of least prompts (SLP) and graduated guidance are important antecedent strategies for interventionists to use. These strategies can help children gain the motor control they need to accomplish self-help tasks. When using the SLP, the adult systematically uses verbal cues, modeling, physical prompting, and physical guidance to help the child through the steps of the task. For example, if a child does not respond to a piece of cracker placed in front of her (and the adult knows that she likes crackers and is hungry), the adult might model the skill by picking up a cracker and eating it (modeling). The adult might then say "Now you try it." If the child still does not respond, the adult might lightly tap the back of her hand and point to the cracker. If all else fails, the adult can gently move the child's hands toward the cracker and physically help her to pick it up.

General Instructional Procedures. During the initial stages of teaching, hand-over-hand guidance may be required (Snell & Farlow, 1993). As the child becomes more proficient, the adult's physical guidance should be diminished and mild prompts, verbal cues, and modeling substituted. Berkowitz, Sherry, and Davis (1971) demonstrated the use of these procedures with young children who had cognitive deficits. They found that each level of assistance (e.g., guidance and prompts) must be systematically diminished once it is no longer of use, and less-intense assistance must be substituted.

Once children learn self-help skills, interventionists should monitor the children's consistent use of those skills. O'Brien, Bugle, and Azrin (1972) found that, even after children with cognitive disabilities learned to eat appropriately with a spoon, they often reverted to eating with their fingers. The researchers incorporated various reinforcement procedures based on intermittent schedules to help the chil-

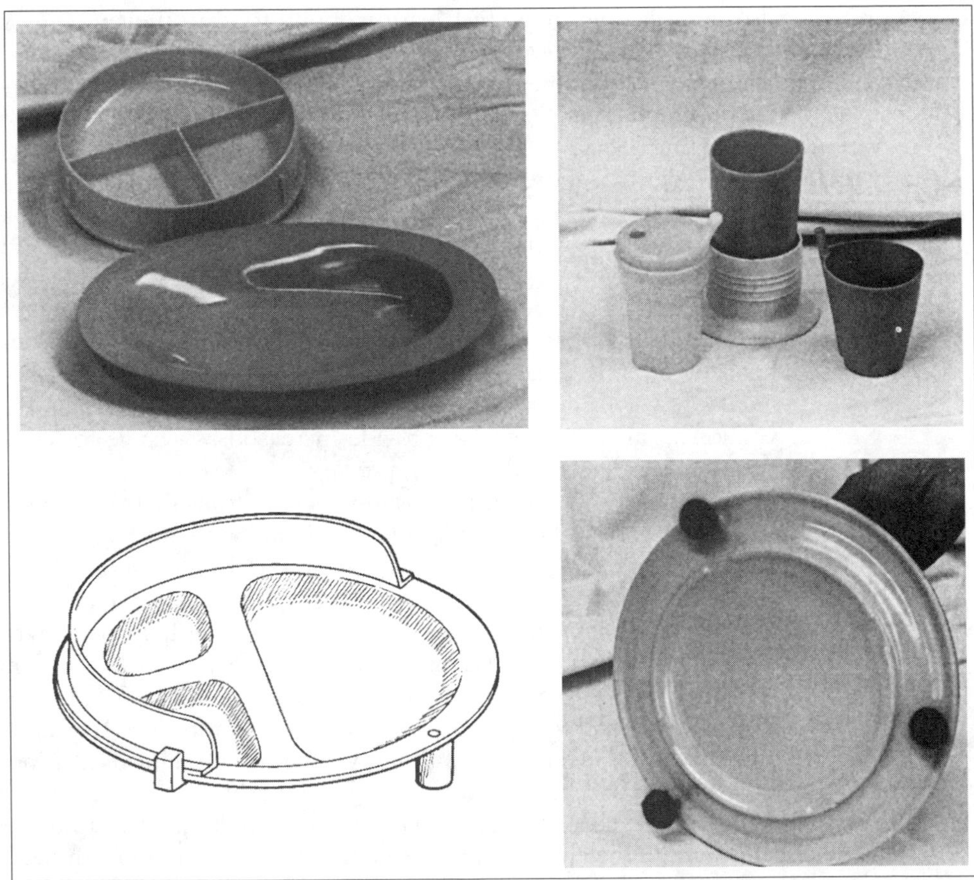

Top, *plates and cups with special features;* bottom left, *plate with guard;* right, *plate with feet.*

dren maintain their performance level. They suggest continuing the social reinforcers (e.g., "good job" or a pat on the arm) after actual instruction is complete. These reinforcers gradually should be diminished on an irregular schedule.

Interventionists who work with children who have multiple disabilities may have to apply specialized strategies designed by PTs, OTs, and SLPs working as a team. Such strategies, which are taught to interventionists by these professionals, help stimulate chewing, swallowing, sucking, and proper tongue movements (Mills & Hedges, 1983; Morris & Klein, 1987). Further strategies also may be necessary to reduce the effects of variable muscle tone or abnormal reflex patterns so that a child can attain more normal patterns of eating. Children with poor muscle control may require special positioning or self-help equipment (Morris & Klein, 1987; Utley, Holvoet, & Barnes, 1977); proper positioning of children during feeding is necessary for safety because it enables them to swallow and chew more easily (Morris & Klein, 1987; Mueller, 1975). Interventionists must consult a PT and OT for assistance in proper positioning and handling for feeding of children with severe and multiple disabilities (see Chapter 4).

Intervention Strategies: Toilet Training

Learning toileting skills can be a big boost to both young children's and parents' independence, and it also plays a role in improving people's attitudes toward children with disabilities. Adults may look more favorably on a child who is toilet trained or has made progress toward that goal.

Readiness. Snell and Farlow (1993) suggest that the first step in the toileting program is to establish whether the child is developmentally able to control bodily functions. Foxx and Azrin (1973a) suggest that this usually occurs at about 2½ years of age. They also suggest that children with more severe disabilities may not be ready to begin active toilet training until 5 years of age. These suggestions do not mean, however, that younger children with severe disabilities cannot begin toilet training earlier. The adult must approach each child as an individual and assess each child's readiness for training. The key is to not push a child with a rigorous training program if she is not developmentally ready. Children who may not be developmentally ready or who do not have the neuromuscular maturity can learn ways to communicate their toileting needs. They also can become familiar with the cause-and-effect relationships that are part of the toileting process (i.e., the connection between the discomfort of wet pants and having urinated).

Assessment. Interventionists must establish the child's pattern of elimination before embarking on a toilet training program. One way of doing this is to check the child's pants every half-hour to determine whether the child is dry, wet, or has soiled. Over several days, a pattern of elimination may emerge if the child's eating and activity levels have remained constant. This pattern directs the interventionist toward a schedule for setting up the training program. Talking to a child about going to the bathroom and sitting her on the potty seat just before an anticipated elimination should be sufficient, over a period of days or weeks, to train her. Calling the child's attention to children who indicate their toileting needs appropriately and allowing the child to accompany a trained child to the toilet also may be effective. Other children may require more systematic training procedures.

General Instructional Strategies. Two alternatives to casual teaching approaches are the forward chaining method described by Mahoney, Van Wagenen, and Meyerson (1971) and the backward chaining program used by Azrin and Foxx (1971). The forward chaining approach guides the child from the first step of a task analysis (e.g., unbuttoning clothing) through all the other steps to completion of the task.

In the backward chaining approach, the adult helps the child with all the beginning skills (e.g., undressing). At that point the adult begins the instruction with the last step in the task analysis sequence (e.g., sitting on the toilet). For children who have not mastered the dressing skills (e.g., toddlers who find it difficult to manipulate buttons and fasteners), the backward chaining approach simplifies teaching the target skills of toileting. Also, if a child cannot undress quickly, backward chaining may serve to decrease accidents.

Prerequisites to training include neuromuscular control and the child's awareness of discomfort when she urinates or soils her diaper or training pants. Parents and interventionists are partners in increasing the child's awareness of the toileting process. For example, each time a young child eliminates, the adult can label the process by saying, "Jenny, you did number one (or two)," using whatever labels the adult is most comfortable with. The terminology, however, should be consistent. Also, if the child urinates in the bath, the parents should be quick to label the process while the child has the multisensory opportunity of seeing, feeling, and hearing about the process. Over time, the hope is that the child will become more aware of the cause of discomfort and of the physiological cues that signal impending elimination.

Adults can help their child's understanding of the cause-effect relationships in toileting by modeling or simulating key behaviors. Many children learn important toileting skills by accompanying their parents to the bathroom and watching them. A simulation might occur when a child wearing diapers or training pants soils them, and her parents bring the soiled clothes into the bathroom, dump the feces into the toilet, and flush. During this process, the adult verbally labels each step.

Modifications. For many children without physical challenges or severe cognitive delays, traditional methods of toilet training are successful. Other children may need special instruction and carefully planned routines. For these children, special equipment may be necessary to help them understand when they need to eliminate and when to express those needs to the adults in their environment. The use of an electronic communication board, for example, can be an important addition to any toilet training program. Electronic communication boards offer a distinct advantage over other forms of communication (e.g., signing and symbol systems) because they demand immediate attention. In a busy classroom or a busy home, a child signing the need to use the bathroom may go unnoticed. When adults fail to respond to a child's attempts to communicate the need to use the bathroom, valuable opportunities are lost for reinforcing communication attempts. Also, opportunities are lost for helping the child learn the cause-effect relationship between feeling the need to eliminate and the actual act. When electronic communication boards are too expensive for a program, other low-technology solutions are available. Children can learn to activate a button connected to a bell or buzzer that will signal their need to eliminate. For children who are not communicating verbally, their ability to immediately express their needs is critical.

To assist in developing toileting skills, there is a variety of self-help equipment, ranging from special chairs (Finnie, 1975) to moisture-signaling devices (Foxx & Azrin, 1973b). Finnie, for example, suggests several ideas involving small potty chairs that are available commercially and can be used with homemade adaptations. Moisture-signaling devices also can be purchased commercially. Such devices can be fastened to the child's underpants or can be inserted into a potty chair and a regular toilet. When the child eliminates, the moisture activates the device, which sounds a tone or plays a song.

Some children with special needs may need devices only to adapt a regular toilet seat. For example, toilet rings are available commercially and attach to any toilet seat. This common adaptation makes the seat small enough to fit a child while providing balance.

Intervention Strategies: Dressing and Grooming Skills

Learning to dress independently or participate in the dressing process can help children to blend into school-based programs. Similarly, being able to wash their hands and to brush their teeth with some degree of independence are positive steps toward entering inclusive environments. As with all areas related to teaching self-help skills, the interventionist should work closely with the parents to coordinate the strategies for teaching these skills. For children who have physical challenges, it is critical that PTs and OTs be consulted for assistance in learning the proper positioning and handling strategies that will facilitate dressing without injuring the child.

Scheduling. As a young child begins to learn new dressing and grooming skills, the interventionist may find it helpful to increase the number of instructional sessions. Attempting to teach a child to brush her teeth in one 10-minute daily session after lunch may not be the most efficient approach. Instead, scheduling 5 or 10 shorter sessions spread throughout the day might be more effective. This allows the child to have multiple opportunities to practice the skill.

Readiness. By 18 to 24 months, a child begins to perform basic dressing and grooming skills. Many children, however, display an understanding of the process involved in these areas even earlier. A child between 12 and 18 months, for example, may pick up a comb and run it through her hair. A child's spontaneous behaviors can be a guide to her readiness for training of more advanced skills.

Assessment. Working closely with parents, interventionists can identify the important dressing skills that need attention. All young children need some help in learning dressing and grooming skills. However, young children with special needs often do not acquire these skills easily. Either commercially produced task analyses or task analyses produced by the parents or the intervention team can provide guidance for the assessment and program planning process.

General Instructional Strategies. Wehman and Goodwyn (1978) provide suggestions for beginning a dressing program with a young child. One suggestion is to begin by teaching a child to undress, because the skills involved are generally easier to perform than those needed for dressing. Other suggestions presented by Wehman and Goodwyn (1978), Westling and Fox (1995), and Snell and Farlow (1993) that may be helpful for interventionists and parents include the following:

- Use clothing one or two sizes too large so the child can remove it with ease.
- Use socks without heels (tube socks) for first sessions. Backward chaining helps the child learn to manipulate the heel area effectively (Reese & Snell, 1991). When the child can pull this type of sock on, introduce a stretchy cotton-blend sock with heels. Follow this with a regular nylon sock.
- For training in putting on or removing crew-neck shirts, first teach the child to raise and lower a hula hoop or similar aid over her head. When the child has learned these hand motions, introduce a dressing shirt that has only a hole for the head. Have the child learn to raise and lower this over her head by modeling and physically helping her. From this, move on to an oversized T-shirt, followed by a regular shirt.
- It is common for a child to have difficulty learning to remove the shirt over her head and then from the arms; therefore, it is better to have the child learn to pull her arms out before raising the shirt over her head. It also is easier to put the arms in the T-shirt before the head.

Modifications. There are more commercially produced materials dealing with dressing and grooming than there are for any of the other self-help areas. For example, Project More (cited in Ferneti et al., 1974) includes task sequences and suggestions for teaching putting on and taking off various items of clothing, combing hair, brushing teeth, and washing the hands and face. Another good resource is *Pre-Dressing Skills* (Klein, 1985), which provides descriptions of practical adaptive techniques and equipment for teaching dressing skills. As with all other self-help areas, children who have motor impairments have more difficulty than nonimpaired children do learning dressing and grooming skills. Finnie (1975) and Klein (1985) present excellent suggestions for facilitating dressing and grooming skills for children with motor impairments:

- Children often have difficulty understanding the task in which they are engaged. They may benefit from dressing or performing certain grooming tasks in front of a mirror.

- Children who have poor balance can perform many dressing tasks while lying down. The child begins by side lying to put on her pants and gradually turns as the pants are raised up to waist level. Alternatively, children can sit in a corner while dressing so that the walls give them support.
- As with all self-help tasks, interventionists and parents should take the opportunity while dressing and grooming the child to label and discuss each step of the process.
- Children can use walls in other ways to provide support. A child can lie on her back with her feet braced against the wall and knees bent. This position allows the child to pull up her pants with the extra stability provided by the floor and the walls. A child also can sit against the wall with knees bent to put on and tie shoes.
- Chairs and stools often can be used for support to help a child while dressing. A chair can be used for support while a child pulls on her pants, first sitting to arrange the pants and get them on her legs, then kneeling to pull them up part way, and finally standing with support to complete the task.
- A child should begin learning to wash and dry her hands and face while seated or standing in front of a basin of water placed on a table. As the child gets older and taller, self-help devices to support the child in front of a sink can be used when necessary.
- Some children with severe disabilities may benefit from self-help aids such as electric toothbrushes. Other aids can make performance of self-help skills possible for even the young child with the most severe disabilities.

Often, using a child's own clothing and establishing a physical positioning routine tailored to the child's needs are more helpful for teaching independent dressing skills than is purchasing special equipment. Clothing can be purchased in styles and sizes that simplify a child's ability to dress. As noted, for example, clothing at least one size too large should be used for children who have difficulty dressing.

Clothing should be simple and include a minimum of fasteners. Stylish clothing may be attractive, but it also may require a series of complex fastening skills. For example, pants with elastic waists are preferable for toddlers learning to dress themselves than are pants with snaps and zippers. A pullover shirt with a large hole for the head avoids the need to manipulate buttons. If the weather permits, shorts are easier than long pants to remove and put on.

Color coding clothes can be an effective method for teaching dressing skills (Langone, 1990). To begin teaching children to match clothes based on color or style, same-color tags can be sewn into the insides of the garments, and children learn to match the like colors. Iron-on pictures of favorite characters can be used to distinguish the front of a garment from the back. Similarly, shoes can be color-coded on the inside to remind children on which foot each belongs.

Velcro can replace buttons and zippers to afford young children an additional measure of independence. Sewing a button over the Velcro will make the garment appear more natural. A zipper can be adapted for easier use by the attachment of a round keyring or large paper clip through the zipper's tab, thus allowing the child an easier grasp of the zipper. Zippers can be made to open and close more easily by being coated with a small amount of soap, either liquid or bar soap.

The best training for self-help skills is modeling of good habits by parents and other children. Most young children do not completely comb their hair, wash their faces and hands, and bathe; however, they should participate actively as much as possible as soon as possible in these tasks. There are many strategies and adaptive aids to help this occur. For example, if a child with disabilities cannot reach her head, a long-handled comb or brush can be used. Also, liquid soap in a small plastic bottle is easier to handle than a bar of soap. Self-help devices such as hand brushes and sponges that attach to the sink with suction cups are available commercially. Tub seats that prevent children from slipping while being bathed are also available commercially. A self-help device that helps children participate in the bathing experience is a washing mitt, which holds a bar of soap that, when moistened, can be rubbed over the body to allow the child to experience the fun of soaping up.

Summary

Self-help skills training enables children to become more independent, thereby allowing them greater opportunities to participate in many normal home, school, and community activities. Including parents in both the design and implementation of self-help skills training is vital: Parents provide insight into their child's present level of performance and have the most opportunities to work on these skills with the child at home. Their participation allows for continuity between home and school efforts and facilitates the child's generalization of learned skills to new settings.

Assessment of self-help skills is performed on two levels: general and specific. Comparing a child to a standard developmental sequence of skills determines whether the child is in need of training. Commercially produced self-help behavior scales are useful as well as a quick reference for deciding in which skill areas the child needs training. Task analysis is the method used to establish a child's specific strengths and weaknesses. By sequencing the subskills of a self-help skill, the interventionist can decide the exact level at which the child needs intervention.

Various strategies, materials, and self-help aids are useful in teaching self-help skills. Use of a specific approach should be based upon the child's level of development and needs, the amount of parental support, and characteristics of the home environment. Whenever possible, self-help aids should be constructed from materials found in the home. This gives parents the sense that expensive special materials are not always needed to meet their child's needs. Resourceful interventionists and caregivers are an asset to every child's program.

 References

Allen, K. E. (1980). *Mainstreaming in early childhood education*. Albany, NY: Delmar.

Anderson, D. R., Hodson, G. D., & Jones, W. G. (1975). *Instructional programming for the handicapped student*. Springfield, IL: Charles C Thomas.

Azrin, N. H., & Armstrong, P. M. (1973). The "minimeal"—A method for teaching eating skills to the profoundly retarded. *Mental Retardation, 71,* 9–13.

Azrin, N. H., & Foxx, R. M. (1971). A rapid method of toilet training in the institutionalized retarded. *Journal of Applied Behavior Analysis, 4,* 89–90.

Bailey, D. B., Harms, T., & Clifford, R. M. (1983). Social and educational aspects of mealtimes for handicapped and nondisabled preschoolers. *Topics in Early Childhood Special Education, 3,* 1–32.

Bailey, D. B., & Wolery, M. (1992). *Teaching infants and preschoolers with disabilities* (2nd ed.). Upper Saddle River, NJ: Merrill/Prentice Hall.

Berkowitz, S., Sherry, P. J., & Davis, B. A. (1971). Teaching self-feeding skills to profound retardates using reinforcement and fading procedures. *Behavior Therapy, 2,* 62–67.

Bigge, J. L. (1991). *Teaching individuals with physical and multiple disabilities* (3rd. ed.). Upper Saddle River, NJ: Merrill/Prentice Hall.

Brown, L., Branston, M. B., Baumgart, D., Vincent, L., Falvey, M., & Schroeder, J. (1979). Utilizing the characteristics of a variety of current and subsequent least restrictive environments as factors in the development of curricular content for severely handicapped students. *AAESHP Review, 4,* 407–424.

Cook, R. E., Tessier, A., & Klein, M. D. (1996). *Adapting early childhood curricula for children in inclusive settings* (4th ed.). Upper Saddle River, NJ: Merrill/Prentice Hall.

Davis, C. A., & Brady, M. (1993). Expanding the utility of behavioral momentum with young children: Where we've been, where we need to go. *Journal of Early Intervention, 17,* 211–223.

Drew, C. J., Hardman, M. L., & Logan, D. R. (1996). *Mental retardation: A life-cycle approach* (6th ed.). Upper Saddle River, NJ: Merrill/Prentice Hall.

Fernetti, C. L., Lent, J. R., & Stevens, C. J. (1974). *Project MORE: Eating*. Bellevue, WA: Edmark Associates.

Finnie, N. R. (1975). *Handling the young cerebral palsied child at home* (2nd ed.). New York: Dutton.

Foxx, R. M., & Azrin, N. H. (1973a). Dry pants: A rapid method of toilet training children. *Behavior Research and Therapy, 11,* 435–442.

Foxx, R. M., & Azrin, N. H. (1973b). *Toilet training the retarded*. Champaign, IL: Research Press.

Helton, G. B., Workman, E. A., & Matuszek, P. A. (1982). *Psychoeducational assessment: Integrating concepts and techniques*. New York: Grune & Stratton.

Howell, K. W., Kaplan, J. S., & O'Connell, C. Y. (1979). *Evaluating exceptional children: A task analysis approach*. Upper Saddle River, NJ: Merrill/Prentice Hall.

Klein, M. D. (1985). *Pre-dressing skills*. (1985). San Antonio, TX: Therapy Skill Builders.

Langone, J. (1990). *Teaching students with mild to moderate learning problems*. Boston: Allyn & Bacon.

Leach, P. (1977). *Your baby and child*. New York: Knopf.

Magnusson, C. J., & Justen, J. E. (1981). Teacher-made adaptive and assistive aids for developing self-help skills in the severely handicapped. *Journal for Special Educators, 17,* 389–400.

Mahoney, K., Van Wagenen, R. K., & Meyerson, L. (1971). Toilet training of normal and retarded children. *Journal of Applied Behavior Analysis, 4,* 173–181.

Mills, Y. L., & Hedges, C. A. (1983). The feeding process and nutritional needs of handicapped infants and preschoolers. *Topics in Early Childhood Special Education, 3,* 33–42.

Morris, S. E., & Klein, M. D. (1987). *Pre-feeding skills: A comprehensive resource for feeding development*. San Antonio, TX: Therapy Skill Builders.

Mueller, H. (1975). Feeding. In N. R. Finnie, *Handling the young cerebral palsied child at home* (2nd ed.). New York: Dutton.

Noonan, M. J., & McCormick, L. (1993). *Early intervention in natural environments*. Pacific Grove, CA: Brooks/Cole.

O'Brien, F., Bugle, C., & Azrin, N. H. (1972). Training and maintaining a retarded child's proper eating. *Journal of Applied Behavior Analysis, 5,* 67–73.

Reese, G. M., & Snell, M. E. (1991). Putting on and removing coats and jackets: The acquisition and maintenance of skills by children with severe multiple disabilities. *Education and Training in Mental Retardation, 26,* 398–410.

Sailor, W., & Guess, D. (1983). *Severely handicapped students: An instructional design.* Boston: Houghton Mifflin.

Snell, M. E., & Farlow, L. J. (1993). Self-care skills. In M. E. Snell (Ed.), *Instruction of students with severe disabilities* (4th ed.) (pp. 380–441). Upper Saddle River, NJ: Merrill/Prentice Hall.

Stainback, S., Healy, H., & Stainback, W. (1977). Teaching eating skills. In M. A. Thomas (Ed.), *Developing skills in severely and profoundly handicapped children* (pp. 129–150). Reston, VA: The Council for Exceptional Children.

Stanhope, L., & Bell, R. Q. (1981). Parents and families. In J. M. Kauffman & D. P. Hallahan (Eds.), *Handbook of special education.* Upper Saddle River, NJ: Prentice Hall.

Thomas, G. E. (1996). *Teaching students with mental retardation: A life goal curriculum planning approach.* Upper Saddle River, NJ: Merrill/Prentice Hall.

Utley, B. L., Holvoet, J. F., & Barnes, K. (1977). Handling, positioning, and feeding the physically handicapped. In E. Sontag (Ed.), *Educational programming for the severely and profoundly handicapped.* Reston, VA: The Council for Exceptional Children.

Wehman, P., & Goodwyn, R. L. (1978). Self-help skill development. In N. H. Fallen & J. E. McGovern (Eds.), *Young children with special needs.* Upper Saddle River, NJ: Merrill/Prentice Hall.

Westling, D. L., & Fox, L. (1995). *Teaching students with severe disabilities.* Upper Saddle River, NJ: Merrill/Prentice Hall.

6

Cognitive Development

Warren Umansky

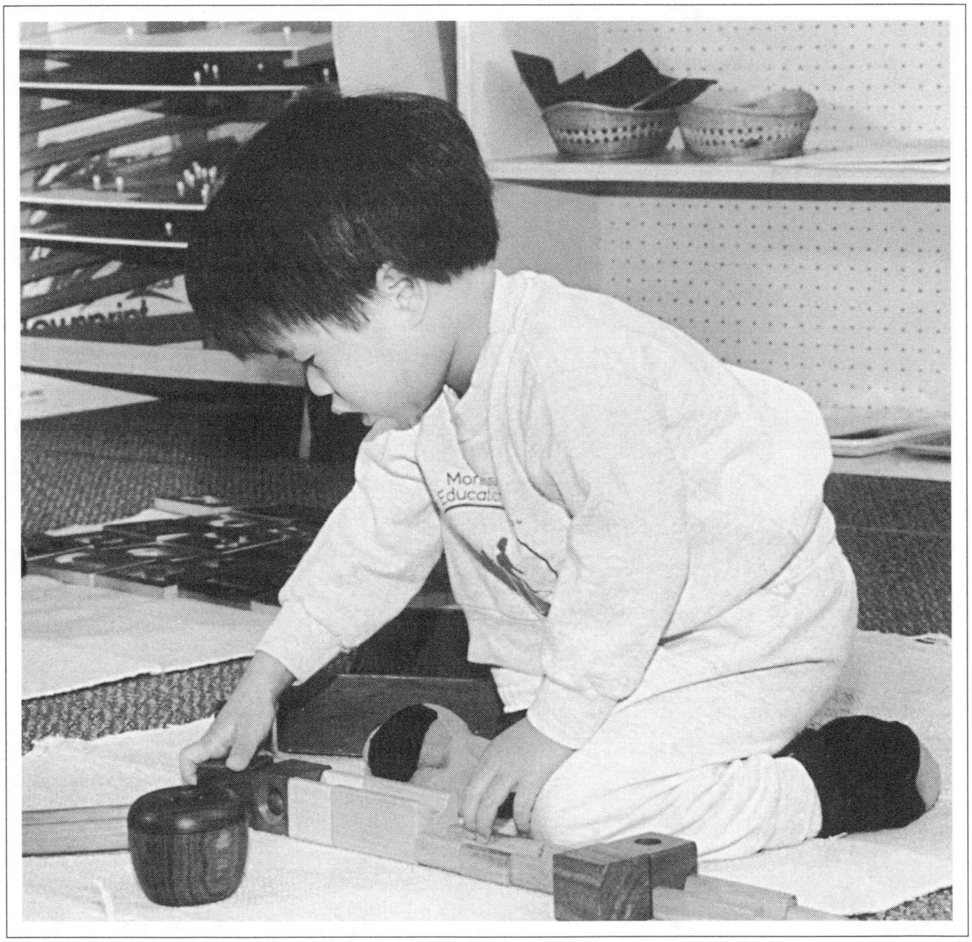

The casual observer of a 5-year-old child hard at play may be mystified by the intensity and variety of the child's behavior: Objects seem to take on life, simple problems evoke interesting attempts at solutions, and newly discovered skills are repeated and applied in different ways. The newborn presents quite another picture—that of a child whose day is spent mostly asleep, whose movements appear to be spontaneous and random, and whose communication repertoire consists only of crying and silence.

The transitions that occur in the normal child during the early years are as exciting to behold as a well-performed ballet is. The acquisition and refinement of skills are evidence that the higher levels of the brain are establishing control and that the child is developing into a cognitive being.

Cognition is difficult to define other than in terms of the many processes it comprises. The word describes mental activity and other behaviors that allow us to understand and participate in events around us. Fundamental to cognitive development is a person's ability to translate objects and events into a symbolic form that can be stored in the brain. The developing thinker is able to store increasingly complex and abstract information, and is able to manipulate the information in a variety of ways. The facility of a child to acquire, store, and manipulate information also is intimately related to development of language, social competence, and purposeful motor skills. For this reason, children who score low on intelligence tests that purport to measure levels of cognition frequently show delays in other areas of development as well.

This chapter examines the development of cognitive processes in young children and the impact that handicapping conditions may have on cognition. By understanding how a child's overt behaviors reflect the unfolding of mental processes, one is better able to interpret a child's performance and thereby plan a developmentally appropriate program.

The chapter concludes with suggestions and principles for providing experiences to children to facilitate cognitive development.

The Range of Cognitive Skills

We receive information through five senses: vision, hearing, taste, smell, and touch. Relating that information to what we have accumulated from past experiences is called *perception*. Perception, then, is sensation with meaning. At yet a higher level of cognitive development, logical thought (the ability to use meaningful information to make decisions and solve problems) emerges. This marks the appearance of conceptual skills.

Even in a newborn, the foundations of cognition are apparent. At birth, a child reveals a varied repertoire of perceptual skills that expands rapidly during the early weeks and months of life. Soon after birth, infants fix briefly on visual stimuli (often the mother's eyes and face because of an attraction to forms with sharp contrasts) and even track moving objects over short distances. They turn away from strong odors, change their sucking patterns for fluids with different tastes, and become quiet in response to certain patterns of sound. Table 6.1 presents an array of perceptual skills present in most normal children during the early years of development.

One must be impressed by the capabilities of a young child, who progresses in about 9 months from the fusion of two cells to a complex and skilled organism. In 9 more months, the child is able to discriminate among information in the environment and remember a few meaningful experiences. He seems to recognize his caregivers, anticipate feeding, and show definite preferences for types and textures of food. During the third 9 months, the child remembers more experiences and begins attaching labels to people and things, permitting finer distinctions among similar stimuli and forming the basis for spoken language. For example, the 18-month-old child is unable to name colors, but he has internal labels for different colors that allow him to distinguish one color from another. The inner language represented by this labeling system is described by Vygotsky (1962). It is the means by which a child manipulates information in more and more complex ways. No longer controlled by the physical characteristics of things, a child suspects that the staunch-looking refrigerator carton might be empty and offer an excellent place to play. He indicates a grasp of temporal concepts by wanting something now rather than later. He anticipates the arrival of his mother from work when the sun begins to set. His spatial awareness and ability to pull together numerous bits of old and new information permit him to think through possible ways to get to the cookie jar on the refrigerator and to try only the solution he thinks is most likely to work. This is quite a change from the infant for whom time and space were dimensions too abstract to

TABLE 6.1 Normal Perceptual Skills

VISUAL	AUDITORY	TACTILE	OLFACTORY	GUSTATORY
Fixing	Localization	Discrimination	Localization	Discrimination
Tracking	Auditory memory	Form Temperature Texture Pressure	Discrimination	
Depth perception	Discrimination: Sound Speech			
Discrimination: Pattern Color Form Size				
Visual memory				
Figure ground				

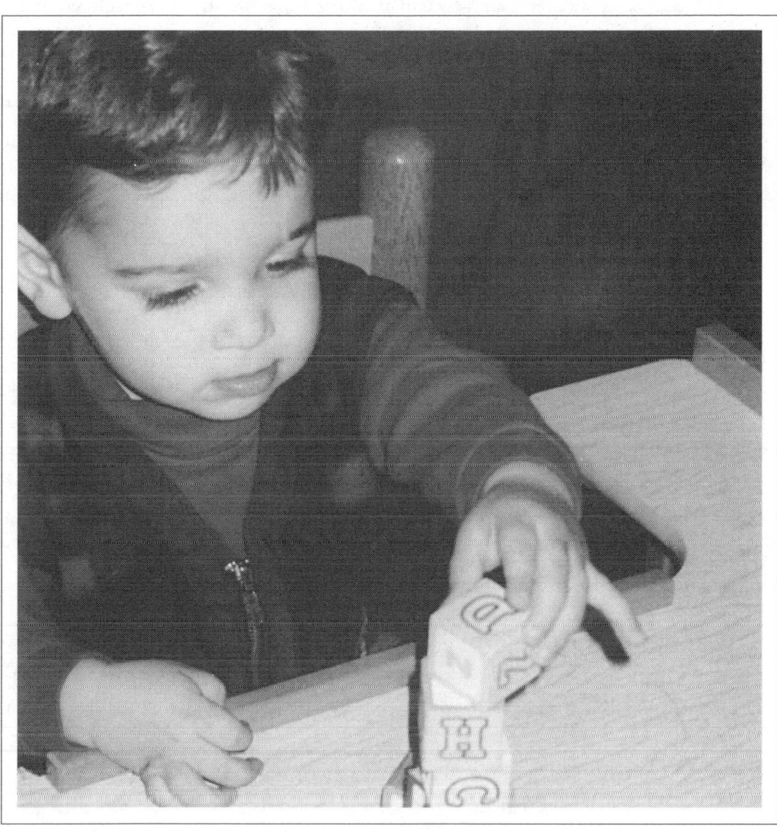

The facility of the child to acquire, store, and manipulate information is intimately related to the development of language, social competence, and purposeful motor skills.

understand. A child who attaches the label "book" to all varieties of books, who knows that there are many kinds of four-legged animals, and who can sort blocks by color or shape or texture also demonstrates a grasp of classification concepts, reflecting another step on the ladder of cognitive skills.

As a child gets older, perceptual skills are refined and integrated into higher-level thought processes. Random scribbling on paper, for example, develops into drawings that reflect a similarity to the model. Piaget and Inhelder (1969) have described children's unique efforts at this stage of emerging conceptual development:

> A face seen in profile will have a second eye because a man has two eyes, or a horseman, in addition to his visible leg, will have a leg which can be seen through the horse. Similarly, one will see potatoes in the ground, if that is where they are, or in a man's stomach. (pp. 64–65)

A child's developing language is also indicative of the expanding range of cognitive skills. He must first sort out the meaningful sounds in his environment. He also must use sound differences to identify and store words for later recognition and speech production (Ferguson, 1978). Initial words tend to be names for people, very familiar objects, and function forms, such as *there, stop, gone,* and *more.* This vocabulary dominates a child's spoken language from approximately 12 to 18 months. When, in the second half of the second year, a child strings words together, it is a demonstration of his capacity to represent relationships between objects and events. There is support for the belief that a child at the stage of one-word utterances actually knows considerably more about sentence structure than he is able to demonstrate. He is prevented from exercising his knowledge by a limited short-term memory and oral-motor control.

Length and complexity of a child's utterances increase within a speaking environment that provides a rich variety of language samples. A child's choice of words in speech then becomes a means to express the ways in which he thinks. Piaget based much of his theory of cognitive development on talks he had with children.

Piaget's Theory of Cognitive Development

Jean Piaget contributed the most comprehensive theory of how cognitive development progresses in children. He viewed development as an unfolding of ever-more complex skills as children modify their mental structures to deal with new experiences.

Development is a continuous process that may vary in the rate at which it occurs in different children, but it always progresses in the same sequence. As with a house, for which the foundation first must be laid, then the outside structures, the wiring, the plumbing, and finally the interior walls, so cognitive development follows an orderly, unchanging progression. Substantial research on children with disabilities has documented the slower rate of development of children with disabilities compared with children who do not have disabilities; however, the same sequence of development as that which nondisabled children have has been documented in children with visual impairments (Fraiberg, 1968, 1975), mental retardation (Kahn, 1976; Silverstein, McLain, Brownless, & Hubbey, 1976; Weisz & Zigler, 1979), hearing impairments (Best & Roberts, 1976), and cerebral palsy (Tessier, 1969/70).

Piaget gave the name *schemata* to the cognitive structures responsible for maintaining a child's internal representations of objects and experiences. As a child engages in different experiences, receives novel sensory input, and is called upon to respond in new ways, new schemata are formed or old ones are modified. A child organizes his experiences, as he develops, into more-complex mental structures. By coordinating schemata, for example, he is capable of generalizing behaviors to new situations. Reaching for an interesting-looking toy might be viewed as the coordination of the schemata of vision, reaching, and wanting a familiar object.

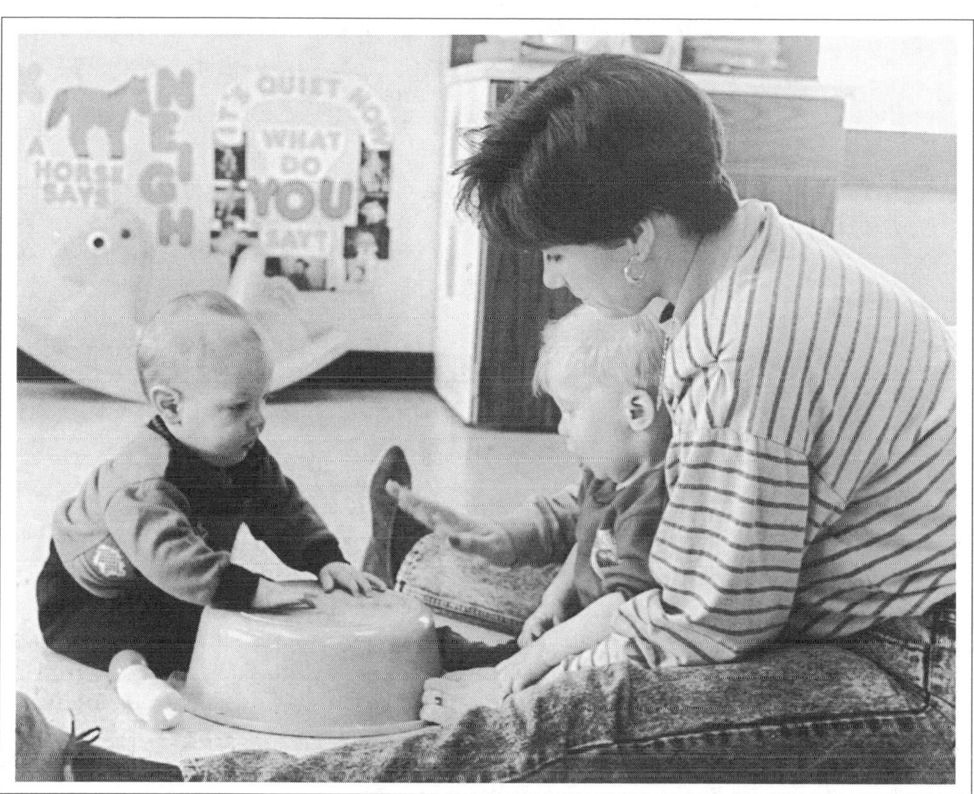

In the early stages of cognitive development, a child is drawn to the surface characteristics of objects. Later, objects become meaningful for what they do or represent.

Piaget described two processes by which a child adapts to new or unique demands from the environment. In *assimilation,* a child interprets new experiences only in terms of schemata that he already has. If, for example, his schema for flying things includes only birds, he may inaccurately identify all flying things as birds. All four-legged animals may be "horses" if someone has once identified a specific four-legged animal for him as a horse. These overgeneralizations that children make are a reflection of how they perceive the world based on a limited store of experiences and information. A second process helps them bring their perspectives more in line with reality. Through *accommodation,* a child's schemata are modified with experience. By being shown a kite or a plane or by having the differences among a kite, a plane, and a bird described, the child expands his schema for flying things to include the new information. He also may begin to expand his store of information about birds to include different types of birds.

Interactions with the environment almost always involve assimilation and accommodation. In the former, it appears that children change the world by fitting new experiences into their understanding. In the latter, the world changes children by altering their understanding to conform to reality. The continuous changing of cognitive structures, or schemata, occurs throughout life.

Young children identify characteristics of the world based upon physical attributes. That is, they cannot comprehend that a large box may be full or empty; they can perceive it based upon its surface qualities only. These percepts often provide erroneous information to a child. As he interacts more with his environment, he may be bound less and less to physical attributes. He may formulate concepts based upon how things are used and of what they are made, and he uses more discrete differences among objects and experiences to solve problems and make logical decisions.

Organization of Development

Qualitative changes mark the development of cognitive abilities in children. Piaget described the *principle of equilibrium* as one of the mechanisms that facilitates change as a child seeks balance in his interactions with the environment. With organization of and adaptation to new experiences through assimilation and accommodation, he achieves stability, or equilibrium.

Piaget presented the significant developmental accomplishments of children in terms of periods and stages. Again, he emphasized the sequence of changes more than the specific ages at which they occur. This explains why we frequently find children with disabilities experiencing a period of cognitive development associated with much younger children. Awareness of this developmental pattern provides valuable direction in program planning for the cognitively young child.

The first two periods of cognitive development—*sensorimotor* and *preoperational thought*—describe a child's progress through a mental age of about 7 or 8 years. The periods of *concrete operations* and *formal operations* describe mental processes of older children.

Piaget's Stages of Development

Sensorimotor Period

A child's earliest behaviors are reflexive in nature; the child gives the same motor response to the same types of stimuli with little understanding of what is happening. A loud noise or sudden movement elicits a startle. Stimulation of the area around the mouth elicits a rooting or suck-swallow response. During the sensorimotor period, mental operations go through a transition from being exclusively overt and motoric to being partially internalized. The child makes more effort at understanding the world. He begins to reflect on sensory information and selects a response from a number of alternatives. He can categorize many stimuli appropriately. Experiences provide the opportunity for the child to recognize the uniqueness of certain stimuli through accommodation. During this period, then, certain people and objects take on greater importance in the child's life.

A child also recognizes his ability to make things happen. He may throw his spoon on the floor and watch its descent intently. He may repeat this over and over, thrilled at his power over matter and at the responses he elicits from his parents.

One of the most significant changes during this period is the development of object permanence, the knowledge that an object continues to exist even though it is out of sight (Ruff, 1982). A keen observer notes that when a very young child drops a rattle out of his crib, he may cry briefly, but does not search for it. At about 12 months, however, he looks for it where he thinks it fell. A child's remembering the existence of an object after it is out of sight indicates that the child has internalized a symbolic representation of the object. The symbolic image is maintained by the child even in the absence of the sensory image. This mental operation is a most significant milestone in a child's development of cognition. The gradual unfolding of object permanence occurs sequentially during the sensorimotor period, as shown in Table 6.2.

Reflexive Stage. Cognitive development begins in a child as a group of invariant reflex behaviors. The cerebral cortex is still immature, permitting lower centers of the central nervous system to maintain dominance over sensorimotor performance. A child sucks, roots, grasps, and startles almost indiscriminately, and often in the absence of a stimulus. A child will suck, for example, even when a nipple is not present. Piaget observed that when a schema of particular importance is present, there is a tendency to exercise it. This process, called *functional assimilation,* allows a child to refine the behavior and to begin extending it to other situations. Thumb sucking, which has been observed even in utero, is one such extension of a schema. Recognitive assimilation also appears early, as the child begins to discriminate among objects to which a schema applies and those to which it does not. A child selects a nipple over other suckable objects when he is hungry, for example.

Infants enter the world prepared to receive and distinguish a variety of sensory information. Refinement of skills occurs quickly. A newborn's explorations and interactions with the environment reflect primitive behaviors, an immature nervous

TABLE 6.2 Stages in Attainment of Object Permanence

AGE	BEHAVIOR
0–4 months	Does not actively search for objects that have moved out of sight
4–8 months	Searches for partially concealed objects
	Anticipates the destination of a moving object that is lost from sight
8–12 months	Searches for objects seen being hidden
12–18 months	Searches for objects hidden in visible changes of location
18–24 months	Searches for objects in hidden displacements by recreating the sequence

system, and schemata that assure the child's survival. These experiences provide the foundation for building more-complex cognitive structures and prepare the child to become more directed in his actions.

Primary Circular Reactions. This stage in a child's development of cognition is characterized by attempts to repeat an action that has been done reflexively or by chance. These actions are described as *primary* because they are limited to basic actions involving a child's own body, and as *circular* because they are repeated. An infant cannot yet initiate new actions. If he by chance brought his thumb to his mouth, he might try to repeat the event. By positioning his hand and head appropriately he may accomplish the task after a number of misses. Through accommodation a child modifies his schemata until he becomes more precise in repeating actions.

A child at this stage also begins to show anticipatory behavior. Whereas a newborn begins purposeful sucking when his lips are in contact with a nipple, a child now may begin to suck when he is placed in a position that he associates with feeding.

Several other important signs appear at this stage indicating a child's growing alertness to stimuli in his surroundings. At approximately 3 months of age, a typical child begins to look in the direction of a sound. He also responds differently to some different visual stimuli. Novel and complex objects or pictures are likely to draw a more lengthy and intent gaze than do things familiar to the child. Continued exploration of novel stimuli in the environment through gross coordination of the senses enables an infant to begin developing schemata for the structure of the environment (Parker, 1993). This then becomes the foundation for relating new information to former experiences and further modifying schemata. This process is the basis for cognitive functioning and is refined during the third stage of the sensorimotor period.

Secondary Circular Reactions. Most parents claim that the most enjoyable stage in infancy comes at about 4 to 8 months of age. By this time, a baby focuses his attention on objects rather than on his own body. He reaches and grasps, providing himself greater freedom in manipulating and exploring objects. His random movements may cause his hand or foot to strike the mobile above the crib, and he begins to refine these movements until he is able to keep the mobile going with purposeful swipes. A child also begins responding in the same way to objects that appear the same to him. This type of primitive classification system develops through recognitive assimilation. A child will swipe at another mobile or something that looks like a mobile until he discovers a more appropriate way to approach the new object. Observing this type of activity and the perception of sameness in his daughter, Lucienne, prompted Piaget's belief (1952) that actions are the precursors of thought processes.

Rattles are interesting toys for children at this age, who are able to reach, grasp, and shake them, and who find the sound pleasing. The significance of specific objects and people signals the development of *object concept,* upon which

Piaget put great emphasis. In the first stages of development, infants perceive an object only in terms of themselves; that is, something to suck, hold, or drop. During this later stage, however, objects begin to gain importance in relation to other objects. They become something with which to learn about spatial relationships and the stability of the universe (Piaget, 1954). Related to this is the concept of object permanence. During the early phase of *object permanence,* children show a fascination for hide-and-seek games. They can find partially hidden objects, and when a toy is moved under a blanket in a predictable trajectory, they may anticipate where it will reappear. The search for hidden objects is likely to be brief, however, perhaps as a function of infants' short memory span and attention (Bower, 1974). Nevertheless, as they develop, the images of objects and experiences beyond their immediate surroundings become more permanent residents of their schemata.

A child's ability to sit independently at this stage and the appearance of teeth afford him a new perspective. Sights, sounds, smells, tastes, and tactile information are likely to increase in quantity and diversity, permitting the child to further refine his schemata for the environment. A child can make finer distinctions between the people and objects nearby. He can distinguish a familiar person or toy from others and can recognize them in different positions or when they are partially hidden from view.

Coordination of Secondary Schemata. This stage is marked by three important characteristics: intention, imitation, and anticipation. A child applies old schemata in new situations to attain a goal. For example, he uses a hitting action for the first time to move a barrier out of his path to get to a toy. He moves his parent's hand to a container that he cannot open himself. This intentional behavior is reflective of the child's beginning awareness of causality, the concept that people and things around him can cause change.

A child at this stage also begins to imitate on two planes, verbal and gestural. At earlier stages, the child tried to imitate sounds that he made and were repeated by someone else. Now, through approximations of his own sounds and then sounds he hears, the child begins to refine his verbal imitation skills. The first imitations to appear are the most closely related to sounds already in the child's repertoire. The same progression is seen in gestural skills. A child first attempts to repeat movements already in his repertoire and then modifies his movements to approximate those of someone else. One of the earliest gestural imitations seen in children is waving bye-bye, which is a modification of children's schemata for reaching, grasping, and releasing.

Children of approximately 10 months of age show rather sophisticated anticipatory behavior. They may begin to cry when adults put on their coats, in anticipation of the adults' departure, or when food is placed before them that they do not like. It is not necessary at this stage for the parents to actually depart or for the child to taste the food in order for the child to cry; he can anticipate the outcome.

Also at this stage, the function of objects assumes greater importance to a child than does merely their appearance. The child is most interested in objects that can be manipulated in different ways, that make sounds, and that have visual fascination when they are explored. The child no longer perceives an object merely by its surface characteristics. He is able to hypothesize what things do by looking at them and, in play, uses the objects in purposeful ways (Zelazo & Kearsley, 1977).

Tertiary Circular Reactions. Primary reactions involve the child's own body. Secondary reactions involve simple exploration with objects. In the stage of tertiary circular reactions, the child approaches objects with an attitude that can be characterized as curiosity. He will repeat the same behavior, then experiment with variations. A child in a high chair might drop his spoon on the tray in the same way several times. He might then begin to drop it from different heights, letting it fall straight or allowing it to spin. The child also begins to use a spoon and can drink from a cup at about this time. Spilling milk on the floor or tossing food across the kitchen is part of a child's exploration. The child may participate in this trial-and-error experimentation until he finds one strategy that is particularly satisfying or effective. In the same way, a child engages other objects in similar unsystematic explorations and continues to broaden his understanding of relationships in his universe.

There is good evidence that, in this stage, *decentration* evolves on the action level, wherein the child learns that events take place in the universe without his involvement or control. He is still limited in interpreting cause-effect relationships for actions but enjoys watching an activity in which he does not participate. When a child watches someone hide an object and then move it to another hiding place, he searches for the object where it has been moved. Formerly, he would have looked in its original position.

Because a normal child usually stands and walks during this stage, his ability to explore sights and sounds in the environment increases dramatically. He can classify objects by function or action in addition to shape. Nelson (1973a) found that children of 15–20 months initially classify objects by form or shape. After they have an opportunity to manipulate the objects, however, they classify them by action or function.

Invention of New Means Through Mental Combinations. Near 2 years of age, a typical child no longer is tied to his actions, but can think through solutions to simple problems without the need for acting them out. The development of symbolic function marks the transition from the sensorimotor to the preoperational period.

The earliest symbols used by a child are probably internal images derived from his perceptual actions. That is, he retains the memory of an experience in some symbolic form. This allows for what Piaget called *deferred imitation.* A child can watch an action, store the image of the action in memory, and repeat it at a later time. A child's ability to imitate also improves, because he is able to work through an action internally before acting it out.

A child's internal symbolic representations are also expressed in his understanding that pictures represent objects. He enjoys looking through a storybook and touching pictures of familiar objects. A child's language also may be a reflection of the experiences he considers most important. Action terms predominate in early language, as do names for objects that children associate with action (Nelson, 1973b).

At the end of this stage, a child perceives objects as permanent and independent. He understands that if an object is out of sight, it may be in one of several other places and he may seek it out in a more systematic way. He recognizes spatial relationships among objects, as when he places forms in a form board correctly or holds a chip in his hand to drop it through a slit in the top of a can.

During the first 2 years of life, then, a child has learned about the physical properties of his environment. Initially, all behavior is overt and related to the child's body. Gradually, the child becomes more interested in other objects and actions and is able to translate these into symbols that he internalizes. More-complex manipulations of symbolic representations characterize the next period of cognitive development.

Preoperational Period

As a child enters this period in cognitive development, thought processes are still immature. A child often is misled by his perceptions of the environment. The broad changes that take place on the action level during the sensorimotor period are matched by similar changes on the level of representational thought during the preoperational period.

Piaget began formulating his theory relating to this period by talking with and observing many different children. He focused on children's egocentrism in relation to communication skills, morality, and reasoning. He later refined his method and gave children specific problems to solve. He then described their thought processes based upon their approaches to problem solving. He called their first attempts at constructing ideas or notions *preconcepts* to signify that children's conceptualization of the universe is still perceptually dominant.

Flavell (1963) described some of the marked changes that take place during the preoperational period. These are presented in the following paragraphs.

Egocentrism. An egocentric child is unable to view things from another perspective. On the three-mountain problem used by Piaget (see Figure 6.1), a child is asked to indicate what a doll would see by looking at the scene from different sides of the table. Not being able to imagine that someone can have a different viewpoint, the child chooses his own point of view.

Children's language also reflects egocentricism. Piaget's daughter Jacqueline, for example, defined *daddy* as "a man who has lots of Jacquelines" (Piaget, 1951). McClinton and Meier (1978) have identified three forms of egocentric speech: monologue, collective monologue, and repetition. In the first, a child talks continuously while working or playing, apparently practicing the synthesis of action, language, and thought. Collective monologue takes place in a group situation. A child speaks with no apparent connection to what another child is saying. Although the social setting is different, the reasons for collective monologue appear to be the same as for simple monologue. Repetition is the third form of egocentric speech. A child repeats what another child has said but presents it as if it were a unique contribution.

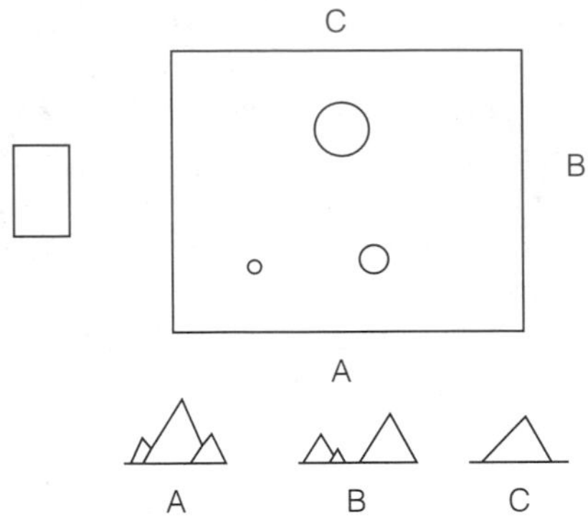

FIGURE 6.1 *Piaget's three-mountain problem*

A child in the preoperational period is unable to anticipate the strategies that another will use in game-playing or problem-solving situations, yet he assumes that others know what he is thinking. In relating a story, for example, he may present it disjointedly or leave out parts, yet believe that the listener understands as he does.

Centration. Successful problem solving requires that a child attend to many attributes of an object at one time. A preoperational child shows centration in thinking. He is unable to consider multiple attributes simultaneously, which causes errors in problem solving. If a child watches while a ball of clay is rolled into a snake, returned to its original form, and rolled again, he focuses only on one dimension when telling why the ball and snake are not equal. One child may say the ball is taller; another may say the snake is longer. Their inability to see the reciprocal changes in dimensions interferes with logical thinking and problem solving. The following problem provides another example of centration.

Given a group of red blocks and blue blocks that are all the same size and shape, a child has little difficulty putting together the blocks that are alike because they differ in only one attribute. However, if the child is given a group of red and blue blocks and red and blue disks, he will be confused. He tends to focus on one attribute at a time; therefore, he may group them all into two piles, or his attention may shift to another attribute during sorting and he may produce a conglomerate of piles.

Similarly, if a child is given seven blue and three white wooden beads, he will correctly name the color of the majority of the beads. But the child will be confused if he is asked whether there are more blue or wooden beads. Again, the child cannot focus on multiple attributes of the whole and its parts.

Irreversibility and Focus on Successive States. A preoperational child does not see that all logical operations are reversible. This is apparent in different types of problems. A child does not understand that if a ball of clay is rolled into a snake, it can just as easily be returned to its original form. Similarly, a child who is

Conservation of substance

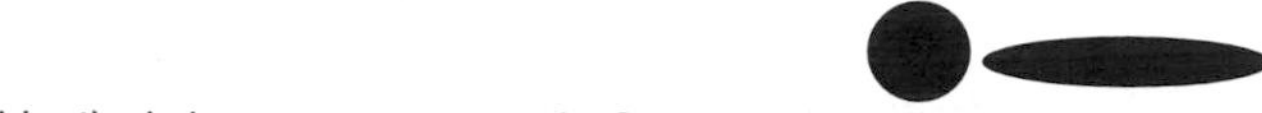

a. The experimenter presents two identical clay balls. The child sees that they have equal amounts.

b. One of the balls is rolled out flat. The child is asked whether they still contain the same amount.

Conservation of length

a. Two sticks are lined up in front of the child. The child sees that they are the same.

b. One of the sticks is moved to the left. The child is asked whether they are still the same.

Conservation of number

a. Two rows of counters are placed in one-to-one correspondence. The child sees that they are equal.

b. One of the rows is elongated (or contracted). The child is asked whether each row still has the same number.

Conservation of area

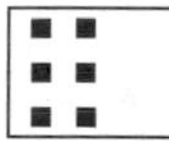

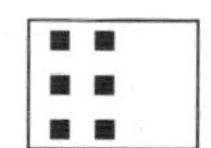

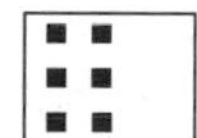

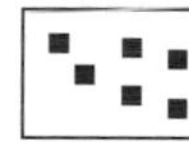

a. The child and the experimenter each have identical sheets of cardboard. Wooden blocks are placed on these in identical positions. The child is asked whether each card has the same amount of empty space.

b. The experimenter moves the blocks around on the card. The child is asked the same question.

Conservation of liquids

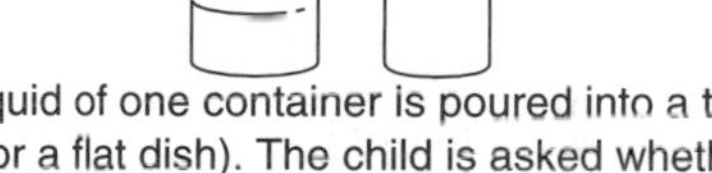

a. Two glass jars are filled to the same level with water. The child sees that they are equal.

b. The liquid of one container is poured into a tall tube (or a flat dish). The child is asked whether each contains the same amount.

FIGURE 6.2 Simple tests of conservation

asked whether he has a brother may say "yes," but when he is asked whether his brother has a brother, he says "no."

This process also is associated with a child's focusing on successive stages of change rather than on the smooth transformation from one state to another. Piaget referred to a child's thought as being like a sequence of individual frames on a film. Flavell (1963) described a child's difficulty in arranging a series of pictures to reconstruct the movement of a stick falling from a vertical to a horizontal position to exemplify a child's view of changed states.

Conservation problems require that a child be able to focus on the transformation from state to state in relation to mass, length, number, volume, and area. Figure 6.2 presents some simple tests of conservation. Conservation of number is usually achieved by age 6. By age 7, a child attains conservation of mass and length; by age 9, weight; and volume after age 11.

Transductive Reasoning. Logical reasoning requires induction and deduction. In inductive reasoning, one generalizes from specific cases. In deductive reasoning, one applies general rules to specific cases. These processes require a child to recognize the stability of attributes despite changing circumstances and differences among attributes under the same circumstances. A preoperational child is not capable of deductive or inductive reasoning. Birds remain birds whether they are perched in a tree in the park or flying in the air. There are distinctive differences between the birds in the two cases. Yet the child who uses transductive reasoning assumes that the two birds he sees are one and the same. He sees relationships at a perceptual level without considering the possibility of higher-order relationships.

The Beginning of Concept Formation. The emergence of logical thought in a child is manifested in problem-solving and decision-making abilities. He begins

TABLE 6.3 Development of Simple Classification, Space and Number, and Seriation Concepts

CLASSIFICATION	SPACE AND NUMBERS	SERIATION
Simple sorting: Groups according to single perceptual attribute.	*One-to-one correspondence:* Establishes equality between two sets of objects that visually correspond.	*Orders objects* according to one property.
True classification: Abstracts common property in group of objects. Finds some property in other objects in group.	*One-to-one correspondence in absence of physical correspondence:* Recognizes equality in absence of spatial equivalence.	*Orders two inversely related series:* Arranges two series at once in inverse order.
Multiplicative classification: Classifies by more than one attribute at a time. Sees that object can belong to several classes at same time.	*Conservation of quality:* Quantity does not vary even when it occupies a different space.	*Seriation and visual representation:* Draws a picture of objects he arranged in series. Then, draws in advance of ordering.
All-Some relation: Distinguishes classes based on property of all members and subclasses based on property of some members.	*Conservation of the whole:* The whole does not vary even when divided into parts.	*Seriation of geometric shapes:* Orders shapes based on area or number of sides.
Class-inclusion relation: Forms subclasses of objects and includes subclasses in larger class.	*Conservation of area:* Area is conserved even if appearance is changed.	
	Transformation of perspective: Pictures objects from different perspective when they are moved.	

Source: From *Piaget's Theory Applied to an Early Childhood Curriculum,* by C. S. Lavatelli, 1973. Nashua, NH: Delta Education Inc. Copyright © 1973 by Delta Education, Inc. Reprinted by permission.

to put things and events into some type of order. Objects show similarities and differences in their physical attributes, in their functions, and in their relationships to other objects. The child begins to group what he sees into classes and subclasses. Lavatelli (1973) summarized the logical processes of classification, space and number, and seriation as they develop in a young child. These processes are presented in Table 6.3.

 *Other Theories of Development*

Vygotsky's Theory

Whereas Piaget focused on the natural laws of intellectual development, Russian psychologist Lev Vygotsky (1978) concentrated on the role of language and culture, describing the roles of instruction, play, help, and learning. He explained cognitive development in terms of social systems comprised of productive interactions between the child and caregiver. Not unlike Piaget, he saw a responsive environment as the key to intellectual development.

Vygotsky used the term *zone of proximal development* to describe the distance between actual and potential development. Actual development is measured by watching a child's independent problem solving. Potential development is what the child does with help or guidance and it becomes actual development through the mechanism of internalization. This mechanism describes the developmental progression of a child from other-regulation, wherein another individual (an adult or more-advanced child) guides the child's activities, to self-regulation, wherein the child initiates purposeful action with other available individuals who provide necessary support only. The successful negotiation of this shift toward greater independence and control requires intersubjectivity. According to Rommetveit (1985), intersubjectivity occurs when both parties share an understanding of the purpose of a given task and each recognizes this of the other. For a productive interaction to occur between an adult and child, there must be a shared social reality such that both are working on the same problem. When shared understanding does not exist, some negotiation between the two parties must occur, requiring communicative interaction or semiotic mediation. Trevarthen (1988) suggests that there is a primary intersubjectivity present at birth between an infant and his caregiver. At 7 to 8 months of age, the infant enters a period of secondary intersubjectivity. At this point, the child and caregiver can share meanings at a higher cognitive level. While Vygotsky stressed the language component of mediation, mechanisms such as joint eye gaze, following other's pointings, and catching other people's attention by using gestures and pointing also can be successful in the formulation of intersubjectivity (Rogoff, Malkin, & Gilbride, 1984). The adult can strive for a new level of intersubjectivity by representing objects and events in different ways, thereby stimulating cognitive development in the infant.

Vygotsky also proposed a sociocultural theory of disability in which compensation comes from cultural enlightment and socialization. He offered a comprehensive and practical approach to educating children with special needs. The foundation of this *theory of disontogenesis,* or distorted development, is that children have two classes of defects. Organic impairments (primary defects) result from both endogenous and exogenous biological causes. Children also experience distortions of higher psychological functions (secondary defects) as a result of social factors. Vygotsky's view was that the development of a child with a disability is determined by the social implications of the organic impairment, but that social support systems can overcome the obstacles imposed by that impairment. The main objective of special education is the application of the principles just described to the development of the child's higher psychological functions by capitalizing on the child's current abilities and by providing meaning to new experiences. Children with caregivers who offer verbal and nonverbal support and who seek a shared understanding with the child of the task to be accomplished, for example, appear to be more motivated to persist with other challenging tasks on their own (Hauser-Cram, 1996; Stremmel & Ru, 1993). The objective of intervention, therefore, must identify a child from the point of strength rather than disability (Gindis, 1995). Social support systems can help children with disabilities overcome obstacles as they evolve processes to adapt to environmental demands.

Behavioral Theories

Not everyone endorses the theory that cognition evolves through developmental changes in the organization of mental structures or that these changes are reflected in children's behavior in learning situations. There are numerous theories about how children learn, or how they ascend to adulthood with growing sophistication in their ability to relate to their environment. From the behaviorist perspective, cognitive development is the result of the method and amount of learning children gain from their surroundings. Although most theories of development emphasize predictable and measurable changes in behavior that are governed by interactions with the environment, the classical research behind the development of these theories took place in the laboratory. The results of these laboratory studies have been applied in natural settings to study particular processes related to learning and the development of cognitive skills.

Attention. A developing child is exposed to a large and diverse group of stimuli at any given time: the sound of a car in the street; the clothes dryer rumbling its tune in the next room; the radio playing; the brightly colored wallpaper; the toys, books, and magazines scattered around the room; the soup and roast cooking in the kitchen; and the family talking.

Very young children sustain attention for only brief periods. When they do attend, it is likely to be to the most intense stimuli in the environment—bright objects, loud noises, and strong smells. As children develop, they begin to concentrate on stimuli with the greatest functional value to the task at hand. They are less apt to be distracted by irrelevant and incidental attributes, and more apt to focus on the relevant details of an object or situation. Kagan and Kogan (1970) postulate that neurological changes contribute to a child's improved attention over time. Attention theory is considered by many to be the critical factor for developmental transitions in perception (Gibson, 1969), memory, thought, and problem solving (Pick, Frankel, & Hess, 1975). Children's ability to focus on the meaningful stimuli in their surroundings plays a significant role in the development of cognition.

Perception. Children differ in how they interpret sensory information. They may perceive the same situation in different ways depending upon their dominant sensory mode and dimension preferences. A newborn may give the same response for many types of stimuli but, as he develops, fewer stimuli elicit the same response. In addition, at different ages an infant shows shifts in the sensory mode he prefers for receiving information. Infants are more tactually attuned to the environment. As they get older, their explorations of the environment shift toward a more visual orientation.

Predictable shifts also occur in a child's preference for characteristics of stimuli during a problem-solving task. For example, a dimension is a category that includes all the variations of an attribute. While color comprises numerous qualities, it is considered a single dimension. Similarly, shape and size are other dimensions in the visual mode. The earliest preference for a stimulus dimension occurs at about age 2, when the child attempts to solve a choice problem by continually selecting the stimulus on the same side (left or right). Older children select stimuli based first on color or size, then based on shape at about 6 years of age.

A child also becomes better able to distinguish among stimuli as he develops. Gibson (1969), in her differentiation theory, proposes that through a child's rich experiences with stimuli, he learns to differentiate attributes of objects and situations and then selects those that are relevant. In addition to becoming aware that different objects and events have different characteristics, he learns through experiences that some attributes are invariant. His toy car is the same whether it is in his hand or across the room, where it appears to be smaller. Similarly, it is the same toy car whether it is viewed from the front, the back, or the side.

Memory. The distinction between perception and conception is often characterized by the quantity of information stored in the brain's data bank and the extent to which a child can take new information and make associations with past knowledge. A child becomes more of a conceptual thinker when the data bank is full of verbal labels for objects and events and there are clusters of related information or symbols to be drawn upon.

Children's retention of information for short and long periods of time follows different paths of development (Liben, 1982). The capacity of short-term memory is small. If we tell a child what to order at a fast-food restaurant, he is likely to forget unless he uses the information quickly. Even then, if the phrase or word string is too long or has little meaning as a whole, he will probably forget it quickly. A 3-year-old child can repeat a string of three numbers presented to him orally. A 7-year-old can recall five numbers; to put this in perspective, most adults do not have a much greater capacity in short-term memory (seven numbers). Short-term memory also allows a child to look for an object that moves out of sight—the skill known as object permanence.

Long-term memory has a greater storage capacity and shows greater differences among ages. It is likely that increased memory capacity over time is a result of a richer abundance of material already in the brain's data bank to which new information can be related. The more meaningful new information is, the easier it is to memorize.

Three strategies used to memorize new information appear to be related to children's use of verbal labels and their ability to group stimuli on the basis of more complex perceptual and conceptual attributes. First, memory through rehearsal increases with age (Flavell, 1970). When children were shown a series of pictures and asked to recall the order in which the examiner pointed to them, Flavell found that younger children who said the words for the pictures to themselves had much better recall. Flavell found the use of verbal mediation to increase with age. Also, when pictures were named for the children who did not use verbal rehearsal, their memory was greatly improved. In fact, very young children were able to point to many named pictures with the same proficiency as adults had! Apparently, the inability to produce the verbal mediators may be a hindrance in certain memory tasks. The acquisition of verbal labels appears to account for age changes in memory capacity. In preverbal children, active manipulation of stimuli may facilitate memory.

Imagery is a second strategy for committing new information to memory. It entails superimposing mental images of one or more stimuli upon each other so that the association of each with the other aids recall. For example, if a child is shown pictures of a dog, a wagon, a toothbrush, and a key, the child might formulate the image of a dog riding in a wagon with a toothbrush in one hand and a key in the other. Although imagery is more effective with concrete stimuli, abstractions may be incorporated into a mental image if they are paired with a concrete object, such as a large orange.

The third strategy reflects some of the more interesting data on developmental progressions. Organization of stimuli into meaningful clusters appears to contribute to their acquisition and recall; however, children organize information in different ways at different ages. Rossi and Wittrock (1971) presented a series of words that could be organized in different ways to children between 2 and 5 years of age. The 2-year-olds tended to cluster together words that rhymed; the 3-year-olds clustered words that had syntactic meaning (such as eat—apple and men—work); the 4-year-olds clustered words by functional similarity (such as hand—leg and peach—apple); and the 5-year-olds recalled the words most often in the order in which they had heard them. Clustering based on more and more complex factors is consistent with what we have already learned about cognitive processes.

Hypothesis Testing. Children under 6 years of age do little systematic testing of hypotheses. Trying to guess the answer in a game of I'm Thinking of Something, a young child's questions are not likely to reflect strategy: "Is it a horse?" "Is it something to eat?" "Is it something I like?" As the child gets older, however, he uses a strategy that involves asking questions that gradually focus in on the answer: "Does it move?" "Does it have wheels?" "Does someone drive it?" "Is it a car?"

Complex techniques of hypothesis testing may not be attained until adulthood. Even then, the problem-solving strategies used may be insufficient or ineffective in producing the correct answer.

Relationships Between Developmental and Cognitive Processing Models

It is important to keep in mind that the differences among the theories of cognitive development are not great. Piaget, representing a developmental approach, focused on the gradual organization of cognitive structures that permits a child to solve problems and perform logical operations. According to Piaget, cognition provides a means to adapt to environmental demands by assimilating new information and modifying cognitive structures—schemata—that are already present. Even a newborn has a basis for interacting with the environment in a motoric, reflexive way.

Proponents of behavioral models focus on the operations involved in receiving, storing, and recalling information. While they do not disavow recognition of internal processes, behaviorists believe that "it is not profitable to speculate about these internal processes since they cannot be directly observed or controlled" (Maccoby & Zellner, 1970, p. 34). They believe that behavior is controlled by stimuli and that development progresses as behaviors are modified to the demands of stimuli.

Kamii (1979) proposed that Piaget's theory explains all phenomena studied by other theorists, while other theories are unable to explain many phenomena described by Piaget. For example, in the situation involving blue and white wooden beads described in the earlier section on centration, Piaget's theory explains that 4-year-olds do not have the ability to consider a part of a class (i.e., only the blue beads) and the whole class (all wooden beads) at the same time. Once they think about a part, the whole no longer exists. By 8 years of age, however, children are able to separate the whole into parts and put them back together as an internal operation. Behavioral models do not explain the development of these types of logical operations (Kamii, 1979).

Furthermore, developmental theorists assert that forcing development to occur by selectively reinforcing behaviors that are chronologically age-appropriate for a child is probably wasteful—if not harmful. Such is the case when children are expected to learn to read because they are 5 years old. If they do not yet have the cognitive structures to assimilate the new information, reading becomes a meaningless exercise for them. To memorize something without understanding it epitomizes teaching without learning. In addition, if a child is force-fed information that his cognitive perspective of the universe says is wrong, it may cause future conflicts in his perspective of reality.

Behaviorism may be viewed as a complement to certain aspects of developmental theory. When the cognitive structures for simple number concepts have developed, for example, repetition is the best way to learn counting and basic skills in arithmetic. Similar strategies from behavioral theory are effective for learning the alphabet and sight words.

Theories of development, while certainly distinct in description, are rarely applied in quite so secular a fashion by educators. Robinson and Robinson (1976) emphasize the utility of a more eclectic approach in relation to children with mental retardation:

> It is probably wise . . . to employ a number of concepts in considering the process of psychological development. Just as it is meaningful to characterize a mentally retarded child from etiological, behavioral, social, and educational perspectives, one need not be impatient if several theoretical systems prove useful in understanding behavior. (p. 242)

 Factors That Affect Cognitive Development

According to developmental theory, cognition unfolds gradually and in a consistent sequence as a function of maturation. Skills are modified and refined, however, as demanded by a child's needs to balance his interactions with the environment. We call this *equilibration*.

Many factors can interfere with the processes involved in the normal cognitive development of a child. Grossman (1977) classified them into nine groups: infection and intoxication, trauma or physical agents, metabolic or nutritional disorders, gross brain disease, unknown prenatal influences, chromosomal abnormalities, psychiatric disorders, gestational disorders, and environment. Some of these factors have a direct influence on the developing brain and may interfere with the transmission or processing of information. Others may impair a child's ability to receive or respond to information. Many of these factors were discussed in Chapter 2. This section addresses only environmental factors.

Cognition and the Environment

In 1961, Pasamanick and Knobloch proposed that children are susceptible to a continuum of damage as a result of reproductive complications. The damage may range from minor and undetectable trauma to significant serious disabilities affecting one's mental, physical, and emotional capacities. The researchers called this a *continuum of reproductive casualty* and identified five disorders related to reproductive casualty: epilepsy, behavior disorders, cerebral palsy, mental retardation, and reading disabilities (Pasamanick & Knobloch, 1966). Several years later, Sameroff and Chandler (1975) presented their continuum of caretaking casualty. They emphasized that a poor caretaking environment may similarly yield a range of deviant development outcomes for children. In fact, the influence of the environment on a child and the transactional nature of a child's relationship with those in the environment (Sameroff, 1979) are generally considered to be more potent and expansive than biological factors are in determining how a child will develop. Several longitudinal studies (Broman, Nichols, & Kennedy, 1975; Duncan, Brooks-Gunn, & Klebanov, 1994; Jordan, 1980; Werner & Smith, 1977) that followed thousands of children found that the effects of perinatal stress on intellectual status was greater in children from low socioeconomic areas. It is not the socioeconomic status itself that contributes to the child's poorer performance, but associated factors—less education of the parent(s), a greater likelihood of a single parent and a less stable home, and fewer educational materials in the child's environment.

A substantive body of research now exists that documents the positive influences on cognitive development when the environment is made more stimulating for the child (Rutter, 1979, 1980). Children moved from poor institutional settings into adoptive homes showed significant IQ gains (Dennis, 1973). Results from the Milwaukee Project (Garber & Heber, 1977) indicate that disadvantaged African-American children made IQ gains of as much as 20 points when an educational intervention program was provided. Other research shows similar consistency in pointing to a strong relationship between a supportive environment and measures of cognitive development (Baydar & Brooks-Gunn, 1991; Brooks-Gunn, Klebanov, & Liaw, 1995).

A child, however, is not a passive learner. A parent's approval and nurturing of the exploratory behavior of a child experimenting with his surroundings facilitate normal cognitive development in the child. A child's early social environment appears to be a better predictor of how development will progress than are biological factors at birth (Jordan, 1980). From the first visual and physical contact a parent has with a child, he asserts his influence on the parent. If the child shows extremes in temperament that conflict with the parent's personality, it creates a more adverse relationship between parent and child. A variety of other family and environmental characteristics also may cause stresses in the home. The traditional nature of parent-child relationships (i.e., the child and caregiver influencing and being influenced by the other) increases the likelihood that a single stress will lead to others (Rutter, 1979). Sameroff (1979, 1982; Sameroff & Fiese, 1990) has concluded that cognitive competence during the early years depends for much of its continuity not on the unfolding of innate capacities, but on environmental constraints.

Kearsley (1979) observed that some children may learn to be cognitively incompetent. He used the term *iatrogenic retardation* to describe children who have the potential for normal development—that is, who are structurally normal—but "whose development (has) taken place in an environment characterized by prolonged parental anxiety and inappropriate caretaking practices" (p. 155). For the past several decades, professionals concerned with early intervention have directed their efforts toward refining procedures and materials for stimulating the development of these children and others who are likely to have disabilities later in life. These efforts have generated programs for applying numerous theoretical and conceptual models that explain how infants develop and learn. The presumption upon which many of the approaches were founded was that the quality of the caregiver (parent or teacher) and the quality of the environment contribute to facilitating development and learning. By improving the input the infant received, the thinking went, development would be maximized within the biological and genetic limits of the child. This thinking had led to a plethora of curricula dedicated to this stimulus-based (or stimulation-oriented) approach (Mori & Neisworth, 1983).

Recently, there have been challenges to what had become the traditional approach to intervention with young children who are developmentally disabled. With the proposal of greater emphasis on co-occurrences in relation to young children's development—that is, the detection by children that two events occurring together or in close temporal proximity are associated—a new conceptual framework for intervention has evolved (Brinker & Lewis, 1982).

Piaget (1952) viewed the influence of co-occurrences on a child as having four aspects: They orient the child to aspects of the environment; they arouse the child and help to modulate his state; their detection provides satisfaction and confidence; and they exercise memory processes as the foundation for development of more-complex mental structures. These influences are most easily viewed within the context of parent-child interactions and, particularly, maternal responsiveness to a child's actions and cues. Recent studies, for example, provide evidence that in infants through 2 years of age, maternal responsiveness is significantly related to a child's development as measured by the Bayley Scales, and significantly more related to development than is maternal stimulation (Jaskir & Lewis, 1981; Lewis & Coates, 1980; Lewis & Goldberg, 1969). In addition, the quality of responsiveness is related to an infant's development (Coates & Lewis, 1980). These studies defined *stimulation* as the quantity of time the mother spent smiling at, holding, and talking to the child and *responsiveness* as the frequency of time the mother performed these behaviors immediately following the infant's actions. Quality was related to the type of responsiveness. Proximal responsiveness (touching, holding, and rocking) was positively correlated to Bayley scores in the youngest children. This relationship lessened as the children got older and the relationship between distal

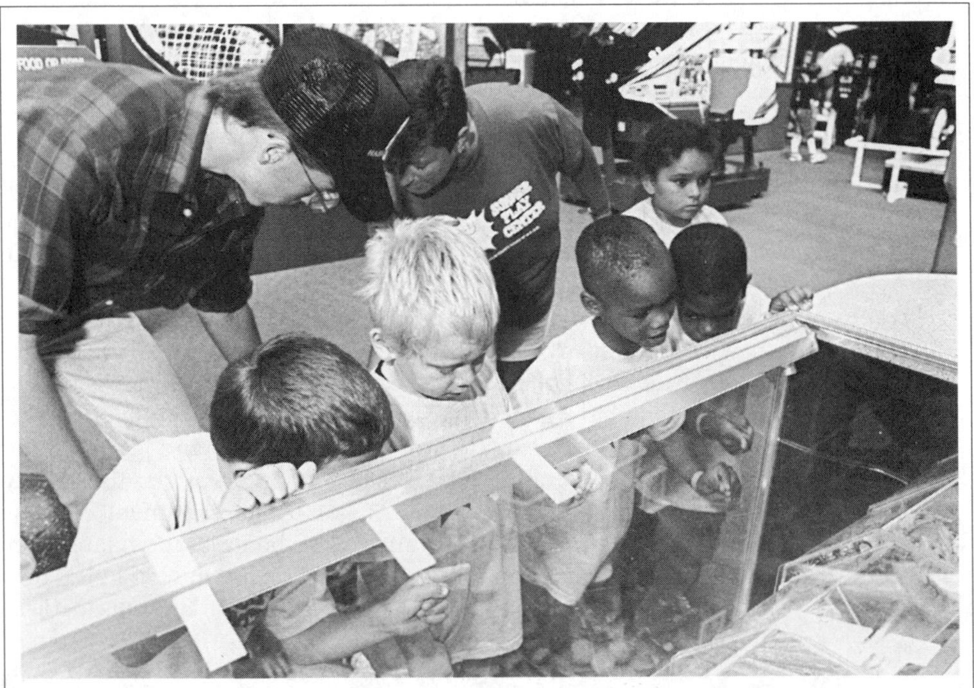

A stimulating environment is a positive influence on cognitive development.

responsiveness of the mother (talking to, looking at, and smiling at) and Bayley scores increased.

Although the relationship between a child's development and maternal responsiveness has not been shown to be causal in nature, a contingent environment facilitates important aspects of a child's cognitive development (Lewis & Rosenblum, 1974). Piaget's emphasis on a child's discovery of the environment during the sensorimotor period is founded on this concept. In the intact child, circular reactions provide the child with information about the nature of objects in the environment and his influence on them. In children with problems, detection of these simple relationships and more-complex relationships may be more fleeting and less available (Brooks-Gunn & Lewis, 1979; Detterman, 1979).

Thus, an unresponsive or stressful environment or one in which the expectations for a child are low may contribute to generalized retardation of cognitive development. A significant number of children with cognitive impairments probably fall into this category.

Cognitive Development and the Child with Special Needs

It is beneficial to consider, from time to time, the amazing ascent of a human being from the union of egg and sperm to a mature, cognitive being. With this perspective, we are better able to appreciate the plight of individuals with disabilities, who must function in a world that makes the same demands upon them as upon intact persons. Imagine a child who is congenitally blind trying to understand what an airplane is or what colors are. Consider how much worldly learning a child who is deaf misses or the social learning opportunities a child with physical disabilities never gets because he cannot participate in games and sports. Developmental theorists look upon the limitations in sensory experiences as restricting the growth and refinement of schemata. Cognitive learning advocates view the same limitations as restricting opportunities for appropriate behaviors to be reinforced, practiced, built upon, and generalized to other situations. From either perspective, a child with an impairment that limits his ability to receive, process, or respond to sensory information is likely to demonstrate delays or gaps in cognitive development.

Considerable research has investigated the effects of various disabilities on cognitive development. However, it contributes little to our understanding of children when they are described in broad categorical terms, such as "retarded" or "delayed." The following discussion therefore looks at the state of our knowledge regarding specific aspects of cognition in young children with disabilities.

Mental Retardation

The term *mental retardation* implies cognitive deficits. Much evidence points to problems in memory and attention being responsible for the subnormal performance of a child with an intellectual disability with that of his normal peers. In addition, differences in brain structure of children with disabilities might create these performance deficits (Raz et al., 1995).

Several theories have been proposed to explain memory deficits. Broadbent's (1958) limited buffer theory suggests that individuals with mental retardation have a smaller than normal capacity to store information, and that the addition of new information requires the purging of "old" information. The "bottleneck" theory was proposed by Tulving (1968); Slamecka (1968), in his elaboration of this theory, asserted that memory is impaired by the inability of a child to retrieve information, not by a limited storage capacity. This theory is supported by the superiority of our recognition memory skills over our recall skills. For example, consider a child who is shown a card with eight pictures on it and told to try to remember all the pictures, then the card is removed. The child will remember more pictures if he is given an opportunity to tell whether a certain picture was present or not (recognition memory) than if he must name the pictures he saw (recall memory). In comparisons of recognition memory of normal children and children with Down syndrome, the latter group still showed significant delays consistent with general developmental lag (Fantz, Fagan, & Miranda, 1975). McDade and Adler (1980) further extended the investigation of this problem by comparing visual and auditory memory skills in preschool-age children with Down syndrome. Their findings revealed limitations in the storage and retrieval of auditory information and severe impairment in the storage of visual information. The differential memory for visual and auditory information was consistent with other findings for young children (Rohwer, 1970), although the subjects with Down syndrome and the control subjects of the same mental age performed significantly worse than did normal subjects of the same chronological age.

Ellis (1970) proposed that memory problems are caused by the absence of rehearsal strategies and an inability to store information. Zeaman (1973) concurred with the rehearsal strategy hypothesis, but argued that the problem is not with storage but with the acquisition of information.

As noted earlier, acquisition of information first requires attention to the relevant stimulus. Some children who are severely impaired may be unaware of their surroundings and be unable to benefit from the stimulation that appears spontaneously in the environment. Environments of low-income children, on the other hand, may be abundant in stimuli that are often ambiguous or excessive (Bernstein, 1960; Wachs, Uzgiris, & Hunt, 1971). The inability of a child to orient and attend to relevant stimuli, particularly if they are complex or demanding, has been implicated as a cause for the poor performance of low-income children on cognitive tasks (Finkelstein, Gallagher, & Farron, 1980) and of infants exposed to cocaine (Mayes, Bornstein, Chawarska, & Granger, 1995). It is likely, however, that early intervention can minimize the impact of these factors.

Similar deficits appear to be inherent in children with mental retardation. Sustained attention to a stimulus requires two components: orientation, or awareness of the stimulus, and comparison and relating of the stimulus to other sensory input or stored information (Laucht, Esser, & Schmidt, 1994; Lewis 1971). From a Piagetian perspective, a child orients to a stimulus through arousal of one or more of the senses. He then compares the input with schemata for similar sensory information.

The inability of a child with mental retardation to retain or recall numerous or complex representations restricts the meaningful interpretation of new stimuli. Consequently, there is no motive for sustaining attention to that stimulus.

Visual Impairments

Piaget and Inhelder (1969) observed a hierarchy of deficits in the cognitive development of children who were blind from birth. Departures from normal development were most obvious during the third stage of the sensorimotor period, when children who were blind failed to reach for objects. Limitations in sensory experiences prevented these children from forming basic sensorimotor schemata. This affected their acquisition of higher-level cognitive skills.

Obviously, children who are blind and partially sighted do not gain the same perceptions of the nature of their environment as do children with sight. Their inability to be lured by objects that promote sustained attention and require them to change their physical position or to judge positions in space delays the development of object concept. Reaching and attaining an object that makes sound may not occur until late in the second year. Only then does a child begin mobility that facilitates his construction of the environment (Adelson & Fraiberg, 1976). Furthermore, pretend play occurs infrequently in children who are blind before 18 months of age, while it is common for their sighted peers (Preisler, 1995). Langley (1980) noted the following:

> Limited in independent mobility until approximately 19 months, the blind child is not able to explore various rooms of the house, to touch objects of interest, and to have them labeled. Unless the blind child is taught systematic scanning and exploration strategies, the similarities between objects and the ability to make generalizations may not develop. The absence of visual opportunities to associate tactual properties with auditory input often leads to meaningless rote verbalization. (p. 18)

Fraiberg (1968) and Warren (1984) found that object concept appears from 1 to 3 years late in children who are blind. Consequently, the lack of knowledge of the permanence of objects in space and critical relationships hinders progress in these children's cognitive development. A child who is unable to use vision to integrate auditory and tactile cues learns much later than sighted children how to maintain contact with his environment. Even very limited vision significantly alters how a child perceives and interacts with the world (Preisler, 1991).

Still, there is evidence that children who are and who are not visually impaired show approximate equivalence in certain concepts (Brekke, Williams, & Tait, 1974; Friedman & Pasnak, 1973). Reynell (1978) indicated that parallel development is most likely to appear at about 3 or 4 years of age, when logical thought begins to replace visual perception as the major learning process. Certainly, the abilities of people such as Helen Keller and Stevie Wonder show that visual impairments from early in life need not limit development of abstract thought. Children who are impaired from birth may develop complex cognitive skills if they are taught to make maximal use of action learning (Piaget & Inhelder, 1969; Rapin, 1979).

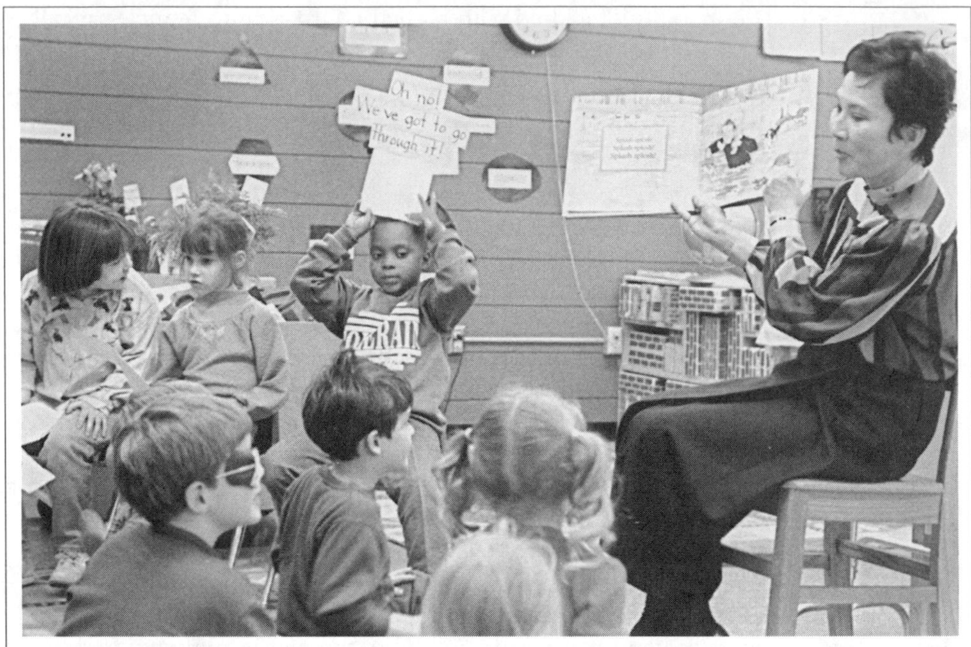

Limitations in visual experiences may prevent a child from forming basic sensorimotor schemata.

Hearing Impairments

Children with hearing impairments are more often identified by their failure to exhibit appropriate language milestones than by difficulties in sensorimotor or preconceptual abilities. This suggests that cognitive development can progress normally in the absence of hearing.

Much of the alienation from the environment of a child with a hearing impairment results from the influence of the impairment on language reception and production. Unfortunately, many tests of intelligence rely on language. Children with hearing impairments, therefore, may be erroneously identified as retarded. The negative reinforcement a child receives based on the lower expectations people have for him as a "retarded" child may contribute to a poorer performance. Blank (1974) found that children with hearing impairments also have the greatest difficulties with tasks for which instructions cannot be easily conveyed with gestures. A widening gap between the performance of children who do and do not have hearing impairments that occurs as they get older may result in part from the increasing complexity of instructions required for tasks at older ages. Meadow (1975) suggested that the cumulative effect of decreased cognitive stimulation and poor interpersonal relations contributes to poorer demonstrated performance by children with hearing impairments. Nevertheless, Best and Roberts (1976) reported that children who are deaf are equal to children who are not in the development of gestural imitation; they may actually be superior in the rate at which they learn to imitate (Wilbur, 1979). Furthermore, Schlesinger (1978) found that young children with deafness develop eye-hand coordination and fine motor skills more quickly than most children do, perhaps because they rely upon gestures for much of their communication.

Can we develop thought processes without language? Piaget (1952) and Vygotsky (1962) believed that the two develop along parallel and independent courses. "At a certain point these lines meet, whereupon thought becomes verbal and speech rational" (Vygotsky, 1962, p. 44). Furth (1966) expounded on the belief that a child does not need a linguistic symbol system to think. Furth's research, based upon Piaget's works, indicates that children with hearing impairments follow a normal course through the early stages of cognitive development. Beyond that, Furth concluded (1973), development is more similar to that of children from impoverished environments. He found no differences between children who did and did not have hearing impairments on simple visual memory tasks involving concrete objects, but greater differences were found when the task involved digits (Furth, 1961). Blair (1957) concurred that children with hearing impairments have greater difficulty on tasks of a more abstract nature. They are able to perform most classification tasks on a par with other children, but they have greater difficulty on tasks requiring analogy and superordinate reasoning in which problem solving requires a combination of concepts (Meadow, 1975).

This discussion demonstrates that doubts remain about how a hearing impairment affects cognitive development. In fact, poor research methodology has prevented a definitive answer. Templin (1950), for example, emphasized the critical nature of experience in determining the debilitating effects of language deficits on cognitive development. If such is the case, the relationship between language and thought must be reexamined. Jamieson (1994) applied Vygotsky's theoretical framework to the interactions between parents and their children who were deaf. She found that parents altered their mediational strategies to meet the child's evolving communicative needs. The degree to which the parent and child can jointly understand a task determines the extent of learning problems the child may have. We can conclude that, in the absence of a linguistic symbol system, children with hearing impairments have the potential to develop normally if their environment is contingently responsive, thereby enabling them to build an alternate system of symbolic representations.

Physical Impairments

A child's first years are ones in which he formulates a perception of the universe through action. A child who is unable to move freely is at a great disadvantage. He may miss the opportunity to see his arms and legs move about—at first, erratically, then in predictable, voluntary ways. He may be unable to manipulate objects or recognize his influence on the universe. He may not change position in order to view his surroundings from different perspectives.

Children with central nervous system damage, as in cerebral palsy and spina bifida, and children with chronic illnesses and orthopedic problems may perceive their universe in a different way from that of the typical child because of the limitations or uniqueness in how they interact with their surroundings. Preschool-age children with physical disabilities display lower levels of persistence on problem-solving tasks than their nondisabled peers do (Jennings, Conners, & Stegman, 1988).

Several British studies (Douglas, 1964; Rutter, Tizard, & Whitmore, 1970) and an American study (Wrightstone, Justman, & Moskovitz, 1953) revealed that children who are chronically ill are significantly behind normal children in academic achievement. Long periods in the hospital, lack of motivation, and negative feedback from environmental interactions account for at least some of the cognitive deficits.

It also has been estimated that approximately 75% of children with cerebral palsy have cognitive deficits; half of children with hydrocephalus and spina bifida have IQs under 80 (Young, Nulsen, Martin, & Thomas, 1973). As with children who are chronically ill, however, the impairment alone probably does not account for the total deficit. Severe language problems combined with limited movement create an atmosphere whereby we perceive children as being disabled because of their inability to communicate or perform appropriately. The insufficiency of traditional test instruments to assess cognitive functioning in the absence of adequate language and movement has led to inaccurate and sometimes harmful judgments about children. Some efforts have been made toward forming more-objective determinations about the cognitive functioning of children with severe physical impairments.

For example, Zelazo (1979; Zelazo, Hopkins, Jacobson, & Kagan, 1974) and Lewis (Brooks-Gunn & Lewis, 1979; Lewis & Baldini, 1979) used an attention paradigm to test children who were unable to respond to test items in traditional ways. *Habituation* is the term for the decrement in an individual's response to a repeatedly presented stimulus. When one is presented with a new or novel stimulus, attention to the stimulus and one's heart rate increase. After repeated presentations, attention wanes and heart rate decreases as one learns to anticipate the event. Monitoring attention and heart rate in children during repeated presentations of the same stimulus, followed by the introduction of a subtle variation and then a return to the original stimulus, enables the examiner to estimate a child's cognitive processing skills (Fagan, 1990). Cognitive level is a function of the speed with which a child habituates to the original stimulus, recognizes and dishabituates to the variation (evidenced by increased attention and heart rate), and recognizes the original stimulus when it is presented again by habituating more quickly (Zelazo, 1979).

Additional research has helped to specify the influence of physical impairment on various perceptual and cognitive tasks. Visual perception problems appear in children who have spent little time in an upright position. These children have difficulties performing form-board tasks (Berko, 1966), discriminating among various shapes, and organizing their spatial environment (Shurtleff, 1966). Poor visual and auditory perceptual skills of children with cerebral palsy have been attributed to the absence of the motor skills that train the visual and auditory systems. Rolling elicits visual pursuit, fusion, and accommodation of the lens to focus on objects at various distances. Poor muscle stability in the neck may inhibit visual fixation; poor stability in the shoulders and arms may cause poor reaching patterns. Similar types of deficits interfere with perceptual development (Rosenbaum, Barnett, & Brand, 1975) and later reading and writing skills (Shurtleff, 1966) of children with spina bifida.

Autism

Children with autism pose an interesting puzzle of perceptual and conceptual skill development. They have difficulty processing sensory input and, as a consequence, may show exaggerated responses or no response to stimuli. They may show no response even to intense auditory or visual stimuli, yet they may engage in rubbing textures, spinning objects, or scratching surfaces. Children with autism appear to show decreased visual fixation and attention, but they can receive information quite well through kinesthetic and tactile means. Ornitz and Rivto (1976) found children with autism to be skillful at tasks requiring fine motor manipulations. However, the fact that they treat very different objects and experiences in stereotyped ways (Rutter, 1978) probably limits the refinement of cognitive processes. The application of more-sophisticated assessment instruments (e.g., the attention paradigm described earlier) to large numbers of children with autism and the examination of behavioral self-regulation, task persistence, and perseverative tendencies (Adrien et al., 1995) may shed more light on the development of cognition.

Facilitating Cognitive Development

Children are born to learn. From their first noisy expression of hearty crying, they are storing and using information to make simple decisions. It is only when new information is no longer available in a form the child can use that cognitive development slows. This may represent an attitude of neglect on the part of the caregiver, for the nature of all children is to take advantage of the learning opportunities in their environment. Infants explore tactual stimuli with their hands, feet, and mouths, and slow their movements to listen to new sounds. Children with visual impairments gravitate toward auditory stimuli and children with hearing impairments toward those visual cues in their environment that carry new information. Children with mental retardation attend to complex stimuli around them when the input is simplified and clarified. In all situations in which a child is in an environment where he is unable to participate independently, the abilities of the teacher and caregiver grow in importance.

Many early intervention programs are founded on the belief that, if children are busy, they are learning. Paper and crayons, puzzles, pegboards, and shape boxes are placed before a child to stimulate learning. The teacher returns periodically to see whether the child has finished the task. When the paper is full of crayon marks, the puzzle pieces are in place, a peg fills each hole, or the shapes rest securely in the container, the child is praised for having learned. Has the teacher missed valuable opportunities to facilitate learning? Unquestionably!

With all young children, but particularly with those who are disabled, learning cannot be left to chance. We know, by studying disadvantaged children, that undesirable consequences result from poor caregiving strategies and a disorganized environment (Brooks-Gunn, Klebanov, & Liaw, 1995; Sameroff, Seifer, Baldwin, & Baldwin, 1993). We also know the benefits of a sound home environment. The distinctions between high and low quality in a child's home life also can be made in an educational program. As goes the parent, so goes the quality of the child's home life. Similarly, as goes the teacher, so goes the quality of the child's educational program. Fancy facilities and elaborate equipment may enhance a good program, but they cannot create one. An orientation toward the way a child does something rather than what he does is the basic approach that provides a cognitively stimulating environment.

In light of the glut of educational materials on the market today—some of which are promoted particularly for young children with disabilities—it is easy to conclude that equipment and curricular materials are the most important factors in facilitating cognition. But such is not the case. Materials are not as important as sound guidance is.

Focusing on the Process

While there are dozens of manuals on the market that contain teaching-learning activities for young children with special needs, they are of limited value to a limited audience. They may be helpful to educational technicians who lack the flexibility or the authority to tailor their approach to individual children's needs. They also may be useful for interventionists seeking ideas around which to develop their own activities. Restricting themselves to teaching by the numbers, however, may mean that interventionists' focus is on accomplishing an activity rather than on how children process information as the activity is presented. Fewell and Sandall (1983) have provided a review of curricula for young children with disabilities that emphasizes how children learn and develop rather than just what they learn.

As the following incident reveals, the facilitation of development depends largely on the interventionist's awareness of how children use learning experiences:

> *Carrie, a 4-year-old with cerebral palsy, was having a grand time painting the carton with blue and yellow paint. In some places on the carton the colors had mixed, producing a vivid green color. "What color is that?" the teacher asked. "It's green," Carrie responded. "Where did you get green paint?" the teacher asked with a smile. Carrie looked at her containers of blue and yellow paint, and her bright eyes reflected the thoughtful activity taking place behind them.*

Education is often more concerned with the product than with the process of learning. Is it any wonder, then, that children have difficulty applying concepts and skills in different appropriate situations? Carrie would have produced a very colorful carton that she might have played with or that might have been hung from the ceiling as a mobile. She would then have gone on to another activity. With the minimal intervention of the teacher in the learning process, however, it is more likely that Carrie will now experiment with mixing other colors of paint. She may mix them in different proportions and begin to experiment with controlling color shades and tones. She may even extend the concept to mixing fluids or different colors of sand, thereby learning other principles about the attributes of matter.

Skills of the Interventionist

Good interventionists and caregivers are notable for their consistent and nurturing approach with children. Beyond that, however, they exhibit specific skills that are particularly effective in facilitating cognitive development. These skills are useful with all children, but their application may differ when the child is disabled (Hawkins, 1979).

Use Materials and Activities That Catch and Sustain a Child's Interest. As discussed earlier, attention is a prerequisite for learning. To attract a child's attention to a specific object or task, we must win the competition with many other stimuli in the environment that are also vying for the child's attention. The primary consideration is appropriate positioning of the child. Equipment should be modified or created to place the child in a position in which he is most free to move and most in contact with his surroundings. Stimuli can then be modified to maximize the child's awareness.

With very young children and children with severe disabilities, increasing the intensity of a stimulus may be sufficient to draw their attention. Loud sounds may improve auditory attention, bright colors and lights may attract visual attention, and varied textures may enhance attention for grasping and manipulation. With older children and children who are less severely disabled, novel variations of familiar activities are most likely to hold their interest. The hazard in using the same familiar tasks over and over is that, although children may retain the skill longer as a result of overlearning, responses reach only the very basic rote level of cognition. There are decreasing incentive and challenge to apply skills in new ways to accomplish the very same task. When an activity is changed slightly during subsequent presentations, benefits may include accelerated cognitive development and better generalization of skills to varied situations. Play at a sand table becomes even more exciting and stimulating when new measuring devices and containers are substituted for the familiar ones. The listening center holds a child's interest when there are new sounds and pictures to match. A new puppet that requires finer manipulations than the old ones do may visit the dress-up area and stimulate many new skills and concepts.

Select Activities with Intrinsic Termination Points. One interventionist prided herself on integrating prevocational skills into her preschool classroom. She had the children sand a block of wood for 10 minutes each day, after which they punched holes in soft leather for 5 minutes. The utter futility of the task would be obvious if one watched the children's attention meander the entire time. The teacher made two fatal errors. First, she provided a task totally out of context to what is meaningful to children. Had she shown the children a toy wagon or a set of blocks that would result from their efforts, the activity might have had some merit. Her second error was not building in a point of successful termination. Time, an extraneous element in the activity, is not an appropriate reason for ending a task. What logic is there for a child when, working through a task, the teacher says that time is up? Each task should be in the form of a problem or challenge for which the child must find a resolution. An activity should not be ended until there is resolution and the child is aware of it. With the sanding task, the teacher could have colored an area on the block with a marker. The children could then have sanded until the marker's color was no longer visible. With the hole punching, she could have outlined holes in geometric patterns, numbers, or letters, and the children could have stopped when the pattern was complete.

In teaching children to control their own behavior, it is desirable that they rely on the teacher as little as possible for continuous directions. While it is good teaching strategy to provide guidance, feedback, and reinforcement to each child, it is equally important to offer developmentally appropriate activities that provide the child with feedback from his own performance and the knowledge of when he has solved the problem. This best occurs, of course, with activities of the self-testing variety. With these, a child knows whether he has performed the task correctly and, if not, he can try another approach immediately. During this phase and at the completion of the task, the teacher can investigate the cognitive processes leading to the child's solution. This is a difficult but necessary skill for interventionists to master.

Use Language as a Cognitive Tool. A substantial body of literature supports the close link between language and thought. For a child to perceive relationships and attain development of concepts, he must have labels to represent objects, people, and feelings. The teacher must provide these word labels for the child until he is able to utilize them to synthesize thoughts and to solve problems. The interventionist who names new objects for a child, describes what that child or other children are doing, gives names to feelings, and discusses the relationships among things and events in the child's environment is contributing to language competence in the child and, therefore, to development of cognitive skills.

Ask the Child Questions That Provide Challenge and Satisfaction. When a child has created a clay structure or paste-up and the teacher responds with "What's that?" it gives the child a clear message. What the child thought to be a realistic imitation of an object or person is not good enough to be identified as such by the teacher. A more reinforcing and thought-provoking response, whether the teacher recognizes the child's creation or not, is "I like what you made. Tell me about it." This approach gives the child a feeling of worth, while allowing the teacher to investigate the development of the child's skills.

The key ingredients in a good teacher's response to a child's task are acknowledgement of the child's efforts and extraction of the child's problem-solving strat-

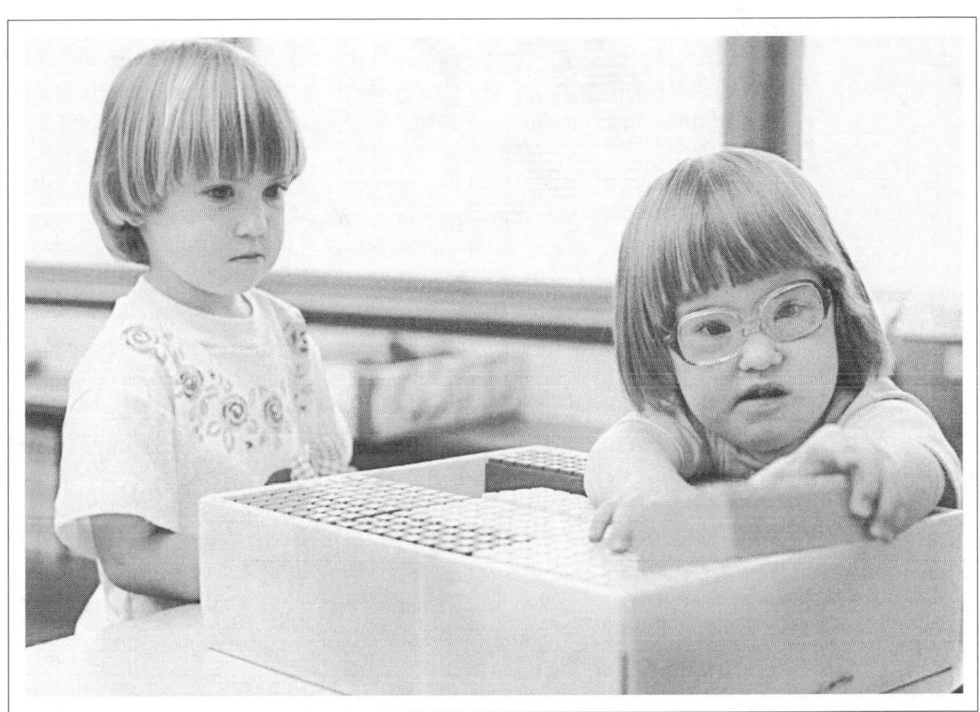

Children learn more quickly and retain information better when a multisensory approach is used—one combining two or more senses in the learning activity.

egy. Was it just luck that allowed a child with a visual impairment to place the round shape in the round slot and not the square or triangular slot, or did the child use a particular strategy to place it correctly? "Good, Joan. Why does that round shape go where you put it?" the teacher should ask.

With children who are nonverbal, the challenge to the teacher is greater. In these cases, the teacher may verbalize through the problem-solving process and demonstrate the strategies leading to a correct response. For example, "Good, this pile has pictures of things we eat and this pile has pictures of things we eat with." Or, "Let's do it again so that one pile has things we eat and another pile has things we eat with. I'll do the first ones; now you do the rest."

Questions should be nonjudgmental and purposeful—not "Why did you do it like that?" but rather "Why do you think those go together?" Put yourself in the place of a child. Given a task to perform, consider the logic involved and the variety of ways to perform the task. Then try to determine the child's approach to performing the task by asking questions that reveal the child's strategy.

Allow for Learning Through Discovery and for the Child to Choose Learning Tasks. In European schools, one rarely finds materials stored away in cabinets or on high shelves. The Montessori approach, begun in Italy, advocates the availability and accessibility of materials to children in the classroom. Through exploration and teacher guidance, children learn what materials are on and off limits to them, how to use new materials, and how to select materials of interest to them.

Discovery is important in the development of cognitive skills. Through exploration, children assimilate information about the order of their surroundings. In many programs, teachers demonstrate how to use new and challenging pieces of equipment, such as graded cylinders or matrix puzzles. They give children an opportunity to work on the task with guidance and then place it in an accessible location so the children may use it at other times. This move toward nurturing independence can work very well with young children with disabilities. However, when interventionists tell children what to do or give them every task to perform, they deprive the children of the rich developmental opportunities that discovery and independent decision making provide.

Some children have difficulty selecting tasks. The following progression indicates how children at different developmental levels can be challenged to participate in activity selection.

1. Let's paint. (noncommunicative child)
2. Do you want to paint? (verbal or nonverbal response acceptable)
3. Do you want to paint or play at the sand table? (verbal, imitative response; the list of choices can be expanded)
4. Show me what you would like to do now. (nonverbal, open-ended response)
5. Tell me what you would like to do now. (verbal, open-ended response)

Children at any level of development can be included in the scheme of selecting and discovering through their own initiative. For this to occur, they must feel secure moving about in their environment (aided by consistency of objects' locations), and materials must be accessible to them. Finally, the interventionist can help children to discover how materials are used, where they are located, and what pleasures they hold. For example, children with visual impairments should be able to expect that their tactual materials are arranged on specific shelves, with the least-difficult items on the lower shelves. Similar patterns may be established for children with other disabilities.

Identify and Utilize Each Child's Primary Input Mode. All learners show a differential preference for receiving and processing information; some learn more effectively from auditory input, and others from tactile or visual input. Children with disabilities are not excluded from this learning characteristic, but if the preferential input mode is the locus of the impairment, learning may be considerably more difficult. The adaptability of young children makes it incumbent upon the interventionist to take advantage of input channels through which accurate information is likely to be received and to nurture and stimulate the secondary input channels that are the site of the impairment.

Young children and children with severe disabilities learn initially through movement. The kinesthetic stimulation of one's arms and legs moving in space, along with watching them move and hearing the sounds of objects they touch or strike, offers the initial learning experiences for a child. Physical movement remains an important mode of learning throughout life.

Education tends to become more and more auditory as a child progresses through formal schooling. Many children discover that they learn more from textbooks or field trips than they do from lectures. Children with disabilities show the same individual differences in how they learn. Consequently, interventionists must be flexible in their approaches. One child may learn a task quickly with a verbal explanation. Another child may require demonstration as well as verbal explanation or may have to be moved through the task, hand-over-hand. Interventionists should, therefore, give careful consideration to how children process different forms of input and use this information in their instructional strategies.

Structuring the Curriculum

The most important criterion for program success is a staff made up of people who know how to teach. Nevertheless, interventionists also must be able to organize the educational program so that it includes aspects that are most beneficial to children's intellectual growth.

Utilizing the structure of Lavatelli (1973) outlined earlier, a program should help children progress from a concrete to a symbolic level in classification, space and number, and seriation operations, from which all concepts are constructed. These may be used as the focus for activities in early intervention programs. The teacher also can organize materials based upon the same principles. Puzzles can be ordered by difficulty based not only on the number of pieces, but also on the spatial complexities of the position of pieces. Different groups of objects and pictures can be available for children to sort or classify. Some groups can contain objects that are very different and other groups can have objects or pictures with only subtle differences. Children can be given dolls to hold that are progressively bigger in size or can be asked to draw another one that is smaller, and then one that's even smaller. Containers at the water table can be color-coded to correspond with the daily color of the water to which food dye has been added. An infant can be given different-sized bottles from which to drink his milk.

If activities are considered in terms of the cognitive processes they require or nurture, program planning can yield more individualization and challenge for children. The works of Lavatelli (1973) and Weikart, Rogers, Adcock, and McClelland (1971) provide more specific activities utilizing this approach.

Summary

For all children, the road to understanding and using complex concepts is quite similar. Children first learn about their worlds by their looks, smells, sounds, tastes, and feel. By seeing how different people and objects in their environments interact, children begin to formulate basic constructs of their worlds based on the simple relationships they perceive. As they add word labels to their experiences and observations, their understanding of the world increases significantly.

A disability may interrupt the cognitive process in four ways: It may interfere with a child's ability to attend to a stimulus, as in a neurological or sensory impairment; it may impede reception of potentially valuable stimuli, as in a visual or hearing impairment; it may disrupt the storage and processing of information, as in brain damage associated with mental retardation; and it may interfere with a child's ability to express his cognitive abilities, as in speech disorders and orthopedic impairments. A Piagetian framework was emphasized in this chapter because it helps us to interpret children's cognitive development even in light of these extreme differences. Furthermore, it provides the interventionist with a foundation from which to plan a program based on a child's current level of performance rather than on his chronological age.

The skills that have been described are caregiver skills and cannot be considered the province of the interventionist alone. Through home visits, parent participation in the classroom, and other broad strategies that include all of the caregivers, the child will be the beneficiary of an environment that has the potential to maximize intellectual development.

References

Adelson, E., & Fraiberg, S. (1976). Sensory deficit and motor development in infants blind from birth. In Z. S. Jastrzembska (Ed.), *The effects of blindness and other impairments on early development*. New York: American Foundation for the Blind.

Adrien, J. L., Matrineau, J., Barthelemy, C., Bruneau, N., Garreau, B., & Sauvage, D. (1995). Disorders of regulation of cognitive activity in autistic children. *Journal of Autism and Developmental Disorders, 24,* 249–263.

Baydar, N., & Brooks-Gunn, J. (1991). Effects of maternal employment and child-care arrangements on preschoolers' cognitive and behavioral outcomes: Evidence from the children of the National Longitudinal Study of Youth. *Developmental Psychology, 27,* 932–945.

Berko, M. J. (1966). Psychological and linguistic implications of brain damage in children. In M. Mecham, F. G. Berko, M. F. Berko, & J. Palmer (Eds.), *Communication training in childhood brain damage*. Springfield, IL: Charles C Thomas.

Bernstein, B. (1960). Language and social class. *British Journal of Sociology, 2,* 271–276.

Best, B., & Roberts, G. (1976). Early cognitive development in hearing impaired children. *American Annals of the Deaf, 121,* 560–564.

Blair, F. X. (1957). A study of the visual memory of deaf and hearing children. *American Annals of the Deaf, 102,* 254–263.

Blank, M. (1974). Cognitive functions of language in the preschool years. *Developmental Psychology, 10,* 229–245.

Bower, T. G. R. (1974). *Development in infancy*. San Francisco: Freeman.

Brekke, B., Williams, J. E., & Tait, P. (1974). The acquisition of conservation of weight by visually impaired children. *Journal of Genetic Psychology, 125,* 89–97.

Brinker, R. P., & Lewis, M. (1982). Discovering the competent handicapped infant: A process approach to assessment and intervention. *Topics in Early Childhood Special Education, 2,* 1–16.

Broadbent, D. (1958). *Perception and communication.* London: Pergamon Press.

Broman, S. H., Nichols, P. L., & Kennedy, W. A. (1975). *Preschool IQ: Prenatal and early developmental correlates.* Hillsdale, NJ: Erlbaum.

Brooks-Gunn, J., Klebanov, P. K., & Liaw, F. (1995). The learning, physical, and emotional environment of the home in the context of poverty: The Infant Health and Development Program. *Children and Youth Services Review, 19,* 251–276.

Brooks-Gunn, J., & Lewis, M. (1979, Sept.). Handicapped infants and their mothers at play. Paper presented at the annual meeting of the American Psychological Association, New York.

Coates, D. L., & Lewis, M. (1980, Apr.). Relationships between cognitive behavior at six years and mother-infant interaction at three months. Paper presented at the International Conference on Infant Studies, New Haven, CT.

Dennis, W. (1973). *Children of the Creche.* New York: Appleton-Century-Crofts.

Detterman, D. K. (1979). Memory in the mentally retarded. In N. R. Ellis (Ed.), *Handbook of mental deficiency, psychological theory and research.* Hillsdale, NJ: Erlbaum.

Douglas, J. W. B. (1964). *The home and the school.* London: Mackgibbon & Kee.

Duncan, G. L., Brooks-Gunn, J., & Klebanov, P. K. (1994). Economic deprivation and early childhood development. *Child Development, 65,* 296–318.

Ellis, N. R. (1970). Memory processes in retardates and normal infants. *International Review of Research in Mental Retardation, 4,* 1–32.

Fagan, J. F. (1990). The paired-comparison paradigm and infant intelligence. *Annals of the New York Academy of Sciences, 608,* 337–364.

Fantz, R. L., Fagan, J. F., & Miranda, S. B. (1975). Early visual selectivity as a function of pattern variables, previous exposure, age from birth and conception, and expected cognitive deficit. In L. B. Cohen & P. Salapatek (Eds.), *Infant perception: From sensation to cognition, Vol. 1.* Basic visual processes. New York: Academic Press.

Ferguson, C. A. (1978). Learning to pronounce: The earliest stages of phonological development in the child. In F. D. Minifie & L. L. Lloyd (Eds.), *Communicative and cognitive abilities: Early behavioral assessment.* Baltimore: University Park Press.

Fewell, R. R. & Sandall, S. R. (1983). Curricula adaptations for young children: Visually impaired, hearing impaired, and physically impaired. *Topics in Early Childhood Special Education, 2,* 51–66.

Finkelstein, N. W., Gallagher, J. J., & Farron, D. C. (1980). Attentiveness and responsiveness to auditory stimuli of children at risk for mental retardation. *American Journal of Mental Deficiency, 85,* 135–144.

Flavell, J. H. (1963). *The developmental psychology of Jean Piaget.* Princeton, NJ: VanNostrand.

Flavell, J. H. (1970). Developmental studies of mediated memory. In H. W. Reese & L. P. Lipsitt (Eds.), *Advances in child development and behavior, Vol. 5.* New York: Academic Press.

Fraiberg, S. (1968). Parallel and divergent patterns in blind and sighted infants. *Psychoanalytic Study of the Child, 23,* 264–300.

Fraiberg, S. (1975). The development of human attachments in infants blind from birth. *Merrill-Palmer Quarterly, 21,* 315–334.

Friedman, J., & Pasnak, S. (1973). Attainment of classification and seriation concepts by blind children. *Education of the Visually Handicapped, 5,* 55–62.

Furth, H. G. (1961). Visual paired-associates task with deaf and hearing children. *Journal of Speech and Hearing Research, 4,* 172–177.

Furth, H. G. (1966). *Thinking without language: Psychological implications of deafness.* New York: Free Press.

Furth, H. G. (1973). *Deafness and learning: A psychosocial approach.* Belmont, CA: Wadsworth.

Garber, H. & Heber, F. R. (1977). The Milwaukee Project: Indications of the effectiveness of early intervention in preventing mental retardation. In P. Mittler (Ed.), *Research to practice in mental retardation, Volume 1.* Care and intervention. Baltimore: University Park Press.

Gibson, E. J. (1969). *Principles of perceptual learning and development.* New York: Appleton-Century-Crofts.

Gindis, B. (1995). The social/cultural implication of disability: Vygotsky's paradigm for special education. *Educational Psychologist, 30,* 77–81.

Grossman, H. J. (Ed.). (1977). *Manual on terminology and classification in mental retardation.* Washington, DC: American Association on Mental Deficiency.

Hauser-Cram, P. (1996). Mastering motivation in toddlers with developmental disabilities. *Child Development, 67,* 236–248.

Hawkins, F. P. (1979). The eye of the beholder. In S. Meisels (Ed.), *Special education and development: Perspectives on young children with special needs.* Baltimore: University Park Press.

Jamieson, J. R. (1994). Teaching as transaction: Vygotskian perspectives on deafness and mother-child interaction. *Exceptional Children, 60,* 434–449.

Jaskir, J., & Lewis, M. (1981, Apr.). A factor analytic study of mother-infant interactions at 3, 12, and 24 months. Paper presented at the annual meeting of the Eastern Psychological Association, New York.

Jennings, K. D., Conners, R. E., & Stegman, C. E. (1988). Does a physical handicap alter the development of mastering motivation during the preschool years? *Journal of the American Academy of Child and Adolescent Psychiatry, 27,* 312–317.

Jordan, T. E. (1980). *Development in the preschool years: Birth to age five.* New York: Academic Press.

Kagan, J., & Kogan, N. (1970). Individual variation in cognitive processes. In P. Mussen (Ed.), *Carmichael's manual of child psychology, Vol. 1.* New York: Wiley.

Kahn, J. (1976). Utility of the Uzgiris and Hunt Scales of sensorimotor development with severely and profoundly retarded children. *American Journal of Mental Deficiency, 80,* 663–665.

Kamii, C. (1979). Piaget's theory, behaviorism, and other theories in education. *Journal of Education, 161,* 13–33.

Kearsley, R. B. (1979). Iatrogenic retardation: A syndrome of learned incompetence. In R. B. Kearsley & I. E. Sigel (Eds.), *Infants at risk: Assessment of cognitive functioning.* Hillsdale, NJ: Erlbaum.

Langley, M. B. (1980). *The teachable moment and the handicapped infant.* Reston, VA: ERIC Clearinghouse on Handicapped and Gifted Children.

Laucht, M., Esser, G., & Schmidt, M. H. (1994). Contrasting infant predictors of later cognitive functioning. *Journal of Child Psychology, Psychiatry, & Allied Disciplines, 35,* 649–662.

Lavatelli, C. S. (1973). *Piaget's theory applied to an early childhood curriculum.* Nashua, NH: Delta Education, Inc.

Lewis, M. (1971). Individual differences in the measurement of early cognitive growth. In T. Hellmuth (Ed.), *Exceptional infants: Studies in abnormality, Vol. 2.* New York: Bruner/Mazel.

Lewis, M., & Baldini, N. (1979). Attention processes and individual differences. In G. Hale & M. Lewis (Eds.), *Attention and cognitive development.* New York: Plenum Press.

Lewis, M., & Coates, D. L. (1980). Mother-infant interactions and cognitive development in 12-week old infants. *Infant Behavior and Development, 3,* 95–105.

Lewis, M., & Goldberg, S. (1969). Perceptual-cognitive development in infancy: A generalized expectancy model as a function of the mother-infant interaction. *Merrill-Palmer Quarterly, 15,* 81–100.

Lewis, M., & Rosenblum, L. (Eds.). (1974). *The effect of the infant on its caregiver.* New York: Wiley.

Liben, L. S. (1982). The developmental study of children's memory. In T. M. Field, A. Huston, H. C. Quay, L. Troll, & G. E. Findley (Eds.), *Review of human development.* New York: Wiley.

Maccoby, E. E., & Zellner, M. (1970). *Experiments in primary education: Aspects of Project Follow-Through.* New York: Harcourt Brace Jovanovich.

Mayes, L. C., Bornstein, M. H., Chawarska, K., & Granger, R. H. (1995). Information processing and developmental assessments in 3-month-old infants exposed prenatally to cocaine. *Pediatrics, 95,* 539–545.

McClinton, B. S., & Meier, B. G. (1978). *Beginnings: Psychology of early childhood.* St. Louis: Mosby.

McDade, H. L. & Adler, S. (1980). Down syndrome and short-term memory impairment: A storage or retrieval deficit? *American Journal of Mental Deficiency, 84,* 561–567.

Meadow, K. P. (1975). The development of deaf children. In E. M. Hetherington (Ed.), *Review of child development research, Vol. 5.* Chicago: University of Chicago Press.

Mori, A. A. & Neisworth, J. T. (1983) Curricula in early childhood special education: Some generic and special considerations. *Topics in Early Childhood Special Education, 2,* 1–8.

Nelson, K. (1973a). Some evidence for the cognitive primacy of categorization and its functional basis. *Merrill-Palmer Quarterly, 19,* 21–39.

Nelson, K. (1973b). Structure and strategy in learning to talk. *Monographs of the Society for Research in Child Development, 38,* (Serial No. 149).

Ornitz, E. M. & Rivto, E. R. (1976). Medical assessment. In E. R. Rivto (Ed.), *Autism: Diagnosis, current research and management*. New York: Spectrum.

Parker, S. T. (1993). Imitation and circular reactions as evolved mechanisms for cognitive construction. *Human Development, 36,* 309–323.

Pasamanick, B., & Knobloch, H. (1961). Epidemiologic studies on the complications of pregnancy and the birth process. In G. Caplan (Ed.), *Prevention of mental disorders in children*. New York: Basic Books.

Pasamanick, B., & Knobloch, H. (1966). Retrospective studies on the epidemiology of reproductive casualty: Old and new. *Merrill-Palmer Quarterly, 12,* 7–26.

Piaget, J. (1951). *Play, dreams and imitation in childhood*. New York: Norton.

Piaget, J. (1952). *The origins of intelligence in children*. New York: International Universities Press.

Piaget, J. (1954). *The construction of reality in the child*. New York: Basic Books.

Piaget, J., & Inhelder, B. (1969). *The psychology of the child*. New York: Basic Books.

Pick, A. D., Frankel, D. G., & Hess, V. L. (1975). Children's attention: The development of selectivity. In E. M. Hetherington (Ed.), *Review of Child Development Research, Vol. 5*. Chicago: The University of Chicago Press.

Preisler, G. M. (1991). Early patterns of interaction between blind infants and their sighted mothers. *Child: Care, Health, and Development, 17,* 65–90.

Preisler, G. M. (1995). The development of communication in blind and deaf infants—similarities and differences. *Child: Care, Health, and Development, 21,* 79–110.

Rapin, I. (1979). Effects of early blindness and deafness on cognition. In R. Katzman (Ed.), *Congenital and acquired cognitive disorders*. New York: Raven Press.

Raz, N., Torres, I. I., Briggs, S. D., Spencer, W. D., Thornton, A. E., Loken, W. J., Gunning, F. M., McQuain, J. D., Driesen, N. R., & Acker, J. D. (1995). Selective neuroanatomic abnormalities in Down's syndrome and their cognitive correlates: Evidence from MRI morphometry. *Neurology, 45,* 356–366.

Reynell, J. (1978). Developmental patterns of visually handicapped children. *Child: Care, Health, and Development, 4,* 291–303.

Robinson, N. M. & Robinson, H. B. (1976). *The mentally retarded child*. New York: McGraw-Hill.

Rogoff, B., Malkin, C., & Gilbride, K. (1984). Instruction with babies as guidance in development. In B. Rogoff & J. V. Wertsch (Eds.), *Children's learning in the "zone of proximal development."* San Francisco: Jossey-Bass.

Rohwer, W. (1970). Images and pictures in children's learning. *Psychological Bulletin, 73,* 393–403.

Rommetveit, R. (1985). Language acquisition as increasing linguistic structuring of experience and symbolic behavior contrast. In J. V. Wertsch (Ed.), *Culture, communication, and cognition: Vygotskian perspectives*. New York, Cambridge University Press.

Rosenbaum, P., Barnett, R., & Brand, H. L. (1975). A developmental intervention program designed to overcome the effects of impaired movement in spina bifida infants. In K. S. Holt (Ed.), *Movement and child development*. Philadelphia: Lippincott.

Rossi, S., & Wittrock, M. C. (1971). Developmental shifts in verbal recall between mental ages two and five. *Child Development, 42,* 333–338.

Ruff, H. A. (1982). The development of object perception in infancy. In T. M. Field, A. Huston, H. C. Quay, L. Troll, & G. E. Finley (Eds.), *Review of human development*. New York: Wiley.

Rutter, M. (1978). Language disorder and infantile autism. In M. Rutter & E. Schopler (Eds.), *Autism: A reappraisal of concepts and treatment*. New York: Plenum Press.

Rutter, M. (1979). Maternal deprivation 1972–1978: New findings, new concepts, new approaches. *Child Development, 50,* 283–305.

Rutter, M. (1980). The long-term effects of early experience. *Developmental Medicine and Child Neurology, 22,* 800–815.

Rutter, M., Tizard, J., & Whitmore, K. (1970). *Education, health, and behavior*. London: Longmans, Green.

Sameroff, A. J. (1979). The etiology of cognitive competence: A systems perspective. In R. B. Kearsley & I. E. Sigel (Eds.), *Infants at risk: Assessment of cognitive functioning,* Hillsdale, NJ: Erlbaum.

Sameroff, A. J. (1982). The environmental context of developmental disabilities. In D. D. Bricker (Ed.), *Intervention with at-risk and handicapped infants: From research to application*. Baltimore: University Park Press.

Sameroff, A. J. & Chandler, M. J. (1975). Reproductive risk and the continuum of caretaking casualty. In F. D. Horowitz (Ed.), *Review of child development research, Vol. 4.* Chicago: University of Chicago Press.

Sameroff, A. J. & Fiese, B. H. (1990). Transactional regulation and early intervention. In S. J. Meisels & J. P. Shonkoff (Eds.), *Handbook of early childhood intervention*. New York, Cambridge University Press.

Sameroff, A. J., Seifer, R., Baldwin, A., & Baldwin, C. (1993). Stability of intelligence from preschool to adolescence: The influence of social and family risk factors. *Child Development, 64,* 80–97.

Schlesinger, H. S. (1978). The hearing impaired. In N. B. Enzer & K. W. Goin (Eds.), *Social and emotional development: The preschooler.* New York: Walker.

Shurtleff, D. T. (1966). Timing of learning in meningomyelocele patients. *Journal of the American Physical Therapy Association, 46,* 136–148.

Silverstein, A. B., McLain, R. E., Brownless, L., & Hubbey, M. (1976). Structure of ordinal scales of psychological development in infancy. *Educational and Psychological Measurement, 36,* 355–359.

Slamecka, N. (1968). An examination of trace storage in free recall. *Journal of Experimental Psychology, 76,* 504–513.

Stremmel, A. J., & Ru, V. R. (1993). Teaching in the zone of proximal development: Implications for responsive teaching practice. *Child and Youth Care Forum, 22,* 337–350.

Templin, M. (1950). *The development of reasoning in children with normal and defective hearing*. Minneapolis: University of Minnesota Press.

Tessier, F. (1969/70). The development of young cerebral palsied children according to Piaget's sensorimotor theory. *Dissertation Abstracts International, 30A,* 4841.

Trevarthen, C. (1988). Infants trying to talk. In R. Söderbergh (Ed.), *Children's Creative Communication*. Lund, Sweden: Lund University Press.

Tulving, E. (1968). Theoretical issues in free recall. In T. Dixon & D. Horton (Eds.), *Verbal behavior and general behavior theory*. Upper Saddle River, NJ: Prentice Hall.

Vygotsky, L. S. (1962). *Thought and language*. Cambridge, MA: MIT Press.

Vygotsky, L. S. (1978). *Mind in society: The development of higher psychological process*. Cambridge, MA: Harvard University Press.

Wachs, T. D., Uzgiris, I. C., & Hunt, J. McV. (1971). Cognitive development in infants of different age levels and from different environmental backgrounds. *Merrill-Palmer Quarterly, 17,* 282–317.

Warren, D. H. (1984). *Blindness and early childhood development (2nd edition: revised).* New York: American Foundation for the Blind.

Weikart, D. P., Rogers, L., Adcock, C., & McClelland, D. (1971). *The cognitively oriented curriculum*. Washington, DC: NAEYC.

Weisz, J. R., & Zigler, E. (1979). Cognitive development in retarded and nonretarded persons: Piagetian tests of the similar sequence hypotheses. *Psychological Bulletin, 86,* 831–851.

Werner, E. E., & Smith, R. S. (1977). *Kauai's children come of age*. Honolulu: University of Hawaii Press.

Wilbur, R. B. (1979). *American sign language and sign systems*. Baltimore: University Park Press.

Wrightstone, J. W., Justman, J., & Moskovitz, S. (1953). *Studies of children with physical handicaps: The child with cardiac limitation*. New York: City Board of Education.

Young, H. F., Nulsen, F. E., Martin, H. W., & Thomas, P. (1973). The relationship of intelligence and the cerebral mantle in treated infantile hydrocephalus. *Pediatrics, 52,* 38–44.

Zeaman, D. (1973). One programmatic approach to retardation. In D. K. Routh (Ed.), *The experimental psychology of mental retardation*. Chicago: Aldine.

Zelazo, P. R. (1979). Reactivity to perceptual-cognitive events: Application for infant assessment. In R. B. Kearsley & I. E. Sigel (Eds.), *Infants at risk: Assessment of cognitive functioning*. Hillsdale, NJ: Erlbaum.

Zelazo, P. R., Hopkins, J. R., Jacobson, S. M., & Kagan, J. (1974). Psychological reactivity to discrepant events: Support for the curvilinear hypothesis. *Cognition, 2,* 385–393.

Zelazo, P. R., & Kearsley, R. B. (1977, March). Functional play: Evidence of a cognitive metamorphosis in the year-old infant. Paper presented at the Biennial Meeting of the Society for Research in Child Development, New Orleans.

7

Communication

Susan R. Easterbrooks

The ability to communicate, like good health, is a trait we take for granted until something goes wrong. Communication permits us to express our basic needs, provides a vehicle through which we can learn about the world, and fosters our functioning as social beings. In order to communicate, we must organize our thoughts and represent them in mutually agreed upon ways that allow us as speakers to share our thoughts with listeners. Children who are delayed in communication, for whatever reason, lack these abilities and are at risk within a demanding and changing world.

Listening to normally developing toddler language is a charming experience, and the errors that an infant or toddler makes during the language development process are a constant source of delight to adults. The preschool years are those during which language acquisition unfolds. By the time children enter school, they are using all the sentence types produced by adults (Menyuk, 1971). According to Chomsky (1957), the critical period for language acquisition is before the age of 5. Youngsters whose parents have recognized their special needs early in childhood are very fortunate, because intervention can be initiated before these precious years of learning have passed.

Language: A Framework and Definitions

Communication

The term *communication* refers to exchanging information and ideas. Communication can occur vocally, nonvocally, gesturally, pictorially through sign language or written language, or through any number of representational systems (e.g., rebus pictures and Blissymbolics). A child who cannot speak may indeed have language, and a child who is not able to use oral language can learn to communicate.

Speech

Speech is defined as the auditory-articulatory code by which we represent spoken languages. Speech includes phonation and articulation of the specific phonemes (the sounds of letters and letter combinations) of a language. Disorders of speech include but are not limited to articulation, dysfluency (stuttering), and voice disorders such as hoarseness or harshness. However, speech is not the only means by which we represent language.

Language

Language, as defined by Bloom and Lahey (1978) is a "code whereby ideas about the world are represented through a conventional system of arbitrary signals for communication" (p. 4). In spoken language, we represent this code through numerous conventional systems, including phonology, morphology, syntax, semantics, and pragmatics. Some children have difficulty mastering a first language because of problems with these systems. Others have difficulty because the language spoken at home differs from the language spoken at school or by the larger community. Others must learn signed or coded forms of English (e.g., Signing Exact English or Cued Speech); still others must learn American Sign Language, which is a distinctly separate language from signed forms of English.

Language is a subject that has both perplexed and fascinated scholars. It has been studied from many perspectives. In the late 1950s, a major change from a structural to a linguistic perspective occurred in the literature, with the appearance of landmark research and publications by such experts as Noam Chomsky (1957) and Jean Berko (1958). Since that time, many authors have written about the areas of phonology, morphology, syntax, semantics, and pragmatics. Historically, the investigation of children's language has differentially emphasized these components in the sequence in which they are listed. Literature on the language of children with disabilities has emphasized different components, depending upon the disabling condition under consideration. This section discusses language used by typical children.

Phonology

In the late 1950s and 1960s, phonological, morphological, and syntactic research was in the forefront of studies on language. Chomsky and Halle (1968) studied the phonological components of language, which are the sound patterns of speech, or the articulatory-acoustic properties that allow us to represent our thoughts. Phonology is speech per se. Jakobson (1968) proposed that the phonemes of any language, that is, the basic units of speech sounds, can be classified in terms of their articulatory and acoustic properties, and that these features are universal. Figure 7.1 indicates the ages by which most children acquire specific use of phonemes. Knowledge of the expected sequence of development is crucial in determining appropriate intervention goals.

Morphology

Morphology is the study of the smallest meaningful units of language, such as *-ed*, *-s,* and *un-*. Berko (1958), in one of the original studies on morphology, devised a task for eliciting grammatical morphemes with nonsense sentences and pictures. For example, in one task, a researcher showed a picture of an animal that looked like a bird to a child, then a picture of two animals. The examiner said "This is a wug. Here are two ____." The examiner then asked the child to supply the missing word. Other tasks based on the cloze procedure were used to study a number of grammatical morphemes and to chart their developmental sequence.

Delineation and development of morphemes were further specified by Brown (1973). The mean length of utterance (MLU), or the average number of morphemes in an utterance, is a popular way of quantifying language (deVilliers & deVilliers,

FIGURE 7.1 Latest ages at which most children acquire specific phoneme use

3 Years
m (mama)
n (nose)
p (pat)
t (toy)
k (kite)
b (baby)
d (duck)
h (hot)
w (water)
g (go)

4 Years
j (yellow)

5 Years
ʤ (jump)

6 Years
r (red)
l (little)
ʧ (choo-choo)
ŋ (ring)

7 Years
θ (this)
ð (think)
s (sun)
ʃ (shock)
v (vase)
z (zipper)

Source: Data from *Oral Communication Problems in Children and Adolescents,* 2nd ed., by S. Adler and D. A. King Eds., 1994, Boston: Allyn & Bacon; "Articulation Development in Children Aged Two to Four Years" by E. M. Prather, D. Hedrick, & A. Kern, 1972, *Journal of Speech and Hearing Disorders, 37,* pp. 55–63; and *Certain Language Skills in Children,* by M. Templin, 1957, Minneapolis: University of Minnesota Press.

1978). The MLU is considered to be a good indicator of potential language problems (Sharf, 1972) because it correlates with many aspects of syntactic development (Brown, 1973). It also is better than age as an indicator of language growth up to the 5-MLU level. Figure 7.2 lists Brown's rules for calculating MLU.

Syntax

Syntax is the aspect of language that pertains to the organizational rules of utterances. We generally equate syntax with grammar and include phrase structure rules (e.g., basic sentence patterns), transformational operations (e.g., passive voice and conjoining), and morphological rules (e.g., pluralization and noun-verb agreement) (Muma, 1978). Lennenberg (1967) postulated that individuals innately possess a *language acquisition device* that permits language development. This device encodes meaning as the deep structure of an utterance. The actual utterance is termed the *surface structure.* The speaker generates certain basic phrase structure rules, which undergo numerous transformations between the deep structure and the surface representation. For example, applying a passive voice transformation to the deep structure "John hit Mary." allows the speaker to generate the sentence "Mary was hit by John." Upon learning these rules, individuals are able to generate an infinite number of utterances according to Lennenberg (1967). Figure 7.3, presented later in this chapter, lists specific syntactic structures.

FIGURE 7.2 *Rules for calculating the MLU of a child's spontaneous production*

Gather a sample of the child's spontaneous production of speech. Start with the second page of the transcription. Count the first 100 utterances that meet the following criteria:

1. Use fully transcribed utterances.
2. Include all repetitions except stuttering. Count each word once in the most complete form produced.
3. Do not count such fillers as *hmm* or *oh,* but do count *uh-huh, yeah,* and *hi.*
4. All compound words (two or more free morphemes), proper names, and ritualized reduplications count as single words. Examples are *birthday, choo-choo, night-night,* and *pocketbook.*
5. Count as one morpheme all irregular past tenses of verbs. Examples are *ran, say,* and *got.*
6. Count as one morpheme all diminuitives. Examples are *doggie* and *blankey.*
7. Count as separate morphemes all auxiliaries. Examples are *is, have, will, could,* and *were.* Also count catenatives, such as *gonna, wanna, hafta,* and *otta.*
8. Count as separate morphemes all verb inflections, including possessive *-s,* third-person singular *-s,* regular past tense *-ed,* and progressive tense *-ing.*

Source: Adapted from *A First Language: The Early Stages* by R. Brown, 1973, Cambridge, MA: Harvard University Press. Copyright 1973 by Harvard University Press. Adapted by permission.

Semantics

With the publication of Bloom's (1970) study of the semantic development of three children, a shift toward a semantic perspective took place (McLean & Snyder, 1977). Semantics deals with the denotative and connotative meanings of words. Bloom found that children talked consistently about certain relationships among people, places, objects, and actions. Semantics is the study of meaning and content; that is, what one is talking about. Researchers call the object, event, or interaction to which we refer the *referent* (Bates, Camaioni, & Volterra, 1975; Bloom & Lahey, 1978; Clark & Clark, 1977; Ervin-Tripp, 1978; Lucas, 1980). Lucas defines *referent* as "an object, action, or event that may be specified and thus denoted or tagged in meaning" and "specifying or marking an object, action, or event through linguistic terms" (p. 244). Bloom and Lahey expand this definition to include words that describe how these objects and events are related both to themselves and to other objects and events. The ways in which a child labels referents differ as the child gets older. However, no matter by what vehicle the child refers to the world, a common core of experiences must occur between the child and significant others (Bruner, 1974). During normal conversations, adults typically label objects, events, and relationships that form the child's lexicon, or vocabulary (Clark, 1974; Ervin-Tripp, 1978). A rich base of experiences with the world is essential to the language acquisition process. Without experiencing objects and events and how they relate, a child has nothing to which a marker or lexical item can be attached. Semantic relationships used at the one- and two-word utterance stage are outlined in Table 7.1. Semantic

TABLE 7.1 Descriptions of Semantic Relationships

TYPE	DEFINITION	EXAMPLE
Agent	Performer or initiator of an action	*Brian* kissed Sara.
Entity	Object or person in a state of being or changing	Sara *is* cute. She *became* tired.
Object/Patient	Receiver of an action	William teased *Chelsea.*
Recipient	Receiver of an object	Lee gave *Chloe* a cookie.
Action	Transitive verb	Victoria *hit* William.
	Intransitive verb	Chloe *cried.*
Process	Transitive verb	Chelsea *wants* a cookie.
	Intransitive verb	Brian *dreams.*
Stative	Verb indicating a state or condition	William *was* hungry.
Possessor	Indicates ownership	It's *Sara's* toy.
Vocative	The person to whom statements are addressed	*Mommy,* watch me.
Existence	Acknowledges that a person or object is noticed	*Hi,* puppy.
Nonexistence	Acknowledges that a person or object is not present	Mommy *not* home.
Recurrence	Indicates repetition	Sandy wants *more* fruit.
Disappearance	Indicates that a person or object previously present is now absent	My headache is *gone.*
Denial	Denies any or all parts of a sentence	I *don't* want a cookie.
Rejection	Indicates rejection of something presented	The baby is *not* wet.
Attribute	Includes such descriptors as size, shape, color, age, quality, quantity, position, function, length, type, hue, weight, and texture	William is *handsome.*
Location/Position	Tells where someone or something is	Put it *there.*
Manner	Tells how something happened	Cheryl drove *quickly.*
Time	Tells when	We went *in the morning.*
Frequency	Tells how many, how often, etc.	Victoria swims *every day.*
Duration	Tells how long something occurred	Chelsea played *all afternoon.*
Purpose	Tells for whom	Sandy baked *Brian* a cake.
Intensifier	Heightens the concept	You are *too* little.
Inclusion	Indicates that current event is to continue	May I go *too?*
Question forms	Asks questions about all semantic cases previously listed	I'm right, *aren't I?*

*This table contains a partial list of the semantic cases that appear most frequently in preschool children's language. A more comprehensive listing can be found by consulting Goldsworthy (1982) and others.

Sources: Data from *Language Development and Language Disorders* by L. Bloom and M. Lahey, 1978, New York: Wiley, *A First Language: The Early Stages* by R. Brown, 1973, Cambridge, MA: Harvard University Press; *Examiner's Manual: Multilevel Informal Language Inventory* by C. Goldsworthy, 1982, Upper Saddle River, NJ: Merrill/Prentice Hall; "Bare Essentials in Assessing Really Little Kids (BEAR): An Approach" by M. S. Hasenstab and J. Laughton, 1982. In M. S. Hasenstab and J. S. Horner, Eds., *Comprehensive Intervention with Hearing-Impaired Infants and Preschool Children* (pp. 203–318), Rockville, MD: Aspen Systems; *Language Development and Intervention with the Hearing Impaired* by R. R. Kretschmer and L. W. Kretschmer, 1978, Baltimore: University Park Press; and *Language Handbook: Concepts, Assessment, Intervention* by J. R. Muma, 1978, Upper Saddle River, NJ: Prentice Hall.

study generally takes the form of observing the repertoire of meaningful referents (things we talk about) as well as the earliest of referent relationships (Lucas, 1980). Semantic study is especially pertinent to the fields of preschool development and special education; thus, the early interventionist should become familiar with this subject.

Pragmatics

Pragmatics refers to the psychosocial dynamics around which we base the use of language (Muma, 1978). The early works of Dore (1974, 1975), Bates (1976), and Halliday (1975) defined pragmatics, and their notions still form the basis for many taxonomies of pragmatic skills today. Pragmatic skills are outlined and defined in Table 7.2. Pragmatics involves teaching a child when and where to use language, not just what or how to say it.

The speech act is considered to be the basic unit of pragmatics, just as the morpheme is the basic unit of morphology and syntax (Austin, 1962; Searle, 1969). The speech act is composed of the doing aspect (utterance act), the meaning component (propositional act), and the function (illocutionary act). Each speech act has an underlying communicative intent that is referred to as the *illocutionary force of the sentence* (Clark & Clark, 1977). For example, when a mother says "Maybe we can do that later." to her child, she has performed an utterance act. Her meaning or proposition is to put a child's request off for later action. The function or illocutionary act of this response is to regulate behaviors. The illocutionary force of the sentence, her underlying intent, is "no."

Several theorists have suggested outlines for common speech acts. According to Dore (1975), children's speech acts include labeling (giving the word for an object), repeating (saying back what an adult has said), answering (responding to an adult's question), requesting (asking for something by gesture, information, or word), calling (loudly addressing someone by name), greeting (showing recognition of a person), protesting (resisting or denying adult action), and practicing (doing or speaking for one's own sake).

An infant uses language in many ways. From 9 to 18 months of age, these uses, as described by Halliday (1975), are instrumental (I want), regulatory (do as I tell you), interactional (implies two people communicating), personal (marking the child's existence), heuristic (indicates curiosity), imaginative (pretending), and informational (providing information to the listener). Halliday described three more uses that emerge between 18 and 24 months of age: interpersonal (or pragmatic), intrapersonal (or mathetic), and ideational (problem solving). From 2 to 3 years of age, a child responds to contingent queries (Gallagher, 1977). A child uses a contingent query to clarify the meaning of what someone has said. Children at this age also can engage in rapid topic change (Shulman, 1985). The 3-year-old is very competent at code switching (Sachs & Devin, 1976), produces contingent queries to maintain conversations (Garvey, 1975), and is temporarily able to assume the perspective of another person through language (Selman, 1971). The concepts of discourse and code switching are relevant to understanding pragmatics. When we speak with another person, our current utterance is tailored by what was previously uttered and by what we are trying verbally to express. This is generally referred to as *discourse,* which Ripich and Creaghead (1994) define as the content needs associated with utterances "the size of any extended stretch of structured language beyond a single unit ranging from pairs of utterances to text structure or classroom lessons" (p. 1). Discourse can take the form of monologues or dialogues.

TABLE 7.2 Aspects of Pragmatic Language

COMMUNICATIVE BEHAVIOR	EXAMPLE
Mutual gaze	Child looks back and forth between mother and object until mother looks at object and labels it.
Repair of failed message	If initial signal does not yield desired results, child repeats, expands, or adds gesture or emotion.
Ritualized gestures	Often accompanied by insistent sounds; child makes mock attempt to reach or engage in some action.
Mutuality	Both partners are mutually engaged in interaction.
Reciprocity	Communicative action of one partner influences communicative action of the other.
Synchronicity	Each partner makes continuous adjustments of timing and intensity.
Turn taking	Mutual give and take in communication.
Whispering	Partners mutually exclude others.
Hints	Child makes round-about request.
Opens conversation	Child initiates communication.
Sustains topic	Child controls the conversation.
Changes topic	Child controls the conversation.
Closes conversation	Child terminates communication.
COMMUNICATIVE INTENTION	EXAMPLE
Attention seeking	Child solicits attention by tugging, imploring, saying “mama,” etc.
Requesting	Child gestures, vocalizes, and verbalizes to demand action, information, or object.
Protesting	Child resists action or object.
Commenting	Child verbally, vocally, or gesturally directs another’s attention.
Greeting	Child ritually notices another.
Answering	Child responds.
Teasing, taunting	Child teases, warns, or conveys emotion.
KNOWLEDGE OF CONTEXT	EXAMPLE
Physical setting	Child changes communication behaviors in different settings.
Audience	Child changes communication behaviors with different partners.

Sources: Data from “The Acquisition of Performatives Prior to Speech” by E. Bates, L. Camaioni, and V. Volterra, 1975, *Merrill-Palmer Quarterly, 21,* pp. 205–206; “The Origins of Reciprocity: The Early Mother-Infant Interaction” by T. B. Brazelton, B. Koslowski, and M. Main, 1974. In M. Lewis and L. A. Rosenblum, Eds., *The Effect of the Infant on Its Caregiver,* New York: Wiley; *A First Language: The Early Stages* by R. Brown, 1973, Cambridge, MA: Harvard University Press; “Facilitation of Mother-Infant Communication” by R. N. Clark and R. Siefer, 1983, *Infant Mental Health Journal, 4,* pp. 67–82; “The Communicative Intention Inventory: A System for Coding Children’s Early Intentional Communication” by R. Coggins and R. Carpenter, 1981, *Applied Psycholinguistics, 2,* pp. 235–252; *Test of Pragmatic Language* by D. Phelps-Terasaki and T. Phelps-Gunn, 1992, Austin, TX: Pro-Ed.; and “Assessing the Pragmatic Abilities of Children, Part I: Organizational Framework and Assessment Parameters” by F. Roth and N. Spekman, 1984, *Journal of Speech and Hearing Disorders, 49,* pp. 2–11.

Conducting a conversation, while seemingly effortless, actually requires a complex set of practical skills. The first of these is turn taking. Before any kind of conversation takes place, the speakers must agree to certain characteristics of an interchange that result in orderliness. If these rules are violated, orderliness ceases, and the result is that we are unable to communicate with our conversational partner. Conversational partners must take turns, and these turns are well specified (Sacks, Schegloff, & Jefferson, 1974).

A set of communicative turns is referred to as an *adjacency pair.* Common, early adjacency pairs include the following:

ADJACENCY PAIRS	EXAMPLE
opening	**Mom:** Good morning. **Child:** Hi.
question-answer	**Mom:** Are you hungry? **Child:** Uh-huh!
greeting-greeting	**Mom:** Hi. **Child:** Hi.
offer-acceptance/rejection	**Mom:** Do you want a cookie? **Child:** No.
assertion/acknowledgement	**Mom:** Sit down. **Child:** No.
compliment-acceptance/rejection	**Mom:** You're my big boy! **Child:** No, I not!
request-grant	**Child:** Want ball. **Mom:** Here it is.
summon-answer	**Child:** Mama! **Mom:** What, sweetie?
closing	**Child:** Nite-nite. **Mom:** Sleep tight.

Each of these pairs serves a unique pragmatic function or purpose. In addition, the opening (Schegloff, 1968) and closing (Schegloff & Sacks, 1973) of a conversation have specific sets of rules for their execution.

To be a competent speaker, a child not only must engage in all the functions of language mentioned in the preceding list but also must code these syntactically in forms that seem appropriate to the recipient of the conversation (Gallagher & Dornton, 1968; Muma, 1978). Adults typically switch the code of their language when talking to young children. For example, one adult might say to another "Where did you find that dress?" but might code the same intention by saying to a child "Oh look! You have a pretty new dress. Did Mommy get it for you?" Comments to an adult and to a child are not always interchangeable.

The effort to deal with pragmatic issues of language has made considerable progress in recent decades. Lucas (1980), Simon (1981), and Gallagher and Prutting (1983), among others, have outlined pragmatic skills and recommended remediation procedures in this area.

Form, Content, and Use

Bloom and Lahey (1978) devised a framework that attempts to organize the components of language in a meaningful and useful fashion. They outlined taxonomies in the areas of language form, content, and use. Bloom and Lahey view language as the interactions among the component parts of form, content, and use. The form of language is comprised of phonology, morphology, and syntax; the content of language is often referred to as *semantics;* and the use of language includes functions and contexts, or pragmatics. The taxonomies of form and content represent fairly accurate compilations of our current knowledge in these areas, although more-recent work in the area of pragmatics requires an update on the taxonomy of use. When the participants in communication can comprehend and produce each of the components in its proper relationship and in an integrated fashion, they are said to have achieved communicative competence (Simon, 1981).

Stages of Normal Language Acquisition

Any discussion of delays must be based on concepts of normalcy, whether the subject is social, emotional, motor, or language development. In order to understand what is different, we first must understand what is normal. Normal language development may be viewed from the perspective of Bloom and Lahey's (1978) concepts of form, content, and use. Traditionally, language has been viewed as developing through a series of stages: the babbling stage, the jargon stage, the holophrastic stage, the telegraphic stage, the stage of overgeneralizations, and the stage of standard form. These forms emerge best when they are developed from a rich base of experiences. A child must experience the world for language to hold any meaning.

Prelinguistic and Babbling Stage

Long before they utter their first words, infants are able to refer to the world around them through their bodies (Bates, Camaioni, & Volterra, 1975). Infants express what they mean by such prelinguistic means as gazing, crying, touching, smiling, laughing, vocalizing, grasping, and sucking, which Bates (1976) calls "perlocutionary acts." Infants also engage in what Bates terms "illocutionary acts" such as vocalizing, using intonation, and grunting, as well as nonverbal behaviors such as giving, pointing, and showing. Bates and Johnston (1977) feel that the number of illocutionary acts an infant uses is a good prognostic indicator of later language ability. Studying an infant's perlocutionary and illocutionary skills is helpful in determining any need for intervention.

One of the first ways in which adults interact with infants beyond meeting their physical needs is to coo and babble back and forth with them. Sharing sounds in this way is an important precursor to further linguistic development. During the babbling period, an infant vocalizes an increasing number of sounds in various combinations. During the first 3 months, an infant produces a variety of vowel-like sounds that are primarily of a reflexive nature (Owens, 1996). Because these early sounds are at the reflex level, most infants with disabilities are able to babble. However, for various reasons, some infants stop babbling and do not move into the next stage. Once a child has developed the cortical ability to inhibit responses, the second stage of babbling occurs, in which we see a peak in the use of labials (*p, b,* and *m*) and dentals (*t, d,* and *n*) combined with vowels. Children's first words are often in the form of reduplications of consonant-vowel combinations (Dale, 1972) such as "mama" for *mother* and "bubu" for *brother.* Children next move into echolalic babbling, in which they begin their attempts at imitating the pitch and contour patterns of other speakers in their environment (deBoysson-Bardies, Sagart, & Durand, 1984).

Jargon

During the jargon stage, which may begin as early as 9 months of age, children continue to develop strings of utterances that carry the stress and intonational patterns of adult speech (Menyuk, 1971). They appear to be talking but say no distinguishable words. In this stage of variegated babbling, children babble a variety of vowel-consonant patterns. Changing experiences influence the continued development of children's babblings (Hilke, 1988). The variegated babbling stage overlaps with both the one-word stage and the telegraphic stage, and children often produce strings of inflected babbling with a real word included. Jargon usually disappears by 2 years of age (Trantham & Pedersen, 1976).

Holophrases

Recognizable words are uttered by children at around 1 year of age (Dale, 1972; Menyuk, 1971; Owens, 1996). A child who uses one-word utterances is said to be in the holophrastic stage. During this phase, a child can say only single words, but each word may represent any number of concepts that adults would typically differentiate in longer sentences. For example, the word *ball* might mean "I want the ball," "I have the ball," or "The dog is chasing the ball." Adults usually recognize the meaning of a word by the context of the situation and by the child's intonation. However, as every parent who has experienced a child screaming "Ball! Ball! Ball!" knows, context and intonation are not always enough to make meaning apparent.

Another characteristic of words at this stage is that they must be able to assist a child in causing change (Nelson, 1973). Words such as *tree* and *chair* are not very common in early vocabularies because children's use of these words is not likely to bring about much change. However, the use of words such as *milk, blanket,* and *ball* are likely to result in some kind of action.

Not only are words in the holophrastic stage associated with change and likely to have a number of referents, but also these words are often overextended. When a child does not know the specific lexical item for a particular referent, she uses familiar words as a substitute, thus overextending the actual meaning of that particular marker (Clark, 1973). For example, the word *Mama* may refer to all the child's caregivers, as well as to her mother. Children often apply concepts of shape when referring to something for which they have no label (Clark & Clark, 1977). For example, the word *ball* may be applied to a toy, an orange, or the moon. Other concepts that form the basis for overextensions are movement, size, sound, texture, and taste. Sometimes overextensions are qualified to foster clearer understanding, as in the case of a young child referring to a horse as a "yeahee cow," whereby "yeahee" is used to describe the horse's whinny and *cow* is the closest word the child knows for the animal.

Shortly after children begin to label objects, they begin to use spatial prepositions and adjectives. Clark (1973) proposed a theoretical model that accounts for the acquisition of spatial terms. Studying this model will assist the early interventionist in understanding why spatial prepositions and adjectives are hard to learn. The model also assists in determining which words to teach first. If a child experiences disruptions in perception of location in space, spatial terminology will be extremely problematic (Lucas, 1980). One reason that time concepts are so difficult for children is that they often are represented by spatial metaphors. For example, one might say to a child "Are you through with your book?" The child, who has only a concrete understanding of the word *through,* may wonder why anyone would expect her to squeeze through a book.

Children who have difficulty learning language also have problems with figurative terms and expressions. In an unpublished study by the author, parents of children as young as 12 months were found to use a variety of figures of speech. The most commonly used figure of speech, noticed in the language of parents of children from 12 to 36 months, was what this author refers to as a presimile. A simile is the use of the structure "The (noun) is/looks like a (noun)." as in the sentences "The fog is like a cloud on the ground." and "The cloud looks like a bunny." Parents of very young children prepare their youngsters for this kind of comparison by using this structure: "The (noun) is/looks like (person) + possessive marker + noun," in which the person in the sentence is someone known well to the child. An example of this is when a mother points to a picture and says, "Look, his tractor is like Paw-Paw's tractor" or "She has shoes like Sissy's shoes." Possession and well-known participants are hallmarks of this structure and were found in the language of virtually every parent of the 27 youngsters studied.

Telegraphic Language

As the jargon and holophrastic stages phase out, the telegraphic stage appears. Brown (1973) and his colleagues (Brown & Fraser, 1963) compared the early word combining of young children with the message in a telegram, in which pronouns, prepositions, articles, conjunctions, and auxiliary verbs are left out to reduce the cost. For example, a sentence such as "I will be arriving at noon on the train from Boston." might be shortened to "Arrive noon Boston train." Likewise, as young children learn to put words together, they leave out extraneous language and preserve the nouns and verbs.

Uninflected verbs are a notable characteristic of the telegraphic stage. Children who use telegraphic speech leave out all the structures of the auxiliary system of the verb. The auxiliary system is comprised of the morphological elements that determine tense and noun-verb agreement. Children also leave out verb expansions and the determiner system (e.g., *a* and *the*) and say, for example, "Baby fall down." or "Puppy chase car."

The auxiliary system develops during the period from 18 months to 3 years of age. This system carries the tense of verbs. In generative and transformational grammar theory, tense is defined as being either past or present. The future tense is carried by structures called *modals,* which include *will, can, may,* and other similar terms. Three small words—*do, be,* and *have*—are actually quite complex because they can function as main verbs or as auxiliary verbs.

Another development that occurs during this period is children's use of the infinitive, often referred to as the *infinitive complement* (e.g., I want to play). The use of the infinitive becomes more and more confusing as the number of subjects and objects in the sentence increases. Table 7.3 charts the development of the verb and auxiliary systems.

Overgeneralizations

Overlapping the stages of telegraphic speech and adult grammar is a period during which children overgeneralize the use of structures they have just learned (Ervin-Tripp, 1964). For example, although children begin to use specific irregular verbs at a very young age, they often overgeneralize the use of the regular marker *-ed,* as in "runned" for *ran,* "bringed" for *brought,* and "hided" for *hid,* and even add an *-ed* to some irregular forms, thereby producing "satted" for *sat* and "sawed" for *saw.* Children also overgeneralize plural forms, as in "foots," "mouses," and "mans."

Basic Sentence Structure

Following the development of all semantic categories and the verb and auxiliary systems, children move into higher-order transformations of basic sentence patterns. Figure 7.3 outlines the five basic sentence patterns and transformations that complete children's journeys toward the use of adult forms.

The normally developing child uses all of these structures by age 4 (Menyuk, 1971). Thus, it requires only 2 or 2 1/2 years from the time the child is uttering telegraphic sentences until she uses complex systems that approximate adult forms. The rapid development of normal communication in such a brief period of time is truly remarkable. Never again does a child learn a skill of such magnitude in so little time.

All the areas of language are closely intertwined. A deficit in one area can lead to a deficit in another. Careful diagnosis of all components is essential in planning appropriate remediation.

Theories of Communication Development

As in all avenues of study, various theories have developed to explain the phenomenon of communication development. While each theory has had its heyday, in fact, children demonstrate various aspects of each as they approach the formidable task of learning to communicate. The four major theories of language acquisition are described in the following paragraphs.

Behavioral Theory

The behavioral theory, associated most notably with Skinner (1957), holds that language is a subset of learned behaviors and, as such, is learned through a process of reinforcement. It begins as a set of mands, or statements, that specify their own reward (e.g. "Want drink!"); tacts, or labels; intraverbals, or replies; and autoclitics, or sentence frames. Through a process of modeling, imitation, practice, and selective reinforcement, a child is said to learn to chain these pieces together to form

TABLE 7.3 Normal Development of the Verb and Its Auxiliary System

PATTERN	EXAMPLE	AGE AT WHICH PATTERN BEGINS TO EMERGE
Uninflected verb (no auxiliaries used)	Doggie eat bone.	By 18 months
Imperative	Jump! Stop!	16–18 months
Agent-Action	Bird fly.	18–26 months
Action-Object	Hit doggie.	18–26 months
Is copula	He is funny.	18–27 months
Is auxiliary	Doggie eating dinner.	Begins using without *is* by 24 months
	Muffy is eating dinner.	Established by 35 months
Irregular past (stabilized later than regular)	I ran.	By 25 months
Simple infinitive (*to* deleted)	I wanna go. (want to)	By 26 months
Am auxiliary	I am running.	By 28 months
Regular past	Kitty jumped.	By 29 months
Will (in answer to questions)	I will.	By 30 months
Modal *will*	He will cry.	By 30 months
Can	I can get it.	By 31 months
Would (in answer to questions)	I would.	By 31 months
Gerund	Swimming is fun.	By 32 months
Are copula	They are cute.	By 33 months
Are auxiliary	They are chasing him.	By 33 months
Have noun	He has got big eyes. (emerges as "He gots big eyes." but becomes refined after 3 years)	By 33 months
Infinitive noun phrase	She's trying to make it.	By 33 months
Alternative subject infinitives	He wants John to play.	By 33 months
Am copula	I am a boy.	By 35 months
Do	I do it!	By 36 months (*don't* comes at least 6 months before *do*)
Did	I did it!	By 36 months
Was copula	It was big.	By 36 months
Should	You should see this.	By 3 years
Could	He could play with me.	By 3 years
Was copula	He was tired.	By 3 years
Were copula	They were old.	By 3 years
Might	I might go.	After 3 years
Must	You must try.	After 3 years
Was auxiliary	Daddy was throwing the ball.	After 3 years
Were auxiliary	They were swimming.	After 3 years
Passive voice	The ball was hit by the bat.	After 36 months
Had better	You had better sit down.	After 36 months

Sources: Data from "The Development of Auditory Comprehension of Language Structure in Children" by M. A. Carrow, 1968, *Journal of Speech and Hearing Disorders, 33,* pp. 99–111; *Psychology and Language* by H. Clark and E. Clark, 1977, New York: Harcourt Brace Jovanovich; "Normal and Retarded Children's Understanding of Semantic Relations in Different Verbal Contexts" by J. Duchan and J. Erickson, 1976, *Journal of Speech and Hearing Research, 19,* pp. 767–776; "Origins of Language Comprehension" by J. Huttenlocher, 1974. In R. Solso, Ed., *Theories in Cognitive Psychology,* Hillsdale, NJ: Erlbaum; *The Acquisition and Development of Language* by P. Menyuk, 1971, Upper Saddle River, NJ: Prentice Hall; *Normal Language Development* by C. R. Trantham and J. K. Pedersen, 1976, Baltimore: Williams & Wilkins; and *Language Assessment and Intervention for the Learning Disabled* by E. H. Wiig and E. M. Semel, 1980, Upper Saddle River, NJ: Merrill/Prentice Hall.

FIGURE 7.3 Sentence types, patterns, and transformations

Sentence Types	**Examples**
Declarative (.)	John is a boy.
Imperative (!)	Pick that up!
Question (?)	What is that?
Basic Sentence Patterns	
1. a. NP + V_1	The baby sleeps.
b. NP + V_1 + adv-m	The baby sleeps softly.
c. NP + V_1 + adv-p	The baby sleeps in the crib.
d. NP + V_1 + adv-t	The baby sleeps at night.
e. NP + V_1 + adv-a	The baby sleeps with a doll.
2. a. NP + V_T + NP	The baby drinks milk.
b. NP + V_T + NP + (adverbials)	The baby drinks milk at the table.
3. a. NP + be + NP	The baby is a boy.
+ (*like* + N)	The baby is like an angel.
+ (*for* + N)	The present is for the baby.
4. a. NP + *be* + adj.	The baby is cute.
5. a. NP + *be* + adv-p	The bottle is on the table.
+ adv-t	Mother is on time.
+ adv-a	The baby is with Father.
Simple Transformations	
Reversible Passive	The boy was hit by the ball.
Nonreversible Passive	The glass was broken.
Dative Movement	The boy gives the baby the toy.
Infinitive NP	The boy likes to play.
For/to complement	He wants the cat to eat.
Negation	
nonexistence	The baby has no teeth.
rejection	I don't want that.
denial	The baby is not wet.
Simple Conjunction	
NP	John and Mary are friends.
VP	John runs and jumps.
S + S	The dog is black and the cat is white.
Adj.	The baby is hot and tired.
T-*there*	There are five children here.
Questions	
Wh- questions	Who, what, where, when, why, how?
Yes/No	Are you happy?
What . . . do	What does a fireman do?
Tag questions	
. . . is it?	That's not right, is it?
. . . right?	He's my age, right?
Subject-Auxiliary Inversion	Can we go?

FIGURE 7.3 Sentence types, patterns, and transformations (continued)

Complex Sentence Level

Adverbial Clauses	
Main clause first	The boy laughed when the clown fell.
Subordinate clause first	When the snow fell, the children went home.
Relative Clauses	
Medial position	The boy who hit John fell down.
Final position	John hit the boy who is crying.
NP Complementation	
Subject	That he is old is obvious.
Object	John thinks that he is old.
Noninitial Subject	It appears that the experiment failed.
Deletions	Sara can't swim, but Brian can.

Verbs That Require Special Syntactic Consideration

Put (requires adv-p)
Have, cost, weigh followed by NP but have no passive form
Seem, appear, become + adj
+ *like* + N
Turn, grow + adj
Stay, remain + adv-p
+ *like* + N
Sense Verbs
feel
smell
taste + adj
sounds like + N
looks

Key:

NP—noun phrase	m—manner	S + S—sentence and sentence
VP—verb phrase	p—place	N—noun
V_1—intransitive verb	t—time	T—transformation
V_T—transitive verb	a—accompaniment	
Adv—adverbial	Adj—adjective	

Sources: Data from *Sentences and Other Systems* by P. Blackwell, E. Engen, J. Fischgrund, and C. Zarcadoolas, 1978, Washington, DC: AG Bell Association for the Deaf; *English Syntax* by C. Hargis, 1977, Springfield, IL: Charles C. Thomas; *Language Development and Intervention with the Hearing Impaired* by R. R. Kretschmer and L. W. Kretschmer, 1978, Baltimore: University Park Press; and *English Syntax* by P. Roberts, 1964, New York: Harcourt Brace & World.

language. Although behavioral theory is now past its heyday, approaches based on it are still used in some situations, especially with children with severe language delays or disorders.

Innatist Theory

The innatist theory has been described under many labels, psycholinguistic theory, syntactic theory, and biological theory among them. Attributed to Chomsky (1957) and Lennenberg (1967), among others, the innatist theory holds that there is a biological basis for language acquisition, and that all humans are prewired to learn language because of the existence of a *language acquisition device;* it is just a matter of what aspect and at what rate language skills develop. Language is processed at two levels or by two sets of rules: phrase structure, or deep structure rules, which are universal from individual to individual, and transformational, or surface structure rules, which govern how each language and each culture rearranges deep structure to surface structure. All infants develop through a series of word pairs as well as developing the sounds of speech in a similar order. This consistency from culture to culture is pointed to as evidence of the existence of the language acquisition device. While this theory fails to consider the importance of meaning and context in language development, it does provide great insight into how we process sentences.

Recently, there has been a resurgence of interest in the biological basis of language as genetic research continues to bring us closer and closer to the understanding of the human sentence processing mechanism (HSPM) (Altman & Steedman, 1988; Crago & Gopnik, 1994; Frazier, 1993). Such a mechanism may be responsible for our ability to process sentences and may be genetically predetermined. Clarification of the existence of such a mechanism would have implications for therapy.

Cognitive Theory

Alternately known as psycholinguistic/semantic theory, case grammar theory, and information processing theory, cognitive theory argues that language development is based on meaning, or semantics, rather than on syntax. Fillmore (1968) and Chafe (1970) argue that the functions of words and their relationships to one another drive grammar. Bloom (1970) argues that there is a set of presyntactic, semantic relationships that precede true syntax (see Table 7.1). The order of their development reflects the order of development of cognitive structures (Bloom, 1973; Brown, 1973). For example, children develop the cognitive skill of object permanence before they talk about the appearance or disappearance of objects.

The semantic/cognitive theory has contributed significantly to our understanding of what young children talk about, and when, and why. It explains language within the overall context of child development and forms the basis for models of intervention that stress active involvement of children with their environment.

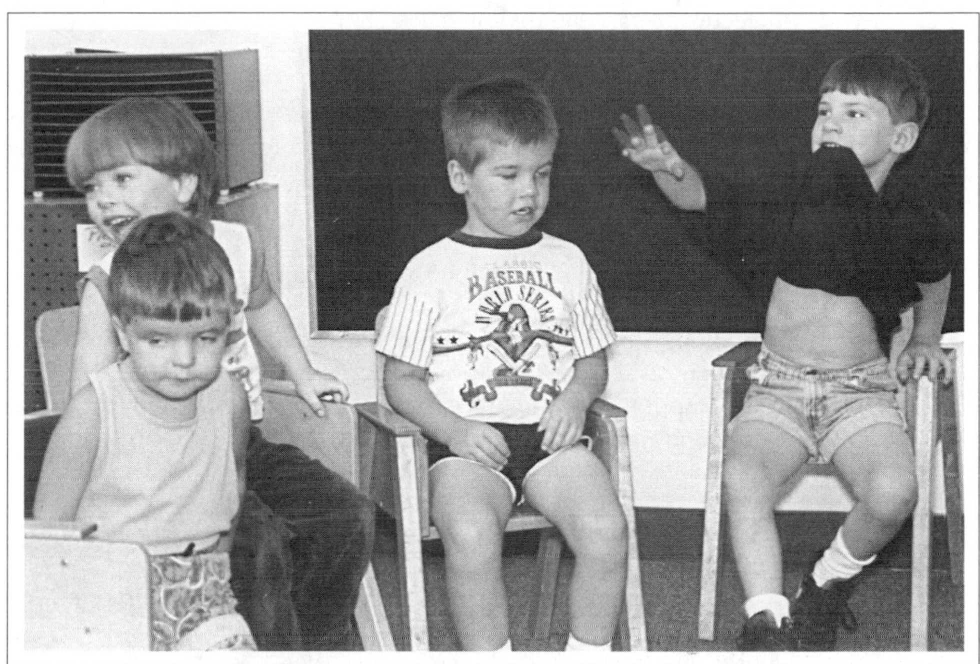

There must be ample time in the preschool day for children to share their personal observations and feelings—and for teachers to listen and respond.

Social Interaction Theory

As a departure from the innatist and cognitive theories, which focus more on the structure of language, the social interaction theory focuses on the social and personal purposes for which we use language. Discussions of structure place language acquisition in a vacuum, while discussions of purpose and function place it squarely in the middle of real life. As first described by Searle (1969), Dore (1974), and Halliday (1975), and later by McLean and Snyder-McLean (1978) and Prutting (1979), language is seen as a means to express intentions. It develops based on the human need to communicate, primarily through parent or caregiver modeling and feedback. Current models or approaches to communication intervention spring from this important contribution to the knowledge base surrounding communication development.

Factors Influencing Communication Development

The process of acquiring language is extremely complex and requires an intact organism that can function in an integrated fashion. Certain prerequisite systems are functioning in the normally developing youngster and, when they are delayed, defective, or absent, they impact significantly on this acquisition process. An inefficient neurophysiological system, a damaged sensory system, limited intellectual potential, and high-risk medical and social environments significantly influence communication development. This section discusses the relationships of hearing, vision, intelligence, memory, and attention to language development.

Early Identification

The age at which intervention begins has a critical impact on a child's development, so much so that PL 99–457 (incorporated under IDEA) requires that states provide preschool services to all children with disabilities. Early intervention allows family members to incorporate appropriate interactions into their daily routines and fosters a supportive communicating environment without which a child's communication development may be permanently delayed. Lack of intervention at this stage significantly limits the influence of later education.

Hearing

A hearing loss represents one of the most serious of all deterrents to spoken language development. We talk because we hear. Youngsters are surrounded by a world that is constantly being labeled, described, and defined by adults. Children with normal hearing experience both environmental and verbal sounds for at least 4,000 hours before they utter their first word (McNeill, 1966), and this does not include the hours when sounds are being processed prenatally.

Parents of a hearing child unconsciously revise their language to meet the child's needs (Snow, 1972). We naturally babble and repeat intonational patterns in a fashion that will support a youngster's comprehension. When hearing is deficient, the natural interaction between adults and infant breaks down and the normal developmental sequence is disrupted (Northcott, 1977). So much occurs linguistically in the first 3 or 4 years of life that even a minor or temporary hearing loss can be very disruptive.

Our sense of hearing is the primary sense by which we detect temporal events (Ling, 1976). Neither vision nor touch provides such sensitive information about time and sequence as does hearing. When a child's perceptions of time are altered, this can influence her acquisition of temporal language and the phrasing and timing of intonational patterns of language. Much information is coded in intonation. A hearing loss also affects the rate of speaking, the appropriate accenting of syllables, the rising and falling of the voice, and the range of speech that conveys emotional messages.

More important than its effects upon speech, however, are the effects of a hearing loss on language. The systems by which children who are deaf code the world vary significantly. While the world can be organized, categorized, and sequenced visually (Bruner, Goodnow, & Austin, 1956), the sense of hearing and the language it supports are a more efficient and reliable means of coding (Ling, 1976). When a child does not have normal hearing, the teacher must present every sound, every concept, every word, and every structure of the spoken language to the child directly and specifically. The skill that develops in others naturally in a few brief years becomes a lifelong task to develop and almost never reaches the same level and precision as that in individuals with normal hearing. The frequent exception to this is the child who is deaf and whose parents are deaf, because this child has the same benefit of access to early comprehensible communication as does the hearing child of hearing parents.

A very mild hearing loss of 25 decibels can be simulated by tightly pressing the cartilaginous flap in front of one's ears into the ear canal (Downs, 1981). By listening to others communicating in various environments (e.g., the hallway, the classroom, or a noisy cafeteria), one begins to understand that a great deal of information is not available. When young children experience mild fluctuating losses that result from colds and ear infections, the interference with language may never be overcome (Ling, 1972). Referring the child with chronic colds, allergies, and ear infections to an otologist may save that child needless problems in developing language as a preschooler and in learning core academic skills.

For children who are learning language, a mild conductive loss (i.e., a loss caused by problems with the outer or middle ear) places them under great stress. Dobie and Berlin (1979) estimated that a loss of this type may be experienced by up to 14% of children. Sarff (1981) reported that an unusually high percentage of students who were labeled as being learning disabled and who were reported to have normal hearing had past histories of medical problems with their ears as well as fluctuating hearing losses. In Sarff's report on an experimental program that screened hearing in a population of 197 subjects with learning disabilities, an astounding 57.2% failed a special screening at 10 decibels. Such a loss, while mild, may still have a significant impact on learning, especially when coupled with a history of problems during the developmental period associated with language acquisition.

Vision

The role of vision in learning language is often discussed in terms of the higher linguistic functions of reading and writing. Visual disorders of perception, discrimination, memory, and the like have been associated with the inability to read and write. Many authors discuss reversal of letters, failure to form sound-symbol correspondences, and poor writing ability in terms of eye-hand coordination (Frostig, 1965; Johnson & Myklebust, 1967); yet the impact of visual impairment becomes far more significant when we review the stages of language development in infants.

One of the first significant developments in language is joint attending. The caregiver and the child view the same object and the caregiver linguistically marks it for the child, thus helping to organize and label the child's world. Joint attending for a child with vision problems must be a more deliberate action, with the caregiver bringing the object to the child's tactile and auditory awareness. At around 9 to 12 months of age, infants develop a gestural system by which they communicate to adults. The assumption is that the adult will see the child's gesture or gaze, follow the direction of the gaze or gesture, and see the object or event that the child intends to share. Visible gestures in language are called *kinesics* and play an important role in the language acquisition process (Bolinger, 1975). Infants who have never been able to see and who have no language skills are unaware that adults can see, so they do not engage in communicative gazing and gesturing in the same fashion as seeing children do. Thus, the language acquisition process for children who are blind is different from that of sighted children.

The same can hold true for a sighted child. Being able to see does not necessarily mean that children are able to look at or to make sense out of what they see. Problems with depth perception, color blindness, uncorrected near- or far-sightedness, nystagmus, and astigmatism interfere with how children perceive and interpret what they see.

While hearing is primarily used to detect temporal aspects and changes, vision is primarily used to detect spatial aspects and changes (Ling, 1972). The sense of touch is not as effective as the eye in dealing with spatial information. Spatial adjectives and prepositions present a major challenge to a child with a vision problem.

Intelligence

The role of intelligence in language has been explored for many years (Luria, 1961; Piaget, 1952; Vygotsky, 1962), yet the relationship is still not fully understood. Language and thought are not synonymous. This is made obvious by children who are deaf and have poor skills in spoken language based on cultural norms, but score well on the performance tasks of intelligence tests. A complex relationship between intelligence and language exists. Environmental factors, social pressures, inadequate sensory experiences, or perceptual problems may diminish the experiences of a youngster and cause poor test performance, because all tests, whether they purport to measure intelligence, aptitude, or achievement, measure what a child has learned (Sattler, 1988). Difficulty in receiving information does not necessarily imply low intelligence. Further, children can develop near-normal ability in some areas of intelligence yet be quite deficient in others.

All other things being equal, language ability increases as mental age increases (Dunn, 1973). However, in the population of youngsters with developmental problems and specific disabilities, all other things are not equal. The variety of factors and their interrelationships are so numerous and complex that we cannot assume a one-to-one correspondence between intelligence and language.

Memory

Memory plays a significant role in the acquisition of language. A child must formulate and hold a visual image in memory so that the auditory symbol used to represent what was perceived will have a point of reference in the child's repertoire of ideas. The process of categorization is extremely important to learning in general and to learning language in particular (Bruner, Goodnow, & Austin, 1956). Children need help seeing likenesses and differences in the world around them to organize their worlds. Efficient organization of experiences assists in the memory and retrieval processes.

Youngsters who are developing language rehearse the language both orally and in their heads. Language rehearsal plays an important role in memory. Children with language problems often have difficulty with language rehearsal (Wiig & Semel, 1984). Further, information that is taken in by a faulty sensory system and/or interpreted by a faulty perceptual system will be coded in the fashion in which it is experienced. Inaccurate, poorly rehearsed, or incomplete concepts and language are stored in that fashion and when they are retrieved for use will be employed in inaccurate and incomplete ways.

Attention

Attention is critical for language development. A child must be able to filter through all the sounds coming in and attach the appropriate sound to the appropriate object or event (Carrow-Woolfolk & Lynch, 1982). Attention deficits are poorly understood by the general public, yet they have a significant impact on language. Attention is a neurobiological process, and attention deficits are real. They are not a result of poor parenting or lack of motivation or ignorance; however, they are difficult to diagnose in preschool children.

More is involved in teaching than just getting a child's attention and providing input. Attention implies the ability to focus actively on a stimulus. Sometimes we are required to focus by choice. In order for children to attend, they must consciously take in specific information while inhibiting a whole array of competing messages. Selection and inhibition require a judgment on the part of the child that a particular piece of information is worthy of attention. Children with problems in selective attention often have problems with language as well as with its impact on interpersonal relationships (Ratner & Harris, 1994).

For children who have not matured neurologically in their ability to inhibit competing stimuli or who have specific neurochemical dysfunctions, it is important that the interventionist assist in the selection and inhibition process by making information more readily accessible. Such factors as pitch, voice quality, loudness, spatial localization, and time of onset affect attentional selection of language (Moray, 1969). Further, the interventionist must assist in the judgment process by making what is to be learned meaningful and worthwhile to the child. To do this, the interventionist must have a good understanding of what is interesting to youngsters at different mental ages and of how to make linguistic information more auditorily and visually salient.

To separate vision, hearing, attention, memory, and intelligence for discussion purposes may be appropriate, but to think of them as individual blocks, stacked neatly one upon the other, is an inaccurate view of the learning process. These aspects are interdependent.

Communication Development in Young Children with Special Needs

Assuming that all the sensory, motor, perceptual, cognitive, and social systems bearing on language are intact, normal children establish the foundation upon which they will develop academic skills by the time they reach school. If children have any of a number of disabilities, language development and, hence, school readiness will be delayed. Different disorders affect language in characteristic ways.

Language Delay Versus Language Disorder

All development occurs in spurts and starts. Some aspects sail ahead while others lag behind, only to catch up later. This is certainly true of the many components of language and is one of the reasons why language assessment in young children is such a challenge. For example, semantic processes may be sufficient, but a child may communicate agrammatically. Children who are delayed in their language development are learning to communicate, but at a slower rate than normal. Children with language disorders have specific problems in coding, storage, and retrieval of their communication skills. Many terms describe true disorders of language. Such terms include specific language impairments and language-learning disabilities (Craig, 1993). Different disabilities influence language in different ways. However, in a child who is language delayed, acquisition of all aspects of language is slower than normal (Reed, 1986).

Mental Retardation

A long-standing question is whether the language of individuals with Down syndrome and with subnormal intellectual development past puberty is different from that of individuals with normal intelligence, or whether it follows similar developmental lines but is merely delayed (Graham, 1976; Sabsay & Kernan, 1993). The bulk of research in this area supports the delay hypothesis. One difference that has been noted is with children with Down syndrome and subnormal intelligence past puberty (deVilliers & deVilliers, 1978). Most studies involving these children have centered around issues regarding language form. However, an alternative perspective provided by surveys of parents show that children with Down syndrome understand what others say to them, even if the words used are not in the child's expressive repertoire (Pueschel & Hopmann, 1993).

Speech delays are typically found in children with mental retardation; however, the severity of retardation cannot be judged either by the degree of intelligibility or by the amount of verbalization. Yoder and Miller (1972) estimated that between 70 and 90% of all children with moderate and severe retardation make articulation errors. Dunn (1973) reported that children with IQs below 25 may never learn to speak.

Numerous studies of the morphological characteristics of the language of children with mental retardation (Dever, 1972; Lovell & Bradbury, 1967; Newfield & Schlanger, 1968) show that children with mental retardation learn all the morphological components of language but do so at a slower rate. Kamhi and Johnston (1982), Graham and Graham (1971), and Krivcher-Winestone (1980) looked at syntax skills and found that, like morphological skills, syntax skills are delayed but not different for children with mental retardation.

Although research in the areas of language form tips the scale in favor of the delay hypothesis, the opposite is true of research on language content and use. Until the mid-1970s, minimal efforts had been made to study semantic development in children with mental retardation (McLean & Snyder, 1977), although there is agreement that these youngsters have difficulty with semantic skills. Difficulties have been noted in the use of nouns and synonyms, in the formation of semantic classes and categories, in adjective use, and with the object relationship classes of space, time, quality, and quantity. With the present emphasis on including children with disabilities in regular school classes, interest in pragmatic language skills has increased as well. Baum, Odom, and Boatman (1975) found that language develops more quickly in children with mental retardation when it is intended for highly functional purposes.

Abbeduto and Rosenberg (1980) found that the turn-taking and illocutionary acts of older children with mental retardation are near normal, while Cunningham, Reuler, Blackwell, and Deck (1981) found the opposite in preschool children with mental retardation. Abbeduto & Rosenberg (1992) found that children with mental retardation have difficulty establishing a referent when they speak, are delayed in all aspects of speech act performance, and cannot repair communication. Pragmatic issues must receive specific program attention with preschool-age children. Environmental approaches that stress the inclusion of a child's natural communication partners seem most effective in enhancing development (Owens, 1995).

Learning Disabilities

Learning disabilities are difficult to diagnose in preschool-age children and are rarely identified as such; however, a look at the histories of older children who have learning disabilities often point to difficulties that existed in the preschool years. A preschooler at risk for learning disabilities (LD) may have numerous auditory and/or visual problems (Roberts, 1995). While children with learning disabilities may have normal vision and hearing, their brains are unable to interpret correctly what they hear and/or see. These processing deficits may result in problems with spatial orientation, sequencing, and discrimination. A child with a learning disability also may have difficulty forming a mental image, holding on to it, and mentally manipulating it (Wiig & Semel, 1984).

Children with learning disabilities often experience word retrieval problems (Wiig & Semel, 1984). To carry on a conversation, a person must be able to pull words from her memory bank on demand. Inefficiency in this area interferes with communicative interaction essential to the language learning process. It also can be quite frustrating, creating a variety of social-behavioral problems.

Children with learning disabilities may have inefficient or immature neurophysiological systems (Arehole, 1995). To pay attention to what others say as well as to one's own thoughts, one's body must cooperate. The bodies of children who have learning disabilities do not cooperate with them, and they may exhibit poor listening skills, hyper- or hypoactivity, distractibility, perseveration, disinhibition, and other qualities, and these may evolve into later problems. Many children with learning disabilities need some extra time to master the basics of oral language before they are ready to handle the kindergarten curriculum. Many will always have language-based problems, and these will contribute to later problems with reading, math, and writing. The semantic and pragmatic aspects of language in particular often are involved as well.

Behavior Disorders

There are numerous reasons why some children have behavior disorders. For example, when children have not matured neurologically to the point at which they can inhibit their responses to stimuli, they may act out. Inability to inhibit a language response may result in a child's blurting out information at inappropriate times. Many children have undetected hearing and vision problems that result in behavioral manifestations and concomitant language problems. Often, a youngster with learning disabilities who does not have the cognitive, motor, speech, or language skills to interact with the world appears to have a behavior disorder because her responses to language and nonlanguage events are inappropriate. Children who have received no supervision or have had inappropriate role models may say and do unexpected things. Providing children with a highly structured, organized environment in which expectations are made clear and natural consequences to actions are meted out firmly but fairly is very helpful in modifying their behavior. It also is essential to provide a structured language environment in which words make sense and are consistently applied to experiences. This helps children assume responsibility for their actions.

Specific Speech Disorders

There are many forms of disordered speech. Each disability impacts on speech development in its own way. However, three categories are recognized as common among children with speech disorders. These are disorders of fluency, articulation, and voice. Physical disabilities such as cleft palate and other anomalies also are found in such children.

Fluency. Fluency involves the forward flow of speech. A child whose speech is dysfluent is often referred to as a stutterer. More males stutter than females do, and the onset of stuttering usually occurs between the ages of 3 and 5. Stuttering cannot be picked up by the imitation of speech patterns of another child. It is often hereditary and may be found in combination with other problems. It almost always influences a child's social and emotional status (Adler & King, 1994). Problems of fluency require real help to overcome, and the speech-language pathologist and parent must work as a team.

Articulation. Articulation disorders are common among young children. Young children typically make articulation errors that adults find charming (e.g., *yap* for *lap*). When babytalk is not outgrown, however, parents may become concerned. It is necessary to be very clear about what articulation errors are normal and what are the result of a delay. Figure 7.1 shows the average rate of acquisition of phonemes and provides a standard with which to judge articulation development. When articulation is severely delayed, professional assistance is needed.

Voice Disorders. Voice disorders include problems with pitch, such as when the voice register is too high or too low, and with loudness, such as when a child is unable to monitor the loudness or softness of her voice. Voice quality features such as harshness, hoarseness, breathiness, hyper- or hyponasality, and problems of resonance may occur in young children with speech disorders. These require professional intervention.

Cleft Palate and Other Craniofacial Anomalies. Cleft palate and other craniofacial anomalies are medical conditions that require specialized care. Often, surgery is involved and, for many newborns, even the act of sucking is affected. Many children with cleft palates may be hesitant to speak, resulting in delayed production. Those with severe impairments may have limited social contacts as a result of either increased illnesses or hospitalizations or fear of rejection by the child or parent. The teacher, parent, and medical professional must work together closely to develop and carry out a program to meet the child's comprehensive needs.

Specific Language Impairment

Specific language impairments are difficult to identify in a young child, but, as with learning disabilities, the case histories of older children with language problems indicate that the problems began in the early years. Language impairments may occur secondary to hearing loss, mental retardation, autism, emotional conflict, learning disabilities, physical disabilities, and lack of English in the home environment. Still, when all these are ruled out, there remains a population of children whose language problems are of unknown etiology. They are said to have a specific language impairment. Fey and Leonard (1983) define *specific language impairment* (SLI) as "a pronounced deficit in the comprehension and/or expression of language in the relative absence of impairments in other areas of development" (p. 65). Traditionally, children received the SLI label based on standard morphological-syntactic criteria. These components of language remain the best predictors of language learning ability (Dale & Cole, 1991). Others have attempted to broaden criteria for referral to include pragmatic areas. Damico and Oller (1980) suggest the following alternative criteria for referral:

1. *LINGUISTIC NONFLUENCY*
   The child's speech is disrupted because of a disproportionately high number of repetitions, unusual pauses, and excessive use of hesitation forms.

2. *REVISIONS*
   Speech production is broken up by numerous false starts or self-interruptions. The child revises what she already has said as if she keeps coming to dead ends in a maze.

3. *DELAYS BEFORE RESPONDING*
   Attempts at communication initiated by others are followed by pauses of inordinate length.

4. *NONSPECIFIC VOCABULARY*
   The child makes frequent use of deictic expressions such as *this, that, then, he, over there,* and the like when the listener has no way of knowing what is being referenced. Also, a child displaying this characteristic tends to use generic terms such as *thing, stuff, these,* and *those* when more specific expressions seem to be required.

5. *INAPPROPRIATE RESPONSES*
   These are easy to recognize but difficult to explain. It is as though the child were operating on an independent discourse agenda, not attending to the prompts of the listener.

6. *NEED FOR REPETITION*
   Multiple repetitions are requested without any indication of improvement in comprehension.

Hearing Loss

In no other group of special children is difficulty with the English language more evident than in the group of children who are deaf or hard of hearing. Problems with the English language appear in all areas of form, content, and use. Bornstein, Saulnier, and Hamilton (1980), who studied 20 children who were prelingually deaf and enrolled in total communication programs for 4 years, found that, although vocalizations increased over time during combined speaking and signing activities, speech intelligibility remained essentially unchanged. Morphological development is typically delayed in children who are deaf or hard of hearing because the morphological components of our language are particularly difficult to hear. By 4 years of age, hearing children are using most morphological elements of language, while children who are deaf or hard of hearing have acquired few or none of these components (Blackwell, Engen, Fischgrund, & Zarcadoolas, 1978). By 10 years of age, when most hearing children are using their reading skills to acquire new knowledge, most children with hearing losses have yet to acquire basic syntactic structures. Hearing losses may be the result of problems with the outer or middle ear, called *conductive losses,* or problems with the inner ear or auditory nerve, called *sensorineural losses*. Problems with the auditory pathways from the inner ear to the brain are referred to as *central auditory processing problems*.

Studies of gestural language development indicate that children who are deaf or hard of hearing tend to organize early language semantically rather than by English word order (Kretschmer & Kretschmer, 1978). From early gestural stages onward, the semantic system and fields represented by specific referents are different and less extensive. Children who are deaf or hard of hearing also are delayed in the pragmatic skills of English.

Pragmatic presuppositions are external conditions that shape a speaker's intention, the grammatical structure used, and other decisions made about the communicative needs of a situation (Kretschmer & Kretschmer, 1978). Pragmatic presuppositions are particularly difficult for youngsters who cannot hear.

Whether a hearing loss is mild or profound, it has a significant impact on the language learning process. One of the most significant ways in which the learning process is altered by lack of hearing is in the mother-child interaction. Language development is an interactive process. Gross (1970) found that mothers of children who are deaf use less humor in their language, use more atypical intonation contours, and are less likely to give verbal praise than are mothers of hearing children. Children who do not hear respond to their mothers' language in different ways, and these changes may cause mothers to alter their language. This pattern, in turn, alters the child's experience with language and perpetuates the cycle of atypical interactions between parent and child.

Children who are hard of hearing are equally at risk for language delays. Many of these youngsters are overlooked and some end up in LD classes or reading entitlement programs. A child with a hearing loss, either mild or profound, must receive language intervention from infancy onward. The sooner the child receives services, the more likely it is that language can develop.

Children who are deaf and whose parents also are deaf have a very different experience. Because they have early access to comprehensible language from infancy, they tend to have better vocabularies and to bring better language skills to the educational process. Problems begin to rise, however, when they approach the task of learning to read, because the grammatical structure of American Sign Language is different from the grammatical structure of English.

Vision Loss

While studies of the language of children with vision losses show that structurally their language is not significantly different (Matsuda, 1984), differences are found in how their language is acquired. Impairment in vision results in an absence of the early gestural language that occurs between a mother and an infant. Further, a child with a vision problem lacks mobility, resulting in fewer experiences with the environment. Limitations on direct experiences result in a child's forming concepts based on insufficient or incomplete perceptual clues that in turn result in only partial understanding of experiences (Warren, 1984). Cutsforth (1951) used the term *verbalism* to refer to the use by children who are blind of terms for which they have no experiential base. Aurally and tactually gathered information is not sufficient to make up for a lack of vision. According to Santin and Simmons (1977), the "early language of the blind child does not seem to mirror his developing knowledge of the world, but rather his knowledge of the language of others" (p. 427).

The preschool teacher must assume a number of roles in relation to the developing language of a child who is visually impaired. First, the teacher must make words as richly meaningful as possible so that they hold semantic loads as close to normal as possible. Second, the teacher must help keep the child in touch with the environment. Because much communication is gestural, children who are blind miss out on many aspects of a daily routine. For example, sighted children see the teacher putting away his materials and know it is time to go to the music circle. They see the juice tray rolled into the room and know it is snack time. Children who are visually impaired must be told that these events are occurring. The teacher must maintain a running dialogue with a child who is blind, describing each event that occurs in the room to give the child an opportunity to interact more naturally with the environment. Keeping a running commentary going can be very tiring, but it is absolutely essential. If aides or parents are in the classroom, rotating turns will keep the child in touch while giving the speaker a rest.

Cerebral Palsy

The language of children with cerebral palsy is difficult to describe because the factors involved are so complex. Some children with this disorder have vision or hearing problems, some have mental retardation, and many have learning disabilities. These subgroups manifest some or all of the types of language problems associated with the additional handicapping condition. According to Wilson (1973), as many as 50% of individuals with cerebral palsy may have speech and language problems resulting from the disorder or in conjunction with an associated secondary handicap.

The language of a young child with cerebral palsy may further be restricted by neuromuscular involvement. Restricted mobility may limit a child's interaction with the environment, resulting in a sparser semantic loading of the language that the child understands and produces. Pragmatically, the child may not have the opportunity to interact with the world in the same fashion as do peers with no motor problems; hence, some of the functions of language may be overused while others are delayed in developing. Neuromotor problems generally interfere with motor planning for speech. Children with cerebral palsy must learn to compensate for structural differences. For this reason, they benefit from speech and language training and often are candidates for alternative communication systems (Adler & King, 1994).

Other Health Impairments and Neurological Problems

The category of other health impairments and neurological problems is so extensive that it cannot be treated adequately in this chapter. Several of the more pervasive problems, however, are described briefly.

Substance Abuse. Maternal ingestion of chemical substances such as alcohol, tobacco, tranquilizers, cocaine, and marijuana can cause disabilities in newborns. Ingestion of a chemical often is taking place before a mother knows she is pregnant (Sparks, 1993), and within the drug culture, trips to the doctor are often infrequent (Kronstadt, 1991). Infants with fetal alcohol syndrome (FAS) have distinct physical features and behavior manifestations, including characteristics of attention deficit disorder, memory problems, and language delays. Children with FAS can be difficult to manage and unresponsive to verbal cautions (Olson, Burgess, & Streissguth, 1992). In addition, their sentence length tends to be reduced and characterized by echolalia (Streissguth, 1986), and their play is unimaginative. These problems interfere with their social interactions.

AIDS/HIV. Approximately 75% of children who are infected with HIV are born to mothers who are intravenous drug users or who were infected through sexual activity (Crites, Fischer, McNeish-Stengel, & Seigel, 1992). Children born with HIV/AIDS have multiple insults associated not only with the disease, but also with the drug used, the poor nutrition usually found in drug users, and the prematurity of infants born to drug users. Prematurity and poor nutrition are related to all aspects of a child's development, including the development of communication.

Autism and Related Disorders. Communication problems are central to autism (Lovaas, 1977) and begin early in the developmental sequence. Disturbances in eye contact (McConnell, 1967), syntax and semantics (Lovaas, 1977), and excessive echolalia have been reported in approximately three fourths of this population (Wing, 1971). In recent years, Pervasive Developmental Disorders have been divided into various subtypes along the spectrum with differentiating features in intelligence and communication. For example, children with Asperger syndrome may have near-normal communication abilities (Frith, 1991).

Remediation attempts in the past endeavored to increase eye contact (McConnell, 1967) and reduce echolalic and other inappropriate behaviors through behavior modification techniques (Lovaas, 1977). More recent views of autism are that it is an inability to achieve intersubjectivity (Kasari, Sigman, Yirmiya, & Mundy, 1993). *Intersubjectivity* is the shared understanding that is based on a common focus of attention. Children with autism have extreme difficulty establishing and maintaining intersubjectivity; therefore, language development is severely impaired because joint attending (intersubjectivity) is a key component to language development.

Research by Bernard-Opitz (1982) and Prizant and Duchan (1981) has shown .. the echolalic language used by children with autism may be more functional than was previously assumed. Prizant and Duchan found that the echolalic patterns of their subjects fell into seven functional categories: nonfocused, turn taking, declarative, rehearsal, self-regulatory, yes-answer, and request. Bernard-Opitz discovered that the pragmatic behavior of her subjects varied across communicative settings and partners but was stable within those settings and with those partners. Communicative intent is difficult to understand in children with autism. Even individuals who are very familiar with a child may have difficulty understanding what various actions mean (Donovan, 1993); however, pragmatic study may prove to be useful in elucidating the needs of this population. Such information suggests that there may be a base of abilities from which to work with children who have autism.

Otitis Media. Many parents have experienced the rapid onset of middle ear infections in their children. Otitis media occurs in almost all children at some time in their young lives. Many children spend months and months of critical language learning time with little or no hearing because of fluid and infections in both ears (Bauer & Mosher, 1990). Teele, Klein, Chase, Menyuk, and Rosner (1990) found that children who had significant ear infections in the first three years of life scored lower on tests of speech and language at age 7 than did their peers whose histories were not significant for otitis media.

Attention Deficit Hyperactivity Disorder. Many of the characteristics of children with central auditory processing disorders are similar in nature to the characteristics of children who have attention deficit hyperactivity disorder (ADHD), although assessment and intervention for these two disorders differ (Tillery & Smoski, 1994). Some of these shared characteristics include inappropriate verbal responses, distraction in the presence of background noise, difficulty sustaining attention for verbal instruction over a period of time, inattention, and difficulty completing multistep tasks. An evaluation of a child with ADHD should include information about her auditory processing skills. This includes assessment of the child's ability to make fine auditory discriminations, to retain and recall auditory sequences, and to be able to focus on an auditory figure against a distracting background.

Speech and Language Assessment

Assessing speech and language is an intensive and time-consuming process. Numerous test instruments provide a quick survey of skills; however, quick surveys offer little direction for formulating the necessary remediation strategies. Language assessment is difficult primarily for two reasons (Kretschmer & Kretschmer, 1978). First, some language components are more easily assessed than others are. Second, with children who have disabilities in general and who have language impairments or delays in particular, one can never be completely sure that the language sampled is truly representative of what the child typically uses. Communication assessment cannot be subsumed under a general psychoeducational evaluation but must be separated and performed in depth and within the context of the world in which the child communicates.

Communication assessment should be ongoing. A variety of strategies should be used, from language sampling and formal tests to observations of the child's behaviors in natural settings. All areas of development should be considered as they relate to communication acquisition. Parents and primary caregivers should be involved actively in the process. Assessment should be tailored to specific communication objectives rather than being determined by a score, and application to intervention should always be considered (Prizant & Bailey, 1992).

All areas of form, content, and use mentioned earlier should be assessed. For each area, information about comprehension and production must be gathered. Comprehension is the child's understanding of language; production is her ability to use language. The comprehension component often is called *receptive language;* the production component often is called *expressive language.* Separate assessments should be made of expressive speech and expressive language.

A few particularly noteworthy tests for preschoolers are presented in Table 7.4. Because new tests appear on the market often and because of the unique needs of young children, it is wise to consult a speech-language pathologist to determine how best to assess current communication skills.

Alternative Augmentative Modes and Technologies

For children with severe mental and motor impairments, oral communication may not be a realistic goal; yet, given the appropriate tools, these children may be able to communicate their needs and wishes through alternative devices that augment communication. McCormick and Shane (1990) defined *augmentative communication* as "the total arrangement for supplementing and enhancing an individual's communication. The arrangement includes (a) the communication device or technique, (b) the representational symbol set or system, and (c) the communication skills necessary for effective use of the system" (p. 429). In recent years, many augmentative devices have been developed. They range from simple home-invented gestural modes to highly sophisticated systems controlled by brain wave patterns.

In the early years of alternative or augmentative communication, communication boards received a lot of attention (McDonald & Schultz, 1973; Silverman, 1980; Vanderheiden & Grilley, 1976). For children who were severely limited in motor functioning, such boards seemed to provide an appropriate avenue for communication, because these devices required only simple skills such as pointing. Children who were able to match actual objects to pictures were candidates for such a device. In recent years, there has been such a proliferation of technology and research, mostly computer driven, that the field of communication augmentation is now quite complex. For example, students who are blind now have access to palm-held word processors. The NOMAD II program by the American Printing House for

TABLE 7.4 Commonly Used Tests of Preschool Communication Development

TEST	AUTHOR/PUBLISHER	DESCRIPTION
Receptive-Expressive Emergent Language Test (2nd ed.)	Bzoch, K., & League, R. (1991). Austin, TX: Pro-Ed.	The REEL–2 is a revision of an earlier tool designed for use in early intervention programs. It assesses both receptive and expressive language via parent interviews of children up to 3 years of age.
Bankson Language Test (2nd ed.)	Bankson, N. (1990). Austin, TX: Pro-Ed.	The BLT–2 assesses the language of children from 3–0 to 6–11 years of age in three categories: semantic knowledge, morphological/syntactical rules, and pragmatics.
Boehm Test of Basic Concepts—Preschool Version	Boehm, A. (1986). New York: The Psychological Corporation.	The Boehm Preschool Version assesses the knowledge in children ages 3 to 5 years of 26 basic relational concepts necessary to begin school.
Sequenced Inventory of Communication Development (rev. ed.)	Hendrick, D., Prather, E., & Tobin, A. (1984). Austin, TX: Pro-Ed.	The SICD–R is a diagnostic battery useful with children whose functional levels range from 4 months to 4 years. The kit comes complete with engaging materials designed to hold even the youngest child's attention.
Test of Early Language Development (2nd ed.)	Hresko, W., Reid, D. K., & Hammill, D. (1991). Austin, TX: Pro-Ed.	The TELD–2 is a diagnostic language test for use with children from 2–0 to 7–11 years in age. It provides data on receptive and expressive language systems and syntactic/semantic language features.
Preschool Language Scale–3	Zimmerman, I., Steiner, V., & Pond, R. (1992). New York: The Psychological Corporation.	The PLS–3 assesses auditory comprehension and expressive communication in children from 2 weeks of age to 6 years 11 months.

the Blind extends the old communication board concept to new heights, with voiced information available simply by touching the screen of a modern communication board. The wide array of advanced technology available today is described in Chapter 9.

New approaches to communication boards stress the importance of social interaction (Reichle, York, & Sigafoos, 1991) and the interactions between the system and a child's environment (Goossens, 1990). The type of augmentative communication system a child uses will depend upon her cognitive level. A child who is extremely limited may need to begin pointing to actual objects before moving into a set of pictures. For a child who is intact cognitively yet limited motorically, the use of symbolic systems such as the written word or Blissymbolics (Bliss, 1965) may be worth considering. However, such symbolically-based communication boards require abstract thinking that may be well beyond the ability of preschoolers with severe mental retardation.

Natural gesture systems such as pantomime, which evolve from a child's own need and ability, may provide a good bridge to oral communication for some children (Balick, Spiegel, & Greene, 1976; Webster, McPherson, Sloman, Evans, & Kuchar, 1973). However, the interventionist must recognize that comprehension and production are two very different skills. In order for children to express communication meaningfully, they must have an understanding of what they are communicating. All too often, language is taught to children with special needs by requiring them to produce words and sentences beyond their understanding. The ability to produce a string of utterances in a rote fashion or through a stimulus-response mode may give a child the appearance of communicating; however, upon investigation, the child's level of understanding may prove to be lacking. Natural gesture, pantomiming, and role-playing may provide a child with a more realistic way of learning and of sharing what has been learned.

One more alternative communication system that has been used successfully with a wide array of communication problems is sign language. It has been used with such disabilities as autism (Bonvillian & Nelson, 1976; Miller & Miller, 1973), mental retardation (Brookner & Murphy, 1975), multiple handicaps (Creedon, 1975), and with individuals who are dysarthric or have had laryngectomies (Chen, 1971). Sign language is an appropriate tool because it can be used with individuals at very young mental ages. Schlesinger and Meadow (1972) reported a case of an 8-month-old child with a hearing impairment whose communication environment and mode consisted of signs. In fact, in normal development, babies of about 9 to 13 months of age rely very heavily on communicative gesturing (Bates, Camaioni, & Volterra, 1975) and develop a pseudosign system to express their wishes and needs. This acts as a tool that allows them to communicate long before they are developmentally ready to utter their first oral words. Therefore, until a child with a disability is developmentally ready to produce words orally, the use of signs may provide the same kind of bridge between understanding and orally communicating as does communicative gesturing in the normally developing child.

When choosing an alternative communication system, the pros and cons of each system must be weighed against the needs of the individual child and the demands of her environment. The following questions must be answered:

1. What level of cognitive ability does the system require and on what level is the child functioning?
2. What level of motor skill is required by the system, and can the child easily perform this level of skill?
3. In what environment can the system be used? Is it something only the teacher can understand or can the child's family use it as well? A communication system is useless if it can be used only during a 15-minute speech lesson. The system must have a broader impact.
4. Will this be used as a permanent communicative approach or is it just a tool until the child is developmentally ready for oral communication?
5. What plans are in place to monitor utility of the system relative to the child's changing developmental and communication needs?

As with all areas of programming for early intervention, the decision regarding alternative communication devices should be made by all those who will be using and developing the system. Such a decision should not be made in haste. It is easier to wait a few extra days or weeks than to put the child through the arduous task of learning one system after another.

Communication Intervention: Issues and Principles

Intervention approaches and practices have changed over the years to reflect the changes in linguistic theory described earlier in this chapter. A discussion of general theories of intervention and some guiding principles for intervention are provided next.

Didactic, Milieu, and Child-Directed Approaches

During the reign of behaviorism, didactic intervention approaches to speech and language development were popular (Harris, Wolchik, & Milch, 1982; MacDonald & Blott, 1974). Didactic approaches involved the direct teaching of a communication goal in a highly structured manner (McCormick & Schiefelbusch, 1990). A child's productions were modified by rewarding closer and closer approximations of the speech or language target with tangible reinforcers, often in the form of food or tokens. Techniques such as reinforcement, shaping, chaining, fading, and prompting were used. In the next decade, emphasis was placed on syntactic development. Modeling, imitation, and expansion were commonly used to develop both speech and language (Yoder & Warren, 1993). In the 1980s, milieu teaching or naturalistic intervention became popular (Alpert & Kaiser, 1992; Kaiser, 1993; Laski, Charlop, & Schreibman, 1988). Milieu teaching focused on the development of functional communication in naturalistic environments, which was driven by the child's interest. Examples of naturalistic approaches are transactional teaching (McLean & Snyder-McLean, 1978), conversational teaching (MacDonald, 1985), developmental interaction teaching (Bricker & Carlson, 1980), and pragmatic intervention (Duchan, 1986).

Caregiver-Child Interactions and the Home Setting

Parents are a child's first language teachers. When a child has an obvious disability or when language is not developing, some parents begin to doubt their effectiveness in guiding their youngsters through the communication environment. Numerous studies support the notion that parents can learn strategies to develop communication in their children (Alpert & Kaiser, 1992; Harris, Wolchik, & Milch, 1982; Tannock, Girolametto, & Siegel, 1989). Instruction for the parents in the home coupled with on-site coaching can build confidence in the parents and skills in both the parents and child (Kaiser, Hemmeter, Ostrosky, Alpert, & Hancock, 1995). This approach yields much better results than training in a workshop format.

Influence of Preschool Inclusion on Language Intervention

The early education classroom can be an excellent environment for assisting children in developing communication skills. For a young child with even the most severe disability, the social environment of a preschool can provide opportunities to learn new ways to communicate and to practice developing skills. Interaction is the key ingredient to communication development (Reike & Lewis, 1984), and most children are often full of ideas and desires that they want to share with adults but can share more easily with their peers.

Principles of Intervention

It is a great challenge to help children who have deviated from the spontaneous and natural process to communicate. The following suggestions will assist the early interventionist in this endeavor:

1. *Use comprehensive assessment results.* Interventionists should base language goals and objectives on a sound assessment of a child's current and unique status. Assessment based on a good understanding of developmental sequences in form, content, and use of language is essential. Chronological and mental ages can give only gross approximations of a child's needs and abilities.

2. *Develop activities that focus on interaction.* Language develops best through interactive use. This means that language should be worked on in the context of communication with others. Computer-assisted instruction, picture cards, and sentence-building cards are useful for reinforcement, but they cannot take the place of human interaction while new forms and uses of language are developing.

3. *Make activities purposeful.* Language must be meaningful and purposeful, not rote and sterile, if a child is to achieve maximum gains. Involving teachers, classmates, parents, siblings, and all possible intervention agents in the interactive process is essential. Create the need to communicate.

4. *Use natural situations.* Language should be taught naturally. Asking the child to repeat "The spoon is in the box" is unrealistic because we rarely place a spoon in a shoe box in real life. Encouraging language in naturalistic settings does not, however, mean that the choice of skills to be taught should be left up to chance occurrence in the communicative exchange. Specific language goals should be outlined, and appropriate situations that allow for the development of these should be fostered.

5. *Allow for variability of development.* Language does not develop in a linear fashion. Some processes develop rapidly while others develop slowly; growth in one area affects growth in another. Children tend to learn language in spurts. The early interventionist must account for this and pace intervention to a child's rhythm, not to what a particular checklist or convention dictates.

6. Take advantage of spontaneous opportunities. While programming decisions must be based on a firm knowledge of the developmental processes, this does not preclude the need to take advantage of vicarious, incidental, and spontaneous learning experiences.

7. Make activities real. Children should become directly involved with the experience to which teaching activities refer. Simply describing or showing pictures of an experience does not ensure that a child has understood the concept.

8. Develop new information within the context of old information. Children need a means of classifying and categorizing what they are learning. They accomplish this most easily when interventionists attach new information to old. New syntax structure should develop within the context of known experiences and known vocabulary. New vocabulary should develop within the context of known syntax. Children need to have their auditory environment organized and consistent in order for it to make sense.

9. Teach vocabulary in depth. Present words to a child in all their contexts and meanings. Using one word in all its contexts and functions is better than using a number of words in a limited context. Also, widening language in this way more

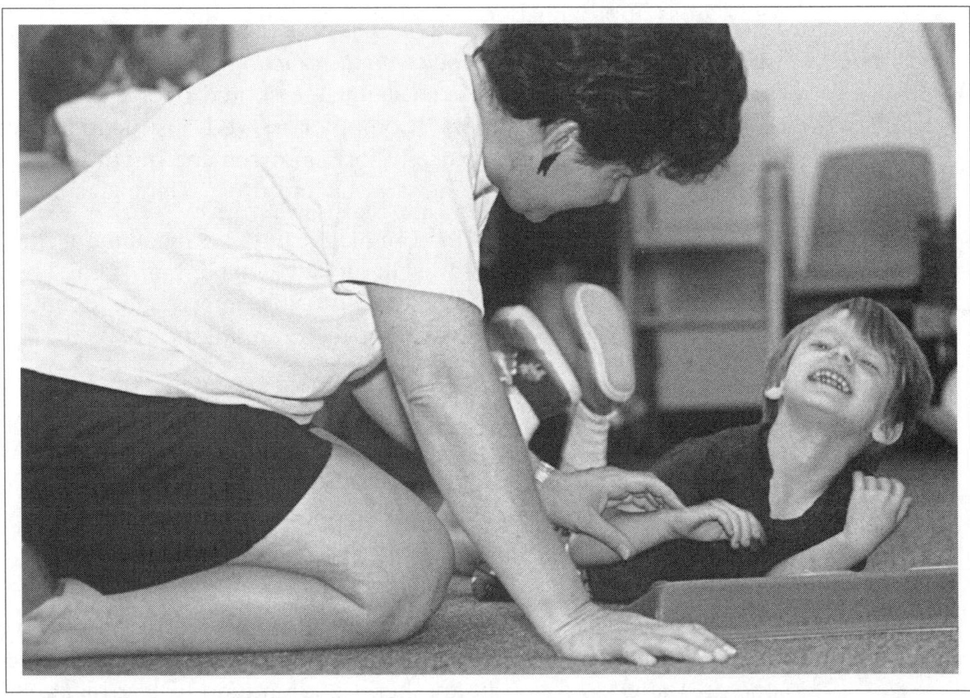

Conducting a conversation, while seemingly effortless, actually requires a complex set of practical skills.

closely approximates natural language development. During the first 6 months of talking, children put most of their efforts into labeling objects and actions, but they rapidly move into broader understanding of those labels. Children try them out in new situations as if they were testing their hypotheses about language. If interventionists are too concerned about adding greater numbers of words to children's vocabularies, the children may stay at the labeling stage far longer than is natural. This does not give children the opportunity to test out and expand the language that they have acquired.

10. Make language experiences fun. Often, what an adult thinks is fun is entirely different from what a child thinks is fun. Knowledge of what children find enjoyable at different ages is essential.

Collaborative Consultation

In the late 1970s and early 1980s, a model of interactions among service providers that focused on taking special education into the regular classroom or educational environment became popular. This collaborative consultation approach stressed the shared responsibility and equal authority of the regular and special educator. Sharing problems, resources, and solutions to enhance outcomes for children is the key to this approach (West & Idol, 1990).

In terms of the youngest children, the early interventionist, the parents, and related personnel become the collaborators. Because the parents have such a central role in the application of information, they must by necessity become the focal point. Parents should be recognized for their expertise. They know their children better than anyone else does, and they know their family's lifestyle better than anyone else does. Mutual respect fosters trust, and trust is the key to involvement. The only way to make a real impact on the life of a child within the context of the family is to be involved with that family. A spirit of openness, sharing of information, and a mutual effort to bring about positive change and growth are the hallmarks of collaborative consultation.

Summary

The acquisition of a system of communication is an achievement of monumental proportion, yet good communication is so central to our existence that we are barely aware of it. Only when communication is delayed does the complexity of its nature become apparent. This chapter discussed development, assessment, disorders, and intervention within the domain of communication.

Current communication theory points to the need on the part of interventionists to understand the complex nature of communication. Communication is multifaceted and tends to develop in a common sequence; however, it does not develop in a linear fashion. Different processes undergo spurts at different times, and delays or growth in one area affect delays or growth in another. By 4 years of age, the average youngster has mastered the basics of adult language. If remediation is not available to children with communication problems before they reach the school years, they may never completely catch up on all their delayed skills. Assessment of communication in children is the first step toward remediation. Depending upon the cause of the deficit, different intervention strategies may be appropriate. In some cases, alternative communication devices may be recommended for a child. The importance of communication in our society demands that its development be a high priority in programs for young children with special needs.

References

Abbeduto, L., & Rosenberg, S. (1980). The communicative competence of mildly retarded adults. *Applied Psycholinguistics, 1,* 405–426.

Abbeduto, L., & Rosenberg, S. (1992). Linguistic communication in persons with mental retardation. In S. Warren & J. Reichle (Eds.), *Causes and effects in communication and language intervention*. Baltimore: Paul H. Brookes.

Adler, S., & King, D. A. (Eds.). (1994). *Oral communication problems in children and adolescents* (2nd ed.). Boston: Allyn & Bacon.

Alpert, C. L., & Kaiser, A. P. (1992). Training parents as milieu language teachers. *Journal of Early Intervention, 16,* 31–52.

Altman, G., & Steedman, M. (1988). Interaction with context during human sentence processing. *Cognition, 30,* 191–238.

American Speech-Language-Hearing Association. (1985). Clinical management of communicatively handicapped minority language populations. *ASHA, 27,* 29–32.

Arehole, S. (1995). Middle latency response in children with learning disabilities: Preliminary findings. *Journal of Communication Disorders, 28*(1), 21–38.

Austin, J. L. (1962). *How to do things with words*. London: Oxford University Press.

Balick, S., Spiegel, D., & Greene, G. (1976). Mime in language therapy and clinician training. *Archives of Physical Medicine and Rehabilitation, 57,* 35–38.

Bankson, N. (1990). *Bankson Language Test* (2nd ed.). Austin, TX: Pro-Ed.

Bates, E. (1976). *Language and context: The acquisition of pragmatics*. New York: Academic Press.

Bates, E., Camaioni, L., & Volterra, V. (1975). The acquisition of performatives prior to speech. *Merrill-Palmer Quarterly, 21,* 205–226.

Bates, E. & Johnston (1977). *Pragmatics in normal and deficient child language*. Paper presented at the annual meeting of the American Speech-Language-Hearing Association, Chicago, IL.

Bauer, H., & Mosher, G. (1990). Ohio infants at risk for communicative disorders. *Journal of the Ohio Speech and Hearing Association, 5,* 43–45.

Baum, D. D., Odom, M., & Boatman, R. (1975). Environment-based language training with mentally retarded children. *Education and Training of the Mentally Retarded, 10,* 68–73.

Berko, J. (1958). The child's learning of English morphology. *Word, 14,* 150–177.

Bernard-Opitz, V. (1982). Pragmatic analysis of the communicative behavior of an autistic child. *Journal of Speech and Hearing Disorders, 47,* 96–99.

Blackwell, P., Engen, E., Fischgrund, J., & Zarcadoolas, C. (1978). *Sentences and other systems*. Washington, DC: AG Bell Association for the Deaf.

Bliss, C. K. (1965). *Semantography (Blissymbolics)* (2nd ed.). Sydney, Australia: Semantography (Blissymbolics) Publications.

Bloom, L. (1970). *Language development: Form and function in emerging grammars*. Cambridge, MA: MIT Press.

Bloom, L. (1973). *One word at a time: The use of single-word utterances before syntax*. The Hague: Mouton.

Bloom, L., & Lahey, M. (1978). *Language development and language disorders*. New York: Wiley.

Boehm, A. (1986). *Boehm Test of Basic Concepts–Preschool Version*. New York: Psychological Corporation.

Bolinger, D. (1975). *Aspects of language* (2nd ed.). New York: Harcourt Brace Jovanovich.

Bonvillian, J. D., & Nelson, K. E. (1976). Sign language acquisition in a mute autistic boy. *Journal of Speech and Hearing Disorders, 41,* 339–347.

Bornstein, H., Saulnier, K. L., & Hamilton, L. G. (1980). Signed English: A first evaluation. *American Annals of the Deaf, 125,* 467–481.

Brazelton, T. B., Koslowski, B., & Main, M. (1974). The origins of reciprocity: The early mother-infant interaction. In M. Lewis & L. A. Rosenblum (Eds.), *The effect of the infant on its caregiver.* New York: Wiley.

Bricker, D., & Carlson, L. (1980, May). *The relationship of object and prelinguistic social communication schemes to the acquisition of early linguistic skills in developmentally delayed infants.* Paper presented at the Conference on Handicapped and At-Risk Infants: Research and Applications, Monterey, CA.

Brookner, S. P., & Murphy, N. O. (1975). The use of a total communication approach with a non-deaf child: A case study. *Language, Speech, and Hearing Services in the Schools, 6,* 131–137.

Brown, R. (1973). *A first language: The early stages.* Cambridge, MA: Harvard University Press.

Brown, R., & Fraser, C. (1963). The acquisition of syntax. In C. Cofer & B. Musgrave (Eds.), *Verbal behavior and learning.* New York: McGraw-Hill.

Bruner, J. (1974). The ontogenesis of speech acts. *Journal of Child Language, 2,* 1–19.

Bruner, J., Goodnow, J., & Austin, G. (1956). *A study of thinking.* New York: Wiley.

Bzoch, K., & League, R. (1991). *Receptive-Expressive Emergent Language Test* (2nd ed.). Austin, TX: Pro-Ed.

Carrow, M. A. (1968). The development of auditory comprehension of language structure in children. *Journal of Speech and Hearing Disorders, 33,* 99–111.

Carrow-Woolfolk, E., & Lynch, J. (1982). An integrative approach to language disorders in children. *Language, Speech, and Hearing Services in Schools, 23,* 198–202.

Chafe, W. (1970). *Meaning and the structure of language.* Chicago: University of Chicago Press.

Chen, L. Y. (1971). Manual communication by combined alphabet and gestures. *Archives of Physical Medicine and Rehabilitation, 58,* 381–384.

Chomsky, N. (1957). *Syntactic structures.* The Hague: Mouton.

Chomsky, N., & Halle, M. (1968). *The sound pattern of English.* New York: Harper & Row.

Clark, E. V. (1973). What's in a word? On the child's acquisition of semantics in his first language. In T. E. Moore (Ed.), *Cognitive development and the acquisition of language.* New York: Academic Press.

Clark, E. V. (1974). Some aspects of the conceptual bases for first language acquisition. In R. L. Schiefelbusch & L. L. Lloyd (Eds.), *Language perspectives, acquisition, and retardation.* Baltimore: University Park Press.

Clark, H. H. (1973). Space, time, semantics and the child. In T. E. Moore (Ed.), *Cognitive development and the acquisition of language.* New York: Academic Press.

Clark, H., & Clark, E. (1977). *Psychology and language.* New York: Harcourt Brace Jovanovich.

Clark, R. N. & Siefer, R. (1983). Facilitation of mother-infant communication. *Infant Mental Health Journal, 4,* 67–82.

Coggins, R. & Carpenter, R. (1981). The Communicative Intention Inventory: A system for coding children's early intentional communication. *Applied Psycholinguistics, 2,* 235–252.

Crago, M. B., & Gopnik, M. (1994). From families to phenotypes: Theoretical and clinical implications of research into the genetic basis of specific language impairment. In R. Watkins & M. Rice (Eds.), *Specific language impairment in children.* Baltimore: Paul H. Brookes.

Craig, H. (1993). Social skills of children with specific language impairment: Peer relationships. *Language, Speech, and Hearing Services in Schools, 24,* 206–215.

Creedon, M. P. (Ed.). (1975). *Appropriate behavior through communication: A new program in simultaneous language.* Chicago: Dysfunctioning Child Center.

Crites, L., Fischer, K., McNeish-Stengel, M., & Seigel, C. (1992). Working with families of drug-exposed children: Three model programs. In L. Rosetti (Ed.), *Developmental problems of drug-exposed infants.* San Diego, CA: Singular Publishing Group.

Cunningham, C. E., Reuler, E., Blackwell, J., & Deck, J. (1981). Behavioral and linguistic developments in the interaction of normal and retarded children with their mothers. *Child Development, 52,* 62–70.

Cutsforth, T. D. (1951). *The blind in school and society.* New York: American Foundation for the Blind.

Dale, D. S. (1972). *Language development: Structure and function.* New York: Holt, Rinehart, & Winston.

Dale, P., and Cole, K. (1991). What's normal: Specific language impairment in an individual differences perspective. *Language, Speech, and Hearing Services in the Schools, 22,* 80–83.

Damico, J., & Oller, J. W., Jr. (1980). Pragmatic versus morphological/syntactic criteria for language referrals. *Language, Speech, and Hearing Services in the Schools, 11,* 85–94.

deBoysson-Bardies, B., Sagart, L., & Durand, C. (1984). Discernible differences in the babbling of infants according to target language. *Journal of Child Language, 11,* 1–15.

Dever, R. B. (1972). A comparison of the results of a revised version of Berko's Test of Morphology with the free speech of mentally retarded children. *Journal of Speech and Hearing Research, 15,* 169–178.

deVilliers, J., & deVilliers, P. (1978). *Language acquisition.* Cambridge, MA: Harvard University Press.

Dobie, R. A., & Berlin, C. I. (1979). Influence of otitis media on hearing and development. *Annals of Otology, Rhinology, and Laryngology, 88,* (Suppl. 60), 48–53.

Donovan, E. (1993). "I NO I NOT EASY TO HELP BUT KEEP HELPING ME." Facilitated communication and behavior management. In D. Smukler (Ed.), *First words: Facilitated communication and the inclusion of young children* (2nd ed.). Syracuse, NY: Jowonio School.

Dore, J. (1974). A pragmatic description of early development. *Journal of Psycholinguistic Research, 3,* 343–350.

Dore, J. (1975). Holophrases, speech acts, and language universals. *Journal of Child Language, 2,* 21–40.

Downs, M. P. (1981). Contribution of mild hearing loss to auditory language learning problems. In R. Roeser & M. Downs (Eds.), *Auditory disorders in school children.* New York: Thieme-Stratton.

Duchan, J. (1986). Learning to describe events. *Topics in Language Disorders, 6,* 27–36.

Duchan, J., & Erickson, J. (1976). Normal and retarded children's understanding of semantic relations in different verbal contexts. *Journal of Speech and Hearing Research, 19,* 767–776.

Dunn, L. M. (Ed.). (1973). *Exceptional children in the schools.* New York: Holt, Rinehart, & Winston.

Ervin-Tripp, S. (1964). Imitation and structural change in children's language. In E. H. Lenneberg (Ed.), *New directions in the study of language.* Cambridge, MA: MIT Press.

Ervin-Tripp, S. (1978). Some features of early child-adult dialogues. *Language in Society, 7,* 357–373.

Fey, M. E., & Leonard, L. G. (1983). Pragmatic skills of children with specific language impairment. In T. M. Gallagher & C. A. Prutting (Eds.), *Pragmatic assessment and intervention issues in language.* San Diego: College-Hill Press.

Fillmore, C. (1968). The case for case. In E. Bach & R. Harmas (Eds.), *Universals of linguistic theory* (pp. 1–90). New York: Holt, Rinehart, & Winston.

Frazier, L. (1993). Processing Dutch sentence structure. *Journal of Psycholinguistic Research, 22,* 85–108.

Frith, U. (1991). Asperger and his syndrome. In U. Frith (Ed.), *Autism and Asperger Syndrome.* New York: Cambridge University Press.

Frostig, M. (1965). Corrective reading in the classroom. *The Reading Teacher, 18,* 573–580.

Gallagher, T. (1977). Revision behavior in the speech of normal children developing language. *Journal of Speech and Hearing Research, 20,* 303–318.

Gallagher, T. & Dornton, B. (1968). Conversational

aspects of the speech of language disordered children: Revision behavior. *Journal of Speech and Hearing Research, 21,* 118–135.

Gallagher, T. & Prutting, C. (Eds.). (1983). *Pragmatic assessment and intervention issues in language.* San Diego: College-Hill Press.

Garvey, C. (1975). *Contingent queries.* Unpublished master's thesis. Johns Hopkins University, Baltimore.

Goldsworthy, C. (1982). Examiner's manual: Multilevel informal language inventory. Upper Saddle River, NJ: Merrill/Prentice Hall.

Goossens, C. (1990). *Engineering the preschool classroom environment for interactive symbolic communication.* Workshop presented at Bradley Hospital, East Providence, Rhode Island, March.

Graham, J. T., & Graham, L. W. (1971). Language behaviors of the mentally retarded: Syntactic characteristics. *American Journal of Mental Deficiency, 75,* 623–629.

Graham, L. W. (1976). Language programming and intervention. In L. L. Lloyd (Ed.), *Communication assessment and intervention strategies.* Baltimore: University Park Press.

Gross, R. (1970). Language used by mothers of deaf children and mothers of hearing children. *American Annals of the Deaf, 115,* 93–96.

Halliday, M. (1975). *Learning how to mean: Explorations in the development of language.* London: Edward Arnold.

Hargis, C. (1977). *English syntax.* Springfield, IL: Charles C Thomas.

Harris, S. L., Wolchik, S. A., & Milch, R. E. (1982). Changing the speech of autistic children and their parents. *Child and Family Behavior Therapy, 4,* 151–173.

Hasenstab, M. S., & Laughton, J. (1982). Bare essentials in assessing really little kids (BEAR): An approach. In M. S. Hasenstab & J. S. Horner (Eds.), *Comprehensive intervention with hearing-impaired infants and preschool children* (pp. 203–318). Rockville, MD: Aspen Systems.

Hendrick, D., Prather, E., & Tobin, A. (1984). *Sequenced Inventory of Communication Development* (rev. ed.). Austin, TX: Pro-Ed.

Hilke, D. (1988). Infant vocalizations and changes in experience. *Journal of Child Language, 15,* 1–15.

Hresko, W., Reid, D. K., & Hammill, D. (1991). *Test of Early Language Development* (2nd ed.). Austin, TX: Pro-Ed.

Huttenlocher, J. (1974). Origins of language comprehension. In R. Solso (Ed.), *Theories in cognitive psychology.* Hillsdale, NJ: Erlbaum.

Jakobson, R. (1968). *Child language, aphasia, and phonological universals.* The Hague: Mouton.

Johnson, D., & Myklebust, H. (1967). *Learning disabilities: Educational principles and practices.* New York: Grune & Stratton.

Kaiser, A. P. (1993). Functional language. In M. Snell (Ed.), *Instructors of students with severe disabilities* (4th ed.). Upper Saddle River, NJ: Prentice Hall.

Kaiser, A. P., Hemmeter, M. L., Ostrosky, M. M., Alpert, C. L., & Hancock, T. B. (1995). The effects of group training and individual feedback on parent use of milieu teaching. *Journal of Childhood Communication Disorders, 16,* 39–48.

Kamhi, A. G., & Johnston, J. R. (1982). Towards an understanding of retarded children's linguistic deficiency. *Journal of Speech and Hearing Research, 25*(3), 435–445.

Kasari, C., Sigman, M, Yirmiya, N., & Mundy, P. (1993). Affective development and communication in young children with autism. In A. Kaiser & D. Gray (Eds.), *Enhancing children's communication.* Baltimore: Paul H. Brookes.

Kretschmer, R. R. & Kretschmer, L. W. (1978). *Language development and intervention with the hearing impaired.* Baltimore: University Park Press.

Krivcher-Winestone, J. (1980). Limits of syntactical development of educable mentally retarded children. (Doctoral dissertation, Yeshiva University, 1979). *Dissertation Abstracts International,* 40, 6230A. (University Microfilms No. 8012676).

Kronstadt, D. (1991). Complex developmental issues of prenatal drug exposure. *The Future of Children, 1,* 36–49.

Laski, K., Charlop, M., & Schreibman, L. (1988). Training parents to use the natural language paradigm to increase their autistic children's speech. *Journal of Applied Behavior Analysis, 21,* 391–400.

Lenneberg, E. (1967). *Biological foundations of language.* New York: Wiley.

Ling, D. (1972). Rehabilitation of cases with deafness secondary to otitis media. In A. Glorig & I. K. Gerwin (Eds.), *Otitis Media Proceedings of the National Conference, Collier Hearing and Speech*

Center, Dallas. Springfield, IL: Charles C Thomas.

Ling, D. (1976). *Speech and the hearing-impaired child*. Washington, DC: A. G. Bell Association for the Deaf.

Lovaas, O. (Ed.). (1977). *The autistic child: Language development through behavior modification*. New York: Halstead Press.

Lovell, K., & Bradbury, B. (1967). The learning of English morphology in educationally subnormal special school children. *American Journal of Mental Deficiency, 71,* 609–615.

Lucas, E. V. (1980). *Semantic and pragmatic language: Assessment and remediation*. Rockville, MD: Aspen Systems.

Luria, A. R. (1961). *Speech and the regulation of behavior*. New York: Liveright.

MacDonald, J. D. (1985). Language through conversation: A model for intervention with language-delayed persons. In S. Warren & A. Rogers-Warren (Eds.), *Teaching functional language*. Baltimore: University Park Press.

MacDonald, J. D., & Blott, J. (1974). Environmental interventions: The rationale for a diagnostic and training strategy through rules, context, and generalizations. *Journal of Speech and Hearing Disorders, 39,* 244–256.

Matsuda, M. M. (1984). Comparative analysis of blind and sighted children's communication skills. *Journal of Visual Impairment and Blindness, 78,* 1–5.

McConnell, O. (1967). Control of eye contact in an autistic child. *Journal of Child Psychology and Psychiatry, 2,* 389–399.

McCormick, L., & Schiefelbusch, R. L. (1990). *Early language intervention: An introduction* (2nd ed.). Upper Saddle River, NJ: Merrill/Prentice Hall.

McCormick, L., & Shane, H. (1990). Communication system options for students who are nonspeaking. In L. McCormick & R. Schiefelbusch (Eds.), *Early language intervention*. Upper Saddle River, NJ: Merrill/Prentice Hall.

McDonald, E. T., & Schultz, A. R. (1973). Communication boards for cerebral palsied children. *Journal of Speech and Hearing Disorders, 38,* 73–78.

McLean, J., & Snyder, L. K. (1977). *A transactional approach to early language training: Derivation of model system. Final Report*. Washington, DC: U.S. Department of Health, Education, and Welfare.

McLean, J. & Snyder-McLean, L. (1978). *A transactional approach to early language training*. Upper Saddle River, NJ: Merrill/Prentice Hall.

McNeill, D. (1966). Developmental psycholinguistics. In F. Smith & G. A. Miller (Eds.), *The genesis of language: A psycholinguistic approach*. Cambridge, MA: MIT Press.

Menyuk, P. (1971). *The acquisition and development of language*. Upper Saddle River, NJ: Prentice Hall.

Miller, A., & Miller, E. (1973). Cognitive development training with elevated boards and sign language. *Journal of Autism and Childhood Schizophrenia, 3,* 65–85.

Moray, N. (1969). *Attention: Selective processes in vision and hearing*. London: Hutchinson Educational Ltd.

Muma, J. R. (1978). *Language handbook: Concepts, assessment, intervention*. Upper Saddle River, NJ: Prentice Hall.

Myklebust, H., & Boshes, B. (1960). Psychoneurological learning disorders in children. *Archives of Pediatrics, 77,* 247–256.

Nelson, I. (1973). Structure and strategy in learning to talk. *Monographs of the Society for Research in Child Development, 38,* No. 149.

Newfield, M. U., & Schlanger, B. B. (1968). The acquisition of English morphology by normal and educable mentally retarded children. *Journal of Speech and Hearing Research, 11,* 693–706.

Northcott, W. (1977). *Curriculum guide for hearing-impaired children (0–3 years) and their parents*. Washington, DC: A. G. Bell Association for the Deaf.

Olson, H., Burgess, D., and Streissguth, A. (1992). Fetal alcohol syndrome (FAS) and fetal alcohol effects (FAE): A lifespan view, with implications for early intervention. *Zero to Three, 13,* 29–33.

Owens, R. (1995). *Language disorders: A functional approach to assessment and intervention* (2nd ed.). Boston: Allyn & Bacon.

Owens, R. (1996). *Language development: An introduction* (4th ed.). Boston: Allyn & Bacon.

Phelps-Terasaki, D., & Phelps-Gunn, T. (1992). *Test of Pragmatic Language*. Austin, TX: Pro-Ed.

Piaget, J. (1952). *The origins of intelligence in children* (M. Cook, Trans.). New York: International University Press.

Prather, E. M., Hedrick, D., & Kern, A. (1972). Articulation development in children aged two to four years. *Journal of Speech and Hearing Disorders,*

37, 55–63.

Prizant, B., & Bailey, D. (1992). Facilitating acquisition and use of communication skills. In D. B. Bailey & M. Wolery (Eds.), *Teaching infants and preschoolers with disabilities.* Upper Saddle River, NJ: Merrill/Prentice Hall.

Prizant, B. M., & Duchan, J. F. (1981). The functions of immediate echolalia in autistic children. *Journal of Speech and Hearing Disorders, 46,* 241–249.

Prutting, C. (1979). Process: The action of moving forward progressively from one point to another on the way to completion. *Journal of Speech and Hearing Disorders, 44,* 1–20.

Pueschel, S. M., & Hopmann, M. R. (1993). Speech and language abilities of children with Down syndrome: A parent's perspective. In A. Kaiser & D. Gray (Eds.), *Enhancing children's communication* (pp. 335–364). Baltimore: Paul H. Brookes.

Ratner, V., & Harris, L. (1994). *Understanding language disorders.* Eau Claire, WI: Thinking Publications.

Reed, V. (1986). *An introduction to children with language disorders.* Upper Saddle River, NJ: Prentice Hall.

Reichle, J., York, J., & Sigafoos, J. (Eds.). (1991). *Implementing augmentative and alternative communication.* Baltimore: Paul H. Brookes.

Reike, J. A., & Lewis, J. (1984). Preschool intervention strategies: The communication game. *Topics in Language Disorders, 5,* 41–57.

Ripich, D., & Creaghead, N. (Eds.). (1994). *School discourse problems* (2nd ed.). San Diego, CA: Singular Publishing Group.

Roberts, J. E. (1995). Otitis media in early childhood and cognitive, academic, and behavior outcomes at 12 years of age. *Journal of Pediatric Psychology, 20*(5), 645–60.

Roberts, P. (1964). *English syntax.* New York: Harcourt, Brace & World.

Roth, F., & Spekman, N. (1984). Assessing the pragmatic abilities of children, Part I: Organizational framework and assessment parameters. *Journal of Speech and Hearing Disorders, 49,* 2–11.

Sabsay, S. & Kernan, K. T. (1993). On the nature of language impairment in Down syndrome. *Topics in Language Disorders, 13*(3), 20–35.

Sachs, J., & Devin, J. (1976). Young children's use of age-appropriate speech styles. *Journal of Child Language, 3,* 81–98.

Sacks, H., Schegloff, E. A., & Jefferson, G. (1974). A simplest systematics for the organization of turn-taking for conversation. *Language, 50,* 696–735.

Santin, S., & Simmons, J. N. (1977). Problems in the construction of reality in congenitally blind children. *Journal of Visual Impairment or Blindness, 71,* 425–429.

Sarff, L. S. (1981). An innovative use of free field amplification in regular classrooms. In R. Roeser & M. Downs (Eds.), *Auditory disorders in school children.* New York: Thieme-Stratton.

Sattler, J. (1988). *Assessment of children's intelligence and special abilities* (3rd ed.). Boston: Allyn & Bacon.

Schegloff, E. A. (1968). Sequencing in conversational openings. *American Anthropologist, 70,* 1075–1095.

Schegloff, E. A. & Sacks, H. (1973). Opening up closings. *Semiotica, 8,* 289–327.

Schlesinger, H., & Meadow, K. (1972). *Sound and sign.* Los Angeles: University of California Press.

Searle, J. R. (1969). *Speech acts: An essay in the philosophy of language.* Cambridge, England: Cambridge University Press.

Selman, R. (1971). The relation of role-taking to the development of moral judgement in children. *Child Development, 42,* 79–92.

Sharf, D. (1972). Some relationships between measures of early language development. *Journal of Speech and Hearing Disorders, 37,* 64–74.

Shulman, B. (1985). *Using play behavior to describe young children's conversational abilities.* Paper presented at the Annual Meeting of the National Association for the Education of Young Children, Los Angeles, CA.

Silverman, F. H. (1980). *Communication for the speechless.* Upper Saddle River, NJ: Prentice Hall.

Simon, C. S. (1981). *Communicative competence: A functional-pragmatic approach to language therapy.* Tucson: Communication Skill Builders.

Skinner, B. (1957). *Verbal behavior.* New York: Appleton-Century-Croft.

Snow, C. (1972). Mother's speech to children learning language. *Child Development, 43,* 549–565.

Sparks, S. (1993). *Children of prenatal substance abuse.* San Diego, CA: Singular Publishing Group.

Streissguth, A. (1986). The behavioral teratology of alcohol: Performance, behavioral, and intellectual deficits in prenatally exposed children. In J. West (Ed.), *Alcohol and brain development* (pp. 3–44). New York: Oxford University Press.

Tannock, R., Girolametto, L., & Siegel, L. (March, 1989). *Efficacy of a conversational model of language intervention.* Paper presented at the American Speech and Hearing Foundation Treatment Efficacy Conference, San Antonio, TX.

Teele, D., Klein, J., Chase, C., Menyuk, P., & Rosner, B. (1990). Otitis media in infancy and intellectual ability, school achievement, speech and language at age 7 years. *Journal of Infectious Diseases, 162,* 685–694.

Templin, M. (1957). *Certain language skills in children.* Minneapolis: University of Minnesota Press.

Tillery, K. L., & Smosky, W. J. (1994). Clinical implications of the auditory processing abilities of children with attention deficit-hyperactivity disorder. In *Central Auditory Processing: Consensus Development Conference.* American Speech-Language-Hearing Association: Rockville, MD.

Trantham, C. R., & Pedersen, J. K. (1976). *Normal language development.* Baltimore: Williams & Wilkins.

Vanderheiden, G. C., & Grilley, K. (Eds.). (1976). *Non-vocal communication techniques and aids for the severely physically handicapped.* Baltimore: University Park Press.

Vygotsky, L (1962). *Thought and language.* Cambridge, MA: MIT Press.

Warren, D. H. (1984). *Blindness and early childhood development.* (2nd ed.). New York: American Foundation for the Blind.

Webster, C. D., McPherson, H., Sloman, L., Evans, M. A., & Kuchar, E. (1973). Communicating with an autistic boy by gestures. *Journal of Autism and Childhood Schizophrenia, 3,* 337–346.

West, J. T., & Idol, L. (1990). Collaborative consultation in the education of mentally retarded and at-risk students. *Remedial and Special Education, 11,* 22–31.

Wiig, E. H., & Semel, E. M. (1980). *Language assessment and intervention for the learning disabled.* Upper Saddle River, NJ: Merrill/Prentice Hall.

Wiig, E. H., & Semel, E. M. (1984). *Language assessment and intervention for the learning disabled.* (2nd ed.). Upper Saddle River, NJ: Merrill/Prentice Hall.

Wilson, M. I. (1973). Children with crippling and health disabilities. In L. M. Dunn (Ed.), *Exceptional Children in the Schools.* New York: Holt, Rinehart, & Winston.

Wing, L. (1971). Perceptual and language development in autistic children: A comparative study. In M. Rutter (Ed.), *Infantile autism: Concepts, characteristics, and treatment.* Edinburgh: Churchill Livingstone.

Yoder, D. W., & Miller, J. F. (1972). What we know and what we can do: Input toward a system. In J. E. McLean, D. E. Yoder, & R. L. Schiefelbusch (Eds.), *Language intervention with the retarded.* Baltimore: University Park Press.

Yoder, P. J. & Warren, S. F. (1993). Can developmentally delayed children's language development be enhanced through prelinguistic intervention? In A. Kaiser & D. Gray (Eds.), *Enhancing children's communication: Research foundations for intervention.* Baltimore, MD: Paul H. Brookes.

Zimmerman, I., Steiner, V., & Pond, R. (1992). *Preschool Language Scale–3.* New York: The Psychological Corporation.

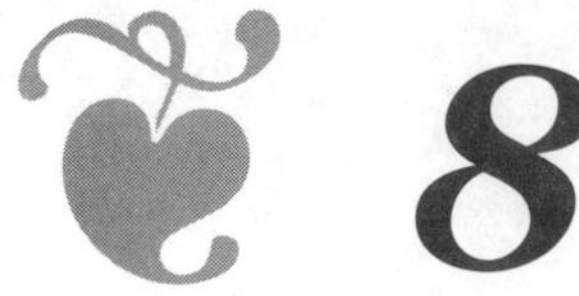

8

Emotional and Social Development

Warren Umansky

A spacecraft leaves Earth and heads out into space, while a young father preparing dinner in Indiana overcooks vegetables in the microwave oven. The spacecraft maintains a perfect course and executes a precise docking with a joint United States–Russian space station. The young father takes his family out for fast food.

Our collective brilliance and simplicity stand in sharp contrast to each other. We often are able and eager to do so much, yet we are limited in so many ways. The development of social and emotional competence in children reflects one area in which modern technology has contributed relatively little. We still grope for reasons to explain why some children are very aggressive and others are passive, or why some seek out playmates and others avoid them.

Under most circumstances, children evolve through a complex system of experiences into emotionally and socially competent individuals. While the development of personality and social skills is not well understood in children with special needs, the factors that enhance personal and social adjustment appear to be the same for all children. For example, for children to enter successful play activities with their peers, resolve social conflicts that occur with peers, or deal with the flow of social exchanges needed to maintain play with peers, a complex set of behaviors is needed. It is understandable, then, why as many as 10% of children with no identified special need have problems establishing friendships and sustaining peer relationships (Asher, 1990). A disability imposes conditions and restrictions on a child that are moderated only by careful planning.

Young children with special needs face challenges in their social worlds. Peers may accept them without reservation or they may be put off by such children's different appearances, language differences, unpredictable responses in social situations, or limitations in their level of participation in typical activities. Adults may be accepting and understanding, or they may reinforce the stigma that a child is nothing more than his disability. In an environment of acceptance, a young child is more likely to feel and to be successful. When a child is rejected, he is more likely to be reluctant to initiate social contact and to suffer from low self-esteem and poor motivation:

> No other child in America can experience such extreme social contrast in a single day, let alone over the course of a childhood: love, understanding, and stimulation at home, intense stigma in the classroom, and, from all too many adults, the tacit message that society's concept of disability is indeed correct, that the child is nothing more than his condition. No other group of disadvantaged children contains so many children who are physically different from their parents and sociologically different as well. Nor does any other group of children contain so many individuals who, because of the physical limitations and social stigma they face, have such powerful incentives for channeling their best mental and emotional energies into learning to manipulate the rules of social interaction to their own advantage. These sociological facts cry out for integration into a broadly based educational strategy for the handicapped child and his parents. (Gliedman, 1979, p. 8–9)

For most children, healthy social and emotional development evolves naturally as a consequence of casual interactions with their environment. For many children with disabilities, however, this is not a natural process, but one requiring careful and deliberate planning. For this reason, social competence is considered by some to be the area deserving greatest emphasis in early childhood programs (Guralnick, 1994).

Influences on Development

Young children with special needs often show unique behaviors in their interactions with others or when they face a problematic task. Yet, as with all children, the range of typical behavior is broad. Some mothers can look back upon the times they were pregnant with their children and describe how each child was different in utero. In some cases, the more active child remained active; in others, there was little relationship between the child's prenatal activity and subsequent behavior.

Temperament

Every child is born with a set of personality characteristics that Thomas and Chess (1977) call *temperament*. These characteristics play an important role in shaping the responses of a child's caregivers and, ultimately, in molding the child's future personality. The easy child, for example, is very adaptable, playful, and responsive to adults. This type of child is likely to receive a great deal of adult attention during the early years because interactions are so pleasant and reinforcing. The difficult child, on the other hand, provides little positive feedback to adults. He is fussy, difficult to soothe, and irregular in sleeping and eating patterns. This type of child is likely to get less positive attention from adults (van den Boom & Hoeksma, 1994). Finally, the temperament of the slow-to-warm-up child is characterized by slow adaptability. Adults who sustain contact with this type of child are usually rewarded by the positive behaviors found in the easy child, but it takes considerably longer to elicit them. An adult's sensitivity and responsiveness to an infant's social cues probably establish the foundation for secure attachment relationships necessary for healthy social and emotional development (van Ijzendoorn, Juffer, & Duyvesteyn, 1995).

Temperament, as a constellation of hereditary qualities, has great implications for a child's future social and emotional development (Ahadi, Rothbart, & Ye, 1993). In formulating his self-concept, a child's evaluation of himself is based upon how others respond to his behavior. Children who are difficult or who have a disability that diverts or distorts their interactions with others appear most likely to develop impaired self-concepts (Lyons-Ruth, Alpern, & Repacholi, 1993).

Early Interactions

Many factors intervene in the process of social and emotional development. A child's temperament exerts a powerful influence on the care that he is given. This

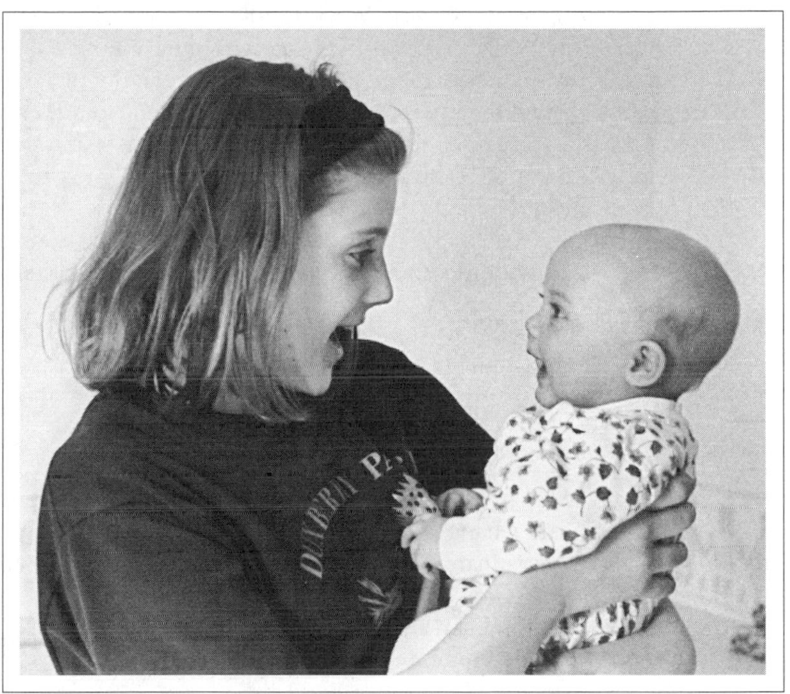

A responsive child is likely to cause caregivers to be responsive, which, in turn, reinforces the child's positive behaviors.

is described by the transactional model (Sameroff & Chandler, 1975; Sameroff & Fiese, 1990), wherein the child is a responder to as well as an initiator of social interactions. A responsive child is more likely to cause caregivers to be responsive, which, in turn, reinforces the child's positive behavior (Lussier, Crimmins, & Alberti, 1994). Similarly, an unresponsive child discourages high-level stimulation by caregivers, which, cyclically, maintains the child's unresponsiveness. This reciprocal process provides an infant with the foundation for understanding how his behavior influences the environment (Bornstein & Lamb, 1992).

Interaction between the caregiver and the young child should produce an empathic bond or secure attachment that promotes a clear concept of self-identity in the child. The empathic bond is strengthened by the physical warmth of the caregiver's body. The bonding process has generated considerable research recently. A precise understanding of what happens during early mother-child interaction, whether biological or psychological in nature, is yet undetermined. Most evidence, however, points to improved outcomes for children who have had physical contact with their mothers shortly after birth (Lozoff, Brittenham, Trause, Kennell, & Klaus, 1977).

When contact is considered in terms of other intervening factors, greater insight into the bonding process may be gained. For example, bonding is a popular topic of consumer magazines and educational television and radio. This has made the information most accessible to middle- and upper-class parents, who may be the group most likely to request contact with their infants following birth. These are also the caregivers most likely to maintain a high quality of care throughout a child's early years of development. It is not surprising, then, that these children tend to do better as they develop. Unfortunately, this hypothesis is clouded by lack of carefully controlled studies (Crouch & Manderson, 1994).

Children may be denied early contact because the caregiver considers it unimportant or because the child requires critical postpartum medical care. Not surprisingly, such children show a higher than normal incidence of emotional disorders and other impairments as they develop. Even when early contact is provided, however, a child who is unresponsive to his caregiver may be contributing to his own social deprivation (Lewis & Rosenblum, 1974).

Personality Development

A child is born with certain personality traits, but his personality is not fixed at the time of birth. Changes occur over time as a result of many factors that influence personality as it is manifested in both emotional expression and social behavior. To differentiate the two, we shall consider *emotion* the expression of feelings, needs, and desires accompanied by specific physiological responses. *Social behavior* describes the general quality of a child's response to people and situations within the boundaries of social and cultural standards.

Newborns have few ways of expressing feelings and show limited discrimination of people and situations. In as short a time as 2 years, however, children have an almost complete store of emotional expressions. Also, depending upon their range of early experiences, they may have an easy or a difficult time adapting to a parent's absence, to long car rides, to spending the weekend with grandparents, or to eating out at a restaurant. Children's early experiences and interactions with their caregivers also have implications for later interactions with other children. There is evidence, for example, that securely attached children interact more with peers than do those who are not securely attached (van den Boom, 1995).

By kindergarten, a child should be a socialized being. Friendliness is an important social behavior because it demonstrates a child's awareness of other people as separate and unique individuals. The importance of the kindergarten social experience has been described by Ladd, Kochenderfer, and Coleman (1996). They found that children who established and maintained positive peer relationships during kindergarten had greater school gains and expressed more favorable school perceptions than did children who were rejected. Many factors contribute to the formation of social behaviors that generate acceptance and success.

Physical Appearance. We often form strong and lasting impressions of other people based on their appearance. By age 5, the social behavior of unattractive children differs from that of children who are considered to be attractive even when no behavior differences were noted at age 3 (Langlois & Downs, 1979). Unattractive children are more active, more aggressive, and more boisterous. Adults have lower expectations for unattractive children (Lerner & Lerner, 1977); adults and other children rate them in less-positive terms (Styczynski & Langlois, 1977).

Name and Gender. Some names elicit more positive responses from children than others do. "The child who bears a generally unpopular or unattractive name may be handicapped in his social interactions with peers" (McDavid & Harari, 1966, p. 458). In addition, males tend to be more vulnerable to family and life stresses than females are (Walker, Cudeck, Mednick, & Schulsinger, 1981; Wolkind & Rutter, 1973). It has been postulated, however, that males are reinforced for more aggressive and competitive behavior by family members and peers, which accounts for increasing differences in their social patterns as they develop (Block, 1982; Serbin, O'Leary, Kent, & Tonick, 1973). This is supported by Maccoby and Jacklin (1974), who reported no differences in activity levels of boys and girls in infancy, but a higher activity level for boys by preschool age.

Sibling Relationships. First-born children receive more attention from their caregivers than do later children (Thomas, Liederman, & Olson, 1972). However, the care they receive from inexperienced caregivers is apt to be inconsistent and experimental. They also miss the opportunities to learn social skills from siblings that later children have. First-born children show less confidence, greater fear of failure, more anxiety, and more social awkwardness than do later children (Schacter, 1959), who are more outgoing and seek the company of peers.

Stress. The formation of a child's personality is closely related to the types of stress to which he is subjected in his early years and to how he deals with the stress. A child who lives in poverty, has multiple hospital stays, or comes from a dysfunctional home is at risk for long-lasting psychosocial disorders. Still, some children handle stresses better than others do, and many progress through adverse early years relatively undamaged (Quinton & Rutter, 1976). Some emerge better able to cope with later stresses, while others are more vulnerable (Rutter, 1980). Rutter (1971, 1978) has indicated that a secure attachment with one parent during the stressful early years may shield a child from later psychosocial disorders.

Parental Style. Parents of large families may show less warmth with individual children and make the development of a close relationship between parent and child difficult. The authoritarian parent, characterized by a "control by power" philosophy, tends to be inconsistent in caregiving and precipitates conflict. This style of parenting is associated with antisocial behavior in children (Garmezy, 1975; Glueck & Glueck, 1950). Authoritative parents tend to be more consistent, to give reasons for their actions, and to be predictable. This type of parenting is associated with more positive social behavior and positive personality traits in children (Baumrind, 1967).

Forms of Social and Emotional Expression

Prosocial Behaviors

Until a child is able to view a situation from another's perspective, it is impossible for him to exhibit the qualities that comprise prosocial behaviors. Sharing, cooperation, turn taking, empathy, and helpfulness require an understanding of another person's needs and feelings. The shift to decreased egocentrism is a cognitive milestone with significant implications for social and emotional development.

Prosocial behaviors increase with age and are closely tied to a child's experiences (Barnett, 1982). Happy children are more willing to share and cooperate than are sad children. In addition, the emphasis placed on certain behaviors in different families or cultures influences a child's expression of these behaviors in social settings (Bryan & London, 1970; Hartup, 1970).

Children as young as 2 years may exhibit sharing behavior. Waldrop and Halverson (1975) noted that children who were socially oriented at this young age were the same 5 years later. However, just as warm and nurturing homes are more likely to promote prosocial behavior in children, inconsistent and nonsupportive homes are more likely to promote antisocial behavior.

Antisocial Behaviors

Numerous types of behavior exhibited by children may interfere with the socialization process. When such behavior occurs rarely, its influence may be insignificant, but frequent or persistent appearance of the behavior may reflect a psychosocial disturbance or contribute to the alienation of the child from the mainstream of society.

Fear. The development of fear seems to occur very early in a child's life. As a child passes through the preschool years, there is usually a decrease in fear of supernatural creatures and imaginary experiences. Then, as the child reaches school age, he gains a better understanding of reality and shows a decrease in unjustified fears. These are often replaced by more permanent fears related to new and specific situations as the child's environment expands and offers new challenges (Wolman, 1978). For example, a fear of the dentist or of returning to an empty house may remain with one throughout life.

Aggression. During the early years of development, it is not uncommon to see children fighting one minute and playing cooperatively the next. Many aggressive episodes among young children erupt primarily because a child is unable to verbalize his needs or wants, and he resorts to the more efficient physical mode of expression. As a child becomes less egocentric and gains a larger verbal repertoire with which to express feelings, however, physical aggression yields to more controlled verbal expression.

Robeck (1969) identified several other reasons for aggressive acts by young children. These include being victimized by other children whose behavior goes unpunished, watching aggressive acts, being punished severely or frequently, and being denied a desired object. Hartup (1974) found a strong relationship between aggression and parental characteristics. Punitive forms of discipline and excessive control of a child's actions are related to higher levels of aggression. Reinforcement of aggressive behavior by parents and by peers may also lead to an increase in aggression and generalization of the behavior to other situations (Caldwell, 1979; Rutter, 1981).

Dependence. Overly dependent children—those who need continuous attention and reassurance—are frequently unpopular with their peers (Martin, 1975). Dependence is a characteristic of infancy, wherein a child has relied on the caregiver to meet all of his needs. The security of this relationship should take a different form as the child becomes more mobile and develops the capabilities for greater self-sufficiency. Passive support by the caregiver facilitates this transition. When support is absent, the child may regress to the use of immature behaviors, such as whining or crying, to solicit assistance for a task he is able to do himself.

Jealousy. Jealousy is a response to undesired competition. It is displayed by a child, for example, when an adult attends to another child or when someone is playing with a prized toy or is chosen to perform a highly regarded task. Jealousy may be manifested in several ways. A child may become aggressive toward the object of his jealousy or may transfer aggression to other children or objects. He may become passive and withdrawn, avoiding contact with others. Or, as often occurs when a new sibling is introduced into the home, the child may regress to immature behaviors. A good talker may start using baby talk. He may begin having toileting accidents and temper tantrums. The quality of and the form in which jealousy is manifested may change with age, but the capacity for jealousy often persists throughout life.

Play

The importance of play in a child's development and learning has received renewed recognition over the past decade. Many years ago, Freud saw play as a way for a child to fulfill his wishes, satisfy his drives, and control events that threaten the stability of his developing personality. Freud considered play to be a means for the child to exercise emerging cognitive abilities. Despite great emphasis having been placed on play by Erikson and others (Erikson, 1968; Piaget, 1954; Vygotsky, 1978), only recently has play received significant attention from early intervention professionals.

In addition to play being important from a developmental perspective, it is being used more and more as an assessment instrument (Linder, 1993). Assessment of young children using a play format may yield more valid results than a standardized assessment procedure does for numerous reasons, as described in Chapter 10.

Play also is used as the foundation for early intervention with young children with special needs.

Play has distinctive characteristics: It is spontaneous and voluntary; it is self-generated and involves active participation; it is intrinsically motivated, that is, performed for its own sake; it is pleasurable; and it differs from child to child (Fewell & Kaminski, 1988). Initially, play is very overt and physical, reflecting a child's immature cognitive structures. Later, however, play becomes more symbolic and social, involving problem solving of real-life situations and acting out roles that the child will take later in life. Play also becomes a mechanism for a child to initiate social interactions with other children. Some consider the establishment of peer relationships to be a child's fundamental social skill (Guralnick, 1993; Putallaz & Wasserman, 1990). For success in this complex endeavor, a child must have knowledge of the current and changing context of the play setting and must be able to use a wide range of cognitive, language, social, and behavior skills to achieve positive interactions with peers (Roberts, Brown, & Richards, 1995). These skills vary with age and with disability. For example, Lieber (1993) found that preschoolers with disabilities in an integrated setting had difficulty gaining entry to a social relationship because they used direct and often disruptive entry behaviors. Children without disabilities, on the other hand, used verbal and nonverbal indirect behaviors to gain acceptance into group play. Indirect entry strategies, such as offering an object, were found by Craig and Washington (1993) as well to be more suc-

Play evolves from being mainly a physical activity to more of a symbolic, social, role-playing, and problem-solving process.

cessful than direct strategies, such as requesting entry into a play situation. There also is evidence that rates of social interaction are higher for children with various types of disabilities in settings with normally developing peers than in settings only with children who have similar disabilities (Field, Roseman, DeStefano, & Koewler, 1981).

Specific studies that have compared the play of young children with disabilities to same-age peers with normal development have found that children with disabilities show less-varied play (Beeghly, Weiss-Perry, & Cicchetti, 1990), less-frequent play (Jennings, Conners, & Stegman, 1988), and lower developmental levels of play (Jennings, Conners, & Stegman, 1988; Li, 1985). However, when compared with children of the same developmental level, few differences are found in their play (Dunst, Mahoney, & Buchan, 1996). Acquisition of play behaviors is delayed in children with disabilities, but these children display similar levels of play intensity and progress through the same levels of play development as do children at the same developmental level (Gowen, Goldman, Johnson-Martin, & Hussey, 1989).

Locus of Control

A very young child is controlled by those around him and by his physical environment. He eats when he is fed; he sleeps when he is put in the crib and the lights are turned off.

As the child gets older, he assumes greater responsibility for his own actions. He should not require directions for every menial task nor expect to be reinforced for every action. The internalization of the locus of control, which is often called *self-control,* reflects the child's increased understanding of the rules of society and social expectations. It requires an ability to delay gratification and to refrain from acting impulsively.

Theories of Social and Emotional Development

Psychosocial Theory

Erikson (1950) described milestones of development in terms of emotional conflicts that a child must resolve to become a socialized individual. He identified three such conflicts during the child's first 5 years: trust versus mistrust, autonomy versus shame and doubt, and initiative versus guilt.

Trust Versus Mistrust. The physical closeness of an infant with his caregiver facilitates the formation of a very strong bond. Consistency of caregiving and physical comfort also creates trust in the child for the caregiver. This prepares him to deal confidently with the experiences that his environment will present. Inconsistent caregiving that leads to frustration and discomfort for the child is liable to interfere with normal development. The child, in this case, has a mistrust of new experiences and relationships. In most children, this conflict is resolved within the first 18 months of life.

Autonomy Versus Shame and Doubt. Society has certain expectations for a toddler. Now that he can move about freely, he must adhere to certain social mores. He will be prepared for encounters with new situations if he has been given the freedom to explore the environment and to initiate his own activities (White, 1975). This contributes to development of self-control and feelings of independence as an autonomous being. Poor caregiving, on the other hand, causes the child to doubt his ability to control his own actions and to feel shame at being so powerless. Most children achieve self-regulation through resolution of this conflict by 3 years of age.

Initiative Versus Guilt. As a child develops, he becomes aware of his power as an initiator of activity. He is more able to control his environment as he gains mastery over his own body. The child understands that people have different motivations and perceptions, and he delights in his ability to figure things out. However, some actions that display initiative lead to feelings of guilt. Such feelings can be inhibiting, contributing to a later lack of initiative. When a child resolves this conflict, he perceives himself as distinctly separate from his parents and free to explore his world.

Social Learning Theory

Learning theory focuses on the influence of the environment on the development of personality and specific behaviors. Bijou and Baer (1979) place great emphasis on interpreting a child's current behaviors based on his history of interactions with the environment. Socialization, then, is viewed as a child's range of experiences from which he develops his personality and learns appropriate behaviors.

Bandura (1977) provided the foundation for explaining social learning theory and for distinguishing it from behavioral theory. Whereas the latter emphasizes the role of reinforcement in maintaining or halting certain behaviors, Bandura proposed that most learning occurs through observation, modeling, and imitation. Consequently, an organized and carefully structured environment is most likely to achieve desired goals. As applied to development of social and emotional skills, sound models and situations that encourage the display of prosocial behaviors are those that facilitate the most normal development.

Assessment of Social and Emotional Development

Social skills and emotions are perhaps the most difficult areas of human development to understand. They are situational in nature; a child may be aggressive in one situation and passive in another. He may cry when confronted with some strangers and befriend others. He may engage in complex imaginary play at the babysitter's house but not at home. How, then, is one to gain an understanding of this complex of behaviors? Systematic assessment of the child may provide some answers.

Multimodal Assessment

The behavior of young children is extremely variable depending upon the setting, the time of day, who is present, and other factors. As a result, there is a shift away from using a single instrument or observation to document a child's behavior. A multimodal approach uses a combination of strategies for collecting information, which may include systematic observations in various settings, interviews, rating scales, and paper-and-pencil tests.

Direct observation of a child in different settings may be the most desirable means by which to evaluate developmental characteristics, because the farther one strays from direct measurements of behavior, the less reliable the results are likely to be. Yarrow (1963), for example, examined the values of the interview as an assessment technique and found that information gathered by interviewing parents tends to follow a pattern of idealized expectations and cultural stereotypes. Parents also frequently confuse a child with siblings or feel obligated to respond to questions in spite of vague recollections. Reliability of information gathered in this way may be improved when the parent is requested to recall recent events, when the behaviors to be recalled are clearly defined, and when response choices are specific and easily quantified.

Interviews with children—a technique that Piaget utilized to discover how they process information—are limited by a child's verbal skills; however, the technique does offer an opportunity for the evaluator to establish a relationship with the child that can assist with more structured assessment at a later time. With older and developmentally normal children, interviews may indeed provide valuable information about their social and emotional development.

What Is Normal?

A basic problem arises with the issue of assessment of social and emotional development. While we have discussed characteristics of normal development in these areas, it is quite difficult to assign expected ages to significant social and emotional milestones. There appears to be some consensus about what abnormal behavior is, so that an observer can identify a child exhibiting inappropriate behavior. But it is considerably more difficult to be precise about what behaviors children should be displaying in various situations and at different ages. Recent varieties of assessment instruments have increased our ability to make comparisons among children and among different situations for a single child.

Types of Assessment Instruments

Systematic Observation. The most reliable information about a child can be gathered by observing him surreptitiously in a naturalistic environment. Several principles guide this type of assessment.

Observations in many settings may be necessary to get a complete impression of how a child interacts with others, how he interacts with objects, and how he deals with challenging situations or conflicts. Furthermore, behaviors may change if the child is aware of being observed. This phenomenon has been well documented in adults (Moustakas, Sigel, & Schalock, 1956; Zegoib, Arnold, & Forehand, 1975), but less so with children. However, it should be expected that one will not see a child's typical behaviors when the naturalism of the setting is disturbed.

Finally, the assessor must have defined specific behaviors to observe and have an objective way of recording the observations. Many electronic coding devices have been developed to record time and frequency data, but little sophistication is necessary to record information reflecting a child's abilities.

Interviews and Questionnaires. Most assessment batteries now include a social and family history in the form of an interview or questionnaire protocol. Valuable information can be gathered through open-ended questioning and through follow-up of vague verbal or written responses. The value depends, however, on the judgment and interpretation of the interviewer. Instruments such as the Vineland Adaptive Behavior Scales (Sparrow, Balla, & Cicchetti, 1984) assist by presenting a format for assessing some skills that fall within the purview of social and emotional development. Asking questions about what the child likes to play with; how he gets along with other children; how often he cries, gets angry, or laughs; and what he does when he's unhappy is likely to provide additional valuable information if the interviewee is a reliable reporter.

Rating Scales. O'Leary and Johnson (1979) have indicated that rating scales are very popular for assessing social development. They suggest four strategies to maximize the reliability and validity of a scale: Use raters who know the child very well, use as many raters as possible, use clearly defined points on the scale, and use several response alternatives. For example, yes-no responses offer little information if one is assessing a child's aggressiveness, while a range of 5 to 7 points along the scale is most desirable. Lorr and McNair (1965) also suggest that a rating for a single characteristic should range from "no appearance of the behavior" to "maximum appearance."

Thomas, Chess, and Korn (1977, pp. 224–227), in their scale for parents and teachers to rate the temperament of young children, offer an example of providing alternative choices to the rater:

When first meeting new children, my child is bashful.	Hardly Ever	1	2	3	4	5	6	7	Almost Always
My child sits still to have a story read or a song sung.	Hardly Ever	1	2	3	4	5	6	7	Almost Always

Projective Tests. The use of projective tests is declining. Some psychologists assert that, through projection, a child expresses impulses that have been unconsciously internalized. Techniques such as drawing, matching pictures with moods or emotions, word association, and creative play were thought to reveal factors that shape and dominate a child's personality. Instruments such as the Draw-A-Person, Rorchach, and Children's Apperception Test have not proven to be valid means of providing insight into young children's behavior (Bradley & Caldwell, 1979), however.

The state of the art in assessment of social and emotional development, then, points in some predictable directions. Greater emphasis must be placed on systematic observation of quantifiable behavior. It is not sufficient to say that "the child is very active." One should be able to document the behavior. For example, one might be interested in knowing the number of times a particularly active child moves from one activity to another. In this case, the teacher could sample the child's movements by charting the number of movements from one activity to another during three 10-minute periods on 5 consecutive days. Or, the teacher might record the amount of time a child spends off-task during selected times of day. In addition, information from parents and other good reporters should be integrated with observational data to identify the child's needs in terms of his interactions with others and his responses to various new and challenging situations.

The Child with Special Needs

It is difficult to separate the direct effects that a disabling condition has on social and emotional development from the effects of the abnormal responses of caregivers to the child. The distinction is of considerable importance and has great implications for the remediation or normalization of differences; and, while it appears that children's development of unusual behaviors may be changed as a result of altered expectations by caregivers, it is worthwhile to consider whether any problems are unique to children with specific impairments. For example, children with communication disorders appear to interact more with adults and often are ignored by their peers (Rice, Sell, & Hadley, 1991). While there are some similarities in the social skills of children with communication disorders and their same-age mates, many differences that place these children at a disadvantage in social settings exist as well (Guralnick, Conner, Hammond, Gottman, & Kinnish, 1996). Similar concerns have been raised for young children with other types of special needs.

Children with Cognitive Differences

This category includes two major groups of children and many subgroups. Children with intellectual disabilities constitute a group about which many false stereotypes have been preserved relative to their personalities and social behavior. These children are not born with feelings of inferiority or inadequacy, but evidence points to their consistent isolation from normal peers. Apparently, the teasing and ridicule to which they often are subjected by peers and adults and the frustration they must face in dealing with life's demands leave their mark on these children's self-concepts, and result in progressively greater social inadequacy and isolation.

If child theorists are correct in emphasizing children's earliest interactions with the environment, then an inability to meet the expectations of the environment early in life may provide a poor beginning. Children with mental retardation often have difficulty giving the cues to their caregivers that elicit nurturance and reinforce the attachment process. If a child is lethargic, does not fix on his caregiver's face or react to being touched or held, as often occurs with children with mental retardation, the attachment between caregiver and child may be weakened. Berger and Cunningham (1981), for example, found delays in eye-contact patterns of children with Down syndrome. In a follow-up study (Berger & Cunningham, 1983), infants with Down syndrome also were found to vocalize less in interactions with their mothers and showed poorer patterns of vocal turn-taking. The difficulties, then, are perpetuated and magnified with the child's continued inability to initiate interactions, unless others are prepared to adjust to the child's decreased signaling capacity.

As a result of a child's early experiences, we might expect him to have difficulty behaving in an age-appropriate way. Development may then be more consistent with mental age than with chronological age. In addition, the consistency for caregiving and expectations that others have for the child determine, to a considerable extent, how the child adapts to new situations and people, how he expresses frustrations in challenging situations, and whether he resorts to physical means to express his feelings, needs, and desires or utilizes speech or a modified communication system.

What do we know about how children with cognitive deficits get along with their peers? Guralnick and Groom (1988) reported an absence of sustained interactions with peers, higher levels of solitary play, fewer friendships, and less interest in social play. Play also is less sophisticated (Beckman & Kohl, 1987). On the other hand, the play of children with cognitive deficits is similar to that of their normal peers relative to engagement in imaginative play, toy choice, and play content (Hellendoorn & Hoekman, 1992).

Another group that is cognitively different and presents unique social and emotional characteristics is gifted children. This group also has been stereotyped, for example, as bookworms, timid individuals, and social introverts. Studies of large groups of gifted people have proven these stereotypes to be false (Newland, 1976; Sears & Barbee, 1977; Terman & Oden, 1947).

Superior ability that provides great success in academic or artistic pursuits also appears to bear on a person's emotional stability and social adjustment. Those who are gifted are especially well prepared for dealing with the demands of life.

Children with Sensory Impairments

Visual Impairments. As with children with mental retardation, not all the difficulties in socialization are the child's (Warren, 1977). The reactions of others to a child's visual impairment may influence the course of his development. Troster and Brombring (1992) reported that children with visual impairments exhibit a more limited repertoire of facial expressions, tend to initiate contact with their mothers less often, and are less compliant with simple requests. The impact on the caregiver is obvious. There often is less desire by a caregiver to interact with a les sive child and more difficulty establishing a secure attachment. According to P (1991), even a very limited amount of vision significantly improves an infa opportunities to engage in interpersonal communication.

Pretend play occurs much later in children with visual impairments than in their sighted peers (Preisler, 1995). Tait (1972) emphasized the relationship of play and exploratory behavior. A visually impaired child is less apt to explore a world that he cannot see—one that holds little of the excitement that color and form present to the seeing child. Furthermore, lack of security emanates from uncertainty about the characteristics of people and things in the environment. All these factors, in toto, interfere with the child's development of self-concept and independent initiation of contacts in his environment (Fraiberg, 1972).

The crucial link between early relationships and later social competence has thus been established. As Scott (1968) and Lukoff and Whiteman (1970) have described, the social competence and emotional maturity of the children with visual impairments in later years depends upon the expectations for them in their earliest years. The incidence of emotional disturbance, for example, has been reported to be higher for children who are visually impaired when they are rejected by the caregiver (Barry & Marshall, 1953) or when they do not establish a secure relationship with an adult in their early years (Hallenbeck, 1954).

Burlingham (1961, 1964) has provided extensive information on the personality development of children who are visually impaired. She noted that greater passivity may follow from feelings of inadequacy and doubts about one's ability to function independently, and she attributed these children's failure to interact with the environment to a dependence-independence conflict and increasing frustration. These may be expressed in self-stimulating behavior (Sandler, 1963) and isolated aggressive acts (Wills, 1970). Fraiberg (1968) also explained this deviant behavior in terms of delayed cognitive development (i.e., the behavior that is displayed is more appropriate for a much younger child) and perpetuation of oral gratification begun in infancy. A child who is visually impaired may continue the oral fixation at later ages with primitive hand clawing and biting behavior (Fraiberg & Freeman, 1964).

Warren (1977) concludes from the evidence:

> It suffices to say that severe emotional disturbance often has its roots in early infancy, and that it is undoubtedly the result of a complex interaction of perceptual, cognitive, and interpersonal factors. The desirability of counseling for parents of blind infants is obvious. (p. 212)

Hearing Impairments. Children who are restricted in their communication with others may share the problems and frustrations experienced by children with other impairments (Altshuler, 1974; Wedell-Monnig & Lumley, 1980). Schlesinger and Meadow (1971) found that parents of children who are deaf are more overbearing and authoritarian than are parents of hearing children. They experience more frustration and resort more to spankings for discipline. Meadow (1975) also found that the children themselves are different. Children who are hearing impaired tend to have more adjustment problems, be more impulsive, and lack empathy.

'ernon (1971) attributed a high incidence of temper tantrums and phys-
on of feelings of children with hearing impairments to their inability to
:ation verbally. These problems often intensify as a child's contact with
lults expands. Misunderstanding, ridicule, alienation, and exploitation
nay do serious damage to a child's self-concept and confidence.

:e from the other extreme also has been presented. Because of the
t verbalization plays in young children's interactions (Garvey & Hogan,
1973), one might anticipate that this is another reason for the alienation of children who are hearing impaired from their normal peers. In fact, studies of school-age children (Darbyshire, 1977; Hus, 1979) support the premise that children who are hearing impaired are rejected by their hearing peers. McCauley, Kennedy, and Bruininks (1976) found that rejection increases with age. However, in one of the few studies done exclusively with preschool children, Vandell and George (1981) reported examples of consistent social competence by children with hearing impairments in their interactions with hearing children. They were persistent initiators of interactions and, in the absence of language, developed alternate communication strategies. Hearing children did not do as well in modifying their communication strategies (i.e., they still used verbal modes), but their social interactions were positive. The implications of these findings support the position that children should be given opportunities for independence and interactions with their environment at an early age.

Children with Emotional Disorders

There have been many attempts to categorize emotional disorders into well-defined groups. However, it remains unclear how the available classification systems apply to preschool children, particularly when normal developmental variations are taken into consideration. Despite the relative lack of data on their application to preschool children, a number of classification systems exist and have been used to diagnose and describe specific emotional and behavioral problems in preschool children. It is important for professionals working with young children with special needs to be familiar with these systems, particularly because some of these systems have measurement devices that may need to be completed by teachers as part of the diagnostic evaluation process.

One of the most commonly recognized systems for classifying child psychopathology is the *Diagnostic and Statistical Manual* (DSM) of the American Psychiatric Association. Now in its fourth revision (DSM–IV), this system provides a multidimensional framework for conceptualizing problem behaviors. The current version of the DSM has more specific diagnoses for children than any previous version, and it requires greater specification for a professional to assign a specific diagnosis. This is the diagnostic system that typically is used by most mental health professionals in the United States.

Another classification system is the *International Classification of Diseases* (ICD), which is published by the World Health Organization and is now approaching its tenth revision. The ICD is similar to the DSM, with an overlap of many of the typically reported childhood disorders.

In contrast to these categorical approaches, a dimensional approach utilizes empirically derived dimensions (i.e., homogeneous groups of behaviors that are statistically related) to classify behavioral and emotional problems of childhood. For example, Achenbach, Edelbrock, and Howell (1987) have identified the dimensions of internalizing behaviors (e.g., sadness, shyness, social withdrawal, depression, and anxiety) and externalizing behaviors (e.g., aggressiveness, delinquency, and acting-out). Similarly, Quay (1979) has presented a dimensional model that identifies four patterns of problematic behaviors: personality disorders, conduct disorders, immaturity, and social delinquency. The first three patterns are appropriate for discussion relative to young children with special needs.

Personality Disorders. A child with personality problems suffers from feelings of inadequacy and, consequently, is uneasy about social interaction. The child's anxiety about others' perceptions of him often have the effect of a self-fulfilling prophecy. Awkwardness in social situations leads to alienation and ridicule, further reinforcing the child's feelings of inadequacy.

This pattern is unlikely to change unless strategies are applied to enhance the child's feelings of worth. In fact, there is evidence that, without intense intervention, personality disorders persist into adulthood, though the manifestations of the disorder may change with increasing age (Robins, 1972; Waldron, 1976).

Conduct Disorders. Children with conduct disorders have difficulty establishing close interpersonal relationships. These children tend to display the most pernicious antisocial behaviors, including disobedience, aggressiveness, irritability, destructiveness, and impertinence. A child who is unable to control his impulses may also evoke punitive behavior from adults, which in turn reinforces attention-seeking behavior or causes the child to transfer the adults' anger and punishment to other children.

Relationships with other children often are guided by egocentric motives. Children with conduct disorders also use their peers as implements with which to combat authority. There is rarely the depth of communication with others that is found in normal relationships. Unfortunately, the manifestations of conduct disorders usually persist into adulthood and even become matters for the legal and judicial systems (Robins, 1972).

Immaturity. A child who has a short attention span; who is lethargic, preoccupied, and clumsy; and who giggles, prefers younger playmates, and is picked on by other children displays another aspect of emotional disturbance. Such children have difficulty dealing with daily demands appropriate for their chronological age and perform inadequately when they are required to do so.

Children with Physical Impairments

A child who is limited in movement, has poor control of voluntary motor acts, and has atypical physical features or other physical impairments suffers the same risks as other disabled children do. For example, they show lower levels of persistence on problem-solving tasks than do their nondisabled peers (Jennings, Conners, & Stegman, 1988). In addition, Graham and Rutter (1968) reported psychiatric disorders in 37.5% of children with brain lesions but without epilepsy, and in 58.3% of children with epilepsy. More than 1 in 10 children that they studied who had a physical handicap exclusive of central nervous system damage displayed an emotional disorder. These findings support the belief that environmental factors, such as the caregiver's expectation for a child and level of acceptance of the child, also contribute to disturbance in the child's social and emotional development. For example, the level of spontaneous play of infants with cerebral palsy can be predicted by the extent to which mothers make necessary adaptations when interacting with their children (Blasco, Hrncir, & Blasco, 1990).

An interesting study reported by Connell and McConnel (1981) provides further insight into the dynamics of the environments of children with disabilities. In a follow-up study of infants with hydrocephalus who had been treated surgically, the researchers found that these children were four times more likely to develop psychiatric disorders by the middle years of childhood than their normal peers were. However, they also reported the following:

> All of the disturbed group came from homes in which there were emotional or social problems and the quality of care left much to be desired. In many cases difficulties in parent-child relationships appeared to be escalating. Lack of parental support resulted in whining, clinging, and "giving-up" behavior on the part of the child; this in turn reflected adversely on parental acceptance. Thus, a most important and probably the deciding factor in the adjustment of the hydrocephalic child would appear to be how his parents cope with the difficulties of his handicap and their own reactions to it. (p. 515)

Similar conclusions were reached for a large group of children with physical disabilities in a British study (Seidel, Chadwick, & Rutter, 1975). It appears that the influence of the environment on a child with a physical impairment can be at least as powerful as that of the impairment itself. This is consistent with information presented about other impairments.

Children with Attention Deficits

Attention deficit disorders (ADD and ADHD) refer to neurologically-based problems wherein a child manifests inattention, distractibility, and impulsivity, and may be hyperactive as well. In fact, it is often the hyperactivity component that contributes to earlier identification of the problem in young children. For children who do not exhibit the hyperactivity component, diagnosis frequently is delayed until the child is in an academic setting.

Alienation from peers, uncompleted school tasks, poor self-esteem, and family conflicts are typical consequences of these children's behaviors. Peer problems result from the young children's impulsiveness and inability to read social cues. Poor self-esteem may result from continuous negative feedback from adults, not being able to meet their own or others' expectations, and an inability to complete tasks or to get along with other children. Family conflicts persist as a result of the stress of a noncompliant young child who rarely sits still, runs off in public places, engages in dangerous activities, won't stay in bed at night, and demands constant attention and supervision. Unfortunately, the child has little voluntary control over these behaviors (Umansky & Smalley, 1994).

In most cases, these problems can be attenuated through a combination of behavior management and medication. With early treatment, the social and academic outcomes can be very positive. However, ADD often coexists with other impairments, which makes effective treatment more challenging (Ingersoll, 1995). The teacher often is part of a team consisting of a physician, therapists, the child's parents, and other professionals to help decide on the best course of treatment and intervention.

Promoting Social and Emotional Development

The need for external controls is important for maintaining order in one's life and in society. That is the fundamental reason for having laws and rules that govern society and its institutions. But external controls do not obviate each individual's need to control his impulses and make independent decisions about his own behavior. Children with special needs often have a particularly difficult time with this responsibility. However, whether they have a cognitive deficit that limits problem-solving and decision-making skills or a sensory or physical impairment that limits the quality of their interactions with the environment, children can learn to be more socially and emotionally competent individuals.

McEvoy and Odom (1996) have delineated recommended practices for promoting social interaction and emotional development for young children with special needs and their families. Interventions for infants and toddlers should focus on supporting positive interactions between the children and their caregivers and on developing secure relationships. The focus on intervention for preschoolers should be social interaction with peers, development of secure peer relationships, and acquisition of specific social skills.

Skills of the Caregiver

The teacher has little control over the skills of the adults who care for a child or the quality of the home environment. The growth of homebound programs and the expansion of parent involvement in activities of early childhood special education programs hold promise for changes. Certainly, in light of the influences that inadequate and inconsistent caregiving have on a young child, opportunities to enhance or support caregiving skills should be welcomed in the educational community.

Positive change requires more than weekly home visits for an hour each, periodic notes sent to parents, or monthly parent meetings. As Chilman (1968) indicates, "Many parents need emotional, social, and intellectual nourishment for themselves. Before they give these life ingredients to their children, they themselves must first receive them. One cannot give what one does not have" (p. 222).

Consistency of Care. A very young child develops trust in a relationship when his needs are met and he gains satisfaction. Subsequently, he begins to feel secure enough to explore the environment and take small risks with new experiences. Caregivers who are consistent in meeting a child's biological needs (e.g., feeding, changing diapers, and attending to scrapes) and subsequent needs for support in his explorations (e.g., through confidence-building hugs and positive words) are likely to find the child becoming confident in his own abilities and secure in relationships with new people.

With a child who has special needs, the caregiver may require help in determining what the child's needs are and how to meet them. The interventionist may find that enhancing the confidence and observation skills of the caregiver are of primary importance. Some caregivers overrespond to a child's cues, never giving the child an opportunity to respond or causing the child to become overstimulated and withdraw (Marfo, 1991). The child may be expressing his needs plainly, but the caregiver expects something different from a child with special needs; and, when interactions between caregiver and child are not fun or at least reinforcing, the caregiver may become less responsive to the child. The interventionist may choose to spend considerable time with the caregiver, at least initially, observing the child and planning ways for the caregiver to respond to the child's different expressions of needs, wants, and feelings.

Providing High-Quality Interactions. The ways in which caregivers and children interact have been the subject of extensive study (Haney & Klein, 1993; Wasserman, Lennon, Allen, & Shilansky, 1987), and the importance of verbal and nonverbal communication between the two is universally acknowledged. Face-to-face interaction helps to establish eye contact and attentional skills in a young child. When tied to supportive verbalizations by the caregiver (e.g., "What a nice smile!" and "I'm going to kiss you on the nose"), the child is encouraged to experiment with vocal play and expressions.

Later, the caregiver provides words for feelings and for important objects in the child's environment. The child is then better able to communicate his own thoughts and feelings without being totally dependent upon adults' interpretations. The interventionist should be prepared to model appropriate ways to interact with a child, observe the caregiver doing it, and provide feedback. For a child with special needs, assistance may be needed to identify the child's signaling system or to help the child develop a consistent way to communicate. Principles of behavior theory may be utilized to shape the responses of a child with a severe disability so that the caregiver can more easily interpret the messages that the child is conveying.

Providing Diverse Experiences. Children can develop quite well without having the latest line of toys on the market, visiting museums weekly, or traveling across the country with the family. These experiences might be indicators of a child's level of care rather than the direct reason for improved development; that is, caregivers who provide such extremely positive experiences are more likely to offer consistently diverse experiences for children. But the extreme is not necessary.

Diverse and rich experiences are available at any socioeconomic level and in any environment.

The interventionist may be able to help a caregiver plan a way to take a child along to the grocery store rather than leave him home with an older child. The local park may not have been utilized before by the family, but the interventionist can show the caregiver how the child and family can enjoy and benefit from a periodic outing. She may also be in a position to bring a group of caregivers and children together regularly for play groups. The interventionist need not be present at these and, in fact, may choose to be absent in order to facilitate spontaneous sharing by the caregivers.

Skills of the Interventionist

Working in a home setting demands that an interventionist be able to modify strategies quickly, be sensitive to and an excellent observer of family dynamics, and know how to suggest and model, while letting the caregiver assume responsibility for interactions with the child. Little is gained from working with a child in the home if the interventionist is not absolutely sure that the caregiver has benefited and that the child will receive those benefits in her absence.

The classroom provides its own challenges to the teacher of young children with special needs. Not the least of these is attempting to meet the individual needs of children in a group setting. The classroom provides the teacher with an opportunity to guide a child's interactions in a minisociety. Although it may be unlike life on the outside, it does offer the child opportunities to learn and practice skills that are transferable to real-world situations and relate to his success in later school experiences (Chandler, Lubek, & Fowler, 1992).

Next, classroom strategies are presented that encourage development of social and emotional skills. Figure 8.1, a teaching skills survey, offers a tool for self-evaluation of strategies and skills in an inclusive or self-contained classroom setting. Normal development in a classroom setting for a child with special needs grows out of the same supportive and nurturing care that is needed at home. Some of the main principles that will assure that children benefit from a classroom experience follow. These are further illustrated in Table 8.1.

Being Consistent. A child learns to control his own behavior and follow social rules when he relates current or anticipated behavior to the consequences of similar situations that have occurred in the past. Teachers can facilitate self-control by providing an environment that allows children to predict accurately whether their behavior will be acceptable or unacceptable. Inconsistency in adult responses makes it difficult for a child to exercise self-control because he cannot predict what the consequences of his behavior will be.

Consistency in responding to behavior is important for another reason. Children need to learn cause and effect in interpersonal relationships. A child learns very early that if he holds an ice-cream cone upside down, the ice cream will fall out. Cause and effect are more difficult to teach in human behavior because people are

FIGURE 8.1 Teaching skills survey

Place a + next to statements with which you agree and a – next to statements with which you disagree. Preferred responses appear on page 307 and should be checked after completing the chapter.

_____ I have something ready for the children to do when they arrive in the morning and help children find things to do during the day.
_____ I give most of my attention to children who misbehave or act out.
_____ Children need to learn that the way the staff behaves may be different from the way children are expected to behave.
_____ An adult needs to explain to children what is acceptable and unacceptable about certain behaviors and to demonstrate appropriate behaviors.
_____ I don't have time to converse with children on an individual basis.
_____ Children are flexible enough to handle new situations easily without guidance.
_____ It's good to keep children wondering what the next activity will be. This keeps them interested.
_____ I like it when children talk with each other at meal and snack times and when they're waiting for the bus or for other activities.
_____ Children need to learn self-control. Sitting at a table or standing in line for long periods helps them learn this.
_____ I like children to wait for me to tell them what to do before they do anything.
_____ The best way for me to get order when the children are noisy is to use my loudest voice.
_____ I take special care to acknowledge children who are behaving appropriately in different activities.
_____ An activity should be challenging to each child without being frustrating.
_____ I take every opportunity during the day to expose children to new information and new skills.
_____ At meal and snack times, and when standing in line, children should not talk.
_____ I expect that children will have trouble staying seated and being quiet for more than 15 or 20 minutes at a time.
_____ I ask children questions that require a verbal response.
_____ The best means to prevent children from misbehaving is to provide firm and consistent punishment.
_____ I make sure that I speak to each child individually for at least 1 or 2 minutes each day.
_____ Staff behavior should be a model for the children. We should behave as we expect children to behave.
_____ Children learn most during the structured activities of the day.
_____ Even if an activity is too easy or too hard for a child, it's more efficient to do the same activity with everyone than to adapt an activity for each and every child.
_____ Children who spend a lot of time wandering around the room are learning important social skills.
_____ I like to tell children what to expect for the next activity or activities.
_____ I expect children in the program to work quietly at a table for an hour or more at a time.
_____ Time spent preventing children from misbehaving is better than time spent punishing those who misbehave.
_____ Keeping children sitting at a table or standing in line too long is asking for trouble and is not very productive.
_____ I spend time explaining to children what I expect from them in new situations.
_____ It's more important to tell children how to behave than for them to see it themselves.

TABLE 8.1 Strategies for Nurturing Social and Emotional Development in the Preschool Classroom

TECHNIQUES THAT ENCOURAGE PROBLEMS	A POSITIVE ALTERNATIVE
Make children sit at the table with nothing to do, or stand in line too long.	Keep children busily engaged in an activity. The wait for lunch or for the bus can be used for story time, singing, or quiet games (for example, "I am thinking of something; what is it?").
Do not tell children what is going to happen next.	Tell children what to expect in ways such as, "We will put our toys away in 2 minutes and get ready for circle time," or "When you are finished with your work, you can find a book and sit quietly in the library corner." Children should not have to deal with unexpected changes.
Let children wander around with nothing to do.	Have work ready for children when they arrive in the morning and have the day planned well. Help children find and engage in an activity during free time. Have something for them to do if they finish an activity early.
Plan activities that are too easy or too hard for the children.	Adapt activities to each child's level so that they provide a challenge without being frustrating.
Do not pay attention to children who are acting appropriately.	Recognize children who are behaving appropriately and say what it is that they are doing right (for example, "I like the way you are eating so nicely, Claudia.").
Attend to "trouble makers" only after they have done something wrong.	Use preventive techniques with children who tend to act inappropriately. Address them by name and touch them periodically during activities to let them know you know they are there. Comment matter-of-factly on the appropriateness of what they are doing (for example, "Roy, you are certainly playing well.").
Provide a poor model for children.	Serve as a good model. Do not shout when children are supposed to control their voices. Respect children and their feelings if you want them to respect you and each other.
Do not understand children's needs to move, talk, and explore.	Provide variation in activities so that children are not required to stay in one place or remain silent too long. Provide physical activities and opportunities for children to talk and ask questions.
Do not explain expectations for children in new situations.	Recognize that children may not know how to act in new situations. Prepare them for new experiences with explanations, stories, role-playing, etc.
Avoid teaching children rules for acting in social settings.	Give children a rationale for acceptable and unacceptable behaviors. Explain to them decisions you make.

inconsistent in how they respond to the same behavior. When adult responses are confusing and misunderstood, children do not relate their own behavior to the effects in their environment. Teachers who take the time to explain the consequences of behaviors and to explain why some behaviors are appropriate and others are inappropriate in different settings are providing valuable support for children.

Exercising Control. Children enjoy the experience of being independent. It makes them feel important, trusted, and strong. If teachers want children to learn to control their own impulses, they must provide opportunities for children to exercise control. The following are examples of planned experiences that accomplish this goal.

1. *Playing.* Children can be allowed to play without adult supervision. A fenced-in play area is a means of allowing a child to play outside without an adult hovering nearby. Young children need the security of knowing that an adult is within calling distance, yet they enjoy the sense of independence with their internal controls as the guiding force. If the adult reappears periodically, children will be reassured. Gradually, children develop the control to manage longer periods of time alone in self-directed play.

2. *Choosing.* Children can be given choices at an early age. Choosing between an apple and a banana allows a child to make a small decision that requires a low level of self-direction. The teacher can suggest that a child select a toy to share in play with the teacher. Statements such as "You made a good choice" reinforce the child's self-concept as a competent person.

3. *Failing.* Constant failure is debilitating, but occasional failure, when the consequences are not severe, helps a child to learn realistically. Some teachers try to protect children from failure and thereby rob them of their chance at discovery learning. Children should have the right to fail in an environment that supports efforts to be independent, creative, industrious, and decisive. One of the greatest barriers to learning self-control is the fear of the external consequences if failure should occur. At early ages, children do not expect themselves to be perfect and therefore approach new tasks with a sense of adventure and excitement. Exposure to adults who are intolerant of failure quickly develops within children a self-critical attitude that may lead to greater dependence on adults rather than self-directed behavior.

Modeling. Young children learn more from what they see practiced than from what they are told is correct behavior. Teachers who interact with children pleasantly, who express a range of emotions at appropriate times, who recognize that the rules of the classroom pertain to staff as well as to children, who share what they have with children as well as expecting children to share with each other—these teachers offer children an example to follow. They make it much easier for children to see how they are expected to behave.

Role-playing is an effective strategy by which to act through social situations with young children, particularly young children with special needs. It offers the opportunity for the teacher to model, observe, and provide feedback to children about the expected consequences of their behavior in a play-practice situation.

Providing Cues. Adults can teach children social skills by providing consistent environmental cues. For example, toys should be stored in the areas of the classroom where they are to be used. It is confusing to children for a toy to be kept on a shelf in the dress-up area when the teacher expects that children use it only in the housekeeping area. The location of objects can signal the child to behave in desirable or undesirable ways.

The teacher who leaves a glass bowl on a table when there is a toddler around has designed the environment for trouble. Not only might the bowl be broken and cause the teacher to become upset, but the toddler also will experience a sense of wrongdoing and guilt for having explored his environment. In this case, the teacher should recognize that the child does not have the self-control to resist handling objects nor the cognitive understanding to recognize which objects are breakable. Teachers must structure the environment to allow children to explore tables and shelves as a natural reward for having learned to pull up and crawl around the room. Later, the teacher can teach children to discriminate objects that are to be looked at from those that may be touched and played with.

Another example of an environmental cue is the type of activity that precedes rest time in school. Quiet activities such as reading a story or listening to music can be helpful cues for children to begin unwinding for a time of rest. Loud, active games prior to a rest period serve to stimulate children and make it difficult for them to exercise self-control when nap time is announced. The planned use of one activity to prepare children for the next event in the day can facilitate the development of self-control. Failure to provide environmental cues for children makes the adult responsible for enforcing the desired behavior and builds dependence on external controls.

Setting Limits. Setting limits develops internal control and understanding in children, and it also provides an environment in which children can freely explore and successfully experience living within established guidelines. Children can then act with some degree of confidence because they are protected from themselves.

One should not place limitations on children that they cannot follow. Limits should match the stage of development and the individual needs of each child. A child with a developmental age of 2 years will have difficulty stopping himself from touching things around the classroom no matter how insistent or forceful the teacher is. By developmental age 5, a child can reasonably be expected to follow a rule related to appropriate use or nonuse of certain objects.

Limitations that are imposed should be necessary. While it is sometimes difficult to know whether a limit is imposed for children's own well-being or for adult comfort, children must understand the limit in order to follow it.

Summary

A child's concept of himself and of the world around him is constantly being shaped. It is changed to some degree by every event in the child's life. For all children, social and emotional development results from being trusted, from being allowed independence, from successfully completing a task, from making a choice, from helping others, and from receiving affection. Disorders evolve from children's being overprotected, from being consistently punished or corrected, from being constantly supervised or ignored, and from always receiving help. Moreover, adults who treat a child's impairment as a totally disabling condition further damage the child's development.

The efforts of the interventionist must follow a consistent pattern: Observe the way a child interacts with the people and things in his environment, then provide the experiences and support that will build feelings of confidence in himself, trust in others, and security in his environment.

Social skills and emotions are perhaps the most elusive areas of human development to comprehend. Maladaptive behaviors evolve over many years, yet they change from day to day and from situation to situation. They contribute to great success in life or to misery and frustration. In this chapter, substantial evidence has been provided that reveals the critical components of social and emotional development in young children with special needs. Interventionists can be optimistic that many of the factors that contribute most to a child's outcome can be influenced by their enlightened approach. By including both child and caregiver in the positive educational process, a socially competent young person can develop.

References

Achenbach, T. M., Edelbrock, C., & Howell, C. T. (1987). Empirically based assessment of the behavioral/emotional problems of 2- and 3-year-old children. *Journal of Abnormal Child Psychology, 15,* 629–650.

Ahadi, S. A., Rothbart, M. K., & Ye, R. (1993). Child temperament in the U.S. and China: Similarities and differences. *European Journal of Personality, 7,* 359–378.

Altshuler, K. Z. (1974). The social and psychological development of the deaf child: Problems, their treatment, and prevention. *American Annals of the Deaf, 119,* 365–376.

American Psychiatric Association (1994). *Diagnostic and statistical manual–Fourth revision*. Washington, DC: Author.

Asher, S. R. (1990). Recent advances in the study of peer rejection. In S. R. Asher & J. D. Coie (Eds.), *Peer rejection in childhood.* (pp. 3–14). Cambridge: Cambridge University Press.

Bandura, A. (1977). *Social learning theory*. Upper Saddle River, NJ: Prentice Hall.

Barnett, M. A. (1982). Empathy and prosocial behavior in children. In T. M. Field, A. Huston, H. C. Quay, L. Troll, & G. E. Finley (Eds.), *Review of human development*. New York: Wiley.

Barry, H., Jr., & Marshall, F. E. (1953). Maladjustment and maternal rejection in retrolental fibroplasia. *Mental Hygiene, 73,* 570–580.

Baumrind, D. (1967). Child care practices anteceding three patterns of preschool behavior. *Genetic Psychology Monographs, 75,* 43–88.

Beckman, P. J. & Kohl, L. (1987). Interactions of preschoolers with and without handicaps in integrated and segregated settings: A longitudinal study. *Mental Retardation, 25,* 5–11.

Beeghly, M., Weiss-Perry, B., & Cicchetti, D. (1990). Beyond sensorimotor functioning: Early communicative and play development of children with Down syndrome. In D. Cicchetti & M. Beeghly (Eds.), *Children with Down syndrome: A developmental perspective.* New York: Cambridge University Press.

Berger, J., & Cunningham, C. C. (1981). The development of eye contact between mothers and normal-versus-Down's syndrome infants. *Developmental Psychology, 17,* 678–689.

Berger, J. & Cunningham, C. C. (1983). Development of early vocal behaviors and interactions in Down's syndrome and nonhandicapped infant-mother pairs. *Developmental Psychology, 19,* 322–331.

Bijou, W. W., & Baer, D. M. (1979). Child development I: A systematic and empirical theory. In B. G. Suran & J. V. Rizzo (Eds.), *Special children: An integrative approach.* Glenview, IL: Scott Foresman.

Blasco, P. M., Hrncir, E. J., & Blasco, P. A. (1990). The contribution of maternal involvement to mastery performance in infants with cerebral palsy. *Journal of Early Intervention, 14,* 161–174.

Block, J. H. (1982). Gender differences in the nature of premises developed about the world. In E. K. Shapiro & E. Weber (Eds.), *Cognitive and affective growth: Developmental interaction.* Hillsdale, NJ: Erlbaum.

Bornstein, M. H., & Lamb, M. E. (1992). *Development in infancy: An introduction.* New York: McGraw-Hill.

Bradley, R. H., & Caldwell, B. M. (1979). Home observation for measurement of the environment: A revision of the preschool scale. *American Journal of Mental Deficiency, 84,* 235–244.

Bryan, J. H., & London, P. (1970). Altruistic behavior by children. *Psychological Bulletin, 73,* 200–211.

Burlingham, D. (1961). Some notes on the development of the blind. *Psychoanalytic Study of the Child, 16,* 121–145.

Burlingham, D. (1964). Hearing and its role in the development of the blind. *Psychoanalytic Study of the Child, 19,* 95–112.

Caldwell, B. M. (1979). Aggression and hostility in young children. In L. Adams and B. Gorelick (Eds.), *Ideas that work with young children (Vol. 2).* Washington, DC: National Association for the Education of Young Children.

Chandler, L. K., Lubek, R. C., & Fowler, S. A. (1992). Generalization and maintenance of preschool children's social skills: A critical review and analysis. *Journal of Applied Behavior Analysis, 25,* 415–428.

Chilman, C. S. (1968). Poor families and their patterns of child care: Some implications for service programs. In L. L. Dittman (Ed.), *Early child care: The new perspective.* New York: Atherton Press.

Connell, H. M., & McConnel, T. S. (1981). Psychiatric sequalae in children treated operatively for hydrocephalus in infancy. *Developmental Medicine and Child Neurology, 23,* 505–517.

Craig, H. K., & Washington, J. A. (1993). Access behaviors of children with specific language impairment. *Journal of Speech and Hearing Research, 36,* 322–337.

Crouch, M., & Manderson, L. (1994). The social life of bonding theory. *Social Science and Medicine, 41,* 837–844.

Darbyshire, J. O. (1977). Play patterns in young children with impaired hearing. *Volta Review, 79,* 19–26.

Dunst, C. J., Mahoney, G., & Buchan, K. (1996). In S. L. Odom & M. E. McLean (Eds.), *Early intervention/early childhood special education: Recommended practices.* Austin, TX: Pro-Ed.

Erikson, E. (1950). *Childhood and society.* New York: Norton.

Erikson, E. (1968). *Identity: Youth and crisis.* London: Faber.

Fewell, R. R., & Kaminski, R. (1988). Play skills development and instruction for young children with handicaps. In S. L. Odom & M. B. Karnes

(Eds.), *Early intervention for infants and children with handicaps: An empirical base*. Baltimore: Paul H. Brookes.

Field, T., Roseman, S., DeStefano, L., & Koewler, J. H. (1981). Play behaviors of handicapped preschool children in the presence and absence of nonhandicapped peers. *Journal of Applied Developmental Psychology, 2,* 49–58.

Fraiberg, S. (1968). Parallel and divergent patterns in blind and sighted infants. *Psychoanalytic Study of the Child, 23,* 264–300.

Fraiberg, S. (1972). Separation crisis in two blind children. *Psychoanalytic Study of the Child, 26,* 355–371.

Fraiberg, S., & Freeman, D. A. (1964). Studies in the ego development of the congenitally blind child. *Psychoanalytic Study of the Child, 19,* 113–169.

Garmezy, N. (1975). The study of competence in children at risk for severe psychopathology. In J. F. Anthony & C. Koupernik (Eds.), *The child in his family at psychiatric risk*. New York: Wiley.

Garvey, C. (1977). *Play*. Cambridge, MA: Harvard University Press.

Garvey, C., & Hogan, R. (1973). Social speech and social interaction: Egocentrism revisited. *Child Development, 44,* 562–568.

Gliedman, J. (1979). Special education and minority education: The path not yet taken. In S. McBride & W. Shuster (Eds.), *Early intervention of developmental disabilities*. Bloomington, IN: Indiana University.

Glueck, S., & Glueck, E. T. (1950). *Unraveling juvenile delinquency*. Cambridge, MA: Harvard University Press.

Gowen, J., Goldman, B., Johnson-Martin, M., & Hussey, B. (1989). Object play and exploration of handicapped and nonhandicapped infants. *Journal of Applied Developmental Psychology, 10,* 53–72.

Graham, P., & Rutter, M. (1968). Organic brain dysfunction and child psychiatric disorder. *British Medical Journal, 2,* 695–700.

Guralnick, M. J. (1993). Developmentally appropriate practice in the assessment and intervention of children's peer relations. *Topics in Early Childhood Special Education, 13,* 334–371.

Guralnick, M. J. (1994). Social competence with peers: Outcome and process in early childhood special education. In P. L. Safford (Ed.), *Early childhood special education*. New York: Teachers College Press.

Guralnick, M. J., Connor, R. T., Hammond, M. A., Gottman, J. M., & Kinnish, K. (1996). The peer relations of preschool children with communication disorders. *Child Development, 67,* 471–489.

Guralnick, M. J., & Groom, J. M. (1988). Friendships of preschool children in mainstreamed play groups. *Developmental Psychology, 24,* 595–604.

Hallenbeck, J. (1954). Two essential factors in the development of young blind children. *New Outlook for the Blind, 48,* 308–315.

Haney, M., & Klein, D. M. (1993). Impact of a program to facilitate mother-infant communication in high-risk families of high-risk infants. *Journal of Communication Disorders, 15,* 15–22.

Hartup, W. W. (1970). Peer interaction and social organization. In P. H. Mussen (Ed.), Carmichael's manual of child psychology (Vol. 2). New York: Wiley.

Hartup, W. W. (1974). Aggression in childhood: Developmental perspectives. *American Psychologist, 29,* 336–341.

Hellendoorn, J., & Hoekman, J. (1992). Imaginative play in children with mental retardation. *Mental Retardation, 30,* 255–263.

Hus, Y. (1979). The socialization process of hearing impaired children in a summer day camp. *Volta Review, 81,* 146–156.

Ingersoll, B. (1995). ADD: Not just another fad. *Attention, 2,* 17–19.

Jennings, K. D., Conners, R. E., & Stegman, C. E. (1988). Does a physical handicap alter the development of mastery motivation during the preschool years? *Journal of the American Academy of Child and Adolescent Psychiatry, 27,* 312–317.

Ladd, G. W., Kochenderfer, B. J., & Coleman, C. C. (1996). Friendship quality as a predictor of young children's early school adjustment. *Child Development, 67,* 1103–1118.

Langlois, D. H., & Downs, C. A. (1979). Peer relations as a function of physical attractiveness: The eye of the beholder or behavioral reality? *Child Development, 50,* 409–418.

Lerner, R. M., & Lerner, J. (1977). Effects of age, sex, and physical attractiveness on child-peer relations, academic performance, and elementary school adjustment. *Developmental Psychology,*

13, 585–590.

Lewis, M., & Rosenblum, L. A. (Eds.), (1974). *The effect of the infant on its caregiver.* New York: Wiley.

Li, A. (1985). Toward more elaborate pretend play. *Mental Retardation, 23,* 131–136.

Lieber, J. (1993). A comparison of social pretend play in young children with and without disabilities. *Early Education and Development, 41,* 148–161.

Lieberman, J. N. (1977a). *Playfulness: Its relationship to imagination and creativity.* New York: Academic Press.

Linder, T. W. (1993). *Transdisciplinary play-based assessment.* Baltimore, Paul H. Brookes.

Lorr, M., & McNair, D. M. (1965). Expansion of the interpersonal behavior circle. *Journal of Personality and Social Psychology, 2,* 823–830.

Lozoff, B., Brittenham, G., Trause, M. A., Kennell, J., & Klaus, M. (1977). The mother-newborn relationship: Limits of adaptability. *Journal of Pediatrics, 91,* 1–12.

Lukoff, I. F., & Whiteman, M. (1970). Socialization and segregated education. *Research Bulletin, American Foundation for the Blind, 20,* 91–107.

Lussier, B. J., Crimmins, D. B., & Alberti, D. (1994). Effects of three adult interaction styles on infant engagement. *Journal of Early Intervention, 18,* 12–24.

Lyons-Ruth, K., Alpern, L., & Repacholi, B. (1993). Disorganized infant attachment classification and maternal psychosocial problems as predictors of hostile-aggressive behavior in preschool children. *Child Development, 64,* 572–585.

Maccoby, E. E., & Jacklin, C. M. (1974). *The psychology of sex differences.* Stanford, CA: Stanford University Press.

Marfo, K. (1991). The maternal directiveness theme in mother-child interaction research: Implications for early intervention. In K. Marfo (Ed.), *Early intervention in transition: Current perspectives on programs for handicapped infants.* New York: Praeger.

Martin, B. (1975). Parent-child relations. In F. D. Horowitz, E. M. Hetherington, S. Scarr-Salapatek, & G. M. Siegel (Eds.), *Review of child development research* (Vol. 4). Chicago: University of Chicago Press.

McCauley, R., Kennedy, P., & Bruininks, R. (1976). Behavioral interactions of hearing impaired children in regular classrooms. *Exceptional Children, 40,* 336–342.

McDavid, J. W., & Harari, H. (1966). Stereotyping of names and popularity in grade school children. *Child Development, 37,* 409–419.

McDowell, J. H. (1979). *Children's riddling.* Bloomington, IN: Indiana University Press.

McEvoy, M. A., & Odom, S. L. (1996). Strategies for promoting social interaction and emotional development of infants and young children with disabilities and their families. In S. L. Odom & M. E. McLean (Eds.), *Early intervention/early childhood special education: Recommended practices.* Austin, TX: Pro-Ed.

Meadow, K. P. (1975). The development of deaf children. In E. M. Hetherington (Ed.), *Review of child development research* (Vol. 5). Chicago: University of Chicago Press.

Mindel, E. G., & Vernon, M. (1971). *They grow in silence: The deaf child and his family.* Silver Spring, MD: National Association for the Deaf.

Moustakas, C. E., Sigel, I. E., & Schalock, N. D. (1956). An objective method for the measurement and analysis of child-adult interaction. *Child Development, 27,* 109–134.

Newland, T. E. (1976). *The gifted in socio-cultural perspective.* Upper Saddle River, NJ: Prentice Hall.

O'Leary, K. D., & Johnson, S. B. (1979). Psychological assessment. In H. C. Quay & J. S. Werry (Eds.), *Psychopathological disorders of childhood.* New York: Wiley.

Piaget, J. (1954). *The origins of intelligence in children.* New York: International Universities Press.

Preisler, G. M. (1991). Early patterns of interaction between blind infants and their sighted mothers. *Child: Care, Health, and Development, 17,* 65–90.

Preisler, G. M. (1995). The development of communication in blind and in deaf infants—similarities and differences. *Child: Care, Health, and Development, 21,* 79–100.

Putallaz, M., & Wasserman, A. (1990). Children's entry behavior. In S. R. Asher & J. D. Coie (Eds.), *Peer rejection in childhood* (pp. 60–89). Cambridge, England: Cambridge University Press.

Quay, H. C. (1979). Classification. In H. C. Quay and J. S. Werry (Eds.), *Psychopathological disorders of childhood.* New York: Wiley.

Quinton, D., & Rutter, M. (1976). Early hospital

admissions and later disturbances of behavior: An attempted replication of Douglas's findings. *Developmental Medicine and Child Neurology, 18,* 447–459.

Rice, M. L., Sell, M. A., & Hadley, P. A. (1991). Social interactions of speech- and language-impaired children. *Journal of Speech and Hearing Research, 34,* 1299–1307.

Robeck, M. D. (1969). Affective learning in the language development of young children. *Journal of Research and Development in Education, 3,* 32–42.

Roberts, S. B., Brown, P. M., & Richards, F. W. (1995). Social pretend play entry behaviors of preschoolers with and without impaired hearing. *Journal of Early Intervention, 20,* 52–83.

Robins, L. N. (1972). Follow-up studies of behavior disorders in children. In H. C. Quay & J. S. Werry (Eds.), *Psychopathological disorders of childhood.* New York: Wiley.

Rutter, M. (1971). Parent-child separation: Psychological effects on children. *Journal of Psychology and Psychiatry, 12,* 233–260.

Rutter, M. (1978). Early sources of security and competence. In J. S. Bruner & A. Garton (Eds.), *Human growth and development.* London: Oxford University Press.

Rutter, M. (1980). The long-term effects of early experience. *Developmental Medicine and Child Neurology, 22,* 800–813.

Rutter, M. (1981). Socio-emotional consequences of day care for preschool children. *Journal of Child Psychology and Psychiatry, 51,* 4–29.

Sameroff, A. J., & Chandler, M. J. (1975). Reproductive risk and the continuum of caretaking casualty. In F. D. Horowitz, E. M. Hetherington, S. Scarr-Salapatek, & G. W. Siegel (Eds.), *Review of child development research* (Vol. 4). Chicago: University of Chicago Press.

Sameroff, A. J., & Fiese, B. H. (1990). Transactional regulation and early intervention. In S. J. Meisels & J. P. Shonkoff (Eds.), *Handbook of early childhood intervention* (pp. 119–149). New York: Cambridge University Press.

Sandler, A. M. (1963). Aspects of passivity and ego development in the blind infant. *Psychoanalytic Study of the Child, 18,* 343–361.

Schacter, S. (1959). *The psychology of affiliation.* Stanford, CA: Stanford University Press.

Schlesinger, H. S., & Meadow, K. P. (1971). *Deafness and mental health: A developmental approach.* San Francisco: Langley Porter Neuropsychiatric Institute.

Schwartzman, H. (1979). *Transformations: The anthropology of children's play.* New York: Plenum.

Scott, R. A. (1968). *The making of blind men.* New York: Russell Sage Foundation.

Sears, P., & Barbee, A. (1977). Career and life satisfaction among Terman's gifted women. In J. Stanley, W. George, & C. Salano (Eds.), *The gifted and creative: A fifty-year perspective.* Baltimore: Johns Hopkins University Press.

Seidel, V. P., Chadwick, O., & Rutter, M. (1975). Psychological disorder in crippled children. *Developmental Medicine and Child Neurology, 17,* 563–573.

Serbin, L. A., O'Leary, D. K., Kent, R. N., & Tonick, I. J. (1973). A comparison of teacher response to the preacademic and problem behavior of boys and girls. *Child Development, 44,* 796–804.

Sparrow, S. S., Balla, D. A., & Cicchetti, D. V. (1984). *The Vineland Adaptive Behavior Scales.* Circle, MN: American Guidance Service.

Styczynski, L. E., & Langlois, J. H. (1977). The effects of familiarity on behavioral stereotypes associated with physical attractiveness in young children. *Child Development, 48,* 1137–1141.

Tait, P. (1972). Play and the intellectual development of blind children. *New Outlook for the Blind, 66,* 361–369.

Terman, L. M., & Oden, M. H. (1947). *The gifted child grows up.* Stanford, CA: Stanford University Press.

Thomas, A., & Chess, S. (1977). *Temperament and development.* New York: Bruner/Mazel.

Thomas, A., Chess, S., & Korn, S. (1977). Parent and teacher temperament questionnaire for children 3–7 years of age. In A. Thomas & S. Chess (Eds.), *Temperament and development.* New York: Bruner/Mazel.

Thomas, E. B., Liederman, P. H., & Olson, J. P. (1972). Neonate-mother interaction during breast feeding. *Developmental Psychology, 6,* 110–118.

Troster, H., & Brombring, M. (1992). Early social-emotional development in blind infants. *Child:*

Care, Health, and Development, 18, 207–227.

Umansky, W., & Smalley, B. S. (1994). *ADD: Helping your child.* New York: Warner Books.

Vandell, D. L., & George, L. B. (1981). Social interactions in hearing and deaf preschoolers. Successes and failures in initiations. *Child Development, 52,* 627–635.

van den Boom, D. C. (1995). Do first-year intervention effects endure? Follow-up during toddlerhood of a sample of Dutch irritable infants. *Child Development, 66,* 1798–1816.

van den Boom, D. C., & Hoeksma, J. B. (1994). The effects of infant irritability on mother-infant interaction: A growth curve analysis. *Developmental Psychology, 30,* 581–590.

van Ijzendoorn, M. H., Juffer, R., & Duyvesteyn, M. G. (1995). Breaking the intergenerational cycle of insecure attachment: A review of the effects of attachment-based intervention on maternal sensitivity and infant security. *Journal of Child Psychology and Psychiatry, 36,* 225–248.

Vygotsky, L. S. (1978). *Mind in society: The development of higher psychological processes.* Cambridge, MA: Harvard University Press.

Waldron, S. (1976). The significance of childhood neurosis for adult mental health: A follow-up study. *American Journal of Psychiatry, 133,* 532–538.

Waldrop, M. F., & Halverson, C. F. (1975). Intensive peer behavior: Longitudinal and cross sectional analysis. *Child Development, 46,* 19–26.

Walker, E. F., Cudeck, R., Mednick, S. A., & Schulsinger, F. (1981). Effects of parental absence and institutionalization on the development of clinical symptoms in high-risk children. *Acta Psychiatrica Scandanavica, 63,* 65–109.

Warren, D. H. (1977). *Blindness and early childhood development.* New York: American Foundation for the Blind.

Wasserman, G. A., Lennon, M. C., Allen, R., & Shilansky, M. (1987). Contributors to attachment in normal and physically handicapped infants. *Journal of the American Academy of Child and Adolescent Psychiatry, 26,* 9–15.

Wedell-Monnig, J., & Lumley, J. M. (1980). Child deafness and mother-child interaction. *Child Development, 51,* 766–774.

White, B. (1975). *The first three years of life.* Upper Saddle River, NJ: Prentice Hall.

Wills, D. M. (1970). Vulnerable periods in the early development of blind children. *Psychoanalytic Study of the Child, 25,* 461–480.

Wolkind, S., & Rutter, M. (1973). Children who have been "in care": An epidemiological study. *Journal of Child Psychology and Psychiatry, 14,* 97–105.

Wolman, B. B. (1978). *Children's fears.* New York: Grosset & Dunlap.

World Health Organization (1995). *International classification of diseases* (9th ed.). Salt Lake City, UT: Medicode Publications.

Yarrow, M. R. (1963). Problems of methods in parent-child research. *Child Development, 34,* 215–226.

Zegoib, L. E., Arnold, S., & Forehand, R. (1975). An examination of observer effects in parent-child interactions. *Child Development, 27,* 109–134.

Preferred responses to Figure 8.1: + – – + – – – + – – – + + + + + – – – + – + + + –

9

Technology

John Langone

Over the past decade, technology solutions to everyday problems have become available at an astounding rate. For people with disabilities, technology has helped to provide independence and assistance in learning and performing skills that previously were thought to be difficult for them. Technology solutions for infants, toddlers, and preschoolers with disabilities are particularly beneficial for attaining optimum intellectual and physical development (Campbell, McGregor, & Nasik, 1994). There is considerable evidence of the positive effects that technology applications can have on typical young children (Haugland, 1992), and, although there are less available data documenting the effects of technology applications for children who have disabilities, that body of literature continues to grow (Howard, Greyrose, Kehr, Espinosa, & Beckwith, 1996).

Technology can benefit young children with disabilities in many ways. For example, technology solutions can help them engage more naturally in play and use imitation as successfully as their typical peers do (Bowe, 1995). Technology applications can supplement high-quality interactions with parents and others by increasing the number of times children are read and spoken to for enrichment. Children with sensory deficits, physical challenges, or more severe cognitive impairments can have access to technology devices that allow them to communicate with their parents, siblings, and friends. Technology makes it possible for these and other children with special needs to play with some toys by making them accessible and by creating new ways to play with them. Technology also can set the stage for meaningful interaction with other children who do not have disabilities and can provide opportunities for learning, exploring, and interacting with the environment (Behrmann, Jones, & Wilds, 1989). In addition, technology opens doors for parents to quickly gain access to information that may be beneficial to their children's development. Finally, technology allows parents to communicate with other parents and professionals quickly and efficiently, and gives them access to support, encouragement, and information.

This chapter discusses how technology can enrich the lives of young children with disabilities. For the purposes of this text, the term *technology* means computers. Computer-based instruction can complement early intervention programs. Many children with disabilities can access the power of computer-based instruction through keyboards and mouse interfaces. Some children with physical impairments require computer access through more sophisticated adaptive equipment, which also will be discussed. This chapter also includes information about how technology can benefit children with sensory impairments and about single-switch technology for use with toys and other devices.

For those who are tuned-in to the latest technology, it will be clear that, of all the chapters in this text, this one will be most vulnerable to time. Technological advances and their applications are quickly advancing; however, the information contained in this chapter should provide important guidance for the interventionist who needs to access such information, particularly given how one Internet Web site, for example, might be linked to other, newer sites.

Cognitive-Social Development and Technology

Technology offers children who have disabilities opportunities that never before were imagined. Technology can help children who have never been able to communicate, control their environment, or play to accomplish these feats. The use of technology also can set the stage for true integration and inclusion to occur by allowing children with and without disabilities to engage in activities together. The first step for using technology effectively is to understand how technology correlates with the developmental stages and learning characteristics of children. The second step is to understand how to integrate technology into a well-balanced curriculum.

Cognitive Development and Technology

While children are playing and exploring their environment, they learn and build a strong foundation for their ability to communicate and to engage in social interactions. For most young children, play and exploration are natural and become a vehicle for improving their motor skills, developing pre-vocationally relevant behaviors, and establishing cognitive abilities that will be the basis for their academic and social successes (Bowe, 1995; Thurman & Widerstrom, 1990).

Children also are natural imitators and processors of information that is presented to them. When parents and other family members read or talk to their children, toddlers and preschoolers can usually process the information for later use or begin to imitate the sounds they hear. Parents and others who present appropriate social models are providing their children with additional opportunities for gaining skills needed for improving social relationships.

When children have disabilities, however, they are hampered in their ability to gain an understanding of their world through play and exploration. The following paragraphs focus on ways that technology can influence such children's attention, perception, information processing, and memory.

Attention. Difficulties in maintaining attention on relevant details of a task and discriminating among important stimuli are common problems faced by children with cognitive impairments (Cook, Tessier, & Klein, 1996). Sensory and motor impairments create similar problems in attention and discrimination skills (Bailey & Wolery, 1992). Children who are hearing impaired, for example, may not be able to attend to unstressed parts of speech or high-pitched sounds (Bowe, 1995).

Technology solutions are available to help learners improve their attention to relevant stimuli regardless of cognitive, sensory, or physical impairments. Computers equipped with speech synthesizers and special software can help children with hearing problems focus their attention on important sounds. When this "speaking software" also includes colorful graphics, visuals, and/or graphic cues, children's attention is drawn to learning tasks.

Perception. Children can perceive visual and auditory stimuli even before birth, and these early perceptions provide a foundation for later learning (Cook, et. al., 1996). However, many children with disabilities demonstrate limitations in their perceptual abilities. Technological advances in hardware and software provide promising strategies to supplement their instruction. Computer-based instruction provides visual images and sounds in combinations that can increase attention and add to a child's perceptual base. Computers can significantly add to the number and variety of stimuli presented to a child; they can tirelessly present the stimuli and begin to help young children understand basic cause-and-effect relationships. Multimedia, or integrated media, instruction also can help young children sample experiences that might otherwise be beyond their personal experiences (e.g., a visit to a farm for children who live in the inner city). Children with hearing problems can see actions on the computer monitor that, when paired with visual images of sounds being made or with words, can facilitate spoken language.

Information Processing. When children analyze and use information that they have perceived, they have processed that information. Piaget posited that children assimilate new information by adding it to existing information. He also believed that children can accommodate their knowledge base by changing their view of information after they add new knowledge. Children with disabilities have more problems processing information than do their typically developing peers.

Overcoming attention and perception problems while providing children with new information are major goals for parents and early interventionists. Technology solutions can enhance their efforts with assistive hardware devices that provide children access to a variety of educational software. Integrated media holds the greatest promise for helping children assimilate and accommodate new information. CD-ROM technology enables software to include a tremendous number of visual images in the form of photos, videos, and graphics to reinforce important informational concepts. Along with sound, children can be exposed to instruction that provides them with interactivity. Such programs not only expose children to information, but also provide opportunities for them to respond. CD-ROM-based programs can direct children to branches of the program where they can receive help or be linked to other information.

Memory. An important component of memory involves the ability to rehearse material that is perceived. When people efficiently rehearse (i.e., repeat or practice) information in their short-term memory, the material is more likely to be stored in long-term memory. When people analyze information in a more detailed way or pair the information with other knowledge, the chances for retention are even better.

Most young children are not efficient at rehearsing information and need a considerable amount of repetition to store information for later retrieval. As typical children get older and reach elementary-school age, they begin to develop rehearsal strategies that serve them in storing, retaining, and being able to retrieve information. Young children with disabilities have considerably more problems learning to use rehearsal strategies and developing independent rehearsal strategies than do their typical peers (Thurman & Widerstrom, 1990).

Social Development and Technology

Social development has many facets and is a result of the complex interaction between biological factors and the environment. Play and its effects on a child appear to stand out as very important aspects of social development (Bruner, Jolly, & Sylva, 1976). When children are limited in their independent or cooperative play, they cannot develop into socially healthy adults or explore the world so that cognitive growth is enhanced.

Technology can be of immediate benefit to children who, because of their limitations, cannot actively engage in play. Low-tech solutions, such as single switches, and high-tech solutions, such as adaptive keyboards, can allow children access to electronic toys and fun computer-based activities. The excitement of electronic toys and computer-based games provides children a common vehicle for engaging in socially rewarding experiences. Parents can enjoy playing with their children and, while doing so, model appropriate social skills and social communication.

Children who may not have had optimal social and learning experiences may be prone to exhibit outer-directed behavior and learned helplessness (Thomas & Patton, 1994). These behaviors may cause such children to develop the outlook that they as individuals have little control over their own lives. Feelings of helplessness often result in a lack of willingness to try anything but the simplest tasks. Some theorists postulate that this behavior is a direct result of a prolonged history of failure and of the effects that these children's disabilities have on how others treat them (Thomas & Patton, 1994).

Technology in general and computer-based instruction specifically can help children overcome the learning and social characteristics that cause them difficulty in acquiring new skills and interacting with their environments. Quality graphics, for example, can highlight important components of a task such as the differences among letters of the alphabet. Computer-based programs that use synthesized or digitized speech can help children to discriminate between and among sounds and can provide many high-quality models. Interventionists can match high-quality computer-based instruction to the individual learning styles of children who need increased visual, auditory, or tactile stimulation.

For children with disabilities, motivation becomes a problem as levels of failure and frustration rise. Technology and computer-based instruction are highly motivational because they provide children with ways to compensate for their limitations while they have fun (Lewis, 1993). The sound, graphics, animation, color, and video components are individually and collectively very exciting for children. In addition, computer-based instruction can provide limitless practice and immediate feedback—instructional qualities that often are necessary for children with special needs. Technology can help to make significant improvements in the cognitive, social, and emotional growth of children who have disabilities. Keeping activities fun while children learn is an integral component of programming for young children with disabilities (Cook et al., 1996). Computer-based instruction can accomplish this goal and be a powerful instructional tool. For all its potential, however, technology cannot replace loving parents and good teachers. Technology is a set of sophisticated tools that, when used to enhance quality learning experiences, can help make significant improvements in the lives of children.

Technology for Parents and Professionals

The development of technology has far outpaced our ability to get these advances into the hands of consumers. There are a variety of reasons why the use of technology is not widespread. One reason is that the flow of funds for purchasing technology is not always evenly spread across school programs. For example, more funds for purchasing technology may be available in elementary and secondary programs than in preschool programs. Another problem that may affect the use of technology with younger children is the lack of exposure that some parents and professionals have to these advances—some even have a "fear" of computers (Bowe, 1995). In any case, the best way to help children have access to these advances in learning is to treat technology as a set of tools. To begin the process of using technology tools, parents and professionals should explore the information that is available about technology solutions.

Technology Skills and Knowledge

Considerable information exists about the competencies teachers should have related to the use of technology (e.g., Church & Bender, 1989; Lewis, 1993). Less information is available on the skills needed by parents for using technology. Figure 9.1 provides a list of basic skills that are generally considered appropriate for professionals who wish to use technology in their work with children who have special needs. Many of these also apply to parents.

Sources of Information About Technology Solutions

The most important step in using technology is to locate appropriate information about hardware devices, software solutions, and financial resources for purchasing technology. There are many books and resource manuals that can help parents and professionals learn more about the applications of technology to teaching young children.

An excellent source of information about technology solutions for children is the Internet. One component of the Internet is the World Wide Web. The Web is user friendly and has become a popular resource for educators and parents. Most schools are provided staff access to the Web through links with commercial services. Households with computers and modems also can access the Web by contracting with

FIGURE 9.1 Technology skills for parents and early intervention professionals

To use technology with young children who have special needs, the parent or professional should be able to do the following:

- Define the terms and concepts related to technology applications in early childhood special education.
- Unpack, identify, and connect the diverse pieces of equipment that make up the technological systems used in early childhood special education (e.g., CPUs, monitors, printers, disk drives, cables, input/output devices, and internal boards such as speech synthesizers, adaptive devices, and augmentative-alternative communication devices).
- Describe various applications of technology in early childhood special education.
- Use a microcomputer and related software to produce signs, posters, overhead transparencies, and other visual aids for the preschool classroom.
- Identify the ways that microcomputers and related technology, such as interactive video, robotics, and augmentative and adaptive devices, can be integrated into the curriculum to meet the educational goals and objectives of children with special needs.
- Identify and explain the use of various forms of adaptive technology.
- Identify the financial resources available to support the use of special education technology.
- Integrate special education technology into effective instructional practices.
- Arrange the physical environment to facilitate the use of technology.
- Teach children with special needs to operate the hardware and software identified for the program.
- Use a microcomputer and related software to produce signs, posters, overhead transparencies, and other visual aids for the preschool classroom.
- Use a computer and appropriate software to manage, monitor, and evaluate instructional activities in the preschool classroom.

commercial services. For those who do not have these opportunities, many public libraries offer their patrons access to the Web's resources.

The Web can provide a variety of information. Interventionists can find examples of lesson plans and sources of instructional materials. They also can join listserves (groups of people having a common interest who can post electronic messages to other members of the group), through which they can discuss with other professionals information about teaching. Parents can find a wealth of information, such as resources for funding assistive technology, product descriptions, services of organizations, and listserves that enable them to share information with other users who have similar interests.

There are hundreds of Web sites that provide information on the topic of technology and young children with special needs. Figure 9.2 provides a short list of some Web sites of interest to early interventionists and parents of young children with special needs. A good place to begin is The National Center to Improve

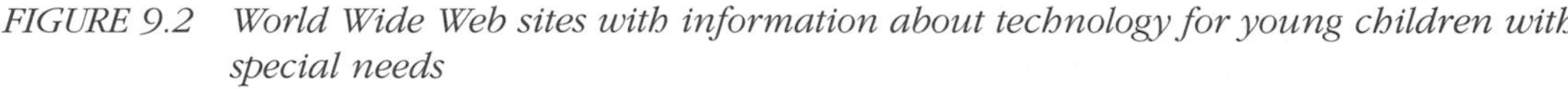

FIGURE 9.2 World Wide Web sites with information about technology for young children with special needs

http://www.edc.org/FSC/NCIP/Library_EC_insights.html

This is the address for the NCIP Web page dedicated to technology in early childhood education. The format of this page is a presentation of conversations taken from NCIPnet and compiled into threaded messages for easy reading and viewing. For example, current postings include discussions about Boardmaker, a software program for Macintosh computers that is used to develop communication board overlays. This Web page also provides an extensive resource list such as the NCIP Profile: Technology Supports Inclusion in Preschool and Resource Files: Technology in Early Childhood Education.

http://www.edc.org/FSC/NCIP/Library_Early_Child.html
NCIP Library: Technology in Early Childhood Education Collection

This Web page presents a variety of low- and high-tech tools for enhancing the learning of young children with disabilities. Information is presented about the use of technology for promoting growth in communication, social interaction, and cognitive development in preschoolers with special needs.

http://www.edc.org/FSC/NCIP/EC_TOC.HTML
NCIP Resources: Early Childhood

This Web page provides a listing of the resources currently contained within NCIP's Early Childhood Resource File. Resources are grouped into six categories: General, Practice, Products, Research, Vignette, and Publications. The following list provides examples of some of the resources available at this site.

- *Baby Power: A Guide for Families for Using Assistive Technology with Their Infants and Toddlers* is edited by Patsy Pierce.
- "Interactive Technology and the Young Child," published by the Center for Learning, Teaching, and Technology, reviews major developments in interactive technology as they pertain to the education of young children.
- "Preparing the Preschool Computer Environment" provides information from the *ACCT Curriculum Guide for Young Children and Technology* and focuses on the importance of developing a learning environment in which computers are integrated for use with young children.
- "Selection of Appropriate Technology for Children with Disabilities," an article first published in *Teaching Exceptional Children,* presents information about selecting appropriate technology for children with disabilities.
- "Technology for Inclusion: Meeting the Special Needs of All Students" describes Mary Male's book about a broad spectrum of issues related to technology for inclusion. The author's recommendations for designing activities and selecting software for young children with disabilities are included.
- "Assistive Technology and Young Children: Getting Off to a Great Start!" shows how assistive technology services and equipment should be an integral part of early intervention and preschool services (Pennsylvania Assistive Technology Project).
- "Computer Environments for Assessing the Strengths of Children with Special Needs" presents three vignettes that illustrate how computers provide an alternative environment for assessing the capabilities of young children with language disorders.
- "Computers for the Very Young: From the Ridiculous to the Sublime" describes how the Kingsway Learning Center's early intervention program uses technology in instructional and therapeutic activities with infants and toddlers who have disabilities. The authors include vignettes of four young children and descriptions of the specific tasks and software used. This document also includes a list of software, adaptive equipment, switches, and goals that can be integrated with a computer.

FIGURE 9.2 World Wide Web sites with information about technology for young children with special needs (continued)

- "Speaking Dynamically" is a description of the Macintosh-based communication software program of the same name for creating on-screen talking communication displays.
- "Storybooks on Computers: An Overview" provides descriptions and information about availability of storybooks for use on computers. This document also focuses on the features to consider when selecting computerized storybooks for students with disabilities. It highlights features such as speech and auditory feedback, graphics, interactivity, and accessibility.
- "Storybook Software: Product List" is an extensive list of electronic storybooks. This document includes a brief description of each storybook's software or CD, a list of titles in a series when appropriate, and a description of special access features that are available.
- "What's Hot for the Computer-Using Tot?" is an article by Warren Buckleitner that describes and evaluates a variety of early childhood software in terms of ease of use, instructional value, appeal, design features, and teacher options.
- "Baby-Babble-Blanket" is a description of the research project that developed the Baby-Babble-Blanket, a switch-activated pad on which infants with severe impairments and multiple handicaps can be placed. When an infant touches various switch locations, software is activated to emit various sounds, and the researchers evaluate the infant's responsiveness to and preferences for sounds.
- "Improving Benefits of Assistive Technology" provides a summary of recommendations for improving the benefits of assistive technology for children with disabilities based on a 2-year study by the Macomb Projects.
- "The Macomb Projects" is a reprint of a brochure that describes the work of a group of projects whose work centers on young children with disabilities, ages 0–8. The group includes one state-funded and six federally funded grant projects at Western Illinois University that focus on assistive technology, teacher training, and curriculum and software development.
- "Providing Public Education Services to Young Children with Disabilities in Community-Based Programs: Who's Responsible for What?" is the first in a series of papers developed by the Research Institute on Preschool Mainstreaming to help policymakers develop preschool mainstreaming policies.
- "Using an Expanded Keyboard to Help Students with Autism Learn to Write" is a brief vignette from an expanded version of the sidebar "Expanded Keyboard Helps Students with Autism Write." This document focuses on Paula Brassil's integrated classroom at the Warren Prescott School in Boston and highlights the benefits of access to an expanded keyboard for James, a student with autism.
- "From Toys to Computers" is a description of a guidebook that provides practical ideas and instructions for adaptations, devices, and techniques that children with disabilities can use to access toys and computers.
- "Simplified Technology for Persons with Severe Disabilities" provides an overview of books and materials for practitioners and parents involved with children who have expressive language disabilities, including both expressive and receptive delays.
- "Southeast Augmentative Communication Publications" describes a series of resource books for teachers, clinicians, therapists, and parents that provide practical information and resources for alternative and augmentative communication.

http://users.aol.com/dreamms/main.htm

DREAMMS for Kids, Inc. (Developmental Research for the Effective Advancement of Memory and Motor Skills) is a nonprofit parent and professional service agency specializing in assistive technology-related research, development, and information dissemination. DREAMMS shares information

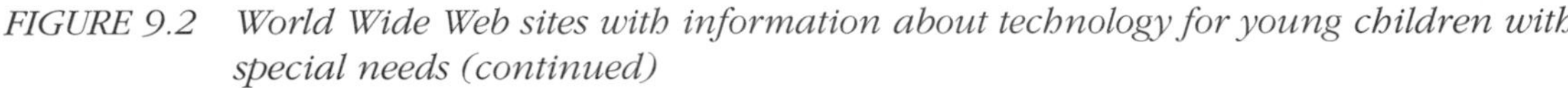

FIGURE 9.2 World Wide Web sites with information about technology for young children with special needs (continued)

for facilitating the use of computers, assistive technologies, and quality instructional technologies for children with special needs in schools, homes, and the community. The services of this group include newsletters, individually prepared Tech Paks, and special programs entitled *Computers for Kids, and Tools for Transition.*

http://www2.apple.com/disability/welcome.html

This Web site by Apple Computer, Inc. presents MAP, the Mac Access Passport, a tool that helps consumers and professionals discover assistive technology solutions for Macintosh computers. MAP provides information about the kinds of products that make it possible for persons who have disabilities to use a Macintosh computer. Users can download the latest version of Apple's product database, link directly with major organizations and manufacturers, and find a collection of access software programs from Apple.

http://interwork.sdsu.edu/ablenet.html

This Web site is managed by ABLE.NET, whose goal is to foster a dynamic exchange of ideas and lifelong learning opportunities. This site provides a great deal of information covering a wide range of ability and disability management system components. This site also allows ABLE.NET to support their goal of providing networking among interested students, people with disabilities, and professionals. Examples of some topics of interest available at this Web site include the following:

- "Forces That Sabotage Return to Work," is a chapter from the book *Return to Work by Design: Managing the Human and Financial Costs of Disability.* Copyright © 1990 by Gene Dent.
- "Creating a World of Opportunities Through Telecommunication Teleconference Text"
- Links to on-line disability information resources
- Calendar of events
- Legal issues, Americans with Disabilities Act legislation
- Prevention of impairment and early intervention strategies
- Rehabilitation options, i.e., re-employment, job retention, and medical separation

http://www.aten.ocps.k12.fl.us/
Assistive Technology Educational Network (ATEN)

- "ATEN Chat Room" allows users to leave messages, add messages, and chat live with others about assistive technology. It also allows users to join monthly conferences on-line.
- "Catalog of Switches" includes specs, ordering information, and color pictures of the devices.
- ATEN's "Device of the Month" profiles devices that may be useful for persons with disabilities. Each month ATEN describes a new device along with statistics, pricing, and ordering information.

http://www.nmia.com/~riattdev/

Assistive Technology Resource Alliance (ATRA) is a resource for participants in the market for assistive technology. ATRA was formed by the Research Institute for Assistive and Training Technologies (RIATT) at the University of New Mexico, Sandia National Laboratories, and Laguna Industries, Inc. in conjunction with the New Mexico Technology Deployment Pilot Project (NMTDP). ATRA links assistive technology product developers and entrepreneurs with technologists, investors, policymakers, and consumers, and helps users decide on needs and find new product ideas, new technologies, funding sources, and key market information.

Practice (NCIP). This Web site (http://www.edc.org/FSC/NCIP/) promotes the effective use of technology for helping students with sensory, cognitive, physical, and social-emotional disabilities. A goal of the NCIP is to link a national community of professionals who use or want to use technology with advocates and consumers. The NCIP also has materials available in print and video, as well as an extensive collection of other resources available through the Web site.

Technology Solutions for Young Children

There is a wide range of computer hardware and software products. This section discusses personal computers, software applications for young children, and adaptive hardware that allows children access to computers and electronic devices.

Personal Computers

Personal computers have become commonplace in homes across the nation. Most programs that provide services to young children with disabilities now have access to computers for instructional purposes. Personal computers can be categorized into two types: those that are made or licensed by Apple Computers, Inc. and those that are produced either by IBM, Inc. or by other companies and are compatible with IBM products. IBM-compatible computers often are referred to as "clones."

There are two types of Apple computers that are commonly found in educational programs. The newer Macintosh computers are user friendly and include a variety of innovations that can be extremely helpful for young children with limitations. For example, Mac computers come with on-board screen magnification for enlarging visual images and lettering that appear on the monitor screen. These computers also come with built-in speech synthesis capability and software solutions that allow children with disabilities to decrease the number of keystrokes they need to complete functions.

The older Apple II series of computers are commonly found in educational settings. These computers have been the workhorses of teachers for more than a decade and still can provide children with high-quality electronic activities. The II series have several limitations, however, including a lack of peripherals (such as built-in voice synthesis, color monitors, and high-speed microprocessors). Voice-production capability and color monitors can be added, but the microprocessor limitations inhibit the use of more-sophisticated multimedia software. Many programs have been developed for these computers that make them still potentially useful. Also, a variety of adaptive devices are available for use with the IIe series of Apple computers.

IBM computers and clones have been the mainstay of business and industry for years. These machines use a different operating system from that of Apple products, so software purchased for one platform usually will not work on the other; however, hardware and software solutions are making the two types of personal computers more compatible.

A computer system for young children should include a CD-ROM player, color monitor, at least 8 megabytes of random access memory (RAM), and the largest hard drive one can afford (at least 540 megabytes). These specifications allow children to take advantage of the new multimedia programs. Many computers available today include these features in the basic package.

The Curriculum and Integration of Technology

Technology provides us with tools for educational use that can increase learning and improve the quality of the lives of children with disabilities and their families. Like other tools, technology can be misused. Using computer-based instruction, communication boards, and adaptive toys in isolation with no link to instructional objectives is a potential misuse of technology (Langone, 1990). For example, a misuse may occur when a teacher places a child at a computer to work with a software program designed to introduce initial nouns, but following the session, the teacher does not structure opportunities for practicing those nouns during other naturally occurring activities. Another example of a possible misuse of technology is when a teacher instructs a child to communicate with an electronic device in an isolated one-on-one activity related to eating (e.g., "May I have a cookie?"), then does not let the child use the board during snack and lunch times.

Early childhood special education curricula generally include goals that are meaningful and relevant to all children and their families. These goals are functional and help children to develop cognitive and social-emotional processes and, eventually, to become better learners (Cook et al., 1996). Teachers should link technology to these same general goals. Thus, for example, a teacher should review a software program designed to help teach first nouns with great care. Then the teacher should make a thoughtful decision about what role the software will play in his overall plan to teach these skills. Similarly, a teacher should carefully analyze different activities and events, and determine what opportunities for communication are available for each child. Using a communication device to produce requests and responses, for example, can be linked to activities and opportunities that occur throughout the day. This approach provides children with practice and natural reinforcement.

Standard Computer-Based Instruction

Most computer software for young children focuses on language skills and on specific preacademic activities such as matching, number recognition, and problem solving (Kinsley & Langone, 1995). Over the years there have been a few research studies that have attempted to measure the success of computer-based instruction with young children who have special needs. These studies have provided evidence of the success that computer-based instruction can have with such learners (Fazio & Rieth, 1986; Lehrer, Harckham, Archer, & Pruzek, 1986; McCormick, 1987; Spiegel-McGill, Zippiroli, & Mistrett, 1989).

Language Development and Communication. Computer-based instruction can be an effective tool in helping children who have disabilities develop and

Technology provides tools for educational use that can increase learning and improve the quality of life for children and their families.

use language and communication skills. When paired with a speech synthesizer and graphics, a computer can provide children with quality models for language use and a method for expressing their messages. These features augment the concepts to be learned and provide a frame of reference for words introduced during instruction. Programs designed to improve receptive language skills introduce new vocabulary, illustrate language concepts, and encourage children to use language by providing exploratory and discovery activities. For example, for the introduction of the word *ball,* a graphic of a ball bounces across the monitor's screen while the speech synthesizer says "ball." The programs that may be the most productive for young children first allow them to explore and discover, then provide opportunities for them to practice the skills that they have learned under new conditions. Such programs provide children with many verbal, graphic, and pictorial cues designed to increase the probability of success. They also provide each child with frequent feedback and reinforcement, often personalized by using the child's name.

Receptive Language Programs. Laureate Learning Systems, Inc. designs and markets a variety of software for teaching cause-effect and receptive language skills to children with delays. These computer-based instructional programs have been carefully researched and designed and are based on the sequences of language development of typically developing children. Laureate markets a series called The Creature Games for children who function below the age level of 9 months. There are six individual programs (*Creature: Antics, Capers, Features, Cartoons, Magic,* and *Chorus*) that allow children to learn the concept of cause and effect, the use of single switches for input and program control, and turn-taking in group activities.

Laureate also markets The Early Vocabulary Development Series, which includes *First Words, First Words II,* and *First Verbs.* These programs offer six instructional levels. The basic level allows a child to activate a switch and cause the computer to identify the picture on the screen. More-advanced levels provide tests for use after a child has mastered the initial levels, at which time cuing and feedback are provided. These programs are available in bilingual versions for young children from Spanish-speaking households. Also available from Laureate is the Exploring Early Vocabulary Series, which reinforces the vocabulary learned during interaction with The Early Vocabulary Development Series; a child who learned the word *drum* in the *First Words II* program, for example, will be asked to "Find the drum."

Young children, under the guidance of adults, learn to express themselves through exploration and play. In traditional classroom settings, teachers may find it difficult to provide many children with all of the opportunities they need to improve their expressive language skills. A solution to this is microcomputer technology, which significantly increases the number of exciting stimuli for children in a variety of instructional situations (Schery & O'Connor, 1992). Colorful graphics, voice support, music, and animation can enhance a variety of activities designed to provide children practice in expressing themselves individually, in small, integrated groups, and with adult assistance.

Software that is designed to help children gain and practice expressive language skills can work in many ways. For example, Laureate Software builds on its receptive language programs by including additional words that children can use to construct phrases and, eventually, sentences. Using the same vocabulary as in the *First Words* program, *Talking Nouns* helps children to use *I, we, show me, like,* and other words and phrases to begin building simple sentences. Basically, programs such as these use overlays placed on the input device (e.g., adapted keyboards and Touch Windows). These overlays, which include pictures and words in combination, help children to choose the words and phrases they wish to use to construct their sentences. The most useful software allows the teacher to set preferences that activate the speech synthesizer to "say" the sentence only after the child has completed its construction. Software by Laureate also has an important feature that corrects the child's grammar and produces the correctly spoken model of the sentence that the child constructed.

Many software programs encourage exploratory play while providing events for children and adults to "talk" about, thereby increasing chances for communication and general language improvement. *McGee* and *Katie's Farm* (Lawrence Productions) are examples of highly motivating programs that stimulate children's language. Adults can encourage children to discuss or describe events that are taking place while they explore the computer-simulated environments (home and farm) with the fictional characters. *Playroom* (Broderbund) is another software program that allows children to discover new things, learn cause and effect, and make choices.

PEAL Software produces many interesting products. *Exploratory Play,* for example, is a language program designed to encourage communication through exploration and play. Using an input device with overlays, a child can press a picture to request a toy, thereby cuing the computer to produce the actual speech. Real toys that match the pictures are available, and children have the opportunity to make increasingly complex requests. Initially, children might request "car" or "I want that" if they have not yet associated the picture with the action. As children gain more-advanced skills, the program helps teach them to use verb-object combinations, more-complex sentences, and more requests for toys.

Expressive Language Programs. A number of companies develop and market software programs designed to help children improve their expressive language skills. For example, Laureate Learning Systems' *Talking Nouns* program can be used as a tool to help children improve their expressive language. A brief list of companies to help early childhood interventionists begin their search follows:

- Don Johnston Developmental Equipment, Inc., P.O. Box 639, 1000 N. Rand Road, Building 115, Wauconda, IL 60084. Telephone: (800) 999-4660. Many programs are available, such as *Day at Play, Eency and Friends,* and *Forgetful and Friends.*
- IntelliTools, 5221 Central Avenue, Suite 205, Richmond, CA 94804. Telephone: (800) 899-6687. Known primarily for its alternative keyboards, IntelliKeys and the Unicorn Expanded Keyboard, IntelliTools also markets software that supports these input devices and allows them, in conjunction with a computer, to become powerful communication devices for expressive language.
- Laureate Learning Systems, Inc., 110 East Spring Street, Winooski, VT 05404. Telephone: (800) 562-6801. This company publishes a variety of receptive and expressive language programs including *Talking Nouns, Talking Nouns II,* and *Talking Verbs.* Laureate also markets computer-based instructional programs for word combinations, early syntax, and syntax mastery. *First Categories,* The Emerging Rules Series, *My Paint and Talking Color Books, Micro-Lads, Let's Go to the Circus,* and The Words and Concepts Series are some of Laureate's programs that can assist teachers.
- PEAL Software, P.O. Box 8188, Calabasas, CA 91372. This company markets expressive language programs such as *Exploratory Play, Representational Play,* and *Action/Music Play.*
- Sunburst Communications, 101 Castleton Street, P.O. Box 100, Pleasantville, NY 10570. Telephone: (800) 321-7511. This company markets the Muppet Learning Keys (an input device) and associated software for use in teaching expressive language skills. *Muppets on Stage* allows children to explore letters and colors, and the *Muppet Word Book* provides opportunities for children to learn upper- and lower-case letters,

word endings and beginnings, consonants, and vowels. The activities are highly reinforcing because children can explore with the Muppet characters from television. The software is available in a Spanish version.

Preacademic Skills. Many programs are available on floppy disks for teaching preacademic skills. One note of caution is warranted, however, in the use of any computer-based instructional program for teaching preacademic skills: Repeated computer drill and practice of reading and arithmetic skills at early ages may create burn out in children rather than strengthen these skills. Thus, requiring children to spend large amounts of time practicing preacademic skills at the computer can be counterproductive. Interventionists should recognize this and emphasize to parents the need to engage children in fun activities that allow them to explore and play while they learn basic, developmentally appropriate skills. Software that captures children's attention while presenting information in a logically sequenced fashion is an asset to interventionists because it allows them to facilitate learning instead of mandating time on task.

A major goal of programs for young children with special needs is to encourage them to develop cognitive skills and literacy. Computer-based instruction can be effective in helping children to strengthen basic cognitive processes, such as attention, perception, discrimination, and memory (Lewis, 1993), while they learn preacademic skills. Following is a brief list of software that can be effective in helping children gain preacademic skills while they engage in fun activities:

- *Stickybear's Early Learning Activities* (Optimum Resource) allows children to discover or be guided through six activities designed to help them gain basic skills for later success in academics. This program is available in Spanish.
- *First Steps Counting and Thinking Games* (Optimum Resource), among other features, allows children to play a block-stacking game, to practice counting, and to begin learning number sets.
- *Muppet Math* (Sunburst) allows children to explore the Muppet Schoolhouse and work with shapes, count, and begin to work with patterns and numbers.
- *Muppetville* (Sunburst) allows children to work on different activities with the Muppet characters. Children have the opportunity to improve their visual-association skills and continue to work with shapes, numbers, and colors.

Educational Resources distributes software from a variety of publishers. Their address is 1550 Executive Drive, P.O. Box 1900, Elgin, IL 60121. Telephone: (800) 860-2009.

CD-ROM- and Videodisc-Based Instruction

The difficulty of placing important concepts and information in the context of meaningful events and activities is a major instructional problem. This difficulty often results in the teaching of skills that children are expected to recall upon command, but that they are never taught to use in problem-solving situations (Hasselbring, Goin, & Bransford, 1991). This phenomenon, described by Whitehead (1929) as the learning of "inert" knowledge, has been the subject of considerable debate among cognitive theorists who believe that our current approach to education presents information to learners that, at best, proliferates the spread of knowledge that has little or no link to practical application (Brown, Collins, & Duguid, 1989; Tripp, 1993). Teaching preacademic skills or basic language concepts in isolation, with no link to common events or concrete applications, may serve to actually impede children's ability to learn these skills and solve problems.

In an attempt to overcome the problem of teaching inert knowledge, the Cognition and Technology Group at Vanderbilt (CTGV) has developed a system they call "anchored instruction." This approach situates learning in videodisc- or CD-ROM-based environments and provides learners with examples of how experts use knowledge as tools to solve problems. Students and their teachers, who act as partners in learning, explore video environments rich in information. Students use video examples cooperatively to solve increasingly complex problems (CTGV, 1993; Young, 1993). The research supporting the effectiveness of situated learning in general (Griffin, 1995), and anchored instruction specifically (CTGV, 1993, 1994), is promising. Anchored instruction provides the opportunity for applying technology-based situated learning to other areas (Hedberg & Alexander, 1994).

Computer-based, multimedia CD-ROM and videodisc software provides and extends anchored instruction by allowing children to experience a variety of stimuli. These stimuli reinforce important concepts and transmit information such that children see concrete examples. CD-ROM technology enables software developers to create significantly more-powerful instructional programs because of the increased storage capacity on the discs. It also makes possible the inclusion of digitized video, animation, sophisticated graphics, and sounds that are designed to enhance the learning of preacademic concepts and language. For example, *The San Diego Zoo Presents . . . The Animals* CD-ROM (Software Toolworks, 60 Leveroni Court, Novato, CA 94949) invites children to take a trip through the San Diego Zoo. Interventionists can use this program to reinforce children's learning the names of animals by pairing the names with the many color photographs and compressed video clips available. Children also can practice problem-solving skills by attempting to navigate around the park. Sound is available to provide children with a verbal description of some of the animals.

Interventionists might wish to use CD-ROM software such as that which portrays author Mercer Mayer's stories *Just Grandma and Me* (Living Books) and *Just Me and My Dad* (Big Tuna New Media) to help children become interested in reading. The adventures of Little Critter, the central character of these books and a favorite of children, present words, phrases, and language concepts using colorful graphics, animation, and sound. For example, one "page" of the *Just Grandma and Me* CD-ROM includes the sentence "I found a nice seashell for Grandma but it was full of a crab." The "page" includes colorful graphics and animation that can be used to reinforce words and concepts such as the animated sequence of the crab popping out of the shell.

Videodisc technology allows for 60 minutes of full-motion video and sound (30 minutes per side) to be pressed onto a videodisc that looks like a cross between an old phonograph record and a large audio compact disc. The video and sound reproductions are superior to those of VHS, and any frame on one side of the disc can be located instantly. This feature is the reason why videodiscs can be a more powerful instructional tool than VHS tapes are, and it is the reason why videodisc technology can be important for implementing anchored instruction in a preschool classroom. For example, one sequence from the videodisc of Walt Disney Productions' *Fantasia* (Buena Vista Video) can be used to introduce and reinforce vocabulary words such as *bucket, water,* and *broom*. The video also can be used to reinforce the action phrases and language concepts of filling the bucket, emptying the bucket, more than one object, and putting on an article of clothing (the hat). All of these words and concepts are vividly and dramatically brought to life as this particular animated sequence's rich visual images show the humorous but problematic results of the main character's actions.

Again, the great advantage of videodisc technology is that, through the use of a remote control or bar-code reader, the particular video clip that will reinforce the word or concept being introduced in a lesson can be retrieved quickly. A VHS tape and VCR player require considerably more time to manipulate, thus breaking the flow of a lesson and possibly losing the attention of the children. The immediate-access feature of videodisc technology also allows interventionists more freedom to retrieve short video clips multiple times when children need more exposure to an animated sequence. Additional viewings may help children form a mental picture that can be associated with the target word or phrase.

Authoring tools, such as *HyperStudio v 3.0* (Roger Wagner Publishing), can be used to create one's own instruction either for presenting information to children or for children's use in cooperative learning groups. *Hyperstudio* can hold a stack of words, phrases, or concepts, which then can be linked to the appropriate video clip via a button provided within the structure of the software. During presentation of the video, a child only has to click on the button to view the desired clip. This tool can make a presentation more natural and eliminate the use of a remote control or bar-code reader, which tend to be more cumbersome. Children can learn to click on the buttons to view the video clip that is anchored to a word or phrase. Authoring programs make possible many options, such as importing sound and animation to support the video clips and the printed words.

Multimedia Instruction. Many quality CD-ROM and videodisc programs are available that can be beneficial for children with special needs. The following list is a representation of a larger universe of products:

- *Let's Start Learning* (The Learning Company) allows children to follow Reader Rabbit through many exploration activities designed to strengthen letter and number skills.
- The Living Books series, including *ABC's by Dr. Seuss* and *The Tortoise and the Hare* (Broderbund Software, P.O. Box 6121, Novato, CA 94948.

Telephone: [800] 521-6263), helps children explore interactive environments that they first experienced in text versions.

- *Mr. Potato Head Saves Veggie Valley* (Playskool) gives children the opportunity to solve problems and strengthen basic language skills and preacademic arithmetic skills by following a story line that takes them through the valley and to the county fair.
- *Tapestry Language Development* (Hartley, 3001 Coolidge Road, Suite 400, East Lansing, MI 48823. Telephone: [800] 247-1380) includes five stories designed to stimulate oral language development, sensory awareness, and problem-solving skills.
- *Tapestry Early Math* (Hartley) also includes five stories designed to help in developing problem solving, decision making, and emerging math skills.
- *A to Zap!* (Sunburst Communications, 101 Castleton Street, P.O. Box 100, Pleasantville, NY 10570. Telephone: [800] 321-7511) provides children with a sophisticated interactive environment that helps them to gain letter, number, and word skills.
- *Hello Kitty Big Fun Deluxe* (Published by Big Top and available through Sunburst) allows children to create their own songs and play number and shape games. An art program also is included.
- *Zurk's Learning Safari* (Published by Soleil Software and available through Sunburst) helps children learn life science, prearithmetic, and prereading concepts using animals in a variety of game activities.
- *Millie's Math House* and *Sammy's Science House* (Published by Edmark and available through Sunburst) use animation with colorful graphics to help children develop early math and science skills, including beginning observation, classification, comparison, and problem-solving skills.
- *Richard Scarry's How Things Work in Busytown* and *Richard Scarry's Busytown* (Published by Computer Curriculum Corporation and available through Educational Resources, 1550 Executive Drive, P.O. Box 1900, Elgin, IL 60121. Telephone: [800] 860-2009) are based on the popular children's books of the same name. Children can engage in interactive activities that explore city life, while the stage is set for interventionists to use these activities as the basis for stimulating language development.
- *Alphabet Blocks* (Published by Sierra and available through Educational Resources) helps children learn letter names, match sounds to written letters, and pronounce them.

Videodisc Programs. Laser Learning Technologies, Inc. (120 Lakeside Avenue, Suite 240, Seattle, WA 98122-6522. Telephone: [800] 722-3505) has a large collection of videodisc instructional packages available (this also is a great source for CD-ROM software). The videodiscs this company sells often come with software that allows students to work individually. The following list is a brief representation of videodiscs that can be useful in working with young children who have special needs. This list does not include the large number of commercially produced movies that are available on videodisc for instructional use:

- *Hi Cat!, Pet Show,* and *Goggles,* based on the book by Ezra Jack Keats, present the adventures of two children in their urban neighborhood. These programs come with bar-code indexes.
- *Curious George, Frog and Toad Are Friends,* and *Ralph S. Mouse* present popular children's stories for use in language development lessons or for recreation. All three videodiscs have bar-code indexes.
- *How the Leopard Got His Spots* and *Pecos Bill* are educational versions of the Rabbit Ears Classics; both come with bar-code indexes and activity guides.

Adaptive Hardware

For most people, a keyboard and mouse are the standard ways to access and control a computer. Young children with physical impairments, however, require alternate methods so that they can benefit from computer-based instruction, communication capabilities, and recreational programs available on computers. Most computer-based instruction designed for typical young children does not require that they make multiple keystrokes using a standard keyboard. Similarly, instruction designed for children with special needs takes into account their limitations. Therefore, this chapter does not provide in-depth information about sophisticated alternate keyboards or low-tech devices such as head pointers, styluses, mouthsticks, or chin/head wands that require specific motor control.

Students with severe disabilities often need assistive tools that allow them to interact with computers and other electronic devices. These assistive tools range in sophistication from simple switches that turn devices on and off to alternate keyboards that have special characteristics matched to individual disabilities. For example, a child who has physical disabilities might need only a single switch to use and play with a toy, while a child with poor motor control might require an adaptive keyboard with large keys or pads, which increase the size of the target and thus allow the child access to a computer. These and other assistive and adaptive tools are discussed next.

Adapted Standard Keyboards. Standard keyboards can be adapted with both hardware and software. Keylocks and keyguards are two low-tech hardware solutions for improving keyboard control. Keylocks are devices that allow the user to lock a specific key, such as the Option key on Macintosh computers. This device allows a person with the use of only one hand to activate multikey functions (e.g., Option + "b" to start the bold command on some word processors). Keyguards overlay the keyboard with raised holes that allow users with poor motor control to find the right keys without hitting other keys by accident. Keyguards also are useful for people with severe physical challenges who require the use of head pointers or other devices that substitute for the ability to make keystrokes with their hands.

Most Macintosh computers come with on-board software for the Stick Keys feature, which allows users to lock specific function keys. Similar software is available for IBM computers. Software also is available to control whether keys repeat when they are held down beyond the initial keystroke. This feature is valuable for those who have difficulty releasing a key once it is activated. Software solutions also allow users who cannot quickly release to set delays in time before keys begin repeating. Macintosh computers come with these features built into the operating system.

Alternative Keyboards. There are many hardware alternatives to the standard keyboard that have a variety of functions based on the needs of individuals with physical disabilities. Although some adaptive devices that provide access to technologies are purely mechanical, such as keyguards and head pointers, most are electronic. Examples of electronic devices include special keyboards and touch pads that typically operate by means of touch-sensitive membranes, and simple switches. These devices generally require some adaptations to the target device, usually the computer.

Three computers often found in today's classrooms are the Apple IIe, the Apple IIGS, and the Apple Macintosh. The IIe and IIGS can be equipped with an insert called the Adaptive Firmware Card (AFC) (Don Johnston Developmental Equipment, Inc., P.O. Box 639, 1000 North Rand Road, Building 115, Wauconda, IL 60084. Telephone: [800] 999-4660), which allows the computer to respond to the input of other devices. The AFC is a hardware card that fits inside the computer and is attached to a control box on its exterior. This device, in conjunction with accompanying software, acts as a substitute for the standard keyboard in the IIe and for the keyboard and mouse in the IIGS. When a variety of alternative keyboards and single switches are connected, a child has access to virtually any software written for these computers. Lewis (1993) provides an excellent description of the use and applications of the AFC. A similar device called the Kemx (Don Johnston Developmental Equipment, Inc.) is available for Macintosh computers; it plugs into the mouse port normally reserved for the standard keyboard.

Computers such as the Apple IIe and IIGS, and some older Macintosh computers, can be equipped with an Echo Speech Synthesizer (Echo Speech Corporation, 6460 Via Real, Carpinteria, CA 93013) to make use of computer-generated speech. Using the Echo, a teacher can make use of "talking" software for instructing students who cannot produce speech to use alternative devices for communication. Speech synthesizers also can be used to improve speech and language skills by providing computer-produced models for speech and allowing children to engage in language development exercises in which the computer "asks" questions, provides auditory feedback, and presents verbal reinforcement. Some newer models of computers come with the on-board ability to produce speech.

There are many sophisticated electronic devices on the market that can provide children access to computers and their many uses. The following list is a representative sample of devices that can help children learn important skills and gain an additional measure of control over their environment.

Unicorn Expanded Keyboard (IntelliTools, 5221 Central Avenue, Suite 205, Richmond, CA 94804. Telephone: [800] 899-6687)

- This is a flat, touch-sensitive device that has a membrane keyboard for the computer capable of being divided into up to 128 squares.
- When attached to a computer, this device can be used as a communication board or an alternative keyboard.
- Squares can be grouped in many different ways, according to the needs of a child, allowing overlays to be created for different uses.
- This device makes it possible to have almost unlimited options for use of computers by children with disabilities.
- A smaller version with similar capabilities is available (Unicorn Model 510)

IntelliKeys (IntelliTools)

- This keyboard does not require an interface device such as the AFC, but plugs directly into the computer.
- The same keyboard can be used with Apple, Macintosh, and IBM computers, thus allowing for more flexibility within programs that have multiple kinds of computers.
- It includes "smart" overlays with bar codes that the board reads, allowing the user to begin typing immediately based on the functions represented on the particular overlay.
- Interventionists can create their own overlays based on individual children's needs.

IntelliKeys utilize overlays that can be adapted to meet an individual child's needs.

IntelliTalk software allows children to type messages that the computer speaks for them.

- IntelliKeys can be used with *IntelliTalk* software that allows children to type messages that they want the computer to speak for them.

Touch Window (Edmark Corporation, P.O. Box 3218, Redmond, WA 98073. Telephone: [800] 426-0856)

- This device is a thin, touch-sensitive overlay that fits over the computer screen and allows input into the computer through the touching of areas on the screen.
- It is available for all computer platforms.
- It operates similarly to a computer mouse.
- The Touch Window is appropriate for children who may have difficulty associating keystrokes on the keyboard with the resulting changes on the computer screen.
- It allows finger tracing of shapes and letters on the screen as a learning activity.
- The Touch Window also can be used as a remote alternative device in a group activity. When it is used as a remote device, overlays are required to replace the prompts normally provided on the computer screen.
- Touch Window-compatible software is required for use. A great deal of quality Touch Window-compatible software is available.

Muppet Learning Keys (Sunburst Communications, 101 Castleton Street, P.O. Box 100, Pleasantville, NY 10570. Telephone: [800] 321-7511)

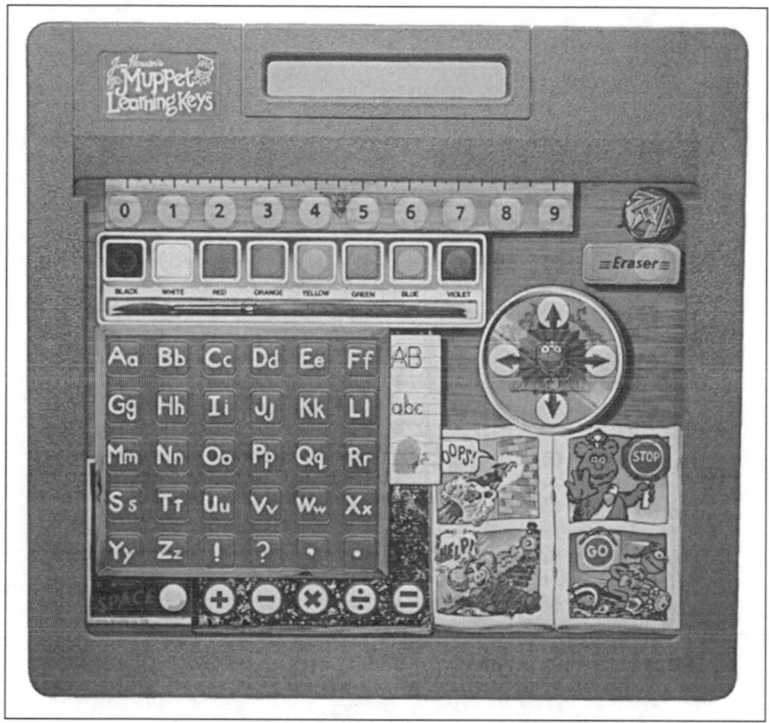

Muppet Learning Keys are attractive and easy for children to access.

- This colorful keyboard is attractive to young children and is meant for use with *Muppet* software.
- It is lightweight for easy use in group activities.
- The keys are arranged in a way that is easy for children to access.
- Arrow keys are arranged in a compass format for ease of understanding.

Power Pad (Dunamis, Inc., 3620 Highway 317, Suwanee, GA 30174. Telephone: [800] 828-2443)

- This device attaches to the game port of a computer.
- Power Pad-compatible software is required for use. Dunamis sells a variety of quality Power Pad-compatible software.
- The Power Pad can be used with software to turn the computer into a communication device.
- It requires more pressure than other devices do to activate its functions.

Switches

- Using plates, levers, or membranes, children can activate electrically controlled devices with very simple muscle movements.
- Switches come in many shapes and sizes.
- Switches can be commercially produced or homemade.

Switches, like these by AbleNet, allow children to activate electrically controlled devices with simple muscle movements.

- Switches can be controlled by hand, arm, foot, head, eyebrow, tongue, or any other muscle over which a child has some control.
- Switches can be used to teach cause and effect to young children.
- Switches can be used with a variety of mechanical toys and devices used for self-care and domestic skills.
- Switches also can be used to operate computers.

Examples of Switches

- *Big Red Switch* (Produced by AbleNet and available through Innocomp, Suite 302, 26210 Emery Road, Warrensville Heights, Ohio 44128. Telephone: [800] 382-8622)
- *Jelly Bean and Specs Switches* (Produced by AbleNet and available through Innocomp)

Technology and Communication

As noted in Chapter 7, the ability to produce speech may not be possible for some children or the production of speech may be delayed to the extent that their speech is unintelligible to others. Technology now provides powerful tools that help children overcome barriers to communication and language development.

Children with the ability to produce speech can benefit from the use of augmentative communication strategies that are designed to support their communication attempts, while alternative communication approaches replace speech for learners who for some reason do not have the ability to speak. Both of these strategies range from low-tech solutions (e.g., picture communication boards, photos, and printed symbol systems) to high-tech solutions (e.g., microcomputers and stand-alone electronic boards) that can either support what a child is trying to say or produce the message completely for the child. Obviously, the high-tech solutions are a must for children who cannot produce speech. These devices also can help children who can produce speech by providing models for pronouncing words and, more importantly, illustrating the cause and effect relationships crucial for early language development (Suddath & Susnik, 1991). A brief description

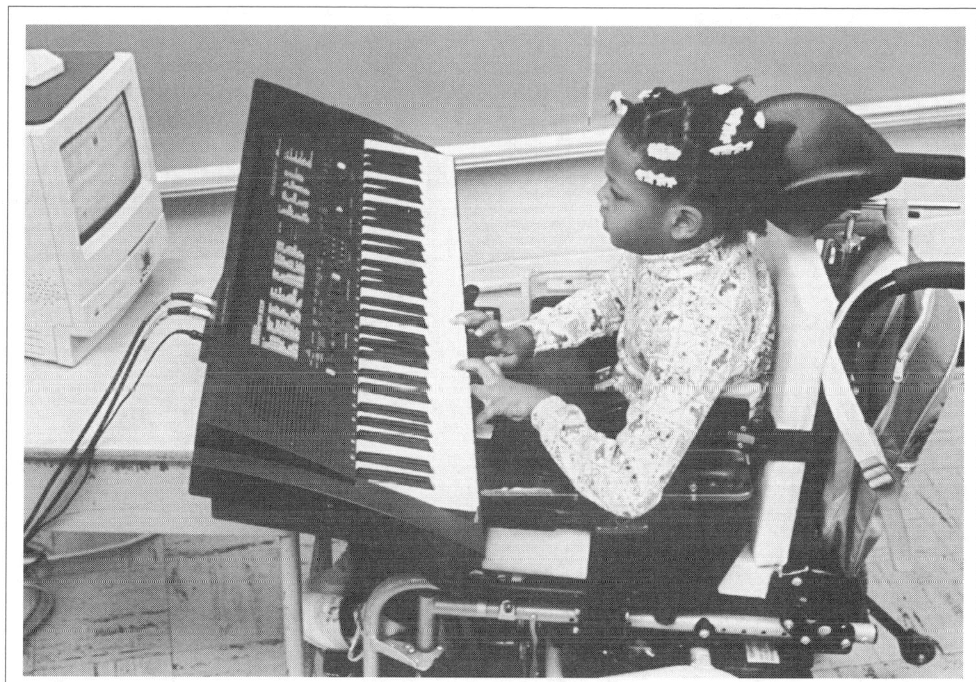

Technology benefits children who, because of their limitations, cannot actively engage in typical play.

of some of the high tech solutions available for augmentative and alternative communication follows.

Stand-alone electronic communication boards and computers with speech production capabilities via software and adaptive devices provide children who have significant speech impairments with the ability to respond to many day-to-day opportunities to communicate (Angelo & Goldstein, 1990). Electronic stand-alone units generally use touch-sensitive membranes as the target surface for pointing. Communication boards use either synthesized speech (computer-produced speech sounds) or digitized speech (digitally recorded natural speech). Digitized speech is immediately more recognizable for most listeners, although listeners can learn to understand synthesized speech in time.

There are a variety of stand-alone electronic devices on the market from which to choose. The type of device one buys usually depends on the amount of money one has to spend, the ability to adapt the device to the needs of children, durability, and ease of use. Generally, the interventionist should not invest in a high-priced device with many features if a lower-priced device will meet the immediate needs of children. As they gain more-advanced skills, more expensive and versatile devices can be obtained. The following list is representative of a larger number of devices that are available. For funding sources, the interventionist should

The Alpha Talker is a stand-alone communication board.

refer to Parette, Hoffman, and Van Biervliet (1994) and *Exceptional Parent* (Vol. 20, 1990; Vol. 25, 1995).

Intro Talker (Prentke Romich Company, 1022 Heyl Road, Wooster, OH 44691. Telephone: [800] 262-1984)

- This is a touch-sensitive board offering 8 to 32 fairly large squares.
- The board is programmable with digitized recordings of natural speech.
- It is suitable for very young children and those with severe disabilities.
- The squares can be labeled with pictures or words.
- Intro Talker is often used as a child's first electronic communication board.

Wolf Board (ADAMLAB)

- The screen can be divided into up to 36 squares or rectangles.
- This device uses lower-quality synthesized speech.
- It has a limited memory of approximately 800 words.
- The Wolf Board can be activated by touch or be connected to switches.
- It is more sophisticated than the Intro Talker.
- This is a less-expensive alternative to high-end devices.

Touch Talker (Prentke Romich Company)

- This is a synthesized speech device with 8 to 32 small keys.
- It generates highly sophisticated synthesized speech.
- The user learns to create words by combining specific keys in sequence.
- More-refined motor skills are required to access these keys than those required for the Intro Talker.
- A liquid crystal display (LCD) is included.

Liberator (Prentke Romich Company)

- This device is similar to the Touch Talker in size and function.
- It uses advanced speech synthesis.
- Phrases and longer messages can be saved in memory for use at a later time.
- The Liberator can be adapted for use with head pointers or other devices.
- In addition to having a liquid crystal display, this device can generate small paper printouts of messages.

Macaw II (ZYGO Industries, Inc., P.O. Box 1008, Portland, OR 97207-1008. Telephone: [800] 234-6006)

- Two models are available: one with direct selection only, and one with direct selection and scanning.
- This device is lightweight and small for easy use.
- It records communication messages.
- It has enlarged key patterns with sensitive keys.

Big Mack Voice Output Communication Aid (Produced by Ablenet and available through Innocomp, Suite 302, 26210 Emery Road, Warrensville Heights, Ohio 44128. Telephone: [800] 382-8622)

- This device allows for 20 seconds of recorded speech.
- One large button activates the message.
- It is easy to use for teaching beginning communication as well as cause and effect.

Speakeasy Voice Output and Communication Aid (Produced by Ablenet and available through Innocomp)

- This device allows for 120 seconds of recorded speech.
- It can adapt for up to 12 switches for group work.
- It allows for auditory scanning and has a keyguard available.

DigiVox and DynaVox (Sentient Systems Technology, Inc., 2100 Wharton Street, Pittsburgh, PA 15203. Telephone: [800] 344-1778)

- These are high-end systems that allow for complex communication.
- Multiple message levels are provided.
- These devices use digital recordings of human voice messages.
- They allow for custom keyboard layout.

Technology and Play

Teaching through the use of fun activities is a critical component of all early intervention programs, and all of the information about technology presented thus far should be viewed in this light. For example, children who cannot produce speech should have access to an electronic communication board that they can use in a play group to request toys or carry on conversations with peers about the activities in which they currently are engaged. Cooperative play groups should include children both with and without disabilities working with exploratory computer-based instruction, such as *Katie's Farm,* so that they can improve their language and social skills while they have fun. Similarly, children who cannot color in traditional ways can do so by using a computer and software such as *KidPix.* In such cases, the interventionist's role becomes that of a facilitator, guiding children in taking turns, sharing, and encouraging one another.

Introducing computer-based instruction into educational programs for young children with special needs should support an existing curriculum (Clements, 1987; Clements, Nastasi, & Swaminathan, 1993; Fallon & Sanders Wann, 1994). For example, activity-based intervention (ABI) is a popular curricular approach for use with young children who have special needs (Bricker & Cripe, 1992). This approach includes both teaching strategies and a curriculum based on a foundation of behavioral and developmental theories. The main thrust of the ABI approach is to use child-directed transactions and build activities within the framework of children's interests. Activities often are presented as units of instruction, and interventionists build each unit around a common theme (Bricker & Cripe, 1992).

Using the ABI approach, an interventionist might choose to develop a unit of instruction around the theme of farm play, for example (Kinsley, Vail, & Langone, 1996). In such a unit, children would be encouraged to play with the materials while practicing language and social skills. They would be encouraged to make requests of each other, share toys, and talk about what they are doing with the toys (e.g., plowing the field with the tractor). The class could construct a barn from a cardboard box and place it near a group of stuffed animals. A mechanical tractor and at least one mechanical animal could be placed in the barn and attached to single switches for access by all children, but for particular use by children with motor challenges. The mechanical toys could be moved in and out of the barn or the children might choose to use them in a variety of ways (Kinsley et al., 1996). Electronic communication could be made available for children needing assistance for full participation in the activities.

Additional technology-based activities might include access to software, such as *Old McDonald* or *Katie's Farm,* that children could play with and explore concurrently while playing with the toys or at other times during the day. Many possible goals could be incorporated in such a unit of instruction, and the interventionist could develop a number of additional activities to complement the farm theme (e.g., a field trip to a farm). Social-skill goals could include children's initiating interaction with peers and responding to their attempts to initiate interactions. Children could learn to express their choices for toys, name animals and objects, and appropriately communicate displeasure. Evidence exists that shows how technology also can improve sensorimotor skills and facilitate movement in children with severe physical impairments (Horn & Warren, 1987; Horn, Warren, & Reith, 1992).

Children with special needs can practice cause-and-effect relationships and practice both parallel and cooperative play as appropriate for their developmental level. The key to the previous examples of activities and others that interventionists develop is that technology levels the playing field between children who have special needs and children who do not. Single switches and adaptive input devices

allow children with disabilities to access toys and computers similarly to the way their peers do. The movement of electronic toys and the effects of powerful graphics, sound, and video embedded in software packages that are reinforcing to children with special needs are equally reinforcing to other children. These conditions set the stage for an environment that fosters true inclusion, one in which children can make friends and learn from one another.

The opportunity to play with toys can be a positive step in the growth and development of young children with special needs. A variety of single switches are available that children can use to access battery-operated toys. Increasingly, commercial distributors are offering a larger variety of toys that come equipped with switches. The following is a brief list of distributors of exciting toys that stimulate children's interest:

- Lekotek is a nonprofit organization with offices in many states. This organization helps to get toys and adaptive devices into the hands of consumers by working directly with parents and teachers.
- The Crestwood Company (6625 North Sidney Place, Milwaukee, WI 53209-3259. Telephone: [414] 352-5678) offers a large variety of switch-operated toys. All of the toys provide action, some provide music and sound, and some include popular characteristics that young children enjoy.
- AbleNet, Inc. (1081 Tenth Avenue S.E., Minneapolis, MN 55414. Telephone: [800] 322-0956) offers toys as well as devices that can be used to adapt toys for use by children with special needs.

Adaptive devices can be used for battery-operated toys that do not come with a single switch but might be appropriate for children with physical disabilities. Such devices can be handy when a child shows a preference for a certain toy and the interventionist would like to use it for teaching cause and effect, and they also allow interventionists to adapt a variety of electrical appliances for use by children who are learning cause and effect. Adaptive devices for toys are an excellent means to teach children to control their environment and participate in a variety of tasks with their peers. A classroom that includes young children with special needs should have many electrical appliances adapted for their use, including switch-activated cassette recorders and radios for music and stories, switch-activated slide projectors for watching slides of favorite photos, and switch-activated kitchen appliances for participation in cooking activities.

Summary

This chapter has provided an overview of available technology and suggestions for using technology to help children with special needs obtain crucial early skills. Technology is not a panacea but can improve independence, learning, and the quality of life for young children who have special needs and their families (Spiegel-McGill, Zippiroli, & Mistrett, 1989). Like all tools, technology can be misused, and

professionals should be diligent in their search for ways to make it effective. One way to ensure the effectiveness of technology is to integrate its use within the framework of a well-planned curriculum. Technology should be used only if it relates to the individual objectives of children as outlined in their IEPs or IFSPs. Technology also should be integrated into all aspects of a child's day and not used only in isolation. Finally, the choice of hardware and software should be made only while working in partnership with families, who are the best judges of their needs and the needs of their children.

References

Angelo, D. H., & Goldstein, H. (1990). Effects of a pragmatic teaching strategy for the requesting of information by communication board users. *Journal of Speech and Hearing Disorders, 55,* 231–243.

Bailey, D. B., & Wolery, M. (1992). *Teaching infants and preschoolers with disabilities* (2nd ed.). Upper Saddle River, NJ: Prentice Hall.

Behrmann, M. M., Jones, J. K., & Wilds, M. L. (1989). Technology intervention for very young children with disabilities. *Infants and Young Children, 1*(4), 66–77.

Bowe, F. (1995). *Birth to 5: Early childhood special education.* New York: Delmar.

Bricker, D., & Cripe, J. (1992). *An activity-based approach to early intervention.* Baltimore: Paul H. Brookes.

Brown, J. S., Collins, A., & Duguid, P. (1989). Situated cognition and the culture of learning. *Educational Researcher, 18,* 32–41.

Bruner, J. S., Jolly, A., & Sylva, K. (1976). *Play: Its role in development and evolution.* New York: Basic Books.

Campbell, P. H., McGregor, G., & Nasik, E. (1994). Promoting development of young children through use of technology. In P. L. Safford (Ed.), *Early childhood special education: Yearbook in early childhood education, Vol. 5* (pp. 192–217). New York: Teachers College Press.

Church, G., & Bender, M. (1989). *Teaching with computers.* Boston: College Hill.

Clements, D. H. (1987). Computers and young children: A review of research. *Young Children, 43*(1), 34–44.

Clements, D. H., Nastasi, B. K., & Swaminathan, S. (1993). Young children and computers: Crossroads and directions from research. *Young Children, 48*(2), 56–64.

Cognition and Technology Group at Vanderbilt. (1994). The relationship between situated cognition and anchored instruction: A response to Tripp. *Educational Technology, 34*(8), 28–32.

Cognition and Technology Group at Vanderbilt. (1993). Integrated media: Toward a theoretical framework for utilizing their potential. *Journal of Special Education Technology, 12,* 71–85.

Cook, R. E., Tessier, A., & Klein, M. D. (1996). *Adapting early childhood curricula for children in inclusive settings* (4th ed.). Upper Saddle River, NJ: Merrill/Prentice Hall.

Exceptional Parent (1990). (20), 6–8. Securing technology funding: Empowering parents.

Exceptional Parent (1990). 25, 43–45. Technology resources.

Fallon, M. A., & Sanders Wann, J. (1994). Incorporating computer technology into activity-based thematic units for young children with disabilities. *Infants and Young Children, 6,* 64–69.

Fazio, B. B., & Rieth, H. J. (1986). Characteristics of preschool handicapped children's microcomputer use during free-choice periods. *Journal of the Division of Early Childhood, 10,* 247–254.

Griffin, M. M. (1995). You can't get there from here: Situated learning, transfer, and map skills. *Contemporary Educational Psychology, 20,* 65–87.

Hasselbring, T. S., Goin, L. I., & Bransford, J. D. (1991, May). Integrated media: Toward a theoretical framework for utilizing their potential. Paper

presented at the Multimedia Technology Seminar, Washington, DC.

Haugland, S. W. (1992). The effect of computer software on preschool children's developmental gains. *Journal of Computing in Childhood Education, 3,* 15–30.

Hedberg, J., & Alexander, S. (1994). Virtual reality in education: Defining researchable issues. *Educational Media International, 31,* 214–220.

Horn, E. M., & Warren, S. F. (1987). Facilitating the acquisition of sensorimotor behavior with a microcomputer-mediated teaching system: An experimental analysis. *Journal of the Association for the Severely Handicapped, 12,* 205–215.

Horn, E. M., Warren, S. F., & Reith, H. J. (1992). Effects of a small group microcomputer-mediated motor skills instructional package. *Journal of the Association for the Severely Handicapped, 17,* 133–144.

Howard, J., Greyrose, E., Kehr, K., Espinosa, M., & Beckwith, L. (1996). Teacher-facilitated microcomputer activities: Enhancing social play and affect in young children with disabilities. *Journal of Special Education Technology, 13,* 36–47.

Kinsley, T., & Langone, J. (1995). Applications of technology for infants, toddlers, and preschoolers with disabilities. *Journal of Special Education Technology, 12,* 312–324.

Kinsley, T., Vail, C., & Langone, J. (1996). The application of technology within an activity-based approach to early intervention. Unpublished manuscript, University of Georgia.

Langone, J. (1990). *Teaching students with mild and moderate learning problems.* Boston: Allyn & Bacon.

Lehrer, R., Harckham, L. D., Archer, P., & Pruzek, R. M. (1986). Microcomputer-based instruction in Special Education. *Journal of Educational Computing Research,* 2, 337–354.

Lewis, R. B. (1993). *Special education technology: Classroom applications.* Pacific Grove, CA: Brooks/Cole.

McCormick, L. (1987). Comparison of the effects of a microcomputer activity and toy play on social and communication behaviors of young children. *Journal of the Division for Early Childhood,* 11, 195–205.

Parette, H. P., Hoffman, A., & Van Biervliet, A. (1994). The professional's role in obtaining funding for assistive technology for infants and toddlers with disabilities. *Teaching Exceptional Children, 26*(3), 22–28.

Schery, T. K., & O'Connor, L. C. (1992). The effectiveness of school-based computer language intervention with severely handicapped children. *Language, Speech, and Hearing Services in Schools, 23,* 43–47.

Spiegel-McGill, P., Zippiroli, S. M., & Mistrett, S. G. (1989). Microcomputers as social facilitators in integrated preschools. *Journal of Early Intervention, 13*(3), 249–260.

Suddath, C., & Susnik, J. (1991). *Augmentative communication devices.* Reston, VA: Council for Exceptional Children, Center for Special Education Technology.

Thomas, C. H., & Patton, J. R., (1994). Characteristics of individuals with milder forms of retardation. In M. Beirne-Smith, J. R. Patton, & R. Ittenbach (Eds.), *Mental Retardation* (4th ed.). (pp. 203–240). Upper Saddle River, NJ: Merrill/Prentice Hall.

Thurman, S. K., & Widerstrom, A. H. (1990). *Infants and young children with special needs: A developmental and ecological approach* (2nd ed.). Baltimore: Paul H. Brookes.

Tripp, S. D. (1993). Theories, traditions, and situated learning. *Educational Technology, 33*(3), 71–77.

Whitehead, A. N. (1929). *The aims of education.* Upper Saddle River, NJ: Prentice Hall.

Young, M. F. (1993). Instructional design for situated learning. *Educational Technology Research and Development, 41,* 43–58.

10

Assessment of Young Children: Standards, Stages, and Approaches

Stephen R. Hooper and Rebecca Edmondson

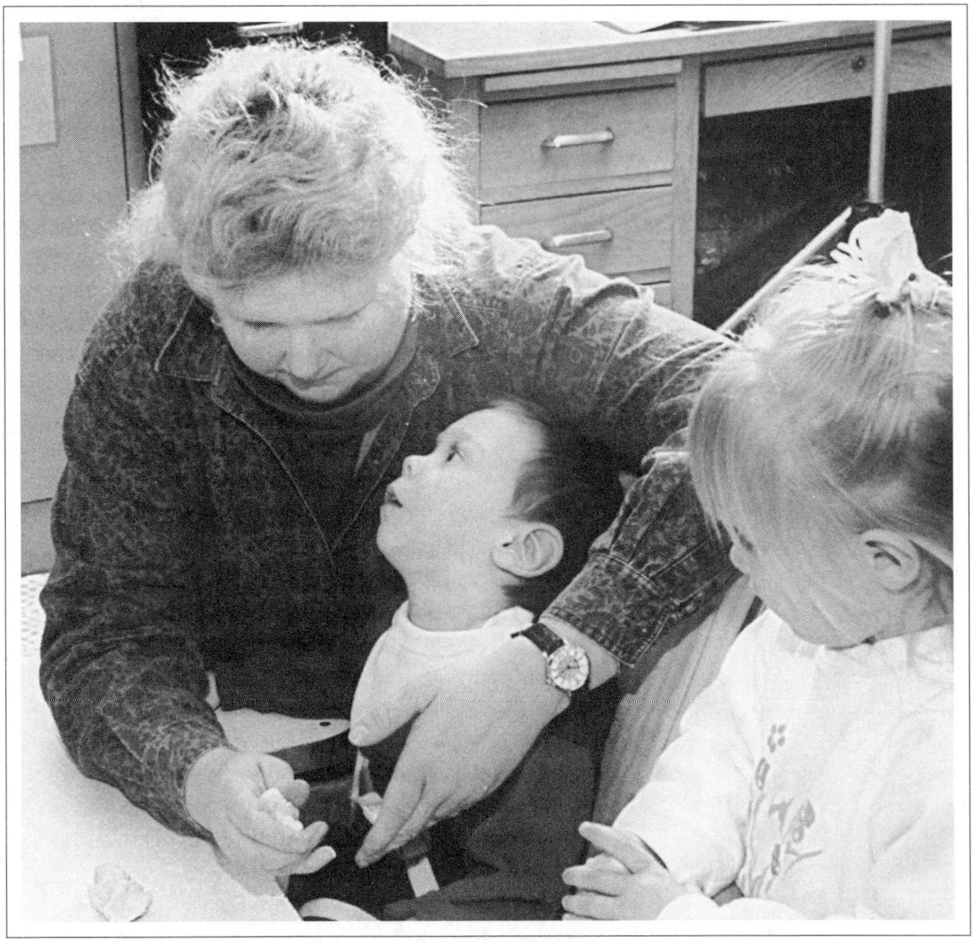

The term *assessment* is broadly defined as "the act of determining the rate or amount of something." More specific to the field of early childhood education, assessment is a goal-oriented problem-solving process that utilizes various measures within a theoretical framework. It is a variable process that depends on the questions being asked, the type of problems encountered by the child, and a myriad of social, developmental, and contextual factors. Thurlow and Ysseldyke (1979) defined *assessment* from an educational perspective as "a data-gathering process for the purpose of decision making." In this sense, assessment applies to all decision-making processes from the earliest diagnosis of a developmental problem through the final determination about a child's program.

This chapter provides an introduction to the complex domain of early childhood assessment. In addition to current standards that impact upon assessment in early childhood, this chapter discusses the different stages of the assessment process, including the specific components to be considered in a comprehensive evaluation, a variety of assessment approaches, and illustrative assessment tools and techniques. Assessment-treatment-tracking linkages also are discussed, particularly in relation to current standards of practice. The chapter concludes with specific considerations for the assessment of young children. This chapter does not contain much description of specific tests, but rather focuses on the standards for testing and the specific approaches that can be employed. An understanding of these aspects of assessment and of child development across the various domains described in this text is far more useful to the interventionist than is being able to identify the latest tests.

Current Standards for the Assessment Process

Many legal mandates have been initiated over the past several decades that have contributed to the evolution of the assessment process for young children with special needs. As discussed in Chapter 1, the Education for All Handicapped Children's Act (P.L. 94–142), and the Education of the Handicapped Act amendments (P.L. 99–457) have provided critical guidelines for the accurate identification, assessment, and treatment of preschool children with special needs. In general, these legal initiatives have mandated specific requirements for the assessment of all children with disabilities. These requirements include the following:

1. Tests must not contain racial and/or cultural bias.
2. Tests must be valid for their intended purpose and should be administered only by appropriately trained professionals.
3. The procedures used should be able to address a variety of educational and developmental needs.

4. A single assessment procedure must not be the sole contributor to a child's treatment plan.
5. A multidisciplinary team or designated group of professionals must participate in the assessment process, and this group must include a teacher with specialized knowledge.
6. A child must be tested in all educational and developmental areas related to the suspected disability.

In addition to these, professional organizations have asserted a number of standards for assessment in the early childhood domain. Organizations such as the American Speech and Hearing Association (ASHA) (1990), the National Association for the Education of Young Children (NAEYC) (1990), the National Association of School Psychologists (Bracken, Bagnato, & Barnett, 1991), and the Division for Early Childhood of the Council for Exceptional Children (DEC) (1993) have offered specific statements pertaining to the assessment and treatment practices for young children with special needs. Neisworth and Bagnato (1996) have distilled these position statements, in conjunction with their perspective of ongoing assessment models and practices, to reflect four major standards: treatment utility, social validity, convergent assessment, and consensual validity. It is important to note that these standards, reasonable as they are, probably have not been applied fully and reliably in most early childhood assessment settings to date (Odom, McLean, Johnson, & LaMontagne, 1995).

Treatment Utility

Treatment utility should be one of the cornerstones of all assessment processes in early childhood (Neisworth & Bagnato, 1996). Many of the traditional types of assessment strategies that have been applied to preschool as well as school-age children have yielded little information about program planning and specific treatment strategies. For example, Bagnato and Neisworth (1994) and others have reported on the relative lack of information that can be gained from determining a child's level of intelligence, particularly in relation to treatment planning. While such traditional assessment tools might well be considered a component of a child's evaluation, they should be augmented routinely with other devices that are more sensitive to treatment utility.

Social Validity

The second standard presented by Neisworth and Bagnato (1996) relates to social validity. Several key questions should be asked in relation to this standard, such as "Is the assessment viewed as valuable for the specific situational constraints presented by a child and his family?" and "Are the assessment methods acceptable to the participants?" Many of the items found on typical early childhood assessment measures require a child to perform tasks that represent skills, but the tasks themselves have little validity with respect to that child's daily functioning. For example, whether or not a child can complete a pegboard may be an important normative finding (i.e., Can the child perform this task at the same level as other children of the same age?), but it may or may not relate to why the child is having trouble with buttoning, zipping, and other functional activities in his daily life.

Social validity considerations in assessment also relate to whether the assessment methods are acceptable to the participants. For example, helping parents of a young child with fine motor disabilities work on buttoning and zipping is far more useful than is helping them to teach their child how to complete a pegboard. Such considerations also increase the probability that the family will become more involved in the assessment, treatment, and developmental monitoring processes.

Convergent Assessment

In tandem with the legal mandate that treatment planning not be based on a single assessment procedure, convergent assessment refers to the process wherein information is obtained from multiple sources. The exact methods by which this information is gathered are less critical than the key concern that the assessment process involve multiple sources of information (McLean & Odom, 1993). Convergent assessment permits examination and discussion of discrepancies in the information (e.g., when one professional notes that a problem exists and another professional disagrees), thus contributing to a better conceptualization of the whole child. As a result, it provides for a firmer foundation upon which to make diagnostic and programmatic decisions about a child, and it establishes multiple mechanisms for monitoring development. This latter advantage is important in that it necessarily requires involvement on the part of the family and encourages their participation in this process.

Consensual Validity

Similar to the convergent assessment standard, the consensual validity standard espoused by Neisworth and Bagnato (1996) reflects the need to reach assessment decisions via consensus by the team members. This generally is much easier said than done. Although the general intent of multidisciplinary teams is to serve the best interests of the child and family, sometimes this intent can become clouded by potential problems in the team's group dynamics. Problems can occur, such as one professional not being able to communicate clearly to another professional because of discipline-specific jargon (i.e., no common language), no common assessment tools (i.e., their "measuring sticks" are different), a lack of clear leadership, or an overpowering of one discipline over another, and little collaboration. These can interfere with the mission of the team. Although a number of assessment models have been proposed to address issues of consensual validity (e.g., System to Plan Early Childhood Services, Bagnato & Neisworth, 1990), the universal application of these models has not yet been achieved.

Stages of Assessment

Mrs. Nelson glanced over at Joey, her 34-month-old son, as they drove to the Developmental Center for his reevaluation prior to starting the preschool program at the local elementary school next year. She couldn't help but think how different it felt going to this evaluation as opposed to his initial assessment when he was 18 months old. She had been so nervous and scared, and really had no idea of what to expect. Mrs. Nelson remembered her initial concerns about Joey being slower to sit, walk, and talk than her other two boys had been. She had talked to Joey's pediatrician about her concerns since Joey was 9 months old, and he had suggested that she wait until he was about a year and a half to see whether he would catch up. When he still was not walking or using single words by that age, the pediatrician referred Joey to the Developmental Center for a comprehensive interdisciplinary evaluation. That evaluation, although quite difficult for both Mrs. Nelson and Joey, not only had confirmed her concerns that he was delayed, but also had helped her access services for him. During the evaluation, Joey was seen by a team of professionals in the fields of audiology, pediatrics, psychology, speech-language pathology, social work, occupational and physical therapy, and nutrition. Mrs. Nelson had been exhausted after providing the team members with the information they needed, but she had realized how well she really knew her child and how important she was in the evaluation process. It had been difficult to hear her suspicions that Joey was developmentally delayed confirmed, but, on the other hand, the team had helped her find a preschool for children with special needs that had been really good. Through the center-based program, Joey had been able to receive speech, occupational, and related educational services. His teacher had monitored his developmental progress by assessing his skills every 4 to 6 months, and everyone was delighted with the gains he had made. Even though Joey was still behind other children his age, Mrs. Nelson was comforted by the knowledge that he continued to make progress and that he enjoyed his classroom activities.

As she turned into the driveway at the center, Mrs. Nelson felt a small twinge of nervousness because she knew she would once again hear about Joey's needs; but she also knew that the team would be able to see Joey's strengths as well. In addition, she was looking forward to sharing with the team the gains Joey had made since the last time he had been there and to helping them plan for his transition to the preschool classroom next year.

In early childhood special education, there are a number of assessment stages through which a child must pass prior to the delivery of early intervention services. Assessment strategies are vital components at each of these stages, although the ultimate goals and objectives at each stage may be different. Further, once services are provided, the assessment process should not end; there should be ongoing tracking of the progress of an individual child as well as program evaluation. The assessment stages are early identification, which includes the components of awareness, Child Find, and related screening procedures; comprehensive evaluation; program planning and implementation; and program evaluation. Figure 10.1 illustrates these stages in a decision-point format.

Stage 1: Early Identification

One of the primary goals of early childhood special education is to identify children with exceptional needs as early as possible so that the formative years may be used to make the most of children's abilities. Identification in early childhood can occur at any point from conception through the first years of formal schooling and typically involves any procedure that leads to the identification of a child with special needs. In fact, research on prenatal diagnostic strategies has evolved to such a point over the past 30 years that early identification can occur quite early in the gestational process (Cheung, Goldberg, & Kan, 1996; Lo et al., 1990).

Awareness. One of the initial components of early identification is awareness. Awareness refers to the various methods used to alert the public and professional community to the needs of young children with special needs. This involves organized efforts to inform and influence the public, especially community leaders, about programs for young children with disabilities. Its purpose is not only to develop sensitivity and promote support for such programs, but also to find children in need of special services. Through these community education mechanisms, community leaders learn to recognize the early signs of delayed or aberrant development. Advocating for awareness also encourages close observation of available services, service needs, and the quality of these services.

Child Find. Another component of early identification is Child Find, which refers to the methods used to locate young children who may exhibit exceptional conditions. Child Find is a community-wide effort involving many agencies that have contact with infants and young children, and it typically occurs within public schools' jurisdiction. The identification of a possible disability may be made by anyone who comes in contact with a child during these early years, including but not limited to the obstetrician, pediatrician, a nurse, dentist, social worker, early childhood educator, or parents.

The medical profession plays a key role in Child Find. The initial identification of a disability often is made by a physician, either the pediatrician or the obstetrician, who may become aware of a disability as early as the first few months of pregnancy through prenatal diagnostic techniques. Some of the more common prenatal screening procedures are presented in Table 10.1. For example, amniocentesis is a process by which a sample of fetal cells is extracted from amniotic fluid. This process typically is conducted at a gestational age of about 15 to 20 weeks, although it can be done earlier (Stripparo et al., 1990). Amniocentesis is usually guided by ultrasound (see Table 10.1) to maximize the success rate of the procedure and to

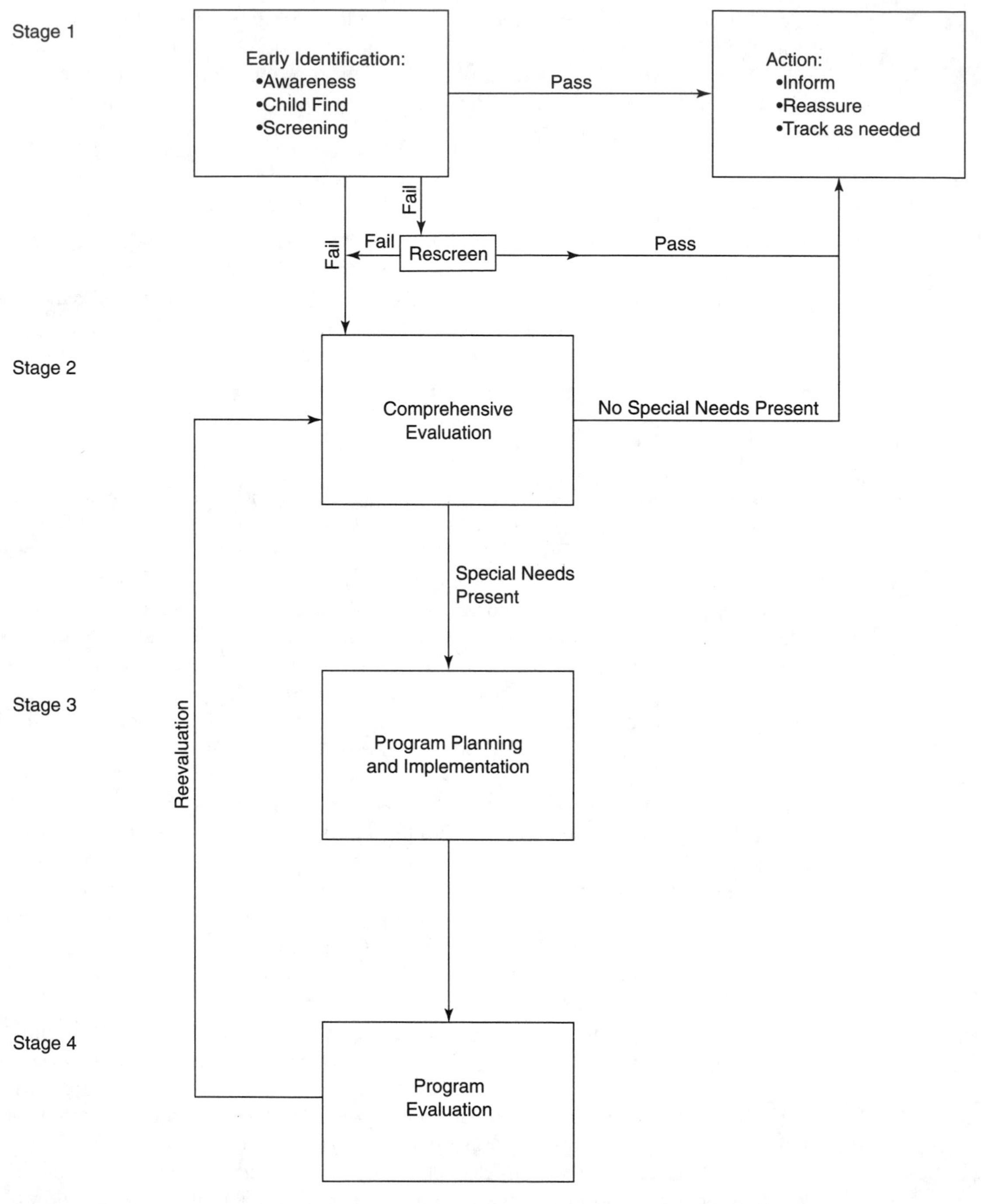

FIGURE 10.1 Stages of the assessment process

TABLE 10.1 Common Prenatal Screening Procedures

SCREENING PROCEDURE	PROCEDURES/UTILITY
Urine Screen	A special stick is inserted in a urine sample at each prenatal visit to identify gestational diabetes. Low levels of sugar may indicate hypoglycemia, while high levels may indicate hyperglycemia. These conditions may affect the developing fetus.
Blood Pressure	Blood pressure is measured with a cuff and stethoscope at each prenatal visit. Abnormal pressure readings may suggest complications such as preeclampsia (maternal hypertension with high levels of protein in the urine and body swelling).
Hemoglobin Screen	Blood is drawn from an arm or finger prick at about 4 months' gestation, and on a regular basis if necessary. The blood is examined for iron levels, with low levels indicating the presence of anemia.
Amniocentesis	A hollow needle is inserted through the abdominal wall into the uterus to withdraw a small amount of amniotic fluid. This procedure usually is done in conjunction with an ultrasound to avoid injuring the fetus, umbilical cord, or placenta. It is conducted at about 13 to 18 weeks' gestation, and typically is performed for high-risk pregnancies (e.g., advanced maternal age and known family history of chromosomal abnormalities). Amniocentesis can provide relatively reliable information about open neural tube defects and genetic defects such as Down syndrome. It also reveals the sex of the fetus.
Alpha-Fetoprotein Test	Blood from a finger prick is used to screen for neural tube defects between 14 and 18 weeks' gestation. A high AFP level is a possible indicator of neural tube defects (e.g., spina bifida and anencephaly), while a low level may suggest an increased risk of Down syndrome or other chromosomal problems. Abnormal levels indicate the need for additional AFP testing, a sonogram, and amniocentesis.
Chorionic Villi Sampling	A needle is inserted into the vagina or abdomen, and then into the uterine wall to the edge of the placenta. Chorionic villi (the fetal components of the developing placenta) are withdrawn and examined. This procedure is generally done between 9 and 12 weeks' gestation. It can reveal chromosomal and genetic abnormalities (e.g., Down syndrome), Tay-Sachs disease and other inborn errors of metabolism, types of cystic fibrosis, and thalessemia (e.g., sickle cell anemia). Testing for other specific disorders and diseases can be done if the family history warrants it.
Ultrasound (Sonography)	Using sonography to generate a live outline of the fetus in utero, this procedure can reveal orthopedic impairment, problems with major organs, and other physical abnormalities. An ultrasound typically is performed between weeks 14 and 20 of the pregnancy.

minimize injury to the fetus (Verp, Simpson, & Ober, 1993). Once the fetal cells are extracted, a genetic analysis can reveal chromosomal aberrations such as trisomy 13, Turner syndrome, Tay-Sachs disease, or 250 other genetic abnormalities (American College of Obstetricians and Gynecologists, 1994). The risk of fetal mortality secondary to this procedure appears to be quite low (approximately 0.5%); the same can be said for fetal injuries (Verp et al., 1993).

Similarly, ultrasound echograms, or sonograms, can reveal orthopedic impairments and physical abnormalities, conditions that may require special treatment at the moment of birth. Ultrasound technology not only has permitted the early identification of some physical anomalies, but also has allowed for surgical correction of problems prior to actual delivery of infants (Vanderwall & Harrison, 1996). Other recent advances in prenatal screening are equally promising. For example, recent procedural advances have been able to show the presence of genetic abnormalities as early as 6 to 10 weeks gestational age using only a single drop of the mother's blood (Cheung et al., 1996; Lo et al., 1990). Prenatal diagnosis is now a routine part of obstetric care, especially in the case of high-risk pregnancies.

An obstetrician sometimes recognizes the presence, or at least the possibility, of a disability at the birth of an infant. Conditions that alert an obstetrician to the possibility of a disability are anoxia (lack of oxygen), possibly caused by a twisted umbilical cord; a prolonged, stressful labor during which the infant may aspirate meconium (fetal waste products) into the lungs; and prematurity and/or very low birth weight.

Other predictors of an abnormality may be observed during a routine examination of an infant immediately following birth. This process generally involves blood and urine tests for metabolic disorders such as PKU, and the Apgar rating (Apgar, 1953), which includes ratings of heart rate, breathing effort, muscle tone, reflex irritability, and color of the skin. More-detailed examinations of a newborn may be accomplished using such tests as the Brazelton Neonatal Behavioral Assessment Scale (Brazelton, 1984), Rosenblith's adaptation of the Graham Scale (Rosenblith, 1973), and a variety of other neurological examinations (Chervenak & Kurjak, 1996; Mindes, Ireton, & Mardell-Czudnowski, 1996). Scales such as the Brazelton allow a pediatrician or another appropriately trained professional to identify possible abnormalities in the central nervous system and in the sensory abilities of a newborn. According to Bergen and Wright (1994), the Brazelton is a more sensitive predictor of later developmental outcomes than is the Apgar score. Further, it offers the opportunity for parents to observe and discuss their infants rather than be directly taught about general infant behavior (Cardone & Gilkerson, 1989). Another similar instrument that can be used with infants 3 to 24 months of age is the Bayley Infant Neurodevelopmental Screener (Aylward, 1995). This screening device taps basic neurological functions, receptive functions, expressive functions, and cognitive processes, and it categorizes performance into low, moderate, or high risk for each domain selected.

If an infant receives medical care from a pediatrician or other primary care provider, deviations from normal development may be identified through observation and from the child's medical history. A pediatrician may suspect possible disabilities if there is a record of stressful birth events, a history of pediatric illnesses, or a family history of developmental problems. Later, if a child does not achieve major developmental milestones (e.g., walking and talking) within normal expectations, then the pediatrician might determine the need for further examination. In addition to having early contact with a child, a pediatrician or other physician has the opportunity to observe the child's development frequently, perhaps through well-child visits, and over an extended period of time. A pediatrician also is the primary source of guidance and assistance when parents believe that their child is experiencing a problem. While it has been estimated that approximately 60% of pediatricians use some type of screening test or procedure to detect developmental abnormalities, unfortunately, most use them inconsistently and/or continue to depend upon clinical judgment (Dobos, Dworkin, & Bernstein, 1994; Glascoe, 1996; Scott, Lingaraju, Kilgo, Kregel, & Lazzari, 1993). In fact, the American Academy of Pediatrics (1986) suggested over a decade ago that pediatricians employ standardized screening procedures to detect developmental problems, and that these procedures be employed at each of the 12 well-child visits planned between birth and 5 years of age.

Another health care professional who may identify a disability in a young child is a nurse. A pediatric nurse may work in a hospital nursery, a child development clinic, or a pediatrician's office, and may observe a child over a period of time. A public health nurse serves a similar role in health clinics, with greater emphasis being placed on family involvement, perhaps via home visitations. Seeing a child in his home setting may reveal factors other than health that could be contributing to the severity of a disability.

Both pediatric and public health nurses have an increasingly critical role in the early identification of young children with special needs. Currently, nurses perform several tasks formerly conducted by pediatricians, including general screening practices to assess a child's development, perhaps even using formal screening instruments such as the Ages and Stages Questionnaire (Bricker & Squires, 1994), the Denver II (Frankenburg et al., 1990), or the Bayley Infant Neurodevelopmental Screener (Aylward, 1995), discussing appropriate health care with the parent, and referring the child to special health services as needed.

Yet another professional who can identify potential health problems in young children is a dentist. Although children rarely see dentists prior to age 3 years, by providing dental care to preschoolers, a dentist can observe the condition of the teeth as well as the structure of the mouth and jaw and is then able to pinpoint specific dental problems such as decayed teeth and malocclusions that can cause speech impairment or eating problems. In addition to early identification, a dentist also can have a role in shaping the oral health of a child and family.

In addition to professionals from the health care fields, social workers may play an important role in the early identification of children with special needs. As a first-hand observer of the family and, perhaps, the home environment, a social worker is in a position to detect inadequacies in the training and intellectual stimulation provided for a child. Such inadequacies may be harmful to a child's physical, cognitive, and social-emotional development. A social worker may recognize abnormalities as well as inappropriate environments and be able to refer children and their families to appropriate resources for assessment and intervention.

Persons involved in day-care services as well as in public and private preschool programs also have a unique vantage point in the early identification of children with special needs; they have the advantage of regular, frequent observation of a child. Early childhood educators also are in a position to observe many

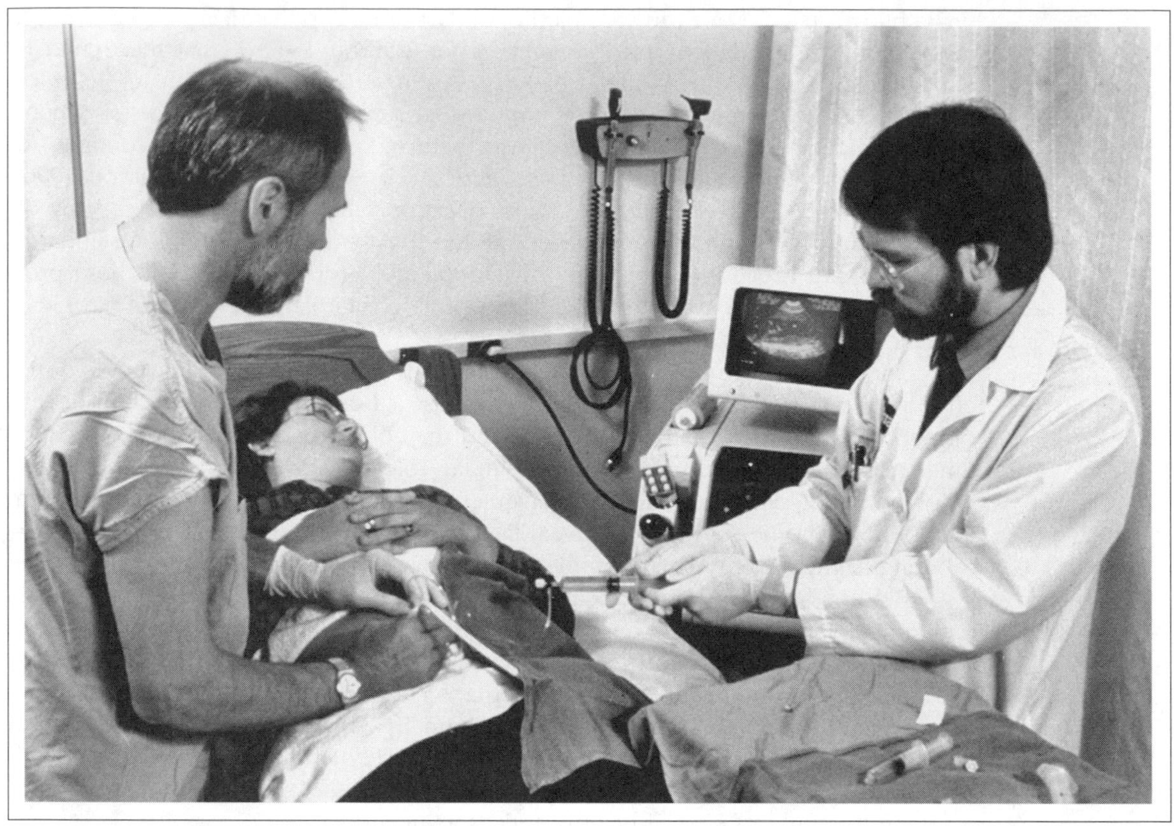

Numerous procedures, such as amniocentesis, can identify prospective medical and developmental problems.

aspects of a child's development. While other professionals are primarily concerned with a specific facet of a child's development, an early childhood educator can observe nearly all developmental facets of a child, thus providing the team with a more holistic viewpoint of that child. This viewpoint, in turn, should be useful in program planning efforts.

Professional expertise is certainly valuable in the early identification of children with disabilities, but even more critical to this process are the parents. In fact, legislation has mandated that the family be involved as active participants in this process. As the primary observers of their child, parents have first-hand knowledge of the child's total development. If a problem is suspected, the parents may be the first to see evidence of it and subsequently seek advice from one or several professionals. Most parents are in a position to confirm, or at least discuss, the clinical suspicions of any professionals who may have expressed concerns. None of these key professionals should operate in a vacuum; thus, the involvement of the family in the early identification process is critical.

Formal Screening. As part of the early identification process, and intimately related to Child Find, young children with special needs can be identified via formal screening procedures. Although professionals in the fields just described conduct formal screening procedures, particularly prenatal screening procedures (see Table 10.1), the Child Find aspects of screening typically contribute to locating infants, toddlers, and preschool children who will participate in a formal screening process and/or comprehensive evaluation to determine their at-risk status for developmental and/or medical disabilities. As Lichtenstein and Ireton (1991) have noted, "The term screening technically refers to the process of selecting out for further study those high-risk individuals whose apparent problems might require special attention or intervention" (p. 487). At this stage, professionals or paraprofessionals typically employ brief, relatively inexpensive measures that are easily administered in an effort to determine which children should be referred to the next stage of assessment (Lichtenstein & Ireton, 1991).

Public laws (e.g., 99–457) have encouraged the implementation of large-scale, early identification screening, or mass screening, wherein a program attempts to screen every child in a specified population. While this type of effort can be expensive, it does increase the chances that young children with special needs will not be overlooked. Further, there tends to be little or no stigma associated with such screening practices because nearly everyone in the specified population participates (Lichtenstein & Ireton, 1991). Some programs may elect to engage in selective screening rather than mass screening. This approach to screening may target specific high-risk groups of children, such as children with a variety of chronic illnesses or children from poverty-stricken areas, or it might be used at specific developmental points in time, such as just prior to kindergarten entry.

Regardless of the type of screening approach, several key assumptions need to be asserted in relation to screening in the early childhood developmental period (Lichtenstein & Ireton, 1991). First, as described in Chapter 1, the basic premise of early childhood services is that early identification and intervention can lessen and/or ameliorate the impact of developmental disabilities. From the classic work of Skeels (1966) to more contemporary efforts devoted to children with environmental (Ramey & Ramey, 1994) and biological (Ramey & Hardin, 1995) risk factors, it does appear that early childhood identification and intervention have had a positive impact on later development.

Second, there is a tacit assumption that professionals can identify developmental problems in young children. According to Lichtenstein and Ireton (1991), this assumption is based on the premise that many of these problems will persist over time. Thus, in a large national collaborative project, Aylward, Gustafson, Verhulst, and Colliver (1987) found that there was a 25% chance that a diagnosis of normal cognitive function at 9 months conceptional age would worsen by 36 months of age, although the presence of motor deficits tended to be more stable. Also, while more-subtle deficits or disabilities may not be identified as readily early in development, perhaps because of a lack of measurement sensitivity, these subtle deficits may show up later in development. For example, certain types of learning problems, such as reading and math disabilities, may not become apparent until some of the early precursors of these functions (e.g., phonology) can be measured (Hooper, 1991; Tramontana, Hooper, & Selzer, 1988).

Third, it is assumed that screening efforts can be conducted without undue constraints on fiscal management in a system. The increase in funding allotted to early intervention by the amendments to Public Law 94–142 has permitted increased activity in Child Find and related screening procedures. These funds also have served to provide more-thorough screening efforts. The early identification of a young child with special needs then requires that these needs be addressed by an intervention program which, in turn, increases the ultimate costs for screening, assessment, and treatment. Consequently, it remains important for professionals to be sensitive to the inclusion of key variables in the decision-making processes involved in screening.

Whether an infant, toddler, or preschooler is referred for further evaluation through Child Find or more formal screening programs, a key issue is whether the decision to refer or not to refer a child for a comprehensive evaluation was accurate. There are several important concepts to consider in this regard: hit-rates, false positives, and false negatives.

Overall hit rates are important to screening in that they provide an index of the accuracy of the screening measure or measures. As shown in Figure 10.2, there are four basic outcomes from a screening decision: two accurate outcomes and two inaccurate outcomes. When a screening decision suggests that a child may be at risk for a medical or developmental problem and the child indeed needs special services, then an accurate referral has been made. This is referred to as *sensitivity*. Ideally, a good screening device or program should capture at least 80% of children with problems (Glascoe, 1996). Conversely, when a screening decision indicates that a child is at low risk for having a medical or developmental problem and the child does not have the target problem, then an accurate nonreferral has been made. This is referred to as *specificity*. Glascoe (1996) suggests that this rate should be at least 90% to minimize overreferrals. Accurate decisions are represented in cells 1 and 4 of Figure 10.2.

Sometimes, a screening decision leads to a referral when in fact the child may not have the medical or developmental problem of concern. This leads to what is called a *false positive* and contributes to overreferrals, as shown in cell 2 of Figure 10.2. Additionally, screening decisions can suggest that a specific problem does not exist, but the child actually may manifest the target problem. This type of decision-making error is shown in cell 3 of Figure 10.2 and is referred to as a *false negative*. False negatives can result in underreferral of children for specific problems which, in turn, may contribute to ongoing difficulties for those children and their families. From an assessment perspective, the frequency of false negatives provides a good rationale for conducting ongoing developmental monitoring, even when a child may not appear to have a problem.

While the overall accuracy of a screening process is important in terms of identifying young children with special needs, it is important to keep in mind the possible consequences that a high rate of false positives and false negatives can

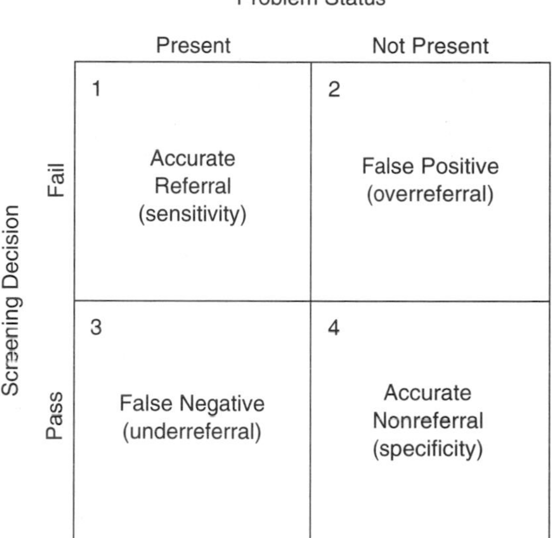

FIGURE 10.2 Types of screening decision outcomes

have on service delivery systems. These types of errors work in tandem with each other such that a decrease in one type of error necessarily results in an increase in the other. A service delivery system needs to determine what kind of error it can tolerate. For example, if too many children are being referred, then the comprehensive evaluation stage may be slowed, and children may not receive the evaluation and any subsequent intervention in a timely fashion. Further, this may place an undue financial burden on a system. If too few children are being referred from the screening process, then many children may be experiencing ongoing medical and/or developmental struggles because they were not identified for further evaluation. A low referral rate also may contribute to alternative interpretations of the presence of apparent developmental problems (e.g., "not motivated," "lazy," or "uninterested parents"), which also may hamper a child's developmental progress. Further, underreferrals to a system can lead to a reduction in funding for necessary services and programs because of the perception that these services are not necessary. Such decisions need to be considered carefully by a screening team, with strong consideration also being given to the base rates (how often they occur) of a disorder (approximately 3% to 10% for most developmental and educational problems), as well as local values, resources, and needs. For example, there may be a selected cutoff score suggested by a specific test; however, this specific cutoff may not be in accordance with local needs, and thus a different cutoff score should be considered. Input from multiple professionals in this regard is extremely useful, particularly in the referral of a youngster to the next stage of assessment, the comprehensive evaluation.

Stage 2: Comprehensive Evaluation

Once a child moves into stage 2, the purpose of the assessment changes from early identification of possible needs and concerns to determining whether a significant problem exists. Obviously, the primary purpose of a comprehensive evaluation can vary, but it can include documentation of a delay, diagnosis of a disability, or the establishment of eligibility for intervention services. In addition, this stage should help to clarify the nature and extent of any problems that might be present, and begin to prepare for stage 3, program planning and implementation.

As was discussed in Chapter 1, federal legislation mandates that the assessment of infants and young children with special needs be conducted with a team approach. An underlying premise of a team evaluation is that it should be comprehensive and cover important domains of development, thus providing critical information for decision making. Most professionals would agree that certain developmental domains should be included in a comprehensive evaluation. These include the cognitive, motor, communication, social and play, and self-care domains (Bailey & Wolery, 1989). Many early intervention programs require information in each of these domains in order to document eligibility for special education services and to plan a child's Individual Education Plan (IEP) or Individual Family Service Plan (IFSP). Medical and family information also is critical at this stage, and should be complementary to information gained from the developmental domains.

Developmental Domains. Again, at least five key developmental domains typically are tapped in a comprehensive evaluation: the cognitive, motor, communication, social and play, and self-care, or adaptive skills, domains.

Cognitive skills are those related to mental and intellectual development (see Chapter 6). In early childhood, these skills include the concepts of object permanence, imitation, means-end or causality, and spatial relationships. As a child reaches preschool age, the assessment of cognitive development includes preacademic skills, such as prereading and prewriting, as well as early quantitative abilities.

Motor skills are related to the use of muscles, joints, and limbs. As discussed in Chapter 4, the assessment of motor skills typically is divided into two areas: gross motor and fine motor skills. Gross motor skills require the use of large muscles and movements such as walking, running, throwing, and jumping. Fine motor skills refer to the use of small muscles and more refined movements such as cutting, writing, grasping, and stacking blocks.

Communication skills are those that allow a child to give and receive information (see Chapter 7). Two types of communication skills that are frequently assessed are receptive and expressive language. Receptive language refers to a child's ability to understand and comprehend information being presented. Expressive language is a child's ability to communicate his thoughts, feelings, or ideas. Communication includes not only the use of words, but also gestures, pictures, facial expressions, and augmentative devices. When communication skills are delayed or impaired, early childhood professionals look for signs of communicative intent, wherein a child may try to communicate a message using a variety of strategies.

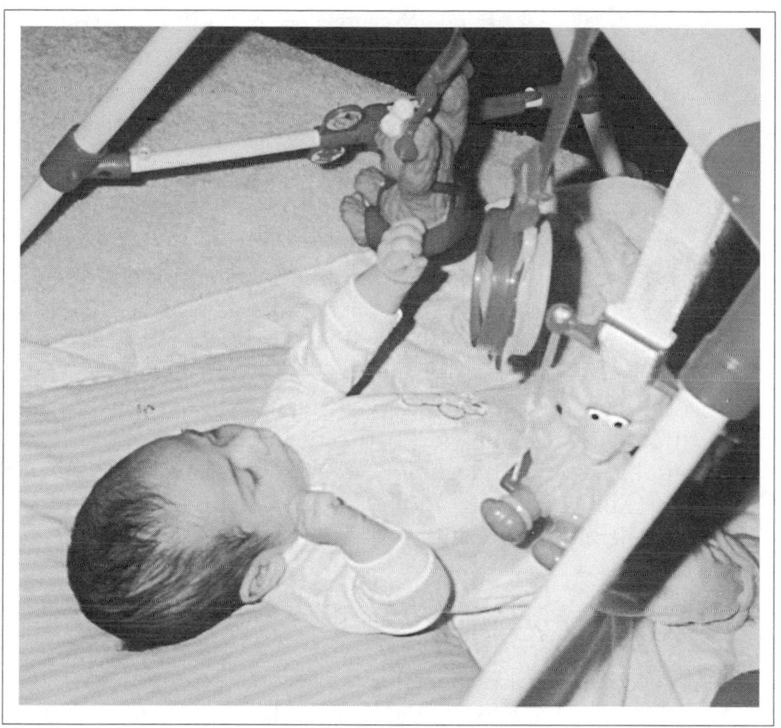

Observing play skills can provide an intervention team with much information about specific aspects of development.

Social and play skills refer to a child's ability to interact with peers, specific behaviors in social situations, and use of toys. Frequently, an informal play assessment is conducted in order to understand a child's cognitive, motor, and communication skills as expressed through the medium of play. As noted in Chapter 8, these skills are critical to children's social and emotional development.

Self-care or adaptive skills are related to a child's ability to function independently in meeting daily needs such as toileting, feeding, and dressing. Understanding a young child's needs for help or assistance during such daily care-taking activities can provide invaluable information for making decisions about placement and the need for individualized assistance.

Medical Issues. Because of the complex nature of many early childhood disabilities and conditions, it is imperative that medical issues receive evaluative consideration. In addition to whatever information can be provided from the prenatal history of a child, including information that has been derived from prenatal tests (such as the ones listed in Table 10.1), a physical examination, which may include laboratory tests, can help determine the nature of a child's disability and lead to a diagnosis (e.g., fragile-X syndrome, neurofibromatosis, or epilepsy). Understanding a child's medical condition also can provide information about the need for specialized attention and assistance within the day-care or preschool setting. It also may prove to be useful for prognostic considerations. Medical factors can significantly impact a child's development and acquisition of new skills. For example, children with infectious diseases, metabolic disorders, and chronic illnesses require ongoing medical monitoring and perhaps medication or frequent hospitalizations.

Family. Gathering information from and about a child's family and home environment can assist professionals in gaining a better understanding of a child's strengths, needs, and overall resources. Most parents know their child better than anyone else does and can provide details about the child's past and current development. In addition, interviewing a child's parents or having them complete questionnaires can provide pertinent information about their parenting skills and attitudes, discipline techniques, and understanding of their child's problems. Having the family involved in the assessment process also serves to elicit their input and cooperation in relation to ongoing developmental surveillance and monitoring.

Stage 3: Program Planning and Implementation

The comprehensive evaluation serves as the prerequisite for stage 3, program planning and implementation. It provides the information needed to discuss placement for a child and to develop his IEP or IFSP. This information is then translated into a plan of action for the preschool teacher or early interventionist. Although more-detailed information about intervention is provided in Chapter 11, it is important to note here that assessment does not stop once intervention begins. The teacher or early interventionist should continue to provide ongoing formal and informal assessment of a child's progress in target developmental domains and behaviors, as specified in the IEP or IFSP; assessment information pertaining to other aspects of growth, general development, and developmental readiness also should be obtained. From an assessment perspective, criterion-referenced types of measures can be quite useful for tracking progress frequently and in a developmentally-sensitive fashion.

Stage 4: Program Evaluation

Similar to stage 3, stage 4 involves assessment procedures that pertain to the success of the intervention plan. The instrumentation used typically is criterion-referenced; norm-referenced tools also can be useful, depending on the questions being asked. The overall goal of this stage is to assess the current developmental levels of a child, to monitor progress related to developmental goals established by the team and family members for the IEP or IFSP, and to determine the need for adjustments and modifications in the child's intervention program. In some instances, a child's developmental gains may have progressed to a point at which they are within age-appropriate levels, and no further services may be needed at that time.

Theoretical Approaches to Assessment

Most early childhood teams have a theoretical approach or philosophy that guides their efforts to move a child through these four stages of assessment. The different theoretical approaches that exist likely have contributed to the differences that can be seen from one early childhood program to another in terms of their assessment and intervention practices; however, as Fewell (1993) has noted, even assessment devices based on different theoretical approaches may show considerable overlap in their item content.

To date, at least four major theoretical perspectives have had an impact upon early childhood assessment and intervention. These include the developmental (e.g., Piaget, 1954; Vygotsky, 1978), behavioral/social-behavioral (e.g., Bandura, 1977), contextual (e.g., Bronfenbrenner, 1986), and a variant of the contextual theory—the transactional model (Sameroff & Chandler, 1975). (An overview of these theoretical models is provided in Chapters 6 and 11.) It is important to note that these theoretical models or their variants form the basic foundation for many early childhood programs. For work in any childhood program, it is important for the professional or paraprofessional to be aware of these theoretical foundations, because they more than likely have contributed to the assessment practices of the program.

Assessment Approaches and Techniques

Related to the theoretical model espoused by an early childhood professional or team, there exists a number of approaches and techniques that can be employed in the assessment process. Indeed, an early intervention team may elect to utilize a combination of these approaches, depending on the nature of the presenting problem (Neisworth & Bagnato, 1996), and it is important for early childhood professionals to be cognizant of these different approaches and techniques. To gain a comprehensive view of a young child, particularly one with delays or documented disabilities, it is especially important to choose a multidimensional assessment approach that employs multiple and often alternative measures, gathers information from multiple sources, examines several developmental and behavioral domains, and fulfills various purposes. While the intent of this section is not to review specific tests and procedures in any detail, it should be noted that Neisworth and Bagnato (1988) have provided an organizational typology of such procedures that can help the early childhood professional make appropriate choices for the assessment process. This typology of measures includes (1) norm-referenced, (2) curriculum-based, (3) adaptive-to-disability, (4) process, (5) judgment-based, (6) ecological, (7) interactive, and (8) systematic observation.

Similarly, Benner (1992) has provided an organization of various approaches and techniques across seven different strands, including formal/informal, normative/criterion-referenced, standardized/adaptive-to-disability, direct/indirect, naturalistic/clinical, product/process, and unidisciplinary/team. Given its importance to the early childhood assessment process, the unidisciplinary/team strand is discussed first.

Unidisciplinary/Team Strand

This strand addresses assessment that involves single disciplines versus several different disciplines. As the term *unidisciplinary assessment* implies, a child is evaluated by a single professional. For example, a child may be seen by an audiologist only to gain an estimate of auditory acuity. Indeed, referral concerns such as these may be handled appropriately by one professional; however, as defined by law, any young child with special needs should be seen by a team of professionals to conduct the assessment and plan whatever interventions might be needed.

Given the many different problems that children with developmental disabilities can have, a team approach clearly is the preferred method of gathering assessment data. The team can include, but not be limited to, a psychologist, social worker, early childhood specialist, audiologist, nurse, speech and language pathologist, nutritionist, occupational therapist, physical therapist, pediatrician, and parents. How this team operates, however, can be quite varied. At present, there are at least three versions of the team process: multidisciplinary, interdisciplinary, and transdisciplinary.

Multidisciplinary Team. In the multidisciplinary team, whose origins are based on the medical model, the number of team members may be set or members may be selected to address the problems presented by the referral source (e.g., one referral problem may demand the presence of a physical therapist while another may not). Regardless of the team make-up, each professional on the team assesses the child and provides verbal and written feedback to the parents and/or referral source, perhaps on different days; however, these professionals do not necessarily discuss their findings with the other team members. Clearly, this type of assessment process can result in conflicting results, perhaps with families and/or early interventionists receiving contradictory findings. Even when a selected professional is deemed responsible for presenting the results from all of the different disciplines involved, concerns may arise related to the comfort of that professional with all of the information being provided, and biases can emerge (Fewell, 1983). For example, such a situation could arise when an early childhood professional is trying to interpret the results of a geneticist or an occupational therapist.

One way to address team-based concerns, which affect all of the variants of the team approach, is to systematize the data collection process. For example, the System to Plan Early Childhood Services (SPECS) (Bagnato & Neisworth, 1990) comprises materials and procedures that assist the early intervention team in reaching consensus in the assessment process. Parents and professionals independently rate a child on 19 developmental and functional dimensions. From these ratings, the dimensions of concern and/or disagreement are identified, and the discrepant ratings are then discussed until a consensus is reached for a rating on each dimension.

Once this occurs, the child's assessment profile can be detailed and appropriate programming options can be pursued.

Interdisciplinary Team. A variant of the multidisciplinary team is the interdisciplinary team. Fewell (1983) notes that, on the surface, the actual number and type of professionals involved in each assessment approach may be exactly the same; the major differences lie in the interdisciplinary team approach's ongoing communication among team members and its attempt to conduct such an evaluation over a day or two. Although the inclusion of ongoing communication in a single session or two may improve the information being provided to families and referral sources, there remain concerns that one professional may take charge and dominate a team meeting. Also, despite the fact that professionals may have the opportunities to talk to one another about their findings, this does not ensure that they will understand one an other.

Transdisciplinary Team. Another variant of the team evaluation is the transdisciplinary assessment, or arena assessment. With this data-gathering approach, a team of professionals observes the child in some type of interaction with another professional and/or facilitator. One way for this process to unfold is for a single professional, such as a speech and language pathologist, to begin her assessment and to have the other professionals observe. The basic premise is that many of the items of the various testing procedures will overlap and/or similar behaviors will be elicited. For example, a speech and language pathologist might be interested in whether a child can follow the directions necessary to perform a motor task, while an occupational therapist may be most concerned with the actual fine motor capabilities of the child. When the transdisciplinary team approach is used, professionals do not have to readminister the same type of item, which should save time, minimize the effects of practice, and preserve the child's stamina for other tasks.

A variant of the transdisciplinary model has a single facilitator work with a child, but this professional is not responsible for any formal evaluation. Thus, the facilitator can provide the child with whatever direction is needed while the other team members collect their data through observation. Family members can be included in this assessment process. Linder (1993) described a play-based assessment model that embodies the transdisciplinary approach. In this model, there are six components to the assessment. The first component involves an unstructured play arrangement wherein the child is encouraged to do whatever he wishes to do. The second component is more structured and begins to envelope the aspects of cognitive and language functioning that were not captured in the initial component. The third component involves the participation of another child for play-based observation. Linder (1993) notes that it is helpful when the other child is slightly older, of the same gender, and not disabled. The fourth component provides an opportunity for the parents to interact with their child in a play situation, much as they would interact with their child in the home setting. The parents initially play with their child in an unstructured fashion, then, after a brief separation, they return

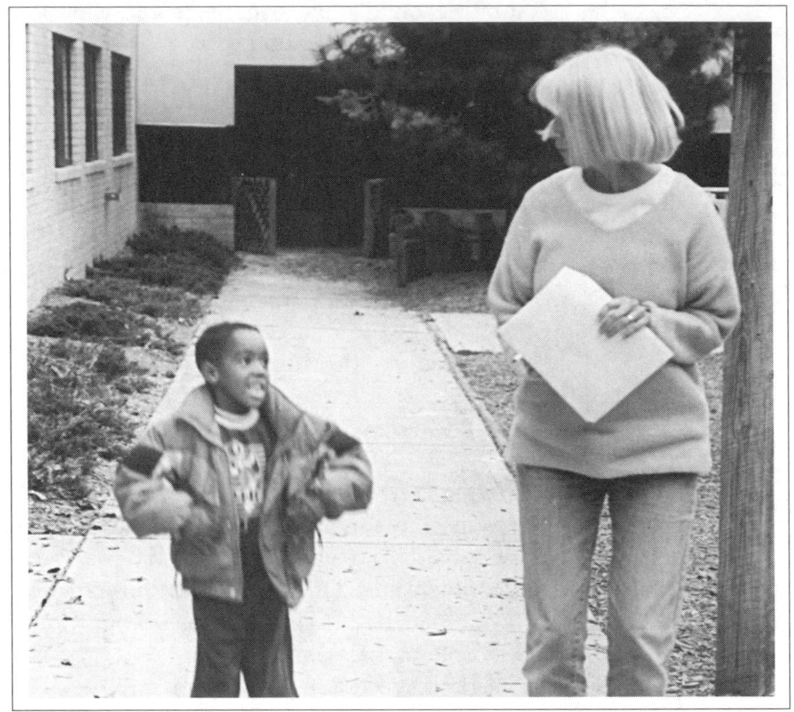

Assessment of young children is most reliable when a number of different approaches are used, including formal testing, observation, and interviews.

to work with their child on more demanding types of activities. The fifth component involves structured and unstructured motor play with the facilitator, and the sixth component is a snack situation wherein eating skills, social behaviors, and other skills can be observed. This assessment model can provide an enormous amount of information to clinicians, early interventionists, and parents across all of the key developmental domains of interest.

Formal/Informal Strand

This strand focuses on the type of information collected in the assessment process. In a formal assessment, the primary strategy for data collection involves the use of standardized tests, which are selected by the examiner(s) with a specific purpose in mind (e.g., screening, comprehensive evaluation, or program evaluation). A specific assessment plan then is set into action. In addition to standardized tests, systematic observations also can be employed; these are discussed next.

At the other end of the continuum are more-informal assessment strategies. Rather than using standardized assessment strategies, the professional or team often uses nonstandardized assessment procedures. For example, a group of professionals may work together to observe the frequency of a specific behavior, and there is a clear structure of systematic data-collection strategies for these observations. An informal data-gathering strategy may indicate the need for and set into motion more-formal data collection.

Normative/Criterion-Referenced Strand

Normative data collection strategies compare a child with his age-level peers. These represent one of the most frequently used strategies in early childhood assessment. The primary emphasis in this approach is on how one child compares with another child of his chronological age rather than whether a child has attained a specific developmental skill. Although this type of data collection produces quantitative information about the overall level of functioning (e.g., developmental quotients and IQs), this information tends to have minimal influence on the selection of specific intervention initiatives. Further, although many normative-based tests have excellent psychometric properties (e.g., reliability), care should be taken when applying them to children with specific disabilities. Indeed, such an approach to assessment may contribute to underestimating a child's abilities if his area(s) of disability are those that primarily are tapped.

Probably the most widely used normative-based instrument in early childhood assessment is the Bayley Scales of Infant Development (Bayley, 1993). The Bayley is designed for children ages 1 month to 42 months and provides a mental and a motor index. These two indices cover such items as imitation, visual-perceptual skills, language, eye-hand coordination, memory, and object permanence. In addition, the Bayley provides a rating scale whereby an examiner can rate a child across a variety of social and temperamental domains.

Criterion-referenced assessment focuses on what specific skills an infant, toddler, or preschooler can demonstrate. In contrast to their norm-referenced counterparts, these types of data-gathering strategies may contribute significant information to a child's IEP or IFSP. Further, they can be quite informal—even created by a preschool teacher or early interventionist—and consequently can be used frequently for ongoing program planning and evaluation. Tying this data-gathering strategy directly into a developmentally sequenced curriculum (curriculum-based assessment) and task analysis also can be quite useful for developmental programming.

Curriculum-based assessment is probably one of the most representative assessment strategies of the criterion-referenced approach. This type of assessment allows the early childhood professional to assess a child's current skills and to monitor progress according to specific program objectives. Curriculum-based assessment even allows a teacher to delineate skills in the curriculum that a child has not yet mastered and to plan accordingly. A weakness of curriculum-based assessment is that the skills assessed are based upon a specific curriculum and may not generalize to another program. The Learning Accomplishment Profile–Revised (LAP–R) (Sanford & Zelman, 1981) is one such instrument that is often used with preschool children with special needs. The LAP–R is designed to assess the skills of children ages birth to 72 months across the domains of cognition, language, fine and gross motor skills, self-help skills, and personal-social skills. Bufkin and Bryde (1996) also have tied this tool to specific programmatic goals and play activities. Similar instruments include the Early Screening Inventory (Meisels & Wiske, 1987), which assesses the visual-motor/adaptive domains, the language and cognitive domains, and gross motor/body awareness; and the Carolina Curriculum for Infants and Toddlers with Special Needs (Johnson-Martin, Jens, Attermeier, & Hacker, 1991).

Standardized/Adaptive-to-Disability Strand

The third strand described by Benner (1992) relates to the standardized nature of the data-gathering process. If an early childhood professional or team employs a standardized assessment, then a fixed set of procedures must be followed during data collection. In fact, some tests, such as many of the intellectual testing measures (e.g., Wechsler Preschool and Primary Scale of Intelligence–Revised and Kaufman Assessment Battery for Children), actually provide specific wording of directions and prompts for the examiners to follow. Standardized procedures also typically include some kind of starting and stopping points at which it is assumed that a child will accurately perform (basal level) or fail (ceiling level) all items below and above these points, respectively. Although this approach may appear to be quite rigid, especially when one considers the wide range of responses and behaviors that any infant or young child may exhibit, many standardized assessment strategies are norm-referenced, and thus it is essential that the standardized procedures be followed to ensure that the data can be interpreted in a valid fashion. As Benner (1992) accurately notes, however, attempting to use these data-gathering strategies with some children with specific disabilities may prove to be invalid (e.g., administering fine motor coordination or fine motor speed tasks to a child with cerebral palsy).

In this regard, adaptive-to-disability data-gathering strategies afford professionals and early childhood teams greater flexibility in attempting to gain a profile of a child's abilities. For example, Benner (1992) has proposed modifying the properties of the objects and materials used in an assessment. Such modifications might include making materials larger and brighter, reducing the number of possible response choices available, and using multidimensional scoring methods that are scaled on a continuum as opposed to having the child respond in a right-versus-wrong fashion. Relatedly, Neisworth and Bagnato (1988) suggest three types of adaptive approaches: (1) the examiner simply modifies the items and procedures as necessary, (2) systematic guidelines are provided for altering the test materials, and (3) the measure is designed for a specific disability. Bagnato, Neisworth, and Munson (1997) also discuss a dynamic modification in which a child might first be tested, then taught the task, and subsequently be retested in an effort to gain an estimate of learning rate. Additionally, Sattler (1992) provides a number of suggestions for testing limits of standardized procedures, particularly for older preschoolers (e.g., eliminating time limits and asking probing questions).

Direct/Indirect Strand

According to Benner (1992), the direct/indirect strand involves how examiners or early intervention teams collect information about a child. Using the direct strategy, a professional works with the child face-to-face. Benner (1992) notes that this strategy is in operation even when a videotape is used to observe and code a child's behaviors. Direct data gathering is likely the most frequently used strategy, and it should be part of every early childhood assessment.

The indirect data-gathering strategy involves the collection of information about a child via other assessment techniques. For example, interviewing parents and other caregivers (e.g., preschool teachers) would serve to provide some index of how a child is functioning in various settings. Rating scales also can be used for indirect data gathering. When indirect data-gathering strategies are combined with direct data-gathering strategies, the assessment process is a richer source of information for the early intervention team. Further, although indirect data-gathering strategies continue to focus on the child, they also can allow the gathering of related information critical to that child's development, such as information about family resources and parental discipline techniques. The Child Development Inventories (Ireton, 1992) fit this mold. These inventories are a multidimensional parent rating system comprising three separate instruments wherein parents answer yes-no items about their child's developmental status. In addition to gaining an appraisal of developmental status, parents are asked to describe their child's behavior and emotional functioning.

Naturalistic/Clinical Observations Strand

Observational data are critical components of all assessment processes. In fact, many of the tests and procedures available for early childhood assessment are little more than structured methods for collecting data on a youngster. With this basic understanding in mind, Benner (1992) describes a continuum of data-gathering strategies that employ observational techniques.

Naturalistic observational strategies require that information be collected in a child's natural setting under routine circumstances. Such strategies can involve observation of the child's overall behavior within the setting or it can focus on more specific types of behaviors (e.g., temper tantrums, social skills during group activities, or fine motor skills during an art activity). Unless there is a good rationale for limiting the observations to specific behaviors—and in many cases this is a preferable type of behavioral observation (e.g., when it is necessary to focus on specific developmental problems)—care should be taken to include other aspects of the setting and/or caregiver so as to minimize bias in the interpretation of the observations. Benner (1992) notes that naturalistic observations can be one of the most ecologically valid data-gathering strategies for a child's actual day-to-day functioning. In fact, many of these assessment strategies are intimately linked to play scales, such as the Play Assessment Scale (Fewell, 1991) and the Symbolic Play Scale (Westby, 1991), and provide observational guidelines for interpreting developmental status (Fewell, 1993; Linder, 1993).

Interactive and ecological types of assessment as described by Neisworth and Bagnato (1988) probably fall on this end of the continuum. In interactive types of measures, the reciprocity between and compatibility of a child and his caregiver(s) are examined. Dimensions of interactions that often are explored include the reading of and response to partner cues, the altering and managing of behaviors, and the ability to initiate and maintain interactions. For example, the Brazelton Neonatal Behavioral Assessment Scale (Brazelton, 1984) examines infant interactive and organizational behaviors by examining elements such as states of arousal, habituation, state regulation, and orientation.

Similarly, ecological assessment techniques examine factors within a child's life that may contribute to developmental status, thus providing a more comprehensive profile of strengths and needs. A child's ecological context includes the home, classroom, and family characteristics such as room layout, materials, available opportunities for stimulation, peer interaction, social responsibility, discipline, and social support. Two ecological assessment tools that can be employed to examine a child's environments are the Home Observation for Measurement of the Environment (HOME) (Caldwell & Bradley, 1978) and the Early Childhood Environment Rating Scale (ECERS) (Harms & Clifford, 1980). More specific measures relating to parenting stress (Parenting Stress Index, Abidin, 1986), parental behaviors (Parent Behavior Checklist, Fox, 1993), and other psychosocial areas also are available (Glascoe, 1996).

On the other end of the continuum is clinical observation. This type of observation occurs when a child is being evaluated in a clinical setting, such as when a pediatrician performs an examination or a child is receiving a comprehensive evaluation at a child development center. Although skilled evaluators can extract reliable and valid behaviors from young children—at least a majority of the time—young children also can become more constricted in their behavioral presentations during a clinic visit. Consequently, the use of different types of observations in tandem provides a more accurate picture of a child's overall functional capabilities.

For example, a formal evaluative process may need to include systematic observation of a specific behavior. Such observation should be objective, quantifiable, and collected over time. Observation may occur in the child's natural setting or in a simulated or staged situation. Systematic observation does not include interpretation of behaviors or judgments but, rather, objective, structured measures of overt behaviors (e.g., the number of times a child hits another child or is off task during an assignment). For formal assessment of a behavior, dimensions that may be included are its frequency, duration, and intensity. Typically, data sheets or coding systems are developed that allow an examiner to observe and record behaviors of concern.

Product-Oriented/Process-Oriented Strand

Similar to the normative/criterion-referenced strand, the product-oriented/process-oriented continuum relates to the type of information that needs to be gathered in the assessment process. A product-oriented data-gathering strategy generally involves administering to a child a battery of tests and procedures with the goals of describing how a child compares to his age-peers and establishing initial developmental or instructional levels for programming. Measures such as the Bayley Scales of Infant Development (Bayley, 1993) and all of the preschool measures of intelligence (e.g., Wechsler Preschool and Primary Scale of Intelligence–Revised) fall under this strand. Similarly, performance-based, or authentic assessment (Meyer, 1992; Wiggins, 1989), and portfolio data-gathering strategies for collecting samples of a child's work over time (e.g., collecting a child's various drawings of a person over the course of a calendar year) (Arter & Spanel, 1991; Meisels, 1993), also are included on the product-oriented side of this continuum. These latter types of product oriented data-gathering strategies are important in that they likely will occur in the child's natural setting.

Process-oriented data-gathering strategies involve *how* a child interacts with the examiner and the environment; they even examine how a child passes *and* fails selected tasks and items. Piagetian types of measures, such as the Uzgiris-Hunt Scales (Uzgiris & Hunt, 1975), which tap many of the Piagetian tasks described in Chapter 6, and dynamic assessment procedures, such as those advocated by Feuerstein (1979), Vygotsky (1978), and Lidz (1987), are data-gathering strategies that are process-oriented. With these types of assessment, children typically are exposed to a task and their performance is observed. If children experience difficulties performing a selected task, they can be taught the task through mediated learning experiences (Tzuriel & Klein, 1987), and then the item is readministered. This test-teach-test type of format can occur as many times as is deemed necessary by the evaluator.

For many young children with significant disabilities (e.g., visual impairment and severe mental retardation), traditional assessment strategies are not appropriate. Consequently, alternative approaches are sorely needed to tap into these children's developmental needs and less-obvious competencies. Process assessment attempts to discover a child's unique capabilities, such as in memory and recall, attention, and information processing through indirect and inferential means. While this is not an ideal method of assessment, it is one alternative when other assessment approaches are not feasible.

Considerations for the Assessment of Young Children

A number of considerations need to be taken into account for work with all young children, but especially young children with special needs. From an assessment perspective, some of these considerations include the selection of assessment approaches and tools, situational constraints including child and environmental variables, the need for strong assessment-treatment linkages, and the involvement of the family.

Selection of Assessment Methods

As has been emphasized over the course of this chapter, assessment of a young child does not, nor should it ever, represent a single point in time; rather, it should be a process that is driven by questions pertinent to a child's development and specific developmental needs. This process notwithstanding, the selection of assessment methods should be guided by basic canons of science (i.e., reliability and validity), cultural sensitivity, and common sense. In fact, many of these standards are described in the *Standards for Educational and Psychological Testing* (American Psychological Association, 1985).

Reliability and validity are critical scientific concepts that must be understood when selecting a specific assessment tool for any part of the assessment process (e.g., screening, diagnostic, or program evaluation). Reliability refers to consistency: Does the test measure what it is supposed to measure in a dependable fashion? Gaining reliable information from any young child is a challenge, and it is imperative that a test assist that process by having adequate reliability.

Validity refers to how well the test measures what it is supposed to measure. The test should have adequate content validity (Does the test reflect the content it is purportedly measuring?), concurrent validity (Does the test correlate with other accepted criteria of performance in each skill area?), predictive validity (To what extent do the obtained scores correlate with some criterion for successful performance in the future?), construct validity (Does the test address the theoretical constructs upon which the test is based?), and discriminate validity (Do subtests measure separate and distinct skills?). While a detailed discussion of these psychometric issues is beyond the scope of this chapter, the early childhood professional should examine test manuals for such information prior to employing any test for screening, diagnostic, or program evaluation purposes.

In addition to the basic psychometric aspects of the assessment tools, it is critical that they be nonbiased and nondiscriminatory. While these issues have been addressed in court cases (*Diana versus State Board of Education,* 1973; *Larry P. versus Riles,* 1979), and subsequently in our federal laws, it is the responsibility of early childhood professionals to be highly sensitive to these issues. Nondiscriminatory assessment refers to the multicultural nature of society and means that any assessment must be equally fair to all children. It is important to note that the nature of any assessment is discriminatory; its overarching purpose is to discriminate among those who need services and those who do not, but it *unfairly* discriminates if it does not allow for cultural differences. Allowing for cultural differences should include administering tests in a child's native language or other modes of communication and providing experiences that are familiar to the child. Closely related to nondiscriminatory assessment is the concept of nonbiased assessment. Duffey, Salvia, Tucker, and Ysseldyke (1981) define a biased assessment as having "constant errors in decisions, predictions, and inferences about members of particular groups" (p. 427). An example of an early childhood professional making a biased assessment is making premature judgments about the child being tested, especially when the child is tested in an unnatural setting.

It is important for the early childhood professional to possess plain old common sense. While it may seem obvious, it is critical that the tests selected actually assist in answering the referral questions. Will the tests provide and/or assist in the assessment-treatment linkages detailed by Neisworth and Bagnato (1996)? If so, how? Further, is the content appropriate for the child? Is the professional administering the test appropriately trained to administer and interpret it? Again, although they are basic, the application of these commonsense considerations lessens the misuse and abuse of assessment tools.

Situational Constraints

Situational constraints can involve any number of concerns that can arise in the assessment process. One of the most common constraints encountered is when a child simply refuses to perform. The child might be frightened, fatigued, slow to warm up to the testing session, or, in the case of an infant, sleeping. Other children may present extreme behavioral difficulties that do not facilitate the assessment process. In all of these situations, it is important for the early childhood professional to be familiar with the many different types of data-gathering methods so as to take advantage of these situational constraints.

For example, when an examiner or team is trying to gain a formal assessment and a child is noncompliant, it might be useful to shift over to more informal (e.g., observation), indirect (e.g., parent ratings or report), and process-oriented (e.g., play) types of data-gathering strategies. If an examiner has a strong background in development and behavioral management strategies, an enormous amount of information could be gained from observation of the child's play and/or other naturalistic observations. If the examiner continues to exert demands to gain the formal assessment information, however, critical time could be lost, not to mention the opportunity to learn more about the functioning of this child.

It will remain helpful for the team of professionals to learn about the child's ecology. This should include gaining knowledge about the child's preschool, the preschool teacher or child-care provider, the home—including other family members, and information pertinent to the individual child. This ecological approach assists interventionists in gaining an increased understanding of the many different behaviors that might be manifested by a child during the assessment process.

Family/Parental Involvement

As discussed in Chapters 1 and 3, the importance of the family in the assessment process cannot be overlooked. Efforts to include family members in the assessment process are ever-increasing, such as in the transdisciplinary play assessment model described earlier, and the input of family members can be absolutely critical to attempts to engage in intervention for a particular child. As noted at the beginning of this chapter, family members need to view the assessment and intervention as consistent with their perceptions of their child as well as with their current familial

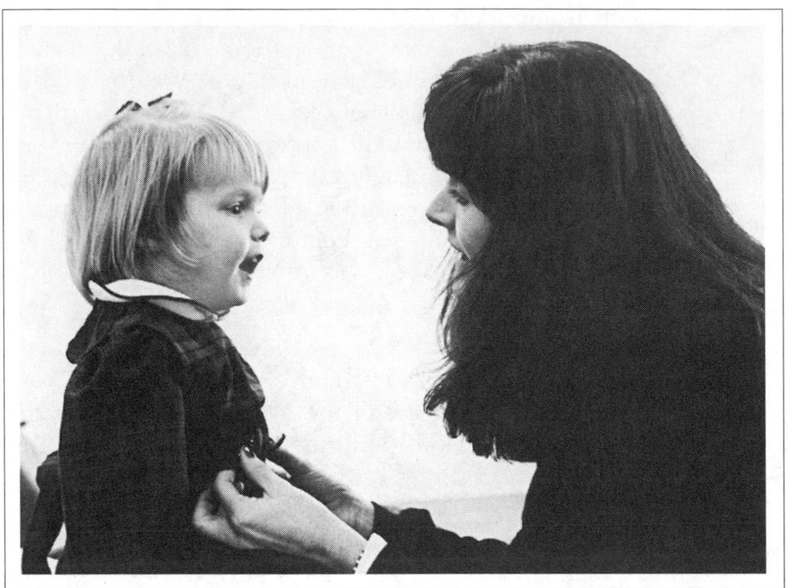

Getting to know a young child is a critical part of every assessment process.

values and needs. Understanding a family's perspective prior to initiating any assessment is useful in constructing the assessment process; it contributes to appropriate decisions about what kind of data-gathering approach as well as what specific tools may be of use. The development of intervention plans also is more collaborative when the family is involved in the assessment process from the beginning.

Summary

This chapter provided an overview of the assessment process in early childhood. Several definitions of the term *assessment* were provided, and contemporary assessment standards were discussed. These included treatment utility, social validity, convergent assessment, and consensual validity, which should be applied to any assessment in early childhood so as to increase the accuracy and utility of the assessment information, and to provide for valid intervention plans. The various stages of assessment were detailed with a particular emphasis on early identification, including issues related to screening and the major components of a comprehensive assessment. The ongoing process of assessment was highlighted, particularly in the intervention and program evaluation phases.

In addition to these aspects of assessment, a number of approaches to assessment were detailed in accordance with a set of strands, or continua, as espoused by Benner (1992). The team approach to assessment in accordance with federal laws was highlighted, with a specific emphasis on transdisciplinary teams. Although the emphasis of this chapter was not on describing the many assessment tools available to the early childhood professional, selected tools were mentioned to illustrate the various strands of assessment. A discussion of some of the issues pertinent to the assessment process, such as test selection, situational constraints, and involvement of the family, also was provided. With a good understanding of the assessment process, in tandem with a firm grounding in basic child development, the interventionist should be able to address the needs of young children with special needs in a sensitive and thoughtful fashion.

References

Abidin, R. R. (1986). *Parenting Stress Index* (2nd ed.). Charlottesville, VA: Pediatric Psychology Press.

American Academy of Pediatrics (1986). Committee on children with disabilities: Screening for developmental disabilities. *Pediatrics, 78,* 526–528.

American College of Obstetricians and Gynecologists (1994). *Maternal serum screening for birth defects.* Washington, DC: Author.

American Psychological Association (1985). *Standards for educational and psychological testing.* Washington, DC: Author.

American Speech and Hearing Association (1990). *Guidelines for practices in early intervention.* Rockville, MD: Author.

Apgar, V. (1953). A proposal for a new method of evaluation of the newborn infant. *Current Research in Anesthesia and Analgesia, 32,* 260–267.

Arter, J. A., & Spanel, V. (1991). *Using portfolios of student work in instruction and assessment.* Portland, OR: Northwest Regional Educational Laboratory.

Aylward, G. P. (1995). *Bayley Infant Neurodevelopmental Screener.* San Antonio, TX: Psychological Corp.

Aylward, G. P., Gustafson, N., Verhulst, S. J., & Colliver, J. A. (1987). Consistency in the diagnosis of cognitive, motor, and neurologic function over the first three years. *Journal of Pediatric Psychology, 12,* 77–98.

Bagnato, S. J., & Neisworth, J. T. (1990). *System to Plan Early Childhood Services.* Circle Pines, MN: American Guidance Services.

Bagnato, S. J., & Neisworth, J. T. (1994). A national study of the social and treatment "invalidity" of intelligence testing for early intervention. *School Psychology Quarterly, 9,* 81–102.

Bagnato, S. J., Neisworth, J. T., & Munson, S. M. (1997). *Linking authentic assessment and early intervention: Advances in curriculum-based evaluation* (3rd ed.). Baltimore: Paul H. Brookes.

Bailey, D. B., & Wolery, M. (1989). *Assessing infants and preschoolers with handicaps.* Upper Saddle River, NJ: Merrill/Prentice Hall.

Bandura, A. (1977). *Social learning theory.* Upper Saddle River, NJ: Prentice Hall.

Bayley, N. (1993). *Bayley Scales of Infant Development* (2nd ed.). San Antonio, TX: Psychological Corp.

Benner, S. M. (1992). *Assessing young children with special needs: An ecological perspective.* New York: Longman.

Bergen, D., & Wright, M. (1994). Medical assessment perspectives. In D. Bergen (Ed.), *Assessment methods for infants and toddlers: Transdisciplinary team approaches* (pp. 40–56). New York: Teachers College Press.

Bracken, B., Bagnato, S. J., & Barnett, D. (1991). *Early childhood assessment* (NASP position statement). Washington, DC: National Association of School Psychologists.

Brazelton, T. B. (1984). *Neonatal assessment scale* (2nd ed.) (Clinics in Developmental Medicine, No. 88). Philadelphia: J. B. Lippincott.

Bricker, D., & Squires, J. (1994). *Ages and Stages Questionnaire.* Baltimore: Paul H. Brookes.

Bronfenbrenner, U. (1986). Ecology of the family as a context for human development. Research perspectives. *Developmental Psychology, 22,* 723–742.

Bufkin, L. J., & Bryde, S. M. (1996). Young children at their best: Linking play to assessment and intervention. *Teaching Exceptional Children, 29,* 50–53.

Caldwell, B. M., & Bradley, R. H. (1978). *HOME Inventory.* Little Rock, AR: University of Arkansas.

Cardone, I., & Gilkerson, L. (1989). Family administrated neonatal activities: An innovative component of family-centered care. *Zero to Three, X(1),* 23–28.

Chervenak, F. A., & Kurjak, A. (Eds.) (1996). *The fetus as a patient.* New York: Parthenon.

Cheung, M. C., Goldberg, J. D., & Kan, Y. W. (1996). Prenatal diagnosis of sickle cell anemia and thalassemia by analysis of fetal cells in maternal blood. *Nature Genetics, 14,* 264–268.

Diana versus Board of Education (1973). C–70, 37 RFP (N.D. Cal.).

Division of Early Childhood Task Force on Recommended Practices (Eds.) (1993). *Recommended practices in early intervention.* Reston, VA: Council for Exceptional Children.

Dobos, A. E., Dworkin, P. H., & Bernstein, B. (1994). Pediatricians' approaches to developmental problems: Has the gap been narrowed? *Journal of Developmental and Behavioral Pediatrics, 15,* 34–39.

Duffey, J., Salvia, J., Tucker, J., & Ysseldyke, J. (1981). Nonbiased assessment: A need for operationalism. *Exceptional Children, 47,* 427–434.

Feuerstein, R. (1979). *The dynamic assessment of retarded performers: The learning potential assessment device, theory, instrument, and techniques.* Baltimore: University Park Press.

Fewell, R. (1983). Assessing handicapped infants. In S. G. Garwood & R. R. Fewell (Eds.), *Educating handicapped infants: Issues in development and intervention* (pp. 257–297). Rockville, MD: Aspen.

Fewell, R. (1991). *Play assessment scale.* Miami, FL: University of Miami.

Fewell, R. (1993). Observing play: An appropriate process for learning and assessment. *Infants and Young Children, 5,* 35–43.

Fox, R. A. (1993). *Parenting Behavior Checklist.* Brandon, VT: Clinical Psychology Press.

Frankenburg, W. K., Dodds, J., Archer, P., Bresnick, B., Maschka, P., Edelman, N., & Shapiro, H. (1990). *Denver–II.* Denver, CO: Denver Developmental Materials.

Glascoe, F. P. (1996). Developmental screening. In M. L. Wolraich (Ed.), *Disorders of development and learning: A practical guide to assessment and management* (2nd. ed.) (pp. 89–128). New York: Mosby.

Harms, T., & Clifford, R. M. (1980). *Early Childhood Environment Rating Scale.* New York: Teachers College Press.

Hooper, S. R. (1991). Neuropsychological assessment of the preschool child. In B. Bracken (Ed.), *The psychoeducational assessment of preschool children* (2nd ed.) (pp. 465–485). Boston: Allyn & Bacon.

Ireton, H. (1992). *Child Development Inventories.* Minneapolis, MN: Behavior Science Systems.

Johnson-Martin, N. M., Jens, K. G., Attermeier, S. M., & Hacker, B. J. (1991). *The Carolina curriculum for infants and toddlers with special needs* (2nd ed.). Baltimore: Paul H. Brookes.

Larry P. versus Riles (1979). 343 F Supp. 1306, 502 F.2d 963 (N.D. Cal.).

Lichtenstein, R., & Ireton, H. (1991). Preschool screening for developmental and educational problems. In B. Bracken (Ed.), *The psychoeducational assessment of preschool children* (2nd ed.) (pp. 486–513). Boston: Allyn & Bacon.

Lidz, C. (Ed.) (1987). *Dynamic assessment: An interactional approach to evaluating learning potential.* New York: Guilford Press.

Linder, T. (1993). *Transdisciplinary play-based assessment: A functional approach to working with young children* (rev. ed.). Baltimore: Paul H. Brookes.

Lo, Y., Patel, P., Sampietro, M., Gillmer, M. D. G., Fleming, K. A., & Wainscoat, J. S. (1990). Detection of single-copy fetal DNA sequence from maternal blood. *Lancet, 1,* 1463–1464.

McLean, M., & Odom, S. (1993). Practices for young children with and without disabilities: A comparison of DEC and NAEYC identified practices. *Topics in Early Childhood Special Education, 13,* 274–292.

Meisels, S. J. (1993). Remaking classroom assessment with the work sampling system. *Young Children, 48,* 34–40.

Meisels, S. J., & Wiske, M. S. (1987). *Early Screening Inventory.* New York: Teachers College Press.

Meyer, C. A. (1992). What's the difference between authentic and performance assessment? *Educational Leadership, 49,* 39–40.

Mindes, G., Ireton, H., & Mardell-Czudnowski, C. (1996). *Assessing young children*. New York: Delmar.

National Association for the Education of Young Children (1990). Position statement on school readiness. *Young Children, 46,* 21–23.

Neisworth, J. T., & Bagnato, S. J. (1988). Assessment in early childhood special education: A typology of dependent measures. In S. L. Odom & M. Karnes (Eds.), *Early intervention for infants and children with handicaps: An empirical base*. Baltimore: Paul H. Brookes.

Neisworth, J. T., & Bagnato, S. J. (1996). Assessment for early intervention: Emerging themes and practices. In S. L. Odom & M. E. McLean (Eds.), *Early intervention/early childhood special education: Recommended practices*. Austin, TX: Pro-Ed.

Odom, S. L., McLean, M. E., Johnson, L., & LaMontagne, M. (1995). Recommended practices in early childhood special education: Validation and current use. *Journal of Early Intervention, 19,* 1–17.

Piaget, J. (1954). *The construction of reality in the child*. New York: Basic Books.

Ramey, C. T., & Hardin, J. M. (1995). Early intervention for low birthweight, premature infants: Participation and intellectual development. *American Journal of Mental Retardation, 99,* 542–554.

Ramey, C. T., & Ramey, S. R. (1994). Which children benefit the most from early intervention? *Pediatrics, 94,* 1064–1066.

Rosenblith, J. (1973, Aug.). *Manual for behavioral examination of the neonate*. Workshop conducted at the Eighty-Third Annual Meeting of the American Psychological Association, Montreal, Canada.

Sameroff, A., & Chandler, M. J. (1975). Reproductive risk and the continuum of caretaking causality. In F. D. Horowitz, M. Hetherington, S. Scarr-Salapetek, & G. Seigel (Eds.), *Review of child development research*. Chicago: University of Chicago Press.

Sanford, A. R., & Zelman, J. G. (1981). *Learning Accomplish Profile–Revised*. Winston-Salem, NC: Kaplan School Supply.

Sattler, J. (1992). *Assessment in children* (3rd ed., rev.). San Diego, CA: Author.

Scott, F. G., Lingaraju, S., Kilgo, J., Kregel, J., & Lazzari, A. (1993). A survey of pediatricians on early identification and early intervention services. *Journal of Early Intervention, 17,* 129–138.

Skeels, H. M. (1966). Adult status of children with contrasting early life experiences: A follow-up study. *Monographs of the Society for Research in Child Development* (Serial No. 105).

Stripparo, L., Buscaglia, M., Longatti, L., Ghisoni, L., Dambrosio, F., Guerneri, S., Rosella, F., Litvania, M., Cardone, M., DeBiasio, P., Passamonti, U., Gimelli, G., & Cuocos, C. (1990). Genetic amniocentesis: 505 cases performed before the sixteenth week of gestation. *Prenatal Diagnosis, 10,* 359–364.

Thurlow, M., & Ysseldyke, J. (1979). Current assessment and decision-making practices in model LD programs. *Learning Disability Quarterly, 2,* 15–24.

Tramontana, M. G., Hooper, S. R., & Selzer, C. (1988). Research on the preschool prediction of later academic achievement. *Developmental Review, 8,* 89–147.

Tzuriel, D., & Klein, P. S. (1987). Assessing the young child: Children's analogical thinking modifiability. In C. S. Lidz (Ed.), *Dynamic assessment: An interactional approach to evaluating learning potential*. New York: Guilford Press.

Uzgiris, I. C., & Hunt, J. M. (Eds.) (1975). *Assessment in infancy: Ordinal scales of psychological development*. Urbana, IL: University of Illinois Press.

Vanderwall, K. J., & Harrison, M. R. (1996). Fetal surgery. In F. A. Chervenak & A. Kurjak (Eds.), *The fetus as patient*. New York: Parthenon.

Verp, M. S., Simpson, J. L., & Ober, C. (1993). Prenatal diagnosis of genetic disorders. In C. C. Lin, M. S. Verp, & R. E. Babbagha (Eds.), *The high-risk fetus. Pathophysiology, diagnosis, and management*. New York: Springer-Verlag.

Vygotsky, L. S. (1978). *Mind in society: The development of higher psychological processes*. Cambridge, MA: Harvard University Press.

Westby, C. (1991). A scale for assessing children's pretend play. In C. Schaefer, K. Gitlin, & A. Sandgrund (Eds.), *Play assessment and diagnosis*. New York: Wiley.

Wiggins, G. (1989). A true test: Toward more authentic and equitable assessment. *Phi Delta Kappan, 70,* 703–713.

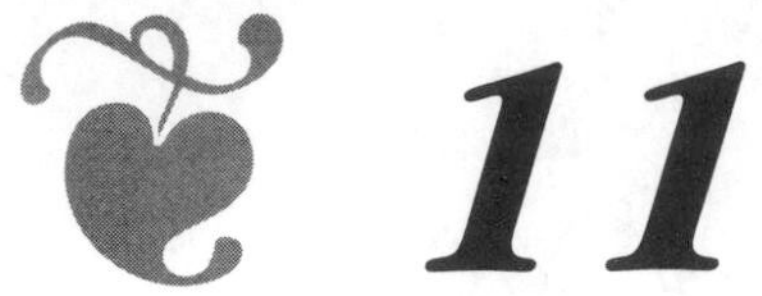

11

Intervention

Tina M. Smith and Harrison D. Kane

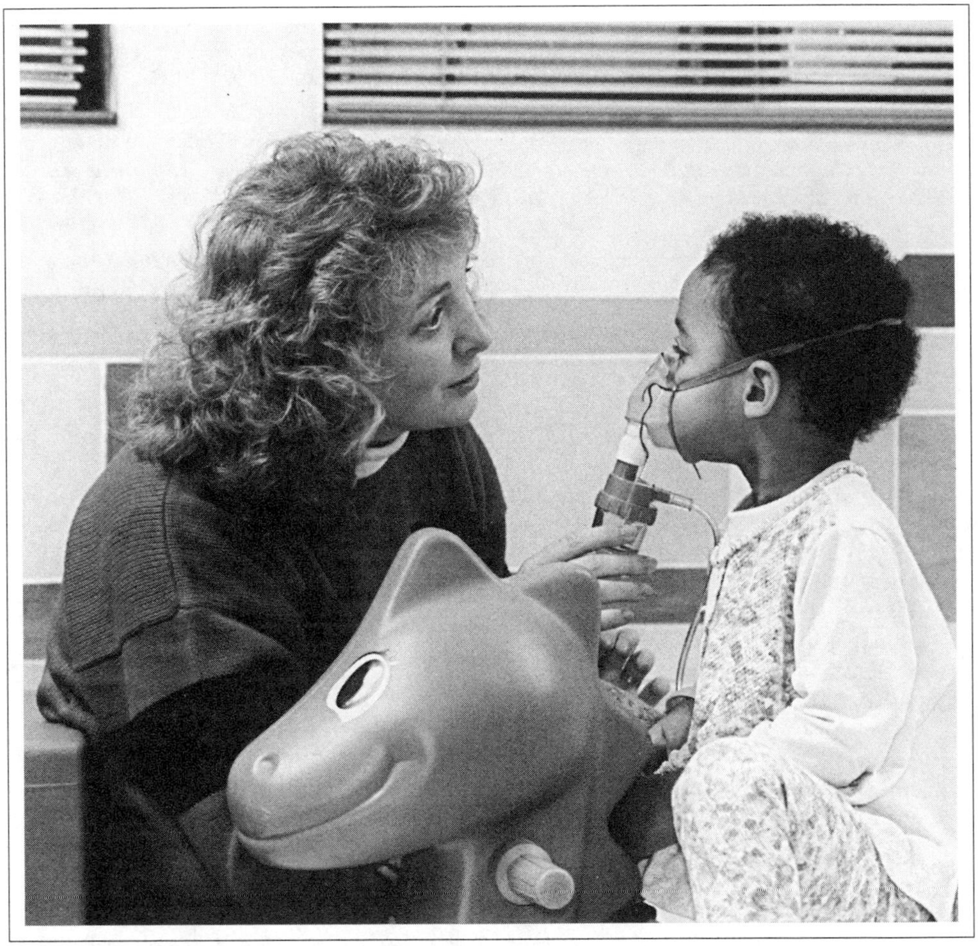

The concept of intervention represents the heart and soul of our work with children. In its broadest sense, intervention includes nearly every interaction that professionals have with children and families. The purpose of this chapter is to discuss intervention as it specifically relates to young children. We begin by offering a general definition of the term *intervention* to put the recent practice of early intervention into a historical context. Next, our discussion turns to more pragmatic aspects specific to early intervention and proceeds through planning, implementing, and evaluating intervention with young children.

Definition of Intervention

Perhaps the most helpful way to begin a discussion of intervention is to define the basic concept. For the professional, a functional definition of the term *intervention* serves three purposes. First, it differentiates intervention from related but different clinical and educational endeavors, such as assessment. Second, a definition provides the framework necessary for formulating individual and program goals. For any field of study to progress, there must be at least some agreement regarding the goals and objectives. In the words of Yogi Berra, "You have to be very careful when you don't know where you're going, or you might never get there." A functional definition of intervention gives the professional an idea of "how to get there." Finally, a definition provides insight into the assumptions underlying professional practice and research.

A number of educational and psychological theorists have attempted to define intervention. Rhodes and Tracey (1972) describe it as any directed action intended to remedy the ill-fit between a child and the environment. Suran and Rizzo (1979) suggest that intervention is any professional effort to facilitate a child's ongoing healthy development. Some researchers (Adelman & Taylor, 1994) emphasize both planned and unplanned outcomes in their definition of early intervention. More recently, Hanson and Lynch have (1995) defined intervention broadly, as "a comprehensive cluster of services that incorporate goals in education, health care, and social service for young children who are disabled or at risk for developing disabilities and their families."

These definitions overlap to a considerable degree, and any of them may serve as a starting point for understanding intervention. However, each is also insufficient in certain respects. For example, Rhodes and Tracey do not address the outcomes of intervention. Intervention can have a multitude of outcomes, some desirable and some undesirable. Although a strong research base helps suggest what the outcomes of a planned intervention will be, there are always unexpected outcomes as well. In this regard, Adelman and Taylor's (1994) emphasis on outcomes is preferable in that the possibility of unintended and even undesirable outcomes is acknowledged along with planned outcomes.

Definitions that consider only problems or disabilities, such as that of Hanson and Lynch, also can be limited. Intervention should not automatically imply the presence of significant problems. While intervention is usually intended to remediate a problem or area of need, it also can be used to establish and maintain positive functioning. For example, prevention is a type of intervention used by everyone at some time to avoid a problem. If we define intervention this broadly, then every person is in need of some form of intervention at some point in development. The essential question is deciding when to intervene, who will be involved in the intervention, and the extent and type of intervention.

Finally, a definition of intervention also should account for the environmental influence of social systems beyond the individual and immediate family, such as school and the local community. Intervention is implemented in environments, not just for individuals. Notably, a person's functioning and development always occur in a given context. For the purposes of this chapter, intervention is broadly defined to refer to outcomes (both positive and negative, intentional and unintentional), conditions eliciting intervention (both positive and negative), and a consideration of the multiple systems affecting and affected by intervention (the individual, family, school, and community). Therefore, we offer the following definition of intervention:

> Intervention is a directed, purposeful process. It is the intentional application of resources with the aim of developing, improving, or changing conditions within an individual, environment, or interactions between an individual and the environment. Intervention always results in both intended and unexpected outcomes, which may be either positive or negative in nature.

Family-Centered Intervention

An important assumption in early intervention for infants and toddlers is that the family is the unit of intervention for services. By taking into account family needs, intervention efforts for infants and toddlers are likely to include goals that go well beyond the educational objectives mandated by special education laws relating to older children. For example, in the case of a family with three children, one of whom has a medical condition that requires constant attention and access to a respirator, one challenge faced by the parents may be how to give the other children the time and attention that they need. For this family, one relevant intervention goal would be the provision of respite services for the child with special needs so that the parents can spend time with their other children. Such needs can and should be addressed by early intervention. Ideally, parents take an active role in the education and development of their children at all ages. With the inclusion of Part H in PL 99–457, Congress acknowledged that families are an integral aspect of a child's life, and worthy of intervention services in their own right.

Multiculturalism and Early Intervention

One aspect of family-centered intervention that is becoming increasingly important and relevant is how to provide services in a multicultural society. American society is a diverse, dynamic, and interactive landscape comprised of communities and individuals. Of course, this was not always the case. In 1970, 12% of the population in the United States under 5 years of age was nonwhite. By 1984, however, 36% of all babies in the United States were born to nonwhite, non-Anglo parents (Research and Policy Committee of the Committee for Economic Development, 1987). By the 1990s, our nation's growing diversity had become even more apparent. For example, the 1990 census recorded that over 380 different languages were actively spoken by American citizens (U.S. Bureau of the Census, 1990). Predictions made by the Children's Defense Fund (1989) were that by the year 2000 there would be "2.4 million more Hispanic children; 1.7 million more African-American children; 483,000 more children of other races, and 66,000 more white non-Hispanic children" than there were in 1985 (p. 116). The predictions for the year 2030 are even more dramatic, projecting a decline of 6.2 million in the population of white, non-Hispanic children. In idealistic terms, this estimate means that future children will be exposed to an enriched, varied, and total human experience. However, in purely practical terms, this prediction also means that nearly half of all school-aged children will be nonwhite. As the number of children of color in the general population increases, there certainly will be a concomitant increase in the number of nonwhite, non-Anglo children requiring early intervention services. However, with so few minorities entering social service professions, the likelihood is that the vast majority of professionals providing early intervention services will continue to be white.

The predicted cultural mismatch between service providers and families offers new challenges for the social service professional. Potential conflicts rooted in culture are likely and unfortunate, because both interventionists and families share the same goal of wanting to help children. These potential cultural misunderstandings arise because people are bathed in a culture from birth. Brown and Lenneberg (1965) found that children may establish a cultural identity as early as 5 years of age. Because our primary culture is a deeply-set part of our values, attitudes, and behavior, we may easily misinterpret a second culture. In any case, the impact of culture on early intervention is indisputable.

Although many teachers, health-care professionals, and psychologists often discuss "cultural issues," surprisingly few sources have attempted to define culture as a facet of early intervention. There are several formalized definitions of the term *culture*. For example, Turnbull, Turnbull, Shank, and Leal (1995) define it as "the many different factors that shape one's sense of group identity: race, ethnicity, religion, geographical locations, income status, gender, and occupations" (p. 8). However, most of us do not rely on textbook definitions. Instead, we operate under the assumption that everyone has an implicit understanding of what is meant by the term *culture;* yet these connotative definitions frequently lead to disagreement and misunderstanding among professionals and between service providers and families. Frisby (1992) found that the term *culture* means different things to different people:

> **Culture A** refers to differences in clothing, lifestyle, values, and traditions associated with a people's level of technological attainment or geographic location. For example, some anthropologists refer to Western or modern culture when discussing societies of Europe or the Americas.
>
> **Culture B** is equated with the humanistic achievement of racial or ethnic groups. For example, when school classrooms celebrate Black History Month, administrators and teachers encourage students to explore the fundamentals of "black culture."
>
> **Culture C** designates common attitudes, values, and beliefs that guide an individual's identification with a particular group. For example, many African-American community leaders garner great support because they are able to articulate the "black experience" in America.

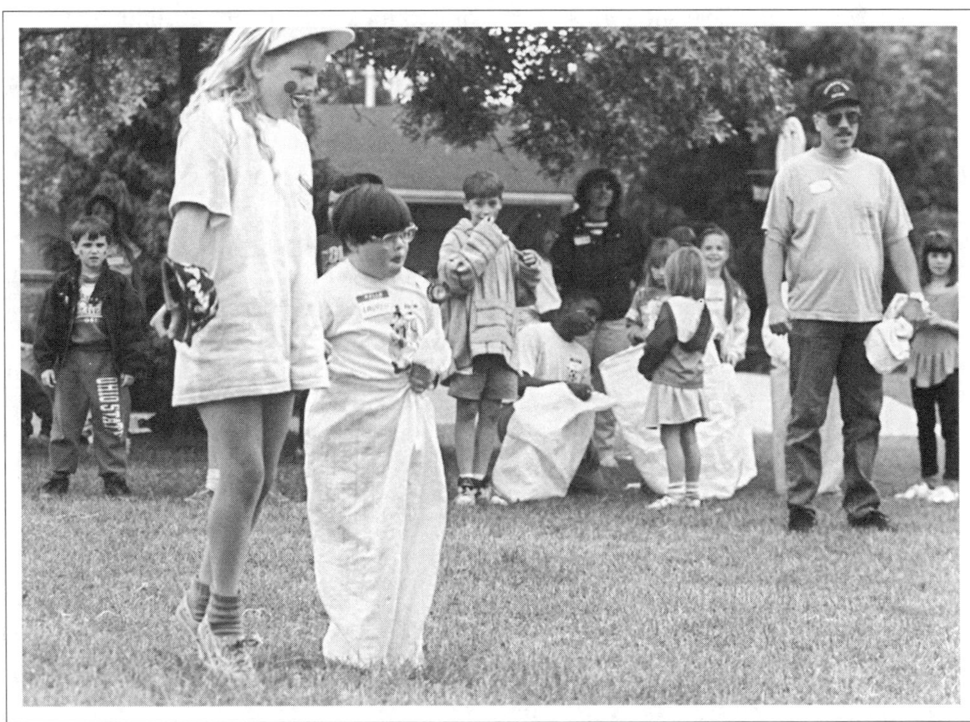

A goal of early intervention is to provide effective and responsible services that are sensitive to the needs of families whose language, culture, and experiences are different from our own.

> **Culture D** refers to the immediate context of an individual. For example, many anthropologists and politicians espouse the ideas of a "culture of poverty" and a "culture of the schools."
>
> **Culture E** is associated with superficial lifestyle choices. For example, in the late 1970s there was a "punk culture" whose members were easily identified by their music, clothing, and appearance. Teachers and linguists use this meaning of culture when they identify certain patterns of speech as "black English."
>
> **Culture F** equates culture with race. This connotative definition of culture is the most superficial and simplistic. Not surprisingly, this definition of culture is also the primary source of misunderstandings between families and professionals. After all, should we assume that a family is culturally different simply because it is racially different?

As early interventionists, one of our primary concerns should be how we will provide an effective and responsible delivery of services that is also sensitive to the needs of families whose language, culture, and experiences are different from our own.

Barriers to Effective Family Involvement

Despite the intent of the law and the best efforts of professionals, parents often are inadvertently left out of the early intervention planning process. Part of the difficulty of including parents stems from the way services were provided in the past. Historically, education professionals have focused intervention efforts on the child. With IDEA's mandates for family-centered intervention, however, came a fundamental shift in the way professionals view themselves and families. Bailey, Buysse, Edmondson, and Smith (1992) outline four basic assumptions underlying family-centered practice that radically shift intervention efforts away from the individual child and onto the entire family:

> 1. Children and families are inextricably intertwined. Intentional or not, intervention with children almost invariably influences families; likewise, intervention with and support of families almost invariably influence children.
> 2. Interventions involving and supporting families are always likely to be more powerful than those focusing exclusively on the child.
> 3. Family members should be able to choose their level of involvement in program planning, decision making, and service delivery.
> 4. Professionals should attend to family priorities for goals and services, even when those priorities differ substantially from professional priorities. (p. 299)

In addition to the paradigm shift from child-centered to family-centered intervention, three types of barriers to full family participation have been identified: family, system, and professional barriers (Bailey et al., 1992). Family barriers include lack of parental skill (e.g., parents who are themselves developmentally disabled), inadequate resources (e.g., lack of time for parents to attend meetings because of the demands of their child's care), and attitudinal problems (e.g., lack of confidence or assertiveness). When these types of barriers exist, it is the responsibility of the professional to help the family overcome them so that fuller and more meaningful participation is possible.

System barriers, perhaps the most frustrating for the professional, are obstacles resulting from the bureaucracy or agency responsible for service provision. System barriers include such difficulties as lack of time and resources, entrenched bureaucracies that are slow to change policies, and inflexible administrative practices. For example, one difficulty frequently encountered when professionals attempt to accommodate families is an inability to schedule meetings after work or on weekends so that working parents can attend. Although system barriers must be addressed at the administrative level, it is important for parents and professionals at all levels to bring their concerns to the attention of policy makers.

Professional barriers result from a lack of knowledge or skills, or from attitudinal problems on the part of the interventionist. Knowledge barriers can arise when professionals are not prepared by their preservice programs or in-service education to work effectively with families, or when they lack experience. Professionals' attitudinal barriers may present an even greater challenge than lack of knowledge or skill, because they involve the fundamental assumptions professionals hold about the ability of families to make decisions about their children's needs. Sometimes, the social service professional approaches intervention with an ethnocentric attitude, using his own culture and experiences as a measure of what is normal, expected, and superior. As one professional reported, "We seem to have the attitude that we know what's best for the child" (Bailey et al., 1992, p. 304).

Program Planning

An underlying principle of IDEA is that all children, including children with disabilities, deserve a meaningful educational experience. This principle was further reinforced in the 1997 Amendments to IDEA (P.L. 105-117). To ensure the quality and richness of this experience for a child with special needs, the educational program must be based on individualized goals and objectives. IDEA requires that these goals and objectives be written down, and that an individualized service plan be created for each child with special needs. This plan is intended to be the blueprint for the child's intervention program. This section of the chapter describes the planning process and the products of this process: the Individualized Educational Plan and the Individualized Family Service Plan.

Step 1: Assessment

The first step in planning an intervention program is to identify areas of strength and need. To a large extent, the success of this process and ultimately the intervention itself is dependent on the success of the first phase, that is, the child's assessment. In early intervention, assessment is always accomplished through a multidisciplinary team evaluation and an in-depth assessment of every aspect of the child's development. By law, professionals from at least two disciplines (e.g., psychology, special education, regular education, and physical therapy) must participate in the assessment.

Many assessment experts recommend a transdisciplinary evaluation as the most thorough and effective means of identifying young children's strengths and needs. As was discussed in Chapter 10, in transdisciplinary assessment, a team of professionals from several disciplines reaches a consensus regarding the unique combination of methods and procedures necessary to assess a child. In practice, the collaborative, transdisciplinary approach reduces overlap of assessment and intervention services because the focus of the assessment is to collect information specifically for the purpose of writing the child's personalized service plan. For example, within the transdisciplinary model, professionals from different disciplines collaborate to obtain the information necessary to plan the child's services.

The transdisciplinary model differs from the more traditional multidisciplinary team assessment in that, within the multidisciplinary model, professionals from each discipline conduct their own assessment independently and without regard for the assessments of other professionals. Because there is naturally occurring overlap among test activities across developmental domains (e.g., language, cognition, and motor domains), there also is overlap in the assessments. For example, a psychologist and a speech-language pathologist would both be interested in a child's ability to respond to the question "What is a cow?" While the speech-language pathologist may be assessing the child's ability to use language to express herself, the psychologist is likely to be interested in the maturity of the child's cognitive abilities. Rather than asking the child the question twice, as would occur in a multidisciplinary assessment, within the transdisciplinary model one of these professionals administers the items and the two then work together to interpret the child's responses.

Multicultural Considerations in Assessment. Families from diverse cultures pose special challenges at this stage in the intervention process. Many of the tests and procedures commonly used to determine a child's developmental and cognitive abilities have been criticized by families, teachers, and psychologists as being biased against ethnic and minority groups. For example, opponents of IQ tests frequently invoke the argument that they measure only skills and abilities valued by the dominant, Western culture and, therefore, children from non-Western or nondominant cultures may be at a unique disadvantage. Test bias is a complex issue, in part simply because we cannot conceive of the number of behaviors and mental processes that we might actually be measuring. For example, in some cultures, children convey respect by acting subdued around adults, especially strangers. Thus, when they are tested, these children may hold back meaningful interaction with their examiners. In such instances, the professionals may never obtain a clear idea of these children's potential or areas of need. Other researchers have found that children who are aware that they are being tested perform better than children who are oblivious to the situational demands of formal testing. Obviously, some cultures—particularly the mainstream culture of the United States—have more experience than others in test situations. Simply stated, a child's cultural experiences may dramatically interact with the testing session. Therefore, the intervention professional should ask some difficult but necessary questions. Have children been referred for early intervention because of an objectively determined real need, or because of a value judgment on the part of social service professionals? Are screening and assessment instruments appropriate to the child's language and cultural background? Are families included in the assessment procedure or are they excluded? Are opportunities provided for reassessment?

Although many service delivery systems still adhere to a one-size-fits-all assessment protocol, a number of researchers and practitioners advocate that assessment be customized to reflect the unique needs, concerns, and priorities of the child and family (Sattler, 1992). Customizing assessment communicates to the family that its cultural differences will be recognized and honored throughout the entire intervention process.

Step 2: The Individualized Service Plan

What Are Individualized Service Plans?

Once a child's needs and the family's strengths, concerns, and priorities have been identified, the intervention plan is outlined in detail. The program plan for most children age 3 and older is called an Individualized Educational Plan (IEP). For infants and toddlers, service goals are outlined in an Individualized Family Service Plan (IFSP). Although most children older than 3 years receive services based on an IEP, federal law does allow states to use IFSPs for preschoolers, and to use IEPs for 2-year-olds who will undergo transitions into preschool programs within the year. IEPs and IFSPs are legal documents, required by IDEA, and the law is very specific regarding their contents. The specific elements of IEPs and IFSPs required by IDEA are outlined in Figures 11.1 and 11.2, and the following paragraphs briefly compare and contrast the two types of program plans. (For a more thorough discussion of IEPs, IFSPs, and the legal requirements for program planning, refer to Chapter 1.)

Similarities Between IEPs and IFSPs. As Figures 11.1 and 11.2 indicate, both IEPs and IFSPs are statements of specific goals and objectives for providing services to children. To this end, both types of plans require that the specific serv-

FIGURE 11.1 Elements of an Individualized Family Service Plan

1. A statement of the child's current functioning in the following areas:
   a. physical development
   b. cognitive development
   c. language development
   d. psychosocial development
   e. self-help skills or adaptive behavior
2. A description of the family's resources, priorities, and concerns.
3. The outcomes expected to be achieved as a result of intervention for the child and family. This should include the criteria that will be used to determine success, time lines for attaining goals, and whether modifications or revisions of the services or outcomes are needed.
4. The specific services—including frequency, intensity, and methods—that will be used to deliver the early intervention services. Also, the specific date that services will begin and the anticipated length of services should be included.
5. A description of where the intervention will take place, including the "natural environments" (i.e., inclusive environments as opposed to specialized clinic or school settings).
6. The name of the service coordinator who is responsible for overseeing the implementation of the plan and coordinating the efforts of various agencies.
7. Anticipated dates when services will begin and end.
8. A statement of the necessary services for the child's successful transition from an early intervention program to a preschool program (from Title I and Title II).

Source: Data from *Birth to Five: Early Childhood Special Education* by F. G. Bowe, 1995, New York: Delmar.

ices the child will receive be identified, along with criteria and procedures that will be used to evaluate the services. Both IEPs and IFSPs specify when the services will begin and how long they are expected to last. In addition, although the wording is somewhat different, both IEPs and IFSPs document the environments in which the services will be provided. Emphasis is placed on providing services in the least restrictive environment (LRE). Placement in a classroom or clinic specifically for children with special needs occurs only when specialized, one-to-one services are deemed necessary to meet the child's educational needs. This is most clearly delineated in the 1997 Amendments to IDEA which require justification when a child does not receive services in a natural setting. Finally, both IEPs and IFSPs contain provisions for making transitions to the next phase of the child's life.

Differences Between IEPs and IFSPs. Although there are many similarities between IEPs and IFSPs, there also are several important differences. Some differences seem minor but have important implications for the ways services are provided. For example, although both plans contain a statement of the child's current functioning,

FIGURE 11.2 Elements of an Individualized Educational Plan for Young Children

1. A description of the current educational performance of the child.
2. Annual goals and short-term instructional objectives.
3. Which specific educational services will be provided to the child.
4. The extent to which the child will be able to participate in regular educational classrooms or activities.
5. When the services will begin, and how long they are expected to last.
6. Objective criteria, evaluation procedures, and schedules for determining whether objectives are being achieved.

Source: Data from *Birth to Five: Early Childhood Special Education* by F. G. Bowe, 1995, New York: Delmar.

IEPs address only educational performance while IFSPs require a broader statement of the child's overall development. This means that IFSPs address the family's concerns, resources, and priorities, as well as five specific domains of child functioning: physical development, cognitive development, language development, psychosocial development, and self-help skills. Because IEPs place less emphasis on the family, only characteristics describing the individual child are included.

Another difference relates to the way program goals are specified. IEPs must include specific short-term objectives, while IFSPs can be more general, including the outcomes that are expected but not specific goals and objectives. In contrast to IEPs, IFSPs allow that early intervention services for infants younger than 3 years may begin before specific details of the program are completed. IFSPs also provide for evaluation of objectives every 6 months rather than annually, as is required for IEPs. These provisions acknowledge the rapid development of infants and the importance of immediate intervention.

Family Involvement in Program Planning. One important difference between IEPs and IFSPs is that professionals are required by law to address families' resources, strengths, and priorities when they are providing early intervention services (usually based on IFSPs) to children younger than 3 years. The implications of this difference for the way services are provided are substantial and reflect fundamental differences in the underlying philosophies of intervention. While the law allows IEPs to include instruction for parents, such instruction is not mandated or even emphasized. However, because IFSPs focus on the family's resources, strengths, and priorities, the plan should specify goals that are designed to build on the family's strengths in order to maximize child functioning.

The omnipresence of the family in the early intervention process highlights the need for the professional to work effectively with family members. As a first step in establishing a family-professional partnership, Lynch and Hanson (1993) suggest that the intervention professional learn culture-specific information about the various groups living in the family's immediate community. With the help of a cultural mediator or community guide, the professional can learn and recognize the family's patterns, beliefs, and practices. Such information is important in discerning which aspects of the family's involvement in the child's intervention result from personal preferences, lack of information, or cultural differences. In fact, what mainstream America views as passive indifference may be considered active, valid participation in some families and cultures (Lynch & Hanson, 1993). However, even if a family is perceived to be totally uninvolved in the planning process, the interventionist should never discount or exclude the family from the decision-making process. To ensure optimal parental participation during program planning meetings, the professional should follow these guidelines:

> - Encourage the family to bring people important to them, including clergy, friends, and relatives.
> - Adapt the meeting to meet the cultural comfort level of the family members. For some families, this may mean holding several preliminary meetings to get to know each member of the family and transdisciplinary team.
> - Be aware that some families may feel intimidated by American bureaucracy. As a result, they may feel uncomfortable contributing in a formal meeting. In these cases, the professional should meet with the family beforehand and be prepared to present the family's perspective to others on the transdisciplinary team. The professional also should anticipate and answer the questions that the family may not even know to ask.
> - Ensure that the goals, objectives, and outcomes are embedded in the family's culture and reflect the family's own perceived needs and priorities.
> - Make use of resources in the community, especially individuals and groups that may share the family's language, unique experiences, and culture. (Lynch & Hanson, 1993, p. 365)

It also is important to note that different families perceive early intervention differently, and their attitudes have a direct impact on the level of family involvement. For some families, the very idea of intervention may be foreign or unacceptable. One of the major tacit assumptions of early intervention is that circumstances for the child and family will change for the better. Some families, especially those new to this country, may resist change and perceive intervention efforts as a threat to the integrity of the family unit. Even families who have been in the United States for generations may perceive an interventionist's well-intended efforts as meddling. If the family has members who are undocumented immigrants, they may even fear the service provider.

Frequently, a family's attitude toward intervention is directly related to its perceptions of handicapping conditions and causation. Hanson, Lynch, and Wayman (1990) found that family perceptions of disabilities fall on a wide continuum, with some families emphasizing the role of fate and other families directly assigning responsibility to family members, essentially blaming themselves for their child's handicap. For example, Vietnamese families often perceive a child's handicap as a stroke of fate, and they resist intervention as being futile (Green, 1982). Other cultures may view a handicap as punishment for past sins, and in some Native American cultures it is thought that the child makes a prenatal choice to be born disabled. By understanding and honoring such cultural differences, the professional may avoid misunderstandings and engender a positive partnership with the child's most important resource: the family.

Who Writes Individualized Service Plans? Individualized service plans, both IFSPs and IEPs, are developed through a collaboration of a child's parents and at least two early intervention professionals. In addition to the child's parents, team members may include other family members (e.g., grandparents or siblings) or individuals designated by the family, a parent advocate, service coordinator, evaluators, and interventionists. For IEPs, the 1997 Amendments to IDEA expanded the number of team members by requiring participation of the special education teacher, the regular education teacher, where appropriate, a person who can interpret the educational implications of evaluation results, and other individuals, at the discretion of the parent or agency, who have expertise relative to the child's needs. For example, a team that is writing a program plan for a child with cerebral palsy would probably include a physical therapist, while a physical therapist might not be needed for a child whose primary problem is speech and language. A wide range of disciplines provide services in early intervention and may be involved in writing IEPs and IFSPs. Team members can include but are not limited to professionals in the areas of audiology, education, medicine, nursing, nutrition, occupational therapy, physical therapy, psychology, social work, special education, and speech-language therapy.

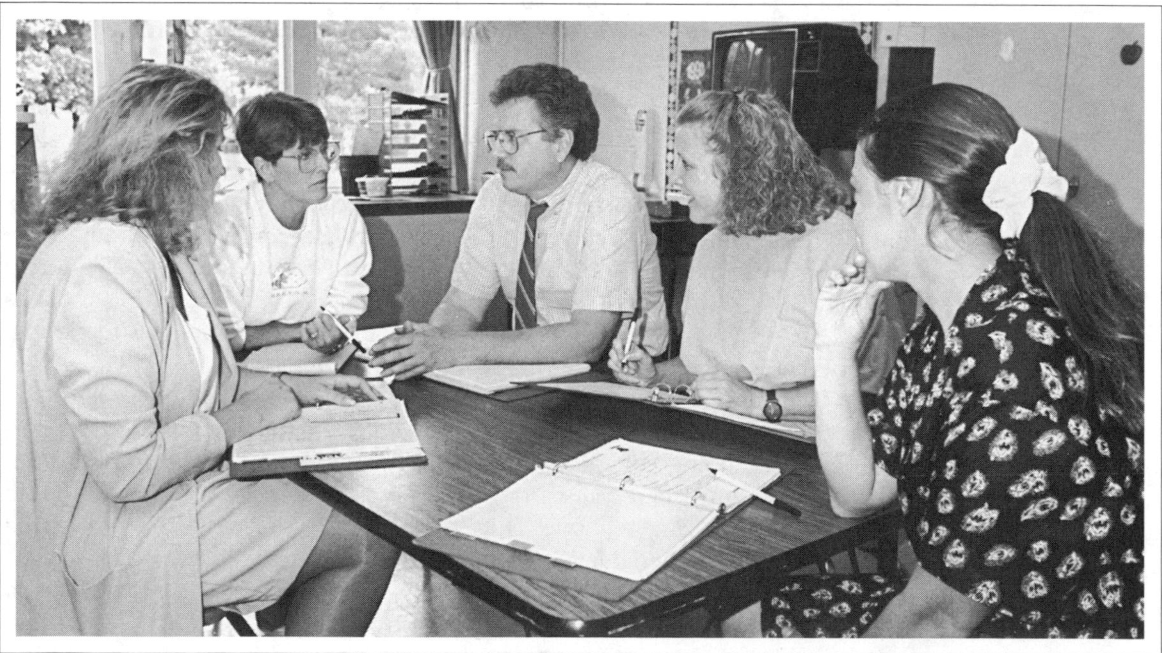

IEPs and IFSPs are developed through collaboration of a child's parents and early intervention professionals.

When Are Individualized Service Plans Written? According to IDEA, an IEP or IFSP should be written within 45 days of a child's being referred for services. Typically, the plan is written at a meeting of the child's parents and the professionals who will work with them. This first official meeting can be very important in that it represents the beginning of the child's involvement with the educational system and, as such, sets the tone for later interactions between parents and professionals. The goal of the meeting is for parents and professionals to agree to a plan of services for the next year (or 6 months, for children under 3 years). This agreement is formalized by all members of the planning team—most importantly the parents—when they sign the written document.

How Are Individualized Service Plans Written? Clearly, an individualized service plan is a very important document in that it determines the nature and level of services that a child will receive. All too often, however, busy professionals view IEPs and IFSPs as nothing more than paperwork to be gotten out of the way. When this attitude is assumed, the writing of the service plan is not taken seriously, which results in a document with little utility and a program of services that has not been well thought out. Because the writing of the service plan has such important implications for effective intervention, strategies for writing practical goals and objectives are described next.

Linking Assessment and Intervention. Goals and objectives of a service plan are framed from the information gathered from the assessment. Thus, the starting point for writing the service plan is the report from the transdisciplinary team evaluation. When thinking about appropriate goals, the team not only should consider the child's needs or areas of weakness, but also should endeavor to create a document that reflects the family's resources and concerns. As each goal is considered, intervention strategies are generated that build on the child's and family's strengths. Effective service plans contain information that enables the team to identify those strengths and resources that can be used to address deficits.

Writing Goals. Goals are intended to describe in practical detail exactly what a child is expected to accomplish within the next 6 months (for IFSPs) or year (for IEPs). They represent observable, incremental steps to intended outcomes, including the maximal degree of participation in natural environments and in a typical curriculum. Although the process may seem straightforward, many professionals find that writing appropriate, helpful goals is among their most difficult tasks. In many respects, the goals of the IEP and IFSP are identical; the basic sequence for establishing and selecting goals is the same for both documents. The fundamental difference is that goals written for the IFSP include family as well as child-centered outcomes. By asking the following questions, professionals increase the likelihood that the goals they write for any service plan will be accomplished and will result in positive changes for the child and family.

1. Were the parents involved in a meaningful way in formulating the goal statements? To ensure optimal parental involvement in program implementation, the goals of the IEP and IFSP must reflect the priorities and concerns of the family. Parents are more likely to participate in early intervention in a meaningful way if the goals of intervention are meaningful to the family. Professionals must be careful not to project their own values and choices onto the family but to address only concerns that are identified by the family (Bailey, 1988). Moreover, goals must consider the unique strengths and limitations of each family member. Child-rearing is a complex task, and certain aspects of caring for a child with special needs may be particularly difficult for some families. For example, many low-socioeconomic-status families struggle with a host of day-to-day survival problems stemming from poverty. Such conditions may make some long-range goals of the individualized plan unattainable. If families are struggling to meet basic survival needs, they will be unable to plan for the future. Therefore, family problems, such as unemployment and lack of adequate clothing and food, need to be incorporated into individualized plans.

Before service plans can target families' needs, professionals and families must work together to identify and prioritize areas for intervention. This process, known in early intervention as family assessment, is crucial to the success of intervention. A number of instruments and techniques have been developed to facilitate the assessment of family needs and priorities. Ideally, professionals use several methods of obtaining information about families' needs and priorities, including interviews and questionnaires.

2. Are the goals functional and age appropriate? Goals and objectives always should be embedded in the functional activities within a child's social system and environment; that is, goals and objectives must be useful. After all, the purpose of early intervention is to enhance children's functioning within the context of their family and environment. Therefore, in relation to the goals of intervention, it is important to include only those activities that will lead to improved functioning in the environment. Obviously, this means considering a child's overall environment as well as the child's specific characteristics. Further, if a child's impairment limits participation in regular educational or social settings, then the intervention plan should be geared toward helping the child move into the most naturalistic environment possible. This means helping to ensure that children in self-contained settings are working toward moving into regular classrooms.

Functional goals also are designed to help make caring for a child easier for the family. For example, in the case of a young girl with fine motor impairments (i.e., problems using her hands), one functional goal might address her ability to help dress herself. On the other hand, a nonfunctional goal might involve working to improve the time it takes her to complete a pegboard. While the second goal may serve to increase her experiences in the fine motor domain, it will have at best a remote relationship to the greater goal of helping her learn to function independently.

3. Are the goals realistic? Goals must be attainable given the specific strengths of a child and the demands of the environment. Achievable goals serve to increase the autonomy of the child and family by improving the caregiver's sense of self-efficacy.

If expectations go unrealized because they were unrealistic, family members may interpret this as evidence of their failure. Worse, if the family of a child with special needs consistently believes that no progress is being made, the family may become either isolated and discouraged about social services or overly dependent on them.

One way to avoid setting goals that are unrealistic is to establish long-term goals as well as short-term objectives. Long-term goals acknowledge family members' dreams for their child and can serve to keep intervention efforts in line with the family's priorities across several years. Short-term objectives, on the other hand, act to keep intervention efforts in the present and help keep families and professionals from becoming discouraged or overwhelmed by goals that may require years of effort before they are realized.

The process of breaking a goal into its component parts is called *task analysis*. Once the family and interventionists have identified a child's current level of functioning and their goals, the next step is task analysis. In this step, every skill necessary to accomplish the ultimate goal is identified. If necessary, these skills may be broken into subskills until the tasks seem manageable. To gain an appreciation for the process of task analysis, consider a simple activity that you do every day, such as brushing your teeth. Next, think about all the steps involved in this seemingly simple routine. First you must find and pick up the toothpaste, then unscrew the cap. Next, you may pick up your toothbrush and then squeeze the toothpaste with the other hand, and so on. Most of us can complete such tasks with a minimum of mental and physical effort, but for a child with fine motor impairment, each step may require intensive preparation and practice.

4. Does the goal account for all levels of learning? The process of learning a new skill can be conceptualized as progressing through five phases: acquisition, fluency, maintenance, generalization, and adaptation (Haring, Whilte, & Liberty, 1980 in Wolery, 1989). Acquisition is the most basic level of learning and means that a child can successfully complete the basic requirements of a skill. Fluency refers to the child's ability to complete the task smoothly and quickly. Maintenance and generalization are related in that maintenance refers to the child's performance of the skill in settings similar to the training situation, while generalization refers to the child's ability to perform the skill in settings different from the training situation. Adaptation represents the highest level of achievement because it reflects the child's ability to modify the skill to fit environmental demands or conditions. All too often, intervention goals stop at the level of acquisition, in that once a child demonstrates accurate task completion, the goal is considered to have been attained. This, however, does not ensure that the child will be able to use the new skill in other settings or that it will actually improve the child's day-to-day functioning. Therefore, Wolery (1989) recommends including goals that address all of these levels of learning.

Step 3: Implementation of Intervention

Once goals have been written, they must be implemented. Intervention implementation involves translating goals and intended outcomes into a planned program of activities. Just as service plans are individualized blueprints for service delivery, the implementation process likewise is unique for each child. Two children may have an identical goal, but the implementation of services to achieve this goal will likely be quite different, depending on each child's unique circumstances and the philosophies and resources of the programs providing the services.

Identifying Resources. The first step in implementation is to identify all the resources needed to accomplish the desired goals and outcomes detailed in the service plan. Resources can take many different forms but always are the tools of the trade for the interventionist. Although the law mandates that a child's needs—not the agency's resources—dictate the services provided, the manner in which a child's needs are addressed is likely to vary according to the resources available.

Family Resources. The most significant resource for a child is the primary caregiver (Gutkin & Curtis, 1990). As such, the caregiver's resources and priorities must be taken into account as intervention is implemented. For example, if the primary caregiver does not have reliable transportation, intervention involving clinic-based therapy is doomed to failure unless the problem of getting the child to the clinic is addressed. Also, the caregiver's resources should be reassessed periodically as family circumstances change. Many unforeseen events can interfere with or enhance family members' ability to support or participate in their child's intervention. Negative events (e.g., illness, sudden unemployment, or a car needing repair) may cause a sudden shift in the family's priorities and necessitate a change in the manner in which services are provided to a child. Likewise, positive events (e.g., extended family members moving nearby or a job promotion) may enable the family to assume additional responsibilities.

In identifying the family's resources, it also is important for the interventionist to understand the family's developmental stage and its impact on perceptions of the child's special needs (Turnbull & Turnbull, 1986). Life-cycle theorists point out that all families go through a series of developmental stages that influence family functioning and needs. Normal life events, such as the birth of a new child or a change in employment, affect in a profound way the family's psychological and material resources. Therefore, it is important for professionals to remain flexible and sensitive to the family's changing needs and resources as they implement intervention.

Professional Resources. To avoid having services provided to a child in a piecemeal fashion or in isolation, the critical task of implementing professional recommendations and treatment must be coordinated by a single person, who is usually known as the service coordinator. The responsibility of the service coordinator is to work with a child's primary caregiver in the integration of intervention services. The importance of a service coordinator is particularly pronounced for children who have multiple needs or whose families are struggling with multiple stressors.

Because program implementation is the most active component of the intervention process, it is also the stage at which a family's cultural differences become most apparent. Any misunderstandings related to the professional-parental collaboration are likely to manifest themselves during implementation. One way to avoid these misunderstandings is through the involvement of community guides. Community guides are respected individuals who are familiar with a family's cultural norms, attitudes, traditions, and perceptions. They may or may not be members of the transdisciplinary team, depending on the wishes of the family. Community guides may be religious leaders, interpreters, elders, or business leaders. They provide the interventionist insight into community norms and expectations and ensure that resources within a family's community are identified and utilized in a meaningful way.

Next, intervention professionals must be identified and their efforts coordinated with those of the primary caregiver. Depending on the needs of a child, these professional resource people may include psychologists, teachers, speech pathologists, physical and occupational therapists, audiologists, physicians, dietitians, or social workers. Within the community, professional resource people may be identified through local schools, day-care programs, Head Start, mental health organizations, governmental agencies, or private nonprofit groups. For the purposes of this discussion, four categories of professional resources are considered: medical, allied health, mental health, and educational resources.

Medical Professionals. For many children with disabilities, particularly those with severe or multiple disabilities, their problems are associated with medical conditions and are usually identified at or not long after birth. In some cases, this identification is made prenatally through amniocentesis, sonograms, or other medical techniques. Families of such children find themselves immediately involved with medical professionals. If a child's condition is identified at birth, it is likely that the child's first physician will be a neonatalogist, a physician who specializes in the care and treatment of newborns.

For most children, however, the primary health care provider is a pediatrician or pediatric nurse practitioner. Depending on a child's particular health care needs, the child may be involved with many types of medical specialists. Some specialists commonly encountered by young children with disabilities include pulmonologists (respiratory system), neurologists (nervous system), orthopedists (skeletal and muscular systems), cardiologists (heart and circulatory system), endocrinologists (endocrine system), and so forth. For children with multiple medical needs, pediatricians often assume the role of medical service coordinators. For nonmedical interventionists such as teachers and psychologists, pediatricians can be an important resource and should be viewed as colleagues in the development of intervention plans for children.

Nurses also are an important professional resource for many children with disabilities. A number of medical conditions require around-the-clock care or frequent medical procedures. Because of financial considerations and families' needs to resume their normal lives, many children, particularly those born prematurely, are released from the hospital with ongoing needs for medical intervention. These children are likely to receive home-based nursing care. In many instances, the nurse becomes one of the primary care providers and, as such, a vital agent of intervention.

Allied Health Professionals. Included in this category are specialized therapists, including speech-language pathologists (SLPs), occupational therapists (OTs), and physical therapists (PTs). As their name implies, SLPs are concerned with disorders related to communication and oral-motor problems. Many young children with disabilities have difficulties with receptive or expressive language that can be addressed by SLPs. In addition, SLPs work with children who have normal language abilities but have difficulty communicating because of unclear speech. There also are SLPs who specialize in the oral-motor structures involved in speech and eating and may be called upon for children with feeding difficulties or structural deformities (e.g., cleft palate) that interfere primarily with eating and speaking.

Physical and occupational therapists are similar in that both are concerned with motor abilities. As a general rule, however, the two professionals can be distinguished by the fact that PTs are primarily concerned with large muscle groups, or gross motor activities, such as walking, sitting, and jumping, while OTs typically address small muscle groups, or fine motor activities, such as writing and tying shoes. OTs also are called upon to assist with daily living tasks and, along with specially trained SLPs, address feeding problems.

Depending on the specialized needs of a child, the expertise of other allied health professionals also may be required. For example, a child with visual impairments may receive services from a vision specialist, who will assess the degree and developmental impact of vision loss, provide early mobility training, and recommend specialized equipment (Correa & Morsink, 1995). Similarly, audiologists and specialists in educational programming for children who are deaf work with children with hearing impairments.

Mental Health Professionals. Families of children with disabilities are likely to encounter a number of mental health professionals as a result of their involvement with early intervention and various forms of social services. Psychologists are likely to be involved in the initial assessment of a child and often are called upon to provide estimates of children's cognitive abilities. Beyond the assessment phase of intervention, psychologists may provide grief counseling services or therapy to address specific problems (e.g., child behavior problems).

Social workers are another type of mental health professional likely to work with families of children with special needs. Social workers' unique understanding of social services and agencies make them a natural choice as service coordinators. Even if social workers are not designated as service coordinators, they often play a vital role in helping a family gain access to social services. Additionally, social workers may provide counseling, parent training, and other mental health services, as their training, interests, and job responsibilities permit.

Educational Professionals. Perhaps the most common professional resource in early intervention is the early childhood educator. Two distinct types of educators can be identified: early childhood educators (ECEs) and early childhood special educators (ECSEs). Whether a child is served primarily by an ECE or ECSE depends in large part on the setting in which services are provided. ECEs commonly work with typically developing preschoolers, usually in a classroom-based early childhood setting. ECSEs, on the other hand, specialize in working with infants and young children with disabilities.

In addition to the different settings in which they work, ECEs and ECSEs are considered to have different philosophies and techniques for working with children. ECEs are more likely to adhere to cognitive models of development, emphasizing developmentally appropriate practices, while ECSEs rely more heavily on behavioral techniques to teach specific skills and behaviors to children with atypical or delayed development (Black & Puckett, 1996). Despite this traditional split among education professionals, as more children with special needs are served in regular educational settings, educators are being called upon to deal with all types of children. Thus, the traditional gap between ECEs and ECSEs may begin to narrow.

Setting Resources. The place where a child with special needs receives services has become a topic of great interest in the past several years. Traditionally, children with special needs of all ages have received educational and therapeutic services in relative isolation. For example, a young child with cerebral palsy might have received educational services in a "preschool class for handicapped children" and received PT services in the therapist's office, rarely if ever interacting with typically developing peers. However, in recent years, the trend toward serving children with special needs in regular settings has gained momentum. The continuum of setting options ranging from clinic- or school-based self-contained classrooms to fully normalized settings is described next.

Self-Contained Settings. Self-contained classrooms are the traditional setting for special education services. Placement in such settings has been based on the assumption that a child's disability prevented her from benefiting from standard classrooms and necessitated intensive, one-to-one instruction (Odom & McEvoy, 1990). Reviews of the research suggest possible advantages of such classrooms for some students, particularly those with severe disabilities such as deafness or autism (Heward, 1996). Similarly, other therapies (e.g., occupational, physical, and speech-language therapy) have traditionally been conducted in isolation, often in hospital-based or clinic settings.

Within the context of self-contained placements, a technique known as reverse mainstreaming has been used to increase contact between children with disabilities and their typically developing peers. With this technique, children without disabilities are brought into the special education classroom or therapy session for varying amounts of time.

Normalized Settings. Federal law requires that intervention be provided in the least restrictive environment (LRE) possible. For infants and toddlers, this often means that services are provided in the child's home. Home-based intervention consists of an interventionist (e.g., an ECSE, SLP, PT, or OT) visiting a child's home on a weekly or biweekly basis, depending on the child's needs and IFSP or IEP goals, and providing direct therapy to the child and consultation with the care providers.

Depending on a family's needs and the age of a child, early intervention services also may be provided in the context of regular child-care settings, such as preschools or day-care centers. In such cases, an interventionist may be called upon to assume a number of roles. For example, an SLP may work with a group of children, only one of whom has a disability, in a day-care classroom. An SLP also may function as a consultant to the regular teachers or assistants. A number of advantages have been identified for this type of service delivery (McWilliam & Bailey, 1994); most notably, by including intervention in a child's regular routine, the child is more likely to use the skills in everyday life. An additional advantage is that the skills addressed are more likely to be functional in nature. However, as the most appropriate setting for providing intervention services is determined, a number of factors must be taken into account. Within the context of family-centered intervention services, the family's preferences must be accommodated to as great a degree as possible, and the decision regarding the setting for service delivery must be made on a case-by-case basis.

For selecting the intervention setting, Bailey and McWilliam (1990) identify two primary considerations: effectiveness and normalization. Effectiveness refers to the intersection between a child's characteristics and environmental demands; that is, given a child's individual characteristics, what is the most effective means of reaching the goals identified by the family? If, for example, the family's priority is that the child develop social skills, the most effective intervention is likely to be in a regular classroom. If, on the other hand, the family identifies learning sign language as the priority, this may best be accomplished in a self-contained classroom for children with hearing impairments.

The Debate Surrounding Inclusion. Few professionals, parents, or individuals with disabilities would dispute that the goal of early intervention and special education is to enable children with special needs to participate fully in all the settings and environments enjoyed by those without special needs. This principle also is reflected in federal law. However, over the past several years, a debate has arisen in special education and related fields as some parents and professionals have begun to call for full inclusion of all children. Although a range of definitions exists, advocates for full inclusion have defined an inclusive school as "a place where everybody belongs, is accepted, supports, and is supported by his or her peers and other members of the school community in the course of having his or her educational needs met" (Stainback & Stainback, 1992, p. 3). Further, within such a school, all types of children learn together, without regard for the nature or severity of their disabilities. Stainback and Stainback argue that, because children with special needs receive services from special educators, regular educators have begun to view special education as a dumping ground for "undesirable" children or children with problems. The only way to correct this, they argue, is to abolish special education completely.

While the ideal of providing support for and acceptance of individuals with disabilities in all settings is appealing, some professionals worry that a small group within the educational community has gone too far on this issue (Fuchs & Fuchs,

1994). By arguing for full inclusion of children with disabilities, the more extreme advocates of inclusion also are calling for the abolition of the range of special services for children with special needs. Other professionals fear not only that such a move is unrealistic, but also that it would threaten the quality of the education that could be obtained by children with special needs.

Clearly, the issues are complex and philosophical, and the debate is likely to be waged for some time. Whether or not schools and the ways in which children with special needs are educated are radically reformed remains to be seen. In the meantime, the Council for Exceptional Children (CEC), the major organization devoted to the education of children with special needs, has issued a middle-of-the-road position statement. The CEC supports inclusion as a meaningful goal but advocates a continuum of services, ranging from full inclusion to specialized settings (Heward, 1996). At this point in the debate, young children and their families are probably best served by professionals who are able to put their own positions on the issue aside and assume a pragmatic approach when developing service plans. Consistent with a family-focused view of early intervention, the setting in which each child receives services should be an individual decision based on the goals and priorities identified by the family.

Developing a Strategy. Once the resources have been identified and the setting selected, the next salient issue is how to use these resources to facilitate the

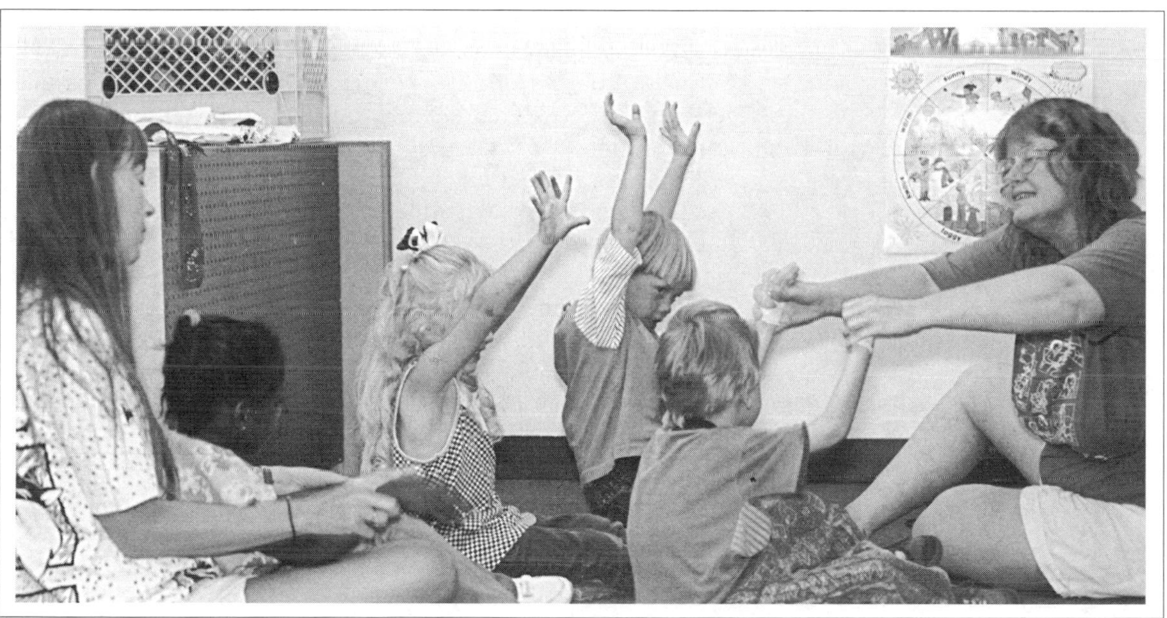

Whenever possible, children with special needs should participate fully in settings enjoyed by children without special needs.

child's optimal development within the framework of the service plan. An instructional, therapeutic strategy is required. Several researchers (Barnett & Carey, 1992; Bricker & Cripe, 1992) suggest that a naturalistic, activity-based approach is the best strategy for program implementation. Naturalistic intervention incorporates environmental variables into service delivery, and training goals are embedded in daily routines. Naturalistic, activity-based intervention is preferred for several reasons. First, intervention is most likely to be successful if it is linked to the caregiver's current living situation. Bricker (1989) reminds us that "the family situation itself dictates where, when, how, and in what areas to begin intervention" (p. 165). Second, skills acquired in naturalistic settings are most likely to generalize to different environments. Generalization of skills is best served by "providing the least artificial, least cumbersome, and most natural positive consequences in programming intervention. Such programming most closely matches naturally occurring consequences" (Stokes & Osnes, 1989, p. 341). Third, naturalistic intervention strategies emphasize the competency and involvement of caregivers. Finally, a naturalistic, activities-based approach ensures that targeted goals and outcomes are likely to be functionally appropriate and valued by the child and family.

Within the structure of naturalistic intervention, short-term, measurable objectives can facilitate the acquisition of new skills. Hanson (1987) advocates task analysis in the teaching of such objectives. Again, in task analysis, a target behavior is first identified and then broken down into a series of smaller tasks required to achieve the target. For example, a target behavior for an infant might be to roll over from her back to her front. The series of behaviors leading to successful completion of the target behavior might be that (a) the infant extends her arm to one side and rolls her shoulders, (b) the infant shifts her leg to align with her shoulders, and (c) the infant completes the roll by turning over to her front. While the primary focus is on the target behavior, task analysis methods also provide the child and family with insight into the process of learning. Moreover, the emphasis on measurable objectives facilitates program evaluation.

Bricker (1989) recommends a combination of home-based and center-based implementation strategies. Home-based strategies are frequently used with infants up to age 3 years. As described earlier in this chapter, professionals visit the home on a regular basis and help the caregiver implement the selected treatments and activities. The advantages of home-based strategies are obvious: Parental involvement is increased and the interventionist is afforded the opportunity to observe parent-child interaction. In addition, home visits become training sessions for the parent.

Center-based models, on the other hand, rely on structured classroom activities and are usually employed with children above age 3 years. Head Start is an example of an intervention program that uses a center-based strategy. Center-based programs may include only children with special needs (self-contained setting) or children both with and without disabilities (inclusive or mainstreamed setting). Although preschools vary in terms of their philosophies, they typically stress the acquisition of developmental, cognitive, social, and self-help skills necessary for success in elementary school.

Center-based models and strategies also afford a child a new setting for practicing skills acquired in the home. A child's ability to generalize skills across settings is crucial for successful transition to new, less restrictive environments. For the family, center-based models also provide the opportunity to interact with other parents as well as needed respite from the child.

Philosophical Approaches and Developmental Theories. One of the crucial ways in which early intervention programs differ from one another is reflected by differences in their philosophical orientations. Early intervention relies on a rich history of developmental theory. Although no one school or theory is right or wrong, different developmental theories support different models of intervention. In addition, different programs focus on different areas of development, based on their underlying theories.

To be effective, intervention should be based on an underlying developmental theory. Not only are programs guided by the theoretical perspectives on which they are based, but professionals working with children and families also are influenced by their own varying beliefs about the ways children develop and the best ways to effect change, which are in turn influenced by their theoretical or philosophical perspectives. Given this central role of developmental theory in intervention, the following paragraphs briefly describe three of the most prevalent theoretical perspectives: those based on developmental, behavioral, and contextual models.

Developmental Models. Developmental models emphasize a child's biological make-up and maturation and are based largely on the theories of Piaget, Dewey, and Erikson. Intervention based on such models rests upon the assumption that development occurs along a natural course internal to a child. As the child encounters new and different experiences, she feels dissatisfied with her current means of solving problems and is motivated to accommodate new information and new ways of thinking.

Interventionists who adhere to developmental models believe that children are internally motivated to explore and master the world around them. For example, Piaget described young children as little scientists who explore the world around them through active manipulation (Bowe, 1995a). Further, this model maintains that the best and most efficient way for children to learn is through hands-on experiences and interactions with the material world. The role of the interventionist, then, is to provide experiences and create environments that support and facilitate a child's individual, self-directed growth. Jerome Bruner describes this process as "discovery learning," whereby children are their own teachers in an environment structured to encourage exploration (Bowe, 1995a).

Professionals who adhere to developmental models such as those based on Piaget's theories often refer to their philosophy as *developmentally appropriate practice* (DAP). Developmental appropriateness refers both to age appropriateness (i.e., the predictable pattern and stages of development described by theorists such as Piaget and Erikson) and to an individual child's pattern of development (Black

& Puckett, 1996). Montessori programs are often cited as examples of programs for young children that adhere to this definition of DAP. As the name suggests, Montessori programs are based on the work of Maria Montessori, an educator who worked in Rome in the early twentieth century. Montessori methods include ungraded classrooms, instruction individualized to meet each child's unique educational needs, material that is ordered sequentially to reflect stages of development, and an absence of punishment (Richmond & Ayoub, 1993).

Behavioral Models. These models are based on the structured principles of behavioral psychology. Unlike developmental models, behavioral models deemphasize the internal motivations of the individual. Instead, specific target behaviors are identified and taught using reinforcement, shaping, and modeling. In its simplest form, behavioral theory relies on the principles of reward and punishment: If a child is rewarded for a behavior, the child is likely to repeat the behavior, while punishing a child following a behavior decreases the chances that the behavior will be repeated. In contrast to programs guided by developmental theories, programs guided by behavioral theory typically rely more heavily on direct, one-on-one instruction.

An adaptation of behavioral theory is social learning theory, an approach emphasizing that children learn by observing and imitating. Within this framework, behavior is believed to be changed because of exposure to models. For example, in the case of a child who cannot play appropriately with other children because of her aggressive behavior, intervention based on social learning theory might include having the child watch other children play together without fighting.

Contextual Models. Contextual models emphasize the role of the environment in shaping the development of a young child. Within such models, the roles of family and community, as well as the greater society, are considered. Urie Bronfenbrenner's ecological model is widely used as an intervention framework. Bronfenbrenner suggests that a child, family, community, and larger society can be viewed as concentric circles of influence that all affect the child's development. Similarly, Lev Vygotsky's sociohistorical theory has been used widely with students who have disabilities (Brown, Evans, Weed, & Owen, 1987). This model is sometimes called the functional model because it emphasizes the importance of social context in the acquisition of domestic, vocational, and communication skills that increase a child's self-sufficiency and independence in daily life. As one might expect, intervention based on this model seeks to facilitate the development of strong, supportive social networks for the family of the target child.

Within the contextual model, Sameroff and Chandler (1975) have developed a transactional approach that examines the intersection between characteristics of the individual and the environment. Because of its sensitivity to both dynamics, this approach provides a framework that is particularly relevant to early intervention. In the transactional model, Sameroff and Chandler suggest that development results from a cycle of ongoing, dynamic, and reciprocal interactions between a child and her environment, which includes parents and other caregivers.

By introducing the notion of reciprocal interactions, the transactional model maintains that a child not only is influenced by her environment but also influences her environment. For example, consider a child who was born with health problems that have caused her to be irritable and to cry most of the time. Because the mother is unable to soothe the child, the mother begins to feel that she is a bad parent. Further, because of the negative feelings the mother experiences around her crying baby, she begins to avoid interacting with the child. Consequently, because the mother rarely talks to or interacts with the child, the child's language does not develop as rapidly as it otherwise would, and as a preschooler she is diagnosed with a language delay. Clearly, the child's language delay was not caused by either the mother's or the child's characteristics alone. Instead, the problem resulted from an interaction, or from the series of dynamic transactions, between the child's characteristics and the mother's feelings and behaviors.

Despite the apparent differences among the three broad kinds of models, all share a single, strong commonality: The thread running through all models of intervention and associated theories is that a child is an active, competent, and social organism. Therefore, although there certainly are biological components to a child's development, there also are interactions between the child and the environment that affect both the child's development and the larger social context. Accordingly, a child's developmental outcome is the result of biological constituents, the environment, and transaction between them. Hanson and Lynch (1995) contend that this is a persuasive argument for early intervention that considers every aspect of a child's environment.

Developmental theories guide our understanding of intervention with children and families by helping us to answer two fundamental questions. **Why** do children behave the way they do? **How** do children develop more-mature behaviors? The following example of Jessica LaSenna, a 4-year-old girl who is having trouble getting along with her peers, is presented to illustrate the differences among developmental, behavioral, and contextual theories:

> *Mr. and Ms. LaSenna are concerned because Jessica has recently begun to hit other children in her preschool. The LaSennas asked three child development experts, each with a different theoretical orientation, to explain why Jessica hits other children and to offer solutions for helping her improve her peer relationships.*
>
> *Jake is a developmental (cognitive) theorist, the first child development expert contacted by Mr. and Ms. LaSenna. Jake believes that children's behavior is best understood in the context of their level of cognitive maturation. Therefore, in order to explain Jessica's behavior, Jake wanted to find out more about Jessica's development; that is, what does Jessica understand about the effects of her behaviors? After spending some time watching Jessica and talking with her, her parents, and her teacher, Jake decided that Jessica has been hitting other children because she does not understand that it hurts others when she hits them. Thus, Jake believes that cognitive immaturity, a deficit in the development of her understanding of the environment, explains*

Jessica's poor peer relationships. Jake believes that the best way to help Jessica learn more appropriate ways of interacting with her peers is to address this lack of understanding by first helping her learn to take the perspective of her peers. Jake recommended that Jessica's parents and teacher talk with Jessica about how her choices (hitting versus not hitting) affect others. Additionally, because Jake believes that children learn from their natural interactions with their environment, he also talked with Jessica's teacher about the classroom and ways to structure Jessica's environment so that she learns how to play appropriately.

Karen is a behavioral theorist. Unlike Jake, Karen does not believe that understanding Jessica's internal thought processes is very important for explaining or changing her behavior. Karen chose instead to focus only on the actual behavior (hitting others). She believes that Jessica hits other children because hitting them is rewarding for Jessica in some way. According to Karen, the key to understanding Jessica's behavior, then, is to discover what leads up to and follows her hitting of others. To determine what is causing the hitting behavior, Karen decided to observe Jessica playing with her peers at school. After watching Jessica for several days and recording what leads up to and follows her hitting behavior, Karen decided that Jessica hits other children when they try to play with a toy she wants. Jessica is rewarded for hitting because, after she hits a child, the child leaves and Jessica can play with the toy of her choice. To help Jessica learn more appropriate play skills, Karen recommended that Jessica be rewarded with a sticker when she shares a toy without hitting other children and that she be sent to time-out when she hits others.

Sara is a contextual theorist, the third child development expert contacted by Mr. and Ms. LaSenna. Sara believes that the environment shapes the way a child behaves. In order to understand why Jessica hits other children, Sara wanted to know about Jessica's environment and about the interactions between Jessica's characteristics and her environment. Not only does Sara want to know about Jessica's classroom, but she also wants to know about Jessica's home life. Sara interviewed Jessica's parents and teacher and observed Jessica at home and at school. Sara decided that Jessica hits others because she hasn't learned social interaction skills from her environment. According to Sara, it is important for all of the people in Jessica's social network (e.g., parents, teachers, grandparents, and peers) to help Jessica learn more adaptive ways of dealing with conflict. Sara also emphasized that if Mr. and Ms. LaSenna are anxious or overwhelmed by parenting responsibilities, Jessica may feel upset and act out at school. Therefore, Sara thinks that an important way for Mr. and Ms. LaSenna to help Jessica is to seek some form of social support.

Types of Programs. In addition to having different theoretical orientations, center-based early intervention programs focus on different areas of child development. Some programs develop their focus as a result of their theoretical orientations. For example, preschools based on developmental theories are likely to focus on children's play because of the belief that play is the most effective and developmentally appropriate way to encourage children's development. However, other programs focus on one area of development because they are specifically designed to serve children who demonstrate particular problems (e.g., language problems). Some of the most commonly encountered types of preschool programs, including play-based, academically-oriented, language-based, and social skills-based programs, are described next.

Play-Based Programs. No matter what their theoretical orientations are, most early interventionists believe in developmentally appropriate practice (Heward, 1996) and therefore agree that play is a vital component of every early childhood program. As the name implies, play-based early intervention programs recognize that children learn best through play. Preschools adhering to this philosophy typically are child-directed, meaning that children are encouraged to select their own activities. By creating a rich learning environment, teachers facilitate development through manipulation of materials and through children's interactions with each other and with adults. Most play-based classrooms are organized around centers (e.g., a housekeeping center, block center, and art center), and children are allowed to rotate among the activities at their own pace.

Academically-Oriented Programs. In contrast to play-based models, there also are traditional, academically-oriented preschools. Academically-oriented preschools strive to teach preacademic skills and prepare children for school. Rather than children being allowed to choose their own activities, as occurs in play-based preschools, children in academically-oriented preschools spend most of their time engaged in teacher-directed activities. Often, these activities involve seatwork or circle time, in which the entire class gathers around the teacher for a lesson. Although some preschoolers may be able to cope with the demands of such a structured setting, most experts in child development agree that large-group activities and teacher-directed programming do not reflect developmentally appropriate practice and are not an efficient way to facilitate the cognitive, language, social, or motor development of young children.

Language-Based Programs. One of the most important developmental tasks of the preschool years is learning language. Language deficits are among the developmental difficulties most frequently encountered by early intervention professionals. For this reason, many preschools are designed specifically to address language deficits. Language-based preschools employ a number of techniques to encourage the use of language, and they often utilize environmental factors, such as the types of toys that are available, to encourage children to use language adaptively. For example, rather than having a large number of toys that encourage solitary play (e.g., puzzles), language-based preschools are likely to contain more social toys (e.g., dramatic play materials and games that require talking or turn taking). Teachers also may wish to set up language-based classrooms in such a way that children are encouraged to ask for help. For example, the most desirable toys may be kept on out-of-reach shelves so that children are motivated to ask for assistance.

Heward (1996) identifies two approaches for systematically promoting language development in the preschool: the incidental teaching model (Hart & Risley, 1975) and the mand model (Rogers-Warren & Warren, 1980). Within the incidental teaching model, the teacher uses naturally occurring opportunities to facilitate language use. Any time that a child wants something from the teacher, the teacher attempts to draw out the conversation. For example, if a child walks up to the teacher on the playground and points to the swings, rather than attempt to anticipate the child's desire to swing, the teacher might say "Can you say *swing?*" If the child says the word, the teacher assists the child with the swing and gives praise. If the child does not say the word, the teacher still provides assistance without reprimand. In the incidental teaching model, it is very important that the child not perceive interactions with the teacher as punitive or unpleasant. This model assumes that language will be learned most effectively if children frequently initiate language opportunities with their teachers.

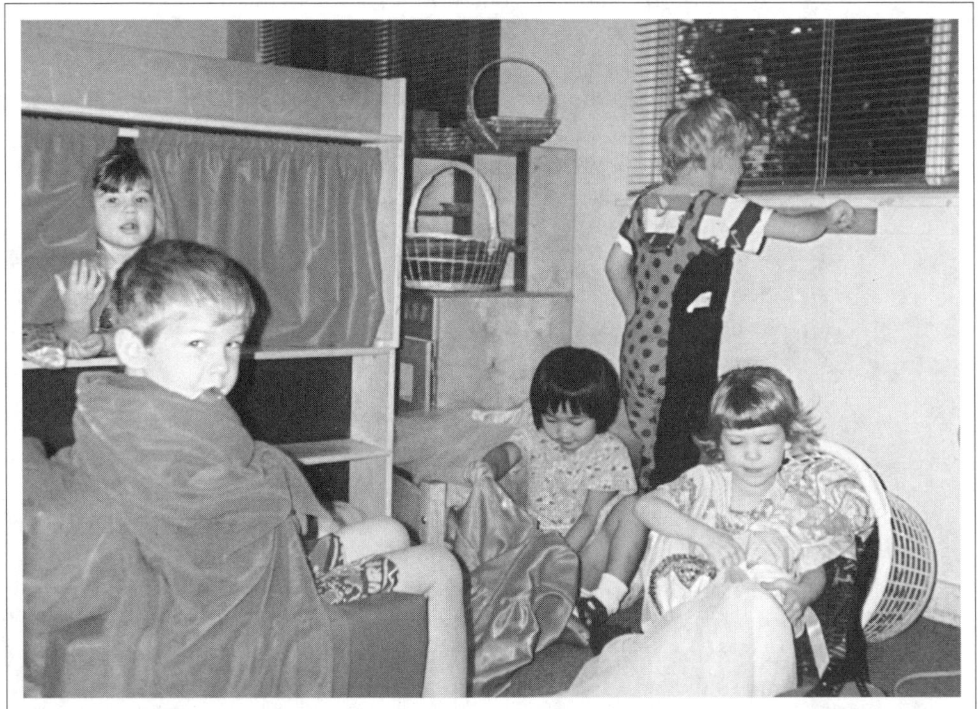

Particularly for children with behavior problems or other difficulties interacting with peers, a social skills-based preschool may be an appropriate form of intervention.

In the mand model, the interactions are typically initiated by the teacher. Within the context of regular activities, the teacher attempts to elicit a target response from a child, usually by asking a question. Using the example of the child who wants to swing, the teacher might say "What do you want to do?" If the child does not respond, the teacher "demands" a response by saying something like "Tell me." The teacher then attempts to elicit a more elaborate response by saying, for example, "Say *Want to swing*."

Social Skills-Based Programs. A developmental task closely associated with language development is social skills development. For many children, preschool is their first opportunity to interact with peers. Particularly for children with behavior problems or other difficulties interacting with peers, a social skills-based preschool may be an appropriate type of intervention. Many such programs use model children, children who are competent social partners, to encourage appropriate play. As with language-based preschools, the environment can be manipulated to increase interaction opportunities. For example, limiting the number of toys available encourages children to play together, and teachers can intervene to encourage appropriate sharing behavior. Therapeutic preschools, programs that incorporate psychological therapy along with educational goals, may be available for young children with severe emotional or behavioral problems.

Best Practices in Early Intervention. To facilitate excellence in program implementation, it helps to have established standards of practice. Such best practices provide a benchmark for measuring the overall quality of any intervention program. Apart from the legal criteria mandated by Part H of IDEA, there are no firmly established standards of practice for early intervention programs. However, several state educational agencies have proposed standards that are believed to be consistent with appropriate practice. Carta, Schwartz, Atwater, and McConnell (1991) and Johnson, Kaufman, and McGonigel (1989) suggest that best practices in early intervention include the following:

- a range of services that vary in intensity based on the needs of the children
- individualized teaching plans consisting of goals and objectives based on careful analyses of children's strengths and weaknesses, and on skills required for future school and nonschool environments
- transdisciplinary assessment that is frequent enough to adequately monitor children's progress
- instructional approaches that are effective, efficient, functional, and normalized
- instructional approaches that actively engage children and their families
- activities that strengthen the abilities of families to "nurture their children's development and promote normalized community adaptation"
- program managers and workers who respect and acknowledge the diversity of patterns and structures within each family

Carta, Schwartz, Atwater, and McConnell (1991) and Johnson, Kaufman, and McGonigel (1989) also offer the following suggestions for best practices in early intervention:

- Families must be permitted to choose their level of involvement with the IFSP process. To help families with decision making, professionals must be clear and honest in their communications with them. Within the framework provided by parental involvement, professionals must respect families' rights to privacy and confidentiality.
- The program manager should strive to form a partnership and collaboration with a child's family. This relationship is fostered by adopting and adapting service delivery strategies that conform to the family's diversity and structure. Professionals also must be accessible and responsive to the family's questions and requests.
- Early intervention services should be flexible, accessible, and responsive to family-identified needs. To address these needs, the family and intervention team should compose goals and objectives that are functional and representative of the family's choices.
- Early intervention services should be provided according to the normalization principle; that is, families should have access to services that are provided in as normal a fashion and environment as possible and that promote the integration of the child and family within the community.
- Planning and service delivery should incorporate multiple agencies and disciplines. This approach acknowledges that no single agency or discipline can entirely meet the complex needs of special children and their families.
- Family members should be present for all decision-making opportunities.

Step 4: Evaluation

Evaluation is an essential but often overlooked component of the intervention process. Snyder and Sheehan (1993) define evaluation as "the process of systematically gathering, synthesizing, and interpreting reliable and valid information about programs for the purpose of aiding with decision making" (p. 269). Program evaluation has two complementary purposes: to examine the effectiveness of a program and to determine the impact of a program on an individual child and family.

At the program level, evaluation is a means of demonstrating accountability (Gabor, 1989; Peterson, 1987). For our purposes, accountability can be loosely defined as the systematic activities through which we seek to demonstrate to our stakeholders that our actions have accomplished the desired outcomes, the "stakeholders" being all parties with an investment in the early intervention program. The most obvious type of investment is financial. Like all state and federally funded programs, early intervention programs have a social and legal obligation to provide proof of their effectiveness. Because administrators, legislators, and other decision makers must determine which programs will receive funding, program evaluation provides vital information. In addition, by evaluating themselves and their programs, professionals help ensure that they will provide the best possible intervention to the families they serve.

Families who participate in early intervention also have investments of time and personal resources in the program and, as such, should be considered an audience for evaluation efforts (Simeonsson et al., in press). Program evaluation thus attempts to determine the impact of early intervention on individual children and their families. Accordingly, evaluation provides an index of program success related to three aspects of service implementation:

1. Efficiency of service delivery: Was intervention implemented as stated in the IEP or IFSP? Were services rendered in a timely and appropriate manner?
2. Overall child outcomes: What changes in the child's behavior occurred and can we demonstrate that they resulted from intervention? What was the quality of these changes? Were any unexpected or undesired outcomes observed? To what extent were the desired outcomes of the IEP or IFSP achieved?
3. Overall family outcomes: Was the family satisfied with intervention? What are their attitudes regarding intervention? To what extent were the family's priorities addressed? (Bricker & Gumerlock, 1988; Peterson, 1987; Snyder & Sheehan, 1993).

The Family's Role in Evaluation. Part II of IDEA formalized the importance of the family in providing early intervention services. Several studies (e.g., Able-Boone, Sandall, Loughry, & Frederick, 1990) have confirmed that families want greater involvement in early intervention programs. Given the importance of the family in formulating objectives and implementing services, it is logical that families also should play a role in program evaluation. An obvious component of program evaluation that directly involves parents is consumer satisfaction. At a minimum, program evaluation should answer the question "Are parents satisfied with the delivery of early intervention services?" Simeonsson et al. (in press) have summarized the importance of family involvement in program evaluation:

> In a comprehensive approach to evaluation, family participation serves as a practical way in which to promote their involvement at each step of the intervention cycle. Their experience is that of a completed encounter for their child and themselves.

Frequently, professionals use specially designed questionnaires and rating scales to assess family satisfaction. One such rating scale used in program evaluation is the Family-Centered Program Rating Scale, or FamPRS (Murphy, Lee, Turnbull, & Tubiville, 1995), a rating scale designed to measure parents' perceptions of and attitudes toward service delivery. Sample items from the FamPRS ask parents to agree or disagree with evaluative statements such as the following:

1. Services can change quickly when my family's or child's needs change.
2. My family is included in all meetings about ourselves and our child.

3. Staff members do not rush my family to make changes until we are ready to.
4. Staff members ask my family's opinion and include us in the process of evaluating our child.

In general, parents who have greater involvement with the delivery of intervention services report greater satisfaction (Caro & Derevensky, 1991). In a recent study designed to isolate the source of parental satisfaction with early intervention programs, McWilliam et al. found that the individual case managers' behaviors were "often directly linked to families' positive impressions of early intervention services" (1995, p. 53). Clearly, from the family's perspective, the individual interventionist is a principal source of their satisfaction. This finding should come as no surprise: The program manager is the primary channel through which the various intervention services flow. The program manager is the professional most visible to the family and represents the concerted efforts of everyone involved in the delivery of services. There is a need for further research to determine the specific personal and professional qualities of early interventionists that relate to parental satisfaction with services.

Not all research fully supports family involvement in early intervention. Innocenti, Hollinger, Escobar, and White (1995) evaluated the impact of parental involvement in the early intervention of 76 toddlers enrolled in a special classroom-based program. The researchers found that parental involvement had a relatively small initial effect on the toddlers' development, and they concluded that parental involvement was not immediately cost-effective. However, the authors also acknowledged that parental involvement may have a cumulative effect that is best evaluated over time. A parent may have the greatest impact not in the short term, but over the course of a child's lifetime. As Skeels (1966) noted more than 30 years ago, more longitudinal research is needed to assess the full impact of early intervention.

Planning the Evaluation. To answer evaluation questions adequately, the interventionist must plan ahead. Because special education law requires that IEPs and IFSPs address evaluation at the program planning stage, evaluation should be a part of the intervention plan. By planning and implementing intervention with an eye toward evaluation, the interventionist can make the process much less time-consuming and more systematic.

A first step in planning program evaluation is to determine the target audience for the evaluation. Who will use the information provided by the evaluation? Different target audiences require that different evaluative questions be answered. For example, if the information is to be used internally (i.e., by service coordinators working in a particular local agency), some questions that may be asked include "Are the children making suitable progress in meeting the objectives of the program plan?" and "Are families satisfied with the behaviors of the case manager?" However, if the information is to be used externally (e.g., by state education agencies), questions such as "What is the cost-effectiveness of service delivery?" and "What percentage of children has been diagnosed with developmental disorders?" might be asked. The expectations and needs of the target audience determine the questions to be answered by the evaluation and thus frame its content.

The next step in planning an evaluation is to develop a design, that is, a systematic method for answering the questions posed for evaluation. This step in evaluation planning is crucial, yet it often is overlooked. One of the major problems in evaluating the effectiveness of early intervention programs occurs when researchers and agencies fail to employ a systematic methodology (Weatherford, 1986). A strong, systematic evaluation design not only provides insight into the overall quality of early intervention, but also helps determine which specific components of an intervention program are most effective. The design should follow logically from the questions to be answered. Some questions, such as those relating to parental satisfaction, are best answered by simple rating scales and questionnaires. Other questions, such as those concerning a child's progress, may be best answered through a series of repeated skills tests. Still other questions, however, are too complex to be answered with a single methodology. For example, a case worker may want to know whether parental involvement is related to the severity of a child's impairment. This question is perhaps best answered with a combination of methods, including natural observations, structured and unstructured interviews, rating scales, and checklists. It may be necessary to further adapt the system of evaluation to the cultural characteristics of the family; for example, the professional may consider a combination of one-on-one interviews and short questionnaires in the family's native language. In all instances, the professional also should seek input from outside sources, especially community members, local advocacy groups, and other human services agencies regarding their perceptions of the program's effectiveness and sensitivity.

Conducting the Evaluation. Once the professional has isolated the target audience, formulated evaluative questions, designed a methodology, and selected the necessary instruments, it is time to conduct the evaluation. This step consists of collecting and analyzing data relevant to the evaluation questions within the framework of the selected design. For the information collected during the evaluation to be useful, the professional must ensure that it is timely, reliable, and valid. Children develop rapidly; therefore, outdated information may simply not be relevant to the needs of the child. In addition, timely information cuts through bureaucratic red tape and facilitates decision making. To be considered reliable, information must be accurate and relatively free from error. For example, an interventionist may wish to evaluate a child's play behaviors. One method of gaining the necessary information is for the professional to ask the mother to report her child's play behaviors. Additionally, the interventionist may decide to observe the child playing with other children and the number of times the child displays positive play behavior in a specified time frame. To be considered valid, information must be relevant to the evaluation question and lead logically to recommendations for practice. The more information that is obtained, the more likely it is that the evaluation will be reliable and valid.

Reporting Results of the Evaluation. The final step in program evaluation is reporting the results to the target audience. The results should be reported in a clear, succinct, and understandable manner. The report also should offer suggestions and recommendations based on the results of the data analysis. An evaluation is worthless if it does not lead to improvements in the quality of intervention. Hanson (1987) recommends providing decision makers with a brief executive summary as a means of calling attention to the significant findings of the evaluation. Naturally, the evaluation should be objective and not influenced by the biases of the interventionists who will be affected by the findings.

It is important to keep in mind that program evaluation is a process rather than a product. Ideally, evaluation should be conducted throughout the intervention program, not just at its conclusion. The purpose of such formative evaluation, occurring throughout program development and implementation, is to monitor the progress of the family and child, and to provide feedback to the family and interventionists on a regular basis. Formative evaluation is particularly important in refining the delivery of services during the initial stages of program implementation (Anastasiow, 1981). Summative evaluation, on the other hand, refers to the measurement of outcomes at the end of the program. Summative evaluation provides an estimate of the overall quality and success of the service delivery. Both formative and summative evaluations are required to accurately assess the effectiveness of an intervention program.

Summary

In this chapter, the process of intervention as it pertains to infants and young children has been discussed. At any given point in history, education and the provision of social services are governed to some extent by the prevailing philosophies and trends of the times. Naturally, notions about what constitutes best practice are constantly changing, and predicting what tomorrow's priorities will be is a bit like fortune-telling. Nonetheless, a review of the literature suggests that a number of trends in practice may influence the provision of services in the next several years.

Now that early intervention is no longer a new field, as it was immediately following the passage of P.L. 99–457, a number of training programs have been developed that are devoted to the systematic training of early intervention professionals. Given the critical role of the individual interventionist in ensuring the success of intervention, the importance of maintaining high-quality professional training cannot be overstated. Reflecting the shift from child-centered to family-centered services, many of these programs are attempting to teach students the skills that are most valued by families.

If current trends continue, we can anticipate that inclusion will be an important force shaping the future of intervention with young children. As was indicated earlier in the chapter, inclusion refers to full incorporation of a child with special needs into normalized settings. If it is fully implemented (as it already has been in some states), not only will inclusion change the setting in which services are likely to be provided in the future, but also, it will change the very nature of children's needs and the ways in which they are met. For example, very different skills are necessary for a child to function appropriately in a regular classroom from those that are necessary to function in a self-contained classroom with only a few other children who also have special needs. To meet these changing needs, intervention programs will need to be more flexible than ever before, and interventionists will be called upon to embrace a spirit of cross-discipline cooperation.

As described earlier in the chapter, some professionals are not content with the current continuum of services and argue for the abolition of all special education for children. Although most early intervention experts agree that inclusion is the goal for all children, the removal of service delivery options infringes on other ideals of early intervention, particularly the legal mandate and commitment of professionals to provide services consistent with family goals and priorities. As the inclusion debate rages on, early interventionists will be called upon to maintain a reasoned approach to the complex—and all too often political—issue of determining the most appropriate setting for service provision.

The spirit and letter of IDEA contain a mandate for service provision that crosses the boundaries of traditional professional disciplines. Increasingly, professionals have been collaborating in early intervention, and this trend seems likely to continue. In particular, the collaboration between medical professionals and other professionals is likely to increase. Improvements in medicine have led not only to increased survival and improved developmental outcomes for medically fragile children, but also to an increase in the number of technology-dependent young children. Given the complexities of such cases, improved collaboration between medical and nonmedical professionals can only contribute to more effective, less fragmented service delivery for children with special needs.

As the number of ethnic and language minorities increase, so will the need for cultural sensitivity in the provision of early intervention services. Recruiting interventionists from minority populations is likely to continue to be a pressing challenge for universities and agencies. In addition, interventionists will be called upon to develop an awareness of their own cultures and values while learning to accept and appreciate the cultures and values of others from diverse backgrounds.

The competition for the ever-shrinking public dollar has forced local and state intervention agencies to prove their effectiveness in concrete and definitive ways. As a result, outcome-based evaluation is becoming more important as agencies struggle to ensure continued funding. Because of the nature of intervention with children with special needs, such evaluation efforts are unlikely to reflect the impact of intervention in valid ways. Therefore, interventionists must approach evaluation proactively and begin to think creatively about efficient and accurate ways of demonstrating the effectiveness of their efforts. Given the current political climate, it seems likely that concerns about accountability will shape the way professionals provide services to children and families.

Despite ever-shifting national priorities and inconsistent funding, children with special needs and their families continue to benefit from intervention services, as indicated by Trohanis (Bowe, 1995):

> Our arrival at Peter's diagnosis of autism has been circuitous and complex, but there is accounting here, for it speaks to the hopes, dreams, and schemes Public Law 99–457 is striving to accomplish for all children and their families. Our family has crawled through an incredulous maze in the last two and a half years, through black holes and windows of light, and we still have a lot of traveling to do. The importance of intervention was a turning point for us. We felt rescued. (p. 369)

References

Able-Boone, H., Sandall, S. R., Loughry, A., & Fredrick, L. L. (1990). An informed, family-centered approach to Public Law 99–457: Parental views. *Topics in Early Childhood Special Education 10*(1), 100–111.

Adelman, H., & Taylor, L. (1994). *On understanding intervention in psychology and education*. Westport, CT: Praeger.

Anastasiow, N. J. (1981). *Socioemotional Development*. San Francisco: Jossey-Bass.

Bailey, D. B. (1988). Considerations in developing family goals. In D. B. Bailey and R. J. Simeonsson, (Eds.), *Family assessment in early intervention* (pp. 229–249). Upper Saddle River, NJ: Merrill/Prentice Hall.

Bailey, D. B, Buysse, V., Edmondson, R., & Smith, T. M. (1992). Creating family-centered services in early intervention: Perceptions of professionals in four states. *Exceptional Children, 58*(4), 298–309.

Bailey, D. B., & McWilliam, R. A. (1990). Normalizing early intervention. *Topics in Early Childhood Special Education, 10*(2) 33–47.

Barnett, D., & Carey, K. T. (1992). *Designing interventions for preschool learning and behavior problems*. The Jossey-Bass Social and Behavioral Science Series and The Jossey-Bass Educational Series. San Francisco: Jossey-Bass.

Black, J. K., & Puckett, M. B. (1996). *The young child: Development from prebirth through age eight*. Upper Saddle River, NJ: Prentice Hall.

Bowe, F. G. (1995a). Birth to five: Early childhood special education. New York: Delmar.

Bowe, F. G. (1995b). Population estimates: Birth to 5: Children with disabilities. *Journal of Special Education 28*(4), 461–471.

Bricker, D. (1989). *Early intervention for at-risk and handicapped infants, toddlers, and preschool children* (2nd ed.). Palo Alto, CA: VORT Corp.

Bricker, D., & Cripe, J. J. (1992). *An activity-based approach to early intervention*. Baltimore: Paul H. Brookes.

Bricker, D., & Gumerlock, S. (1988). Application of a three-level evaluation plan for monitoring child progress and program effects. *Journal of Special Education 22*(1), 66–81.

Bronfenbrenner, U. (1986). Ecology of the family as a context for human development: Research perspectives. *Developmental Psychologist, 22*, 723–742.

Brown, F., Evans, I. M., Weed, K. A., & Owen, V. (1987). Delineating functional competencies: A component approach. *Journal of the Association for Persons with Severe Handicaps, 12*(2), 117–124.

Brown, R. W., and Lenneberg, E. (1965). Studies in linguistic relativity. In H. Proshansky & B. Seidenberg (Eds.), *Basic studies in social psychology* (pp. 244–252). New York: Holt, Rinehart, and Winston.

Caro, P., & Derevensky, J. L. (1991). Family-focused intervention models: Implementation and research findings. *Topics in Early Childhood Special Education, 11*(3), 66–80.

Carta, J. J., Schwartz, I. S., Atwater, J. B., & McConnell, S. R. (1991). Developmentally appropriate practice:

Appraising its usefulness for young children with disabilities. *Topics in Early Childhood Special Education, 11*(1), 1–20.

Children's Defense Fund (1989). *A vision of America's future.* Washington, DC: Author.

Correa, V. I., & Morsink, C. V. (1995). *Interactive teaming: Consultation and collaboration in special programs.* Upper Saddle River, NJ: Merrill/Prentice Hall.

Frisby, C. L. (1992). Issues and problems in the influence of culture on the psychoeducational needs of African-American children. *School Psychology Review, 21*(4), 532–551.

Fuchs, D., & Fuchs, L. S. (1994). Inclusive schools movement and the radicalization of special education reform. *Exceptional Children, 60,* 294–309.

Gabor, P. (1989). Increasing accountability in child care practice through the use of single case evaluation. *Child and Youth Care Quarterly, 18* (2), 93–109.

Green, J. W. (1982). *Cultural awareness in the human services.* Upper Saddle River, NJ: Prentice Hall.

Gutkin, T. B., & Curtis, J. (1990). School-based consultation: Theory, techniques, and research. In T. B. Gutllin & C. R. Reynolds, (Eds.), *The handbook of school psychology* (pp. 577–611). New York: John Wiley and Sons.

Hanson, M. (1987). *Teaching the infant with Down syndrome: A guide for parents and professionals.* Austin, TX: PRO-ED.

Hanson, M., & Lynch, E. W. (1995). *Early intervention: Implementing child and family services for infants and toddlers who are at risk or disabled* (2nd ed.). Austin, TX: PRO-ED.

Hanson, M. J., Lynch, E. W., & Wayman, K. (1990). Honoring the cultural diversity of families when gathering data. *Teaching of Exceptional Children in Special Education, 10*(1), 112–131.

Hart, B., & Risley, T. R. (1975). Incidental teaching of language in the preschool. *Journal of Applied Behavior Analysis, 8,* 411–420.

Heward, W. L. (1996). *Exceptional children* (5th ed.). Upper Saddle River, NJ: Merrill/Prentice Hall.

Innocenti, M. S., Hollinger, D. D., Escobar, C. M., & White, K. R. (1995). The cost-effectiveness of adding one type of parent involvement to an early intervention program. *Early Education and Development, 4*(4), 306–326.

Johnson, B. H., Kaufman, R. K., & McGonigel, M. J. (1989). *Guidelines and recommended practices for the Individualized Family Service Plan.* Bethesda, MD: Association for the Care of Children's Health.

Lynch, E. W., & Hanson, M. J. (1993). *Developing cross-cultural competence: A guide for working with young children and their families.* Baltimore: Paul H. Brookes.

McWilliam, R. A., & Bailey, D. B. (1994). Predictors of service delivery models in center-based early intervention. *Exceptional Children, 61*(1), 56–71.

McWilliam, R. A., Lang, I., Vandiviere, P., Angell, R., Collins, L., & Underdown, G. (1995). Satisfaction and struggles: Family perceptions of early intervention. *Journal of Early Intervention, 19*(1), 43–60.

Murphy, D. L., Lee, I. M., Tunbull, A., & Turbiville, V. (1995). The Family-Centered Program Rating Scale: An instrument for program evaluation and change. *Journal of Early Intervention, 19*(6), 24–42.

Odom, S. L., & McEvoy, M. A. (1990). Mainstreaming at the preschool level: Potential barriers and risks for the field. *Topics in Early Childhood Special Education, 10*(2), 48–61.

Peterson, N. L. (1987). *Early intervention: An introduction to early childhood-special education.* Denver: Love.

Research and Policy Committee of the Committee for Economic Development (1987). *Children in need: Investment strategies for the educationally disadvantaged.* New York: Author.

Rhodes, W. C., & Tracey, M. C. (1972). *A study of child variance: Intervention, Vol. 2.* Ann Arbor: University of Michigan Press.

Richmond, J., & Ayoub, C. (1993). Evolution of early intervention philosophy. In D. M. Bryant & M. A. Graham (Eds.), *Implementing early intervention: From research to effective practice.* New York: Guilfford Press.

Rogers-Warren, A., & Warren, S. (1980). Mands for verbalization: Facilitating the generalization of newly trained language in children. *Behavior Modification, 4,* 220–245.

Sameroff, A., & Chandler, M. J. (1975). Reproductive risk and the continuum of caretaking casuality. In F. D. Horowith, M. Hetherington, S. Scarr-Salapetek, & G. Seigal (Eds.), *Review of Child Development Research* (pp. 187–244). Chicago: University of Chicago Press.

Sattler, J. (1992). *Assessment in children* (3rd ed., rev.). San Diego, CA: Author.

Schorr, L. B., & Schorr, D. (1988). *Within our reach: Breaking the cycle of disadvantage*. New York: Doubleday.

Simeonsson, R. J., Huntington, G. S., McMillen, J. S., Dodds, A. H., Halperin, D., Zipper, I. N., Leskinen, M., & Langmeyer, D. (in press). Services for young children and families: Evaluating intervention cycles. *Infants and young children*.

Skeels, H. M. (1966). Adult status of children with contrasting early life experiences: A follow-up study. *Monographs of the Society for Research in Child Development, 31*(3, Serial No. 105).

Snyder, S., & Sheehan, R. (1993). *Family-centered early intervention with infants and toddlers: Innovative cross-disciplinary approaches*. Baltimore: Paul H. Brookes.

Stainback, S., & Stainback, W. (1992). *Curriculum considerations in inclusive classrooms: Facilitating learning for all students*. Baltimore: Paul H. Brookes.

Stokes, T. F., & Osnes, P. G. (1989). An operant pursuit of generalization. *Behavior Therapy, 20*(3), 337–355.

Suran, B. G., & Rizzo, J. V. (1979). *Special children: An integrative approach*. Glenville, IL: Scott, Foresman.

Turnbull, A. P., Turnbull, H. R., Shank, M., & Leal, D. (1995). *Exceptional lives: Special education in today's schools*. Upper Saddle River, NJ: Prentice Hall.

Turnbull, S. K., & Turnbull, J. M. (1986). *Families, professionals, and exceptionality: A special partnership*. Upper Saddle River, NJ: Merrill/Prentice Hall.

U.S. Bureau of the Census (1990). Characteristics of the population: Vol. 1. Washington, DC: United States Department of Commerce.

Weatherford, D. L. (1986). The challenge of evaluation: Early intervention programs for severely handicapped children and their families. In L. Brickman & D. L. Weatherford (Eds.), *Evaluation: Early intervention programs for severely handicapped children and their families* (pp. 1–17). Austin, TX: PRO-ED.

Wolery, M. (1989). Using assessment information to plan instructional programs. In D. Bailey & M. Wolery (Eds.), *Assessing infants and preschoolers with handicaps*. Upper Saddle River, NJ: Merrill/Prentice Hall.

Epilogue

We have sought in this text to provide a thorough overview of early childhood issues that are pertinent to infants, toddlers, and preschoolers with special developmental needs. Early childhood special education has witnessed an explosion in knowledge since the previous edition of this text was published. Although the direct application of new knowledge generally lags behind best clinical practices in most fields of study, we have tried to provide current information in a form that we hope encourages rapid application with children and families. We hope that students and professionals working in the field of early childhood special education will strive for best practices and that the information provided in this text will facilitate those efforts. As we close, there are many remaining questions and issues that confront professionals in this field. A brief discussion of the most important of these follows.

Terminology. We have attempted to standardize the terminology used in this text from one chapter to the next; this was a compromise of semantics and principles. For example, in a world that attaches status and importance to titles, what title best characterizes what we do? What title or titles are more appropriate and desirable? We decided to use the term *early interventionist* or *interventionist* in most cases rather than *early childhood special educator, teacher, educator,* or *therapist.* While all these terms refer to professionals who work with infants, toddlers, and/or preschoolers, not all have special education training, college degrees, or training in specialized aspects of intervention (e.g., feeding, play, and positioning). We settled on a term that appears to encompass all professionals who offer early intervention programming.

We also struggled with the terms used to describe the children. *Handicapped children, mentally retarded children,* and similar terms have been out of favor for several years. We also avoided using the term *developmentally delayed* because, although federal and state legislators endorse the use of this term, the concept of delay suggests that these children will catch up. In fact, most will continue to show a wide range of developmental problems throughout their life spans. We opted for the terms *children with disabilities* and *children with special needs* for clarity and consistency; however, do other terms define the population as clearly or more clearly?

Inclusion. Some advocates for children with disabilities believe that all these children should be educated in integrated settings with their nondisabled peers. The logistics of this approach pose one dilemma; the benefits pose another. It is relatively easy to integrate school-aged children in classes within a school building; however, given that early childhood programs are rarely mandatory in states, particularly for children under 4 years of age, finding programs in which young children with special needs can be included poses a problem. Another concern is the training of staff members in programs that do include children with special needs and the availability of specialized staff members to provide support at times when such support is most needed. Also, should all young children with special needs be included in regular classes without regard to the type or intensity of their disabilities? Should consideration be given to the effects of such children's inclusion on the learning of the nondisabled children in the class? Is the inclusion strategy supported by research data? Is inclusion more beneficial for children with certain types or degrees of disabilities than others?

We extend the definition of inclusion to mean the involvement of families in the entire early childhood special education process. Indeed, family matters and issues have been discussed in nearly every chapter of this text. Although the inclusion of families in this process has been discussed for years, it has been only recently that models have attempted to incorporate a family perspective. Family thoughts, feelings, ideas, and observations have been addressed relative to their importance to assessment; they also are critical to intervention and developmental monitoring. Family involvement, however, is not a program component with which many professionals in the field feel very secure and comfortable. It will remain an ongoing challenge for professionals who work with young children with special needs to keep other family members appropriately involved. What role, for example, should parents have in their child's program? How prepared are professionals now entering the field of early intervention to analyze family needs and to work productively with family members who show very diverse characteristics?

Training. The primary emphasis of this text has been on understanding child development and applying it within the context of the individual needs of a child and family. Those who have observed their own children or younger siblings growing up begin their formal training with an enriched perspective of how children develop. We cannot overstate the importance of the best practices model, which is built on a sound knowledge of what makes children tick. At the same time, training programs should orient early interventionists to a team approach to assessment and intervention, with special consideration being given to matters of family, culture, and socioeconomic status. Still, questions remain: Should training programs in early childhood special education reflect a single philosophical orientation or should they be more eclectic in their make-up? How can diverse training needs be integrated into a college-based training program? What other training components might be needed? One thing is certain: Working with children with special needs requires familiarity with many different disciplines. Training programs for early interventionists must address the multidisciplinary and transdisciplinary facets of assessment and treatment. Such training improves the quality of services that these professionals provide to young children with special needs and their families.

Technology. These are great times in which to live. Computers, microwave ovens, compact disc players, and computer-chip-based toys all make life easier, but only because we know what we want and buy what we can. When a technological aid is recommended as being of benefit to a young child with special needs, the child's caregivers must appreciate the importance of the aid, know how to use it, understand when to use it, and get support to continue to use it with or for the child. In addition, the need for the technological aid must be evaluated regularly to determine whether the approach is working and the child has progressed, or whether the child has regressed and a new approach or different technological aid is required. Computers have served to improve certain aspects of assessment and intervention for children with special needs (e.g., by offering other vehicles for play), and they have contributed to the dissemination of information in a more rapid and thorough fashion. For example, the information superhighway is now a reality and can be used by nearly anyone.

Medical technology has shared in an abundance of significant advances that will continue to have a dramatic impact on early childhood special education. For example, more infants are surviving birth trauma and very low birthweight than ever before, which may add to the population of children who need early intervention. On the other hand, prenatal surgery holds promise for correcting problems even before infants are born. In addition, new medications and surgical treatments can cure or correct problems that otherwise would cause serious, lifelong impairments.

Technology undoubtedly will continue to expand. It is not possible for a textbook to keep pace with the rapid rate at which advances are evolving, but suffice it to say that technology is here to stay and it likely will be an ever-growing component in the early childhood domain with which interventionists must keep pace. It is unproductive, however, for technology to be dumped on caregivers without the support necessary to help make it successful. Technology creates questions as well as solutions: Should technology be withheld from a child or family if a program cannot provide the necessary ongoing support? Should more efforts be made to enlist the most sophisticated technological approaches with children regardless of cost? How can ongoing training be provided to teachers so that they can stay on top of technology? How does a program keep from relying too heavily on instructional technology to the detriment of person-to-person instruction?

Keeping Pace. It is important for early interventionists to remain aware of the rapidly changing information base related to new clinical findings, scientific breakthroughs, and legislative activities. What resources are available to help early interventionists keep up with scientific, legislative, and other relevant events in the field? What vehicles are available for interventionists to have an impact on decision making in their communities and states? Given the fiscal pressures at all governmental levels, funding for early intervention services may determine what progress is made in the field. Logical, rational, and informed professionals can tilt the legislative and fiscal scales in favor of necessary support for programs.

We hope that this text has provided professionals and students interested in early intervention with a clear picture of the current state of the field. Just as this third edition reflects the marked changes that have occurred in the progress of early childhood special education since the publication of the prior edition, we look forward to reporting on future significant changes in the next edition—changes in which the reader well may have played a role.

Name Index

Subject Index